Church as the Bride of Christ

Christian Heritage Rediscovered

The Series, as the name suggests, is meant to focus on Christian Faith & Living vis-à-vis topics like Literature & Poetry, Indigenous Philosophizing, Ethical response towards Agriculture, Health & Healing, Science & Technology, Ecofeminist Theology, Sociological approach towards Human Rights, Law & Politics, Arts, History of Ideas, Ancient Civilizations, Cultural Contiguity, Religious Cosmologies & Mysticism, Footsteps of famous Theologians, World Peace & Harmony, Global Capitalism, Network Marketing, Cybertheology, Population & Demographics, Epigraphic Studies, Contextualized Education, and many others. We welcome a Mss. on any topic/s mentioned, whether they are original works, scholarly monographs, collections of conference papers, revised dissertations, or translations of historical documents. Through the Series we, the Publishers, are striving to put forward published works that may help Institutions, Academic Bodies, Researchers, Scholars and the World at large in furthering their respective knowledge and understanding on the concerned subject. We welcome your comments on our efforts and further suggestions on how we can foster the upcoming thoughtful theologically grounded books.

Christian Heritage Rediscovered - 77

Church as the Bride of Christ

Ecclesiological & Societal Understanding
of the Early Syriac Church
based on the
Select Homilies of Mar Jacob of Serugh

Santhosh K. Joshua

CWI
Christian World Imprints

First Published in 2020 by

Christian World Imprints
Christian Publishing & Books from India
C-3, Shop No. 14, Ground Floor
Wazirpur Industrial Area, **Delhi-110052**
cwidelhi2017@gmail.com
www.ChristianWorldImprints.com
Phone: +91 11 41526079

ISBN: 978-93-5148-349-6

Printed in India

Contents

Acknowledgement

It is my committed duty to remember and express my profound gratitude to those who helped and encouraged me in the process of writing this dissertation. Prof. Dr. Thomas Kollamparampil CMI, Dean of Studies in the Faculty of Theology (2013-2015) at Dharmaram Vidya Kshethram, Bangalore, and my Director who took an unprecedented interest in my work and an untiring pursuance of the progress of my study. Father, please accept my unfeigned gratitude. I am wordless and mute when I think of my mentor and spiritual guru late lamented Ghevarghese Mar Ivanios Metropolitan who has been my inspiration for a study on Church Fathers. My sincere gratitude to Dr. Pualachen Kochappally CMI, and Dr. Geo Pallikkunnel CMI have greatly encouraged and supported me during my studies at DVK, Banglore. It is my privilege to acknowledge Dr. Joy Philip Kakkanattu CMI the present Dean of the Faculty of Theology, Fr. John Neelankavil CMI, Librarian, and all staff community of the DVK without their whole hearted support the work would not have been completed. I owe them more than many. Mr. K. C. Jacob Mavelikara, whose support is invaluable, a big thanks from the bottom of my heart. Finally, most important are my brothers in my monastery who have been exemplary in servicing me during the time of need.

My sincere thanks to all those who have been helpful in completing this study. Once again I remember everyone and acknowledge with gratitude their cooperation.

Santhosh K. Joshua
Bangalore

Abbreviations

AAA	*Apocryphal Acts of the Apostles*, London: Gilbert and Rivington, Whitefriars City.
AAS	*Acta Apostolica Sedis*, Romae: Polyglottis Vaticanis.
ABD	*The Anchor Yale Bible Dictionary*, in six volumes, New Haven: Yale University Press.
AJSL	*American Journal for Semitic Literature*, Chicago: University of Chicago.
AMS	*Acta Martyrum et Sanctorum,* Vols. 1-VII, (ed.) P. Bedjan, Paris 1890-1897. [Reference to these volumes are indicated with the abbreviation *AMS* + Volume no. in Roman numerals + page(s) + lines.
ANF	*Ante-Nicene Fathers*, in 10 Volumes, NY: T&T Clark.
ASPD	*Aphraatis Sapientis Persae Demonstrationes*, PO 2.
BO	*Bibliotheca Orientalis Clementino Vaticana*, Vols. 1-4, (ed,) J. S. Assemani, Roma 1719-1728.
CBQ	*The Catholic Biblical Quarterly*, LA: Catholic Biblical Association of America.
CH	*Des heiligen Ephraem des Syrers Hymnen contra Haereses*, E. Beck, (ed.) CSCO 169-70, Syr. 76-77. Louvain: L. Durbecq, 1957.
CJul	*Des heiligen Ephrem des Syrers Hymnen de Paradiso und Contra Julianum,* (ed.) E. Beck, CSCO 174/175 (Syri 78/79), Louvain, 1957.
CNis	*Des heiligen Ephraem des Syrers Carmina Nisibena* I, (ed.) E. Beck, CSCO 218-219, (Syr. 92-93.), Louvain: Secretariat du CorpusSCO, 1961, and *Des heiligen Ephraem des Syrers Carmina Nisibena* II, (ed.) E. Beck, CSCO 240-241, (Syr. 102-103), Louvain: Secretariat du CorpusSCO, 1963.

Crucif	*Des heiligen Ephraem des Syrers Paschahymnen: De azymnis, de crucifixione, de resurrection*, (ed.) E. Beck, CSCO 248-249, (Syri. 108-109), Louvain: Secretariat du CorpusSCO, 1964.
CSCO	*Corpus Scriptorum Christianorum Orientalium*: Louvain.
DR	*The Downside Review*, Radstock, Bath: The Monks of Downside Abbey.
EncJud	*Encyclopedia Judaica*, NY; Macmillan Company.
Ep	*Epistulae Quotquot Suprnunt 1.* SARUGENSIS, *Epistulae quotquot supersunt*, (ed.) G. Olinder, Paris 1937, CSCO 110, Louvain, Imprimerie Orinetaliste, Durbecq, 1965. [All references regarding this source in this dissertation is from *CSCO* 110; References to this volume will be indicated with the abbreviation *Ep* +Number of the letter in Roman numerals + page(s) + line(s)].
Epiph	*Des heiligen Ephraem des Syrers Hymnen de Nativitate (Epiphania)*, (ed.) E. Beck, CSCO 186-187, (Syr. 82-83), Louvain: Secretariat du CorpusSCO, 1959.
ER	*The Encyclopedia of Religion*, NY: Macmillan Company.
ET	English Translation
Fasc	Fascicule
FH	Thomas Kollamparampil, (ET) *Jacob of Serugh Select Festal Homilies*, Rome & Bangalore, Dharmaram Publications, 1997. [References to these homilies are indicated with abbreviation *FH* + Number of the homily in Roman numerals + page(s) + line(s).
FT	French Translation
HCJ	Jacques De Saroug: *Homelies Contre Les Jufis*, M. Albert (ed.) *PO* Tome XXXVIII, (Fac. 1, No 174), Turnhout: Diffusion Mondiale, 1976. [Critical edition with FT. References to these homilies are indicated with the abbreviation *HCJ* + Number of the homily in Roman numerals + line(s)].
HEcc	*Des heiligen Ephraem des Syrers Hymnen de Ecclesia*, (ed.) E. Beck, CSCO 198-199, (Syr. 84-85), Louvain: Secretariat du CorpusSCO, 1960.
HFid	*Des heiligen Ephraem des Syrers Hymnen de Fide*, (ed.) E. Beck, CSCO 154-155, (Syr. 73-74), Louvain: L. Durbecq, 1955.
HNat	*Des heiligen Ephraem des Syrers Hymnen de Nativitate (Epiphania)*, (ed.) E. Beck, CSCO 186-187, (Syr. 82-83), Louvain: Secretariat du CorpusSCO, 1959.
HPar	*Des heiligen Ephraem des Syrers Hymnen de Paradiso und contra Julianum*, (ed.) E. Beck, CSCO 174-175, (Syr. 78-79), Louvain: Peeters, 1957.

HR	*History of Religions: An International Journal for Comparative Historical Studies*, Chicago: Chicago University Press.
HS	*Homiliae Selectae Mar Jacobi Sarugensis,* Vols. I-V, (ed.) P. Bedjan, Paris-Leipzig 1905-1910, [References to these volumes are indicated with the abbreviation *HS* + Volume no. in Roman Numerals + Page(s) + Line(s)]
HTM	Holy Transfiguration Monastery, MA, USA.
HTR	*Harvard Theological Review*, Cambridge, MA: Harvard Divinity School.
Hugoye	*Hugoye Journal for Syriac Studies*, Online Journal by Bethmardutho.
HVir	*Des heiligen Ephraem des Syrers Hymnen de Virginitate*, (ed.) E. Beck, CSCO 223-224, Syr. 94-95. Louvain: Secretariat du CorpusSCO, 1962.
IDB	*The Interpreter's Dictionary of the Bible: An Illustrated Encyclopedia*, in 4 Volumes, Nashville: Abington Press.
IT	Italian Translation
JANES	*Journal of the Ancient Near Eastern Society of Columbia University*, NY: Jewish Theological Seminary.
JBL	*Journal of Biblical Literature*, Atlanta.
JCSSS	*Journal of the Canadian Society for Syriac Studies*, Toronto: University of Toronto.
JSP	*Journal for the Study of the Pseudepigrapha*, NY: Sage Publications.
Jul	G. E. Hoffmann, *Iulianos der Abiruennige, Syrische Ezraehlungen,* Lieden, 1880; English Translation: H. Gollancz, *Julian the Apostate,* Oxford & London, 1928.
LP	*Liber Perfectionis*, ed by Paul Bedjan.
MOSC	Malankara Orthodox Syrian Church
MT	Malayalam Translation
NIDB	*The New Interpreters Dictionary of the Bible*, 5 Volumes, Nashville: Abingdon Press.
NIDNT	*New International Dictionary of the New Testament*, 4 Volumes, NY: Zondervan.
NIDOTT	*New International Dictionary of the Old Testament and Theology*, 5 Volumes, NY: Zondervan.
NPNF	*A Select Library of Nicene and Post Nicene Fathers of the Christian Church*, NY: T&T Clark.

OCP	*Orientalia Christiana Periodica*, Roma: Pontificio Istituto Orientale.
OLA	*Orientalia Lovaniensia Analecta*, Louvain: Peters Press.
OrSyr	*L'Orient Syrien*, France: Vernon.
ParOr	*Parole de l'Orient*
PG	*Patralogia Greca*, 161 Volumes, Paris: J. P. Migne's Imprimerie Catholique.
PO	*Patrologia Orientalis*, in 41 Volumes, R. Graffin (ed.), Paris.
POB	*Pontifical Biblical Commission*, Rome.
PS	*Patrologia Syriaca*, in 2 Volumes, R. Graffin (ed.) Rome: Pont. Institutum Orientalium Studiorum.
QHC	Jacqes De Sarough: *Quarte Homelies Metriques sur La Creation,* Alwan Khalil (ed. & tr.),in *CSCO* Vols 508/509, (Syri 214/215), [Critical edition with FT, References to these homilies are indicated with abbreviation *QHC* + Number of the homily in Roman Numerals + Line(s) + Page number].
Resur	*Des Heiligen Ephraem Des Syrers Paschahymnen: De azymnis, de crucifixione, de resurrection,* (ed.) E. Beck, CSCO 248/249, (Syri. 108-109), Louvain, 1964.
SHF	*Jacques de Saroug: Six Homilies Festals en Prose,* (ed.) F. Rilliet, *Patrologia Orientalis* 43 (Fascicule 4, No 196), Turnhout 1986, [Critical edition with FT; References to these homilies are indicated with the abbreviation *SHF* + Number of Homily in Roman Numerals + Paragraph(s)]; E.T. of the following homilies IV, VII, IX, XI, XII, XV in T. Kollamparampil, *FH.*
SMS	*Martyrii, qui wr Sahadona, quae supersunt omnia*, Paris / Leipzig: Otto Harrassowitz, 1902.
SVTQ	*St. Vladimir Theological Quarterly*, Crestwood, NY: St. Vladimir Seminary.
Syri.	Scriptores Syriac
TDNT	*The Theological Dictionary of the New Testament*, Grand Rapids: W.M.B. Eerdmanns.
tr.	Translation
TV	*The True Vine*, Boston, MA: Holy Trnasfiguration Monastery.
VC	*Vigiliae Christianae,* Amsterdam
Vol.	Volume

Transliteration Table

Syriac Alphabets	English Transliteration
ܐ	’/a
ܒ	B
ܓ	G
ܕ	D
ܗ	h
ܘ	w
ܙ	z
ܚ	ḥ
ܛ	ṭ
ܝ	y/i
ܟ	k
ܠ	l
ܡ	m
ܢ	n
ܣ	s
ܥ	′/a
ܦ	p
ܨ	ṣ
ܩ	q
ܪ	r
ܫ	š
ܬ	t
Vowels	
ܰ	a
ܳ	o
ܶ	e
ܺ	ee
ܽ	u/oo

General Introduction

Syriac is one of the major dialects of Aramaic. At least from the sixth century BC Syriac was the *lingua franca* of the whole West Asia till it gave way to Arabic in the seventh century AD.[1] Syriac language was developed in and around the city of Edessa or Urhai, a city of the little kingdom Osrhoene, in successive stages. Syriac language produced a large number of works in various disciplines such as religion, science, medicine, astronomy and so on. Theological genre contributes a lion's share of Syriac literature and is truly a great treasure house of knowledge of the East. Syriac is the liturgical language of the Syriac speaking Churches and of some of the Churches in the Indian subcontinent. For many centuries the Western Christian scholars were either unaware of this rich treasure or ignored them.

Jacob of Serugh[2] is one of the prominent Syriac religious poets. He was, for a long time, a Corepiscopos and finally the bishop of Betnan of Serugh in modern Turkey. The scholarly world has accepted his prodigy in religious teachings and his interpretation of the Scripture and started serious studies on his works. Most of the early studies were made on his Christology and Christological position. Now it is generally accepted that in spite of his strong independent stand in Christological debates of his times, he was not a controversialist but only a spiritual theologian and a teacher. The Lazarist priest Paul Bedjan[3] edited a good number of his homilies. The recent translations of his *Memre* (verse homilies) brought more insights into his teachings. These made him popular like his predecessor Mar Ephrem. His typological interpretation received much attention from the ordinary believers and made his homilies popular. Unlike those who look for rational interpretation, the twentieth century postmodernists, who prefer life experience, are attracted by the fluid and unsystematic but deeper and penetrating spiritual interpretation of the Semitic Church. Such a shift in the reading of the academic world is a

[1] Murray, *Symbols of Church and Kingdom*, 3.

[2] From here onwards mostly he will be mentioned Mar Jacob.

[3] Van den Berg, "Bedjan, Paul," 65.

blessing to the Syriac theology too. As a result many scholars, especially from the West, have started studying the writings of Mar Jacob and became popular among the orientalists.

1. Theme of the Study

The present study is based on one of the favorite themes of Mar Jacob, "the Church as the Bride of Christ." This is a typological interpretation, which expounds the God-human-nature relationship.[4] Through this theme he elaborates the understanding of the early Syriac Church on creation, sin, Holy dispensation of Jesus Christ and the salvation of humankind. The paradigm of God-human-nature relationship is at stake in the present world due to several reasons. The present era of consumerism[5] and globalization[6] has brought about changes in the perspectives of the ideological and pragmatic areas.[7] This has created breakups in the harmonious relationships and the elimination of many local, aboriginal and indigenous cultures. At this juncture, the researcher finds Jacob of Serugh's exhortations "the Church as the Bride of Christ" a refreshing paradigm capable of reinvigorating the relationship hazards.

2. Importance of the Theme

Through this theme Mar Jacob delineates God-human relationship from the time of creation. And this relationship is built upon the rock of love of God towards humankind. On the other hand the chosen bride, the Israelites, were unfaithful and rejected the Bridegroom, Christ; therefore, He elected another bride, the Church, who was 'blackened with the fume of idolatry.' Through this theme Mar Jacob portrays the loving, forgiving, and self-emptying God who is a model for today's selfish and disintegrated world.

Human society has undergone considerable changes in life and environment due to the rapid growth of science and technology which contracted the world into a global village. Invention of new commodities, added the softness and comfort to living. Aggressive campaign and unethical marketing throughout the world at large produced globalization and spread

[4] In this study 'the bride-bridegroom' imagery is often named as spousal imagery, nuptial imagery, marriage imagery, etc.

[5] Consumerism is a term that defines the modern tendency to consume goods and service. Here the writer is a critique of this tendency and term; through which Multi-National Companies compel people to buy their products through different strategies and earn maximum profit without any morale. Here people buy goods even though they are not necessary for their daily needs. This over consumption is creating imbalance in social order, the gap between the haves and the have-nots are increasing, through the over exploitation of the natural resources creates ecological crisis also.

[6] Globalization is a later 20th century phenomena in which world became a global village and a global market.

[7] The shift in the time of globalization will be discussed in elaboration of the problem.

of consumerism, which are the two major threats to the contemporary world. The holistic rhythm that existed in human society gave way to materialism and embraced the epicurean concept of life. Profit and accumulation of wealth became the motto of life. Self centered enjoyments and pleasures gained prominence in human life. The situation warranted a shift in the relation between God and Human, Human and Human and Human and Nature. In the God-Human relationship, with the new approach, people opted for a materialistic and prosperity-oriented theology and spirituality whereas they disregarded the loving, selfless, austere, and sacrificial models of Jesus. They relegated Jesus as a wonder worker and the fulfiller of their material needs. This understanding made the faithful to go to cults and some desperate and dispirited ones completely estranged themselves from faith itself. Thus the new perspective created a serious flaw in the human understanding of the Divine. On the human-human relationship plane, people became more selfish and individualistic. Suspicion and hatred grow foster by day among human beings more than ever before. This subscribes to deterioration in interpersonal relations and causes the flattering of family value system. Due to the aberration in the family value system, families are separating. But children bear the brunt of this separation. The basic social system in the society is in jeopardy. Unrest and violence enter in the society. They further extend to terrorism and wars in the world. The fragmentation in the relationships damages peaceful co-existence in a society. Human relation to Mother Nature has also been disturbed. The greed of humans leads to the ruthless exploitation of Mother Earth. It has emerged into devastating level creating ecological crisis that challenges the very existence of the natural world order.

This situation challenges the society to develop a new value system; a bridge of divine and novel relationship that would bring a harmonious co-existence in this world. Several options may be available to overcome this disturbing situation. This researcher favors a biblical pattern of relationship of the bride and the bridegroom to fill in this gap, used by Jacob of Serugh. This imagery explains how the Bridegroom, Christ, brought peace and harmony in the world by means of His marriage to the earthly bride, the Church. Though his predecessors used this imagery to delineate a strong God-human relationship, Mar Jacob is the one who brought it into broader perspectives by the repeated use of this imagery to connect various episodes in the Bible. Mar Jacob lived in a hotpot of Christological controversies; but he chose a moderate path against the opposites. He gently taught his faith in a sublime manner. He was genuine, tolerant, and ecumenical in his dealings and therefore he is acceptable to all. However, the writings of Mar Jacob have not gained much scholarly attention and there is a great need to bring his wisdom before the light of the world. In this context a study on Mar Jacob's favorite theme "Church as the Bride of Christ" is worthy and relevant.

3. Scope and Limitations of the Study

This study intent to learn Mar Jacob of Serugh's teachings on the Divine Love and the salvific act of Jesus, the Bridegroom, in the 'bride-bridegroom' imagery where the Church is depicted as the new bride of the heavenly Bridegroom, portrayed in his select homilies. The study further explores the different aspects of the marriage imagery and its various implications including the relevance of this imagery in the ecclesiological, soteriological, spiritual, eschatological, ecumenical, anthropological, and social areas from the modern life situation. This study will also enquire into the effect of this imagery in the liturgy and ecclesiology of the West Syriac Church tradition and its importance in the current theological discussions. Since this imagery is not used to explain the divinity of Jesus Christ but to explain the relation between God and human beings, this would not be a Christological or doctrinal study of Mar Jacob. Around 760 homilies of Mar Jacob which have already been found and many of them are yet to be edited and published. It is beyond reach to evaluate all these writings and to discus on the various aspects of them. Hence, this study is concentrated on select homilies of Mar Jacob, in particular on the ecclesiological homilies. Since this study is particularly based on the writings of Mar Jacob this would not go deep into its biblical foundations.

4. Importance of the Study

The rich trail of Syriac theology was in oblivion till the late nineteenth century for various reasons. The new cultural exploration found these hidden treasures and initiated a new awakening in the study of Syriac writings. Jacob of Serugh with his commendable writings and theology hold a position, according to the Syriac scholars, next to Mar Ephrem. His homilies were tools for evangelization, worship, and teachings. An erudite study of his works would lead to new dimensions of their meaning.

Secondly, as mentioned above, the present world needs a holistic relation between God and human beings and between human beings and Mother Nature. Mar Jacob's interpretation of the love of God through the 'bride-bridegroom' imagery will help the world to reexamine its value systems in a new frame and in a holistic way. Such a study is very important in this postmodern world. In this sense, Mar Jacob's writings and his theology is a major area of discussion among the contemporary oriental theologians. Also, this study is important in two ways: (1) this work will enhance interest in the studies of the forgotten Syriac theology and the Church Fathers, (2) this would give a model for a holistic approach towards God-human-nature relationship and thereby open a chance to create a new vision of the world.

5. Previous Works

Paul Bedjan edited many of Mar Jacob's homilies and almost six of which deal directly about Church and its various imageries. A detailed study of this particular theme in the writings of Mar Jacob might not have been conducted in the past. But, Robert Murray's *Symbols of Church and the Kingdom*[8] is a beacon for many Syriac scholars, and the bride-bridegroom imagery is an important theme in this renowned work. Sebastian Brock conducted much studies particularly on Mar Jacob, as well as the Syriac theology as a whole, where the same theme is dealt with. Thomas Kollamparampil, Johns Abraham Konat, and James Puthuparampil are the Indian scholars who studied on Mar Jacob closely and the observations have been helpful in this study.

6. Hypothesis

The hypothesizes of this research are: (a) the ethical values that existed among the interrelationship (both horizontal and vertical) of God, Human, and mother-nature have been distorted on account of faithlessness and egocentrism of humans; (b) the bride and Bridegroom imagery is a judicious paradigm for recreating the distorted relationship in its original frame. The Bible states "Therefore a man leaves his father and mother and clings to his wife and they become one flesh" (Gen 2:24). This law implies the union of two bodies to become one 'in will and praxis'; (c) St. Paul compares the union between Christ, the Bridegroom, and the Church, the bride, with that of the husband-wife union in this world. Sacrificial love of Christ, the Bridegroom, and the unfailing love and loyalty of the bride, Church, just as is found in a true marriage union, are the adhesive that make this relation unbreakable and indissoluble; (d) a perfect and unbreakable bond is created through sacrificial love and loyalty in the union of man and woman; (e) this selfless love should not be contained within themselves but need to be extended beyond themselves to the human society at large for healthy co-existence. This is a great call for the people of God, the bride, to offer selfless love to bring peace and harmony in the world.

7. Method of the Study

The aim of this study is to find out Jacob's interpretation on the salvific act of Jesus Christ through the bride-bridegroom imagery and show how it would help in the modern world to solve its depravation in ethical values caused by the deterioration of relationships as explained above. The first aspect is to observe closely in the various homilies and systematically arrange them in the main chapters of this study. Many of his important terminologies will also be analyzed. Among the published homilies I have selected seven homilies which may be called ecclesiological homilies of Mar Jacob. Though this theme is

---

[8] See the bibliography, Murray, *Symbols of the Church and the Kingdom*.

present in almost all of his homilies, an extensive study shall be made only from his ecclesiological homilies and few other homilies which are mentioned in the study. Unless it is specifically mentioned all translations of the original texts are translated by the researcher only. Since his predecessors and successors used this imagery to explain the same theme the researcher will compare and analyze their interpretations with those of Mar Jacob. Therefore, it will be a critical and analytical study. On the other hand, unlike other critical studies this would not analyze literally the flaws and merits of the theme but examine how Mar Jacob finds this theme to explain the God-human relationship in a spiritual atmosphere.

The first chapter is a discussion on Mar Jacob's life, works, and his basic theological approach and insights. The second chapter discusses the ecclesiological homilies and his methodology. The third chapter describes the marriage imagery and its cultural and social backgrounds. The fourth chapter portrays how Mar Jacob has seen Jesus as the Bridegroom of the Church and His relation to the Synagogue or the nation. The fifth chapter discusses how the Church became the bride of the heavenly Bridegroom and how she differs from the old bride, the synagogue. Sixth chapter is a portrayal of Mar Jacob's eschatological vision. Finally, the seventh chapter discusses the relevance or application of the 'bride-bridegroom' imagery in the contemporary world for a more relevant ecclesial vision and guidance.

Chapter 1

Mar Jacob of Serugh
A Theological Investigation

Introduction

Mar Jacob of Serugh (AD 451-521) is one of the greatest Syriac poet theologians of all times. Scholars consider him second after Mar Ephrem (c373) and equal to Narsai (c502). While his predecessor Mar Ephrem was known as the "harp of the Holy Spirit" Mar Jacob was known as the "flute of the Holy Spirit and harp of the believing Church."[1] He is known for not his theological refutations and contending attitude but known for his voluminous spiritual exhortations and his ardent faith in God. He is one of the less Hellenized Syriac theologians of his times. The scriptural and typological characteristics of his writings are the perfect examples of his Semitic interpretation. He considered, like Paul the apostle, preaching of the Gospel as his duty and considered it a debt if he failed in the mission[2] (1 Cor 9:16). He had a special talent to interpret the scripture. B. Sony quotes a Syriac manuscript source which describes him: "The Holy Spirit revealed to him and explained all the secrets of the Holy Scriptures. This doctor became the vase of the Spirit and filled the Holy Church with his wisdom by commenting on the Sacred Scriptures."[3] The chronicle attributed to

---

[1] Wright, *A Short History of the Syriac Literature*, 67.

[2] Bedjan, *HS* V, 332.15; ET. "A Homily on Samson," *TV* 11(1992), *TV* 11(1992), 53.31.

[3] Sony, "La méthode exégétique de Jacques de Saroug," 67. The English translation is from McCarron, "An Epiphany of the Mystical Symbols," 57. McCarron gives the details of the source that it is found in Paris Syr. 177 Col, 147a- 148b and it is written by an anonymous author. Vööbus, also mentions this document; see Vööbus, *Handschriftliche Überlieferung*, 13–16.

Joshua the Stylite,[4] composed in Jacobs's own time describes Mar Jacob as a strong man of faith and consoler and an encouraging figure of his time against the persecution of Persian Sha Kawad. It says that:

> (People) prepared to flee westwards, but the respected Jacob, the *perideutes,* who composed *memre* on sections of the Scriptures and *sughyotho* and songs (*zimrotho*) on the time of the locusts, did not neglect his duty at that time. He wrote letters of exhortation to all the cities, encouraging people to trust in divine salvation, and not to flee.[5]

A Modern scholar called him a conservative in thoughts and practice.[6] But it would be apt to call him as an Orthodox teacher of his time. Unlike the modern scholarly approach to scriptural interpretation, he had no double standing or inconsistency of faith. Most of the modern scholars depend on their reason and empirical knowledge to interpret the scripture. However, the Church Fathers like Mar Jacob were not simply scholars but teachers of faith with staunch conviction. Their tool for explaining the mysteries of God was not reason but cognitive and intuitive understanding of the scripture. They interpreted the scripture more spiritually as against the literal interpretation of the modern scholarship. They had strong faith in God; as a result, they were very affirmative in their teaching. Therefore, one should understand their interpretation of the scripture from their point of view. Hence, it is better to call Mar Jacob positively as an 'orthodox' rather than with the negative connotation of 'conservative.' This chapter is a discussion on the life and works of Mar Jacob as well as his basic theological understanding.

1.1. Jacob of Serugh: Life and Works

More than two biographies are available on Mar Jacob of Serugh.[7] Wright argues that not less than three biographies are available: first one by his name sake Jacob of Edessa, second one is by an anonymous author, and the third one is a lengthy panegyric written by his disciple George.[8] Bickell says that the last one would be a composition by most probably George, the Bishop of Serugh, and a contemporary of Jacob of Edessa.[9] Most of these biographies are described by Vööbus, *Handschriftliche Überlieferung Der Memre-*

---

[4] Wright, *The Chronicle of Pseudo-Joshua the Stylite,* 63-64.

[5] Wright, *The Chronicle of Pseudo-Joshua the Stylite,* 63-64. Cited in, Brock, "Jacob's Forgotten *Sugitho,*" 39.

[6] McCarron, "An Epiphany of the Mystical Symbols," 58.

[7] Brock, "Jacob of Serugh: A Select Bibliographical Guide," 237-239.

[8] Wright, *A Short History of Syriac Literature*, 67.

[9] Bickell, *Bibliothek,* 198.

Dichtung Des Jaqob Von Serug I.[10] Kollamparampil argues that all these are not historically reliable. However, he agrees the historicity of Mar Jacob's studies at the school of Edessa between the years 466-473,[11] his appointment as *Chorepiscopo* during the year between 502-503,[12] his consecration as the bishop of Batnan in Serugh at the age of 68 in June 519 (830 Greek year),[13] and his death in the year 520/521.[14] A biography translated in Latin by Abbeloos[15] describes that his father was from Kurtam, on the Euphrates. Wright sites that his father was a priest of the village. And his parents were childless for many years.[16] By the intercession of Mari of Barhadat they got a son and his name was Jacob. None of the manuscripts offers his birth date. Hence, his date of birth is deduced from the date of his death and it is considered to be 451.[17] Wright gives the date of death as 29 November 521.[18] Abbeloos narrates a fascinating story about Mar Jacob: when he was three years old his parents brought him to the feast of Mar Moqim and the shrine was crowded with faithful people including many priests. At the time of epiclesis, during the Holy *Qurbono*, the child Jacob ran to the holy altar and at that time an angel of God descended and blessed him. Again the biography describes that, just like Ezekiel ate from the scroll, the child stretched his hands and took the cup and drank from it three times. And from that moment the Holy Spirit alighted on him and he started to make discourses, which was an abnormal thing. Another manuscript edited by Assemani also says fairly the same thing.[19] The above story looks like a fiction; sometimes there would be no facts behind this; but

---

[10] Brock, "Jacob of Serugh: A Select Bibliographical Guide," 237-239.

[11] Kollamparampil, *Salvation in Christ,* 25-26; Cf. Olinder, *Ep* XIV 58-61. Kollamparampil gives other references of: *Histore nestorienne*, 121; Barhadbsabba Arbaia, *L'histore ecclesiastique,* 612.

[12] Kollamparampil, *Salvation in Christ,* 25-26; Cf. Olinder, *Ep*, XV 62-63; Kollamparampil gives references of: *Chronicon Pseudo-Dionasianum,* I syr. 280-281, tr. 206-207; *Chroniqe de Michel,* t. IV, 268-269, tr. T. II, 261-262; Barhebraeus, *Chronicon ecclesiasticum,* t. I col 189-192.

[13] Cf. Assemani, *BO*, Vol. I, 286-289; Abbeloos, *De Vita et scriptis,* 90.

[14] Kollamparampil, *Salvation in Christ,* 25-26.

[15] Abbeloos, *De Vita et Scriptis*, 86-104.

[16] Wright, *A Short History of Syriac Literature*, 68; cf. Kollamparampil, *Salvation in Christ*, 27.

[17] Kollamparampil, *Salvation in Christ,* 27; The manuscript sources give the date of his death varyingly. Yet researchers came to a conclusion as the year 833 (Greek year) corresponding to 521. As Jacob died at the age of 71 his birth might probably be in the year 451. See more on Kollamparampil, *Salvation in Christ*, 26.

[18] Wright, *A Short History of Syriac Literature*, 68. The church calendar uses in Malankara Orthodox Church reminds his feast day as November 29.

[19] Assemani, *Bibliotheca Orinetalis* I, 206-209 (I have no acces to this one but I quoted from the translation by Brock). Brock, "Jacob of Serugh: A Select Bibliographical Guide," 238.

these types of narration was common among the Syriac hagiography of the time to elevate a person's holiness.[20]

Assemani's translation portrays that Mar Jacob started writing *memre* at the age of 22. It says, once the bishops heard about this prodigy they summoned him and asked him to utter a *memre* on the vision of Ezekiel. He began to sing "O Exalted One who is seated upon the Chariot of the Heavenly Beings…"[21] and by seeing this they accepted his charisma. Abbeloos' translation numbered his *memre* as 763 and says that he is equivalent to fifty prophets.[22] His prose writings will not come to level of his *memre*. Olinder published most of his letters.[23] A liturgy is ascribed to him, an order of baptism, and many other prose and poetical writings could be found in his name.[24] Bar Hebraeus says that he appointed seventy amanuenses to copy his 760 metrical homilies.[25] Jacob of Edessa says that they were 763, among which that on the Chariot of Ezekiel was the first one, and that on Mary and Golgotha is the last, which he left unfinished.[26] However, many of them were destroyed or not edited yet, but Paul Bedjan edited and published around 200 homilies.[27] Though most of these homilies are written by Mar Jacob all of them may not be his own. Some of them may be written by later authors and attributed to him or compilation of his own works. Many scholars support this argument.[28]

1.2. Edessa at the Time of Mar Jacob

The life situation of a person will reflect her/his physical and mental factors. Mar Jacob spent most of his life time in modern Urfa, Syriac Urhay, and ancient Adme, on the Balikh River, northwest of Harran which is in southeastern Turkey today.[29] At his time this was a disturbed area, both politically and

[20] For example the martyrdom of Mar Kuriakose and his mother Yulithy says that Mar Kuriakose, a boy, at the age of three and half encouraged his mother to receive martyrdom (Voragine, *The Golden Lengend*, 323-324). Another example is Mar Jacob's writings on "On the Sleepers of Ephesus," which narrates about children who woke into life after many centuries sleep (Brock, "On the Sleepers of Ephesus").

[21] Brock, "Jacob of Serugh: A Select Bibliographical Guide," 238.

[22] Brock, "Jacob of Serugh: A Select Bibliographical Guide," 237.

[23] Olinder, *Ep*, 1952. Please see in the bibliography

[24] See a detailed description on them in, Wright, *A Short History of Syriac Literature*, 68-72.

[25] Wright, *A Short History of Syriac Literature*, 70.

[26] Abbeloos, *De Vita.* 312; cited, Wright, *A Short History of Syriac Literature*, 70.

[27] Bedjan, *HS* 5 Vols. Please see in the bibliography

[28] See more in Konat, "A Metrical Homily of Jacob of Serugh on the Mysteries, Types and Figures of Christ: Authentic or Compilation, 71.

[29] For more information on the early developments and struggles of Edessa and Persian Christianity and its background see: Baumer, *The Church of the East*, 1-30.

religiously.[30] Politically Edessa was a buffer zone between Persia and Rome where war occurred constantly between these rival Empires.[31] Until 213 AD the city was under various rulers but since then it came under the Roman rule. It is believed that Christianity spread out in Mesopotamia through Edessa.[32] During the 3rd and 4th centuries many heretics like Bardisan, Marcion, and Mani interrupted Christianity.[33] The fifth and sixth centuries witnessed the fierce fight between Nestorians and non-Chalcedonians.[34] Nestorius studied in the Antiochene School under Theodore of Mopsuestia. When Sisinnius of Constantinople died on 24 Dec 427 (AD), by the personal interest of Emperor Theodosius, Nestorius became the bishop of Constantinople. In AD 428 he started teaching that Mary as mother of Christ (Christotokos) and not mother of God (Theotokos). Cyril of Alexandria fought against this heresy and the council of Ephesus condemned him. Then Nestorius was exiled to Persian Syria.[35] Nestorians made a rapid growth in the Eastern part of Syria.[36] Following Cyril, in Syria, Mar Jacob and others contended against Nestorianism. In AD 489 emperor Zeno closed the school of Edessa accusing of Nestorianism.

The council of Chalcedon made another unpleasant situation in this area. The fight between the Chalcedonians and the non-Chalcedonians not only affected the theological and the political milieu of the Roman Empire but also the Edessan Mesopotamia, outside the Roman Empire. The after-effect of this fight has percolated even in the translation of the Bible. Wright says that Philoxenus of Mabbug revised the Peshitta version because of dissatisfaction and resentment.[37] In Syria, under Emperor Justin and his follower Justinian, the persecution of the Monophysites turned violent during the years 518-521.[38] Edessa was in total unrest both theologically and politically in Mar Jacob's time. Schisms and heresies inflamed the atmosphere of Persia, especially in Edessa because it was the center of Christianity in Persia. Being an orthodox teacher Mar Jacob tried to teach the right faith, but unlike Mar Ephrem, Severius of Antioch and Philoxenus of Mabbug, he was not a violent attacker against the heterodoxy.

[30] Baumer, *The Church of the East,* 53.

[31] Moffet, *A History of Christianity in Asia* I, 6, 46.

[32] Baumer, *The Church of the East,* 11-17.

[33] Baumer, *The Church of the East,* 16.

[34] Baumer, *The Church of the East,* 14.

[35] Baumer, *The Church of the East,* 49.

[36] Wright, *A Short History of Syriac Literature*, 65.

[37] Wright, *A Short History of Syriac Literature*, 13-14.

[38] Wright, *A Short History of Syriac Literature*, 66.

1.3. Christological Controversy at the Time of Mar Jacob

Christological controversy that aroused with the council of Ephesus (AD 431) in the Roman Empire translated into the Persian Empire due to the exile of Nestorius to Pershia. Therefore, Syrian Mesopotamia was also became a place of controversy. In the Roman Empire Antiochenes, who supported Nestorius, and the Alexandrians, who supported Cyril, fought against each other. The same was the situation in the Persian Empire where a split could be traced in the school of Edessa also.[39] The Nestorian controversy led the way to the Eutycan controversy. In this controversy Dioscoros was the leader of Alexandrian school and Flavian was the leader of the Antiochene School. The Antiochenes accused that, Eutycus, an Alexandrian monk, taught that Christ has only one nature. But his advocates say that he actually taught the Cyrillian formula of "one Incarnated nature of God the Word."[40] Cyril taught that the Word was united to flesh unconfusedly and hypostatically.[41] When he emphasized the humanity of Jesus Christ the Antiochene party found Docetism in his teaching.[42] The Eutychan schism fired the way to the Chalcedonian council and the heresy over the nature of Christ. Mar Jacob was born into this religious turmoil.

1.4. Mar Jacob's Influence in the Liturgical Theology of the West Syriac Church

Mar Jacob is one of the most influential persons in the West Syriac liturgical tradition. The Church considers him along with Ephrem, Isaac, Balai, and Barsauma as *malphono* (teacher) of the Church.[43] Most of the canonical offices and other liturgical rites of the Malankara Orthodox Syrian Church, which follows the liturgy and theology of the Syriac Orthodox Church, use his *bo'uto*.[44] This underlines his prominence in the liturgical life of the Church. (To find out these *bo'ute* from his homilies is a laborious task and it is not aimed at in this work.) Further the Church uses an anaphora and an order of baptism,[45] which are ascribed in his name. Though the West Syriac liturgical rites are formed out of a common liturgical and theological collection, many of his literal expressions of theology and typological interpretations are used in the various compositions of its liturgical rites. It is a very tedious task to

---

[39] Kollamparampil, *Salvation in Christ*, 15.

[40] Samuel, *The Council of Chalcedon Re-examined*, 14, 236-244.

[41] Jurgens, *The Faith of the Early Fathers* III, 228.

[42] Frances, *From Nicaea to Chalcedon*, 261.

[43] *Vishuddha Qurbanakramam*, 44.

[44] The same could be seen in all West Syriac rites in India.

[45] Brock by interpreting the act of epiclesis in the Antiochene baptismal rites says that the epiclesis of Philoxenus' baptismal rite is formed by somebody who closely related to Mar Jacob. See, Brock, "The Epiklesis in the Antiochene Baptismal Ordines," 211.

trace all such theological interpretations in the West Syriac liturgical rites and it does not fall in this work. Yet, this part is small discussion in this regard.

The long prayer, called *sedro*, which is used in the West Syriac liturgical prayers, most often contains theological expressions of either Mar Ephrem or Mar Jacob. One of the *sedre* for Nativity starts like this:

> Praise to the God-child who has no beginning or end born as a man to the virgin who has beginning; the Lord of the shining stars who dawned from the womb and enlightened whole creation by his rays; since he raises children in the womb became a child in the womb; the one who had been before the beginning of the world, in the fullness of time, born as the son of David from the daughter of David; for a particular time he was showed as a child who was older than generations and clans; the one who sends rain and snow to the earth sucked milk from the daughter of man; …[46]

Almost the same wordings could be seen in Mar Jacob's homily on Nativity.[47] Moreover, many other phrases and usages which are of Mar Jacob is described in the nativity rite; for example: when he was glorified in the eternal holy place with the Father and the Holy Spirit, entered and dwelt in the holy womb of virgin; though, in nature, being rich by his humility he was wrapped in swaddling cloth; sucked milk from the breast of a human lady;[48] today God appeared in the world and enlightened the world;[49] the ancient of the days became a baby etc.[50]

His Homily *on Communion of Holy Mysteries* witnesses several phrases which are found in the present West Syriac Eucharistic order; see an example:

> All gathering along with the priest will pray to the Father
> to send His Son to descend and dwell upon the offering.
> And the Holy Spirit with his power hovers over the bread and wine and
> sanctify it and make his body and blood.[51]

This phrase is commonly found in all anaphoros. The anaphora of Mar Jacob says: "May the Holy Spirit indwells on this bread and makes it the

---

[46] *Promiyon* I, 143.

[47] Bedjan, *SMS*, 741.8ff; ET. *FH* I, 62.449ff.

[48] Bedjan, *SMS*, 775.9-10; ET. *FH* II, 96.9-10.

[49] Bedjan, *SMS*, 777.13-16; ET. *FH* II, 97.53-54.

[50] Bedjan, *SMS*, 791.14; ET. *FH* III, 111.23. The order of Nativity describes; "… the One who born from the daughter of David as a son of David; the One who had been before the worlds and creations; aged one than generations and clans and appeared for a particular time…" (*Promiyon* I, 143).

[51] Bedjan, *HS* III, 657.6-9. This would be seen in the post epiclesis sanctus of the West Syriac anaphora. (*Ktobo d-Takso d-Anoporo*, 162-163). A study on Mar Jacob and Syriac anaphora in Harak, "The Syriac Orthodox Celebration of the Eucharist in the Light of Jacob of Serugh's *Memro* 95," 91-113.

body of Christ. May the Holy Spirit indwells in this cup and makes this as the blood of Christ our Savior."[52] One of the hymns sung before starting the Holy *Qurbono* publically says about the offerings of Abel, Noah, and Abraham;[53] Mar Jacob in his homily *on the Reposed* says the same about the offerings of the above mentioned righteous men and finally prays to God to receive the oblations, commemorations, and prayers of sinners:

> Abel offered the firstlings of his flock and chief fatlings,
> and righteous Noah sacrificed the clean beasts of those that were left.
> Abraham gave three three-yearlings in the sacrifices he sent up,
> and unto the Godhead Jacob tithed all that he possessed…
> in sacrifice, vows, tithes and precious gifts,
> the just made their offerings to God.
> But today it hath fallen to thee to offer a loaf…
> He that has divine love in his soul
> shows his love for him after he is dead, and forgets him not. With
> commemorations, oblations, and prayers,
> he brings the remembrance of him before God in the holy temple.[54]

Through these lines Mar Jacob speaks about the mercy of God who absolves the sins of His flock in reciprocation for their pure sacrifice and prayers. The passage describes the story of those who received forgiveness and blessings through their oblations and prayers and the present sinful state of humankind. In it he asks, even though they are in sinfulness, if they return from their sinfulness and offer prayers for forgiveness and offer pure sacrifice, forgive them just as you received the sacrifices of Abel, Noah, Abraham, Jacob, and others and bless them.

The 'Church from the nations' is a commonly used phrase of Mar Jacob;[55] same could be seen in the West Syriac rites very often.

> Glory be to the Heavenly Bridegroom, who has chosen the daughter of the gentiles as a bride for Himself and has, by His victorious blood, cleansed her from all sins and iniquities, and has betrothed Himself to Her and has redeemed Her from the slavery of Satan and has set Her free from all Her debts and sins."[56]

---

[52] *Ktobo d-Takso d-Anoporo*, 106.

[53] God who dids't receive the lamb
blameless Abel brought.
Who the gift of Noah took,
Abraham's sacrifice;
See our fast and hear our prayers
answer by thy grace our please (*Vishuddah Qurbana Kramam*, 168).

[54] Bedjan, *HS* I, 541.18-543.21; ET. "On the Reposed," *TV* 5(1990), 46.127-48.164.

[55] Infra 5.3.9.

[56] *Koodasha Kramangal*, 62; cf. *Vishuddha Qurbanakramam*, 105.

Mar Jacob always praises the Son of God for His sacrifice for the humanity and His saving activity through the sacrifice of His own blood. "This Church, that I bought with all Mine own Precious Blood, thou keep safe."[57] Again, "You gave her the pure gift of your victorious body and blood which is your ring, …"[58] In the wedding rite the Church sings:

> With the ring the Holy Church was married to Messiah.
> She received His holy body and His holy blood.[59]
> Messiah by dispensing ring His Church betrothed
> sacred, most, His body and blood she receiveth.
> Tamar, truly was rescued from death by the ring
> we may so receive remission of debts and sins.[60]

> You gave her the pure gift of your victorious body and blood which is your ring, and have made her rejoice and shine in your glorious light; and giving her the divine gift of your ring, have made her abide with You forever.[61]

All these passages emphasize the sacrificial aspect of Jesus Christ. Through His sacrifice He saved the descendants of Adam from sin and death and gave life and the 'robe of glory.' Moreover, through His death Christ presented His body and blood as pledge which saves men from the eternal punishment. See another passage from a *sedro* which shows Mar Jacob's influence in the West Syriac liturgy:

> Welcome to the new day that by its authority who removed old darkness. Welcome the first day which enlightened and adorned the two worlds. Welcome the dawn which dawned and rejoiced the universe. Welcome the flower of resurrection which shattered the death, the murderer of Adam. Welcome the treasure house which gathers together all nations to the joy and happiness. Welcome the pure and mighty Sunday which resolved the iniquity of Friday… Welcome the resplendent day star of righteousness which shone us by lifting us from the darkness of sin. Welcome the comfort of the mournful and joy of the sad.[62]

The above passage is taken from the *sedro* of Sunday of Resurrection. The entire *sedro* is almost a replica of Mar Jacob's prose homily on *Sunday of Resurrection*.[63] Sebastian Brock found a *Madrošo* "On the Soul" by Mar Jacob

---

[57] *Koodasha Kramangal*, 68. See Mar Jacob's interpretation on this infra 4.3.13.

[58] *Koodasha Kramangal*, 66. Bedjan, *HS* II, 287-288, Brock, "The Wedding Feast of Blood on Golgotha…," 587-588; cf. Brock, "Mysteries in the Hidden Side of Christ," 466-467.

[59] *Koodasha Kramangal*, 60.

[60] *Koodasha Kramangal*, 60.

[61] *Koodasha Kramangal*, 66.

[62] *Promiyon* I, 12.

[63] Rilliet, *SHF* VI, 630.9ff; ET. *FH* XV, 320.1ff.

in both Pampakuda and Mosul *Penkitos* and gives a very good translation in an article titled *A Prayer Song by St. Jacob of Serugh Recovered*.[64] He found that both *penkitos* are abbreviations of the original manuscript found in the British Library (Add. 14592) which is dated as early as sixth century.[65] Thus, in this way it could prove that Mar Jacob influenced the liturgical theology of the West Syriac Church to a great extent.

1.5. Theology of Mar Jacob

Mar Jacob will be known for four elements of his theologizing: as a Spiritual Theologian, a Christo-centric theologian, a Scripture based theologian, and as a typological exegete. First of all, his exhortations are aimed at the spiritual nourishment of his people. Though refutations against the heresies can be seen in his homilies, he had written most of them not solely for refutation, but to educate his people the right faith. Therefore, by interpreting the true faith he is a prophet and teacher of Orthodoxy. He was not courteous like Aphrahat against the heretics or a sharp opponent like Ephrem. But by his systematic approach on biblical topics and apostolic teaching he taught the true faith to his Church; in this way he was an apologist against the heretics and a defender of the faith. He saw everything in a spiritual way and travelled through the road of unconditional faith. His faith vision guided him more than reasoning and empirical knowledge in evaluating the mysteries of God. In his homily *On Faith* he emphatically discusses this:

> I wandered by scrutinizing you and I did not find you among the wise
> I took refuge in faith and I found out you.[66]
> I set out to search you with the wise and I stumbled
> I turned to walk with ignorant without stumbling.[67]
> I know him, he is ever God of all
> without search I believe him that he is the Son of God.[68]

These are some of the examples of his faith over reason. Therefore, he uses the term *rozo* (mystery) to explain the exalted mysteries of God. Also, in his homilies, he often describes the role of spiritual beings to explain the same. He believed in the unworthiness of human nature in this regard. He says, "no one is able to speak of God; even the wisest man, who tries to enquire about

[64] Brock, "A Prayer Song by St. Jacob of Serugh Recovered," 29-37. The abbreviated form of the *madrošo* is available in Mosul *Penkitho* Vol. IV, 658-659 attributed in the name of Mar Ephrem and in Pampakuda *Penkitho* Vol. II, 362-363.

[65] Brock, "A Prayer Song by St. Jacob of Serugh Recovered," 30.

[66] Bedjan, *HS* III, 587.9-10.

[67] Bedjan, *HS* III, 587.11-12.

[68] Bedjan, *HS* III, 630.20-631.1.

God, would not know what he is searching for."[69] A person who tries to learn of the Divine is like a swimmer who swims in the vast sea without slightest idea of how long he should swim to reach shore. Neither silence, nor voice, or discourse contains Him.[70] Therefore, he is a spiritual theologian, who finds the inner meaning of the Word of God.

Secondly, the locus of his theological interpretation is the life of Jesus Christ and His redemptive works. Though he upholds the faith in the Holy Trinity, Christ is the focal point. He wanted to speak and teach about the salvific act of the Father through the life of Jesus Christ in this world. Because He is the One who made reconciliation between the heaven and the earth by His atoning sacrifice.[71] According to Mar Jacob, in both Testaments Christ is the central figure; every word and incident of the Old Testament says about Him. To him the Old and New Testaments are the two arms that stretched out to the two sides on the cross.[72]

Thirdly, unlike his Greek and some Syriac contemporary theologians, who use philosophy to explain the scripture, Mar Jacob's theology is based mainly on the Scripture. Scripture is the divine revelation of the Word of God. Without the revelation nobody can learn about God; if God did not Incarnate no one could interpret Him.[73] Therefore, he saw the Scripture as the foundation and mirror of faith. Each and every verse of his homilies is based on the scriptural references.

Finally, his biblical interpretations are mainly typological. He believed that typology is an appropriate vehicle to interpret the mysteries of God. He sees the Old Testament as the shadow of the New Testament. According to him each and every incident and each and every verse of the Old Testament speaks about Jesus and His works.[74] He sees the incidents and persons of the Old Testament prefigure the incidents in the life of Jesus Christ, hence, he taught his Church accordingly. Modern authors are of the opinion that Mar Jacob and Mar Ephrem believed that theological interpretation could be possible through the Incarnated Jesus, the scripture, as well as nature. He says, both the Scripture and nature are revelations of God.[75]

---

[69] Bedjan, *SMS*, 792.8-793.2; ET. *FH* III, 112.39-113.54.

[70] Bedjan, *SMS,* 792.8-9; ET. *FH* III, 112.39-40.

[71] Bedjan, *SMS*, 789.8-9; ET. *FH* II, 107.295-296.

[72] Bedjan, *HS* II, 362.11-12; ET. *FH* VIII, 219.317-318.

[73] Bedjan, *SMS,* 790.11-12; ET. *FH* III, 111.11-12.

[74] Infra. 2.2.7.

[75] Shemunkasho, "Jacob of Serugh and His Influence on John of Dara", 163; cf. Griffith, *Faith Adoring Mystery*, 19-20.

He believed in the one Holy Trinity and its perfect union,[76] Incarnation of Jesus Christ, the virgin birth, atoning sacrifice, death, resurrection, and ascension, the Second Coming, procession of the Holy Spirit, in the holy Church, in the apostolic succession, holy priesthood, sacraments, communion of saints, etc. He believed in the exalted power and authority of God. He accepted the incomprehensibility of the Divine by the meager knowledge of human being. He believed in the divine creation of the universe and everything in it including the creation of human beings. He found that God created man out of His love. God descended to earth to create man and to save him from eternal damnation.

1.6. Christology

Christology was an important matter of controversy in the early Church, especially between the Antiochene and the Alexandrian theological schools in the Roman Empire. But in the Persian Empire, following the above mentioned schools, there were two streams of teachings, whose medium of liturgy and teaching was Syriac, and engaged in raging debates regarding the nature of Christ. Controversies over interpreting Christ were the main reason behind almost all the divisions in the early Church. The Church Fathers considered themselves as the defenders of the true faith. In the West Syriac tradition, Severius of Antioch and Philoxenus of Mabbug were the shining stars in the debates on theological issues. But at the same time the teachers like Ephrem, Jacob of Serugh, Balai, Isaac of Antioch, Jacob of Edessa played significant role to teach the right faith of the Church.

Until the recent past Mar Jacob's position in the Christological controversies were not defined well; but now-a-days it is confirmed that he stood with the non-Chalcedonian party.[77] Though Mar Jacob had studied in the school of Edessa he never followed the Nestorian or Antiochene Christologies. According to B. Sony Mar Jacob's theological position is to be ascertained from his spiritual exegesis, which is Alexandrian in nature.[78] He further says that Mar Jacob combined the Alexandrian tradition with the Ephremean tradition. The following is a discussion about Mar Jacob's part in the Christological controversies and how he fought against the heresies.

1.6.1. Mar Jacob against Heresies

The fathers, through their homilies, not only taught the true faith but also they engaged in an intellectual war against the heretics and schismatics. Mar Jacob

[76] Bedjan, *HS* II, 232.8-9; Bedjan, *HS* I, 182.18-22; ET. *FH* VI, 177.315-319.

[77] Konat, "Christological Insights in Jacob of Serugh's Typology," 47. See the footnote 7 in the same article for more discussion.

[78] Sony, "La Methode exegetique de Jacquesde Saroug," 90.

also used to confront heresies like Docetism,[79] Arianism,[80] Marcionism,[81] etc. The following is a brief study on Mar Jacob's teachings against the heresies.

1.6.1.1. Against Jews

Mar Jacob wrote homilies against Jews and systematically challenged their arguments against the divinity of Christ. Murray says that the Syriac fathers, especially, Aphrahat and Ephrem, use this theme to express their anti-Jewish bitterness.[82] Benin comments that Aphrahat is courteous and Ephrem is castigating the Jews but Jacob of Serugh slowly and methodologically sets up his Jewish straw men in order to knock them down all the more efficiently.

> He is neither the courteous disputant nor the vehement antagonist; he is the professional polemicist, he takes every positive attitude towards the Law, calling it a medicinal herb, a nursemaid, a light in the world; for him the problem is the Jews who refuse to let go. They are the children who never grew up.[83]

The orthodox Jews always questioned the divinity of Jesus Christ. They taught that He is not the Messiah and He is only Jesus, the son of Joseph and Mary (Mt 13:55-56; Mk 6:3). But, against this, Mar Jacob taught that Jesus is the Messiah who was prophesied about.[84] Therefore, he wrote commentaries against Jews. He asks them:

> O Jew, whom are you looking for to come the earth?
> for none other will come again because there is none, keep yourself silent.
> The Father had a single (Son) and He sent Him as He promised …
> and because it (prophecy) saw that the Son had come, behold, it is silent.[85]

St. Paul condemns Jews and the Greeks who use wisdom and reason to inquire the divinity of Jesus Christ. He says "For Jews demand a signs and Greek desire wisdom, but we proclaim Christ crucified" (1 Cor 1:22). Mar Jacob also condemns the reason seekers regarding the Divine origin and the Virgin birth of Jesus Christ. He says that nobody knows other than the Father,

---

79 Bedjan, *HS* II, 361.1; ET. *FH* VIII, 218.286.

80 Rilliet, *SHF* II, 564.19-566.17; ET. *FH* VII, 199.34-200.35; Bedjan, *HS* II, 374.5-6; ET. *FH* VIII, 229.565-57.

81 Bedjan, *HS* II, 364.13-14; ET. *FH* VIII, 221.361-362.

82 Murray, *Symbols of Church and Kingdom,* 41.

83 Benin, "Commands, Covenants and the Jews," 145.

84 Bedjan, *SMS,* 688.2-15; ET. Puthuparampil, "Homily on the Perpetual Virginity of Mary," in *Mariological Thought of Mar Jacob of Serugh,* iii.53-66.

85 Bedjan, *SMS,* 798.18-799.2; ET. *FH* III, 119.171-176. See another good example in which Mar Jacob wrote against Jews who says that Jesus was not from the Father. Bedjan, *SMS,* 688.2-15; ET. Puthuparampil, "Homily on the Perpetual Virginity of Mary," in *Mariological Thoughts in Mar Jacob of Serugh,* iii.53-66.

even the watchers or seraphs cannot be inquired (*meṣ'n*).[86] He explains: The first birth of the Son is from eternity and it is hidden from the fiery ones, cherubs, etc.[87] Investigators cannot find the nature of the Divine One.[88] Regarding the divinity of Jesus Christ Mar Jacob writes:

> My Lord is concealed (*kso*) from all and His place is hidden (*gnaz*) and His name is secret (*steero*).
> He is exalted above us and He is concealed from you and hidden from all.
> He is distant with His Father, and He dwells with you, and how can you investigate?
> I have not seen Him, but to you who are His mother, behold He will be made manifest.
> He is concealed from our race and how I should speak of him, I do not know.
> His voice is heard by me but as for His appearance, I am not capable of seeing it.[89]
> He dwelt in the pure woman while remaining glorious in the bosom of His Father
> He shone forth in the young girl but his light was bright over the chariot.
> In the womb is His conception but wings of the watchers are set on fire from Him.
> He is totally in Mary and He is fully in His Father and He is in all (*bmaryam kooleh wbabooh kooleh wabkul aetavh*).
> He stirs (*mze'*)the Cherubs, He is clothed (*aṭep*) with the members (of body), He is found with all.[90]

These lines affirm the hidden as well as the exalted nature of Jesus Christ. Mar Jacob answers how He acts as God and a man at the same time. The divine things are beyond our imagination. Nobody can comprehend Him with his/her reason. There were many in Mar Jacob's time who did not believe in the Virgin Birth and Divinity of Jesus Christ. Therefore, he frequently asserts the true faith throughout his discourses. Often he condemned the unbelievers, who suspected on the Divinity of Jesus. When the Jews argued against the Virgin Birth of Jesus Christ he was a confessor against them and argued for the Virgin Birth of Jesus Christ.[91] He says both scripture and nature proclaims testimony:

> Who was united (*zuog*) to the virgin earth that gave birth to Adam
> and even Adam, with whom was he joined (*nqpo*) for the birth of Eve?
> Who was united (*zuog*) (in marriage) with tree when it gave birth to the lamb

[86] Bedjan, *SMS* 723.12; ET. *FH* I, 45.71.

[87] Bedjan, *SMS*, 723.4-724.10; ET. *FH* I, 44.63-45.90.

[88] Bedjan, *SMS*, 724.7-8; *SMS*, 793.3-4; ET. *FH* I, 45.87-88; *FH* III, 113.55-56.

[89] Bedjan, *SMS*, 729.19-730.4; ET. *FH* I, 51.211-216.

[90] Bedjan, *SMS*, 740.14-19; ET. *FH* I, 61.433-438.

[91] Bedjan, *SMS*, 784.19-20, 788.6; ET. *FH* II, 103.207-208, 106.274.

or who knew (the rock when it gave birth to rivers?
By what spirit did the staff sprout forth in an unusual manner
or by what marital union did a lifeless jawbone bring out water?
In these wombs who has generated these offsprings,
for, is this alone, that which happened in me, untrue?[92]

All these unnatural incidents are narrated in the scripture and the Jews believed in them but they are reluctant to accept the unnatural birth of Jesus Christ. He argues that if earth can give birth to Adam, a virgin can give birth to a baby; if Adam without intercourse with a woman could produce Eve, a virgin could conceive; if a tree can give a lamb as a fruit, or rock could give water or dry stick could blossom, a virgin could give birth to a child. He says all these examples support the Virgin Birth of Jesus Christ. See another example where Mary requests Simeon to be an advocate of the divine birth of her child, Jesus.

It is fair for you to be an advocate among the unbelievers.
Raise your voice, let all hear what you are saying.
Raise your voice, O aged one, as a trumpet
so that the world may learn that the Fruit which I have given birth to is the Lord of the times.
O aged one, call out and give witness to the Son who is from eternity,
because I had been reckoned as an adulteress on account of Him.
Speak, Simeon, to the Jews and do not be afraid;
and reprove them, as how much they have accused me on account of your Lord.
Speak here at length, without ceasing,
so that the whole earth may receive proclamation from you.
Be moved and say everything public about the child,
so that the universe shall perceive who He is and whose Son I carry.
Be a herald among the unbelievers and reprove them,
because I am falsely accused at the hidden birth (*yeldeh kesio*) of Son of God.[93]

Here, Mary asks Simeon to proclaim his divine knowledge about the Virgin Birth and refute the Jews who doubt the divinity of Jesus Christ. Through these kinds of interpretations Mar Jacob becomes the advocate of the right faith and condemns the Jews who argue that Jesus Christ is not true God of true God.

1.6.1.2. Against Arianism

Arianism was a 4th century Christian heresy promulgated by Arius denying the divinity of the Son of God. He taught that the Son does not have the same

[92] Bedjan, *SMS*, 750.12-19; ET. *FH* I, 70.641-71.648.

[93] Bedjan, *HS* V, 461.20-462.10; ET. *FH* V, 154.291-306.

divine status of the Father. And there was a time when the Son was not there.[94] But the Church condemned his teachings in the council of Nicaea in AD 325. The Church taught that the Son has the same divinity of the Father and the Son was eternally born to the Father. When the Father created the world the Son was with Him. Mar Jacob taught the same in his homilies. He tried to display the equality of Son of God with the Father. Against Arianism he taught that "there was no (time) when the Father is without you (Son) (*lo it a'mt 'itawh abo men bel'odayk*)."[95] Again, "I know He is ever God and believe without a search that He is the Son of God."[96] He is equal (*šwo*) to His Father.[97] The Father-Son relationship is perfect. When the Son became man His divinity was not damaged. When He was fashioned in the womb of Mary He was with His Father.[98] He was perfect before and after His descent and the Father had the confidence to acknowledge His Son.[99] Through the repeated use of Son's Lordship,[100] divinity, and co-eternity[101] with the Father in creation Mar Jacob preached Orthodox theology and wants to affirm Christ's equality with the Father and Holy Spirit. When he explains the glory of the Son on the occasion of His transfiguration, Mar Jacob says that the reason for the display of the glory of the Son is that the Father wants to prove that the Son is equal to Him.[102] Regarding the birth of Christ he states that He was there with the Father beyond the eternity:

> When and where is His history capable of explanation?
> for speech has no place to speak about His manifestation.
> Beyond the ages, beyond bounds and times,
> beyond distances, beyond the compass of all created things,
> beyond beginning of all creation, the Father begot Him.[103]
> Having been born without beginning, He was hidden in His Father,
> And in these last times He came openly and was not received.[104]

---

[94] Berkouwer, *Studies in Dogmatics: The Person of Christ*, 60.

[95] Bedjan, *HS* V, 455.13; ET. *FH* V, 148.165.

[96] Bedjan, *HS* III, 630.20-631.1.

[97] Bedjan, *HS* V, 460.15; ET. *FH* V, 153.268.

[98] Bedjan, *SMS*, 733.21; ET. *FH*, 55.295.

[99] Bedjan, *HS* I, 191.15; ET. *FH* VI, 185.496.

[100] Bedjan, *HS* V, 450.1; ET. *FH* V, 143.48.

[101] Bedjan, *HS* V, 448.11-14; ET. *FH* V, 141.13-16.

[102] Bedjan, *HS* II, 374.1-6; ET. *FH* VIII, 229.561-564.

[103] Bedjan, *HS* III, 321.34; ET. "Why our Lord Abode upon the Earth," *TV* 4 (1990), 38.29-33.

[104] Bedjan, *HS* III, 321.7-8; ET. "Why Our Lord Abode upon the Earth," *TV* 4 (1990), 37.7-8.

In the homily on the *Baptism of our Redeemer* Mar Jacob points out that the Holy Spirit manifested in the form of a dove is not to perfect the Son but to bear witness with the Father. The Spirit descended and rested upon Him in a holy manner not because holiness was insufficient in Him, and it had to be made perfect in Him…The Father and the Spirit together bore witness to the Only Begotten so that legally they might give what is due to the same True God.[105] Again he affirms the equality of the Father and the Son:

> The disciples saw that all that the Father has, the Son too has:
> power and glory, and the great light, as His Father.[106]

Thus all these examples show Mar Jacob's defense against the Arianism and taught that Jesus is the Son of God and He has no deficiency in His divinity and He is co-eternal with the Father. Everything was made by and through Him.[107]

1.6.1.3. Against Nestorianism

Nestorius who followed the Antiochene theology taught that Mary is only the mother of Christ (*Christotokos*) and not the mother of God (*Theotokos*); therefore, he denied the Alexandrian Logos-Sarx Christology.[108] But the council of Ephesus (431 AD) under the leadership of Cyril of Alexandria condemned Nestorius and his teachings.[109] Mar Jacob being a follower of the Alexandrian school was against the teachings of Nestorius and taught that Jesus Christ is true God and true human. Moreover, he emphasized the divinity of Jesus Christ; therefore, he often called the virgin as the mother of God (*yoldat aloho*). He used to teach his Church that the child born in the womb of Mary is the Son of God.[110] It is noteworthy that, in the words of Jansma, the only person against whom Mar Jacob repeatedly spoke was Nestorius.[111] In a homily *On the Perpetual Virginity of Mary*, Mar Jacob says:

> Mary is calumniated by those who are far and near,
> and her homily is swallowed up by the Jews and pagans.
> The foreigners as well as the familiar ones talk foolishly about her
> and friends and adversaries speak about her according to their pleasure.

---

[105] Bedjan, *HS* I, 186.9-14; ET. *FH* VI, 180.389-181.396.

[106] Bedjan, *HS* II, 374.4-6; ET. *FH* VIII, 229.565-566.

[107] For more discussion see Konat, "Christological Insights in Jacob of Serugh's Typology," 48ff.

[108] For a more independent study see Grillmeier, *Christ in Christian Tradition,* 447ff; cf. Schwarz, *Christology*, 154-155.

[109] Grillmeier, *Christ in Christian Tradition,* 484-487.

[110] Bedjan, *HS* V, 462.10; ET. *FH* V, 154.305.

[111] Jansma, "Credo of Mar Jacob," 28.

> The Jews calumniate her Child (saying) that (He) is not from the Father,
> neither did she conceive nor did she give birth in her virginity.
> They blaspheme about her that she conceived the Son as a result of sexual union,
> and the Son who dwelt in her is not the Power of the hidden Father.
> The pagan who is far, (says) neither did she give birth, nor that she exists,
> he does not even know that the blessed woman has a Son.
> Another fool, who is neither a Jew nor a pagan,
> talks idly about her, that the body of the Son is not from her.
> One wicked person says that she did not give birth to God,
> but Messiah, since the Messiah is not God.[112]

The above passage shows Mar Jacob's response to various heretical groups who denied the divinity of Jesus as well as who refused to call Mary as the mother of God. In the last two lines he expresses his displeasure against Nestorian teachings.

1.6.1.4. Against Chalcedonians

Some scholars argued that Mar Jacob is a dyophysite.[113] Some others say he is a monophysite. Yet others say he is a miaphysite. Chesnut says that in Jacob there is no adequate notion of whether Christ was a perfect union of man and God. She says:

> While he (Jacob) actually uses the language of Monophysite side of the Christological controversy, the Monophysitism to which he holds is incomplete if judged by the standards of both Severus and Philoxenus… Further, Jacob does not have an adequate version of the union between God and man in Christ, relying as he does on an unclear notion of mixture between two.[114]

But a thorough reader of Mar Jacob could understand that the divine-human nature of Christ is well-defined in his writings. He asserts the Divine and the human natures of Christ.[115] Therefore, he answers to many of the early century Christological controversies that questioned the divine and human natures of Christ. It could be proved that Mar Jacob evidently followed the

---

[112] Bedjan, *SMS,* 688.2-15; ET. Puthuparampil, "Homily on the Perpetual Virginity of Mary," in *Mariological Thought of Mar Jacob of Serugh,* iii.53-66.

[113] Krüger, "*Le caractère monophysite de la troisième lettere de Saroug,*" 301-302; Chesnust, *Three Monophysite Christologies*, 120. Modern scholars like V. C. Samuel rejected the argument that there was monophysitism in the teachings of Alexandrian school. According to them the controversy in the council of Chalcedon was due the terminological misunderstanding; both parties intended to say are the same. (Samuel, *The Council of Chalcedon Reexamined* 293-302).

[114] Chesnut, *Three Monophysite Christologies,* 141.

[115] Bedjan, *SMS*, 784.15-16; ET. *FH* II, 103.203-204; Bedjan, *HS* I. 59.7-14; ET. "On the Serpent of Brass," *TV* 6(1990), 49.215-222.

Alexandrian Christology[116] and he was from the non-Chalcedonian or Cyrillian tradition: "One Incarnated nature of God the Word."[117] Mar Jacob says that Jesus Christ is fully God and fully man. He writes: "The Word who came and became flesh but was not changed."[118] He states:

> His birth is divine as well as human
> and it is not to be investigated because His wonder is without limit.
> He is divine and in a virgin manner the womb bore Him.
> He is human too because the womb gave birth to Him corporeally.
> One alone is the Child, the true Son, perfect and wondrous,
> begotten from the Father, hidden from the watchers, adored by men.
> From the divine essence and from humanity, single is the Only begotten.
> Son of Majesty and son of Mary, a single redeemer.[119]

Mar Jacob was a non-Chalcedonian and teaches that Jesus Christ is fully human and fully divine and He cannot be divided into two natures. He is both the Only Begotten of the heavenly Father and the son of Virgin Mary.

1.6.1.5. Against Docetism

Docetism was another heresy in the early Church. It taught that the physical body of Jesus was an illusion or an appearance only. Hence God cannot die, He only seem to have a physical body, but in reality He is a pure spirit.[120] Mar Jacob along with other orthodox teachers condemned this teaching and affirmed humanity of Jesus Christ and He truly died on the cross. Mar Jacob said, "And as for the fool who denies that the body of the Son was from her, she also hates him and his teaching and flees away from him."[121] "For me He is God, born in the flesh, from the house of David, even as He suffered on the Cross."[122] "He came to circumcision so that no one might deny his humanity."[123] Thus he affirmed the bodily appearance of Jesus Christ.

1.6.2. Mar Jacob on Christological Titles

The following part is a discussion on Mar Jacob's usage of various Christological titles.

---

[116] Jansma, "The Credo of Mar Jacob of Serugh," 24.

[117] Samuel, "One Incarnate Nature of God the Word," 114.

[118] Bedjan, *SMS*, 725.14; ET. *FH* I, 47.116.

[119] Bedjan, *SMS*, 760.3-10; ET. *FH* I, 79.843-850.

[120] McGrath, *Heresy: A History of Defending the Truth*, 114ff.

[121] Bedjan, *SMS*, 690.11-12; ET. Puthuparampil, "Homily on Perpetual Virginity of Mary," in *Mariological Thought of Mar Jacob of Serugh*, v.105-106.

[122] Bedjan, *HS* III, 631.6-7.

[123] Bedjan, *HS* V, 448.18; ET. *FH* V, 142.25.

1.6.2.1. Messiah

Literally the term Messiah (*mšiḥo*) 'the anointed one' shows the position of a certain person who is appointed to carry out a mission. This 'messiah' may not be God.[124] In the Old Testament kings, prophets, and priests were anointed with oil to appoint to their respective positions. The prophets prophesied about the arrival of a Messiah to deliver Israel from their enemies and this prophecy was fulfilled in Jesus, the Christ. It is significant to note that Mar Jacob uses the term 'Messiah' and 'Son of God' frequently. Though it seems that he uses these terms as synonyms, a sharp examination would prove that he has a clear distinction between these terms. He uses the term 'Messiah' only when he directly and particularly says about the redemption through Jesus or Jesus as a redeemer. On the other hand, most of the time, he uses the term 'Son of God' to say simply the Incarnation of Jesus, to explain His divinity, and various deeds of miracles, which reveals His superhuman power, in His public ministry. See an example where Mar Jacob uses these terms in adjacent lines:

> Every one whose lot it has been to escort the procession of the Son of God
> hath been honored with revelations and with visitations of angels.
> Fair was Samson when he portrayed the type of the Messiah,
> and made the riddle that the sweet came out of bitter.[125]

Mar Jacob here portrays that Samson was a 'type' of Messiah. At first, he uses the title 'Son of God' who was adored by the angels, prophets and the human beings to emphasize His divinity. Secondly, he uses the title 'Messiah' when he finds a 'type' of a real 'Messiah' (Jesus Christ) in Samson who was a 'messiah' or a 'redeemer' of Israelites from the Philistines. It says in other terms, Mar Jacob portrays Jesus as both the Son of God and the redeemer of the world. By using the title 'Messiah' Mar Jacob upholds the Jewish heritage and expectations.[126] The Church believes that Jesus is the Messiah who has been prophesied in the scripture and through Him the salvation of the human race was fulfilled. In the homily *On the Baptism of Our Redeemer* he writes:

> She began to gazing until she would perceive Him who was coming to her,
> as she was examining the baptized one after another.
> She herself was casting her eye for a moment upon many
> so that she might perceive among them the Only-Begotten to whom she is betrothed.
> When someone was descending for baptism the crowds surrounded him

[124] Bedjan, *SMS*, 688.2-15; ET. Puthuparampil "Homily on the Perpetual Virginity of Mary," in *Mariological Thought of Mar Jacob of Serugh,* iii. 65-66.

[125] Bedjan, *HS* V, 339.1-6; ET. "A Homily on Samson," *TV* 11(1992), 58.165-168.

[126] Rilliet, *SHF* II, 560.5-562.6; ET. *FH* VI, 196.22-197.26.

in order to take notice of him lest perchance he might be Messiah who is coming.[127]

Just as announced in the prophecy the Messiah was born in Judea, in the city of David, but until the announcement of John at Jordan the Messiah was hidden among the crowd. At the time of His baptism Jesus was revealed to the world that He is the Messiah (Jn 1:29, 41) by the testimony of John. From the day of His baptism, He was recognized and was revealed to the world and what had been hidden was manifested as it was spoken by one person to another, saying: "We have found him about whom Moses in the Law and also the prophets wrote, Jesus the son of Joseph, from Nazareth" (Jn 1:41; Deut 18:15; Acts 3:22).[128] Mar Jacob perceives "Messiah is the Power of the Father as it is written."[129]

He also used to call Jesus as the Son of David[130] and Mary as the daughter of David. The Davidic succession has an important place in the prophetic tradition of Israel. They believed the salvation of Israel will come from the house of David. Therefore, he affirms the Old Testament's prophetic fulfillment through Jesus Christ, because the Old Testament prophesied Messiah would come from the clan of David (2 Sam 7: 12; 1 Chron 17:11-14; Ps 89:35-36; Isa 9:6-7; 11:1; Jer 33:14-26; Jn 7:42). Mar Jacob depicted Messiah as the "light of the nation" (Isa 60:1) who by His dawn trampled the idols of the nations and liberated Israel from the slavery of idols.[131] He again says that all through His works Jesus Himself manifested to the world that He is the expected Messiah.[132] Finally, Messiah liberated Barabbas, the son of Adam, by His death.[133] Here, Mar Jacob elucidates that Barabbas as *Bar Abba*, which means 'son of the Father,' that is, Adam, who was created by God. By liberating Barabbas and crucifying Christ, the Messiah, the Jews did not know that they are fulfilling the prophecy and desire of the Father. Therefore, by His death Messiah liberated the son of the Father (Adam) and his descendants from the slavery of *Sheol*.[134] Mar Jacob delineates Jesus as the Messiah and teaches that Jesus is the Messiah prophesied in the Old Testament. He was born and manifested in this world and by His atoning sacrifice He liberated the sons of Adam from the slavery of sin and death.

---

[127] Bedjan, *HS* I, 171.5-10; ET. *FH* VI, 166.75-80.

[128] Rilliet, *SHF* II, 560.5-562.6; ET. *FH* VII, 196.22-197.26.

[129] Bedjan, *LP*; ET. "Homily on the Blessed Virgin Mary," *TV* 5.1(1993), 22.369.

[130] Bedjan, *SMS*, 743.19; ET. *FH* I, 64.506.

[131] Rilliet, *SHF* IV, 596.3-9; ET. *FH* XI, 269.23.

[132] Rilliet, *SHF* III, 578.1-2; ET. *FH* IX, 240.27.

[133] Rilliet, *SHF* V, 626.22-628:13; ET. *FH* XII, 290.32-291.34.

[134] Rilliet, *SHF* V, 626.22-628:13; ET. *FH* XII, 290.32-291.34.

1.6.2.2. Son of God

Son of God (*bar aloho*) is another biblical Christological title that Mar Jacob regularly uses in his homilies. Mar Jacob's basic theology is centered on Christ, "Son of God," who saved the world. In other words his theology is Christo-centric. In order to elaborate this theme he uses all the possible biblical imageries and interpreted in a typical way that his predecessors followed. He uses the "Son of God" title in this context. Through this title he affirms that Christ is really the Son of God the Father. "Behold, this is my Son, this is truly my beloved."[135] He was with the Father even before the creation of the universe and He was with the Father in the creation. The Father created everything with the Son. Even before the time of creation, the Son was appointed as the Savior of the universe. Therefore, in the fullness of time He came down to the earth and liberated Adam and his children from the slavery of sin and death. Various functions of the Son of God will be discussed in the following section.

1.6.2.2.1. Son of God: The Savior

Mar Jacob of Serugh uses the Christological title 'Son of God' to elaborate the *kenosis* as well as God's initiation for the salvation of humanity.[136] According to this theology Son of God out of His love for men,[137] left all His heavenly glories, and descended to earth.[138] The Son of God became the second Adam (human) in order to make humankind the spiritual Adam (*Adam rooḥonoit*).[139] Son of God mingled (*ḥlat*) with the humankind as one among them.[140] The primary duty of the Son of God is to cast down Satan from his rule over the humankind.[141] In order to liberate human being from the slavery of Satan the Son of God died on behalf of all[142] on the cross.[143] It is interesting to note that, in most cases, where he depicts the battle with Satan, Mar Jacob uses the

[135] Bedjan, *HS* I, 185.9; ET. *FH* VI, 179.368.

[136] Bedjan, *HS* I, 299.1-2; ET. "On the Publican and the Pharisee," *TV* 9(1991), 19.1-2.

[137] Bedjan, *HS* II, 762.11; ET. "On Paul the Apostle," *TV* 10(1991), 68.298.

[138] Bedjan, *HS* III, 321.2-23; ET. "Why Our Lord Abode upon the Earth," *TV* 4(1990), 37.2-38.23. Here, Mar Jacob says that the Son of God descended to the earth in order to abolish the darkness on the earth and renew and restore the ruined creation.

[139] Bedjan, *HS* III, 326.1-6; ET. "Why Our Lord Abode upon the Earth," *TV* 4(1990), 41.90-96.

[140] Bedjan, *HS* III, 411.3; ET. "Parable of the Leaven," *TV* 3(1989), 45.3. In his *Homily on Samson* Mar Jacob said, "The *Son of God* stirred from His place and came to our Land to espouse the Church of the nations." Bedjan, *HS* V, 336.14-15; ET. "Homily on Samson," *TV* 11(1992), 56.113-114.

[141] Bedjan, *HS* III, 413.5; ET. "The Parable of the Leaven," *TV* 3(1989), 47.29.

[142] Bedjan, *HS* I, 465.10; ET. "On Paul the Apostle," *TV* 10(1991), 70.357.

[143] Bedjan, *HS* III, 322.3-4; ET. "Why Our Lord Abode upon the Earth," *TV* 4(1990), 38.12-13.

Son of God title. He uses the title Son of God upon the confidence that only God could defeat Satan and his army. Moreover, after defeating gods of the nations, it is the right of the Son of God to establish the Kingdom of God by establishing the Church in the world.[144]

The Father ordained the Son as the Savior of the world even before the creation of the universe.[145] Before creating Adam the Father had the foreknowledge that he would have failures. The Father want to save His creation and He knew that if He created in His own Image His Son would be able to save Adam from perdition, therefore He created Adam in His own Image and Likeness. Therefore, the Son of God is appointed as the Savior of humanity even before the creation of Adam.

Mar Jacob finds that Jesus saved the world not at a particular point of His life but it was a process throughout His life. It is commonly believed that the Son of God saved the world by His atoning sacrifice on Golgotha. But according to his writings, this process of liberation started with the nativity of our Lord. It is interesting to note that the salvation is achieved through the birth of Jesus Christ. He finds the nativity day as a day of liberation of Adam:

> On this day He drove out Zion who had persecuted Him
> and He invited that despised woman who had deserted Him, to enter.
> On this day the head of the barren woman is lifted up
> because she was cast down in abandonment among strangers.
> On this there is exaltation to the humiliated woman
> who had been thrust down, of her own will, in the shrine of demons.
> On this day the sorrowful woman who had been repudiated has exulted
> because the bridegroom has come and collected and gathered her from among the idols.
> On this day the lamenting woman has exulted
> because there was the marriage feast at which she has been comforted from her distresses.
> Today freedom has come for the enslaved woman
> who had been bound to minister to idolatry.
> Today the one who was persecuted for a long time has been released,
> because the mighty one stood up and broke the fetters of her imprisonment.
> Today the maid-servant of the demons has obtained freedom
> because the great Lord has put them to fight and lead out what belongs to him.
> Today the imprisoned (woman) has gone out of darkness
> because the light has shone out and shattered the gates of the house of darkness.
> Today the painter restored the image of Adam:

---

144 Bedjan, *HS* III, 321.1, 322.11; ET. "Why Our Lord Abode upon the Earth," *TV* 4(1990), 37.1- 38.25. Here, Mar Jacob uses the terms darkness and manslayer to mention Satan. Bedjan, *HS* III, 413.5-21; ET. "The Parable of the Leaven," *TV* 3(1989), 47.29-30.

145 Alwan, *QHC* I, 12.10-11.

because it had worn out, He mingled with it pigment that it might not get corrupted.
Today the master builder has rebuilt the house that had fallen,
and so that it might not fall, the support of divinity entered in.
Today this Lord has reconciled Himself with Adam
because the Son who shone forth has set peace between the two sides.
Today the Shepherd has found sheep that had gone astray,
and put upon His shoulders He lifted up and carried it into Paradise…
Today the outsiders have entered and became inmates
and behold, the household members have gone out
and parted in anger from the King's palace.[146]

This redeeming action of the Son of God continued through baptism, teaching and healing, passion and death, descent into the *Sheol*, Resurrection, and ascension. It is imperative that the Son of God to receive sacrifices and to provide propitiation, redemption and salvation to all.[147]

1.6.2.2.2. Pre-existent Son

Another character of the Son of God, according to Mar Jacob, is His pre-existence. He has neither beginning nor end.[148] Regarding the nativity of the Son of God he writes: "Yesterday and today He is Jesus, Son of God, the One without beginning who wished to become subject to a beginning."[149] He is the Son of God who was there from eternity[150] and it was through him the Father created everything.[151] Mar Jacob writes:

The supplication of the old man bears witness to the Son indeed,
because in a mystical manner His name had existed before the sun.
That supplication of the old man in the presence of the child
would reveal the story of the Son of God, how he is from eternity.[152]
Simeon says: "He is Almighty for eternity and it is easy for Him;
and He is more exalted than you; you shall learn from Him how He is.
Eve, your mother, is immensely younger than He
for He is the one who governs all times and their ordering.
Behold, by the hands of your Son the creation came into existence long before,

[146] Bedjan, *SMS*, 769.14-770.21; ET. *FH* I, 88.1039-89.1068.

[147] Bedjan, *HS* V, 454.21; ET. *FH* V, 148.152.

[148] Bedjan, *HS* II, 205.14; ET. Thekeparampil, "Jacob of Sarugh's Homily on Malkizadeq," *Harp* 6(1993), 61.180.

[149] Bedjan, 803.14; ET. *FH* I, 124.277.

[150] Bedjan, *HS* V, 454.20; ET. *FH* V, 148.146; Bedjan, *HS* III, 321.7; ET. "Why Our Lord Abode upon the Earth," *TV* 4(1990), 37.7.

[151] Bedjan, *HS* V, 459.12-18; ET. *FH* V, 152.245-254.

[152] Bedjan, *HS* V, 453.17-20; ET. *FH* V, 147.127-132.

and He was with His Father when He was making the walls of the universe.
Through Him the world was generated to come into being from nothing.[153]

These passages from the homily on *Presentation of Our Lord* witness Mar Jacob's idea of the pre-existence of the Son of God. He was before the sun and the earth were created. He was with the Father during the creation process. Nothing was created without His knowledge. And through this pre-existence Mar Jacob visualizes the Son of God's authority with the Father over the created world and co-eternity with the Father as well as His redeeming power.

1.6.2.2.3. Royal Nature of the Son

Mar Jacob sometimes describes Christ as a Royal Son (*bar-malko*) and it attributes Him a kind of authority over creation just like the princes of the world have authority over their people. Just as the people fear the kings of the world the creation trembles before the Son of God. Mar Jacob portrayed the Son of God on a high pedestal, unapproachable, incomprehensible, a high-ranking state, where entry is restricted. Like a victorious king the Son of God defeated the authority of death and liberated the children of Adam. However, this great King humbled Himself and identified with the dust of the earth in order to redeem them. Regarding the Royal nature of the Son of God Mar Jacob writes:

John shrank back trembled and he was terrified by the Royal Son.
He adored Him and confessed, as he passionately made supplication[154]
Go, Royal Son, redeem the captives, for behold, they are looking for you,
you need to take no armor for yourself from the water.
Your crown is eternal and is not changed;
from the treasury of baptism you are not going to be fulfilled...
You are born upon the purple of the Father from His essence;
and you do not need to be clothed from this place and thus to redeem.[155]

Through the title 'Son of God' Mar Jacob wished to proclaim the powerful and Almighty Jesus. He sees the royal nature in His form, dress, deeds, etc.; everybody adore Him, tremble at His sight, He flies on His fiery vehicle driven by angels and spiritual beings, His authority expands all over the world: on earth, sky, and on seas, and even has the authority over the dead ones. He called the dead and they came out from their places and Mar Jacob says that He has authority over heaven and earth and commands all, living and dead.[156] He continues:

---

[153] Bedjan, *HS* V, 459.12-18; ET. *FH* V, 152.245-256.

[154] Bedjan, *HS* I, 179.3-4; ET. *FH* VI, 173.237-238.

[155] Bedjan, *HS* I, 179.13-20; ET. *FH* VI, 174.247-254.

[156] Bedjan, *HS* II, 359.15-360.12; ET. *FH* VIII, 216.255-217.275.

From the mountain of Nebo He called Moses and he obeyed Him
then He beckoned to him Elijah by the whirlwind and he came.
One from the earth and another from the air, they presented themselves,
so that they might be witnesses to the Son on the mountain that He is the Son of God.[157]

Thus, through the Royal Son Mar Jacob portrays the divine as well as powerful Son of God, who is Almighty and every animate and inanimate tremble before Him. But this Son God became a simple human being in order to save His creation from sin and death. He put on humility because of His love for His creation.

1.6.2.2.4. Son of God the Eternal Priest

Mar Jacob calls Jesus as the priest who came to become a sacrifice on behalf of the sinners.[158] In the homily *On Malkizedeq* Mar Jacob asks, why David compared the Son of God with Malkizedeq and did not compare others like Abel, Noah, Abraham, Levi, because all these offered animals or its blood but Malkizedeq did not offer anything other than his own sufferings. He says:

It was through these noble, spiritual and exalted thoughts
that the renowned Malkizedeq became a priest.
Without sacrifices, through his own suffering, he was made a priest,
and because of this the Son of God was compared to him.
Who became priest and did not bring in any alien blood
but through His own blood He made atonement for the whole world.[159]

This reflects the duty of the Son of God. The Son of God's primary duty was to become human and offer Himself for the atonement of human beings. Mar Jacob calls Him as "The Priest who came to become a sacrifice on behalf of the sinners."[160] He is the eternal High Priest and the source of pardon and absolution of the sins but He became the offertory lamb for the absolution of humanity.

If it is pardon (*ḥusoyo*), it proceeds from you for mankind
and if it is forgiveness (*šubqono*) the forgiveness of debts too is yours.
If it is priesthood (*kumarooto*), the whole of it is in you because you are the High Priest
and if it is Kingship (*malkooto*), you are the one who fastens the crowns for the kings.
Holiness proceeds from you to mankind:

---

[157] Bedjan, *HS* II, 359.5-8; ET. *FH* VIII, 216.245-249.

[158] Bedjan, *SMS*, 725.10; ET. *FH* I, 46.112.

[159] Bedjan, *HS* II, 202.7-12; ET. "Jacob of Sarugh's Homily on Malkizadeq," 58.107-112.

[160] Bedjan, *SMS*, 725.10; ET. *FH* I, 46.112.

and if it is priesthood, behold the world exists by your right hand.
And seeing that the fullness of divinity is with you,
and what is there for the small river to accomplish in you?[161]

Since He is the Son of God He is eternally the High Priest. By His own sacrifice He absolves the sins of the world. He, the One, who receives the oblation from the hands of earthly priests (whose priesthood is flowed from Him) became oblation.

Thus through the Christological title 'Son of God' Mar Jacob conveys and affirms the divinity of Jesus Christ. He is Almighty, eternal, creator of all, and the Savior of the world who offered Himself as a sacrifice for many.

1.6.2.3. Lord

Let every tongue confess that Jesus Christ is Lord (*moryo*), to the glory of God to the Father! (Phil 2:11; Rom 14:11). 'Lord' is another Christological title used in the homilies of Mar Jacob to depict the Almighty Son. The term 'Lord' is theologically as well as culturally fecund and it widely uses in his homilies. The term Lord and its usage should be defined from the cultural settings of the time. Slavery was common at the time of Jesus and his disciples. The term Lord is a familiar form of addressing people of higher echelon to express unconditional loyalty. Angel Gabriel uses the term in a cultural sense, "Behold, my Lord is with you, she learned that he was a servant."[162] Here he uses it to denote the master-slave relationship. Apostle Thomas' declaration of "my Lord and my God" (Jn 20:28) has significant theological importance. In his homily *On New Sunday and on Thomas the Apostle* Mar Jacob uses this term completely in a theological sense, where, he uses in a post-resurrection mood. In this homily he uses this term to denote a celestial authority of resurrected Christ.[163]

Jesus is the Lord in the highest who descended into the depth (world) to save the world which was immersed in sin and death. This idea of *kenosis* is one of the major virtues of Jesus, the Lord in the heights. The title 'Lord' indicates that Jesus is the ruler of the heavenly and the earthly ones[164] (who are holy in nature) but descended to the depth (to the sinful world) to teach humankind that they shall attain the lost heights of Paradise.[165] The title 'Lord' also indicates the power of God who is the Lord of all created beings.[166]

---

[161] Bedjan, *HS* I, 177.2-9; ET. *FH* VI, 172.193-200.

[162] Bedjan, *SMS*, 728.9; ET. *FH* I, 50.175.

[163] Bedjan, *HS* II, 654.13; 657.8; 662.15; ET. "On New Sunday and on Apostle Thomas," *TV* 4.2(1992), 54.106, 56.185, 60.280.

[164] Bedjan, *SMS*, 745.20-746.10; ET. *FH,* 66.545-67.554.

[165] Bedjan, *HS* III, 412.4-5; "The Parable of the Leaven," *TV* 3(1989), 46.7-8.

[166] Bedjan, *SMS*, 742.7; ET. *FH,* 63.469.

Therefore, the usage of Lord by the Syriac fathers to address Jesus Christ must be viewed in these perspectives. Mar Jacob uses the term by giving complete respect of this understanding. Sometimes he referred to Christ as King. In some cases he interchanges the words *King* and *Lord*.[167] Both express the authority over all created beings while He adorns the throne.[168] Again the title 'Lord' denotes Jesus as the controller of all, and who can decide the birth and death of a human being.[169] Mar Jacob calls Him the Lord of the creation.[170] Sometimes, he uses the term Lord to show the heavenly authority of Jesus Christ who gives victory to the kings of the world and controls the world.[171] He is the Lord of all both in heaven and on earth. Jesus was often addressed as the King of kings or simply King.[172] Lord of the ancient and Lord of the New.[173]

> Yes, in truth He is your Lord come approach and adore Him
> do not be wavering about the Redeemer who has come to you.[174]
> It is He whom the Cherubs bless with trembling as they stand in awe,
> then in truth His pure yoke is placed upon their neck.
> Many thousands of heavenly beings are standing in His presence
> and it is He whom myriads of the sons of the light bless.
> Seraphs call out towards Him with the song 'Holy, Holy, Holy'
> and before His brightness, 'Holy, Holy, Holy' issues from their mouth.
> Three times they reveal their mouth with hallowing
> and then they call The Lord by His name with fear.[175]

On occasions the title 'Lord' is used to exemplify the splendor and majesty of Jesus Christ. When he describes the dialogue between Mary and the angel Gabriel, Mar Jacob compares the angel's figure and appearance with that of his Lord's.[176] Here he tells this Lord is beyond the understanding and nobody can see Him in His original nature. If the servant is so fiery in nature how much more be the Lord of the servant? By seeing the angel Gabriel Virgin Mary marveled and said, "if you are servant, clothed lightning upon your members,

---

[167] Bedjan, *HS* III, 718.1-19; ET. "A Homily on Stephen," *TV* 7(1990), 49.151.50.169.

[168] Bedjan, *HS* III, 718.20-21; ET. "A Homily on Stephen," *TV* 7(1990), 50.170-171.

[169] Bedjan, *HS* V, 452.11-16; ET. *FH* V, 146.99-104.

[170] Bedjan, *HS* I, 454.2; ET. *FH* X, 256.187.

[171] Bedjan, *HS* IV, 286.6; ET. "The King of Moab," *TV* 1(1989), 58.87.

[172] Bedjan, *HS* I, 447.18; *FH* X, 250.55.

[173] Rilliet, *SHF* III, 576.13; ET. *FH* IX, 240.26.

[174] Bedjan, *HS* I, 176.5-6; ET. *FH* VI, 171.175-176.

[175] Bedjan, *HS* V, 460.3-10; ET. *FH* V, 152.259-153.266.

[176] Bedjan, *SMS*, 728.17-729.19; ET. *FH* I, 50.185-51.208.

then your Lord is entirely fire as you say."[177] Even angels cannot see Him or comprehend Him; but they can hear Him.[178]

Again the term is used to contrast with the exalted position of Jesus Christ, the Son of God, the Lord, and the Creator of all with that of His humility which was clothed for the salvation of humanity. In order to show this contrast He writes: "Blessed is the king who comes in the name of the Lord" (Lk 19:38).[179] He who wears Royal Crown asked for a colt.[180] "The Lord of kings was riding upon a colt."[181] The Christological title 'Lord' is used to show the exalted nature and his overwhelming authority over the created world.

1.7. Pneumatology

The noun Spirit (*rooḥo*) is used as feminine in Syriac language. Sebastian Brock, in his article entitled *Holy Spirit in Syriac Baptismal Themes* discussed this aspect in detail. According to him the word for 'spirit' or 'wind' happens to be feminine in Semitic languages and this made some ramification when using the term *rooḥo* to the Holy Spirit. "Early Syriac writers consistently construe *ruaha d-qudsha* as a feminine, and it is clear from a few oft-quoted texts that the Holy Spirit was actually regarded as mother in some circles."[182] He gives the examples of gospel quotes preserved by Origen and Jerome, and some usages in the *Acts of Judas Thomas* and *Aphrahat* and other later writings like *Sahadona* and Mohse Barkepha.[183] (Mar Jacob also uses 'spirit' in feminine gender[184]). After verifying these texts he concludes that poets like Mar Jacob used the term for the sake of versification and not strictly in grammatical sense.[185] At the same time, Mar Jacob very purposefully calls the Holy Spirit as 'Mistress of heaven' (*morat rome*)[186] This area needs further studies.

In his faith on the doctrine on the Holy Spirit, Mar Jacob adheres to the Nicaeo-Constantinople creed. He believes in the same divinity of the Spirit with the Father and the Son. They are One and undivided:

> If you are baptized in the name of Spirit, how is it possible
> that I shall sign the water separately because you are with the Spirit.

---

[177] Bedjan, *SMS*, 728.19-20; ET. *FH* I, 50.187-188.

[178] Bedjan, *SMS*, 730.2-5; ET. *FH* I, 51.213-214.

[179] Bedjan, *HS* I, 448.4; ET. *FH* X, 250.63.

[180] Bedjan, *HS* I, 447.11; ET. *FH* X, 250.49.

[181] Bedjan, *HS* I, 453.16; ET. *FH* X, 255.179.

[182] Brock, *Holy Spirit in Syriac Baptismal Tradition*, 3.

[183] Brock, *Holy Spirit in Syriac Baptismal Tradition*, 3-5.

[184] Bedjan, *HS* I, 185.12-186.20; ET. *FH* VI, 180.371, 181.396.

[185] Brock, *Holy Spirit in Syriac Baptismal Tradition*, 6, 21; cf. Brock, "Come Compassionate Mother," 250.

[186] Bedjan, *HS* I, 172.7; ET. *FH* VI, 167.97.

The Father is in His Son and the Son is wholly in His Father,
and the Spirit who is from Him is one power without confusion (*wrooḥo dmeneh ḥad uḥdono dlo bulbolo*).
And how shall I, the poor one, perform this,
and set a division in that undivided harmony (*lo metplag*)?[187]

He believes that the Holy Spirit proceeds from the Father and is equal in divinity with the Father and the Son; therefore, he writes: The Spirit floated from the Father in a great wonder and flew down descended, rested upon and abode in His Beloved.[188] At the same time he believes that the Son has the authority to send the Holy Spirit to the world: "I am your flute, breath in me Your Spirit, O Son of God."[189] On another occasion he writes: "The life-giving spirit is to be found in the Son of God; He suffices for the human race, for whomever issues from it."[190] Again, "The Spirit poured forth from the Holy One upon the aged sterile woman."[191] All these usages show the Son's right of sending the Holy Spirit. These lines witness his pneumatology which comply with the scriptural narrations (Jn 15:26; 16:7). In the homily on "Pentecost" Mar Jacob reminds the same: "The Son of the King ascended to his Father in order to send the armor of the Spirit from His Father to his servants."[192] He argues:

Before his ascension, while being elevated, he gathered them
and breathed upon them so that they might receive the Spirit from him.
And again when he was going he assured them that he would send
the Holy Spirit who would teach them the truth.[193]

It shows that the Son has the power to send the Holy Spirit and secondly, it shows that the Father will agree with Him.[194]

Mar Jacob also writes about the sanctifying character of the Holy Spirit. He sanctifies the world and everything in it. Perfecting the sacraments is the primary example for the sanctifying power of the Holy Spirit. John the Baptist taught Israelites that when the Bridegroom comes He will baptize

---

[187] Bedjan, *HS* I, 182.18-22; ET. *FH* VI, 177.315-318.

[188] Bedjan, *HS* I, 185.10-11; ET. *FH* VI, 180.369-370.

[189] Bedjan, *AMS* IV, 650.7; E.T. Harvey, "On Simeon the Stylite," in *Ascetic Behavior in Greco-Roman Antiquity*, 17.6.

[190] Bedjan, *HS* IV, 819.1ff.

[191] Bedjan, *SMS*, 743.21; ET. *FH* I, 64.503.

[192] Bedjan, *HS* II, 676.18-19; ET. *FH* XVII, 360.135-136.

[193] Bedjan, *HS* II, 676.20-677.2; ET. *FH* XVII, 360.137-140.

[194] Bedjan, *HS* II, 677.5-6; ET. *FH* XVII, 360.143-144.

you with Holy Spirit and fire.[195] Through the baptism the unholy will become holy and become the bride of the heavenly Bridegroom. In the Homily on the *Baptism of Our Redeemer* Mar Jacob says that the Holy Spirit descended not to sanctify the Son but to give witness to the Son.[196] This asserts that one of the characteristics of the Holy Spirit is the sanctification. Regarding the sanctification of the ordinary bread and wine into the body and blood of Jesus Christ Mar Jacob says:

> The Holy Spirit makes his power descend on the bread and wine
> sanctifying them and turning them into the Body and Blood.
> And through hovering he mixes them in a holy way,
> and sacramentally they become one with him, as is written (Jn 17:11, 21)[197]

It is not the priest or the Son of God who sanctifies the offerings, but the Holy Spirit who proceeds from the Father and descends, overshadows and resides in the bread, transform it into the body of Christ and makes it reassured pearls to adorn the souls that are betrothed by him.[198] While writing on the conception of the Virgin Mary, Mar Jacob says: "The Holy Spirit will come to you and the power of the Exalted One will abide upon you lovingly."[199] Usually this passage is explained with the Holy Spirit as the source of Mary's conception (Mt 1:20). But here he affirmatively differentiates the duty of Holy Spirit and the indwelling of the Word of God. It could be explained that Holy Spirit is only a sanctifier and the Word was the power who indwelled in her.[200] In another occasion Mar Jacob says that "the exalted power is the true Son."[201] In another place he states that the Royal Son might enter through the ear of the pure virgin.[202] But yet another homily Mar Jacob very explicitly declares the duty of Holy Spirit in the event of conception:

> That the Spirit would come and then the Power of the
> Most High would dwell within her.
> The Holy Spirit came unto Mary to loose from her
> that first sentence of Eve and Adam.

---

[195] Bedjan, *HS* I, 181.20; ET. *FH* VI, 177.294; Bedjan, *HS* II, 679.11-12; ET. *FH* XVII, 362.192.

[196] Bedjan, *HS* I, 185.1-19; ET. *FH* VI, 179.360-180.380.

[197] Harak, "The Syriac Orthodox Celebration," 99.

[198] Bedjan, *HS* IV, 597.8-13.

[199] Bedjan, *SMS,* 733.7-8; ET. *FH* I, 54.281-282.

[200] Bedjan, *SMS*, 733:7-8; ET. *FH* I, 54.281-282.

[201] Bedjan, *SMS*, 737.5-8; ET. *FH* I, 58.362-365.

[202] Bedjan, *SMS*, 739.9; ET. *FH* I, 60.408.

He sanctified her and purified her, and made her blessed among women,
and set free from Eve her mother's curse of pains.[203]

When Virgin Mary conceived the Son of God, it was the Holy Spirit who sanctified and purified the virgin to become an abode of the Holy One. Therefore, one of the main functions of the Holy Spirit is sanctification.

The Holy Spirit gives men all kinds of virtues: In one place Mar Jacob says that Jesus came to this world to send or give the Holy Spirit to the world. It purifies the men from their sins. It is gentle and reconciling; it can burn and kindle souls with many graces. Thus the sanctification makes a person to produce the fruit of Spirit (Gal 5:22-23):

He became a temple wherein the Holy Spirit was ministered to,
and he was altogether filled with grace in every way.
Wisdom, understanding, perception, and an untainted life, were his,
and sanctify and love, the treasury of the virtues,
and forthright speech and a mouth that preached the truth.[204]

Thus Mar Jacob portrays the Holy Spirit as the giver of all virtues. In many occasions He portrays the Holy Spirit as the power house: When the Holy Spirit indwells upon somebody he/she will get an unusual power and courage to do the will of God.

The Spirit poured forth from the Holy One upon the aged sterile woman,
infused into her the power to proclaim the truths to His mother.
A flood of prophecy surged out upon the daughter of Aaron
to supply streams of hidden things to that Daughter of David."[205]

While speaking on the experiences of Pentecost Mar Jacob says that the resurrected Christ clothed His disciples with armor and the power of Spirit.[206] the Holy Spirit was a teacher to them and it taught them a new speech without any training and filled people with wisdom.[207] Again he says the Spirit as a great school for the sons of light and from where they learned the speech of the nations.[208] From this school the disciples, the uneducated fishermen, filled with wisdom, were enlightened and spoken in different languages.[209] The power of the Spirit gave them the courage to tread upon the evil.[210] All through these

---

[203] Bedjan, *LP*; "Homily on the Blessed Virgin Mary," *TV* 5.1(1993), 22.73-75.

[204] Bedjan, *HS* III, 712.11-16; ET. "A Homily on Stephen," *TV* 7(1990), 45.41-45.

[205] Bedjan, *SMS*, 744.22-745.3; ET. *FH* I, 64.503-506.

[206] Bedjan, *HS* II, 677.3-4; ET. *FH* XVII, 360.141-142.

[207] Bedjan, *HS* II, 678.2-3; ET. *FH* XVII, 361.161-162.

[208] Bedjan, *HS* II, 678.18-19; ET. *FH* XVII, 361.177-178.

[209] Bedjan, *HS* II, 678.6-10; ET. *FH* XVII, 361.165-168.

[210] Bedjan, *HS* II, 679.3-4; ET. *FH* XVII, 361.183-184.

references Mar Jacob portrays the Holy Spirit as power house and a source of courage to face any eventuality.

Mar Jacob compared the Holy Spirit to Fire. In the homily on *Pentecost* he gives a vivid account of this kind of interpretation. "From the house of the Father tongues of living fire went out and it kindled in the Apostles and all of them were illuminated to speak."[211] This fire kindled and enlightened the souls of the disciples. Mar Jacob gives different biblical imageries of the Holy Spirit such as dove,[212] fire, tongues of fire[213] and so on. He calls it as a gift of the Father.[214]

Thus, according Mar Jacob, Holy Spirit is one of the Persons in the Holy Trinity who proceeds from the Father and equal to the Father and the Son in divinity. He sanctifies and perfects the human beings. On His arrival the ordinary people will become wise and eloquent and source of all virtues.

1.8. Eschatology

Mar Jacob portrays the eschatological events through the imagery of wedding (Mt 25:1-10). In this imagery main characters are Christ as the Bridegroom, the faithful Church as the bride, and the Kingdom of God is the bridal chamber. Since the sixth chapter is devoted for this topic it will be discussed later.

1.9. Ecclesiology

Mar Jacob taught the pre-existent nature of the Church. He found mainly two instances as the inauguration of the Church in this world: during the creation and in the form of tabernacle in the wilderness. Both these concepts are prominent in his teachings. In his homily *On the Veil of Moses* he says that when the prophet uttered the union of man and his wife (Gen 2:24) he declared the origin of the Church.[215] Two homilies[216] are dedicated to propound the theory of the erection of the Church at the wilderness through the tabernacle. He says it was not Moses who built the tabernacle but God himself made it.[217] He called the Church as free woman which resembles Apostle Paul's comparison of the Church (Gal 4:22-29).[218]

---

[211] Bedjan, *HS* II, 677.13-14; ET. *FH* XVII, 360.151-152.

[212] Bedjan, *HS* I, 185.12; ET. *FH* VI, 180.373.

[213] Bedjan, *HS* II, 677.10; ET. *FH* XVII, 360.151.

[214] Bedjan, *HS* II, 673.15; 677.7; ET. *FH* XVII, 357.71, 360.145.

[215] Bedjan, *HS* III, 291.14; ET. Brock, "On the Veil of Moses," in *Studies in Syriac Spirituality*, 79.164.

[216] Bedjan *HS* I, 3-38 & 38-46.

[217] Bedjan, *HS* I, 40.7-44.3.

[218] Bedjan, *HS* I, 41.2-3; 43.1.

The favorite ecclesiological theme of Mar Jacob is the 'bride of Christ' but other themes are also seen in his writings. Church as the body of Christ is one of the biblical imageries that Mar Jacob uses in his homilies to speak on the Church. While addressing the suffering of Paul Mar Jacob quotes this analogy mentioned by St. Paul (1Col 1:24; 1Cor12:12-24).[219] Jesus taught his disciples that "abide in me and I in you...I am the Vine and you are the branches... (Jn 15:4-5). St. Paul gives the imagery in details (Eph 4:11-16). Here, Mar Jacob also follows his great tradition and calls himself as the part of that large body of which Christ is the head. Like Christ bought his beloved Church by His blood[220] Paul also says that he suffered that which is lacking in the sufferings of Christ in his body for the sake of the Church.[221] In his teachings, the departed has an important place in the Church.[222] Church is a community which offers the true sacrifice of the body and blood of her Lord.[223]

At Pentecost the Church became the second Babel.[224] While in the first Babel the tongue scattered the assembly into different languages, on the other hand in the second Babel the tongue unified the people of different languages and regions into one (Gen 11:1-8). Church is also mentioned as 'pure one'.[225] As against the synagogue Mar Jacob often describes Church as the pure one who declined the friendship with idols (adultery). The reason for attaining the purity, he observes, is the love of Christ, the Bridegroom. The old bride has been defiled due to adultery or worship of the foreign gods but the Church the new bride, rejected her earlier friendship with idols and was betrothed to the real Bridegroom. After the betrothal she never looked back to her earlier life. He says that the Church is the only earthly one who loved Christ more than anyone else.[226] Mar Jacob calls the Church as the Daughter of King,[227] Daughter of light,[228] the Daughter of the day,[229] or the Church of light[230] of two

---

[219] Bedjan, *HS* II, 755.20-756.1ff; ET. "On Paul the Apostle," *TV* 10(1991), 63.167-182ff.

[220] Bedjan, *HS* II, 758.14; ET. "On Paul the Apostle," *TV* 10(1991), 65.221.

[221] Bedjan, *HS* II, 756.19-757.1; ET. "On Paul the Apostle," *TV* 10(1991), 64.185-188.

[222] Bedjan, *HS* I, 544.1; ET. "On the Reposed," *TV* 5(1990), 48.165.

[223] Bedjan, *HS* I, 545.6ff. ET. "On the Reposed," *TV* 5(1990), 49.189ff.

[224] Bedjan, *HS* II, 674.3-8; ET. *FH* XVII, 357.79-358.85.

[225] Bedjan, *HS* II, 757.13; ET. "On Paul the Apostle," *TV* 10(1991), 64.199.

[226] Bedjan, *HS* II, 757.17; ET. "On Paul the Apostle," *TV* 10(1991), 64.203-204.

[227] Bedjan, *HS* I, 538.6; ET. "On the Reposed," *TV* 5(1990), 43.55.

[228] Bedjan, *HS* I, 329.3; cf. Kollamparampil, *Salvation in Christ,* 88; Bedjan, *SMS,* 799.6; ET. *FH* III, 119.180; Bedjan, *HS* II, 374.17; ET. *FH* VIII, 230.575; Brock, "Jacob of Serugh: A Poem on Soul," 43.*qoph.*

[229] Bedjan, *HS* III, 290.3; ET. Brock, "On the Veil of Moses," in *Studies in Syriac Spirituality*, 78.132.

[230] Bedjan, *HS* V, 336.8; ET. "A Homily on Samson," *TV* 11(1992), 56.107.

reasons: firstly she is the enlightened one by the light of the Bridegroom who is full of light.[231]

Secondly she washes her impurities in the water of baptism and tears of repentance and now she is effulgent bright and there is no spot of darkness in her.[232] Therefore, he addresses the Church as the pure and daughter of light, daughter of the day, the Church of Light. Here the Light always represents Christ, the Sun of righteousness, in Him there is no spot.[233] Son of God is portrayed as the ray of the Light or Sun.[234] Sometimes mentioned the Holy Spirit as the ray of light. Church from the nations or Daughter of the nations is a prominent theme in his homilies.[235] Church from the nations is another important theme and it will be discussed in the fourth chapter.[236]

1.10. Soteriology

Soteriology comes from the Greek word *sōtēre* which means salvation. The word 'soteriology' comes from the verb *zozo* and its adjective *zoe* corresponds to the Latin sanus which means return to good health which was lost.[237] The corresponding Syriac term is (*purqono*), means salvation, and Jesus Christ is addressed by *porooqo*, the Savior. Mar Jacob comprehends salvation as the experience of life with the Son of God, the Bridegroom, in His bridal chamber.

In Mar Jacob's view soteriology has three stages: pre-creation plan, post- creation till the ascension, and finally, the execution of salvation in the eschatological times. According to him the salvation history starts even before the creation of human beings. Out of His love God wished to create human beings but since He had the foreknowledge that creation will fall down from its nature so God created man in His own Image.[238] Mar Jacob, in his homilies, repeatedly says about the love of God towards mankind. It is by His love He created man in His Image and Likeness, and by the same love from the beginning God foreseen the Incarnation of His Only Begotten Son.

The post creation scenario has different levels: Adam and Eve transgressed and fell from their position and therefore, were expelled from Paradise. But God appointed 'just men' to teach and guide His creation but the creation did not obey them.

---

[231] Infra, 4.3.8.

[232] Infra.5.1.1.1.

[233] Mal 4:2.

[234] Bedjan, *HS* III, 287.1; ET. Brock, "On the Veil of Moses," in *Studies in Syriac Spirituality*, 76.69.

[235] Infra. 5.3.3.

[236] Infra. 5.3.9.

[237] Evdokimov, *In the World, of the Church*, 12.

[238] Infra. 3.5.1.

The king wished to send His Son to rehabilitate the earth,
which the evil one had led away captive with the rows of idols, that he had brought along and (so) subjugated it.
His ambassadors resounded to inform the earth before His advent,
so that the Son of the virgin should be announced by His messengers.
The ambassadors made an assault on the persecutor but he was not terrified.
They shot at him arrows but he did not move away from the captives.
The merciful One saw that the world was wearied and the evil one had got the upper hand,
and He sent His Son to snatch the prey away from the captor.[239]

The same love that created human beings compelled God to come down to renew him.[240] According to His mercy the Father sent His only Begotten Son to save humanity.[241] The Son took the image of human being and became man[242] to save Adam, who fell from his noble rank.[243]

Your Father sent you and so you came to bear these things
excellent is your will perfect is your work and do accomplish your way.
Descend, my Lord, and effect the way on account of which you have come.
Bind the sin and liberate Adam by your crucifixion.
Ascend on the cross and put to shame principalities and powers
unmask them because the rulers were in error.[244]

By His grace the Lord came down for nativity to restore the Image of Adam that had been corrupted.[245] Through various sacraments the Son of God saved the world. Mar Jacob says that, through the birth of the Son of God, He fixed the distorted nature of humanity. He writes: "On that coin which the evil one damaged He will imprint His being and through it He will ransom the whole world from servitude."[246] When the rebellious one wanted to become God bodily he made up the great image. Therefore, the Son of the Magnificent One took human body to elevate the fallen ones. Through this act He overthrew the rebellious one and redeemed the lost ones.[247] He instituted the sacrament of baptism for cleansing[248] and served His own body as a pledge for salvation and

---

239 Bedjan, *SMS,* 725:19-726:4; ET. *FH* I, 47.121-128.

240 Bedjan, *SMS*, 725:15-16; ET. *FH* I, 47.116-117.

241 Bedjan, *SMS*, 725:15-16; ET. *FH* I, 47.116-117.

242 Bedjan, *SMS*, 725:15-16; ET. *FH* I, 47.116-117.

243 Bedjan, *SMS*, 776.7-8; ET. *FH* II, 96.23-24.

244 Bedjan, *HS* II, 367.17-22; ET. *FH* VIII, 224.429-434.

245 Bedjan, *SMS*, 725:1; ET. *FH* I, 46.103.

246 Bedjan, *SMS*, 733.15-16; ET. *FH* I, 55.291-292.

247 Bedjan, *SMS*, 775.11-77.1; ET. *FH* II, 96.11-97.38.

248 Bedjan, *HS* I, 181.6-15; ET. *FH* VI, 176.281-285.

union with His nature. Mar Jacob writes about the salvation process through birth and baptism:

> The loving kindness summoned me to come to birth.
> That has again called me to come to baptism too.
> The great mercy has drawn me to descend to become new born babe,
> it is that (mercy) which drew me to descend to become baptized.[249]
> While I do not need the furnace of the waters, behold, I am entering
> so that humanity that is worn out should be recast with that stamp of mine.
> I am stimulating them so that they should come the fountain like me
> in order that with the coin of mine they shall be stamped spiritually.
> To the tomb of water I am bringing down humanity,
> so that I may make them immortal in the resurrection.
> I am making them enter into the moist womb so that it will conceive them
> and give them the new birth without birth pangs.
> And again it is righteousness that I should be baptized by you, do not delay.
> Come, open the road because the world is expecting to be renewed by me.[250]

After the baptism, in order to restore the Image of Adam, the Son of God walked in this world with the sinful man and taught them His precepts. According to the will of God[251] He died for the sake of fallen Adam and killed the death by His death.

> Go, descend, accept the lance and the nails that are reserved for you
> because that also is the very purpose of your way and for it you have come.
> Behold, the cross which the daughter of Hebrew has fabricated gazes at you,
> go, be adorned and be glorified by it, as it is proper for you.
> Your death is the crown of life for humanity
> die as you willed and let all live by you, as it pleased you.[252]

After, all the above mentioned preparations are done He descended into the *Sheol* and rescued the prisoners who were imprisoned from the time of Adam.[253] He strengthened His disciples, gave them the authority of forgiveness of sins and gave them the Holy Spirit to be with them until the second coming.

The eschatological culmination is the final stage of salvation. In that great event the good will be taken to the bridal chamber of light to enjoy with the bridegroom and the wicked will be thrown outside in the darkness of *gehenna*.[254] Thus, According to Mar Jacob, Jesus is the Savior of the fallen

---

[249] Bedjan, *HS* I, 178.1-4; *FH* VI, 172.213-173.216.

[250] Bedjan, *HS* I, 181.6-15; ET. *FH* VI, 176.281-290.

[251] Bedjan, *HS* II, 367.18; ET. *FH* VIII, 224.430.

[252] Bedjan, *HS* II, 369.8-13; ET. *FH* VIII, 225.363-468.

[253] Bedjan, *SMS,* 725.19-726.4; ET. *FH* I, 47.121-128.

[254] Infra.1.7.11.

humanity. He found that salvation is a process; each and every act of Jesus Christ was a part of that saving work. Through those acts he saved humanity from sin and death. But, even after the ascension of Jesus through the Holy Spirit, the apostles and the Church, and through various sacraments this act of salvation will continue until the Second Coming.

1.11. Anthropology

Mar Jacob says about three kinds of beings: Supreme Being, Angels, and human beings. Supreme Being is the creator of all and He created the world out of nothing. Nobody could see the Supreme Being with their naked eyes but can hear and experience Him. He is unapproachable to earthly and heavenly beings.[255] Another terrestrial being is portrayed as the servant or messenger (*malako*), of the Supreme Being. Satan will also come under this group. They are neither God nor human but the middle ones. They are fiery in nature.[256] Human beings are the third type of being below the status of God. Human nature and God's nature are different; when Eve desires to become a goddess, which is beyond her nature, she fell.[257] Though human beings seem to be lower in nature than the angels they have several other peculiarities and prominence than the angels. The more prominent one is the right to carry the body and blood of the Son of God which is not permitted to the angels.[258]

God created Adam by harmoniously synchronizing the four elements of the nature which are against one another.[259] God formed man from the very dust of the earth,[260] which he took and kneaded with water to form mud; added air and fire, united them like colors to make a beautiful picture.[261] He mixed

[255] Bedjan, *SMS*, 729.20-730.7; ET. *FH* I, 51.211-218.

[256] Bedjan, *SMS*, 729.7-8; ET. *FH* I, 50.195-196.

[257] Bedjan, *SMS*, 731:5; ET. *FH* I, 52.237.

[258] *Vishuddha Qurbanakramam*, 223.

[259] Rilliet, *SHF* III, 580.1; ET. *FH* IX, 242.32; *Promiyon* II, 226. There were five eternal principles each in its own religion: light in East, wind in the West, fire in the South, water in the North, while darkness inhabited in the lower regions. The Lord of all occupied the region above. Due to the some sort of mingling of these eternal elements chaos ensued, and from mixture of the elements the Lord of all made the world and set it into order. See Mathews, *Introduction to Commentary on Genesis,* 61. The Greek philosophy does not propose fire as one of the elements of creation. cf. Possekel, *Evidence of Greek Philosophical Concepts in the Writings of Ephrem the Syrian*, 95.

[260] Bedjan, *HS* IV, 815.9-12; Bedjan, *HS* III, 863.1-2.

[261] Bedjan, *HS* I, 159.14-19; See Jansma, *L'Hexameron,* 4,14, 134, 154, 260. You gave him an immortal soul and destructible body, the one emerging from nothingness, the other from the four elements. (Air, water, fire and earth). The stoic philosophy also supports this argument. You gave him a soul endowed with reason and judgment, capable of distinguishing between godliness and ungodliness, of perceiving justice and injustice. You gave him a body endowed with five senses and with movement. *The Apostolic Constitutions* XII.

them together under one yoke,[262] they formed as it were, a chariot, upon which the five senses stand as a driver.[263] Then He breathed the life-giving spirit in him (Gen 2:7).[264] Adam was filled with light and life and many other beautiful gifts.[265]

With his five bodily senses and five spiritual senses, man is a ten-stringed harp, a vocal vessel, singing praise and glory of God[266] {five bodily senses are sight (*ḥzto*), hearing (*šm΄a*), taste (*ṭ'm*), feeling (*gešto*), and smell (*sooqo*) and the spiritual senses are understanding (*mad'o*), mind (*havno*), discernment (*puršono*), intelligence (*sookolo*), and knowledge (*yid'to*)}. Mar Jacob states about this ten senses:

> Wake up, my harp, and praise the Son
> with discernment, with many tunes full of love.
> Praise externally with five senses of the body,
> and praise in secret with the five senses of the spirit.
> With smell, touch, taste, hearing, and sight,
> with these five senses, praise with your body.
> And then praise with the hidden senses of the soul;
> knowledge, understanding, awareness, mind, and thought.[267]

Thus, when God created man He adorned him with spiritual and divine beauties: with rationality,[268] with free-will,[269] and with the grace of immortality.[270] God gave him a beautiful and desirable dwelling-place, the Paradise, which is planted towards the east, and this entire visible world: parts of which he would be beholder at its wonders, and parts of which, he would be a ruler.[271]

God created man as the crown of creation with all of his body and senses to perceive and appreciate God's handiwork. All the beauty and color of the rest of creation are summed up in him.[272] According to Mar Jacob, human beings are made of three parts: body soul and spirit and these are put together into one unit. Just as Jesus said, "where two or three are gathered together,

---

[262] Bedjan, *HS* III, 154.5-15.

[263] Bedjan, *HS* III, 155.15-18.

[264] Bedjan, *HS* III, 113.14-17.

[265] Bedjan, *HS* V, 796.6-8, 797.2-21.

[266] Bedjan, *HS* II, 77.9-14; *HS* V, 796.5, 797.4-10.

[267] Bedjan, *HS* II, 77.1-14.

[268] Rilliet, *SHF* III, 578.25; ET. *FH* IX, 241.32.

[269] Bedjan, *HS* I, 270.3-10.

[270] Alwan, *QHC* II, 23.129-24.166.

[271] Bichery, "Repentance and Fasting,"18.

[272] Bedjan, *HS* III, 152-155, 157-159.

there am I in their midst (Mt 18:20). Man with his three parts jointly is a temple of God with Christ in his midst.[273] His head represents the heights, and his feet the depths below the earth. Another beautiful observation of Mar Jacob is that human being is a small world, a microcosm, whose soul fills all parts of his body just as the power of God fills all over the world. And just as the body cannot limit the mind, so the world cannot limit the power of God.[274]

Another important aspect of Jacob's anthropological vision is that the Image of God is indwelt in human beings. Man is created in the Image of God. Like a coin stamped with the image of the king, the soul, the highest part of creation[275] is stamped with the Image of the great King.[276] And the Image is not simply that of the Father, but also, specifically, that of Christ. Christ was with the Father when Adam was formed and because the Father wished to send Christ to earth as a man, He prefigured Him in Adam.[277] Also, he writes that man has been created in a union of mortal and immortal.[278] He uses mainly two expressions to show the nature of man in relation to God. He used *şalmo* and *dmooto* for 'Image;' which are same terms are used in the Genesis account. In another occasion Mar Jacob uses these terms to show the 'type' of something or somebody as well as to show the anthropological significance of man. In the anthropological context he said, "When the Father fashioned Adam, He fashioned him by the Son, and in the likeness (*dmooto*) of His corporality itself He made his appearance (*şoorto*)."[279] It is clear that he uses these expressions to denote the external appearance of man; on the other hand *şalmo* is used to denote the internal nature of man. [He uses the term (*yuqno*), which means Image, as a synonym to *şalmo*].[280] Therefore, Mar Jacob says:

> It is the creator who with his skillfulness juxtaposed the natures
> in making the same man as of life and as of death.
> He established an image half dead and half alive,
> so that he should be subjected to two estates independently.
> He poured out the soul into a vase of clay mixed of dust
> and he mingled them together intelligibly.

---

273 Bedjan, *HS* II, 232.4-20.

274 Bedjan, *HS* IV, 553-556.

275 Bedjan, *HS* IV, 334.8-9.

276 Bedjan, *HS* III, 374.5.

277 Bedjan, *HS* III, 11.2-11; 611:4, 591:11ff.

278 Alwan, *QHC* II, 23.131-25.186; Mar Ephrem also having the same concept: "For when God created Adam, He did not make him mortal, nor did He fashion him as immortal, so that Adam, either by keeping or transgressing the commandment, might acquire from one of the trees, the (life) that he perfected." McVey, *Homily on Our Lord,* 108-109.

279 Alwan, *QHC* I, 11.214.

280 Konat, "*Old Testament Types of Christ,*" 72.

The wisdom inserted the living nature in the mortal clay
and the image was constituted to live or die easily.
Moreover, he gave that reasonable freedom
to choose according to its will, equality, life or death.
It is for this reason that he is mortal or immortal;
in this way towards where he himself inclines there to he turns himself...[281]

God mixed[282] his Image with dust and He mixed two different natures (divine and human) in the *ṣalmo* of Adam.[283] The verb *mixed* receives special importance. The word he uses for mixing is *leeš* which means 'to knead'. Thus, here mixing is like how flour is kneaded to make dough.[284] Therefore, mixing is an internal organically combining process and not an external adding process. Thus, man created within the immortality of God, which is His essential nature, with the mortality of dust or a created thing. It can be deduced from the above passage that human beings are created with both chances of mortality or immortality.

1.12. Mariology

In the Syriac Church there are no separate Mariological thoughts as such, but it is all related to the Christology of the Church. On the other hand Mary was a fascinating figure in the Early Churches as a whole, including its Syrian form. She holds the first place among the saints of the West Syriac Christian tradition. Every liturgical order intercedes to the Mother of God. The Fathers of the Church praised and glorified her place in the history of salvation. Even from the end of the first century or from the early second century itself Mary was glorified in the Church. The *protoevengelium* of James on Mary is the best example of this veneration. The fathers of the Church considered, just as Christ was prefigured in the Old Testament, Mary was prefigured in the Old Testament. In order to praise and glorify the part played by Mary in the salvation history the Fathers found and used several 'types' of Mary in the Old Testament. Perhaps these types interpret as the mariological thoughts of the Syriac Church.

The most important controversy over Mary in the Church of the Roman Empire was whether she is the Mother of Christ (κριστοτοκος) or Mother of God (θεοτοκος). The controversy began with the discussion of the nature of Christ. Nestorius, an Antiochene priest taught that Mary was only the mother of Christ and not the mother of God. Finally, the Church officially settled that Mary is the Mother of God and not simply the mother of Christ and the so

[281] Alwan, *QHC* II, 23.133-24.144.

[282] Alwan, *QHC* II, 23.137.

[283] Konat, "Old Testament Types of Christ," 72.

[284] Smith, *Syriac Dictionary,* 241.

called Nestorianism was condemned and Nestorius was exiled to Pershia. Mar Jacob also had no hesitation to call her Mother of God (*yoldat aloho*).[285]

Depicting Mary's qualities is very difficult just as depicting the mysteries of her Son Jesus Christ. Mar Jacob rightly asks: "How shall I paint the image of this most fair Maiden with dull colors of a blending unfit for her?"[286] Her position and devotion was magnificent; therefore, the Fathers of the Church found several imageries to depict the picture of the Virgin. They called her by using several titles such as, virgin, young girl, the second heaven,[287] daughter of poor, Mother of the Lord of Kings,[288] Virgin soil,[289] the ship bearing the treasures,[290] good field,[291] second Eve,[292] virgin mother, the fair palace, chariot of celestial being,[293] daughter of David,[294] second/new heaven,[295] tabernacle,[296] heavenly throne,[297] guarded ship,[298] honorable dove,[299] powerful city,[300] guarded field,[301] Mother of the King[302] dove,[303] enviable ewe,[304] chaste woman,[305] etc. The one and only quality that leads her to all these characteristics is her motherhood of the Son of God. The daughter of the lowly is ascended to a candidature of the mother of God. It was the greatest of all graces that was ever bestowed upon a human being. The quality of Virgin Mary to become the Mother of God is her humility, purity, sincerity and holiness. He writes:

---

[285] Bedjan, *LP*; "Homily on the Blessed Virgin Mary," *TV* 5.1(1993), 13.153; 22.377.

[286] Bedjan, *LP*; "Homily on the Blessed Virgin Mary," *TV* 5.1(1993), 9.59.

[287] Bedjan, *LP*; "Homily on the Blessed Virgin Mary," *TV* 5.1(1993), 8.43.

[288] Bedjan, *LP*; "Homily on the Blessed Virgin Mary," *TV* 5.1(1993), 8.39.

[289] Bedjan, *HS* III, 413.15; ET. "The Parable of the Leaven," *TV* 3(1989), 47.38.

[290] Bedjan, *LP*; "Homily on the Blessed Virgin Mary," *TV* 5.1(1993), 8.41.

[291] Bedjan, *LP*; "Homily on the Blessed Virgin Mary," *TV* 5.1(1993), 8.43.

[292] Bedjan, *LP*; "Homily on the Blessed Virgin Mary," *TV* 5.1(1993), 9.45.

[293] Bedjan, *SMS*, 744.12; ET. *FH* I, 65.515; Bedjan, *LP*, "Homily on the Blessed Virgin Mary," *TV* 5.1(1993), 9.55.

[294] Bedjan, *SMS*, 732.13; 744.3; *FH* I, 53.265; 64.505.

[295] Bedjan, *SMS*, 744.11; ET. *FH* I, 65. Bedjan, *LP*, "Homily on the Blessed Virgin Mary," *TV* 5.1(1993), 8.34.

[296] Bedjan, *SMS,* 744.17, ET. *FH* I, 65.520.

[297] Bedjan, *SMS,* 744.18, ET. *FH* I, 65.521.

[298] Bedjan, *SMS*, 747.8; ET. *FH* I, 68.575.

[299] Bedjan, *SMS*, 747.12; ET. *FH* I, 68.579.

[300] Bedjan, *SMS*, 747.18; ET. *FH* I, 68.585.

[301] Bedjan, *SMS*, 747.20; ET. *FH* I, 68.587.

[302] Bedjan, *SMS*, 727:21; ET. *FH* I, 49.165.

[303] Bedjan, *SMS*, 728:4; ET. *FH* I, 49.171.

[304] Bedjan, *SMS*, 747.10; ET. *FH* I, 68.577.

[305] Bedjan, *SMS*, 747.14; ET. *FH* I, 68.581.

When our Lord came down to earth, He regarded all women,
but chose one only, who was the most well-pleasing of them all.
He searched her out and found in her humility and holiness,
guileless motions and a God-loving soul.
A pure heart and all the thoughts of perfection;
and by reason of these He chose that pure Maiden full of all beauty.
He stirred from His place and couched in that most glorious among women,
for there was none like her in the world who might be compared with her:
One humble, pure, innocent, and without spot:
for she and none other was worthy to become His Mother.[306]

It is not proved that Mar Jacob ever considered that Mary is sinless by birth to support the immaculate doctrine of the Roman Church. But several times he says that she is guileless, innocent, pure, untainted, spotless, without worldly and fleshly desires, untainted womb, etc.[307] In one occasion he said "From her infancy the impulses of holiness stirred within her."[308] It is very important to note that it does not say anywhere that she is holy from her mother's womb. Again in another occasion he says that, "the Son of God refined His Mother in the Holy Spirit when He dwelt in her, that without sin He might receive a pure body from her." And again, "By the Spirit He rendered her body free from sin beforehand the Word came down to become flesh."[309] All these references do not support her sinless birth. But they say about her purification. Therefore, it could be assumed that Mar Jacob does not believe in the immaculate concept.

Mary was ever virgin: Mar Jacob believes in the virgin birth of Jesus Christ and Mary remained virgin even after the birth of Jesus. An answer to the demons' question to the Evil One, regarding the birth of Jesus Christ, the evil one says that, he has never see such a birth from the time of Cain. Every woman gives birth with birth pangs but this young girl remains virgin and still she gave birth to a child. It is a mystery to him how did she conceive and how she gave birth to child without breaking her virginity.[310] Supporting this argument Mar Jacob again says: "hidden child did not lose the seal of virginity at his birth… virginity he preserved intact… The young Mary continued on in her virginity."[311] He again writes: "The seal of virginity were ever in her body,

---

[306] Bedjan, *LP*; "Homily on the Blessed Virgin Mary," *TV* 5.1(1993), 12.121-130.

[307] Bedjan, *SMS*, 738.14; 739.1, 11; 742.4; ET. *FH* I, 59.392; 60.400, 410; 62.466; Bedjan, *LP*; "Homily on the Blessed Virgin Mary," *TV* 5.1(1993), 23.400.

[308] Bedjan, *LP*; "Homily on the Blessed Virgin Mary," *TV* 5.1(1993), 13.159.

[309] Bedjan, *LP*; "Homily on the Blessed Virgin Mary," *TV* 5.1(1993), 22.286-287.

[310] Bedjan, *SMS*, 783.19-784.12; ET. *FH* II, 103.185-200.

[311] Bedjan, *HS* III, 300.19-301.5; ET. Brock, "On the Veil of Moses," in *Studies in Syriac Spirituality*, 84.361-85.371.

and sanctity in her soul."[312] Regarding the birth of Jesus he said, like Adam gave birth to Eve through Holy Spirit without any fleshly desire Virgin gave birth to the Son of God.[313] He calls Mary as the mother of the King.[314]

He compares Mary with Eve; and calls her second Eve. Just as Eve became the "Mother of all living" Mary became the mother of the Living.[315] If Eve, by her disobedience, brought enmity between God and humanity; Mary by her obedience brought peace between God and humanity. She made peace between earth and heaven. Instead of the serpent, angel Gabriel rose up to speak and instead of Eve, Mary came forth to receive him. On behalf of her mother the daughter repaid the debt of Adam. "The edifice that the serpent had torn down, Gabriel built up anew, and Mary arighted the foundations that Eve had pulled down in Eden."[316] Eve brought wrath to earth but Mary brought peace to earth.[317] Eve brought disturbance by trying to become a goddess; whereas, Mary by her humility brought peace on the earth. By the silence of Eve came condemnation and infamy and by the speech of Mary, life, light, and innocence restored.[318] In short, Mar Jacob teaches about Mary that she is truly the Mother of God, ever virgin, second Eve, etc.

1.13. Free Will

Mar Jacob teaches that God created Adam with free will (*ḥirooto*)[319] and it was his choice to select what to do, say or think.[320] In one occasion he says that God created Adam as a rational being and created him with four elements of nature which are opposite to one another and put wisdom over it.[321] And among all other creatures only human beings have free will. In one of his homilies he writes: "I (Adam) alone have the free will from creatures."[322] He calls the free will as 'a driver or a charioteer (*henyooko*).[323] When God gave free will to man it was not aimed to commit sin but to glorify God always and it is his duty to grow in spirit. Those who do not glorify God will come under the rod of

---

[312] Bedjan, *LP*; "Homily on the Blessed Virgin Mary," *TV* 5.1(1993), 13.150.

[313] Bedjan, *LP*; "Homily on the Blessed Virgin Mary," *TV* 5.1(1993), 24.417-418.

[314] Bedjan, *SMS*, 727.21; ET. *FH* I, 49.167.

[315] Bedjan, *LP*; "Homily on the Blessed Virgin Mary," *TV* 5.1(1993), 24.41-429.

[316] Bedjan, *LP*; "Homily on the Blessed Virgin Mary," *TV* 5.1(1993), 18.283-284.

[317] Bedjan, *LP*; "Homily on the Blessed Virgin Mary," *TV* 5.1(1993), 19.305, 315.

[318] Bedjan, *LP*; "Homily on the Blessed Virgin Mary," *TV* 5.1(1993), 21.333-334.

[319] Alwan, *QHC* II, 24.141.

[320] Bedjan, *LP*; "Homily on the Blessed Virgin Mary," *TV* 5.1(1993), 14.173-180.

[321] Rilliet, *SHF* III, 578.5; ET. *FH* IX, 241.29.

[322] Bedjan, *HS* I, 270:9.

[323] Alwan, *QHC* II, 24.145.

justice.[324] However, Adam used his free will to sin and therefore, he fell from his high position.[325] In another occasion he describes the same: "You created me to live, but I by my own will tasted death, by my own will I went out from the great height of Eden."[326] Regarding the free will Mar Jacob opines that doing vice is not free will but it is the act of Satan.

> God has given free will to the sons of men,
> and with his free will, man acquires righteousness.
> Free will likewise worketh also iniquity,
> it is not hindered; were it hindered, it would not be free will.
> And that the sons of men all possess free will equally…
> And that one man is not without free will, while another has it;
> for all men are equal both in nature and in free will.[327]
> He that desires to work iniquity has power to do so;
> and him that works righteousness, God does not hold back.[328]

From the words of Mar Jacob it could be inferred that doing vice is not free will. Free will is given to choose good, to obey the precepts of the Creator and keep away from evil. But Satan misled man and fell from free will. He says every man has been created with free will: angel Gabriel, Simon Peter, Judah Iscariot, and John.[329] They have the power within them to choose what to do or not. Some desires to do the will of God or good, others do wickedness or the will of Satan. Mary did the will of God than what the world wishes; therefore, her free will kept her virginity.[330] Both the prodigal son and his brother had the free will. The younger one used his free will to get away from his father's presence and ruined his life. But the elder son used his free will to stay with his father and serve him; therefore, he was beloved to his father.[331]

---

324 Bedjan, *HS* I, 270.17; ET, "On the Prodigal Son," *TV* 5.4(1994), 13.57.

325 Bedjan, *HS* III, 152.1-4.

326 Bedjan, *HS* V, 796.7; 798.13.

327 Bedjan, *HS* I, 276.13-21; ET, "On the Prodigal Son," *TV* 5.4(1994), 18.181-19.190.

328 Bedjan, *HS* I, 277.1-4; ET, "On the Prodigal Son," *TV* 5.4(1994), 19.191-194.

329 Alwan, *QHC* III, 33.65-68.

330 Bedjan, *SMS*, 739.11-19; ET. *FH* I, 60.411-418.

331 Bedjan, *HS* I, 277.1-12; cf.
For our freedom is like a soul for desires, and by it they live,
but if it sheds them, it is as if they were dead.
Therefore (our freedom) is self governing since by its will debts stand
and by its will sins fall.
It is like the Heavenly One Whose power contains the universe,
and if He retracted it, all would fall. *HVir* III.8; ET. McVey, *Ephrem the Syrian*. 273.

1.14. Sin

Mar Jacob uses different words for sin such as (*ḥṭo*),[332] (*ḥbo*), etc. Sinfulness is described by darkness (2 Cor 6:14; Eph 5:11; 1 Jn 1:5-6) and holiness is portrayed by light. The sinners live in dark (*ḥešooko*) or night (*lilyo*) and fade with the fume of sins but the holy ones live in the light. Jesus was always pictured as day (*imomo*) or light) *nuḥro*) and when light enters into a dark place the darkness will disappear. Therefore, the bridal chamber of Christ is always portrayed as lighted chamber. Syriac theology defines redemption as the washing of the ugly dark deposit of sin from a person. When one is in sin she/he will emit stinky odor from him/her; and when he/she washes away his/her sins he/she emits fragrance.

Mar Jacob's doctrine of sin is not an alienated one from his tradition. Following the scripture and his predecessors, he says, Man/Adam was created in the Image and glory of God and he was free from sin and corruption. But since Adam was created as a rational being, Mar Jacob argues that, Satan was jealous of him.[333] Therefore, Satan planned a plot against man to put him into sin and to alienate him from communion with God. In order to execute his plot he enticed the woman. He continues, "then snake (Satan) entered to break up the joyful banquet and drag Adam down to the grave."[334] The snake slithered around, whispering to the bride, deceiving her into sin and she fell in his treachery. Eve thought that she could achieve the divinity of God. "Behold, she wanted (to become) a goddess which would be beyond (her) nature." [335] "Like an eagle among the simple doves, he would force Adam and Eve to fly from the nest of Eden."[336] Adam and Eve transgressed the Law of God and therefore sinned. Due to the sin at Eden humanity lost its glory.[337] Mar Jacob depicts this story of fall in the dialogue *Poem on the Soul*. An answer to the question how did the soul lose its place in the luminous bridal chamber, the soul says, the transgressor enticed to transgress the commandment of God and offered the kingdom but she was cheated and she ended up in the *sheol* where it is full of darkness and hardship.[338]

It is noteworthy to mention Mar Jacob's right interpretation of the creation story. Many of the modern scholars accuse that the cause of the environmental problem is the wrong medieval Judeo-Christian understanding of Genesis 1:28. They read this passage, "God ordained man and woman to subdue and

---

[332] Bedjan, *HS* I, 278.18; ET, "On the Prodigal Son," *TV* 5.4(1994), 20.230.

[333] Rilliet, *SHF* III, 578.24; ET. *FH* IX, 242.34.

[334] Bedjan, *HS* V, 797.5-6, 10-14.

[335] Bedjan, *SMS*, 731.6; ET. *FH* I, 52.237.

[336] Bedjan, *HS* III, 160.17-20.

[337] Bedjan, *SMS*, 731.1-6; ET. *FH* I, 54.275-280.

[338] Brock, "Jacob of Serugh: A Poem on the Soul," 42.*yud-kop*.

domain over the earth". Therefore, human beings are ordained to subdue and domain over the created world to their own benefit and this understanding made human beings to exploit nature ruthlessly and enjoy it for themselves. This anthropocentric theology of the middle ages devastated the eco system.[339] But Mar Jacob very clearly interprets that this passage is not giving the license to subdue the earth but to keep it and protect it. Therefore he says; "He made me a guardian for paradise but I failed to guard it."[340]

Mar Jacob views that sin is alienation from God.[341] He states: "Whenever a man sins, he is far from God."[342] The one who sins go away from God to where he thinks he is not visible to God and he wipes away the thoughts of God from his mind.[343] Another marvelous interpretation is that those who sin will be far from himself, because as soon as a man forgets God he forgets his own soul.[344] See his interpretation:

> The faraway country whither that he journeyed
> is an evil will that is far from God.
> He takes his heart far from God, and then he sins;
> for he journeyed as it were to another country, to sin there.
> As long as the Lord is not there for him to see,
> he sins, and the Lord is not in his mind.
> Therefore it is written that he journeyed to a far country
> and scattered his wealth in prodigal living.
> He distanced his soul from God while he sinned
> and subjugated his freedom to laboring for vanities.
> Virginity, the great treasure that nature possesses,
> he ruined with adultery and fornication, and perished from him…
> set him at a great remove from God when he sinned.[345]

When a person sins his/her glory will lose and will fall from son-ship.[346] The reward of sin is habitation in darkness and hardships.[347] They will be abandoned from the rays of light and will put on the leaves of shame and they will lose the protection of the seal of King.[348]And finally, sin brought death.[349]

---

339 White, "The Historical Roots of Our Ecological Crisis," 1024.

340 Brock, "Jacob of Serugh: A Poem on the Soul," 42.*nun*.

341 Rilliet, *SHF* III, 578.19; ET. *FH* IX, 241.29.

342 Bedjan, *HS* I, 278.16; 281.3; ET, "On the Prodigal Son," *TV* 5.4(1994), 20.228; 22.278.

343 Bedjan, *HS* I, 278.19-20; ET, "On the Prodigal Son," *TV* 5.4(1994), 20.229-230.

344 Bedjan, *HS* I, 284.16; ET, "On the Prodigal Son," *TV* 5.4(1994), 24.348-349.

345 Bedjan, *HS* I, 278.15-271.19; ET, "On the Prodigal Son," *TV* 5.4(1994), 20.227-21.253.

346 Rilliet, *SHF* I, 540.11-20; ET. *FH* IV, 131.7.

347 Brock, "Jacob of Serugh: A Poem on the Soul," 41. *dalath*.

348 Brock, "Jacob of Serugh: A Poem on the Soul," 41.*zayin*.

349 Bedjan, *SMS*, 730.16; Bedjan, *FH* I, 52.228.

Mar Jacob says that free will and sin are closely interrelated. It is free will that decides a person to sin or not to sin. For example, the prodigal son had the free will to take his portion and went away from his father's house. And he used his free will and went away from his father's house and lived wantonly.[350] Therefore, Mar Jacob has a clear vision of sin. Guinan, from a western view point blames that Mar Jacob's theology on sin has not fully been developed. He says, "… but this is true of all Monophysite theologians. Since no controversy on original sin or grace ever arose among them, their doctrine in these areas always remained "in its infancy," in a somewhat rudimentary form."[351] In a Western juridical understanding of sin he is right that the Eastern theologians are at the infancy state on the understanding of sin. But in the Eastern Christian thinkers give importance to Adamic sin; therefore, Mar Jacob is right.

1.15. Sheol

The Hebrew word *Sheol* is found sixty-five times in the Hebrew bible. The Greek parallel translated as 'Hades,' used twenty-six times in Apocrypha and ten times in New Testament. Both *Sheol* and Hades refer a place where the dead ones are summoned. It was also called 'the pit' (Isa 38:18), "the bottomless place" (Lk 8:31; Rom 10:7), "the lower parts" (Ps 63:10; Eph 4:9). The post exilic Judaism portrayed *Sheol* as a place of punishment of sinners. The synoptic gospels and James used to denote it as a place of pain.

The cosmology of the ancient locates three worlds: the heaven in the upper part, the earth in the middle, and *Sheol* in the underworld. The Syriac Fathers also refer three-tier cosmological regions: paradise, *Gehenna*,[352] and *Sheol*. The concept of (*Sheol*) has an important place in the Syriac theology. Some scholars are of the opinion that the concept of *Sheol* is not based on cosmology but rather on concern for the destiny of the dead.[353] Mar Jacob also supports the three-tier world. Paradise: which Adam lost, but Christ regained; *Sheol*: is an under-worldly place where the departed inhabited; *Gehenna*: is an eschatological fiery place where torments are waiting for the wicked. It is said

[350] God has given free will to the sons of men,
and with his free will, man acquires righteousness.
Fee will likewise worketh also iniquity;
it is not hindered; were it hindered, it would not be free will.
And that the sons of men all possess free will equally,
thou mayest understand from the reaching of the Son of God. (Bedjan, *HS* I, 276.13-21; ET, "On the Prodigal Son," *TV* 5.4(1994), 18.181-19.186).

[351] Gunian, *Eschatology of Jacob of Serugh*, 25-26.

[352] *Gehenna* is coming from Hebrew which means tormenting place. Smith, *Syriac Dictionary,* 68. The same word is uses in Greek also. Cf. Sokoloff, *A Syriac Lexicon*, 229.

[353] Reicke, "Hell," 198.

that *Gehenna* is an unpopulated place until the Day of Judgment.[354] *Didascalia Apostolurum* portrays *Sheol* as underground. When says regarding the sin of Dathan, Korah, and Abiram it uses the term *Sheol* simply as underneath the earth. "And the earth opened her mouth and swallowed Dathan and Korah and Abiram and their tents and their vessels and all that were with them, and they went down alive to *Sheol*."[355] Mar Jacob uses this term very usefully in his homilies. In its very broad usage Mar Jacob and other writers used the term *Sheol* as the tomb of the dead. But in popular spiritual sense it is the place where the dead assembled before the death of Christ. He directly and without any confusion refers the tomb of Jesus is *Sheol*.

The following are some of the usages of *Sheol* in Mar Jacob. *Sheol* is a place where the captives were gathered.[356] It is the place beyond the limits of the inhabited land.[357] It located below the recesses[358] in the heart of the earth[359] in the caves in the depths of the earth,[360] it is the underworld.[361] *Sheol* is a place of darkness[362] (Job 10:21-22; 17:13; Ps 88:6, 12; 143:3) and silence (Ps 6:5; 30:9; 88:10-12; 115:17; Isa 38:18). Its inhabitants are called dark or gloomy ones.[363] Jacob calls it as the land of dead (*ar'o dmooto*) the house of perdition (*bet abedno*), house of the deceased (*bet aneede*), the place of the dead (*ataro dmeeto*), belly of death (*karso dmauto*), where the men who have been swallowed down are corrupted and decay.[364] *Sheol* is a great city of the captor (Isa 38:10). It has bars and bolts on its gates, and high walls around it to keep its treasures (prisoners).[365]

It can be evaluated from the writings of the Syriac Fathers that they found *Sheol* as a place of perdition and moreover, the place which is assigned for transgressors. However, Jesus broke the doors of the *Sheol* and liberated the departed from the custody of *Sheol* and saved them. This reminds the promise of Jesus to his disciples that, "You are Peter, and on this rock I will build my Church; and the gates of hades will not prevail against it" (Mt 16:18). Through the transgression Adam stripped life and put-on death. Transgression of the

---

[354] Buchan, *Blessed is He Who Brought Adam from Sheol,* 35.

[355] *The Didascalia Apostolorum in English*, 103.

[356] Bedjan, *HS* I, 179.13; ET. *FH* VI,174.247.

[357] Bedjan, *HS* I, 180.4; ET. *FH* VI, 174.259.

[358] Bedjan, *HS* II, 881.12.

[359] Bedjan, *HS* II, 880.22.

[360] Bedjan, *HS* V, 791.17.

[361] Bedjan, *HS* V, 800.11.

[362] Bedjan, *HS* I, 497.3; ET. McCollum, "Homily on Peter," in *MHMJS*, Fasc. 22, 38.288.

[363] Bedjan, *HS* V, 798.1-2.

[364] Bedjan, *HS* II, 344.1, 18; *HS* III, 430.8-9; 559.4.

[365] Bedjan, *HS* V, 786.7; 787.19; 788.6; 796.6; 800.6-7.

commandments had put them to shame and they became strangers at the house of the Father, they were cast out from the heights of the Garden of Eden; *Sheol*, the abyss of the dead, received them.[366] They were deprived of the table of the King and became dust, and the food of the dragon. In the *Sheol*, the webs of spider covered them, they were cast down, they stumbled and fell and became devoid of hope.[367]

For Mar Jacob it is a place of bondage and once a person enter there, nobody can escape from there. By taking the example of the story of Samson he compared it like a harlot. Just as the harlots *Sheol* puts all those came from the generation of Adam under her custody,[368] whereas Jesus shattered the doors (usually Syriac fathers used the term *bars*) and liberated them from the bondage of *Sheol*, Satan. According to Mar Jacob *Sheol* is a place where all the departed from Adam till the time of Jesus' death waited eagerly for the arrival of Jesus and wait for the good news of resurrection. They expected that the Messiah will come and open the door of Paradise for them.[369] In his view it can be deduced that until the entrance of Jesus there is no difference between righteous and unrighteous in *Sheol*, everyone from the time of Adam including Abel, Noah, Abraham, Moses, Joseph and other righteous people waited resurrection.[370]

> Go die and redeem, for behold, all the dead look at you.
> Visit the prisoners and make your light shine forth among the dead.
> Behold, in the caves of the tombs all the captives are shut up.
> Go, enter into it and make return the bereaved to their place.
> As you will it, thus accomplish, because it is fair for you.
> Conquer the victorious one, and grant victory to Adam who had been condemned.[371]

Mar Jacob compares Jesus' redemptive act with that of Samson. Just as Samson went to the harlot's house and destroyed its walls and killed the enemies, in order to regain the generations from Adam Son of God descent and slept in the *Sheol* broke its bars and victoriously came out of it with the slaves. He says:

> *Sheol* is a harlot and all the generations were her men;
> and she seized our Lord, that He should be with her like rest.
> So He went in, and slept, and the door of the tomb was shut upon Him,
> and in their madness they stood guarding Him as they did Samson.
> But the Savior rose from the grave and broke down

[366] Rilliet, *SHF* I, 540.12-14; ET. *FH* IV, 131.7.

[367] Rilliet, *SHF* I, 540.25; ET. *FH* IV, 132.7.

[368] Bedjan, *HS* V, 346.4; ET. "A Homily on Samson," *TV* 11(1992), 64.309.

[369] Bedjan, *HS* V, 463.19-20; ET. *FH* V, 156.337-338.

[370] Bedjan, *HS* V, 463.11-466.8; ET. *FH* V, 155.329-158.388.

[371] Bedjan, *HS* II, 368.2-7; ET. *FH* VIII, 224.435-440.

all the bulwarks of *Sheol* as He departed, and they stood not before Him.
And this likeness brought Samson in unto the harlot,
for she too is *Sheol*, being perdition to all that draw near her.
This type which was depicted in Samson gave him the strength
to lift up the gates and the iron bars and to depart as he did.
Many had gone in unto that harlot of the Philistines,
no man save but Samson broke down the gates of her town.
All generations went in unto *Sheol*, the ravager of all,
but excepting our Lord, no man threw down its walls and quickened its dead.
This mystery was kindled in this Hebrew,
and he pulled up the gates of the fortress after going in unto the harlot.
He confounded the Philistines by his mighty deed,
and depicted an image of them that guarded the tomb of the Son.[372]
He upended and cast down all the high walls of *Sheol*,
and brought out thence the spoils of the generations that had been imprisoned.
Sheol's bolts and bars and gates, He broke,
and emptied the stronghold of the captivity imprisoned therein.[373]

Therefore, *Sheol* has a deeper meaning, primarily it is a tomb, and secondly it was the place where all generations from Adam were captives until the arrival of Jesus Christ. Jesus went there, lied down there like an ordinary man as a captive. When he resurrected from the dead he shattered its wall and liberated the children of Adam from the captivity of *Sheol.*

Conclusion

This chapter is an introduction to Mar Jacob of Serugh, his life, works, and major theological understanding. He lived in Syrian Edessa during the second part of the fifth century and early quarter of the sixth century. He was a prodigy and powerful writer. Above all, he was a man of ardent faith in God Jesus Christ. He was a spiritual father with strong conviction that he was called for preaching the word of God. He lived in a period of controversies and schisms, therefore, he taught the right faith to his countrymen.

The latter part of this chapter discussed Mar Jacob's theological interpretation in general. It is found that his writings are spiritual interpretation rather than theological refutations. He is spiritually oriented and scripture based theologian. He uses types and images to elucidate the mysteries of God. Though he studied in the school of Edessa he is inclined to the Alexandrian theology. He followed and upheld the faith and teachings of Mar Ephrem. He is orthodox in his theological understanding and taught the right faith against the heretics. His acceptance of the entire Christendom, like his predecessor Mar Ephrem, underlines his orthodoxy in teachings.

---

[372] Bedjan, *HS* V, 346.4-347.2; ET. "A Homily on Samson," *TV* 11(1992), 64.309-326.

[373] Bedjan, *HS* III, 419.19-22; ET. "The Parable of the Leaven," *TV* 3(1989), 53.167-170.

Chapter 2

Mar Jacob's Ecclesiological Homilies and Exegetical Methodology

Introduction

Church has an important place in the theology of Mar Jacob of Serugh. He considered the Church as the vehicle for salvation. Many of his homilies concentrated on the entity of Church. Through these homilies Mar Jacob tried to establish the pre-existent nature of the Church. In these homilies he compares the Church with the Synagogue or Israel, the chosen people Israel as the prototype of the Church. Before God created the world He had the image of the Church in His mind. Mar Jacob brings images of Eve and the people of Israel, whom God brought from Egypt, as the bride of the Most High. The Bridegroom, Christ, instituted sacraments for the salvation of the world. And He appointed priesthood as the authority to dispense the mysteries. This chapter introduces some of the homilies of Mar Jacob and their main arguments. These homilies shall be the foundation of ongoing discussions in this study. The second part of this chapter is a discussion on the methodological approaches of Mar Jacob in his biblical interpretation. Unlike other traditions Mar Jacob followed the symbolic and typological interpretation to elucidate the biblical truths.

2.1. Ecclesiological Homilies of Mar Jacob

In the category of ecclesiological homilies I have selected seven homilies from the available sources; mainly from the Bedjan's edition. There would be many such homilies which discuss purely on Church but all of them are not considered in this study. Among those homilies which I have selected some of them with their title itself declares ecclesiological character, but some of them are not. In some cases though the title hold the term 'Church' there would not be many references on the particular typology of 'bride-bridegroom' imagery. Even though by its title it may seems like a festal homily, "On the Baptism of Our Redeemer in the Jordan"[1] is fully devoted to this theme. Therefore, I have much depended on this homily to bring out his theology. Other than these homilies I partially or fully depend on many homilies of Mar Jacob by various editors like Bedjan,[2] Rilliet,[3] Alwan,[4] Albert,[5] and others. Because, in their interpretation of the Scripture, the Syriac Church Fathers may not go for systematic rational cross reference as the modern historical critical interpreters. Rather, they find interconnection of the salvation history through the texts used by repeted, cyclic interpretation. They made use of the advantage of the polyvalence of the symbolic theology. They could insert any theme of salvation history in any of their homilies. So that each and every homily of Mar Jacob is important in interpreting the imagery.

2.1.1. The Descent of the Most High on Sinai, and Mystery of the Church

The homily on "The Descent of the Most High on Sinai, and Mystery of the Church" is the second homily in Bedjan's edition (*HS* I, 3-37). This homily describes the Mount Sinai event (Ex 19-34). In this homily Mar Jacob portrays the entire Sinai event as an administration of the establishment of Church. As usual the author of the *memro* envisages the greatness of the Almighty God and his own weakness to interpret the mysteries of God. From the first section[6] itself Mar Jacob portrays the 'bride-bridegroom' imagery[7] and calls Israel as an adulterous wife.[8] In the second section[9] he says about the love God and the pre-Sinai event; how God saved Israel from Pharaoh. Because of his love for his creation God chose synagogue or Israel as the bride.[10] From the early sections of the homily he portrays different aspects nuptial imagery

[1] Bedjan *HS* I, 167-193, homily number 8.

[2] *Homiliae Selectae Mar Jacobi Sarugensis*, Vols. I-V, (ed.) P. Bedjan, Paris-Leipzig 1905-1910; *Martyrii, qui wr Sahadona, quae supersunt omnia*, P. Bedjan, (ed.), Paris 1902.

[3] *Jacques de Saroug: Six Homilies Festals en Prose*, (ed.) F. Rilliet, *Patrologia Orientalis* 43 (Fascicule 4, No 196), Turnhout 1986.

[4] *Jacqes De Sarough, Quarte Homelies Metriques sur La Creation*, (ed. & tr.) Khalil Alwan, in *CSCO* Vols 508/509, (Syri 214/215).

[5] Albert, *HCJ* =Albert, Micheline., "Jacques De Saroug Homelies Contre Les Jufis," *PO* Tome XXXVIII, Fac. 1, No 174. Turnhout: Diffusion Mondiale, 1976.

[6] Bedjan, *HS* I, 3.-6.2.

[7] Bedjan, *HS* I, 4.3-4.

[8] Bedjan, *HS* I, 4.5.

[9] Bedjan, *HS* I, 6.3-8.12.

[10] Bedjan, *HS* I, 6.17-18.

like betrothal, wedding ring, crown, wedding feast, etc.[11] He gave ransom, and brought the bride out from Egypt. He guided her through the Red Sea and the wilderness, fattened her with quails and water.[12] In the third section[13] he describes Moses' ascent to Sinai and dramatically envisions various events on the mountain. Again, he describes many virtues of the bride.[14] He called Moses as the friend of the bridegroom, the mediator who made possible the covenant between the bridegroom and the bride.[15]

The next section[16] shows that God chose Moses as the mediator between the Bridegroom and bride. The Bridegroom sent His friend to prepare the bride for betrothal. He came down from the mountain and taught the glorious nature of the Bridegroom and exhorted her to be pure just as the Bridegroom is pure. He gave instructions about how she should behave. In the fifth section[17] Moses, the friend of the Bridegroom, educated her further. He sanctified her to become the bride of the heavenly Bridegroom.[18] The sixth section[19] also speaks about the efforts of Moses to prepare the bride of the heavenly Bridegroom. Moses took three days to educate the bride about her call and election.[20] He filled her with wisdom and holiness. Then Mar Jacob describes about the heavenly beings' preparation for the betrothal.

In the seventh section[21] he romanticizes the descent of the Bridegroom to Sinai. He beautifully portrays the different responses of the heavenly and earthly, animate and inanimate things. The eighth section[22] starts with the description of descend of God on the mountain of Sinai. He narrates the magnificence of God. He tells that cloud is a bridal chamber and the entire event was a banquet.[23] In the ninth section[24] Mar Jacob raises some questions regarding the unnatural events on and around Mount Sinai. In the conclusion of this section he assumed that these are pointing to the birth of the Church.

---

[11] Bedjan, *HS* I, 7.8-11.

[12] Bedjan, *HS* I, 7.1-8.12.

[13] Bedjan, *HS* I, 8.13-10.18.

[14] Bedjan, *HS* I, 9.7ff.

[15] Bedjan, *HS* I, 10.19-20.

[16] Bedjan, *HS* I, 10.19-12.13.

[17] Bedjan, *HS* I, 12.14-14.16.

[18] Bedjan, *HS* I, 13.13-14.

[19] Bedjan, *HS* I, 14.17-16.12.

[20] Bedjan, *HS* I, 14.21.

[21] Bedjan, *HS* I, 16.13-18.14.

[22] Bedjan, *HS* I, 18.15-20.17.

[23] Bedjan, *HS* I, 20.5-8.

[24] Bedjan, *HS* I, 20.18-22.13.

The tenth section[25] is a discussion on various attitudes of Moses, the friend of the Bridegroom, the nation, and corruptor. The corruptor made confusion in the bride but Moses encourages her by telling about the power and holiness of her Bridegroom. The eleventh section[26] deals with the wedding on the top of the Mountain. The Bridegroom is ready; the marriage chamber, the marriage settlement (dowry), the wedding garments, and the wedding feast are also ready. Sounds of thunder, veil of clouds, and light of glory make a magnificent setting for the betrothal.

In the twelfth section[27] Mar Jacob portrays his incomprehensibility to understand the Bridegroom. Heavenly beings wondered about his descent to the earthly mountain. He says that the throne of the Bridegroom is covered to both the earthly and the heavenly. The vision of the earthly are covered with fire and the heavenly by his glory.[28] Thirteenth section[29] describes Moses' ascend to the Most Holy One in the cloud. The Bridegroom sits in the bridal chamber and a curtain of cloud is set before the Bridegroom. Moses entered in the bridal chamber and receives the cut stone that containing the instructions.[30] Then he instructed the bride compassionately and purged her from corruptions. In the fourteenth section[31] he concludes the homily.

2.1.2. Consecration of the Church, and Prophet Moses

This is the third homily in Bedjan's edition (*HS* I, 38-46). This is comparatively a small homily. Mar Jacob tries to prove that the Tabernacle which Moses pitched in the wilderness is a 'type' of the Church. In it he compares Moses and Jesus, Church and the tabernacle, seventy preachers and seventy elders of Moses, twelve apostles and leaders of twelve tribes of Israel and so on.

The homily starts with regular introduction which narrates his weakness to delineate the incomprehensible God and His glories. The first section[32] comprises thirty six lines. The second section[33] starts with the mystery of the Church which is foreseen through the establishment of the tabernacle at the wilderness by the hands of Moses. He says that the tent was not made by Moses but by God Himself.[34] He built the Church which was chosen from

[25] Bedjan, *HS* I, 22.14-24.2.

[26] Bedjan, *HS* I, 24.3-27.5.

[27] Bedjan, *HS* I, 30.3-33.5.

[28] Bedjan, *HS* I, 32.3-6.

[29] Bedjan, *HS* I, 33.6-35.16.

[30] Bedjan, *HS* I, 33.14-17.

[31] Bedjan, *HS* I, 35.17.38.2.

[32] Bedjan, *HS* I, 38.8-40.6.

[33] Bedjan, *HS* I, 40.7-41.18.

[34] Bedjan, *HS* I, 40.9.

eternity and Moses was only a witness to this event.[35] Then he writes that Moses saw "New Jerusalem" in the darkness on Mount Sinai.[36]

In the beginning of the third section[37] Mar Jacob mentions that God showed Moses the typical image of the Church in the darkness of Mount Sinai and he descended from the mountain and established exactly what God showed him.[38] In the same part he states about the crown of the Church which reminds the crown of the bride. The rest of the third section deals with the high ranking position of the Church, the place of angels, and its adornments are described. The fourth section[39] begins with a comparison between Jesus and Moses. Here he says Moses exactly resembles our Lord.[40] Then he goes to the revelations of David about the bride Church. He compares twelve apostles with the seventy elected men from the tribes of Israel.[41] Thus he adorned the proto Church with several adornments and entrusted it to the nation. The fifth section[42] describes marvelously about the confrontation between God and Moses. Mysterious things were going on and finally Moses came down with a veiled face and the mysteries of the Church were hidden in him.

2.1.3. A Homily on the Baptism of Our Redeemer

This is the eighth homily in the Bedjan's edition (Bedjan, *HS* I, 167-193). An English translation is available in the *Select Festal Homilies* by Thomas Kollamparampil.[43] Though this homily, by its title, will fall under festal homilies the bride-bridegroom imagery is the main theme of this homily. The homily starts with the discussion of the Bridegroom's preparation of bridal feast to His bride, the Church. The immediate line says the Royal Son wished to betroth the afflicted one and He sent her to the fountain (baptism) to wash her dust.[44] The bride was weak and wearied and her beauty was altered due to her idol worship. By His loving kindness the Bridegroom prepared the wholesome water and sent her to wash her filth so that she would be purified

---

[35] Bedjan, *HS* I, 40.10-11.

[36] Bedjan, *HS* I, 41.4.

[37] Bedjan, *HS* I, 41.19-44.3.

[38] Bedjan, *HS* I, 41.21-42.1.

[39] Bedjan, *HS* I, 44.4-46.16.

[40] Bedjan, *HS* I, 44.5-6.

[41] Bedjan, *HS* I, 44.22-45.13.

[42] Bedjan, *HS* I, 46.17-48.5.

[43] Kollamparampil, *FH* VI, Bangalore: Dharmaram Publications, 1997, 159-186. Some of these translations are re-published by Gorgias press with Sertho Syriac script in *MHMJS* Fascicules. 2, 3, 8, 18-20, 21, (Texts from Christian Late Antiquity vols. 4, 5, 13, 23, 24), Piscataway, NJ: Gorgias Press, 2008-2010.

[44] Bedjan, *HS* I, 167.1-4; ET. *FH* VI, 162.1-4.

to become the bride of the heavenly Bridegroom. The whole section[45] deals with the foul nature of the Church and Christ's saving activity by sending her to the baptismal water which He specially prepared for her. When He prepared baptismal water He placed the robe of glory into it[46] therefore, the bride could retain it through baptism.

The second section[47] tells about the commissioning of the friend of the Bridegroom to adorn the bride. The Bridegroom sent His friend, son of the barren woman (John the Baptist), before Him to adorn the bride. John came with the dress of the Holy Spirit and talked to her beautifully about the Royal Bridegroom who comes to betroth her and exhorted her to adorn herself in order to receive her promised Bridegroom. The third section[48] is an exhortation from the book of Isaiah about the Bridegroom. The Church asked Isaiah to teach her about John the Baptist; because she knows Isaiah and his promise beforehand. The Church asks, though in his appearance he is very poor his words are magnificent; therefore, tell me whether he is genuine or not. Then Isaiah speaks that he is genuine. He is the one who makes smooth the steep ways of your Bridegroom. Go and descend into the water and be purified.

In the fourth section[49] Mar Jacob portrayed that the bride believed in the Baptist and purified herself by listening to him. After hearing from Isaiah the bride approached the Baptist by thinking that he is the Bridegroom; because, Messiah was concealed from her among the tribes.[50] But the Baptist revealed that he is not the Bridegroom but only a faithful servant of her Bridegroom and made her wait for the Bridegroom. In the fifth section[51] Mar Jacob portrays the bride's waiting for the Bridegroom. When she heard from the Baptist about her Bridegroom she was eagerly waiting for her betrothed. She was earnestly looking upon each one who descended for the baptism in the hope that whether he would be her Bridegroom. Here, Mar Jacob portrays her as a 'comely woman' (ܦܐܝܬܐ *p'yto*)[52] Just few minutes ago she was black, weak, and wearied but now she became beautiful by the washing of her filth from her body. Mar Jacob here introduces another new concept: the womb of waters. This reminds the rebirth through the baptism. Sixth[53] and seventh[54] sections are

---

[45] Bedjan, *HS* I, 167.1-168.9; ET. *FH* VI, 162.1-163.16.

[46] Bedjan, *HS* I, 168.8-9; ET. *FH* VI, 163.15-16.

[47] Bedjan, *HS* I, 169.10-169.2; ET. *FH* VI, 163.17-164.30.

[48] Bedjan, *HS* I, 169.3-170.7; ET. *FH* VI, 164.31-165.56.

[49] Bedjan, *HS* I, 170.8-171.5; ET. *FH* VI, 165.57-166.74.

[50] Bedjan, *HS* I, 170.15; ET. *FH* VI, 165.64.

[51] Bedjan, *HS* I, 171.6-19; ET. *FH* VI, 166.75-88.

[52] Bedjan, *HS* I, 171.15; ET. *FH* VI, 166.85.

[53] Bedjan, *HS* I, 171.20-173.5; ET. *FH* VI, 167.89-168.114.

[54] Bedjan, *HS* I, 173.6-174.4; ET. *FH* VI, 168.115-169.134.

also portrayals of waiting for the Bridegroom. Here many biblical passages are explained. In his narration it is sure that the Baptist knows beforehand that the Holy Spirit would come upon the Son and the Father would give confirmation. Mar Jacob calls the Church as the 'bride of Light' (*kalat nuḥro*). Thousands and ten thousands were baptized, but neither the Spirit nor the voice of the Father did come and still the Church is awaited the Bridegroom. Now the adorned Church, with the ornament of repentance, is ready to receive the Bridegroom and the wedding feast is also ready, but the Bridegroom has not arrived yet.[55] They are waiting for the Spirit and the white garment which the Bridegroom may bring.

In the eighth section[56] Mar Jacob delineates the changes in the water at the Bridegroom's arrival. Finally, the Bridegroom arrived and even when He was far away from the river the water became fervent and fire kindled the stream as a preparation for his arrival and made itself clean and sanctified its womb. He says that the Bridegroom's power kindled the water and the Holy Spirit stood above the water. He came to the baptism not to sanctify himself but the water may be sanctified by his descent. In the ninth section John the Baptist and David are introducing the Bridegroom to the bride. John says that, this is your Bridegroom from the beginning, He is betrothed to you.[57] He is the Lamb who carries the sin of the world. Then David came and exhorted the bride to forget her people and adore this Bridegroom. The next few sections are a conversation between the Bridegroom and the friend of the Bridegroom. Mar Jacob separated the tenth section for John's argument against Christ's demand to baptize Him.[58] When Christ approached John to be baptized by his hands, John replied that he wish to be baptized by Him, He is rich, His is governorship and authority. He is not lacking anything to be baptized by his hands because pardon and forgiveness belong to Him.

Eleventh section[59] is Christ's reply to John. He said that, He is not lacking anything to gain from the baptism but His loving kindness and mercy compelled Him to receive birth and baptism. He wants to recover the image of Adam; that is His mission. The twelfth section[60] is a confession of John. John was trembled on hearing the words of Christ: he compared himself to husk and straw and

[55] Here, he reminds three baptismal practices of his church that: they practiced Chrismation or anointing immediately after the baptism of water (Bedjan, *HS* I, 173.10; ET. *FH* VI, 168.119) and during the baptism the candidates will be naked (Bedjan, *HS* I, 173.20; ET. *FH* VI, 169.129). Immediately after the baptism the candidates will be dressed in white clothes as representation of the robe of glory.

[56] Bedjan, *HS* I, 174.5-175.10; ET. *FH* VI, 169.135-170.160.

[57] This shows that the Church is a preexistent one.

[58] Bedjan, *HS* I, 176.11-177.9; ET. *FH* VI, 171.181-172.200.

[59] Bedjan, *HS* I, 177.10-179.2; ET. *FH* VI, 172.201-173.236.

[60] Bedjan, *HS* I, 179.3-180.9; ET. *FH* VI, 173.237-175.264.

not fit to approach the Fire. Since the Bridegroom is not lacking anything it is not necessary to be baptized by him and therefore, avoid a schism from the world (the author may be mentioning about Arianism which argued that the Son of God is not equal with the Father in His divinity). John requests the Bridegroom to rush to the captives and liberate them from captivity because His is the kingdom and power. The thirteenth section[61] is a reply of Christ about the reason of His baptism. He says that, He does not lack anything so that He may gain nothing from the water but to redeem the Church. If He does not descend into the waters He could not be able to place armor in the waters. If He forges armor in waters the Church may put it on through baptism and they could armor themselves for the battle against the evil. As a commander in the war zone He should be an example in the contest. If He keeps away from this battle the followers would not go for the battle. Moreover, He is recasting humanity with His stamp, so that, they may be spiritually strengthened. And He is bringing them to the tomb of water so that He may lead them to immortality in the resurrection and to the new birth without birth pangs.

Fourteenth section[62] also is a reply from John. In the first part he argues that how he could act against his preaching. He already preached to the Church about the Bridegroom that He is older to him and He will baptize the Church in Holy Spirit. Secondly, what shall he say when he baptize the forgiver of debts; in whose name he shall baptize Him? If it is in the name of the Father You are in His bosom. Whom shall he invoke to sanctify water, he cannot invoke Holy Spirit to baptize in His name because he cannot separate Holy Spirit from the Son. And finally, he gives a Trinitarian doctrine that "the Father is in the Son and Son is wholly in His Father, and the Spirit who is from Him is one power without confusion."[63] In the following section[64] Christ commands to John to baptize Him. And according to His command John puts his hand on the head of the Bridegroom.

In the sixteenth section[65] Mar Jacob marvelously portrays the descent of the Bridegroom into the baptismal water of Jordan. When He approached the water His fire kindled the water and inflamed it. The river leaped like the baby in the womb of Elizabeth. Ordinary water was mixed with the splendor of holiness. The coal of Fire came and descended into the water and took off his cloth and placed into the womb of baptism. The seventeenth section[66] deals about the changes in the atmosphere and the witnessing of the Father and the

[61] Bedjan, *HS* I, 180.10-181.15; ET. *FH* VI, 175.264-176.290.

[62] Bedjan, *HS* I, 181.16-182.21; ET. *FH* VI, 176.291-177.319.

[63] Bedjan, *HS* I, 182.18-19; ET. *FH* VI, 177.315-316.

[64] Bedjan, *HS* I, 183.1-8; ET. *FH* VI, 177.319-178.326.

[65] Bedjan, *HS* I, 183.9-184.15; ET. *FH* VI, 178.327-179.354.

[66] Bedjan, *HS* I, 184.16-186.21; ET. *FH* VI, 179.335-181.400.

Holy Spirit. The glory of God spread all around the atmosphere, clouds of light came from the extremities and stood still like a bridal chamber, dark clouds appeared and made a veil of the royal palace on the waters of Jordan, and different colors surrounded the river turned the atmosphere in to fascinating mood. The Father's sound rent the sky and witnessed the Son, "This is my Son, this is truly my Beloved." The Holy Spirit floated from above like a dove and besprinkled her Holiness into the baptismal water and rested upon the Son not to sanctify Him but to bear witness because the Law requires two witness (Deut 19:15).

The eighteenth section describes the Church's attitude. By seeing the baptism of the Bridegroom the bride was marveled. She remembered the song of David that, "When the waters saw you, O God, they were afraid... (Ps 77:16-17). Mar Jacob again says that through the sanctification of the waters of Jordan the whole waters of the earth were sanctified. Section nineteen[67] describes the astonishment of the heavenly beings by seeing a feeble man's hands lay upon the Fiery One and says about the love of the Father toward His beloved Son. The last section[68] deals the handing over of the priesthood of Levi to the Redeemer.

2.1.4. A Homily on Our Lord and Jacob on the Church and Rachel and on Leah and the Synagogue

This is the 75th homily in the Bedjan's edition (*HS* III, 208-223).[69] In this homily Mar Jacob describes the mystery of the Church which was revealed in the Old Testament through the patriarch Jacob and his wives. The primary argument of this homily is that the nation, the bride who was betrothed to the heavenly Bridegroom, betrayed her Bridegroom and went after others. Then the Bridegroom took the bride from among nations. The details are as follows. His hypothesis is shown in the opening section[70] of the homily. His hypothesis is "He (the Son of God) set His face to come to espouse the Church from the nations."[71] He says that the Son of God's action was portrayed in every page of the Scripture as 'types.' And through their actions they symbolized the Son of God from the ancient times. The second section[72] starts with the statement that from the beginning of the creation the Son of God was eager to take off His journey to the world. His shadow is visible in all generations. Then Mar Jacob directly come to the story of Jacob, the patriarch, and says that he was a

[67] Bedjan, *HS* I, 189.4-191.13; ET. *FH* VI, 183.445-185.496.

[68] Bedjan, *HS* I, 191.14-193.10; ET. *FH* VI, 185.497-186.533.

[69] An English translation of the homily is available in *True Vine* 16, 4(1993), 51-64.

[70] Bedjan, *HS* III, 208.1-209.2; ET, "On Our Lord and Jacob," *TV* 4.4(1993), 51.1-52.18.

[71] Bedjan, *HS* III, 208.5; ET. "On Our Lord and Jacob," *TV* 4.4(1993), 51.5.

[72] Bedjan, *HS* III, 209.3-210.9; ET. "On Our Lord and Jacob," *TV* 4.4(1993), 52.19-53.46.

'type' of the Bridegroom. When Jacob went to his uncle's house in search of his future wife he was typified Jesus Christ's Incarnation to betroth the new wife from among the nations. He describes, that Jacob travelled from poverty to poverty and suffering which resembles the Son of God's self emptying. As Jacob brought his wives from among the idols, on the other hand Jesus saved the nations from the idol worship and sanctified them. Then he portrays and differentiates between Leah and Rachel and the nation and the nations. As Leah was disfigured, the nation, the synagogue, was disfigured through its adultery and as Rachel was beautiful, the nations, the Church, was beautiful through her commitment to the Bridegroom.

In the third section[73] he further goes with the similarities of Jacob's and Jesus' journeys. Just as Jacob found his wife at the well Jesus betrothed the Church at the river Jordan. Just like Jacob opened the cover stone of the cistern by himself (Gen 29:10), which was not able to be moved by many, Jesus opened up the baptism at Jordan. In the next section[74] he compares Jesus' suffering with that of Jacob's. When Jacob found Rachel and kissed her with tears, Mar Jacob argues that this kiss was not of carnal desire. If it was with carnal desire he would not have wept but he was typified the Son of God who betrothed the Church by the suffering of His body. Again he says about the stone on the mouth of the well and baptism in the fifth section.[75] Even a mighty man could not move the stone single handedly but Jacob moved it because the mystery of the Son shadowed upon him. Jacob served Laban for seven years to get Rachel and Jesus also suffered for the sake of His betrothed.

The sixth section[76] also deals with the toil of Jacob. He served Laban for seven years in view of marrying Rachel but Laban beguiled him. Instead of Rachel Laban gave him Leah whose eyes were not beautiful. When the day break arrived he understood that his bride is not Rachel but Leah. He was not dispirited but labored another seven years for Rachel and made her his own. Mar Jacob finds the same in the life of Jesus also. He says that the bride deceived him and perceived a plot against him. The seventh section[77] is a debate between Jacob and Laban. Jacob asked Laban, why he deceived him by giving Leah instead of Rachel for whom he served Laban. Laban replied that it is the custom of their land that the younger will not be given to marriage when an unmarried sister is there. Here, Mar Jacob introduces another custom of his time; thus it is very precious to the historians and social scientists.

---

[73] Bedjan, *HS* III, 210.10-211.18; ET. "On Our Lord and Jacob," *TV* 4.4(1993), 53.47-54.76.

[74] Bedjan, *HS* III, 211.19-213.12; ET. "On Our Lord and Jacob," *TV* 4.4(1993), 54.77-56.112.

[75] Bedjan, *HS* III, 213.13-216.2; ET. "On Our Lord and Jacob," *TV* 4.4(1993), 56.113-58.166.

[76] Bedjan, *HS* III, 216.3-218.15; ET. "On Our Lord and Jacob," *TV* 4.4(1993), 58.167-60.222.

[77] Bedjan, *HS* III, 218.16-219.8; ET. "On Our Lord and Jacob," *TV* 4.4(1993), 60.223-60.238.

In the eighth section[78] Mar Jacob is very successful to end up his hypothesis that the Bridegroom is having two wives: from nation and from nations. Leah became his first wife who resembles the Church from the nation or synagogue and beautiful Rachel became his second wife and she resembles the Church from nations. The ninth section[79] portrays the love of God towards humankind. According to Mar Jacob every nation is dear to the Creator, so that He toiled and gained them. His bride, the Church, is even beautiful than Rachel. By puting on the veil of Moses the nation went before the Adonai. Onlookers thought that she is beautiful but she was hateful than Leah, because her eyesight was not clear; therefore, she thought the calf is her Lord. The ill-favored and abominable one who remained among the nations brought near to the house of God and for the Church's sake God saved her.

The tenth section[80] is more ecclesiological in its bride-bridegroom imagery. Here, Mar Jacob says that the Bridegroom betrothed both the nation and the nations. In the shadow of darkness Leah became his wife and she was not beautiful because her eyes were odious, the light was feeble, wearisome in appearance, sullen of countenance, and covered with blemish. But Rachel was beautiful like the Church who knew the Father, worshipped the Son, and received the Holy Spirit. The Church and Rachel were without guile and loved their husbands. Rachel and the Church appeared before their husbands without the veil. Leah entered in the bridal chamber in the dark but Rachel entered in the morning. At the morning Jacob saw Leah and at daybreak the Son saw the double-minded Synagogue. And in the concluding session Mar Jacob reiterates his earlier statements and says that in the patriarch Jacob the Lord was hidden and in Leah and Rachel the synagogue and the Church were mysteriously laid. Leah was blameworthy and deceptive like the Synagogue and Rachel was righteous and beautiful like the Church.

2.1.5. Homily on the Veil on the Face of Moses

Mar Jacob's *memro* "On the Veil on the Face of Moses" is 79 *memro* Bedjan's editions (volume III, 283-305).[81] Through this homily Mar Jacob tries to contend the Jews who did not accept Jesus, the sun of righteousness, as their savior and purports that He is the One who was prophesied in their Law. He says that the veil of Moses' face was a symbol and it coved the Son of God from the Jews. In this homily Mar Jacob portrays the saving work of the Son of God in the light of nuptial imagery. The details of the homily are as follows.

---

[78] Bedjan, *HS* III, 219.9-221.19; ET. "On Our Lord and Jacob," *TV* 4.4(1993), 60.239-62.270.

[79] Bedjan, *HS* III, 221.20-222.10; ET. "On Our Lord and Jacob," *TV* 4.4(1993), 62.271-63.304.

[80] Bedjan, *HS* III, 222.11-223.16; ET. "On Our Lord and Jacob," *TV* 4.4(1993), 63.305-64.330.

[81] Sebastian Brock translated this homily into English and it is published in various sources (see in the bibliography).

The first section[82] says why he intended to write this homily. The reason is: once a man asked him what is the symbolic relevance of the veil on the face of Moses? Thus he asks God to come and explain through him the meaning of the veil.

In the second section[83] he suggests that the veil on the face of Moses is a 'type' of prophecy. Through this veil Lord proclaims to the world that "I have a secret." He says that this is a prophecy about the Son of God. The third section[84] also deals with the Son's secret. He says that Christ's radiance itself was shown on the face of Moses. Therefore, it is the Son himself. Since the Hebrew people were not ready to understand God's mysteries the Son was hidden on the face of Moses. He again says that every prophecy was about the Son. The fourth section[85] explains that when the Son arrived, everything that which was hidden in the prophecy was revealed.

Fifth section[86] brings the nuptial imagery into the discussion. In this imagery he portrays Christ as the Bridegroom of the Church. From eternity itself the Father found a bride and betrothed her to His Son. This was known to the Prophet Moses and he proclaimed this through his prophecy; "Therefore, a man leaves his father and his mother and clings to his wife, and they become one flesh" (Gen 2:24). In this prophecy he aimed the betrothal between the Son and the Church. When the wedding had been done Paul brought the news of the wedding between Christ and the Church into the light; hitherto, this was a mystery. The Bridegroom made his betrothed enter through the water and made her pure and finally He gave His blood as bride price and bought her. He sealed the marriage with a cross and placed His body as the wedding feast. In the sixth section[87] Mar Jacob explains the Son's saving work which was portrayed through the slaughter of the lamb. He argues that a mere lamb was not able to save anyone from death, but it was originally portrayed the saving activity of the Son of God. When they sprinkled the blood over the lintels and door posts it depicted a 'type' of the cross of the Son. David was aware of

[82] Bedjan, *HS* III, 283.1-284.15; ET. Brock, "On the Veil of Moses," in *Studies in Syriac Spirituality*, 74.1-75.20.

[83] Bedjan, *HS* III, 284.16-285.20; ET. Brock, "On the Veil of Moses," in *Studies in Syriac Spirituality*, 75.21-46.

[84] Bedjan, *HS* III, 285.21-286.21; ET. Brock, "On the Veil of Moses," in *Studies in Syriac Spirituality*, 75.47-76.68.

[85] Bedjan, *HS* III, 287.1-16; ET. Brock, "On the Veil of Moses," in *Studies in Syriac Spirituality*, 76.69-84.

[86] Bedjan, *HS* III, 287.17-291.14; ET. Brock, "On the Veil of Moses," in *Studies in Syriac Spirituality*, 76.85-79.164.

[87] Bedjan, *HS* III, 291.15-293.14; ET. Brock, "On the Veil of Moses," in *Studies in Syriac Spirituality*, 79.165-80.208.

this therefore, he said "set things a guard over my mouth" (Ps 141:3). He says "Great mystery is expounded in this small matter."

The seventh section[88] depicts many instances of the Passover events. Mar Jacob compares the Passover through the Red Sea with the baptism of the Son. Then he compares cross with the stick which Moses struck on the sea; manna with bread; rock with Christ, etc. The eighth section[89] shows Mar Jacob's versatile ability to find Christ in everything in the wilderness events. He compares the bronze serpent with Christ who was suspended on the cross. The ninth section[90] is a description of how Moses got the radiance on his face and how the Son has uncovered it. When Moses asked the Father to look at Him the Father showed His face's backside,[91] therefore, His brightness rested on Moses' face. Mar Jacob teaches that this radiance was the Son Himself. Since the Levites were not worthy to look upon it Moses veiled his face from them. Again, he symbolically says that when the groom of prophecy arrived he removed the veil from the face of prophecy. Here he calls the cross as the groom of prophecy.

The tenth section[92] discusses one of the greatest imaginations of the Syriac mystical theology; here he delineates a picture of the Bridegroom betrothed to the bride on the cross and the bride was born from the pierced side of the Bridegroom. Mar Jacob portrays that just like Eve was taken from the side of Adam, the Bridegroom, Christ, gave birth to his bride, the Church, from his pierced side. Eve was born with a mortal body but here, the Church was born with an immortal spiritual body. Like the sounds of Joshua and his company broke down the walls of Jericho, the cries of the Bridegroom pulled down the walls of *Sheol* and recovered its captives.

In the eleventh section[93] Mar Jacob compares the virginity of Mary and the veil of prophecy. The twelfth[94] is a refutation against the Jews who did not accept the Bridegroom. He says that the Jews hardened their heart and were

---

[88] Bedjan, 293.15-295.16; ET. Brock, "On the Veil of Moses," in *Studies in Syriac Spirituality*, 80.209-81.252.

[89] Bedjan, *HS* III, 295.17-297.16; ET. Brock, "On the Veil of Moses," in *Studies in Syriac Spirituality*, 81.253-82.294.

[90] Bedjan, *HS* III, 297.17-299.8; ET. Brock, "On the Veil of Moses," in *Studies in Syriac Spirituality*, 83.295-330.

[91] To this explanation he has his own reasons. See Brock, "On the Veil of Moses," in *Studies in Syriac Spirituality*, 83.297-302.

[92] Bedjan, *HS* III, 299.9-300.16; ET. Brock, "On the Veil of Moses," in *Studies in Syriac Spirituality*, 84.331-360.

[93] Bedjan, *HS* III, 300.17-301.20; ET. Brock, "On the Veil of Moses," in *Studies in Syriac Spirituality*, 84.361-85.386.

[94] Bedjan, *HS* III, 301.21-305.7; ET. Brock, "On the Veil of Moses," in *Studies in Syriac Spirituality*, 85.387-87.460.

not willing to remove the veil from the face of prophecy. He compares Jesus with the sun and the Law as lamp. When the Jews depend on the Law even after the arrival of Jesus, he says that, they use the Law like a lamp in the noon time even after the Sun of Righteousness has arrived. There is no use of the lamp in the mid-day, the lamp is helpful when it is dark, now the sun of righteousness appeared and there is no need of the lamp.

2.1.6. (Theological) Investigation and the Consecration of the Church

This is the 135th homily in the Bedjan's edition (Vol. IV.767-789). As described in the title this is a refutation against the investigators who investigated the place of the Church and her Bridegroom, Jesus Christ. The chief accusers are the Pharisees. They tried to inflict suspicion in the minds of the faithful by asking crooked questions. The first part[95] is a setting of debate and the Church declares her conviction about her Betrothed. She says to enquirers, "I am betrothed, you should not enter with me because I love my betrothed." "...and without investigation I love the one who died for me." "I know that He is truly the Son of God." And Mar Jacob accepts the divinity and humanity of Jesus Christ. He says that the cross is the wedding feast of the Church. The second part[96] is mostly the Church's declaration on the synagogue who investigated the Bridegroom. In the third part[97] Jacob portrays the prophecy of Isaiah about the Bridegroom and His name is Immanuel. He descended from His exalted place and mingled His superior nature with the nature of human beings. The third part[98] says about the exalted place of the Bridegroom. The fourth part[99] is also an argument against the investigators. He says the Church will not enquire about her betrothed. Paul also believed in Him without investigation.

The fifth part[100] demonstrates the curses of the investigators. The sixth part[101] is also Church's affirmation of her Bridegroom. In the seventh part[102] he describes the descent of the Bridegroom who was taken from Abraham, Moses, and David but He is from above. He says about the humanity and divinity of the Bridegroom. He was born from the virgin's womb without breaking her virginity. The eighth part[103] says about the Incarnation of the

[95] Bedjan, *HS* IV, 767.1-769.5.

[96] Bedjan, *HS* IV, 769.6-770.7.

[97] Bedjan, *HS* IV, 770.8-771.16.

[98] Bedjan, *HS* IV, 771.17-773-7.

[99] Bedjan, *HS* IV, 773.8-775.10.

[100] Bedjan, *HS* IV, 775.11-776.21.

[101] Bedjan, *HS* IV, 777.1-778.4.

[102] Bedjan, *HS* IV, 778.5-780.6.

[103] Bedjan, *HS* IV, 780.7-782.3.

Bridegroom. Though He was exalted above all, in order to exalt the Image of Adam, he became an ordinary human being. He was exiled to Egypt and returned to Nazareth and was known as Nazarene. He was baptized in the womb of Jordan not to be sanctified by it but to sanctify the entire waters of earth. He received the priesthood from John which His Father had given to Aaron through the hands of Moses. He closed the old and opened a new way. In the ninth part[104] Mar Jacob says about various deeds in the public ministry of the Bridegroom. The tenth part[105] offers more spousal images. Here the Church says to the Pharisees that she knows her betrothed well and she does not need to make an enquiry of Him. She says that the Bridegroom made the marriage settlement at baptism; He offered His own soul as a marriage gift to her. The Church says to the Pharisees that she is married to Him and nobody can separate her from Him. The eleventh and twelfth parts[106] speak about Mar Jacob's response after hearing the speech of the Church. He marveled about her conviction, he praises her, and he curses the investigators.

2.1.7. A Verse Homily on Tamar

"On Tamar and on the Symbol of the Church" is another homily of Mar Jacob. The present translation is taken from Joseph Zingrele's (1831-1891) edition. Zingrele published the text on the basis of the *Vatican Syr*. 117, a three columned manuscript of the 12th/13th century containing a large number of Jacob's *memre*.[107] Since Zingrele's text is not of easy acccss Brock gave the original text with the translation. Like many other homilies the introduction[108] of this homily also narrates the majesty of God and his own inadequacy to explain the divine mysteries. The second section[109] describes the loving kindness of God. According to His love He created man in His Image. The creation of man in His Image proclaims the Son of God's advent to the world to save human beings. Thus, from eternity the Father planned the Incarnation of the Son for the salvation of His creation. Since the human beings are created in the Image of the Son of God they received honor. The prophecy to Abraham, "Your seeds shall be blessed" is an expectation of the Son of God. According to Mar Jacob since then the discerning women were yearningly looking for the blessed child. Leah and Rachel are examples of these women. They learned that from the seed of Abraham all generations were going to be blessed. Therefore,

---

[104] Bedjan, *HS* IV, 782.4-783.11.

[105] Bedjan, *HS* IV, 783.12-784.13.

[106] Bedjan, *HS* IV, 784.14-787.10-787.11-789.4.

[107] See more about the manuscript at the introduction of article; Brock, "Jacob of Serugh's Verse Homily on Tamar (Gen 38)," 279-280.

[108] Brock, "Jacob of Serugh's Verse Homily on Tamar (Gen 38)," 280.1-281.36.

[109] Brock, "Jacob of Serugh's Verse Homily on Tamar (Gen 38)," 281.37-283.96.

though they were chaste they acted as impudent ladies and asked children from Jacob, the stock of Abraham. Ruth also was such a lady who went to Boaz in the dark to get a seed from him.

The third section[110] describes about the discernment of the chaste women who acted like wanton women. Mar Jacob here justifies them that their actions were not adultery but they yearningly desired the blessed seed of Abraham through whom the world shall be blessed. He says the "mistress of mysteries incited them." Here he uses the term "mistress" to indicate the Holy Spirit. In the fourth section[111] he again refers to Ruth who rushed to Boaz in the dark with a desire of a seed from Abraham and thus she begot the father of Jesse and from him king David was born. In the fifth section[112] Mar Jacob comes down to Tamar who was chaste and an honorable woman who acted as a prostitute with the desire of Son of God. The sixth section[113] elaborates the above theme. Why did Moses, who hates and reproves all adulterous put the story of Tamar, a prostitute, as a jewel among his writings? Mar Jacob says, "Her action was (indeed) ugly, but her faith made it beautiful, and it was resplendent and dear because of the Mystery that was performed in her." Moses even did not blame Judah who went to a prostitute because he acted according to the Spirit. That is why Jacob and Moses extol Judah. Mar Jacob lauds Tamar's faith in the seventh part. She took pride in the house of Abraham and had faith in God. Her husband died without leaving a child to her and her second husband also cheated her and God punished him and was taken to the tomb. She was considered as a cursed one and sent to her father's house. But the discerning woman did not fail in her love and faith in God. Being in desire of the seed she acted as a prostitute and trapped Judah and plundered the seed from him. Mar Jacob writes:

> The soul, heart, and eyes of Tamar, so full of beauty,
> were raised up to God as she supplicated Him;
> while from the outside was clothed in the garb of loose women.
> From the exterior, a prostitute, vexed and full of faults,
> but within, a soul which was radiant with the (future) shining forth of the Only Begotten.[114]

The seventh section[115] describes Tamar's confrontation with Judah to get the seed of Abraham. She acted like prostitute and stopped Judah on his way

---

[110] Brock, "Jacob of Serugh's Verse Homily on Tamar (Gen 38)," 283.97-114.

[111] Brock, "Jacob of Serugh's Verse Homily on Tamar (Gen 38)," 283.115-284.124.

[112] Brock, "Jacob of Serugh's Verse Homily on Tamar (Gen 38)," 284.125-136.

[113] Brock, "Jacob of Serugh's Verse Homily on Tamar (Gen 38)," 284.137-285.178.

[114] Brock, "Jacob of Serugh's Verse Homily on Tamar (Gen 38)," 287.233-238.

[115] Brock, "Jacob of Serugh's Verse Homily on Tamar (Gen 38)," 285.179-287.258.

and engaged in a conjugal union with him under veil. In the eighth section[116] Mar Jacob says that because of her prayer and her good intention she was victorious to get what she desired. She took Judah's ring, staff, and scarf as pledge to witness her sincerity. The ninth section[117] speaks of the pride of Tamar on getting the seed of Abraham. In the tenth and eleventh section[118] Mar Jacob portrays the anger of Judah while he heard the news of pregnancy of his daughter-in-law. The executioners came to execute the verdict of Judah but the noble woman took out the pledges and asked them to show these things to their master and say the owner of these things is the father of my child. Twelfth, thirteenth, and fourteenth,[119] are three short sections describing the aftermath of the incident. Judah understood those things are his own and ordered to withdraw his condemnation against the chaste woman and acknowledged openly "She is more innocent than I; let her not be abused."

In the last three sections[120] Mar Jacob compares Judah and Son of God and Tamar and the Church. Tamar on her way to the crossroads resembles the Church. Once she found the savior she seized three pledges which resemble Faith, Baptism, and Cross of Light to the Church. These pledges will rescue her from the torment of *gehenna*.

2.2. Methodology of Mar Jacob

Mar Jacob was a versatile genius in interpreting the scripture in his own style. He is primarily a spiritual (*roohonoyo*) and literal (*šooronoyo*) interpreter.[121] As an interpreter of the scripture he followed a combination of the Alexandrian and the Ephremean traditions. Which means, he followed the Alexandrian Christology and when he comes to the interpretation of the scripture he adopted the method of Mar Ephrem. He seldom used the philosophy of the Greek and allegorical method of Alexandrians but he used symbols and types for his biblical interpretation. Most of his homilies are based on the biblical themes or characters. As it was said in the earlier chapter he was a spiritual interpreter and his interpretation is centered on Christ; in other words he was a spiritual-Christo-centric theologian. Mostly he depended on metrical homilies (*memre*) as a vehicle of his theological lessons. He uses different methods of interpretations. He used the negation method, parallel and paradox method, symbolic, allegorical and typological methods to convey the mystery of the

[116] Brock, "Jacob of Serugh's Verse Homily on Tamar (Gen 38)," 287.259-289.298.

[117] Brock, "Jacob of Serugh's Verse Homily on Tamar (Gen 38)," 289.299-320.

[118] Brock, "Jacob of Serugh's Verse Homily on Tamar (Gen 38),"289.321-290.348.

[119] Brock, "Jacob of Serugh's Verse Homily on Tamar (Gen 38)," 290.349-291.368.

[120] Brock, "Jacob of Serugh's Verse Homily on Tamar (Gen 38)," 291.369-292.420.

[121] See more supra, 1.5.

scripture. He depended on prose and poetry as medium of his theological elucidation. Kollamparampil writes:

> Syriac biblical literature is rich with the perusal of Semitico-biblical literary genre. In many respects, Mar Jacob stands in that milieu in which the sacred Scriptures themselves had their origin, and he shares their Semitic vocabulary, structures, figures, and more prominently their world-view.[122]

His knowledge in biblical passages is sublime. Through his homilies he interconnects many biblical passages which have no relationship at first sight. But, very dramatically and seriously, he finds relationship between them. This was rare in other traditions. The following are some of the methods which he used to teach the Scripture.

2.2.1. Method of Negation

Modernism, which is deeply rooted in the West, believes that as a Supreme Being, human being, with empirical knowledge or science, could control the universe. It even tried to comprehend God within the limits of their reasoning and understanding. On the other hand the Eastern world never supported this idea. To them human beings and their intellect have limitations and they cannot go beyond certain limits. Also, they believed that words are inadequate to explain the divine mysteries of God.[123] They never believe that it is a weakness, rather considered it a strength. According to Evagrius, theology is not a mere cerebral exercise and he taught that a theologian is a man of prayer. He says, "If you are a theologian you will pray in truth; if you pray in truth you will be a theologian."[124] They tried to seek the mysteries of God in their continuous meditation of the scripture. They read and digested and found all possible passages which were coherent to their particular topics and gave spiritual interpretations. Therefore, they were well versed in the scripture. For this reason they were able to dispense the mysteries of God very marvelously to their audience. Therefore, they are spiritual exegetes and their hermeneutics are not all-too-easy.

In order to explain the incomprehensible and the ineffable God, the Alexandrian School followed the platonic trajectory of interpretation; this system of theologizing is also called *apophatic* theology.[125] The word meaning

[122] Kollamparampil, *Salvation in Christ*, 40.

[123] Mar Jacob is a good example of this kind of thoughts. Most of his homilies begin with this kind of statement telling the human feebleness before the ineffable divine. See some examples (Bedjan, *SMS* 720.1-16; ET. *FH* I, 41.1-15; Bedjan, *HS* V, 447.9-10; ET. *FH* V, 141.9-10; Bedjan, *HS* II, 348.3-349.3; ET. *FH* VIII, 204.11-205.33.

[124] PG 79, col. 1180B.

[125] Placher, *A History of Christian Theology: An Introduction*, 94ff. cf. "Christianity" in *The New Encyclopedia Britannica*, Vol. 16, 331b.

is "turning away from speech."[126] According to this principle, they believed that the creation cannot define or comprehend the Creator;[127] there is an ontological chasm between the Creator and the creation.[128] So that, they avoided the emphatic affirmation about the divine; in other words they simply adapted the method of negation. On the other hand, the West followed the Aristotelian method of interpretation, which brought everything under a definition. It is known as the *kataphatic* theology. They mainly followed a critical method and explained the scripture literally.

The Antiochene School followed *kataphatic* method to interpret the scripture. At the same time, as said earlier, the Alexandrians adapted the Jewish-Semitic-style of allegorical and typological method of interpretation.[129] They gave importance to the inner meaning of the scripture rather than word by word literal meaning. In their inner-self they have a pastoral mind and they interpret the scripture accordingly. Therefore, DeSimone rightly describes that patristic interpretation of scripture is always theological, pastoral in nature, and relevant to man's relationship with God.[130] They read the bible theologically, within the heart of the living tradition, with authentic Christian tradition.[131] Though they are not following the allegorical method as such, through the symbolic interpretation, the Syriac Orient was also very close to the Alexandrian school. Mar Jacob also followed the same methodology in his homilies.[132] B. B. Sony argues that he was a follower of Alexandrian School of thoughts,

---

[126] McGuckin, "Apophaticism," 23.

[127] Placher, *A History of Christian Theology: An Introduction*, 95. Cf. Bundy, "Language and the Knowledge of God in Ephrem Syrus," 60. If, then, our knowledge cannot even achieve a knowledge of itself, how does it dare to investigate the birth of Him who knows all things? How can the servant, who does not properly know himself, pry into the nature of his Maker? (*Hfid*, 9.16; ET. Brock, *The Luminous Eye,* 26-27).

[128] *Hfid* 15.3-5, 64. Cf. Koonammakal, "Ephrem's Imagery of Chasm," 176; cf. Griffith, *Faith Adoring Mystery,* 21-23.

[129] Maloney, "Apophatic Theology," 568.

[130] DeSimone, *The Bride and the Bridegroom of the Fathers*, 9.

[131] POB, *The Interpretation of the Bible in the Church*, Rome, 1993, 96-97. Cited DeSimone, *The Bride and the Bridegroom of the Fathers*, 10.

[132] Your nativity, O Son of God, is wonder and my mouth is inadequate
to narrate your great story with my enfeebled tongue.
Your revelation is exalted above all human mouths and how is it possible
that I who am feeble should narrate your story?
And how shall I, an unworthy, hasten (to narrate) your story?
Your Father alone knows how your birth (took place)...
Cherubs, the servants, have never learned where your abode is,
and to which place shall my mind proceed to speak about you? (Bedjan, *SMS*, 720.1-16; ET. *FH* I, 41.1-15).

> His exegesis is a reaction, although he does not say so *expressis verbis,* against the Judaizing 'textual' exegesis of Theodorians who, according to him, had divided Christ. Jacob succeeds in uniting the Ephremean tradition with the Alexandrian tradition in the exegetical domain: finding Christ throughout the Bible.[133]

Thus negation is an important and effective method that Mar Jacob uses in his homilies to explain about the Almighty God.

2.2.2. Paradoxical and Parallel Method

Paradoxical and parallel are the other two effective methods which Mar Jacob and the other fathers used to interpret the scripture. In paradoxical type of interpretation, they use diametrically opposite events or themes to present their ideas. This is a form of comparison; through this comparison the author creates a virtual image of the thing, person, or an instance in the mind of the reader. This will help the reader to comprehend the idea than a monotonous interpretation. For example:

> The Mighty One knocked and the ambassador trembled inside the house of his father.
> The King spoke and the servant fell down and adored Him.
> The Creator gave a gesture and the offspring, the son of the barren woman, exulted.[134]

Here, 'the Mighty One and the ambassador,' the King and the servant,' and the creator and the offspring' are served to denote two opposite poles of actions. Here, Mar Jacob tried to differentiate a certain relationship pattern through action-response medium. An example of paradoxical method of interpretation is seen when he very effectively communicated the difference in stature between Jesus and John the Baptist. On the other hand in parallelism they bring together events, ideas, actions or words of same or contrasting nature simultaneously. This is a kind of rhetoric pattern. Repeated usage of sounds, meaning, and structure serves the order. Parallelism is a prominent feature in Hebrew poetry as well as in most literatures of the West Asia.[135] Adele Berlin defined parallelism as "the repetition of the same or related semantic content and/or grammatical structure in consecutive lines or verses."[136] But he says there is no consensus on precisely what parallelism is. Through this method one passage may spread light to the other one. In other words one may consider

---

[133] Sony, "La Methode exegetique de Jacques de Saroug," 90; cited from McCarron, "An Epiphany of Mystical symbols," 58-59.

[134] Bedjan, *SMS*, 743.4-6; ET. *FH* I, 63.485-487.

[135] "Parallelism," in *The New Encyclopedia Britannica*, Vol. 9, 15th Edition, 142.3c.

[136] Berlin, "Parallelism," 155.

as the shadow of the other. Through these methods they affirm whatever they want to convey. Mar Jacob is a good user of this technique. He used to affirm the pre-Christian nature of the Christ event or used to affirm importance of the theme which he proposes through this method. In every two lines he compares or contrasts an idea. See an example from Mar Jacob's homily:

> Yesterday He had mounted the wood of crucifixion
> but today there is strength, resurrection of the dead and power.
> The day before yesterday Simon repeatedly renounced (saying) he does not know Him
> but today he runs to see His tomb because He was raised up.
> The Friday of the sufferings prepared ambushes for the apostolic group;
> but on Sunday, a new vision and cheerfulness.
> Yesterday the King was seized up in sleep in *Sheol*
> but today he woke up and stood like a man who shook of his wine.[137]

In the above verses he made combination between yesterday and today. Yesterday was a day of pain and confusion but today is a day of victory and joy. By this pattern he affirms and asserts what he is going to tell. Through the repeated voices he attracts the audience's attention. This kind of parallelism is visible in many liturgical songs and prayers of the West Syriac Church.[138]

2.2.3. Exclamatory and Interrogative Method

Exclamations and interrogations are other patterns of Mar Jacob's methodology. In this pattern he uses to ask a series of question to the readers or to one of the characters in the homily. He affirms what he wants to say through this method:

> O guarded ship, where has your swift (prow) sunk?
> And which sea snatched away your merchandise amidst its waves?
> O enviable ewe, in which place did they take off your load (of treasure),
> and once despoiled they dismissed and left you as it were in a desert?
> O honorable dove, who has cut off the wings of your beauty
> and plucked and carried off the sound feathers of your virginity?[139]

2.2.4. Alphabetic Acrostic Method

Another pattern of interpretation is to start every line with alphabetic acrostic.[140] The first part of the stanza will starts with the same word or phrase. Sometimes, it may seems like parallelism but in this method unlike the other one he deals with the same thing and there is no comparison or contrast.

---

[137] Bedjan, *HS* II, 614.8-16; ET. *FH* XIII, 296.65-297.72.

[138] *Kashtanubhavazhcha Namaskaram.*

[139] Bedjan, *SMS*, 7478-13; ET. *FH* I, 68.575-580.

[140] Brock, *Studies in Syriac Spirituality*, 211.

On this day let the earth with everything in it exult
and instead of thorns let it bring forth the blessings from your nativity.
On this day let Adam, the head of the race, rejoice
because he has acquired divinity from your birth, as he had sought.
On this day let Eve give thanks more than Adam
because the infant who will remove the pains of her suffering has shone forth from her.
On this day let the garden exult together with its trees
because in you the expelled heir has returned to Eden, his habitation.[141]

2.2.5. Dialogue Method or Dispute Method

The method of dialogue is another hermeneutic form which he uses in Semitic circle. Sometimes, it was called dispute poems. Murray describes that there is confusion among the scholars regarding the classification whether it will fall under *madraše* or under *soogito*.[142] But Brock published several articles on this subject[143] and in one of them he clarifies this as the *soogito* which will come under the subsection of *madraše*.[144] In this method two characters, especially biblical, will argue with each other. "The argument takes the form of a precedence dispute or contest which takes place before a judge."[145]

In the early Mesopotamian tradition this genre of poems are quiet popular. In one of his articles R. Murray gives the details of such genre poems.[146] He says: "It involves a different kind of activity and of personification, its dialogue frequently concerns the usefulness or moral superiority of the contending subjects, and it has a remarkably constant structural pattern."[147] Brock says about this: "Ephrem is simply following a pattern already well exemplified in earlier Mesopotamian literature, where similar precedence of disputes between two parties (normally personifications) survive in Middle Iranian, in Akkadian

141 Bedjan, *SMS*, 767.3-8; ET. *FH* I, 85.985-86.992.

142 Murray, "Aramaic and Syriac dispute poems and their connections," 157.

143 Brock, in "Dispute Poems and Dialogues in the Ancient and Mediaeval Near East," 109-120; Brock, "The Dispute Between the Cherub and the Thief," Brock, "The Dispute Poem from Sumer to Syriac," 1-10; Brock, "Syriac Dispute Poems: Various Types," 110-119; Brock, *Sogitha, Syriac Dialogue Hymns*, Jacob Vellian, ed., Syrian Churches Series XI, Kottayam: Jacob Vellian, 1987; Brock, "Dramatic Dialogue Poems," 135-147; Brock, "Syriac Dialogue Poems: Marginalia to a Recent Edition," 29-58; Brock, "Dialogue Hymns of the Syriac Churches," 35-45.

144 Brock, in "Dispute Poems and Dialogues in the Ancient and Mediaeval Near East," 110.

145 Brock, *Studies in Syriac Spirituality*, 212.

146 Murray, "The Syriac Contest-Poems and their connections," 157-187.

147 Murray, "The Syriac Contest-Poems and their connections," 159.

and in Sumerian."[148] Homily six in "Against Jews,"[149] "Cherub and Thief,"[150] "Dialogue Poem of Soul,"[151] etc., are good examples of dialogue poems of Mar Jacob. Such a dialogue poem could be seen in the Good Friday service of the Malankara Orthodox Syrian Church. Brock writes that he has seen around forty such kind of poems in the liturgical circle of the Syriac Churches.[152] Thus the dialogue form is another method of theological exposition of Mar Jacob.

2.2.6. Symbolic Interpretation

According to the Webster's Dictionary the word symbol is made up of two Greek words 'syn' means 'together' and 'ballein' means 'to throw.' Literally it means "thrown together," and denotes an object used to represent something abstract.[153] Brock defines "Types and symbols are a means of expressing relationships and connections, of instilling meaning ways, between the Old Testament and the New, between this world and the heavenly, between the New Testament and the Sacraments, between the sacraments and the eschaton. In every case they "reveal" something of what is otherwise "hidden."[154] Therefore, symbols give ideas on abstract or hidden meanings into a concrete form. The symbols can carry a bundle of ideas in a single expression. For example, wound on the side of Christ and the water and the blood flowing from it[155] represents many things: this symbolizes the Eucharist, wedding feast, dowry or bride price, baptism, fountain of Paradise, and re-entry into the Paradise by avoiding the lance of Cherub. Scholars named it as *polysemous nature*.[156]

Unlike most of the western scholars, who stand for logical understanding, the Semitic authors are neither philosophical nor systematic in their biblical interpretation. But they use simple method of symbolic interpretation; therefore, they can easily communicate the inner meaning of the scripture to their audience. Möhler emphasized the importance of symbolism for theology: "Symbols, like the word, mediate inner movement. They are not only the unifying point of all but are also the organ through which the interiority of the

---

148 Brock, *Studies in Syriac Spirituality*, 212.

149 Albert, *HCJ* IV, 112-135.

150 Brock, Sebastian, "The Dispute Between the Cherub and the Thief," *Hugoye* 5.2 (July 2002).

151 Brock, Sebastian P., "An Acrostic Poem on the Soul by Jacob of Serugh," *Sobornost* 23.1(2001), 40-44.

152 Brock, *Studies in Syriac Spirituality*, 215.

153 *Merriam-Webster's Collegiate Dictionary,* 1994.

154 Brock, *Hymns on Paradise*, 42.

155 Bedjan, *HS* III, 299-300.

156 Beisen, *Simple and Bold*, 37.

one flows out into totality and back from it again."[157] Valenziano suggests, "In theological language symbolism refines and enhances theological discourse in a manner far beyond the refinement and enhancement it brings to any other type of discourse. This involves the formation of a full theological language, pregnant with every semiological and ontic potential for human discourse about God."[158] Therefore, the Eastern theologian(s) heavily depend upon symbols to interpret the Divine. Brock explains that according to Mar Ephrem all religious languages are metaphorical because no language is adequate to convey about God; rather, it is a sign of God's loving compassion for us that the incarnation took place not only into the body, but into language as well. Just as God put-on the "garment of flesh," so, too, did God put-on the "garment of names," entering into human language as in to the body so that we might approach and in our limited way know about God.[159] Since nothing can content the Divine the vast chance of semiotic potentiality with the linguistic potentiality will widen the epistemological horizon of a person and this will be the best tool to know the ineffable.

At the same time it should be noted that the symbols are only a preliminary and an elementary means of revelation and it is not the reality.[160] Brock says; "Types and symbols are definitely not to be seen as proof texts whose aim is to compel assent; rather, they are just invitations, offering the possibility of acquiring some knowledge of divine reality."[161] Again, "Types and symbols serve as pointers. From the subjective human perspective a type or symbol can be seen as a revelation of some aspect of the divine mystery (whether or not that aspect may one day be more fully revealed)."[162] Dulles says, "These images communicate through their evocative power. They transform the horizons of man's life, integrate his perception of reality, alter his scale of values, reorient his loyalties, attachments and aspirations in a manner far exceeding the powers of abstract conceptual thought."[163]

Another salient feature of symbols is their fluidity. Since the symbols are fluid and subjective in character and there is no strict juridical sense of linear definition, each person who goes through it will receive a message according to his own perception. Murray rightly says when the Church Fathers interpret, "An argument proceeds not by exhausting topics successively but with frequent *inclusio,* circling round on itself like a conversation round a fire, gradually

[157] Möhler, *Unity in the Church,* 200.

[158] Valenziano, "Liturgy and Symbolism," 32.

[159] *HFid* 31. ET. Brock, *The Luminous Eye,* 43.

[160] Murray, "The Theory of Symbolism in Ephrem's Theology," 6.

[161] Brock, *The Luminous Eye,* 54.

[162] Brock, *The Luminous Eye*, 41; cf. Brock, *The Bible in the Syriac Tradition*, 56-63.

[163] Dulles, *Models of the Church*, 20.

advancing and going deeper."[164] Therefore, Crispino Valenziano's comment is clearer in this respect:

> The symbols of the great ecclesial tradition is not to repeat it what has been done before just as it was done in the past; it is to make one's own the fullness of ecclesial memory and recreate it in an original manner, not stamping it out of the same mold. This whole subject leads beyond the epistemological category and is open to other issues as well.[165]

Symbols are subjective and they convey the message according to the situation and the perception of the observer; it opens new avenues in front of the visionaries. Commenting on Ephraim's biblical interpretation style Brock also feels the same. He says that Ephrem has the awareness that every scripture reading has two meaning: internal spiritual meaning and external literal meaning.[166] Symbolism caters the internal spiritual meaning and it is simple.

In the light of the above discussion, it is clear that the Eastern Church Fathers use symbols to teach the divine mysteries because God is indefinable and incomprehensible. When faith conjoins with the symbols, spiritual interpretation would be easy. For a critical interpreter symbols and types may be absurd things. But for the spiritual interpreters like Mar Ephrem and Mar Jacob symbols and types are perfect tools for interpreting the scripture. Mar Jacob points out that the symbols have their own meaning and they are telling something indirectly to its onlookers. In other words meanings are hidden in symbols. He calls even prophecy as symbols.[167]

> The daysprings of thy symbols has appeared amidst the readings
> open my eyes for me, O Son of God, that I may see its beauty.
> Thy great image is borne by the books of prophecy,
> which carry thee in solemn procession, for the world to see how fair Thou art.
> From generation to generation Thy type has peered out like a luminary,
> and gladdened with its rising whoever say Thee and marveled.
> With the allegories and dark sayings in scriptures,
> the just in sundry places portrayed thee through their revelations…[168]

---

[164] Murray, *Symbols of Church and Kingdom*, 2.

[165] Valenziano, "Liturgy and Symbolism," 31.

[166] Brock, *The Luminous Eye*, 46.

[167] Bedjan *HS* III, 285.8; ET. Brock, "On the Veil of Moses," in *Studies in Syriac Spirituality*, 75.21-46.

[168] Bedjan, *HS* V, 331.1-332.8; ET. "A Homily on Samson," *TV* 11(1992), 51.1-52.24. See what Ephrem says about symbols in his hymns:

> Wherever you turn your eyes, there is God's symbol
> Whatever you read, there you will find His types. (*HVir* 20:12; ET. McVey, *Ephrem the Syrian* 348).
>
> Lord, Your symbols are everywhere,

Symbols of divine things always carry mysteries because they are multivalent in nature. A complete interpretation is impossible. Therefore, it is mysterious or *rozaic*. Paul speaks about this mystery when he interprets the bride and bridegroom, which is above the human perception (Eph 5:32).

2.2.7. Typological Interpretation

The word 'type' is derived from the Greek word τυπος. In Syriac language the fathers borrowed the same term from Greek *tupso* to denote the term 'type.' Other terms that Mar Jacob uses similar to *tupso* are *rozo(e) dmuto, şalmo*, etc. In Christian tradition typology is a method of biblical interpretation which Jesus and Paul used on several occasions.[169] It tells and uses to explain the Divine plan which happened in the recent past was shown to the men of God through different incidents in remote times; or it correlates the past and the present. For example, the crucified Christ was proclaimed at the time of Moses through the brass serpent raised in the wilderness (Jn 3:14), Adam as the type of Christ (Rom 5:13-14), Old Israel as the type of Church (Gal 4:21-28), regarding the sacraments of Baptism and Eucharist Paul says:

> I do not want you to be ignorant of the fact, brothers, that our forefathers were all under the cloud and that they all passed through the sea. They were all baptized into Moses in the cloud and in the sea. They all ate the same spiritual food and drank the same spiritual drink; for they drank from the spiritual rock that accompanied them, and that rock was Christ
> (1Cor 10:1-3).

There are several other episodes which indirectly are the typological exegesis, such as, Eucharist (Jn 6:30-31), Priesthood of Melchizadek (Heb 5:6), etc. Thus typological interpretation was well known in the biblical and Semitic world. But Joseph Fitzmyer clarifies that this hermeneutic was known to the pre-Judeo-Christian world. In a study on "Old Testament Quotations in Qumran and New Testament" Fitzmyer writes:

Yet you are hidden from everywhere.
Though your symbol is on high,
Yet the height does not perceive that your are;
Though your symbol is in the depth.
It does not comprehend who you are;
Though your symbol is in the sea,
You are hidden from the sea;
Though your symbol is on dry land,
It is not aware what you are.
Blessed is the hidden One shining out. (*HFid*, 4.9; ET. Brock, *The Lumious Eye*, 55)

[169] Froehlich, ET. *Biblical Interpretation in the Early Church*, 8-9.

> A. von Harnack once maintained that Paul was the originator of the typological exegesis. E. E. Ellis has shown, however, that such typological interpretation of the Old Testament existed in pre-Pauline strata of the New Testament. But many of the examples cited in classes B and C above will show that this type of interpretation was also pre-Christian, being practiced by contemporary Jews as well, even though we do not find in the Qumran material any Semitic equivalent of the Pauline *typos* or *typikōs*.[170]

Biblical typology receives many definitions from the scholars: J.N.D. Kelly defines typology that "the method of exegesis presupposed in the preceding section, has in modern times been given the convenient name typology."[171] In the typological exegesis both the Old and the New Testaments are closely interrelated. The events and persons of the Old Testament prefigured and anticipated the New. The typology took history seriously. It was the scene of progressive unfolding of God's consistent redemptive purpose.[172] Cahill observes that the Bible is permeated with reinterpretations of a past tradition in the light of a new experience. "Typology, however, is but one specific mode of the larger category of interpretation, one in which a present event, person, situation, or thing suggests a likeness to an event, person, situation, or thing of the past."[173] Woollcombe describes that, "Typological exegesis is the search for linkages between events, persons or things within the historical framework of revelation, whereas allegorism is the search for a secondary and hidden meaning underlying the primary and obvious meaning of a narrative."[174] Griffith points out that typology bridges the chasm between God and man: "And this catechesis consisted in poetic meditations on the symbols and types which God distributed in nature and scripture to lead people across the chasm separating creatures from their Creator."[175] Mircea Eliade says that the typology is a creation of certain vision: he says, "… the great originality of Judaeo-Christianity was the transfiguration of History into theophany."[176]

From the above discussion of the scholars the following features could be deduced. The biblical typological interpretation always tells the story of a fulfillment of the past experience of prophecy or there will be an intimation of eschatological character.[177] Typology can take place in two different planes,

---

170 Fitzmyer, *Essays on the Semitic Background of the New Testament*, 55.

171 Kelly, *Early Christian Doctrines*, 69.

172 Kelly, *Early Christian Doctrines,* 71.

173 Cahill, "Hermeneutical Implications of Typology," 268.

174 Lampe and K. J. Woolcombe, *Essays in Typology*, 40.

175 Griffith, "Spirit in the Bread and Fire in the Wine," 227.

176 Eliade, *Images and Symbols: Studies in Religious Symbolism*, 164.

177 Goppelt, "Typos," 252.

sometimes simultaneously; a horizontal plane, Old Testament, New Testament, and a vertical plane, this world- the heavenly world.[178] In typology there will be a 'type' and an 'antitype.' Another feature of typology is that there is a cause behind the explanation; i.e., the antitype will be related to a particular act or acts of the type. For example the synagogue's disobedience and disloyalty to God caused the election of an obedient and loyal Church as the bride. Here, loyalty and obedience are the basic cause of the action. External and literal similarity is not necessary in typological interpretation. Gopplet suggests that "this correspondence does not lie merely in the external similarities between the events. It is to be seen primarily in the essential similarity in God's acts."[179] The message of typology may be understood only to those who have faith in God and believes that God not only intervenes in history but He is Incarnated in a historical time to confirm his former interventions in history.[180] Northrop Frye suggests that typology comes from "faith, hope, and vision,"[181] and that typology proceeds from a particular "vision of historical process."[182] Cahill calls them as insiders.[183] It is a grace of the writer to find and articulate the details of divine intervention.

On the other hand, in the allegorical exegetical method the sacred text is treated as a mere symbol, or allegory, of spiritual truths. The literal, historical sense, if it is regarded at all, plays a relatively minor role, and the aim of the exegete is to elicit the moral, theological, or mystical meaning which each passage, indeed each verse and even each word, is presumed to contain.[184] When the Eastern Church and theologians uphold these kinds of interpretation the West, especially from the reformed and liberals, deny these methods categorically, yet Thomas Aquinas and other likeminded theologians made use of it. Martin Luther criticizes the allegorical interpretation and said, "Immature and strange." According to him scripture is "to teach, reprove, correct, and train in righteousness, so that the man of God may be perfect for every good work."[185]

In the East the Church Fathers like Mar Ephrem uses this method to interpret the scripture. But Mar Jacob is the one who uses typology profusely in his homilies. In his opinion each and every passage of the Old Testament

---

[178] Brock, *Studies in Syriac Spirituality*, 4.

[179] Goppelt, "Typos," 251.

[180] Eliade, *Images and Symbols*, 170.

[181] Northrop, *Creation and Recreation*, 60.

[182] Northrop, *Creation and Recreation,* 60.

[183] Cahill, "Hermeneutical Implications of Typology," 268.

[184] Kelly, *Early Christian Doctrines*, 70.

[185] Martin Luther, "Lectures to Song of Solomon," 15:194.

talks about the Son of God. So that wherever you look you see the image of the Son:[186]

> In all those books, where is the Son of God not depicted?
> Seek, if thou canst, what cannot be found at all!
> There is no page that the Son's figure does not overshadow,
> nor any reading which speaks not of Him plainly.
> Every letter in the Scriptures is written in the Name of the Lord,
> and every saying, it is He that is to be richly expounded.
> In every time, He was spoken of, that He was coming to the earth,
> even till He came and His heralds rested from the good tidings.[187]

Another word which Mar Jacob uses simultaneously instead of 'type' is '*rozo*' (mystery). Mar Jacob found typology and allegory as tools for describing the mysteries of the Lord.[188] When he is comparing Rachel and the Church he says that, "The mystery of the Church lay on her face like a jewel."[189] In another homily he writes: The homilies, O Son of God, have plunged me into the sea of Thy Types... waves of Thy narrations have dashed vehemently upon me: sweep me, O Pilot, into the harbor of the truths prefigured by the types.[190] In short Mar Jacob made use of the typology throughout his homilies to interpret the mysteries of God. He found this as a simple and efficient tool to comprehend the incomprehensible God; because proper words and definitions are insufficient to explain the nature of God and His plans. Mar Jacob believed that God loved His creations from the very beginning of their creation and He has a plan in His mind to save them from perdition. Both the Old and the New Testaments speaks about the same plan and its various implementations. In fact they are the two sides of the same coin and inter-related to each other. One is the shadow of the other and one stands for the other. Therefore, through the typological interpretation Mar Jacob underlines the unity of the scripture. In conclusion, Mar Jacob and other Eastern Christian fathers used typology at great length in their writings to interpret the scripture effectively and through this they proved that the New Testament is the fulfillment of the Old.

---

[186] Bedjan, *HS* III, 285.21-286.3; ET. Brock, "On the Veil of Moses," in *Studies in Syriac Spirituality*, 75.47-50.

[187] Bedjan, *HS* III, 208.11-209.2; ET. "A Homily On Our Lord and Jacob," *TV* 4.4(1993), 52.11-19.

[188] Bedjan, *HS* V, 332, 10; ET. "A Homily on Samson," *TV* 11(1992), 53; Bedjan, *HS* I, 537.15-16, 538.5-6; ET. "On the Reposed," *TV* 5(1990), 43.45-46, 53-54.

[189] Bedjan, *HS* III, 211.11; ET. "On Our Lord and Jacob," *TV* 4.4(1993), 54.69.

[190] Bedjan, *HS* I, 49.1-4; ET. "On the Serpent of Brass," 41.1-4.

2.3. Bride-Bridegroom Imagery Prior to Mar Jacob

The Bride-Bridegroom imagery was well established in the Christian circles many centuries before Mar Jacob. Fathers of the Church from both the Greek East and Latin West along with the Syriac Fathers used this biblical imagery to teach the divine mysteries to their Churches. Scholars have the opinion that the Bride-Bridegroom imagery has roots in the Canaanite and Mesopotamian cultural backgrounds. Baab writes:

> Since Israel's faith was fashioned in the fires of the religious and cultural tensions, the prominence of the concept of sacred marriage in the Canaanite culture made an Israelite adaptation of this concept a most effective weapon for defending the faith. In the Canaanite world the cycle of the seasons was believed to be intimately associated with sexual relations between gods and goddesses. These relations were momentous for the welfare of an agricultural community.[191]

There are plenty of examples from many pre-Christian traditions regarding the sacred marriage to point out the influence behind the concept of marriage imagery of Jewish and Christian theology. In Egypt Osiris and Isis (Inanna), in Babylon Tammuz and Ishtar, and in Canaan Baal and Ashtart are some of the sacred marriage epics. Pagoulatos points out that "In the ancient West Asia spiritual marriage between humans (kings and Priests) and gods took place in temples."[192] Again he brings forth the ancient Greek mythology of the wedding between Zeus (god of heaven) and Hera (goddess of earth): "On the Island of Crete, in the area near by Knossos, the marriage of Zeus and Hera was celebrated by mean of "an evening bridal procession followed by a nocturnal festival."[193] Thus this predominant cultural background of the neighboring countries was adapted in the religious realm of Israel to expound a strong divine-human relationship.

The Old Testament and the New Testament refer to this imagery to delineate God-human relationship. The Christian analogy of the heavenly nuptial imagery goes back to the Old Testament, where God appears as the Bridegroom, and Israel appears as the bride. When God Incarnated in Christ, He called Himself, and was called, the Bridegroom (Mk 2:19; Jn 3:29). Though the gospel narratives mention that Jesus called himself as Bridegroom it never tells that Jesus called anybody as bride. But Paul the apostle called the Church as the bride of Christ. It is from this foundation that the Fathers of the Church constructed the 'bride-bridegroom' imagery. Nevertheless, through this imagery they instilled in their believers the mystery of the Incarnation of Jesus Christ, His selfless love, sacrificial death, redemption of mankind from

---

[191] Baab, "Marriage" 286.

[192] Pagoulatos, *Tracing the Bridegroom in Dura,* 42.

[193] Pagoulatos, *Tracing the Bridegroom in Dura,* 42.

sin and death, glorious Second Coming and Eternal life with Jesus Christ the Bridegroom.

In the Greek Christian tradition Origen is considered as the first organized theologian of nuptial mysticism in Christian patrology.[194] The bride imagery is predominant in his interpretation of the *Song of Songs*. Rush says that, "his (Origen) Logos-mysticism is a bridal or marriage mysticism."[195] He speaks of the beauty of the bride, the soul, loved by the Bridegroom, the Word of God.[196] In the *Commentary on Canticles* he says that, "Let us bring in the soul whose every desire it is to be joined in fellowship with the Word of God and to enter into the mysteries of His wisdom and knowledge, as into the chamber of a heavenly bridegroom."[197] Several other Greek and Latin Church Fathers discussed the theme prior to Mar Jacob.[198] One of the prayers in the Byzantine tradition says: "Behold the Bridegroom comes in the middle of the night; … I see Thy bridal chamber adorned, O my Savior, and I have no wedding garment that I may enter there. Make the robe of my soul to shine, O giver of Light, and save me."[199] Discussing on *Gospel of Philip*, Van Eijk suggests that according to the *Gospel of Philip* salvation is equivalent to marriage and marriage is the archetype of salvation.[200]

Bible is a sea of mystery and the Syriac Church Fathers are blessed fishers in the deep sea. They are masters of Biblical interpretation. Their knowledge in the Scripture facilitates them to go deep down to the mysteries of the Scripture and snatch and endow with the precious pearls of the Scripture towards the readers. Mostly they used symbolic and typological languages to enhance the depth of the mysteries of Scripture to their poor faithful. They delve into the New Testament themes and figures out their 'type' in the Old Testament and they explained the mysteries of the Scripture in their homilies in symbolic languages. This edified their poor audience to be instructed in the mysteries and became ardent followers of Christ Jesus.

Early Syriac writings such as *Odes of Solomon*, *Acts of Judas Thomas*, and *Book of Steps*, and authors like Aphrahat, Mar Ephrem discussed this imagery. Among which the *Acts of Judas Thomas* and Mar Ephrem discuss this very

---

194 Quasten, *Patrology* Vol. 2, 98-100.

195 Rush, "Death as Spiritual Marriage," 82.

196 Origen, *De oratione* 17,2; Cited Rush, "Death as Spiritual Marriage," 82.

197 Origen, *Canicle,*1; cited Quasten, Patrology Vol. 2, 99.

198 Clement, Stromateis, 3. 6, 11, 49, 74; Origen, Canticles 11, 15, 19; Tertullian, De Corona 14, Cyprian, The Treatises of S. Cælius Cyprian, 2.19; Jerome, Ep. 123. 12; Methodius, Symposium 38; Ambrose, Commentary on Luke, 6.38; Chrysostom, Hom 20, On Ephesians; Augustine, On Marriage and Concupiscence, I.10, 11, 17, 19.

199 Ware, and Mother Mary, (eds.), *The Lenten Triodion*, 510.

200 Eijk, "The Gospel of Philip and Clement of Alexandria," 104.

deep and well. Acts of Thomas discourages the wedding in this world and asks to the faithful to be ready for the heavenly bridegroom. "…that was a bridal chamber which was taken down, this is a bridal-chamber which remaineth forever. …Thou art a bridegroom who passeth away and is changed; Jesus is the true bridegroom who enduredth forever. …"[201] Aphrahat, the Persian sage says to *bnai qyomo* on the spiritual marriage:

> All those who are betrothed to Christ are far removed from the curse of the Law, and are redeemed from the condemnation of the daughters of Eve; for they are not wedded to men so as to receive the curses and come into the pains. They take no thought of death, because they do not deliver children to him. And in place of a mortal husband, they are betrothed to Christ.[202]

Mar Ephrem is another fourth century author who praises the bride-bridegroom Imagery. He sung:

> Cana herself may speak;
> I am grateful to be found worthy to invite him among my guests-
> That Heavenly Bridegroom Who descended and invited all.
> To enter His pure feast I am invited.
> Among the generations I shall confess that He is the Bridegroom and there is no other.
> And His bridal chamber is prior to the ages,
> and His feast is rich and not wanting-
> unlike my banquet that was lacking and He filled it.[203]

Mar Jacob occupies these authors in his homilies but he uses this theological theme in a deeper manner. According to S. P. Brock the bride imagery is introduced in the web of typology in the fifth century. "In the fifth- and sixth- century poets (but not yet in Ephrem) a new strand of imagery was introduced into this web of typology namely the image of bride."[204]

In the Syriac Churches, along with the aim of worship, the liturgy is used as good theological lessons. The marriage liturgy of the West Syriac tradition has a dense theological reflection. It is more than a petition or prayer, rather it teaches how a couple should live in this world by pleasing God their Creator and Eternal Husband. A prayer describes about the sacrificial act of Jesus Christ, the Bridegroom to save His bride, the Church:

> Glory be to the Heavenly Bridegroom, who has chosen the daughter of the gentiles as a Church for Himself and has, by His victorious blood, cleansed her

---

[201] *AAA,* 132.

[202] Parisot, *Demo* VI.6. 269.10-15; E.T. Valavanolickal, *Aphrahat*, *Demonstrations* VI. 6. p. 141.

[203] *HVir* 33.4. E.T. McVey, *Ephrem the Syrian Hymns,* 408.

[204] Brock, "The Wedding Feast of the Blood on Golgotha…" 121.

> from all sins and iniquities, and has betrothed Himself to Her and has redeemed Her from the slavery of Satan and has set Her free from all Her debts and sins.[205]

In one of the hymns in the West Syriac Marriage rite sings:

> Church am I, the holy Church; Bride of Heavenly- Bridegroom
> Holy Church thus speaketh, "who; Is my groom! Blessed am I
> Worship I my groom who came; And was betrothed to me
> "That day I was betrothed; Veil'd me anon nobleness
> Creatures were all astounded; Dressed in glory, great am I![206]

One of the East Syriac prayers describes almost the same: "O Thou heavenly Bridegroom, Who espousedst Thy Church through the priest, the son of the priests, John Thy bride-man and messenger; we pray to Thee to have mercy upon us."[207] Thus the bride-bridegroom imagery was an important imagery to express the God-human relationship from pre-Christian era. In the Syriac theological and liturgical tradition it is used widely to praise the Almighty God for his loving kindness and remind the faithful of the eternal mercy of the Savior.

Conclusion

This chapter has discussed seven ecclesiological homilies of Mar Jacob which widely describe the spousal imagery as a pedagogical instrument. These homilies serve as the mainstay of the present study. The second part of this chapter discussed various hermeneutical methods which Mar Jacob used to interpret the scripture effectively. In the Oriental and the Eastern understanding God is ineffable to human beings. He is even hidden to the heavenly beings. Therefore, strict definitions by human beings out of their limited understanding cannot contain the Almighty God and the divine mysteries. In other words, creation cannot define the Creator because He is above the creation. Therefore, the Oriental and the Eastern Theologians are content with symbols and types to interpret the Divine Nature. Following Mar Ephrem Mar Jacob used symbols and types widely in his theological and scriptural interpretation. Symbols of nature proclaim the glory of God, their creator. Put it in other words, the creation is a representation of its creator. It reveals the power and the wisdom of its creator. Therefore, by seeing the creation one could evaluate its creator. Also a symbol could provide unexplainable meanings to the observer. But 'types' are more powerful than the symbol because they are the real replica of the original. Similarities of the real in the distant past make a 'type.' That means there is a direct relationship between the 'type' and real. Both the

205 *Koodasha Kramangal,* 62.

206 *Koodasha Kramangal,* 78.

207 Badger, *The Nestorians and Their Rituals II,* 266.

symbols and 'types' were created from the subjective cognizance of a person. Therefore, their meaning, especially of the symbols', may be varied according to the person and environment that he/she lives. Finally, this chapter discussed the use of the nuptial imagery prior to Mar Jacob. The marriage imagery was well known to almost all neighboring cultures of Semitic and Canaanite world. Mar Jacob used this advantage very fruitfully. While remaining in the community of the Church the marriage imagery offers a personal relation with God. This personal relationship with God is important and relevant in the present compartmentalized and secluded world.[208]

[208] I mean, in the present world, due to the establishment of modern amenities people are self content. The need of others in one's life is comparatively less. Though people are communicating each other most of them are living a life of retreat; retreat into one's own personal life or the basic pattern of the modern life style is selfish. But they need help when they go through painful situation or any situations when they need to share their feelings. Then they often found asylum in God's grace. It is very common tendency in the modern world. Thus the personal relationship of the bride imagery is very relevant.

Chapter 3

Betrothal and Marriage Imagery in Mar Jacob of Serugh

Introduction

The last part of the second chapter of this study has briefly discussed Mar Jacob's predecessors' usage of betrothal and marriage imagery. This chapter elaborates the various aspects of betrothal and marriage imagery in Mar Jacob's homilies. It is imperative to note that the marriage imagery is well rooted in the Scripture. Both the Old Testament and the New Testament portrayed this imagery to show the relation between God and His people. Through this imagery the Old Testament shows the relation between Yahweh and the people of Israel. The prophets used to portray Yahweh as husband and Israel as the wife.[1] This is mostly in connection with the worship of God. The first two of the 'Ten Commandments' exhibit the covenantal relation between Yahweh and His people, Israel. Yahweh states, I am your God, you shall not have any other gods. You shall not make image of any or worship them (Ex 20:1-6). When God commanded "I am your God" the immediate meaning is "you are (not) my people" (Hos 1:9). Thus, a close personal relationship is drawn in this commandment. But, when the people of Israel entered Canaan and mingled with them, the Israelites gradually began to worship the gods of the Canaanites and took wives from among them going against the commandments of Yahweh.

The later prophets like Isaiah, Jeremiah, Ezekiel, and Hosea rose up and rebuked the people of their practice of idolatry. The prophets took the imagery of marriage to teach the true relationship with Yahweh. They placed

[1] Bedjan, *HS* III, 288.3-4; ET. Brock, "On the Veil of Moses," in *Studies in Syriac Spirituality*, 77.93-94.

Yahweh as the true Bridegroom with whom the people of Israel had entered into a covenantal relationship. They depicted Israelites as adulteress since they worshiped other gods and had broke the covenantal relationship with Yahweh, their true Bridegroom (Isa 50:1; 62:5; Jer 2:1; Ezek Chapter 16; Hos 2:2-3). They called Israel to turn back to their God, Yahweh, their true husband (Hos 3:5; 6:1). In the New Testament, Christ compared Himself as the Bridegroom. It rightly used the bridal imagery to explain the eschatological events several times (Mt 9:15; 25:1-10; Mk 2:19-20; Lk 5:34). But Paul is the one who explicitly used this imagery in connection with Christ and the Church (Eph 2:22-32).

Ensuing the Scriptural depiction of the marriage imagery, the Church Fathers, especially from the Syriac tradition, like Mar Ephrem and Mar Jacob taught the salvation history through this imagery. This great tradition visualized the goal of Christian life as to live with Jesus, the real Bridegroom, in His bridal chamber; which is the eternal life in the kingdom of God. They used this theme as a parallel to the Greek theological understanding of *theosis* or divinization.[2] The Greek fathers always found the goal of Christian life as the participation in the divinity of God. They called this as divinization or *theosis*.[3]

Mar Jacob says that all creations were betrothed to God in the blood of His Son.[4] According to him the main reason for the Divine Marriage is to rehabilitate or retrieve humankind from corruption and death of their old nature.[5] Due to the transgression, Adam and Eve became corrupted, their image and likeness of God were distorted, and they became mortals.[6] Consequently, they were expelled from the Garden of Eden, the Paradise, and God set a Cherub with the revolving sword to guard the gates of Eden from mortals entering into it.[7] Later, God in His infinite mercy decided to reclaim them from corruption and death.[8] Therefore, God sent His ambassadors, the prophets, to

---

[2] Beggiani, *Introduction to Eastern Christian Spirituality*, 13.

[3] Lossky, *The Mystical Theology of the Eastern Church,* 196.

[4] Bedjan, *HS* II, 386.12; ET. "Homily on the Ten Virgins," *TV* 4.1(1992), 49.219-220.

[5] Bedjan, *SMS*, 725.19; ET. *FH* I, 47.121.

[6] Rilliet, *SHF* I, 540.1-18; ET. *FH* IV, 131.5-132.7; cf. Rilliet, *SHF* III, 578.17-21; ET. *FH* IX, 241.31.

[7] Rilliet, *SHF* I, 540.17-542.6; ET. *FH* IV, 132.8; cf. Bedjan, *SMS*, 813.3-4; ET. *FH* XVI, 335.93-94.

[8] The Apocryphal *Life of Adam and Eve* says that Adam and Eve repented and observed forty days fast by standing forty days into the water of river *Gihon* up to his neck. One commentator says while he was completing forty days God accepted his repentance and his body was transformed into sieve. See Anderson, "Adam and Even in *The Life of* Adam" (7-33) in *Biblical Figures Outside the Bible,* 18. *The First Book of Adam* witnesses the coming of Jesus Christ to save the human kind from its sins. This document claims it as the first prophecy of the Christ's coming (XIV. 4-5, XXIV. 4-6, online).

educate and cleanse the descendants of Adam.[9] However, they rebelled against God and rejected the counsel of the prophets.[10] Finally, God sent His Only Son to save His creation but they not only rejected him but also killed him.[11] Then the Bridegroom elected the Church as His bride. This is the basic hypothesis of the salvation history of the Fathers and through the marriage imagery they elaborate it dramatically.

In order to develop the above mentioned salvation account, the Syriac Fathers used to relate every act in the life of Jesus Christ under the marriage imagery. They portrayed Christ as the Heavenly Bridegroom who descended from His heavenly abode to marry the adulteress wife, Israel, who was betrothed to Him eternally.[12] When the betrothed rejected and crucified Him[13] the Bridegroom selected a new bride, the Church, from the nations and betrothed her.[14] By this act Christ redeemed the bride and made her entrance possible into the eternal bridal chamber, which was barred through the transgression of Adam. The essence of the marriage imagery is the history of salvation. The rest of this chapter explores how far Mar Jacob envisioned the marriage imagery to educate his audience on the glorious event of salvation and thereby states how far the Church is indebted to the Heavenly Bridegroom and how far she kept the marriage covenant intact.

3.1. The Staging Posts

The term 'way'[15] (*'urho*) has a prominent role in the saving works of Jesus Christ. In his interpretation Mar Jacob compared Christ's Incarnation to a journey. Christ had to undergo three staging posts or milestones before reaching the destination.[16] Sebastian P. Brock sees three staging posts in Mar Ephrem's homilies: Mary's womb, womb of Jordan, and womb of *Sheol*.[17] Mar Jacob also discuses these three staging posts in his homily:

> He completed His whole course by three staging posts (*awone*):
> He resided in the Virgin and came to birth, though he was God;

[9] Bedjan, *HS* III, 707.1-4; cf. Sony, "La Methode Exegetique de Jaques de Sarugh," 73.

[10] Rilliet, *SHF* IV, 594.13-596.9; ET. *FH* XI, 268-269.22.

[11] Bedjan, *HS* II, 614.8; ET. *FH* XIII, 296.65.

[12] Alwan, *QHC* I, 3.49.

[13] Bedjan, II, 624.19-626.1; ET. *FH* XIV, 308.13-309.38.

[14] Bedjan, *HS* I, 167.1; ET. *FH* VI, 162.1; cf. Bedjan, *HS* I, 458.17-20; ET. *FH* X, 260.281-282.

[15] See other usages of 'way' in Syriac theology in, Murray, *Symbols of Church,* 246-249.

[16] Bedjan, *HS* III, 295.1-2; ET. "On the Veil on Moses," 81.237; cf. Bedjan, *HS* III, 208.1-4; 210.4-11; ET. "On Our Lord and Jacob," *TV* 4.4(1993), 51.1-4, 53.41-48.

[17] Brock, *The Luminous Eye,* 92.

> again, baptism received him, and yet he was God,
> and he descended to *Sheol*, and the world recognized that he was God.[18]

Sebastian P. Brock brings out the same idea in two other West Syrian services which asserts its place in the early Syriac Churches:

> Your Son, Lord, by his own will and by your will dwelt in the world for our sake in three different staging posts, in the womb made of flesh, in the womb of baptism, and the gloomy abode of *Sheol.*[19]

By the staging posts Mar Jacob refers to the important events in the life of Jesus Christ, the Bridegroom.[20] The birth, baptism, and descend into the *Sheol* are the three stages through which Jesus Christ traveled to liberate and betroth the Church. By His nature He is incorruptible and unapproachable even to the angels of heaven.[21] But through the birth He identified with His bride in image (*ṣalmo*),[22] walked along in her paths and became approachable to the human beings. Another reason for the Incarnation of the Son is that, without taking the form of human being (that is His own Image) He could not save human beings from sin and death.[23] Mar Jacob says that this has to be done because this is the fulfillment of God's will.[24] Therefore, birth from the womb of the daughter of Adam is important in the process of salvation. Baptism of Jesus is the second staging post through which Christ betrothed the Church. Although He has no sin and had no need of baptism, He received it from the hands of His servant. Through the baptism Jesus Christ purified the source of the water and instituted baptism, the great sacrament for the purification and salvation of humankind. Descent into the *Sheol* is another staging post where the dead from the time of Adam were imprisoned. The Bridegroom descended into the *Sheol* and liberated the children of Adam from fetters, which is also a betrothal event.

The interpretation made by Mar Jacob on three stages carry equal importance. It could be deduced that each staging post has its own relevance and uniqueness in the way of salvation. The fundamental difference between a spiritual interpretation and historical-critical interpretation of the Scripture

---

[18] Bedjan, *HS* III, 593.11-13; cf. Brock, "Some Important Baptismal Themes," 197.

[19] *Anonimous Syrian Orthodox Service,* 32; cited in Brock, "Some Important Baptismal Themes," 197.

[20] Vellian categorically says that according to the East Syrian liturgical texts Jesus betrothed the Church at the time of his baptism. Vellian, "The Church as the Bride," 498. But Mar Jacob's interpretation all the staging posts are betrothal.

[21] Bedjan, *SMS*, 723.10-21; 728.17-729.11; ET. *FH* I, 44.69-45.80, 50.185-200.

[22] Bedjan, *SMS*, 733.15; ET. *FH* I, 55.289.

[23] Alwan, *QHC* I, 3.37.

[24] Bedjan, *SMS*, 754.12-21; ET. *FH* I, 74.725-734.

is seen here. In the former the interpreter is totally free to make his version and have no barrier of time and space or to be metered with scientific methodologies; the concern is only effective communication of ideas. But the other is bound with many poetical constrains. He/she has only one aim that is to effectively interpret what he/she wants. On the other hand, the latter will be bound with many things related to it. In this kind of interpretation the time and space and the methodology play their own contributions and has limitations. In the case of the betrothal imagery, though Mar Jacob sees three staging posts, not as contrary in itself but complementary. Therefore, the staging posts are very important, for it is through this that the Bridegroom betrothed the bride and saved her from desolation.

3.2. The Concept of Time

Mar Jacob explains that the 'type' of the betrothal was announced in the Old Testament events; especially through the covenantal agreement of Mount Sinai. The readers may wonder how he can imagine the same event in such a variety of historical times and events! Also, he uses the same incident to interpret different themes; which can also create doubts in the minds of a normal reader. But in the spiritual interpretation these things are very easy; because they believe in the sacred time which can surpass all barriers. On the other hand a person who is oriented in the scientific and modern educational system that uses reason as the tool and canon or a modern theologian who uses redaction or historical methods to analyze an event or a passage may not approve of this kind of exegetical work. But Brock says:

> Sacred time, however, is not concerned at all with the sequence of events in ordinary time (indeed it can reverse them); rather the concern of sacred time lies in the salvific content and meaning of an event or events that take place either in primordial time, 'in the beginning,' or (and this is particularly characteristic of Judaism and Christianity) at a point or points in historical time. These salvific events continue to be effective throughout history, and can be 'recaptured' at any point of historical time, since they are eternally present in sacred time.[25]

The Syriac Church Fathers used cyclic, sacramental, or sacred time to interpret the salvation history rather than the historical, linier time concept. For the oriental theologians of the ancient times, it was not an impossible task, because they lived in a luminous world where time and space were not barriers to them. They were conscious of a transcendent world that is beyond the dimensions of space and time, so they visualized many concepts to interpret the divine mysteries which the empiricists may not agree. The one who lives within the sphere of this world cannot go beyond the linier time or historical time. But, for those who live in the spiritual world believe that nothing is

[25] Brock, *Holy Spirit in Syriac Baptismal Tradition*, 10.

impossible for God and time and space will not be a barrier to Him. Therefore, they saw the salvation history in sacred time. For them the divine things are not run through the concept of linier time. Sebastian P. Brock says about the meaning of sacred time:

> It is of course totally mistaken to see this matter in terms of historical time, known to historians of religion and to anthropologists as 'sacred time': in sacred time what is important is the salvific content of an event, and not the relationship of that event to other events before and after in historical, or linear time. This means that events of the same salvific content can come together in sacred time, even though they may be separate in linear time.[26]

Before the Oriental Christians the Semitics were aware of this kind of concept of time; Piotr Michalowski suggests that "… in ancient Mesopotamia there is absolutely no trace of any apocalyptic vision and thus the linear axis of time is not so strongly determined."[27] Mar Jacob was also not an exception to this peculiar time concept of the Eastern world. He followed the great stream in which his predecessors were guided. The greatest blessing of this form of interpretation is that they can transcend the time-space barrier. Therefore, he interpreted the birth, baptism, crucifixion, etc., as betrothal.

3.3. Understanding the Major Term

This section discusses the major term *mkr*, that is used by Mar Jacob in his marriage imagery. The Hebrew term for betrothal is *'rś*, which means betroth a wife. The act of betrothal in ancient Israel seems to have been a public, legally binding undertaking upon which the validity of marriage rested. Betrothal has been considered as the final step in concluding marriage, following which the only thing remaining was the consummation of marriage.[28] Its *Akkadian* form is *mkāru* and its simple meaning is to do business and its *peal* form means to buy. 2 Samuel 3:14 explicitly uses the term with meaning 'wife' means "give my wife whom I *espoused*". Another meaning is 'a promise' or 'a pledge.' The third type of meaning is "promise a woman in marriage to" Exodus 22:16 says: "the virgin who was not *betrothed*." Or 'betroth' Mathew 1:18 is an example: "when his mother Mary *betrothed* to Joseph, before they came together."[29] Passive participle form (*mkeerto*) or (*mkeer*) means bride and bridegroom.[30] Therefore, often this term is found to be used as both in modern sense of betrothal and marriage.

---

[26] Brock, "Some Important themes," 191.

[27] Michalowski, "Presence and the Creation," 384.

[28] Mays, *Hosea: A Commentary,* 50.

[29] Sokoloff, *A Syriac Lexicon*, 761.

[30] Smith, *Syriac Dictionary*, 272.

3.4. Betrothal According to the Jewish and Biblical Understanding

The Church holds a strong background of Jewish and Biblical traditions. Since it is closely indebted to both, it would be useful to understand the betrothal in these two traditions. This part of the chapter is an inquiry that how the Jewish and the Biblical traditions see betrothal and marriage image in relation to God, particularly how it can be associated to the Christ-Church relationship.

3.4.1. Betrothal in Jewish Tradition

The basic theology and system of marriage in the Jewish tradition is based on the Genesis account "Therefore a man leaves his father and his mother and clings to his wife, and they become one flesh" (Gen 2:24). Mar Jacob also takes this passage to explain his idea of Christ's betrothal to the Church and thereby the event of the salvation history through the Son of God.[31] The following section is a discussion on the Jewish custom of marriage ceremony and theological understanding of marriage.

There are two main parts in the Jewish marriage custom: betrothal and marriage. According to the Jewish custom the marriage was usually arranged by the elders of the two families. The minimum age for marriage, in the rabbinic time, was thirteen for male and twelve for female. It was customary to marry within the tribes or families, but outside the forbidden degrees of kinship (Lev 18:6-24). Fathers gave daughters to approved husbands (Ex 2:21; Josh 15:16-17) and often, if not always, the exchange involves "a marriage price" (Ex 22:16; Deut 22:29; Josh 15:18-19). In the betrothal events of Jewish tradition an agreement will be made between the families of the bride and the bridegroom. This does not imply that she became his wife proper, but a pre-marital agreement only. This may occur between two persons or with the witness of a community of friends and relatives belonging to both bride and bridegroom. Usually, the engagement takes place at the home of the bride's father. At betrothal ceremony the husband presents the wife (and her father) with the marriage contract and the bride-price.[32] Betrothal was understood to have legal consequences (Deut 20:7; 22:23-27). One or even more than a year may be taken to execute the marriage proper (Mt 1:18-25). Before the

[31] Bedjan, *HS* III, 288.1ff; ET. Brock, "On the Veil of Moses," in *Studies in Syriac Spirituality*, 77.89ff. But Aphrahat gives a quite different interpretation on this passage; He states: "Who is it who leaves father and mother to take a wife? The meaning is as follows: as long as a man has not taken a wife, he loves and reveres God his Father and the Holy Spirit his Mother, and he has no other love. But when a man takes a wife, then he leaves his (true) Father and his Mother." Parisot, *Demo.* XVIII.10, 840.5-9; ET. Valavanolickal, *Demonstrations* II, 162.

[32] The same thing can be seen in the Ugarit texts where husband will gives a bride-money and writes a contract with the bride's father. After the marriage the wife will leave his father's home and stay in his husband's house. See, (Marsman, *Women in Ugarit and Ancient Israel*, 99-101).

marriage if the wife shows unfaithfulness to the husband, he can divorce her either publicly (Deut 22:23-27) or privately by signing a divorce notice in the presence of two witnesses (Deut 24:1; Mt 1:19).

The Babylonian Talmud also recommends that, the betrothal can be enacted by money, by contract, or by living together. In the betrothal with the presence of two witnesses the bridegroom hands over any object of value (more than a *Petura*) to the bride and recites the marriage formula, "Behold, you are consecrated unto me with this ring according the law of Moses and Israel."[33] After this two short *berakah,* or prayer for the of blessing God, are recited to ratify the betrothal: one over the wine and the second is the actual prayer for the function. It says:

> Blessed art Thou, O Lord our God, King of the universe, who has hallowed us by Thy commandments, and hast given us command concerning forbidden marriages; who hast disallowed unto us those that are betrothed, but hast sanctioned unto us such as are wedded to us by the rite of the nuptial canopy and the sacred covenant of wedlock.[34]

This is the first part of the betrothal called *Kiddushin* or *erusin.* The living together is forbidden until the second part, which is the marriage proper, *nissu'in,* is over; which is also known as *huppah.* The couple fast all-day and confess their sins, as on the Day of Atonement; they wear crowns of myrtle, and the bride, if a virgin, also wears a long veil as she proceeds with her retinue to the bridegroom's house for the everlasting feast. At the threshold, the contract is written down. After the feast, the bridegroom himself recites the seven blessings, which, later the tradition was passed to the rabbis to be said.[35] During the approximate year between the betrothal and nuptial ceremonies, the betrothed girl was legally the man's wife even though she was still a virgin, since the marital relation did not begin until the nuptial ceremony.[36] Joachim Jeremias said, "According to later Jewish law the betrothal effects the "acquisition" of the bride by the bridegroom and is thus a valid marriage. Though the bride still stands under the *parira potestas* until the marriage, she is legally a married woman from the time of the betrothal."[37] The betrothal could be abrogated only by formal written divorce or by death.[38]

---

[33] Hertz, *Daily Prayer Book*, 1011; cited in Posner, "Marriage Ceremony," 565.

[34] Hertz, *Daily Prayer Book*, 1011; cited in Posner, "Marriage Ceremony," 565.

[35] Stevenson, *To Join Together the Rite of Marriage*, 13-14.

[36] *Ketuboth* 5.2; *Midrash Rabbah Songs* iv. 8. 1. Cited in Belkin, "The Problem of Paul's Background," 51.

[37] Jeremias, "νύμφη, ωυμφίος," 1099.

[38] *Kiddushin* 3.7, Cited in Mielziner, *The Jewish Law of Marriage and Divorce,* 51.

There is a strong tradition among the Jewish mystics regarding the spiritual realm of marriage relationship between God and the individual soul. The Jewish mystical tradition tells the background of spiritual marriage between individual soul and heavenly Bridegroom. As early as the formative period of the Talmud (fifth and sixth centuries AD) the relations between God and Israel were conceptualized as a spiritual marriage.[39] This idea is especially prominent in the interpretations of the Song of Songs. Though there is an erotic overtone in the metaphorical description, there is no physical intercourse involved like in the Sumerian tradition. Lapinkivi describes about the Jewish mystical interpretation:

> In Jewish mysticism, the sacred marriage is an ecstatic union between an individual human soul and God and, although it is described with erotic metaphors, no one is required to play the part of the divine Bridegroom; thus there is no actual sexual intercourse involved. This would in fact be impossible, because the bride-soul belongs to a male saddiq (righteous man) indentified with the *Sefirah* of the *Shekhinah.* The *Shekhinah,* the tenth *Sefirah* (also known as *Malkut*), is viewed as the feminine partner of the system of the other (nine) *Sefirot* regarded as the "world of the male"; or she is the bride of God, namely, the *Sefirah* of *Tiferet* or *Yesod,* the bridegrooms. On the other hand, real intercourse is taking place in the case of *mitation dei*, when the righteous has sexual relations with his wife on the Sabbath night and is, in this way, imitating the divine sexual act of the *Sefirot* of the *Shekhinah* and *Tiferet* that occurs in heaven. In this case, however, the *Shekhinah* does not take the place of the wife, nor does the *Saddiq* play God's role as the divine Bridegroom.[40]

The above description reveals the concept of spiritual marriage in the Jewish mystical tradition and its theological understanding. This purports the closeness of the divine human relationship in the nuptial metaphor. They believe that man and woman cannot be one (Gen 2:24) without divine intervention, so that, they attribute God's spiritual union to human sexual intercourse. This illustrates the Jewish convention that, betrothal is an agreement between two families in which bridegroom will agree that he will take the girl as his bride. He will give a bride price to the bride's parent. And in the spiritual tradition the human soul is considered as the bride of God. Many of these aspects have been used by Mar Jacob in the bride-bridegroom imagery.

3.4.2. Betrothal in the Old Testament

Betrothal in the Old Testament can be divided into two: betrothal announced in Torah and the betrothal announced in the Prophetical books. The betrothal announced in the Torah can also be called covenantal betrothal or indirect

[39] Matter, "Mystical Marriage," 31.

[40] Lapinkivi, "The Sumerian Sacred Marriage and its Aftermath," 25.

betrothal, because there is no direct declaration about the marriage but a covenantal agreement only. Zimmerman rightly says about the reason for the absence of direct reference of male-female imagery in relation to Yahweh-people of God relationship:

> Unlike the acceptance of other pairs of deities that were known in the religious environment that surrounded Israel, strict monotheistic belief in YHWH initially avoided any mention of a female figure at YHWH's side. No references to a "sacred marriage" can be found in the Hebrew Bible. Indeed, it seems that the language and theology of this concept is intentionally avoided by the biblical authors. Nevertheless, gender specific metaphors have been used since the time of the prophets to lend form and expression to Israel's belief in God. However, gender metaphors were used in the literature of YHWH cult neither to describe the power of God in terms of masculine potency nor to present an exemplary divine love relationship between a god and a goddess. Instead, the language of human love was used to describe a person's relationship to God: more specifically, the relationship of the people of Israel to God. Israel's relationship to God was characterized as a passionate and jealous love liaison, marked by the ruptures and reconciliations found in relationships between man and a woman.[41]

Therefore, it could be understood from the background where the name of the Almighty is not pronounced the explicit reference of this imagery cannot be expected. But it is not difficult for a later interpreter to envision a nuptial imagery in the covenantal relationship between the Yahweh and His people. On the other hand the prophets very clearly use the marriage imagery to explain divine-human relationship. This imagery shows the passionate love of God towards His people. The prophecy of Hosea is a good example of this kind of love.

3.4.2.1. Yahweh Betrothed Israel: In Torah

The prophetical books of the Old Testament explicitly mention the bride-bridegroom imagery to depict the divine-human relationship. But as said earlier, a glimpse of this imagery can be traced in the Torah. The Torah itself declares the covenantal agreement between Yahweh and His people. In the course of time various covenants were made between Yahweh and the people: The covenant with Noah, Abraham, and Moses. But even before them a covenant could be seen in the Garden of Eden; where God made a covenant with Adam and said that "but of the tree of the knowledge of good and evil you shall not eat, for in the day that you eat of it you shall die" (Gen 2:17). Since marriage enacts through a covenant between the bridegroom and bride or between their families, the covenant between God and His people is apparent though not visible.

---

[41] Zimmerman, "The Love Triangle of Lady Wisdom," 243.

Therefore, the covenantal relationships with Adam, Noah (Gen 9: 1-17), and Abraham are the archaic forms of betrothal. Nonetheless, the covenant made with Abraham that "And I will make of you a great nation" (Gen 12:2, 13:16) is the beginning of the covenant in historical time. Again, the extension of this covenant can be seen in another form:

> I am God Almighty; walk before me, and be blameless. And I will make my covenant between me and you, and will make you exceedingly numerous." Then Abram fell on his face; and God said to him. "As for me, this is my covenant with you: you shall be the ancestor of a multitude of nations. No longer shall your name be Abram. But your name shall be Abraham; for I have made you the ancestor of a multitude of nations. I will make you exceedingly fruitful; and I will make nations of you, and kings shall come from you. I will establish my covenant between me and you, and your offspring after you throughout their generations, for an everlasting covenant to be God to you and to your offspring after you. And I will give to you and to your offspring after you, the land where you are now an alien, all the land of Canaan, for a perpetual holding; and I will be their God." God said to Abraham, "As for you, you shall keep my covenant, you and your offspring after you throughout their generations. This is my covenant, which you shall keep, between me and you and your offspring after you; every male among you shall be circumcised. You shall circumcise the flesh of your foreskins, and it shall be a sign of the covenant between me and you (Gen 17: 1-12).

The final covenant in Torah is the Ten Commandments, given to Moses at Mount Sinai, which will be discussed later. This covenantal agreement is a symbol of God's loving care and protection towards His people, for they should not perish; and therefore, it is a betrothal. In Jewish tradition, after the betrothal the wife will be under the protection of her husband. This might be a reflection of the protection of Yahweh.

3.4.2.2. Yahweh Betrothed Israel: In the Prophetical Books

The following part will explore the hidden reminiscent prophecy of the Christ-Church's divine betrothal in the prophetic books. Hosea may be the first explicit user of the marriage imagery in connection with the People of God. He says: Rebuke your mother, rebuke her, for she is not my wife, and I am not her husband. Let her remove the adulterous look from her face and the unfaithfulness from between her breasts (Hos 2:2). Prophet Ezekiel dedicated chapters 16 and 23 to discuss the adulteress nature of Israel. He compares Samaria and Jerusalem with two sisters: Oholah and Oholibah. These sisters became prostitutes in Egypt, where "Thus you longed for the lewdness of your youth, when the Egyptians fondled your bosom and caressed your young breasts" (Ezek 23:21). Jeremiah remembers the good times of Israel as faithful wife of Yahweh: "I remember the devotion of your youth, your love as a bride, how you followed me in the wilderness, in a land not sown" (Jer 2:1). But later he says about the unfaithful bride, Israel: Have you seen what she did, that faithless one, Israel, how she went up on every high hill and under every green tree, and played the whore there?" (Jer 3:6). Regarding the relationship between Yahweh and the people of Israel prophet Isaiah says: "Your maker will be your husband" (Isa 54:5). When they were in trouble the prophet again says: "Where is your mother's bill of divorce with which I put her away? Or which of my creditors is it to whom I have sold you? No, because of your sins you were sold" (Isa 50:1). All these Bible references denote the prophetic interpretation of the bride imagery. Mar Jacob made use of this imagery either explicitly or implicitly to explain the God-human relationship.[42]

3.4.2.3. Church as the Betrothed in the New Testament

Though mentioned covertly, the Gospel texts are very rich in relation to the bride-bridegroom concept between Jesus and the Church. Most of these are mentioned in an eschatological context. Several times Jesus has called himself as 'Bridegroom' (Mt 9:15; 22:2-14; Mk 2:19; Lk 5:34; 14:8, 16-24; Jn 3:29). On another occasion Jesus symbolically explains the second coming using the imagery of the wedding chamber (Mt 25:1-12). But Paul explicitly mentioned the bride imagery in connection with Christ-Church relationship (Eph 5:22-33). He explains it as a great 'mystery' (*rozo* ܪܐܙܐ). This term recurs in his homilies to explain the divine nature and divine-human relationship.[43] Paul reminds the Church of Corinthians as "betrothed to Christ as pure virgin" (2 Cor 11:2). In the Book of Revelations, the author sees the "the wedding of the Lamb" (Rev 19:7-8). The Lamb is betrothed to the Church and the heavenly Jerusalem (Rev 19:7; 21:2-3, 9-10).

3.5. Betrothal of the Church According to Mar Jacob

As a teacher and a pastor of his Church Mar Jacob has interpreted the Word of God to his flock in a spiritual manner. Though his homilies are theological in nature they are plain enough to a lay person. His mind was full of Jesus and His saving activities. Therefore, he had read the Scripture in the understanding that entire scripture passages are leading to one point: Jesus and His saving works. He tried to make his flocks understand that Jesus is the Savior of the world and He saved it from sin and death. To explain this mystery he used the Biblical imagery of bride and bridegroom; because, marriage was considered as an

[42] Rilliet, *SHF* IV, 596-600; ET. *FH* XI, 270.26- 271.30.

[43] In his Homily on the Veil of Moses itself uses the term ܪܐܙܐ 7 times. Other than that this he uses veil (ܚܦܝܐ) and hidden (ܡܟܣܝܐ) several times. Bedjan, HS III, 285.7; 288.13; ET. Brock, "On the Veil of Moses," in Studies in Syriac Spirituality, 75.33, 77.101. In the homily On Our Lord and Jacob, he uses the term 13 times.

indissoluble relationship pattern around him.[44] The church documents and his predecessors influenced him to develop the imagery. The Canons 9 of the West Syriac Church says that: "If any of the Christians leaves his wife- without the cause of adultery or fornication, or takes another one- the synod has ordered that he shall be excommunicated from the church and from the mysteries, and from intercourse with Christians..." Canon 10 says that: "If any of the Christians betroths and then abandons his betrothed to look upon another- the synod has ordered that they shall be excommunicated from the Church of God; the same shall be the case with wives of men who abandon their husbands."[45] Moreover, his predecessors like Mar Aphrahat and Mar Ephrem successfully used this Biblically based imagery to educate their flocks. Therefore, whenever he wants to talk about the saving works of Jesus he used the imagery in its full meaning. He uses every act of marriage; cleansing before the betrothal, the betrothal event, betrothal by giving bride price, betrothal agreement, etc., marriage, marriage adornment, marriage feast, marriage chamber, nuptial life with the Bridegroom, etc. Through the marriage imagery Mar Jacob affirms the loving kindness of God and salvation of humankind through Jesus Christ.

Mar Jacob's interpretation alludes that, unlike the regular human betrothal the heavenly betrothal is a unilateral; the betrothal is fully conceived, initiated, and executed by the Father through the Son of God. In the homily on *Creation* he clearly says that, it was there in the Father's mind even at the time of creation or before the creation of man. Otherwise the Father would not give His Image to dust.[46]

Just as in the Jewish betrothal custom, where parents find and proposes the bride to their son, Mar Jacob says that, the Father betrothed (selected) a bride to His Only-Begotten Son.[47] Through the prophecies in the Old Testament He taught and prepared her for His Son.[48] But this Bridegroom, as against the usual one, is an iconoclastic one, who emptied Himself and descended to earth from his high and sublime profile, identified with the ordinary sinful bride, humiliated, and gave his body and blood as the bride-money and

[44] Mar Ephrem sees the bridal chamber in the heaven is indissoluble; therefore the marriage in this earth is also indissoluble. He writes: "The bridal chamber which he prepares is not subject to divorce. There are no days there, for these is no sun. There is no change there, for there are no stars. Eternity is seated with... rest; sorrow and joy disappear when he enters the fortress or rest (Graffin, "Hymnes inedites de Saint Ephrem sur la virginite," 63-103; Cited Nir, *Joseph and Asneth.* 83).

[45] Vööbus, *The Synodicon in the West Syriac Tradition,* 5.

[46] Alwan, *QHC* I, 2.30-3.40.

[47] Bedjan, *HS* III, 287.17; ET. Brock, "On the Veil of Moses," in *Studies in Syriac Spirituality*, 76.85.

[48] Bedjan, *HS* III, 285.21-287.16; ET, Brock, "On the Veil of Moses," in *Studies in Syriac Spirituality*, 75.47-76.86.

wedding-feast.[49] Through the imagery of betrothal Mar Jacob explains the saving act of Jesus Christ; by which he says how Christ, the Bridegroom, saved the Church, the bride, in effect the world itself, from sin, death, and eternal damnation. Through this act He retrieved the robe of glory which was lost at the Garden of Eden through the sin of Adam. By receiving the lance on His side the Bridegroom removed the revolving lance which guarded the gates of the Garden of Eden and made possible the Church's reentry into the Paradise, which he refers as the eternal bridal chamber to enjoy with the eternal Bridegroom.

3.5.1. Betrothal Announced in the Old Testament

Mar Jacob has the conviction that the betrothal between Christ and the Church was hidden in the prophecies.[50] This section is a discussion of how he envisages the Old Testament background of the betrothal of Christ and the Church.[51] According to him the Old Testament is a huge house in which Moses entered and delineated the picture of Son of God and covered it with a veil. Every action in the Old Testament is pointing to the Son of God.[52] When Paul entered in the ministry of the Church, he saw the mystery and proclaimed that the Old Testament mysteriously proclaims the Son of God as the Bridegroom. Most of his vision on this theme is seen in the *Homily on the Baptism of our Redeemer* and *Homily on the Veil of Moses*. In his homily *On the Baptism of Our redeemer* Mar Jacob says that, "O Church from the beginning I betrothed to you this Bridegroom; in the hope of this One I have held you from the time

---

[49] Mar Jacob uses both these aspects in his homilies. Bedjan, *HS* III, 290.15-18; ET. Brock, Brock, "On the Veil of Moses," in *Studies in Syriac Spirituality*, in *Studies in Syriac Spirituality*, 78.144-148.

[50] Bedjan, *HS* III, 284.20; ET. Brock, "On the Veil of Moses," in *Studies in Syriac Spirituality*, 75.24; Bedjan, *HS* I, 40.7-12.

[51] The same can be seen in the writings of Mar Ephrem. In *Contra Heresies* he wrote:

In the Torah Moses prepared
The way of symbols before that people
That was straying on all ways.
Our Lord, however, in his testaments
Completed, established the way of truth
For the peoples that came to the way of life. (*CH.* 25.3).

[52] Bedjan, *HS* III, 286.13-16; ET, Brock, "On the Veil of Moses," in *Studies in Syriac Spirituality*, 76.60-64. Mar Ephrem also says the same in his hymns. He states:

The apostles-mere fishermen-with his colors
were able to fashion prototypes of his symbols
the prophets, as painters, painted him
because he taught them whom he resembled (Walters, *Hymn on the Unleavened Bread,* 66).

I came."[53] The foundation of his argument is Genesis 2:24. Still it is scattered all over the Old Testament. The direct reference to the betrothal is professed by the later prophets like Isaiah, Jeremiah, Ezekiel, and Hosea.

In Mar Jacob's opinion God betrothed His people to His Only Son even at their creation. This most interesting interpretation on the betrothal imagery is given in his first homily *On Creation*. He describes that before the creation the Father foreknew that human beings will fall and thus they will perish. With the same love that God the Father intended to create human beings, He decided to create human being in His own Image (Gen 1:26); so that, He could save them from the fall. Therefore, the betrothal happened even before the creation of man. Mar Jacob said this is a 'type' of betrothal between Son of God and the Church.[54] He argues that Moses not says about an ordinary man and woman, because they cannot become one.[55] But this is a prophecy about the betrothal of the Son of God with the Church. The 'type' of this betrothal has been announced and renewed in the prophecies from time to time through the covenants.[56] In every age, the law and the covenant have been changed. At first, God changed the covenant of Adam and gave another one to Noah. And once again He gave (another) to Abraham. And He changed that of Abraham, and gave yet another one to Moses. And when that of Moses was not observed, He gave another covenant to the last generation, a covenant that does not change.[57] Mar Jacob enumerates and scrutinizes the five covenants the Lord enacted and observes that God advanced the world in stages. Humankind progressed from infancy through adolescence youth, maturity, and perfection.[58] He again portrays the five covenants to a didactic exercise. He expands the metaphor, noting that the five covenants correspond to the five books of the Law and five human senses. He says like different stages of human life God revealed the truth to the Israelites in different stages according to their capacity to understand:

---

[53] Bedjan, *HS* 1, 175.13-16; ET. *FH* VI, 170.63-64.

[54] Alwan, *QHC* I, 2.21-3.50; The same idea would be visible in Aphrahat. He says before God created other creations He had the full image of man in His mind; therefore, in a sense, man was created even before all other creations. Moreover, God made a marriage feast by creating woman for him. *Demo*, 797. 1-19; cf. Gavin, *Aphraates and the Jews*, 37. The Jewish teachings also hold the same opinion. For more discussion see Gavin, *Aphraates and the Jews*, 38.

[55] Bedjan, *HS* III, 290.10; ET. Brock, "On the Veil of Moses," in *Studies in Syriac Spirituality*, 78.139.

[56] Aphrahat, the Persian Sage in his *Demonstrations* mentions five covenants in human history: the covenants to Adam, Noah, Abraham, Moses, and Christ. (Parisot, *Demo,* 961. XI, 11-12. 407.17-501.10; ET. Valavanolickal, *Aphrahat Demonstrations* II, 14-15). According Benin, "each step in human history marked the progressive unfolding of the truth" (Benin, "Command Covenants and Jews," 145).

[57] Benin, "Commandments, Covenants, and Jews," 142.

[58] Albert, *HCJ*, 122.151-170.

> (As a master) does not at first grant a complete book to a youth
> to read, but first commences with the syllables,
> he starts with the letters, to write them and show them (to the youth).
> With the syllables he progresses to words and then further
> and when he reads well, and has formed the letters fully he gives him.
> the large tome where one may find all wisdom.
> God also, who is a good Teacher for humanity
> raises them up, little by little, to perfection.[59]

Mar Ephrem describes that the Old Testament is filled with symbols of the Son:

> In every place, if you look, His symbol is there,
> and when you read, you will find His types.
> For by Him were created all creatures,
> and He engraved His symbols upon His possessions.
> When He created the world, He gazed at it and adorned it with His images.
> Streams of His symbols opened, flowed and poured forth
> His symbols on His members.[60]

The *Gospel of Philip* also describes at length about the hidden mysteries of the Son of God under the veil of the Old Testament:

> The mysteries of truth are revealed, though in type and image. The bridal chamber, however, remains hidden. It is the Holy of the Holy. The veil at first concealed how God controlled the creation, but when the veil is rent and the things inside are revealed, this house will be left desolate, or rather will be destroyed. [61]

The above quotation says that the prophecy about the Bridegroom, Son of God, was hidden in the Old Testament but revealed to everybody after the death and resurrection of the Son of God. The author compared the veil that covered the Son of God in the Old Testament with the temple veil. When the veil of the temple was torn from top to bottom at the death of the Son (Mt 27:51) the mysteries were unveiled and published to the Church. Also, through this event, the priesthood of the Old Testament vanished and the Shekina, the place of glory, was desolated. Thus, Mar Jacob and other Church Fathers have no doubt that the Church was betrothed to the Son from the beginning of the creation.[62] Through the prophecies the prophets taught this mystery but it was hidden.

[59] Albert, *HCJ*, 120.120-122; cf. Benin, "Commands, Covenants, and Jews," 148.

[60] *HVir* XX.12, 70; ET. McVey, *Ephrem the Syrian*, 70-71.

[61] Isenberg, *Gospel of Philip*, 84.15-85.20, 150.

[62] Alwan, *QHC* I, 2. 21-22.

3.5.2. Betrothal at Mount Sinai

Mar Jacob found the Covenant of Mount Sinai as a 'type' of Jesus' betrothal.[63] Mar Jacob uses many of the Jewish marriage customs and practices in this comparison between the betrothal at Mount Sinai and Golgotha. The Jewish marriage has a purification rite before the marriage proper.[64] He saw this purification rite in the betrothal at Mount Sinai. He compares Israel's Passover through the Dead Sea and the Church's baptism at Jordan and describes these as act of purification.[65] In his *Homily on Mar Ephrem*, Mar Jacob says: "Long ago, a boastful bride came up out of the sea, while the Hebrew women played tambourine to give praise. And now, the redeemed Church bathed in baptism, our sisters plays the melodies of Ephrem to make a joyful sound."[66] Since a deliverance aspect is involved in the betrothal, it is a joyful occasion too. He compares joy of the Nation and nations.

Richard Batey gives a wonderful explanation on the pre-cleansing process before Moses' meeting Yahweh at Sinai. In Exodus 19:10 God commanded Moses, "Go to the people and consecrate them today and tomorrow, and let them wash their garments." Batey assumes that this is a pre-betrothal cleansing. More over "The Hebrew word for consecrate or sanctify (*qudaš*) was also the term used for formal betrothal and was so understood by the rabbis in this text."[67] Mar Jacob portrays this purification of the people of Israel as a purification rite before the betrothal at Mount Sinai. Moses instructed the bride the about the splendor of the Bridegroom,[68] washed her and adorned her.

> You sanctify me today and tomorrow mystically
> and third day I will come towards her vigorously.
> Moses descended and began to adorn the bride;
> she was wearied and was torn asundered by the troubled one.
> He taught the impudent one not to feel lowly
> and he admonished her that the invisible bridegroom may not despise you.
> The holiness poured out to him in the way so that He may exalt her;

---

[63] Alwan, *QHC* I, 7.105-9:144; Rilliet, *SHF,* 602:2; Bedjan, *HS* I, 14.1-16; 40:7-12.

[64] Supra 3.4.1.

[65] Bedjan, *HS* I, 167.2-168.3; ET. *FH* VI, 162.2-10.

[66] Amar, "A metrical Homily on Holy Mar Ephrem," 39.58-59.

[67] Batey, *The New Testament Nuptial Imagery.* 16. Rationalizing this notion a little more, Batey again brought another derivation of vocalization of the Hebrew term *kekallotho* and interprets that the Sinai covenant was a betrothal. He said, citing Exodus 31:18, "And he gave Moses, when he had made and end (*kekallotho*) of speaking with him on Mount Sinai, the two tablets of the testimony." Using rabbinic technique *derash* he re-reads the term to *kekallatho*, which means, as his bride. Thus the given meaning will be: "When Yahweh had made (Israel) as his bride, while speaking to Moses on Mount Sinai, he gave Moses the two tables of the testimony" (Batey, *The New Testament Nuptial Imagery.* 16-17).

[68] Bedjan, *HS* I, 14.1-16.

so that she may see his face in purity when you receive Him.
When He sees you He will put the holy crown upon your head;
you will enter with him luminous bridal chamber with splendor.[69]

Mar Jacob saw the betrothal at Mount Sinai as a mysterious picture drawn by the great prophet Moses on the spiritual wall.[70] When Yahweh betrothed Israel on Mount Sinai, He put up the bridal chamber with a cloud of light on the mountain.[71] He summoned seventy elders along with Moses, the friend of the Bridegroom,[72] to the betrothal and betrothed the despised and tiered girl (Ex 24:9).[73] Our author repeatedly affirms the event on Mount Sinai as a prefiguration of Christ's betrothal of the Church.[74] He compares the event on Mount Sinai with the betrothal at Golgotha and states: "It was the same for the elders of Israel, when they were invited to Mount Sinai for a banquet without bread and there burst out a delightful drink which was not of wine… for more than a royal table which is adorned with very many delicious dishes."[75]

The details of Sinai Covenant and the sacrifice followed draws a parallel to the sacrifice on the Mount of Golgotha. Mar Jacob sees the former as a 'type' of the latter. He calls them as two covenants belonging to Son:

> Because the two covenants, old and new, belong to the Son, because of this, two mountains have become celebrated through Him. Your residence at Sinai is testimony that the two mountains are fellows of one another. For if the disciples of the Cross were to live on Golgotha alone, and the disciples of Moses were to live today on Mount Sinai the place of Moses, there would be an opportunity for them to speak against each other, and those who were at Mount Sinai would be thought to be followers of Moses, and those who were at Golgotha to be followers of Jesus. But the Only Begotten of the Father, to whom both mountains belong, has driven the crucifiers from both of them, and has established you to be heirs of Golgotha and Sinai, and for you to love and cherish the glorious presence of the Father and the Cross of the Son.[76]

---

[69] Bedjan, *HS* I, 12.4-13.

[70] Bedjan, *HS* III, 287.20-21; ET. Brock, "On the Veil of Moses," in *Studies in Syriac Spirituality*, 77.87-88.

[71] Bedjan, *HS* I.

[72] Friends of the bridegroom has an important role in the marriage ceremony in Jewish tradition. See more in 4.4.

[73] Bedjan, *HS* I, 10.21-11.7; Bedjan, *HS* II, 358.20-21; ET, *FH* VIII, 215.239-240.

[74] Mar Jacob deals this issue alone in his homily *Descent of the Most High on Mount Sinai and the Mystery of the Church*. See an example; Bedjan, *HS* I, 12.14-20.

[75] Rilliet, *SHF* III, 582.23-25; ET. *FH* IX, 244.40; Bedjan, *HS* I, 13.1-4.

[76] Olinder, *Ep,* 36; ET. Brock, "Jacob of Serugh, Letter VII, to the Monks of Sinai," 244. See more discussion in Bedjan, *HS* I, 14.14-19.

Mar Jacob contends that the two covenants belong to the Son and that both happened on the same mountain. The following discussion on the Sinai incident would substantiate the above statement of Mar Jacob. After the descent, Moses offered a sacrifice to God and it was a Covenantal sacrifice: And Moses took the blood and threw it upon the people, and said, "Moses took the blood and dashed it on the covenant that the Lord has made with you in accordance with all these words" (Ex 24:8). A parallel could be seen in the upper room; Jesus took the wine and said: "Then he took a cup, and after giving thanks he gave it to them, saying, drink from it, all of you; for this is my blood of the covenant, which is poured out for many for the forgiveness of sins" (Mt 26:27-28). And it was fulfilled at the top of Golgotha. A cultural element also involves in this act. The Semitic culture demands a visible action with the vocal agreement which binds the agreement intact. There were number of possible forms of covenant; covenant of blood was one of such covenants (Jer 34:18; Gen 15:9-12; 17-18).[77] In the Sinai covenant Moses cut the animal and poured the blood as a sacrifice; it was a deed of covenant. When the soldiers struck on Jesus' side and water and blood flowed from Him (Jn 19:34), Mar Jacob says, He signed an agreement with the bride.[78]

Another common factor between the covenant at Mount Sinai and Golgotha is the 'covenant meal.' This can be seen often in the Old Testament (Gen 31:46, 54; Josh 9:14; 2 Sam 3:20; Ex 24:9-11). The common meal among the Semites was a usual sign of community fraternity. For example, when Isaac and Abimelek made their covenant of friendship, the pact was sealed by a meal (Gen 26:28-30). In the Sinai covenant Yahweh made a covenant meal with seventy elders, who were the representatives of the tribes of Israel

---

[77] The essential covenant rite at Sinai, however, had to do with a sprinkling of blood on both altar and people. It would be useful to understand the exact significance of this blood-rite. As a covenant and as a means of expiation the blood right provides the background for the Eucharistic chalice (Bedjan, *HS* III, 296.8-297.4; ET. Brock, "On the Veil of Moses," in *Studies in Syriac Spirituality*, 82.260-283), and thereby, the betrothal at Golgotha. "The life of all flesh is its blood" (Lev 17:14). The *nephes* or vital principle was thought to reside in the blood, therefore, the blood of a human victim was thought to be more holy than the animal victim itself, because blood was a sign of life or even contained life. Various rites of blood-sharing were looked upon as a sign of a sharing of a common life, those who mingled their blood in a covenant laceration rite became symbolically blood brothers. The symbolism of the Sinai blood rite is more subtle. Moses took half of the blood and threw it against the altar. That which is placed upon the altar is thought to pass from the sphere of the profane to the sphere of the divine. The throwing of the blood against the altar indicated that the life symbolized by the blood had somehow become a divinized life. It had passed over from the sphere of the profane to the sacred. Only afterwards was the remaining blood sprinkled on the people. The rite thus performed indicated not only that a community of life had been established between God and his people, but that the people received this new life from God.

[78] Bedjan, *HS* III, 290.14-15; ET. Brock, "On the Veil of Moses," in *Studies in Syriac Spirituality*, 78.143-144.

(Ex 24:9-11). When Jesus made a covenant with the Church he made a meal for the Church. This is also a sign of the consummation of the eschatological meal with the Bridegroom (Isa 25:6-8). Here the scene is the same with that of Exodus 24:9-11, but now it is not only the seventy elders representing Israel who were called to the top of the Mountain of God, but all the nations of the earth, who come streaming into the great covenant banquet. The Rabbinic legend says that the Torah promulgated on the Mount of Sinai in seventy languages in order that it might eventually be brought to all the people of the world.[79] Thus, all these factors are the external supporting documents to Mar Jacob's typological interpretation of Sinai covenant as betrothal and its relation with the sacrifice on Golgotha.

The cultural and ecclesiological backgrounds are very important in making the above interpretations. Modern scholars have the opinion that the covenantal agreement originated against the fertility cult of ancient Israel. People of the ancient West Asia believed in the fertility gods that they were natural forces.[80] They thought that progeny and abundance in the agriculture are the gift of these fertility gods. Therefore, they worshiped and pleased the fertility gods by making intercourse before their idols (Jer 2: 20); and this led to the origin of temple prostitution. Over against this defiled rite or ritual prostitution, Yahweh made first command that I am your God (Ex 20:2). Thus, Yahweh entered into a covenantal relationship with the people of Israel.[81] Through this betrothal Yahweh made her His own, for He redeemed her from the slavery of the Pharaoh.[82] Through this covenantal agreement Yahweh taught, and reminded of the old covenantal agreement (covenant with Noah and Abraham), and entered into a renewed contract with the people of Israel, His bride, out of His unending love.

Mar Jacob's predecessor, Mar Ephrem, the great theologian and poet reminded the same covenantal agreement of Sinai through his *memro*:

---

[79] Plastaras, *Creation and Covenant*, 178.

[80] Schillebeeckx, *Marriage: Human Reality Saving Mystery*, 13; Herbert, "The Fertility Cult in Hosea," 73; Nissinen, Martti, and Uro, Risto, "Sacred Marriages, or the Divine-Human Sexual Metaphor: Introducing the Project," 1. Main aim of the sacred marriage was understood as: "Fertility, coronation ceremony, legitimization of kingship, involving deification of the king, obtaining blessings for the king, producing an heir for the throne, installation of *en* or *nin-dingir* priestesses, carrying out the religious duties of the en-priest of Inanna, composing secular love songs, (rite of passage songs), and finally, composing royal poetry. However, Lapinkivi suggests that main object of the sacred marriage was fertility. The sacred marriage was existed at least the time of Hamurapi of the first Babylonian dynasty (ca. 1792- 1759 BCE.). Lapinkivi, "The Sumerian Sacred Marriage and its Aftermath," 9-11.

[81] Bedjan, *HS* III, 285.17-18; ET. Brock, "On the Veil of Moses," in *Studies in Syriac Spirituality*, 75.44.

[82] Amar, "A Metrical Homily on Holy Mar Ephrem," 36:52-39:58. Here, Mar Jacob calls the people of Israel as the bride redeemed through the water.

Nissan the victorious month, which was sent by victorious One
was resplendent and victorious in Egypt,
delivering and escorting out the Royal bride.
It sprinkled the ground before her with its abundance,
filling it with flowers scattered everywhere;
lighting served as torches that gave illumination.
While thunder roared its acclaim;
the mountain slipped before her.
Blessed is the exalted One who escorted the despised girl.
A chaste wedding feast took place in the wilderness,
with bridal chamber set on Mount Sinai.
The Holy One descended and took in betrothal
the daughter of Abraham His beloved friend.[83]

Mar Ephrem very beautifully interpreted the Biblical covenant of the olden times in a novel way. The month of Nisan is very important to the Jewish and Aramaic Christians, because the month of Nisan witnessed several important events in the history of Israel and the Church.[84] Here he is praising the month

---

[83] *Resur* 83; cf. Brock, *The Luminous Eye*, 93-94.

[84] "Nisan, the post-Exilic name of the first month of the Jewish year. Its pentateuchal name is *hodesh ha-aviv* (lit. "month of spring," Ex. 13:4 and parallels) and it is also referred to as the month of the ripening ears of barley. The post-Exilic name, occurring in the biblical and apocryphal records (Esth 3:7; Neh 2:1; 1Esd 5:6) and frequently in Josephus and rabbinic literature (e.g., Megillar Taanit), is linked with the Babylonian first month, *Nisannu* (derived from *nasa* "to start"). The Mishnah calls the first of Nisan the "new year for kings and festivals" (RH 1:1). Reigns of monarchs in biblical times were reckoned from that time, but later it was made the seventh month of the civil year (RH loc.cit.). The zodiacal sign of this month is *Aries*. In the present fixed Jewish calendar it invariably consists of 30 days, and the 1st of Nisan never falls on a Monday, Wednesday, or Friday (See Calendar). In the 20th century Nisan, in its earliest occurrence, extended from March 13 to April 11, and in its latest from April 11 to May 10. According R. Joshua, this is the month during which the world was created and the Patriarchs were born (R.H. 11a). It was in Nisan that God spoke to Moses from the burning bush. In this month redemption will occur in the time to come (*ibid.*).The tabernacle was erected in Nisan (Ex 40:17), and the princes brought their offerings then (Num 7:1-2). Because the 12 princes offered their gifts to the tabernacle every day beginning with the first of Nisan, each day was considered a festival day. All public mourning is prohibited in Nisan. "*Tahanun* and *Zidduk Ha-Din* are not recited, nor are eulogies allowed (Sh. Ar., OH 429:2). As "the greater part of the month was thus sanctified, the entire month is deemed holy" (*ibid.,* comm.. of *Magen Avraham,* 3).

Memorable days of Nisan include the Passover period: the 14th of Nisan, the eve of the biblical feast of Passover when all leaven is cleared from Jewish households, and in Temple time, the Paschal lamb was sacrificed (Ex 12); and the festivals of Passover from the 15th and 21st of Nisan (in the Diaspora 22nd) of Nisan. The 15th and 21st of Nisan (in the Diaspora 15th-16th and 21st-22nd), the first and last days of Passover, respectively, are full of holydays. 16th – 20th of Nisan (in the DIaspora 17th -20th) are the intervening days of the festival, "*hol ha-moed.* The 16th of Nisan is the controversial "morrow of Sabbath" (see Lev 23:11,15,16) when an *omer* of barley was offered in the Temple and marked the commencement of the counting of the *omer.* Other

of Nisan in which the victorious Moses liberated Israel, the despised girl, from the bondage of Egypt. The month of Nisan is the month of spring, when the seeds that lay buried in the earth sprouts and flowers blossom especially the Lilly.[85] Thunders and lightning is the characteristic feature of the month of Nisan. Thunders and lightening were also the signs of marriage feast.[86] In this month God spoke to Moses in the burning-bush. And it was in this month that God liberated his beloved from the slavery of the Pharaoh. In the same month Yahweh entered into a covenant with Israel on the Mount of Sinai, which is a betrothal. And it was in this month that Jesus gave his life as ransom for the liberation of the Church from the slavery of sin and death. Mar Jacob finds the liberation of Israel from the bondage of Pharaoh and other incidents followed by it as a prefiguration of the redemption through Christ, the Bridegroom, on Golgotha and he called it as betrothal.[87]

The Sinai covenant is important in two aspects: firstly, it shows a liberation aspect and secondly, it shows a commitment. The liberation from Egypt has both social and spiritual aspects. In the social aspect it is a liberation or freedom from the persecution and torture of foreigners. The Israelites, as slaves of Egyptians had no freedom to execute their own will or had not enjoyed any social justice. They were under tyranny and oppression. They were marginalized socially, economically, politically, and they did not even have the right to progeny, because, the Pharaoh ordered to kill all the male children of Israelites (Ex 1:16). The God of their fathers saw their grievances and send His prophet to liberate them from their physical slavery and He liberated them from the slavery of the Pharaoh. He comfort the people from their distress which was an integral part of Jesus' public ministry. He liberated the lepers from the marginalization of the society; He liberated the demon possessed people from the slavery of demons, etc. Theologically the betrothal is liberation, liberation from the sickness of the souls and the sickness of the society at large and applicable to any society past, present, and future. It is not an exception in contemporary India. Caste system in India is an example. Some are of the higher caste, some are lower and still some are untouchables by birth and it is a prevailing truth in the Indian society. Likewise the whole world is sick in one way or other or in a combination of all evils. Monopoly of wealth

---

traditional dates in this months are 1st-7th of Nisan, the defeat by the Pharisees of the Sadducees' claim that the *tamid* (Ex 29:38-42), Num 28:1-8) was to be defrayed by private donations (Meg. Taan.1), 8th -21st of Nisan, a Pharisaic victory over the Sadducees in a dispute concerning "the morrow of the Sabbath" and the day of the month on which Shavuot falls (Meg. Taan.1); 1st (or 8th), 10th, and 26th of Nisan, the respective anniversaries of the death of Nadab and Abihu, of Miriam, and of Joshua, once observed as fasts (Meg. Taan.13). Wiesenberg, "Nisan," 275.

85 Walters, *Hymns on the Unleavened Bread,* 47.

86 Bedjan, *HS* II. 358.20-359.8; Bedjan *HS* I, 188.17-18; ET. *FH* VI, 182.437-438.

87 Rilliet, *SHF* IV, 596.10-19; ET, *FH* XI, 269.24.

by a few is another evil. Exploitation of human power is rampant. Unethical exploitation of nature and indiscriminate misuse and conscious destruction of ecological balance are the major evils, which our society is encountering. The liberation which Jesus extended to humankind is comprehensive and inclusive of those mentioned above. Therefore, one of the important missions of the Church in this modern world is to liberate such people or nation from contemporary forms of slavery.

In the spiritual realms, the Israelites were in a foreign land and worshipping their true God was a real trial for them. Also, since they were a minority living among the majority Egyptian gentiles, naturally, the poor minority were compelled to incline to the gods of the dominant Egyptians by authority and coercion. The liberation of the Israelites from Egypt by Moses was also liberation from spiritual slavery. This enabled them to worship the God of their fathers. In this modern world though most of the people are physically free many of them are spiritually slaves. Spiritual exploitation is a major problem in this world. The ignorance of the common people and the various other problems they encounter in life are exploited today. Spiritual empowerment is necessary in this world. It is imperative of the Church to take cognizance to imparting the right knowledge to the faithful to liberate from spiritual exploitation and anarchy.

Secondly, the covenant of Sinai implies a commitment with each other in the society. God came down and gave a set of commandments. It is a covenant, in which first party says, "I am Your God," and the second party was withheld from making or worshipping other gods. Then said you keep my commandments you will be my people and I will be your God (Ex 20:2-4). A mutual agreement of love and care can be seen here. Also by signing this covenant they entered into a commitment. This kind of commitment has disappeared from the current society. Selfishness and exploitation are the face of the society. Family relations, individual relations, inter-religious relations and international relations have deteriorated. The Sinai betrothal is a model for committed relationship.

3.5.3. Betrothal at Jordan

The betrothal event at Jordan envisions the liberation of the bride from the slavery of sins and makes her as the pure bride of Christ. This is the second staging post in the journey of the Bridegroom. In this stage Christ betrothed the Church through his immersion in the River Jordan and made her blameless and spotless (Eph 5:26-28). The following is an introduction to Mar Jacob's background to build up his theology on the betrothal at Jordan.

In the Syriac understanding, the serpent, which deceived Eve, inhabited under the water and through His descent into water Christ defeated it. The

Semitic Leviathan[88] (Job 41:1; Ps 74:14; 104:26; Isa 27:1) was characterized as a giant, crooked, and devourer serpent. Many of the liturgical prayers of the West Syriac Church refer to this serpent and say it is the killer of the human race and Jesus by his descent killed this serpent. A prayer of the West Syriac Church says: "O Lord, may the head of the dragon which kills the children of men be crushed under the sign of your cross."[89] Thus Jesus' descent was a victory over the death. A hymn of an anonymous author about the betrothal at Jordan says:

> He made me His bride from the Jordan's water;
> He gave me freedom from the water,
> He showed me His Father's riches,
> and look, His kingdom awaits me.
> In the womb of the Virgin He betrothed me
> and He received me in pure union of marriage;
> He mingled me with His exalted nature
> and made me an heir of Life.
> From the womb of Jesus is mine,
> and I am His from the water.
> A pure virgin has given Him to me,
> and baptism has given me to Him.[90]

This hymn speaks that Christ purified and redeemed the bride through immersion in the river Jordan. Moreover, through the immersion she mingled with the exalted nature of Christ and united to Him and achieved salvation. The salvation is attained but not perfected. The real salvation will be obtained in the eschatological Kingdom of God only. The above hymn states about four elements that happen through baptism: purification, redemption, participation in the nature of Christ, and the union with Christ. *Gospel of Philip* states it is redemption and resurrection from death, but the real redemption takes place only at the bridal chamber.[91] According to it Jesus retained the bride from death: "By perfecting the water of baptism, Jesus emptied it of death. Thus we go down into the water, but we do not go down into death, in order that we may not be poured out into the spirit of the world. When that spirit blows, it brings the winter. When the Holy Spirit breathes, the summer comes."[92] St. John Chrysostom says:

---

[88] Bedjan, *HS* III, 294.7; ET. Brock, "On the Veil of Moses," in *Studies in Syriac Spirituality*, 81.223.

[89] *Koodashakramangal,* 37; cf. *Anduthaksa*, 217.

[90] Epiphany Hymn: Anonymous Author, ET. Brock, *The Treasure House of Mysteries*. 256-257.

[91] Isenberg, *Gospel of Philip* 69.25-30, 142.

[92] Isenberg, *Gospel of Philip* 77.5-15, 146.

> Thou art called to a marriage, beloved: enter not in clad in sordid raiment, but take a robe suitable to the marriage. For if when men are called to a material marriage, though they be poorer than all other, they often possess themselves of or by clean raiment, and so go to meet those who called them. Do Thou too who hast been called to a spiritual marriage, and to a royal banquet...[93]

Rush, a modern thinker says: "Bridal mysticism ... is of the sacramental order, originating in the initiation of baptism. It is baptism that makes everyone the spouse of Christ that brings about the sacred marriage between the Christian and Christ."[94] Daniélou Jean states: Baptism is seen in its fullness as a nuptial mystery. The soul until now which is a simple creature becomes the Bride of Christ. When she comes out of the baptismal water in which he has purified her by His blood, He welcomes her in her white bridal robe and receives the promise which binds her to him forever.[95] The following part is a discussion on Mar Jacob's understanding of the betrothal at the River of Jordan.

3.5.3.1. Sanctification of Cosmic Waters through the Baptism of the Bridegroom

Sanctification of the waters of Jordan through the immersion of Jesus is a prominent subject since first century.[96] The Bridegroom is special in character; He loved His future bride and He Himself initiated the betrothal and made her pure, who was lying in filth. In order to purify her He cleansed the waters of Jordan first, because the sin of Adam not only corrupted Adam but the entire universe. Through His descent into the waters of Jordan Jesus purified all waters of the earth.[97] On the first day of creation the spirit of God blew upon the water and made an order in creation (Gen 1:2).[98] When Adam sinned the Holy Spirit departed not only from Adam but departed from the whole creation. The sin had weakened, enfeebled, and deprived the grace of the Spirit, and deteriorated earthly matters.[99] When the serpent defeated Eve, Satan spit its venom onto earth and thus earth was poisoned. For this reason the water and

---

[93] Chrysostom, "Instructions to Catechumens," 167.

[94] Rush, "Death as a Spiritual Marriage," 83.

[95] Daniélou, *Bible and the Liturgy,* 200.

[96] Ignatius of Antioch says: "Our Lord Jesus Christ was, according to God's dispensation, the fruit of Mary's womb, of the seed of David; He was born and baptized in order that He might make the water holy by His passion" (Ignatius, *Epistle to Ephesians,* 18).

[97] Bedjan, *HS* I, 180.10-11; ET. *FH* VI, 175.265-266.

[98] In Syriac has two meanings: spirit and wind. Mar Jacob says that the spirit of God is not the Holy Spirit but it was regular wind; he calls it created wind. Bedjan, HS III, 23.10; ET. Young, "Six Days on Creation, Fist Day," in Message of the Fathers of the Church, 54.338. According to Sebastian P. Brock, for many Syriac father the spirit referred in Genesis 1:2 is not Holy Spirit but the wind only. Brock, Bible in Syriac Tradition, 92.

[99] McDonnell, "Jesus' Baptism in the Jordan," 217.

earth was contaminated and unfit for habitation. In the *Homily on the Leaven* Mar Jacob mentions about the defiled water and says that:

> But the world's waters were at that time not fit for dough.
> The serpent had vomited into the source of the spring, pouring death therein,[100]
> she took the meal and placed it in the font of baptism,
> and, taking oil and water, She kneaded it bountifully.[101]

In this homily Mar Jacob compared Jesus to a piece of leaven which ferments the whole bread that is the Church. The water was not good for fermentation of the dough. When Jesus entered into the font of baptism the water became rich by the descent of Jesus. Thus, Syriac theology, especially Mar Jacob, teaches that the descent of Jesus into the waters of Jordan caused the purification of the whole waters of earth.[102]

The creation account describes the purification of water. However, the Holy Spirit is the agent of purification,[103] on the other hand, in the baptism, Jesus is the agent of purification. Mar Jacob very emphatically says that Jesus does not need any sanctification from the Holy Spirit because He does not lack anything,[104] because He is equal to the Father and the Holy Spirit in His divinity. Ignatius of Antioch has mentioned this earlier, "He was born and has been baptized in order to purify the water by his passion."[105] Jacob of Serugh emphasizes this: "The entire nature of the waters perceived that you had visited

---

[100] Bedjan, *HS,* III, 416.9-10; ET. "The Parable on the Leaven," *TV* 3(1989), 49.96-97.

[101] Bedjan, *HS,* III, 416.14-15; ET. "The Parable on the Leaven," *TV* 3(1989), 50.101-102.

[102] *The Teaching of St Gregory,* an early Armenian catechism, compares the baptism of Jesus at the Jordan with context of creation account (Gen 1:2). In the beginning the Spirit transformed chaos into cosmos, "moving over the waters, and thence set out the order of the creatures," including the ornamenting of the heavens where the angels dwell (Thompson, *The Teaching of Gregory,* 413). According this teaching the Spirit has a larger role in creation. "He came down to the waters and sanctified the lower waters of the earth" (Thompson, *The Teaching of Gregory,* 413). It says, the same happened in the baptism event of Jesus Christ. When Christ stepped down into the water of Jordan and "by treading the waters with His own footsteps, He sanctified them and made them purifying (waters)" (Thompson, *The Teaching of Gregory,* 414; compare, Bedjan, *HS* I, 183.9-184.15; ET. *FH* VI, 178.327-179.354), and restored the lower and the upper waters (McDonnell, "Jesus' Baptism in the Jordan," 217). Following this tradition feast of baptism of Christ has an important place in the Syriac Church. During the liturgy the priest bless the water in connection with the purification of the waters of Jordan by the descent of Jesus in the River Jordan. Kilian McDonnell, by quoting various texts says, "In Syria (and Armenia), where the baptism of Jesus would play a role unequaled in either the Latin or Greek traditions, the feast is not known until the second half of the third century. By the time of Ephrem (ca. 306-373) it was the greatest feast in Syria. In the West there is no trace of the feast until the fourth century." (McDonnell, "Jesus' Baptism in the Jordan," 211).

[103] Cited in Brock, "Some Important Baptismal Themes," 192.

[104] Bedjan, *HS* I, 184.15. ET, *FH* VI, 179.354.

[105] Ignatius, *Letter to Ephesians,* 83.

them- seas, deeps, rivers, springs and pools all thronged together to receive the blessing from your footsteps."[106] It is explicit that by stepping down into Jordan Jesus consecrated entire waters of the earth. He interprets Jesus as the Coal of Fire (Isa 6:6) which is pure in its nature and purifies all that touches it.[107] Another passage says that, such a Coal of Fire descended into the waters of Jordan and the water was inflamed with the divine heat of the Holy One and got warmed up. He set the water of Jordan at the pinnacle of all the waters of the universe and thus it purified all waters of earth far and near, and in the summit, middle, and in the abyss. Since he places it as the top of all waters, symbolically he places Jordan as the mother of all waters. He says:

> The heavenly beings marveled at that ablution of the Flame
> when its glorious body was rinsed to sanctify the waters.
> The rushing streams of water were mingled with rays of light
> and the river had been set on fire with the brightness that dwelt in it…
> The whole air grew warm and became inflamed in a holy manner
> because the Son of the Holy One descended for baptism though He was not lacking.[108]
> You stepped upon Jordan as upon the summit of all seas;
> and the extremities of the abysses and of the floods trembled at your power.
> The whole nature of the waters was stirred by your descent,
> because by your baptism you made everyone worthy of pardon.
> The waters of seas, although distant, are not distant
> because the power of your holiness has stirred mystically and visited them.[109]

3.5.3.2. Sanctification of the Bride through the Baptism of the Bridegroom

Sanctification of the bride through the baptism is presented in two ways: by the baptism of John the Baptist and through the baptism of Jesus Christ. By the baptism of John, the bride was cleansed from filthiness of her body, which had accumulated through idolatry and its rituals. Again, John cleansed her mind with his teaching about the Bridegroom, therefore, she abstained all evil thoughts from her mind. Still she was imperfect because the bride did not receive the robe of glory that was lost at Eden. Therefore, the Church, the bride of the Heavenly Bridegroom, waited for His descent into the water, so that she would be sanctified through the womb of the waters. "John also eagerly waited for Him to come, so that through Him his (John's) baptism would be

[106] Brock, "Baptismal Themes in the Writings of Jacob of Serugh," 327.

[107] Bedjan, *HS* I, 184.2; ET. *FH* VI, 178.341.

[108] Bedjan, *HS* I, 184.6-15; ET. *FH* VI, 179.345-354.

[109] Bedjan, *HS* I, 188.5-10; *FH* VI, 182.425-430.

made perfect as it was imperfect."[110] He came and made the imperfect water into a perfect one; therefore, everyone who is baptized in it would be cleansed without any doubt. Mar Jacob describes the process of cleansing the water through the descent of Jesus in it; he says:

> The Royal Son came out from among the crowds to come to the river
> and when He was far off, the baptismal water became fervent in response to Him,
> and the river overflowed and silently proclaimed Him.
> The Holy Spirit came out by itself and stood above the water
> and the heat of His power kindled them ...
> It was not that it became fervently heated at His arrival so as to render Him holy, for He is holy.
> It embraced Him so that its womb might be sanctified by Him.
> It exulted in Him because He was its accomplishment and consummation
> and it stretched out its arm so that the holiness of the Son might be received into it.[111]

Thus, according to Mar Jacob, the betrothal of the Bridegroom is very significant in the process of salvation. Through His baptism Jesus cleansed and purified the unclean waters for the purification of all. To Mar Jacob baptism is a rebirth by healing the sick. He writes:

> The Son of God descended and stirred the baptismal water,
> so that it might give birth to all kinds of beautiful creatures everyday.
> A new creation has begun, having come from our Lord.[112]

3.5.3.3. Reasons for Jesus' Baptism at Jordan

First of all Jesus' baptism is the fulfillment of the prophecy. Jesus had no necessity of baptism but He received it to fulfill the prophecy. He waited until the fulfillment of prophecy of Moses and received the baptism from John.[113] The betrothal at Jordan reminds the preplan of the Father before the creation of human being. Mar Jacob in his homilies *On the Baptism of Our Redeemer* and *A Prose Homily on Epiphany* brought out the prophecies concerning the arrival of the Messiah. Mar Narsai has the same opinion when he was writing the *Homily on the Epiphany of Our Lord.* "Let it be so now," the King replied to the herald. "it is thus fitting that justice be fulfilled in me."[114]

---

[110] Bedjan, *HS* I, 171.21; ET. *FH* VI, 167.89-90.

[111] Bedjan, *HS* I, 174.5-17; *FH* VI,169-170.135-145.

[112] Bedjan, *HS* IV, 702.17-19; cited in Brock, "The Epiklesis in the Antiochene Baptismal Ordines," 210.

[113] Rilliet, *SHF* II. 558.8; ET. *FH* VII, 195.18.

[114] Graffin, *Narsai's Metrical Homilies*, II, 84.241-85.242.

Secondly, He wanted to be one among them, needy and poor, like His bride otherwise He could not save her: Mar Jacob states, "It was right for the rich Bridegroom that He took upon himself to bathe in the waters that were mixed for the poor bride. It was important for the true friend of the Bridegroom as well, showing before the guests that he was needy and deficient, because he made petition that his need might be filled by the perfect riches of the Bridegroom who has sent him."[115] Mar Jacob, in his homilies dramatically, points out that Jesus prevented John the Baptist from disclosing His divinity. In the gospel texts several times Jesus prevented his disciple from disclosing His identity (Mt 8:4; 16:20; 17:9; Mk 7:36; 8:30; 9:9; Lk 5:14; LK 8:56; 9:21). Mar Narsai also has the same opinion.[116]

Thirdly, the Bridegroom wanted to purify the bride from filth by cleansing the waters of the earth.[117] In order to purify her he descended into the waters of Jordan and through his descend he purified the waters of whole earth from the poison of the serpent which vomited in the water of Eden.[118] In the Syriac theology there is a beautiful interpretation regarding the baptism of Jesus Christ. Through the descent into the waters of Jordan the Son of God did a heroic act to crush the head of the serpent (Gen 3:15) who poisoned the waters of the earth through the sin of man at Eden.[119] Until this time nobody was able to defeat Satan but it was only the Son of God who could do that. In this tradition Jesus Christ saved the Church through his descent into the waters of Jordan. Meanwhile, according to Mar Jacob, this story was foretold in the prophecy through the episode of Jacob's removal of the stone from the mouth of the well and provided water to the flock of Rachel. He said, the river was not filled with water, but mysteries, the mysteries of the Church.[120] Finally,

---

[115] Rilliet, *SHF* II. 558.14-17; FH VII, 195.19.

[116] Let it be so, Do not reveal my majesty and my honor in the sight of on-lookers.
Until I perform and fulfill everything that is written.
Let it be so! I am being baptized as one deficient and in need of mercy,
so that I may fill up in my person lacking to the human race.
From the race that has succumbed to sin I am also.
Let it be so I am paying for the bond that Adam wrote in Eden.
From the clay that passions have overwhelmed is my structure.
I am from the lineage that death has swallowed and defrauded of its life.
Let it be so I am descending in mystery into the eater and raising it up (*Narsai's Metrical Homilies*, II, 84.241-87.252).

[117] Supra, 3.5.3.1.

[118] Bedjan, *HS,* I, 174.5-175.10; ET, *FH* VI, 169.135-170.160.

[119] Bedjan, *HS* III, 416.11; ET. "The Parable on the Leaven," *TV* 3(1989), 49.97.

[120] Bedjan, *HS* III, 210.15-16; ET. "On Our Lord and Jacob," *TV* 4.4(1993), 53.51-52.

through the descent the Bridegroom placed the robe of glory into the waters of Jordan so that whoever enters into it could clothe it.[121]

3.5.3.4. Jacob's Meeting with Rachel: A Prefiguration of Christ's Betrothal at Jordan

Mar Jacob sees a 'type' of Jesus, who betrothed the Church through his baptism, in Jacob, the patriarch, who betrothed Rachel at the well. When Jacob on his way to his uncle Laban to seek a wife saw two maidens near a well and he helped them by lifting the cover stone from the mouth of the well not knowing they were daughters of his uncle and fell in love with the younger Rachel (Gen 29:1-12). Mar Jacob says this is a 'type' of Jesus' betrothal at the River Jordan.

> As flocks of sheep and shepherds stood round about it,
> he found a great stone there laid upon its mouth,
> and thirsty sheep gazing at the stone, that it might be lifted away.[122]

The homily narrates that, before the arrival of Jacob many shepherds tried to remove the heavy stone from the mouth of the well, but they were incompetent to remove it. When Jacob arrived Rachel was waiting for somebody to remove the stone from the mouth of the well so that she could take water for the flock. Inspired by the Holy Spirit, though it cannot be done by a single person, Jacob removed it and gave water to the flock of Rachel.[123] Mar Jacob alludes this incident to the process of salvation through Jesus Christ, the Bridegroom. Just as Rachel was looking for someone to quench the thirst of her flock, when Jesus arrived for baptism the Church was eagerly waiting for someone to quench her thirst for salvation. Like Jacob who arrived and removed the stone from the mouth of the well; finally, the Son of God, the real Bridegroom came out and washed the sins of the bride and purified her. Jacob betrothed Rachel at the well and Christ betrothed the Church at Jordan.

Mar Jacob compares the well (*beere*) with the river (*nahro*) Jordan, Jacob with Jesus, Rachel with the Church, and the removal of the cover stone with that of the cleansing of sin of the Church. Since the comparison of Jacob to Jesus and Rachel to the Church is set apart for discussion later the similarities of the well and Jordan and sin is discussed here. Both of them contain water and it has a significant role in Christian theology. Water is the source of life

---

[121] See more infra, 6.3.2.

[122] Bedjan, *HS* III, 210.17-19; ET. "On Our Lord and Jacob," *TV* 4.4(1993), 53.53-54.

[123] Bedjan, *HS* III, 210.18-211:7; ET. "On Our Lord and Jacob," *TV* 4.4(1993), 53.55-54.64. There is no such indication in the bible. The bible tells that Jacob saw a well and shepherds whom water the sheep and asked them about Laban and they showed Rachel, Laban's daughter. And when he heard it was his cousin he removed the stone from the top of the well and helped to water the sheep of Rachel. All other narrations are he may be received it from extra-biblical traditions.

and salvation. The primordial water had no quality in itself, but, when the spirit of God) *rooḥo daloho*) hovered (*mraḥpo*) on it, drove away the darkness from it (Gen 1:2).[124] Then God commanded let there be light (Gen 1:3) and light came in.[125] Then, from water the first living creatures came out (Gen 1: 20).[126] The beauty of Mar Jacob's interpretation can be seen here. Thus, when compare the sanctification of the primordial water with that of Jordan; the Genesis account says that day dawned over the dark water and it became life-giving water. Mar Jacob often interprets Christ as the Flash Light,[127] the Sun,[128] the Sun of Righteousness,[129] etc. Therefore, it can be interpreted that the same Son of God, the second Person in the Holy Trinity, was the day dawned upon the primordial water (Gen 1:3) and the One who manifested in the waters of Jordan. It would be substantiated with Mar Jacob's own words. He divides the duty of the Trinity in creation process and says: "The Father signals, the Son creates, and the Spirit perfects."[130] Thus when the Son, Light, dawned on the water the darkness disappeared from it.[131] Darkness represents sin and evil; so that, in the creation and in the baptism darkness or sin was the stumbling block before the Son of God and therefore, in both occasions the Son purifies the water and made it into life-giving water.

During the baptism of the Bridegroom, Mar Jacob says that, "the Holy Spirit came out by itself and stood above the water and heat of His (Son) power kindled them (waters)...it was not that it became fervently heated at His arrival so as to render Him holy, for He is holy; It embraced Him so that

---

[124] Mar Jacob says that when God created the universe it was dark and void and the spirit of God blew on it and the darkness disappeared. He uses the term darkness of the water. Bedjan, *HS* III, 23.7; ET. Young, "Six Days on Creation, Fist Day," in *Message of the Fathers of the Church*, 54.435.

[125] Bedjan, *HS* III, 24.17-18; ET. Young, "Six Days on Creation, Fist Day," in *Message of the Fathers of the Church*, 56.465-466.

[126] Ephrem says:
At creation the Spirit hovered over the waters.
They conceived and gave birth to reptiles, fishes and birds;
The Holy Spirit hovered over the baptismal water
And it gave birth to symbolic eagles- the virgins and leaders,
And to symbolic fishes-the chaste and the intercessors,
And to symbolic reptiles
The cunning who have become as simple as doves *HEpi* 8.15.

[127] Bedjan, *SMS*, 778.7-8; ET. *FH* II, 98.71.

[128] Bedjan, *SMS*, 778.9-10; ET. *FH* II, 98.72-73.

[129] Bedjan, *SMS*, 814.18; ET. *FH* XVI, 336.123.

[130] Bedjan, *HS* III, 13.14; ET. Young, "Six Days on Creation, Fist Day," in *Message of the Fathers of the Church*, 34.243.

[131] Bedjan, *HS* III, 287.13; ET. Brock, "On the Veil of Moses," in *Studies in Syriac Spirituality*, 76.81.

its womb might be sanctified by Him."[132] Again water caused the destruction and salvation of the world (Gen 7:21, Ex 14:23, 27); water is the way of salvation (1Cor 1:1-4); without baptism through water nobody can enter into the kingdom of God (Jn 3:5). Finally, Jesus offered living water to the people who were in hunger and thirst (Jn 4:10). From the well Jacob made Rachel and her sheep drink water and on the other hand through the institution of baptism at Jordan, or by making the life-giving water, Jesus gave eternal life to the Church. In the former case they drank the water and in the latter they immersed in it. But the end results of both are salvation. If Rachel is saved from carnal thirst and rejoined to the salvation history by becoming a great grandmother of Jesus, the Church was saved from its former sins and became the bride of the heavenly Bridegroom.

The second relation pattern is rock (*keepo*) and sin (*ḥto*). Theologically, rock has an important role. From the rock the Israelites drank water in the wilderness (Ex 17:6). Later Paul compared the rock as Jesus Christ (1Cor 10:4).[133] St Ephrem and others gave further interpretation and compare with that of flowing of water and blood from Christ's side at Golgotha.[134] Then Christ was compared to the corner stone (Acts 4:11; Eph 2:20; 1Pet 2:6);[135] the stone hewn without hand (Dan 2:35).[136] Again Christ acclaimed the faith of Peter and referred him as *Kepha* (Mt. 16:18).[137] Paul used stone as stumbling blocks (1Cor 1:22-23)[138] a stumbling and a rock of offence (1Pt 2:8). The Book of Revelation 2:14 clearly says sins of adultery, fornication etc as stumbling blocks. In *Peshita* the word used for the stumbling block is (*kšl*) basically means an offence or block but it also means rock.[139] Paul sees the Law as a stumbling stone (Rom 9:32). Therefore, in the scripture, rock is found as parallel to sin. Here, Mar Jacob intent to compare the patriarch Jacob's removal of the stone from the mouth of the well with Jesus Christ's removal (cleansing) of the sins of the people who approached Him. Therefore, Mar Jacob says that just as patriarch Jacob rolled the stone from over the well, by the institution of

---

132 Bedjan, *HS* I, 174.9-16; ET. *FH* VI, 169.139-144.

133 Bedjan, *HS* III, 295.9; ET. Brock, "On the Veil of Moses," in *Studies in Syriac Spirituality*, 81.245; cf, *HPar.* V.I, 15; ET. Brock, *Hymn on Paradise*, 102.

134 Bedjan, *HS* V, 344.2-3; ET. "A Homily on Samson," *TV* 11(1992), 62.367-368; Bedjan, *HS* III, 295.7-10; ET. Brock, "On the Veil of Moses," in *Studies in Syriac Spirituality*, 81; cf. Ephrem, *Commentary on Pauline Epistles*, 68. Cited in Brock, *The Luminous Eye,* 81-82.

135 Bedjan, HS III, 295.14; ET. Brock, "On the Veil of Moses," in *Studies in Syriac Spirituality*, 81.249.

136 Bedjan, HS III, 295.11; ET. Brock, "On the Veil of Moses," in *Studies in Syriac Spirituality*, 81.247.

137 For more reference see. Murray, *Symbols of Church and Kingdom*, 205-239.

138 Bedjan, *HS* II, 751.18; ET. "On Paul the Apostle," *TV* 10(1991), 61.105.

139 Smith, *Syriac Dictionary*, 229.

baptism Jesus removed the sins of the Church. Patriarch Jacob's act culminated in the betrothal to Rachel, who is a 'type' of Church, likewise, Mar Jacob says that, the act of Jesus is a betrothal to Church:

> And, like the stone, He rolled away sin, which was a heavy thing,
> He opened the baptismal font for His betrothed, that she might bathe there,
> and He drew, and let the nations of the earth drink like those flocks
> He lifted the weight of sins by His mighty strength.[140]

In the eyes of an ordinary person there is no allusion to baptism in the meeting of Jacob and Rachel; but for men of discernment, in the meeting of the two pairs (Jacob and Rachel; Christ and the Church), can see that one person of each pair (Jacob and Christ) liberates the other one. Here the deftness of the Syriac Fathers should be appreciated. They make use of the every meager speck to buildup ideas and interpret them in greater dimensions. The Syriac Fathers read the Bible and meditated on it to know the Son of God and fathom his works. They accepted everything in the Bible in relation to Him. In the homily *On Our Lord and Jacob*, Mar Jacob found that the well is not full of water but mysteries; mysteries hidden about the Son of God.

Origen in his *Homily on Genesis* compares Rebecca's and Abraham's servant's meeting (Gen 24:18) and Jesus' and Samaritan woman's (Jn 4:28) meeting[141] as well as Jacob's and Rachel's (Gen 29:1-20) meeting and Moses' and Zipporah's (Ex 2:15-22) meeting. Then he said, "There, one comes to the wells and the waters so that brides may be found; and the Church is united to Christ in the bath of water."[142]

It is seen that several dissimilarities between the Sinai betrothal and the betrothal at Jordan. The Son of God betrothed the nations (Church) at the waters of Jordan and liberated her from the bondage of Satan. At the betrothal on Mount Sinai Yahweh appeared to Moses on Mount Sinai and thereby to the Nation, people of Israel, became the bride of Yahweh. Here in the River Jordan God descended and made Himself visible to John and to the Church. On that summit of Sinai Yahweh came down in a hidden manner and reminded and warned the people and gave a written document to remember forever that "I am the Lord (husband) thy God... Thou shalt have no other gods (man) before me." Here on the plains of Jordan the Son of God came and preached the Kingdom of God and repentance through His friend, John the Baptist. If the pinnacle of Sinai witnessed the father of the Bridegroom, here at the valley of Jordan the Church confronts the real Bridegroom. If at the Mountain the Father showed only His back to His friend, Moses, here in the wilderness the

---

[140] Bedjan, *HS* III, 213.6-9; ET. "On Our Lord and Jacob," *TV* 4.4(1993), 55.106-109.

[141] Origen, *Commentary on the Gospel According to John: Book 13-32,* 105-106.

[142] Origen, *Com. Gen.* 10.5.

Trinity manifested to John, the friend of the Bridegroom. If in the Mountain, God had revealed His great glory; here in the valley of wilderness, the Lord of the heights bowed his head before the servant like an obedient servant.

In the betrothal at Jordan the mode of agreement is different from the earlier betrothal. In the Old Testament betrothal with Abraham God established circumcision as a mark of covenantal contract between Yahweh and His people. In Jordan the Bridegroom established a new sign of covenantal agreement: the baptism of the water. Later he affirms the validity and necessity of regeneration from the water to enter into the Kingdom of God [bridal chamber (Jn 3:5)].

Universal salvation is another main significance of the betrothal between Christ and the Church. Salvation, in betrothals prior to this one is solely for the people of Israel, but here this betrothal is for the whole universe. The representatives from all nations witnessed the baptism of the Bridegroom.[143] The betrothal represents salvation from sin, universal salvation is the main thrust of betrothal at Jordan.

Through this brave act of baptism, the Bridegroom snatched the bond of Adam and liberated the bride and retrieved the robe of glory which was lost in the Garden of Eden.[144] The bond of Adam was recompensed by the heavenly Bridegroom, emptying Himself and took the form of the dust, liberated the bride and retained her for Himself. He portrayed this act very magnificently in various homilies.

3.5.4. Betrothal at Golgotha

> Would that I were an eagle, my Son,
> that I might fly to the four quarters of the earth
> to invite and bring in all the nations
> to the great wedding feast of your death.
> Who is it who has been moved by envy against you, my sweet one?[145]

This is a profound example of the faith upheld in the Church on the death of Christ for her salvation. It proclaims the evangelical enthusiasm of the Fathers of the Church to proclaim the awe-inspiring love of Christ towards the Church, His bride. It is the faith of the Church that the Son of God died for her sins and betrothed her and made her His own.[146] In his homily on the *Ten*

---

[143] Bedjan, *HS* I, 167.1-168.9; ET. *FH* VI, 162.1-163.16.

[144] Bedjan, *HS* I, 168.10-17; ET. *FH* VI, 163.17-24.

[145] Brock, *Bride of Light,* 40.3-6, 137. cf. Mathews, "Jacob of Serugh, Homily on Good Friday," 147.

[146] Philoxenus of Mabbug says: "There came forth blood and water": baptismal water together with the blood that brings absolution; by the 'water' the font was indicated, by 'blood' the Holy Mysteries which cleanse us from sin every time we receive them (De Halleux, *Philiene de Mabbog, Lettre aux monies de Senoun,* 6).

Virgins Mar Jacob says: "All creation was betrothed to God in the blood of His Son."[147] The humanity as well as all creations are betrothed to the Bridegroom, Christ. The crucifixion of the Bridegroom brings forth a universal salvation. He says: He likened all creation to the ten virgins, for if it so His will, all creation can shine in the new age.[148]

Thus, forgiveness of sins and liberation from the bondage of Satan are the main thrusts of betrothal at Golgotha. In his epistle to Ephesians Paul reminds this aspect; "In him we have redemption through his blood, the forgiveness of our trespasses, according to his riches of his grace that he lavished on us" (Eph 1:7). In the following verse Paul tells that in the fullness of time He will bring the entire universe, both in heaven and earth, under a single head, in Christ (Eph 1:10). Since man is the head of woman (1Cor 11:3; Eph 5:23) and Christ is the husband of the Church (Eph 5:23) the mystery is revealed on the cross at Golgotha.

According to Mar Jacob Golgotha is another staging post of the betrothal of the heavenly Bridegroom, Christ, who sacrificed his life for his bride. He says it as unusual. The Bridegroom gave up his life to betroth the bride. Never again has this kind of betrothal been repeated in history. In the Indian context, a custom called *sati* was practiced where the wife (bride) jumped into the funeral pyre of her deceased husband to immolate herself.[149] This was observed as a sign of loyalty to the husband. Usually, through the death, a person will be physically removed from his or her spouse.[150] In the unusual betrothal at Golgotha the bride betrothed herself to a slain Bridegroom and through the death of the Bridegroom the bride joins him.

3.5.4.1. Love of God and Betrothal at Golgotha

Love of the Bridegroom for his betrothed is sublime. In the words of Mar Jacob this love can be found in the Bridegroom even before the creation of the universe.[151] Because of His love God created human beings in His Image, because of His love God descended to the world to create Adam, because of His love He again came down for the second time to save humankind, and because of the same love, He ascended to the cross.[152] In the *Homily on Samson*

[147] Bedjan, *HS* II, 386.11-12; ET. "Homily on Ten Virgins," *TV* 4.1(1992), 49.226. One of the prayers of the West Syriac Church states; "She became a betrothed through the slaughter of her Bridegroom; adorned with his crown of thorns, and saved by his wounds" (*Promiyon* I, 4).

[148] Bedjan, *HS* II, 286.19-20; ET. "Homily on Ten Virgins," *TV* 4.1(1992), 49.233-234.

[149] Lord William Bentick in 1829 banned SATI by enacting law.

[150] Bedjan, *HS* III, 290.19-20; ET, Brock, "On the Veil of Moses," in *Studies in Syriac Spirituality*, 78.149.

[151] Alwan, *QHC* I, 3.39-45.

[152] Alwan, *QHC* I, 3.33.

Mar Jacob says: "He continued His way and by His Cross He betrothed, and took a wife her for whose sake He came down to the home of the earthborn."[153] The Son of God, by His love for the Church, gave Himself up to shame and dishonor, He betrothed her by giving a wedding ring made out of the iron nails which were fastened on his hands; he served a wedding banquet with His own blood. By receiving the lance on His side removed the lance of the Cherub which had been protecting the Garden, Paradise, from the entrance of the transgressor into it. Through these gallant acts the Bridegroom, he purged the corrupted bride, betrothed her, and made her entrance possible into the wedding banquet that was denied to her because of her corruption. See how Mar Jacob pictured the event of betrothal at Golgotha:

> The bride went mad and crucified the Bridegroom thus angering the Father,...
> The King's Son made a wedding banquet of blood on Golgotha,
> and their he betrothed the daughter of Light so that she should be his;
> the royal ring was forged with the nail of his hands
> and the betrothal was given with his holy blood.
> He betrothed her there, because she had shown him love at the time of his dishonor;
> He moved her over and placed her at his right hand, so that she might be with him:...
> The guard heard the commotion of someone entering Paradise,
> so brought along the sword, for he was standing alert on watch;
> as the bride of Light was entering the Bridegroom was wounded
> those who struck him did not know who it was who it was struck.
> He received in his side the sword, and seized it from the guard,
> he let him go off, and opened up the door for all to enter.
> The Lord of the garden was struck with the sword as he opened it up,
> it was having been carefully guarded ever since Adam,
> instead of the robber (Adam) who left it, their entered a thief,
> while his master was wounded as he opened it up before him, to let him in.[154]

Thus the sacrifice of the Son of God is another betrothal or another staging post through which the Bridegroom saved his beloved from death and perdition. Through this betrothal, out of His love, the Bridegroom gave Himself as a ransom to His father and killed the death which had killed the man from the beginning. By receiving the lance on His side the Bridegroom removed the Cherub's lance from the gate of Paradise and thus made the entry of His bride possible.

---

[153] Bedjan, *HS* V, 336.18-19; ET. "Homily on Samson," *TV* 11(1992), 56.117-118.

[154] Bedjan, *HS* II, 587.8-588.16; cf. Brock, "The Wedding Feast of Blood on Golgotha," 587-588; cf. Brock, "Mysteries in the Hidden Side of Christ," 466-467.

Conclusion

Betrothal at Golgotha is the pinnacle of all other betrothal events. The other betrothals did not witness a direct confrontation with Satan, but the Bridegroom liberated and purified her by cleansing her mind. However, here in Golgotha, the Bridegroom had a direct fight with the enemy and defeated him. Here it is not a war with regular soldiers but a spiritual war in which the Bridegroom died for the bride and defeated the death that defeated her at Eden. He became a ransom to the Father. All these happened because of the love of God towards His creation. He does not like His creation to perish. So He sent His Only Begotten and He died for His bride. The love of God must become the source of meditation in the contemporary world. There is no replacement for His love. The Father's love was unconditional. We are facing lots of problems in our daily life. The society and individuals confront many problems in the present world. Knowing Christ and his sacrifice is the panacea to attain peace and harmony.

This chapter discussed the love of God towards His creation. To fulfill this love the Son of God descended to earth and saved the Church from sin and death. This sacrificial act of love is delineated in the Bible as betrothal and marriage. Jacob of Serugh and other Fathers of the Church took this imagery to teach their fellow Christians the love of God. No other imagery could substantiate this Divine love other than marriage.

The unusual feature of Biblical interpretation of Syriac Fathers is seen here. They gave more importance to the spiritual meaning of the text rather than the literal or historical. They had a synchronic view of the history of salvation. They prefer sacred time rather than linier time to interpret the Scripture. They found each event in Christ's life unique and accomplished. The Syriac Fathers were spiritually enlightened and they saw each and every person or incident in the Old Testament as in anticipation of Jesus.

Mar Jacob found three occasions in the life of Jesus as betrothal events. Sinai covenant, baptism at Jordan, and Sacrifice at Golgotha. Each one of them indicates the liberation events. Jesus liberated the betrothed from sin through these stages. Earlier the bride was taken from the nations (Israel) but later He chooses nations (whole word) as the Nation rejected and killed Him. The betrothal of Christ is revealing to every Christian who is a bride of Christ.

Chapter 4

Christ as the Bridegroom

Introduction

> Praise be to the heavenly Bridegroom Who by His love betrothed the soiled daughter of the gentiles and by his hyssop washed and cleansed and made her a pure bride and invited the prophets, evangelists, and martyrs to her wedding feast.[1]

The above passage, which describes the salvific act of Jesus Christ, is taken from one of the prayers of the West Syriac Church. This is the hallmark of the great tradition, which describes Christ as the Bridegroom of the Church. Through this imagery the Church taught her Children the sacrificial love of Jesus Christ who descended and saved her through His atoning sacrifice. The Church found several Old Testament and New Testament passages to support her arguments. Mar Jacob, the bishop of Batnan, also holds the same tradition and believes that Jesus Christ by His eternal mercy saved the Church. Moreover, the Incarnated Son of God is a model for humankind to make an intimate relationship with God just as a bride with her bridegroom. This chapter is an elaboration of Mar Jacob's contention on Christ as the Bridegroom of the Church.

4.1. Etymological Interpretation

Mar Jacob uses the word 'Bridegroom' (*ḥatno*) to depict Christ as the 'Bridegroom' of the Church. The Hebrew root for the term 'bridegroom' is '*ḥtn*'. In *hitpael* form it means to become intermarried. Noun *ḥōtēn* means become a male relative like father-in-law or brother-in-law. The term *ḥātān*

[1] *Promiyon* I, 1-2.

means son-in-law (daughter's husband). Ugaritic verb *ḫtn* means to marry. Noun cognates of Hebrew *ḥātān* include Ugaritic *ḫtn*, son-in-law.[2] Noun *ḥ^atunnâ* means wedding. The word *ḫatnûtu,* wedding, may be a Canaanite loanword.[3] In Hellenism, especially in the Gnostic understanding, the image of bridegroom and bride is used to denote the relationship of a *sōtēr*, savior, to humanity, and is taken into the concept of *hieros gamos*, sacred marriage.[4] Three words are used in the New Testament to denote the bridegroom/husband: *ḥatno* {(Mk 2:19,20; Mt 9:15 (two occurrences); Lk 5:31-32; and Mt 25:1-10; Jn 3:29; Rev 18:23)} are in relation with Christ and John 2:9 in relation with normal bridegroom; *gabro* (Mt 1:16, 19; Lk 16:19; Rom 7:2ff; 1Cor 7:2ff; 2Cor 11:2; Eph 5:22ff; Rev 21:2) which is mostly used in relation with husband and wife in common and in some instances indirectly mentions the divine-human relationship; and *b^aalo* (Mk 10:12; Lk 2:36; Jn 4:16ff; Acts 5:9; Col 3:18; 1Tim 3:2ff; Titus 1:6; 1Pet 3:1,5,7) which is explicitly denoting the regular husband-wife relationship.

4.2. Old Testament 'Types' of the Bridegroom

The third chapter dealt on how Mar Jacob visualized the events of the Old Testament and persons as 'types' of Jesus or related to Jesus; because his mind was filled with the images of Christ. In his homilies when he portrays Jesus Christ, he saw several 'types' of Jesus in the Old Testament. The first part of this chapter introduces some important Old Testament personalities whom Mar Jacob portrayed as the 'types' of the Bridegroom, Jesus Christ.

4.2.1. Isaac: A 'Type' of the Bridegroom

> I shall proclaim to Isaac, the child who escaped from the knife,
> I have carried that One, in a symbol of whom, your father bound you.[5]

The homily *On Abraham and his Types* portrays Isaac as a 'type' of Jesus Christ who was sacrificed on the top of the mountain of Golgotha.[6] He observes several symbols and typological events to compare Isaac with Jesus. Isaac was miraculously born to an old woman who is considered sterile; on the other hand, Jesus was miraculously born to a virgin. Isaac was innocent and Jesus was also without corruption. Isaac faced an ordeal; Jesus suffered and died in his body. In this homily Mar Jacob portrayed the ordeal of the Father

---

[2] O'Connell, "ḥtn," 325-326.

[3] Wakely, "*hatunnâ*," 328.

[4] Günther, "Bride," 584.

[5] Bedjan, *HS* V, 465.7-8; ET. *FH* V, 157.367-368.

[6] Bedjan, *HS* VI, 64.6-7; cf. "An Epiphany of Mystical Symbols," 65.

who loved His Only Son and He asked Abraham to sacrifice his only son if he loves Him:

> I have only one and I did not prevent Him from becoming a sacrifice;
> (you) fulfill (*šmlo,* (like Me and do as I did if you are My friend.
> Come, resemble Me and bind) *, pkoor*) your son if you love (me);
> that the whole resemblance may be fulfilled in you, in that you are pleased at.[7]

To unravel the meaning of these verses, the reader ought to know the mindset of Mar Jacob. He considers that all the figures of the Old Testament are related to Jesus Christ and they pre-figured Jesus Christ in a distant time. Here, Mar Jacob composes a dialogue between God the Father and Abraham, who was chosen by God as the father of the faithful; and the motivation of the election of Abraham was redemption of humankind. Even before the trial of Abraham (Gen 22:1-13) the slaughter of His Only Begotten was conceived in the mind of the Father. It was pre-figured in history through Abraham and Isaac. Therefore, He told Abraham that, "I have only one and I did not prevent him from becoming a sacrifice." And now, it is your turn to fulfill my will on the earth; therefore I know that you love me.

In Mar Jacob's opinion, God demanded Abraham to sacrifice his boy not to kill him[8] but to publish the mystery of the Messiah.[9] He wanted to reveal that Abraham must know that He sent mysteries with Isaac; and that He had not forsaken Abraham. Through this act Abraham might know that he was fulfilling a 'type' through his only begotten (*iḥeedoyo*) which is fitting to the Only Begotten of God the Father. And this may make Abraham happy when he saw the days of the crucifixion of Jesus Christ.[10] Mar Jacob says; "Mysteries flown abundantly in His mind and it was kindled in him. Until Isaac was spared from the knife (*sakeeno*) I (Mar Jacob) did not find it."[11] Through such events Moses reminded Israel that the Son of God will be sacrificed on the Mount of Golgotha. But nobody dared to investigate these 'types'. Even Abraham did not investigate more about the imagery of Isaac. He describes: the image (ܨܘܪܬܐ, *ṣoorto)* of Jesus expelled (*dohio*) Isaac against the killing and his father (Abraham) he saw it and marveled. He was silent and did not interfere, because these are the mysteries of God. Isaac carried the image (*neešo*) of our Lord

---

[7] Bedjan, *HS* IV, 68.1-4.

[8] The escape of Isaac from the knife is also a pre-figuration of the Son. Because, though the Son died on the Cross the death and Sheol cannot conquer Him. Therefore, the escape of Isaac from the knife is a pre-figuration of Jesus' victory over death.

[9] Bedjan, *HS* IV, 63.13-14.

[10] Bedjan, *HS* IV, 64.7-8.

[11] Bedjan, *HS* IV, 66.9-10.

and it continued to be obscure in his sufferings.[12] He again portrays various aspects of the image of the Son of God in Isaac and says: Look Abraham saw the mountain which he walked on; from thence the aged one was given the beckon of the image of the Son. While he was pounding the road of killing in its entire miles; only one inn (*had awono*) was there and that was the altar. The symbol invited him; come here, ascend and see these mountains, upon them made the salvation of the world. Come ascend and behold the life-giving slaughter which is placed on the altar; and the sacrifice of slaughter while not come through the knife...[13] See the following passage from *On Mysteries, Types and Figures of Christ* which describes the comparison between Christ and Isaac.

> For, as they say Golgotha was the mountain of Isaac,
> and at the place of crucifixion his father bound him.
> Where Zion fixed the wood to crucify the Son,
> there sprouted that tree which carried mysteries.
> In secret He indicated to him, that on Golgotha he will sacrifice Isaac,
> that the mystery may be served on the mountain of crucifixion.
> Three days Isaac was concerned for his father,
> to offer an image for the death of the Son, and then he is raised.
> On the third (day) he defeated death and was set free from it,
> this is the (image) of the Son, who rose from the tomb on the third (day).
> Isaac bore the wood for his sacrifice to that mountain,
> this is the Son who carried His cross when He was coming out.[14]

Mar Jacob found parallels of place and incidents in both cases and tried to establish the pre-figuration of Jesus' death with the travel of Isaac. He says, Mount Moriah[15] where Isaac was taken for sacrifice not only represents Golgotha on which Jesus was crucified, but exactly it is the same place where Abraham's sacrifice occurred and Christ was sacrificed.[16] Isaac carried the wood for his sacrifice and the Son of God also carried wood (cross) for his

---

[12] Bedjan, *HS* IV, 66.13-18.

[13] Bedjan, HS IV, 74.21-75:3.

[14] Bedjan, HS III, 311.17-312.12; ET. Konat "On the Mysteries, Types, and Figures of Christ," *Le Museon* 118(2005), 79.133-144.

[15] According to James R. Davila, in the OT history, two Moriahs are referred. One is at Genesis 22 which is three day's journey from Bersheba. He says that itself is wrong information. The second one is mentioned in 2 Chronicles 3:1 and this Hill of Moriah is situated in Jerusalem where Solomon built the Temple. He says Jerusalem is a woody place and not necessary carry firewood for sacrifice. After thorough discussion he suggests that Moriah is originally the temple place and in order to associate this place with the patriarch some scribes knowingly suppressed the original place of Genesis 22 and given the name of Moriah there. Davila, "Moriah," 905.

[16] In one of the prayers on West Syriac Church in the *Liturgy of Passion Week* says both Moriah and Golgotha are exactly the same place. *Kashtanubhavazhcha Namaskaram*, 23.

sacrifice. Abraham prepared an altar on the top of the earth to sacrifice Isaac; Zion (sons of Abraham) prepared another altar (cross) to sacrifice the Son of God. Isaac was bounded on the altar and Jesus was bounded on the cross with nails. Isaac was the only begotten to his father; Jesus was also the Only Begotten[17] to His Father. The mystery springs-forth on the top of the mountain like a ram[18] and mysteries[19] went-forth on the top of the mountain from the side of the Only Begotten. Isaac was concerned for three days about his father regarding the sacrificial lamb and he asked, father we have fire and wood, where is the lamb for sacrifice? Three days Jesus was under the earth and victoriously He came out after breaking the bars of *Sheol.*

In an anonymous dialogue poem, *On the Sacrifice of Isaac*, the author starts with the poem that "Abraham and Isaac who marked out between them a 'type' of the Father and the Son."[20] This dialogue poem is a typical replica

---

[17] In both occasions Mar Jacob uses the term *iheedoyo*. This term has a major theological significance in biblical literature; it represents Jesus Christ the Only Begotten Son of the Father. Meanwhile, in Syriac literature the term is used to denote others too. Also the same term is used to call the hermits or the single ones in Syrian asceticism.

[18] With the example of ram Jacob and other Syriac fathers explains the mystery of virgin birth. Mar Jacob compares Jesus' birth and death with the birth and death of ram on the top of the mountain. He said, "The sacrifice of Isaac and the ram which came down from the tree, depicts there mystically His birth and death" of the Only Begotten. There is only one tree gave birth to a ram (in this world) which is a mystery. (And) there is only one virgin (in this world) gave birth (to a child) in her virginity (is also a mystery). Bedjan, *HS* III, 311.17-19. In the West Syriac liturgy, which is used by Malankara Orthodox Church in the Wednesday third hour service that praises the Mother of God and several other places uses this imagery this imagery as a refutation against those who question the virgin birth of Jesus Christ.

The Church shows three things
The tree that gave marvelous fruit
The hard rock, and the fish
To refute against the heretics
The tree gave the ram
The fire stone gave water
The fish gave *estiro* (coin)
These three belittle the heretics who suspect the virgin birth (*Vishuddha Qurbanakramam*,56).

Ephrem also gives the same interpretation. Though its focus is on Mary Mar Ephrem discuss the very same theme here:

Never before, and never again,
Has a tree given birth to a lamb here on earth (Gen 22:13),
And no other virgin has given birth without any man's help.
Mary and the tree are one; the lamb was hung up in its branches,
As our Lord was on Golgotha;
The Lamb saved Isaac, as our Lord saved creation (Brock, *Bride of Light,* 57).

[19] Water and blood which came out from the side of Jesus is considered as symbols of baptism, Eucharist, and the Church.

[20] Brock, "A dialogue Poem on the Sacrifice of Isaac," 63.

of Mar Jacob's ideas with the above mentioned elaboration.[21] The same interpretation can be seen in various liturgical texts of the Syriac Churches. Third watch of the Tuesday *Lilyo* in Passion Week is dedicated to the story of Isaac. "Great is the mystery performed by the child Isaac by carrying the wood for his sacrifice. He represented the 'type' of the Son of God, who carried His cross and left Jerusalem."[22]

> Isaac the child was bound and was placed on the altar. He rejoiced to die and to fulfill the will of his Creator. He indicated the mystery of the Son who died for our sake in order to fulfill the will of the Father who sent Him for our salvation. Glory to the Lord of the types who fulfilled the words of the upright who saw His images with the eyes of the Holy Spirit.[23]

Therefore, it can be concluded that Isaac was a favorite typological figure of the Syriac Churches to educate about the salvific death of Jesus Christ.

---

[21] Abrahaṃ left the tent,
And Isaac mounted upon the donkey,
A type of the Son who rode the colt
As entered Jerusalem (Brock, "A dialogue Poem on the Sacrifice of Isaac," 63).
Abraham and Isaac travelled on the journey,
Taking with them two young men,
Just as Christ went up to the mountain
Taking with him two stripped men (Brock, "A dialogue Poem on the Sacrifice of Isaac," 64).
Three days shall the Son be
In the heart of the earth, with those who sleep.
Like Sarah shall Mary his mother
Be comforted at his resurrection. (Brock, "A dialogue Poem on the Sacrifice of Isaac," 66).
Death of your son is quite important
To deliver the Peoples from the curse;
My Son shall come down, and he will be sacrificed
In the body he has put on from the womb. (Brock, "A dialogue Poem on the Sacrifice of Isaac," 67).
Great is the mystery, and utterly glorious,
Which Abraham's son performed on the mountain:
He carried the wood with which to be burnt,
He went out to die, unaware.
A great act of discernment, and much to be wondered at,
Did the Son of God perform on earth:
He carried the wood whereon he was to be crucified,
And He went forth to die, to deliver all. (Brock, "A dialogue Poem on the Sacrifice of Isaac," 68-69).

[22] *Kashtanubhavazhcha Namaskaram,* 80.

[23] *Kashtanubhavazhcha Namaskaram,* 68.

4.2.2. Jacob: A 'Type' of the Bridegroom

> I shall see Jacob, the younger one who became great because of your type.
> I shall also boast that I have carried you, escorting you in honor.[24]

The betrothal of Jacob and Rachel performed as a 'type' of the Son of God's betrothal to Church in the previous chapter.[25] This section deals with Mar Jacob's interpretation of the patriarch Jacob as a 'type' of Jesus, the Bridegroom. He has no hesitation to accept that Jacob, the patriarch, as an Old Testament 'type' for Jesus Christ. Every act of Jacob including his journey to Laban's house resembles the Incarnated Jesus. As Jacob travelled and bought Leah and Rachel from a pagan's house, so also the Son of God came down from his lofty place and bought the Church from among the nations. Beyond that, Jacob's wedding to two wives, Rachel and Leah, represent betrothal of two Churches, the Church from nations and the Church from the nation respectively.[26] In the homily *On Our Lord and Jacob* Mar Jacob very dramatically describes the betrothal event and how Jacob and Rachel were represented as Christ and Church. The following lines well explained the great journey of patriarch Jacob to Haran.

> Tidings of his road took Jacob to the house of Haran, when He, the Just Prince, came down to espouse to himself the daughter of the pagans:
> she who was brought up among idols.[27]

At the outset Mar Jacob makes it clear that, as Jacob, the patriarch, went and betrothed the daughter of a pagan, the Just Prince (Jesus Christ) came to the world and espoused the daughter of a pagan who lived among the idols. The end result of both Jacob's and Jesus' acts were redemption. In the Old Testament Yahweh planned to redeem the world through the descendants of Abraham and in the New Testament God willed to redeem the world at large through His Only Begotten. Moreover, through the 'just men' of the Old Testament, God prefigured the Son of God's works of salvation.[28] Here, on the way to Haran Jacob had a vision at Bethel and where God spoke to him, as promised to Abraham that He will make Jacob's seed like the dust of the earth; you shall be spread over the four quarters of the earth and with your seed all families of the earth shall be blessed (Gen 28:14). Jacob proceeded to Haran to see the girl/s in whom the seeds were to be born. This is a pre-figuration of Jesus' journey to save earth from damnation; because, Jesus came from

---

[24] Bedjan, *HS* V, 465.9-10; ET. *FH* V, 157.369-370.

[25] Supra, 3.5.3.3.

[26] Infra 5.3.2.

[27] Bedjan, *HS* III, 209.7-8; ET. "On Our Lord and Jacob," *TV* 4.4(1993), 52.23-24.

[28] Infra, 4.2.2.

heaven and Jacob also covered lots of miles; at the time of Jesus' birth the angels gave the message to shepherds that, "Do not be afraid: for see, I am bringing you good news of great joy for all the people" (Lk 2:10). Both Jesus and Jacob were rich, but both of them acted like servants in their work places (Gen 29:15ff. Phil 2:7). Both journeys were in search of the nations. Mar Jacob reiterates that Jacob, the patriarch is an image of the Son. He states:

> For if Jacob had not borne in the image of the Son,
> he would not have been so famous in his deeds.[29]
> How lofty is the tale of this Jacob, who was altogether wondrous!
> for he resembles his Lord, and hence he is exalted in the Scriptures.
> Consider Jacob's journey, how much it resembles the Messiah's,
> and understand from this that he walked no path but His.
> He was foreshadowing our Lord in his deeds;
> for he came down, was betrothed, waxed rich, and ascended to his Father.
> Consider how much Jacob, when he journeyed in poverty,
> resembled the Son, Who emptied himself and came down.[30]

The prophecy of Isaiah calls Jesus as a wonder (Isa 9:6); Mar Jacob calls patriarch Jacob as a wonder in his deeds. Jacob resembles Jesus in all his ways. Both of them found their spouses and betrothed them. Through the betrothals both Jacob and Jesus increased their wealth and returned to their own places. Jacob was a great shepherd who increased his flock than that of his father-in-law (Gen 30:43); Jesus called Himself as the good shepherd (Jn 10:11). Mar Jacob says, "The shadow of the great shepherd rested upon him."[31] In order to betroth Rachel Jacob entered into a covenant with Laban;[32] Jesus wrote a covenant with His blood in order to betroth His loved one. Mar Jacob uses not a contract but the term 'covenant' and it receives special attention. The covenantal relationship between Yahweh and Israel is a special type of agreement; a divine notion lies in it.

Mar Jacob compares Messiah's sufferings with that of Jacob, the patriarch. He said, when Jacob betrothed Rachel he wept. A man who has lust would not weep but engenders gaiety with its heating. His weeping prefigures Christ's sufferings. He raises this idea very descriptively:

> Think not, my son, that Jacob desired her after a carnal manner (*pagaronoito*
> (for even when he kissed (*nqeš*) her, he wept sore with great suffering.
> Were it lust, he would not then have shed tears,
> since lust engenders gaiety with its heating.

---

[29] Bedjan, *HS* III, 209.17-18; ET. "On Our Lord and Jacob," *TV* 4.4(1993), 52.33-34.

[30] Bedjan, *HS* III, 210.2-9; ET. "On Our Lord and Jacob," *TV* 4.4(1993), 53.39-46.

[31] Bedjan, *HS* III, 213.21; ET. "On Our Lord and Jacob," *TV* 4.4(1993), 56.121.

[32] Bedjan, *HS* III, 214.4; ET. "On Our Lord and Jacob," *TV* 4.4(1993), 56.126.

For weeping is begotten of suffering and sorrow,
and wherever there is weeping, there is no lust at all.
Therefore Jacob was not with lust enkindled,
but the suffering of the Son's mysteries were fallen upon him.
Whoever kissed his betrothed while weeping, except Jacob?
For he beheld the mystery of the Church in Rachel at her betrothal.
It was fitting that he wept and suffered when he kissed her,
to signify in his betrothal the sufferings of the Son.
With his tears he painted an image of the Son of God's passion;
for when he betrothed the Church, He suffered, and only then was she betrothed.[33]

Mar Jacob contented that Jacob's betrothal was a pre-figuration of Jesus' betrothal of the Church at Golgotha. Jesus betrothed the Church out of His love and this love is not in a carnal manner but love for the redemption of His betrothed. Jesus betrothed the Church through His passion and sufferings however, the regular betrothal is an occasion of joy with full of dispensation of food and drink. Here, unlike the normal betrothal which is full of joy, in the betrothal of Jacob he kissed Rachel by weeping and in tears (Gen 29:11). Mar Jacob interprets that this betrothal was none other than a 'type' of Jesus' betrothal of the Church. He points out that never before or even after this, a bridegroom wept when he betrothed a woman.

Again, Jacob betrothed two wives: Leah and Rachel; Jesus also betrothed two: the nation and the nations.[34] Jacob opened up the stone, which resembles the sin, from the face of the well, Jesus opened the baptism for the remission of sin.[35] Jacob saw the ladder at Bethel on which the fiery beings were ascending and descending. Mar Jacob explains that, the heavenly beings do not have the need of a ladder to come down and go up but the ladder represents the cross of the only begotten. Therefore it foreshadowed the divine wedding of Jesus on the cross.[36]

Mar Ephrem held the same findings. In his commentary on Genesis he says about the love between Jacob and Rachel. He compares Jesus with Jacob and the Church of nations with Rachel.[37] In the Armenian Commentary on Genesis Mar Ephrem says:

> Divinity led Jacob to a well in order to make manifest His compassion, and both the strength of [Jacob] with respect to the rock and his compassion by his

---

[33] Bedjan, *HS* III, 211.19-212.10; ET. "On Our Lord and Jacob," *TV* 4.4(1993), 54.77-55.90.

[34] Bedjan, *HS* III, 218.17-219.9; ET. "On Our Lord and Jacob," *TV* 4.4(1993), 60.223-238.

[35] Bedjan, *HS* III, 213.6-7; ET. "On Our Lord and Jacob," *TV* 4.4(1993), 55.

[36] Bedjan, III, 310.9-22; ET. Konat "On the Mysteries, Types, and Figures of Christ," *Le Museon* 118(2005), 78.99-112.

[37] Tonneau, *Gen.et Exo.* XXIX.4, 93; ET. Mathews, *Comm. on Gen.,* 179.

> watering [of the flock]... in order to manifest that there was to come forth from him the Shepherd who feeds His sheep with His flesh and with His blood and when Jacob threw his arms around [that stone], his limbs gladly gave relief to his soul, for he saw the sign of that One who would remove the burden from the shoulders of the nations (Mt 11:28-30; Rev 2:24-29), the types [church].[38]

Thus according to Mar Ephrem, Jacob fore-figures Jesus by his acts on the well at the land of Haran. Again, Ephrem in the *Hymns on Virginity* compares Jacob as the 'type' of Jesus, the True Lamb and betrothed.[39] In short Mar Jacob and other Syriac Church Fathers observe that the patriarch Jacob is a 'type' of the Son of God.

4.2.3. Samson: A 'Type' of the Bridegroom

Samson is another 'type' from the Old Testament figures (Judg 13-16). He was born to a barren woman after having a vision from an angel of God. She kept away from wine, beer, and unclean things until she gave birth to a child and the child also lived as a Nazirite and the power of the Lord was with him until his death. The name 'Samson' is related to the Hebrew word *šemeš*,[40] and *šemšo* in Syriac both mean 'sun.' He violated the commands of God. Israelites engaged in marriages with foreigners which led to worship of idols and condemnation by God (Judg 3:6). Samson loved and married a foreign a prostitute (Judg 14:1-4). His marriage violated the Law of God; "For your part, do not make a covenant with the inhabitants of this land" (Judg 2:2). The term which used in Judges for 'prostitute' {Heb. *zōnâ,* Syr. *znee*} is used to describe Israel's prostitution.[41] Though Samson did all those violations of the Law, Mar Jacob found a 'type' of Christ,[42] a savior,[43] deliverer,[44] and a bridegroom of the daughter of the nations[45] in him. He did not consider Samson's misdeeds or negative sides but takes only his Christ-like characters and actions.[46] Just

---

[38] Mathews, *Armenian Commentary on Gen.,* 120.

[39] *HVir,* XX.2, 67-68; XXI.11, 74; ET. McVey, *Ephrem the Syrian,* 346, 353.

[40] Robert, "Judges," 225.

[41] Olson, "The Book of Judges," 841.

[42] Bedjan, *HS* V, 336.4; ET. "A Homily on Samson," *TV* 11(1992), 56.103.

[43] Bedjan, *HS* V, 333.4, 8; ET. "A Homily on Samson," *TV* 11(1992), 53.39,45.

[44] Bedjan, *HS* V, 334.17; ET. "A Homily on Samson," *TV* 11(1992), 54.74. See the prophecy of Isaiah 40 and Luke 4:18.

[45] Bedjan, *HS* V, 336.21; ET. "A Homily on Samson," *TV* 11(1992), 56.120.

[46] Bedjan, *HS* V, 333.3; ET. "A Homily on Samson," *TV* 11(1992), 53.39. Mar Jacob says "He did foolish deeds time to time yet I ought not for of this". Again Mar Jacob writes:

> Why did Lord's Nazirite go in unto the harlot?
> His tale confuses me, and I know not what to say of it.
> The Lord is very meek and forbearing towards the sons of men,
> And where they fall, it is not He that seeks to cast them down.

like Messiah was appointed to redeem the Israelites, Samson was an appointed man of God. Samson was appointed to rule and deliver Israel from the hands of Philistines. His betrothal to a Philistine woman was a pre-figuration of Christ's betrothal to the Church from the nations. Mar Jacob very emphatically says:

> Whom does Samson resembles if not our Lord, who came to espouse
> the Church of the nations, and death met Him like a mighty foe?
> Samson went down to take wife that daughter of the uncircumcised,
> hereby depicting our Lord, Who betrothed with His Gospel, the daughter
> of the pagans.[47]

Mar Jacob again asserts his argument using the very word 'type' and said; "The types of his Lord blazed in him like luminaries,[48] and they gave him power and strength to slay the lion."[49] These luminaries might be his predecessors like Jacob, Joseph, Moses, and Joshua who did overcome all the hindrances through the power of God, which was mysteriously bestowed upon them.

Mar Jacob sees several resemblances between Christ and Samson; both were Nazirite,[50] though they were innocent both Christ and Samson had enemies but they slew their enemies; Samson slew the lion's whelp and Christ killed the death itself. Samson went in search of a bride from pagans; our Lord also descended in search of a new bride from gentiles.[51] The (Holy) Spirit guided both of them; Samson defeated the lion and the Philistines and our Lord defeated death through his death.[52] As of the lion was unable to stop Samson's march towards his espousal of the daughter of pagans, so also, the cross was not a hindrance in the way of the Son of God to betroth the daughter of nations.[53] Mar Jacob said, as Jesus was filled with Spirit before he went to the wilderness to encounter Satan, Samson was filled with the Spirit of God that enabled him to slay the whelp of the lion:

> His mighty deeds that Samson wrought were God's.
> But the others which were not good were his own.
> It was not that God told him to go in unto harlot;
> He himself wished to go in, and the Lord did not constrain him, since he was free (Bedjan, *HS* V, 344.14-345.1; ET. "A Homily on Samson," *TV* 11(1992), 63.279-286).

[47] Bedjan, *HS* V, 335.5-10; ET. "A Homily on Samson," *TV* 11(1992), 55.83-86.

[48] There is no exact references to these luminaries.

[49] Bedjan, *HS* V, 336.4; ET. "A Homily on Samson," *TV* 11(1992), 56.103.

[50] Bedjan, *HS* V, 333.2, 335.17; ET. "A Homily on Samson," *TV* 11(1992), 53.38, 55.95.

[51] The daughter of the nations was prefigured in the daughter of the pagans (Bedjan, *HS* V, 336.10; ET. "A Homily on Samson," *TV* 11(1992), 56.109).

[52] Bedjan, *HS* V, 336.11-12; ET. "A Homily on Samson," *TV* 11(1992), 56.110-111.

[53] Bedjan, *HS* V, 336.17; ET. "A Homily on Samson," *TV* 11(1992), 56.117.

The Son's mystery dawned upon that Nazirite,
and gave him power to fashion an image full of wondrousness;
then the Spirit of the Lord took possession of him mightily.[54]

Mar Jacob compared Samson's journey to the land of Philistines as the descent of Jesus for Incarnation and considered him as the Son of God and the Messiah who redeemed the Israelites from the hands of Philistines.

He raised up an image of our Lord in the land of Philistines,
for it was Samson's lot to raise it up there.
The Son of God stirred from his place and came to our land
to espouse the Church of the nations, as we have said.
But death met Him, the lion that ate all generations,
and He slew death as Samson slew the lion.
He continued His way, and by His Cross He betrothed and took to wife
her for whose sake He was come down to the home of the earthborn.
The lion was unable to stay Samson's journey,
for he espoused and took a wife as he pleased and them departed.
Nor was the journey of the Son of God stayed by the death,
for He took the Church, made her His own, and then ascended.
These mysteries blazed in that Hebrew,
wherefore he ripped open and slew the lion, as ye have heard.
He rent the lion asunder, went his way, and made the betrothal as he desired;
and as he returned, the mystery plainly went another step forward in him.[55]
Death, (which is) the lion which devoured all generations, met Him,
and He killed death as Samson killed the lion.
The riddle which the Hebrew held fast, concerning the Philistines,
was not interpreted until Christ came to the world.
Death is bitter[56] and our Lord is the sweet honey,
and it enlightened and stood up, that sweet came out of bitter.[57]

According to Mar Jacob the riddle of Samson was fulfilled when Christ became food for all generations. Mar Jacob interprets the incident of honey from the lion as a symbol of Eucharist. There is confusion in comprehending this comparison; the problem is, the lion is the attacker in the former story and death is the attacker in the latter one; Samson is the defender in the former and Christ in the latter. In the former story the offender was killed but in the latter the defender was killed; in the former the offender gave honey from

---

[54] Bedjan, *HS* V, 335.21-336.2; ET. "A Homily on Samson," *TV* 11(1992), 55.99-56.101.

[55] Bedjan, *HS* V. 336.12-337.6; ET. "A Homily on Samson," *TV* 11(1992), 56.111-57.126.

[56] In the West Syriac funeral service calls death as bitter: "This drink of death is bitter (ܡܪܝܪ) to those who drink it" (*Savasamskarakramam*, 25).

[57] Bedjan, *HS* III, 316.22-317.3; ET. Konat "On the Mysteries, Types, and Figures of Christ," *Le Museon* 118(2005), 82.239-83.244.

its carcass but against this offender gives the sweet fruit in the latter one. This is the contradiction; while the representative of death gave honey in the former one; the representative of life produces honey in the latter case. This is a *prima fasciae* contradiction. But the solution is; according to the Christian interpretation, in general, through the death of Christ, the death was killed. Therefore, the problem is solved and in the Samson incident and Christ event ultimately the attacker, lion/death, were annihilated. Mar Jacob says; death was the consumer of generations from Adam till Christ; when Christ was eaten by the death He became the food of life for all generations. Therefore, the riddle "eatable came forth from the eater" fulfilled through the death of Christ.

Again, Jesus went to the *Sheol*, where all the dead were under capture, and liberated them from the bondage of death. In Samson's episode Mar Jacob compares the harlot with *Sheol*. He said, like Christ willingly descended into the *Sheol* to liberate the captured ones Samson himself went to the harlot, the *Sheol*, and triumphed over them.[58] Therefore, according to Mar Jacob, God purposefully raised Samson as His image in a remote time to show the mystery of the Son; to teach that the Son of God will come to save nations from idolatry. Just like Samson killed his enemy, the lion's whelp, Son of God would kill the enemy of the humankind, the death. Samson's riddle had remained as a mystery until Jesus defeated the enemy of generations.

Ephrem says that Samson is a 'type' of Jesus Christ who was also a Nazirite and courageous. Just as Samson brought sweet from bitter Jesus brought life to the humanity that was under the bitterness of death.[59] Comparison of various events of Samson's life with that of Jesus Christ by Mar Jacob and other Syriac fathers assert that Samson as a 'type' of Jesus Christ.

4.3. Christ the Real Bridegroom

This section is on how Mar Jacob sees Christ as the Bridegroom of the Church and how He differs from the gods of Gentiles. Mar Jacob and other Syriac Fathers teach that Jesus Christ is the real bridegroom and all other gods of the nations (Gentiles) are paramours. This conclusion is derived from a dual background; the Church was brought forth from two backgrounds: from the people or the Nation and from the peoples or nations. Often they are called daughter of the nation (*bart-amo*) (and daughter of nations (*bart-amme*) or daughter of the gentiles (*bart-hanpo*). To the Nation/Israelites the Fathers used to teach them that Jesus is the Messiah whom they were looking for. And

---

[58] Bedjan, *HS* V, 345.10-346.19; ET. "A Homily on Samson," *TV* 11(1992), 63.295-64.324.

[59] The Nazirite, Samson, gazed at the type
of your courage. He tore the lion apart,
and made the sweet life emerge
from its bitterness for human beings. (HNat, XIII.4, 74; ET. McVey, St Ephrem the Syrian, 137).

when they turn to the nations/non-Israelites, they taught that Jesus Christ is the true God and the idols are false gods. As a pedagogical tool they used the marriage imagery to teach their faithful that Christ is the Bridegroom and the Church as the bride. They inherited this imagery from the eighth century BC Israelite prophets, who have instructed the people of Israel that Yahweh is the true Bridegroom. When the Israelite people have started to worship the foreign gods the prophets taught that there is only one true God/Bridegroom that is the God of their fathers who redeemed them from Egypt and from their enemies. Since they worship the foreign gods they are committing adultery. When the Fathers of the Church faced the same predicament in the Church they employed this imagery and taught Christ as the true Bridegroom/God and all other heretics are false.

Mar Jacob often uses the imagery of the bridegroom to teach the right faith of the Church in a time of skepticism and heresy. When the Jews rejected the divinity of Jesus, Mar Jacob writes:

> (Jewish) Elder, you come! You come! Who suckle milk and see
> the blessed bread and leave the breast of your childishness.
> Christ is the bread, the Law is only milk without firmness;
> and milk alone never makes a person mature.
> The time for milk is past, and (the person) does not agree
> to be weaned from the Law, which is not only milk.[60]

In this part of the homily, refuting the Jews, Mar Jacob teaches that the time of the milk, Law, is over, and it is the time of bread, Christ. Therefore, the Church should follow Christ rather than Law. A strong influence of St. Paul can be seen in this teaching. He uses the imagery of milk to educate the Corinthian Church that it is the food of babies. "And so, brothers and sisters, I could not speak to you as spiritual people, but rather as people of the flesh, as infants in Christ. I fed you with milk, not solid food, for you are not ready for solid food. Even now you are not ready" (1Cor 3:1-2). Babies cannot consume hard food; likewise the Church in Corinth is in infancy to understand the mysteries of God. In this part, instead of solid food, Mar Jacob uses bread; because it is purely Christological in nature. Christ Himself declared that "I am the true bread from heaven" (Jn 6: 32). Another reference is to the Law. Here also Mar Jacob follows St. Paul: In Romans Chapters 3 and 4 Paul refuted the Judaizers of the Roman Church who insisted on practicing the Law and circumcision and he gave importance to faith rather than Law and circumcision of the heart than to circumcision of the flesh. The same can be seen in his homily on Epiphany:

> Moses made gush out from the cloud of Sinai the fountain of milk, the nurse of little children, so that the world might suck and grow up in the knowledge which

[60] Albert, *HCJ*, 194.195-200; cf. Benin, Command Covenants, 147.

would make it (the world) arrive to rise up to the nourishment of the perfect. For, John weaned the world from milk, and showed forth and set before it the true[61] bread, Christ, manifesting Him who said: *I am the bread* (Jn 6:35) appropriate for the full stature of man. The law, that is to say, is the milk, but, *I am the bread,* that is to say, be weaned from the milk of the children and come and live by the bread, the food of the strong [62] (1 Cor 3:2; Heb 5:12-14).

This is also a refutation against the Jews as well as a teaching regarding the salvation through Messiah, the True Bridegroom. In short, Mar Jacob establishes that Jesus Christ is the true Messiah whom prophets preached about. The Law is a shadow of Messiah and after the arrival of Messiah the Law has no existence.

When he confronts the non-Jewish teachings he uses the Christological term, 'Son of God,' to denote Jesus Christ who came for the salvation of the world. The Son of God came to the world and uprooted all thorns of idolatry from the face of the world.[63]

> The diligent Son [of God] uprooted and cast down the temples of the demons,
> and lo, He planted churches at the ends of the entire world.
> He uprooted the thorny tangle of idolatry from every quarter,
> and planted cedars[64] to give shade to the world.
> He built up the creation with gold and precious stones,[65]
> and brought forth hymns of praise from desolate lands.
> He made the world into a kings' palace full of lovely things,
> and set the cross therein like a pearl column.
> He burned incense to sweeten the earth with a sweet fragrance
> form a root that Virgin Soil gave the world.
> The smoke of the high places, which had smothered all creation with its stench
> has passed from the world.
> The air that was troubled by the fumes of sacrificial victims,
> which ascended through it to polluted demons, is become clear and pure and sweet.
> The head of the Son of God was lifted up on Golgotha,
> and all the corrupted world saw it and was restored.[66]

Here Mar Jacob reminds the Church that Jesus is the annihilator of the idols and false worship. Idolatry was a common feature among the gentiles and when Jesus started his public ministry He cleared the world from idol

[61] This is not appeared in the text of Albert but Kollamparampil referring other manuscripts added.

[62] Rilliet, *SHF* II, 550.9-15; ET. *FH* VII, 189-190.2.

[63] Rilliet, *SHF* I, 540.1-5; Bedjan, *SMS*, 819.16; ET. *FH* XVI, 341.231.

[64] Cedar here represents the local churches.

[65] It is referring to sacraments.

[66] Bedjan, *HS* III, 413.5-20; ET. "The Parable of Leaven," *TV* 3(1989), 47.29-44.

worship and planted churches in the place of temples which polluted the world through its stinky fumes of sacrifice of idol worship.[67] Cedar is a precious, tall, and strong tree[68] of the hills of Lebanon; Solomon used this wood to construct the temple of Jerusalem (1Kings 6:9). The places of gentiles were barren and desolate, now it is filled with beautiful churches with precious stones and gold. Materially it was true that during the time of Mar Jacob persecution had almost ended and the Church had flourished and was cherished in a peaceful atmosphere. Many churches were wealthy and they were adorned with precious metals and pictures. Cross erected on the top and inside of the churches like flag-posts, symbol of victory and salvation. On the other hand, spiritually, the gold and precious stones represent the sacraments of baptism, and Eucharist. Abundance of the Church internally means that the gentiles became members of the Church and thereby received Jesus as their Bridegroom.

In another homily Mar Jacob uses the parable of the true shepherd, in which Christ says that, He is the true shepherd and all others are thieves and robbers (Jn 10:1-6) and the real Shepherd gave His life for His sheep (Jn 10:1).

> For thirty years He walked with her in the land of evil men,
> so that she might be trained with Him, and He could then take her up to the place of His Father.
> He was to her a companion, and by His intimacy He trained her,
> lest she flee when He led her back with Him to His realm.
> He came to her father's house and was tried by poverty,
> yet He was not loath to show her how much He loved her.[69]
> So that she, as the daughter of that race, would be with Him in one mingling,
> since it is written that the two of them shall be one, He became embodied in her;
> He became one with her, made her one with Himself, and behold, they are one.
> He became the Son of man and made her, the Church, the daughter of God
> and by His commingling, the saying is established that the two are one.[70]

Here Mar Jacob depicts, as a true shepherd, how much Jesus loved His Church, how He trained her to become one with Him, and how much He suffered for the sake of His bride. In many of his homilies Mar Jacob used to call Christ as the Light[71] of the world, Day time, Sun of righteousness, Dawn

---

[67] Bedjan, *HS* IV, 286.1-3; ET. "Homily on the King of Moab," *TV* 1(1989), 58.81-84.

[68] Mar Jacob compares Samson into a strong high Cedar. Bedjan, *HS* V, 350.6; ET. "Homily on Samson," *TV* 11(1992), 67.390. One of the West Syriac worship song says that, "Righteous will prosper like palm trees and thrive like cedars of Lebanon" (*Vishuddha Qurbanakramam*, 35).

[69] Bedjan, *HS* III, 331.203ff.; ET. "Why Our Lord Abode upon the Earth for Thirty Years," *TV* 4(1990), 45.203-207.

[70] Bedjan, *HS* III, 333.9-13; ET. "Why Our Lord Abode upon the Earth for Thirty Years," *TV* 4(1990), 48.42-46.

[71] Brock, "Jacob of Serugh's Homily on Tamar (Gen 38)," 281.39.

etc.[72] All these imageries show that Christ is the one who dissipate the darkness of the world. By the term darkness he reminds of the sin and idolatry of the gentiles. This is another example which tells that Christ is a true Bridegroom and Savior.[73] Through these types of explanations Mar Jacob tries to establish that Christ is the true Bridegroom. Many of his predecessors also use the same theme to argue that Jesus is the true God who came to save the world.[74] Mar Jacob used to teach that Jesus Christ is the true bridegroom and all others are paramours. Through this he proves that Jesus is the true God who saved the world by His atoning sacrifice of His body.

The prefiguration of Christ indicates God's plan for the salvation of the nations. It denotes the love of God towards the Church (nations) in the Old Testament. Once it was believed that the salvation belongs to the Nation and nations were ignored by many respects. This dilemma is now proved unnecessary. God never shun His creation and they are beloved to Him. God sent His Only Begotten to redeem nations by His death. This providence of God gives confidence to the minds of the faithful. Even in the contemporary situation this saving mystery of God spreads hope among the people who are in suffering and despair and they believe that He would not despise them. This interpretation is relevant even today. The following part will describe how Mar Jacob substantiates that Jesus Christ is the true bridegroom of the Church.

4.3.1. Veiled Bridegroom

The messianic expectation was fulfilled in Christ Jesus; and this is another well developed Christology in Paul and other New Testament writers. In the Acts, Luke quotes the preaching of Peter as to Messianic prophecy being fulfilled in Jesus (Acts 3: 22). "The Lord your God will rise up for you a prophet like me

---

[72] Brock, "Jacob of Serugh's Homily on Tamar (Gen 38)," 281.25-29; Bedjan, *SMS,* VII, 781.1-782.10; ET. *FH,* II, 100.125-101.154.

[73] Bedjan, *SMS,* 781.15; ET. *FH,* II, 101.142; Rilliet, *SHF* II, 560.20; ET. *FH,* VII, 196.24.

[74] Acts of Thomas deals with true bridegroom, true marriage and true bridal chamber and says that the bridegroom, wedding, and bridal chamber of this world are passing and corrupted. There only one eternal and true Bridegroom and that is Jesus Christ. Throughout the text we can see this aspect of teaching: Remember my children, what my brother said to you, as to whom he commanded you; and know this that if you abandon this filthy intercourse you become holy temples, pure and free from afflictions and pains both manifest and hidden…but you will be persuaded by me. And keep yourselves purely unto God, you shall have living children… and you shall be hoping when you shall see the true wedding feast; and you shall be in it praisers (of God), and shall be numbered with those who enter into the bridal chamber (*AAA*, 70-71).

Aphrahat, in his demonstration on Covenanters exhorts for the need of virginity to receive the true bridegroom therefore, to abandon the bridegroom of this world. "For let us be aroused from our sleep at this time (Rom 13:11)… Let us keep the appointed meeting with the glorious bridegroom so that we may enter with him to his bridal chamber" (Parisot, *Demo*, VI.1, 240.10-15; ET. Valavanolickal, *Demonstrations* I, 122-123).

among your own people; you shall heed such a prophet"[75] (Deut 18:15). Paul depicts that the rock in the wilderness represents Christ.[76] He said: "I do not want you to be unaware, brothers and sisters that our ancestors were all under the cloud, and all passed through the sea, and all were baptized into Moses in the cloud and in the sea, and all ate the same spiritual food, and all drank the same spiritual drink. For they drank from the spiritual rock that followed them, and the rock was Christ" (1Cor 10:1-4). Thus pre-figuration of Christ in the Old Testament was lively in the minds of apostle and the early Church; being influenced by this idea Mar Jacob and other writers moved their pen to find and interpret Christ in the Old Testament.

Mar Jacob, without any doubts, affirms that the images of the Son of God were depicted in the Old Testament. But they were veiled under the prophecy.[77] The spiritual eyes of Mar Jacob envisions the Bridegroom of the Church even from the Genesis account (2:24). To him the 'man' is a personification of Christ the Bridegroom. When the Father created the Son was hidden in the Father and revealed and in Adam[78] (*kso hweeth babook waglok bAdam kad bar leh. Wzar beh dmootho dpagaronoothok wgaliyonek*) Thus, even from the time of creation the bodily presence of the Son was there in the earth with His people in a hidden manner.

> The Hidden Father betrothed a bride to his Only-Begotten,
> having instructed her through prophecy in a symbolic way.
> In his love he built a great palace for the bride of light
> and depicted the bridegroom in various ways in her royal home.
> Moses entered in and, like a skilled artist, delineated
> the bridegroom and the bride, and then covered a great picture with a veil.[79]

In another homily Mar Jacob brings out the same thing and says:

> Moses entered, and like a skilled painter depicted Him,
> the bridegroom and the bride, and hide the great image in the crown.
> He set down in his book that man will leave his father and mother,
> and cling to his wife, and both will become one body.[80]

---

[75] Alwan, *QHC* I, 9.139.

[76] Bedjan, *HS* V, 295.9-16; ET. Brock, "On the Veil of Moses," in *Studies in Syriac Spirituality*, 81. 247-252.

[77] Supra 3.4.4. ff. cf. Bedjan, *HS* III, 286.12; ET. Brock, "On the Veil of Moses," in *Studies in Syriac Spirituality*, 76.60.

[78] Brock, "Jacob of Serugh's Homily on Tamar (Gen 38)," 281.47-48.

[79] Bedjan, *HS* III, 287.20-288.2; ET. Brock, "On the Veil of Moses," in *Studies in Syriac Spirituality,* 76.85-77.90.

[80] Bedjan, *HS* III, 309.17-20; ET. Konat "On the Mysteries, Types, and Figures of Christ," *Le Museon* 118(2005), 77.87-90. Mar Jacob uses three terms to interpret the unrevealing of the Bridegroom: hidden (ܡܛܫܝ), veiled (ܡܟܣܝ), and mystery (ܐܪܙܐ). All these terms are used to

He found that all prophecies proclaim the mystery of the heavenly Bridegroom.[81] Events and luminaries of the Old Testament depict Jesus Christ typologically; but they are above the human comprehension.[82] Only with the help of lamp, the doctrines, one can expound this mystery.[83] He has the opinion that Moses and other prophets were aware of presence of the Bridegroom, the Only Begotten of the Father. He writes:

> He set His face to come to espouse the Church of the nations,
> and in divers times He was revealed in allegories.
> Examine the scriptures; behold, thou wilt find His path there,
> for there is not one title in the readings that does not proclaim Him.
> Take doctrine as a lamp and enter the Scriptures;
> by it thou canst see the beauty of hidden things.
> In all those books, where is the Son of God not depicted?
> Seek, if thou canst, what cannot be found at all!
> There is no page that the Son's figure does not overshadow,
> nor any reading which speaks not of Him plainly.
> Every letter in the Scriptures is written in the Name of the Lord,
> and in every saying, it is He that is to be richly expounded.
> In every time, He was spoken of, that He was coming to the earth,
> even till He came and His heralds rested from the good tidings.[84]

In the opinion of Mar Jacob, the 'types' and their acts were pedagogical;[85] through them the Father wanted to teach and mend the people of Israel to receive the Son of God, the heavenly Bridegroom.[86] Meanwhile, the Father wanted His Son to be veiled. He said "the Father kept the Son in concealment, without anyone knowing and he wanted to reveal this matter to the world in

---

denote something intangible to human perception. He uses the term *mystery* ܐܪܙܐ (Bedjan, *HS* III, 286.8; 288.13; 289.8, 14; 291.10; 292.4, 10; 295.15; 30.4.) time to time to fill up the gap of his incomprehensibility, which is a common tool to interpret the Divine aspects which is above the comprehension of human beings.

[81] Brock, "Jacob of Serugh's Homily on Tamar," 294.51-55.

[82] Mar Jacob says the Son was hidden in luminaries. Since the Son is light and Coal of Fire and when He indwells in another person, that person also shares the light of Christ (Bedjan, *HS* I, 487.13.103; ET. McCollum, "Homily on Peter," in *MHMJS*, Fasc. 22, 18. Further discussions see 4.2.8). The Son was hidden in Moses, therefore, his face was shone and in order to cover the Son from the world he covered his face (Bedjan, *HS* I, 46.5-6; Bedjan, *HS* III, 286.1-13; ET. Brock, "On the Veil of Moses," in *Studies in Syriac Spirituality*, 75.48-76. 60).

[83] Bedjan, *HS* III, 208.10; ET. "On Our Lord and Jacob," *TV* 4.4(1993), 51.10.

[84] Bedjan, *HS* III, 208.5-209.2; ET. "On Our Lord and Jacob," *TV* 4.4(1993), 51.5-52.18.

[85] According to Mar Jacob God through the prophets educated Israelites the true worship of God. In time to time He gave five covenants with Israel, which says how would be the relation between God and the people. See five covenants: supra: 3.2.

[86] Brock, "Jacob of Serugh's Homily on Tamar (Gen 38)," 294.52-53.

symbolic terms."[87] Even Jesus Christ Himself, in His public ministry, restrained His disciples from disclosing that He is the Messiah and He is going to be a sacrifice; because his time was not yet come (Mt 16:20).

Mar Jacob finds the following reasons for the veiling. First of all the Hebrew people were not ready to see the Son.[88] Therefore God, through the prophets who are the friends of God, taught the People symbolically. Secondly, the primary nature of prophecy itself is hidden or veiled; therefore, the 'types' also were hidden.[89] Also, the Father wants to keep the Son under the veil and liked to reveal the Incarnation of the Son in Symbolic way.[90] In short, the veiling is a divine will and the question of 'why' does not arise. He said Moses himself is a figure of prophecy so that He covered the face of Moses. The following passage describes the decision of God to hide the story of Son of God from the people of God:

> So that whenever a prophet arouse on the earth to speak, it might be recognized
> that his words were veiled from those who heard them
> that there was something hidden in the matter of which he spoke,
> and his words to be understood, required an awareness of what they symbolized.
> Thus he cries out in the prophet, I have a secret, I have a secret
> So that the world might be aware that the prophecy contained secrets hidden
> in symbolic language.
> The words and actions of prophecy are veiled;
> it hides its contents in parables so that they might not be recognized.
> It devises figures and utters its wonders as if in secret,
> so that the world might not become openly aware of the Son of God.[91]

Therefore, according to Mar Jacob, veiling the mystery of the Son from the people is a divine plan. But, in the fullness of time[92] , the Son of God, the eternal light, through His revelation uncovered the mystery of Moses and the other prophecies to the world (Heb 1:1-2). He said, if the Son of God was not Incarnated these treasures of mysteries would not be uncovered.[93] "Our Lord

---

[87] Bedjan, *HS* III, 284.20-21; ET. Brock, "On the Veil of Moses," in *Studies in Syriac Spirituality,* 75.25-26.

[88] Bedjan, *HS* III, 286.6, ET. Brock, "On the Veil of Moses," in *Studies in Syriac Spirituality,* 76.53.

[89] Bedjan, *HS* III, 284.16-19; ET. Brock, "On the Veil of Moses," in *Studies in Syriac Spirituality*, 75.21-24.

[90] Bedjan, *HS* III, 284.20-21, ET. Brock, "On the Veil of Moses," in *Studies in Syriac Spirituality*, 75.24-25.

[91] Bedjan, *HS* III, 285.3-12, ET. Brock, "On the Veil of Moses," in *Studies in Syriac Spirituality*, 75.29-38.

[92] Albert, *HCJ*, 118.107; Bedjan, *HS* III, 112.21.

[93] Bedjan, *HS* V, 338.18-19; "A Homily on Samson," *TV* 11(1992), 58.159-160.

shone out as the sun in the world, and all received light: symbols and figures and parables were all explained."[94] For thirty-three years the Bridegroom walked with the bride and taught His ways.[95] Even then, the bride did not understand the meaning of "Therefore a man leaves his father and his mother and clings to his wife, and they become one flesh" (Gen 2:24). But it was Paul who removed the veil and explained the mystery completely to the Church (Eph 5:30-32).[96] The idea of the hidden Christ in the Old Testament was a favorite theme to Ephrem too.[97]

4.3.2. Just Men are the Images of the Bridegroom

This section is a discussion on Mar Jacob's rendering of the *just men* as the images of the Bridegroom. The two words Mar Jacob uses for the 'just men' are *keene* and *zadeeqe*. Both carry the same meaning in the noun form 'upright,' 'right,' 'just,' etc. The noun *keene* is used as 'true' (Gen 42:11) and 'righteous' (Rom 3:10). The adverb *keenooto* represent justice, righteousness, etc.[98] Mar Jacob very categorically says that the prophets, the kings, the righteous, and the patriarchs are the images of the Bridegroom.[99] One of his homilies starts with the following thought:

> The path of the Son has been marked out by all manner of mysteries,
> and with their steps they have measured the earth as they journeyed.
> Behold, since the world began, He had been borne in procession, to come to the earth,
> and righteous persons heralded Him by their deeds.[100]

---

[94] Bedjan, *HS* III, 287.13-14; ET. Brock, "On the Veil of Moses," in *Studies in Syriac Spirituality*, 76.81.

[95] Bedjan, *HS* III, 331.11-12; ET. "Why Our Lord Abode upon the Earth for Thirty Years," *TV* 4(1990), 45.203-204.

[96] Bedjan, *HS* III, 289.4; ET. Brock, "On the Veil of Moses," in *Studies in Syriac Spirituality*, 77.113.

[97] His entire reason for preserving the flock
was because of something hidden in its midst.
The something which was hidden in it has come forth
and has become the Shepherd of mankind.
In the contemptible flock, He hid
the Prince of the shepherds.
He has left the foolish flock
for the nations have become his pasture. (Stanley Kazan, "Isaac of Antioch's Homily against
Jews," in *Oriens Christianus*, 46(1962), 95-98; cited in, Benin, *Command, Covenants*, 143).

[98] Sokoloff, *A Syriac Lexicon,* 594; cf. Smith, *Syriac Dictionary,* 202.

[99] Bedjan, *HS* III, 209.4-8; ET. "On Our Lord and Jacob," *TV* 4.4(1993), 52.21-22.

[100] Bedjan, *HS* III, 208.1-4; ET. "On Our Lord and Jacob," *TV* 4.4(1993), 51.1-4.

In the *Homily on Creation* Mar Jacob says that the Father had a pre-knowledge that He would send His Only Son for the salvation of the creation.[101] But the Father willed to send His husbandmen or 'types' before the Son to prepare the way of the Son (Mt 21: 33-39); however, Christ is hidden in them. In the opening part of *A Homily on Samson* Mar Jacob found that all just men were like the beads of a chain, which connects each other. He writes that Noah, Seth, Abraham, Isaac, Jacob, Joseph, Moses, Aaron, Joshua, Gideon, Jephthah, Samson, etc., bore images of the Son.[102]

In one way or the other all of them followed the path of the Son of God at their times.[103] Through the allegories and 'types' they represented the Bridegroom; however, they were veiled. Jacob has his own reasons why they are veiled.[104] Noah and Abraham depicted the Son, for they were righteous. Isaac prefigured Him through the journey to the place of sacrifice carrying the firewood, which represents Son of God's journey to Golgotha. Jacob, the earthly bridegroom, and Christ, the heavenly Bridegroom, snatched their brides from the nations and saved them.[105] Joseph remained pure in the foreign land matches with the Son of God's pure Image. Moses saw the Bridegroom within His Father at Sinai. Aaron was the earthly representative of His priesthood and through his sacrifices announced the sacrifice of the Son of God for the salvation of humankind. Joshua carried His name before the arrival of the heavenly Bridegroom and did miracles as He did later. Both Gideon and Jesus were born after angelic visions and both were conquerors. Jephthah through his offering of his daughter had fore-shadowed the slaughter of the heavenly Bridegroom. Through these comparisons Mar Jacob wanted to say that they are the archetypes of Christ. Through these comparisons or finding the prototypes of Christ in the ancient just men Mar Jacob wants to proclaim that, all the prophesies of the Old Testament prophecies are fulfilled in the New Testament or all Old Testament figures are the shadow of Jesus Christ.[106]

On Moses Mar Jacob says: "At every stage and milestone that Moses passed through, his entire journey he depicted an image of God's Son."[107]

---

[101] Alwan, *QHC* I, 9.149-150.

[102] Bedjan, *HS* V, 331.1-332.9. ET. "A Homily on Samson," *TV* 11(1992), 51.1-52.24.

[103] Bedjan, *HS* V, 333.3; ET. "A Homily on Samson," *TV* 11(1992), 53.39.

[104] Supra 4.3.1.

[105] Church from the nations is a favorite theme for Mar Jacob. But Mar Ephreme seems to be introduced in the Syriac Theology.

[106] Bedjan, *HS* III, 287.11-16; ET. Brock, "On the Veil of Moses," in *Studies in Syriac Spirituality*, 76.79-84.

[107] Bedjan, *HS* III, 295.1-2 ET. Brock, "On the Veil of Moses," in *Studies in Syriac Spirituality*, 81.237-238.

Many other Fathers of the Church have the same opinion.[108] Through these interpretations Mar Jacob affirms the importance of Old Testament, because all just men in the Old Testament represent the Bridegroom.

4.3.3. Bridegroom: The fulfillment of Prophecy

This section is closely related to the former ones. But this part analyzes how Mar Jacob saw the theme, "in Christ the Bridegroom, all the prophecies were fulfilled."[109] Mar Jacob believed that Christ is the fulfillment of the prophecy (Mt 1:22). In fact the basis of the typological interpretation itself is the Old Testament prophetical pre-figuration of Christ. He finds the parallels of Jesus' birth in Old Testament: in the birth of Adam who was born without a human father or mother; lamb from the tree (Gen 22:13);[110] River from the rock (Ex 17:5-7);[111] sprouted staff (Num 17:8);[112] Isaiah's Prophecy of virgin birth (Isa 7:14; Mt 1:23);[113] Jacob's blessing of Judah that "the scepter shall not depart from Judah" (Gen 49:10);[114] the prophecy of Isaiah regarding the governance (Isa 9:6),[115] etc. Stone hewed without hand (Dan 2:34);[116] the new pitcher of Elisha (2Kings 2:20);[117] the salt that purified the fountain (2Kings 2:21);[118] shining star of Jacob (Gen 24:17);[119] shoot of Jesse (Isa 11:1).[120] These are some of his prophetical references that prove the virgin birth of the Son of God, the heavenly Bridegroom.

Mar Jacob teaches that the prophets were the mouth of God and through them He pronounced His commandments. And everything that a prophet

---

[108] Hypolytus of Rome said: "The bridegroom's fragrance delighted all the Just of the Old Testament who longed for Him: Noah, Abraham, Jacob, Tamar, Joseph, Moses, Aaron, Phinehas, Joshua, David, Solomon, Daniel, and the three young men of Babylon" (Hypolytus, *Cant.*, 2.5.8). Origen says: "The Law and prophets present their revelations of the Bridegroom but the bride longs for the direct words of his real presence." (Origen *Cant.* 1; cited in Desimone, *Bride and Bridegroom,* 44).

[109] Bedjan, *SMS*, 794.18-19; ET. *FH* III, 115.91-92.

[110] Bedjan, *SMS,* 750.14; ET. *FH* I, 71.643.

[111] Bedjan, *SMS,* 750.15; ET. *FH* I, 71.644.

[112] Bedjan, *SMS,* 750.16; ET. *FH* I, 71.645.

[113] Bedjan, *SMS,* 751.2; ET. *FH* I, 71.653-654.

[114] Bedjan, *SMS,* 754.2-3; ET. *FH* I, 74.715-716.

[115] Bedjan, *SMS,* 754.9; ET. *FH* I, 74.722.

[116] Bedjan, *SMS,* 794.20; ET. *FH* III, 115.93.

[117] Bedjan, *SMS,* 795.1; ET. *FH* III, 115.95.

[118] Bedjan, *SMS,* 795.3; ET. *FH* III, 115.97.

[119] Bedjan, *SMS,* 795.5; ET. *FH* III, 115.99.

[120] Bedjan, *SMS,* 796.2; ET. *FH* III, 116.115.

prophesied was with the knowledge of the Son of God and the prophecy bore the Son on her face.[121]

> It was He who spoke through Moses' mouth when He spoke,
> for He is the Word who provides every word of prophecy;
> without Him there is no word, no revelation
> in prophets, for He is the treasure store of prophecy.[122]

Thus, Mar Jacob underlines the divine origin of the prophecy. Moreover, he observes that all the prophets are divine counselors and prophesies are beautiful lessons. From this understanding Mar Jacob says: "The hidden Father betrothed a bride to his Only Begotten and instructed her through prophecy in a symbolic way."[123] Therefore, after the betrothal at the creation (Mt 13:35),[124] through the prophecies, the Father instructed the bride how to behave and the nature of her Bridegroom.

In his homily *On Creation* Mar Jacob elaborates the reason for the descent of God for the second time.[125] And this descent for the second time was prefigured through various prophecies. He explains a 'type' of Christ's restoration of the world can be seen through the second tablets of Moses at Sinai. The first tablets (Ex 32:15) represent the first descent of God to make Adam and the second tablets (Ex 24:28-29) represent the descent of the second time, i.e., Incarnation of Christ.[126] Again, in the same homily Mar Jacob finds the 'type' of Christ in the broken pot of Jeremiah. Through the first pot God typified the corrupted Adam and second one represented Christ (Jer 18:4).[127] Through the Incarnation or God's descent of the second time the prophecy of David was fulfilled (Ps 22). Through the arrival of the Son the following prophecies were fulfilled. Thou hang him on the tree (Deut 21:22); they will pierce my hands

---

[121] Bedjan, *HS* III, 298.5-15; ET. Brock, "On the Veil of Moses," in *Studies in Syriac Spirituality*, 83.305-314.; cf. Bedjan, *SMS,* 799.9-800.17; ET. *FH* III, 120.183-121.214.

[122] Bedjan, *HS* III, 298.7-11; ET. Brock, "On the Veil of Moses," in *Studies in Syriac Spirituality,* 83.307-311.

[123] Bedjan, *HS* III, 298.7-11; ET. Brock, "On the Veil of Moses," in *Studies in Syriac Spirituality,* 83.307-311.

[124] Alwan, *QHC* I, 4.57 following says the reason for the descent of God for the second time. For the first God descended to create Adam from the dust. But He knew that Adam will be transgressed and eternally perished if He does not make him in His Image. If He make him in His Image God can save him from perdition through the descent of a second time. Mar Jacob elaborates this episode in a beautiful manner and said the reason of creation of man in His Image is out of His love for the mankind. Thus here, Mar Jacob's hypothesis is seems that God confirmed the betrothal of His Son with the bride [Church] even before the creation of mankind.

[125] Cf. Bedjan, *SMS*, 775.13-14; ET. *FH* II, 96. 13-14.

[126] Alwan, *QHC* I, 7.105-9.140.

[127] Alwan, *QHC* I, 10.167-171.

and feet (Ps 22:17); they will give me vinegar and gall to drink (Ps 69:21); they will divide my garments (Ps 22:19); they will lead me like lamb for slaughter (Isa 53:7); they will make wound on my hands (Zach 12:6), etc.[128]

Mar Jacob finds that after the arrival of the Bridegroom there is no place for prophecy; therefore, it ended with the Incarnation of the Son of God. He said:

> The resonance of the prophets and that of the heralds became silent because the King has come and He caused the voices that were premature to come to an end.
> The Bridegroom himself entered and received the bride, the daughter of Light, and prophecy will not resound again concerning the good tidings.[129]
> Till He came the horns of prophecy called out,
> but once He has come, behold, silence is extended over the heralds.[130]

Mar Jacob confirms the arrival of the Messiah in Jesus Christ through these assertions. He defended Jesus and condemned Jews for their further expectation of the future Messiah after the arrival of the Expected One and their rejection of the divinity of Jesus as the Son of God. He said: "O Jew, whom are you looking for to come to the earth? For, none other will come again because there is none; keep yourself silent."[131] Thus through these arguments Mar Jacob confirms that Jesus is the Son of God, the expected Messiah and the Bridegroom of the Church. And through Him all prophesies were fulfilled.

4.3.4. Attested Bridegroom

The title 'attested bridegroom,' implies that the Bridegroom was confirmed or indicated by somebody that He is truly the heavenly Bridegroom. In the gospel texts there are seven attestations: the angelic attestation to Mary (Lk 1:35), the angelic attestation to Joseph (Mt 1:20), Elizabeth's attestation (Lk 1:43), the Divine Counterparts (Mt 3:16 17; 17:5; Mk 9:7; Lk 9:35), Simeon Lk 2: 29-32), John the Baptist (twice) (Mt 3:11; Mk 1:7; Lk 3:16; Jn 1:36), and Peter (Mt 16:16).

Before the elaboration of the theme it would be better to know the term which is used by Mar Jacob to express the idea. The term which Mar Jacob used to denote attestation is *audee* which is the *aphel* form of the root *yad* which means love, confess, acknowledge, profess, assert, belief, praise, etc. In the

---

[128] Bedjan, *HS* I, 499.15-500.19; ET. McCollum, "Homily on Peter," in *MHMJS*, Fasc. 22, 46.337-48.364. A long list of the prophecy and the depiction of its fulfillment can be seen in Jacob's Homily *On the Nativity of Our Lord.* See, (Bedjan, SMS 794.18-800.17; ET. *FH* III, 115-121).

[129] Bedjan, *SMS*, 799.3-6; ET. *FH* III, 119.177-180.

[130] Bedjan, *SMS*, 799.15-16; ET. *FH* III, 120.189-190.

[131] Bedjan, *SMS*, 798.18-19; ET. *FH* III, 119.171-172.

early Church those who confess the faith against persecution or against heresy was known as *maudyone*. Thus confessing the faith before others received an important place in the early Church. By the term attestation the Bridegroom was acknowledged or confessed before the bride who doubted in Him or who was unknown to her.

Since the birth of the Bridegroom was in a concealed[132] manner the attestation is necessary to confirm the identity of the Bridegroom. The Jews expected Messiah as a king who will be born in a palace but He was born in a manger like a pauper.[133] Therefore, the popular acceptance was absent in the birth of this heavenly Bridegroom. Thus, the Jews continuously questioned His divine origin. Moreover, the Bridegroom Himself did not wish to reveal his identity. The following attestations proclaim the legitimacy of the Son of God, the Bridegroom of the Church.

Virgin Mary had doubt in the annunciation of Angel Gabriel; and asked how a virgin will be conceived? She asked: "O fiery one, if you are not propounding any explanation in my ears the story that you are telling will not be accepted… I am not an infant like her (Eve) who became snare to her husband, for unless I have learned the truth, you shall not depart."[134] In reply angel said: "My Lord is true and I am announcing the truth to you … the Holy Spirit will come to you in a holy manner and the power of the Exalted One will abide upon you lovingly … In the furnace of your womb He will cast and prepare an image for Adam; and into it the God of all will lower Himself to come to birth."[135] This is the first attestation about the Bridegroom Christ. Second attestation comes from Elizabeth; with the fullness of Holy Spirit she said: "Who would grant to me that my Lord would come to me with His mother and the Son of the Mighty One would visit the son of the feeble one in his house."[136] Mar Jacob found this as a prophecy. The third attestation is again by the angel; but to Joseph. When Joseph doubted on the virgin and prepared to abandon her secretly the angel of Lord appeared and said: "O Son of David, do not doubt."[137] "Do not be alarmed or doubtfully afraid of her because the one who dwells in her is truly the Son of the Exalted One."[138] In the third attestation God convinced the suspecting Joseph and as a result, the one who tried to abandon the virgin mother received her with fear and honor.

---

[132] Bedjan, *SMS*, 723.18-724.4, 763.1-2; ET. *FH* I, 45.77-84, 82.899-900.

[133] Bedjan, *SMS*, 781.16-19; ET. *FH* II, 101.139-142.

[134] Bedjan, *SMS,* 730.12-13, 731.4-5; ET. *FH* I, 52.223-224, 235-236.

[135] Bedjan, *SMS,* 733.7-8, 15-16; ET. *FH* I, 54.281-282, 55.289-290.

[136] Bedjan, *SMS,* 744.8-9; ET. *FH* I, 64.511-512.

[137] Bedjan, *SMS,* 753.22; ET; *FH* I, 73.713.

[138] Bedjan, *SMS,* 754.10-11; ET. *FH* I, 74.723-724.

The fourth attestation is from the old prophet Simeon who was waiting for the arrival of the Messiah.[139] He said: "Release me henceforth, for I have seen You, my Lord… Behold, my eyes have seen Your great mercy as You promised. Set me free and let me be at rest on the earth until resurrection."[140] Fifthly, John the Baptist attested the bridegroom twice: once at Jordan and the other to his disciples. But in the baptism, John the betrother, the Law, and the other two persons of Trinity attested Him that He is the true Bridegroom of the Church.[141] Mar Jacob's opinion is that the primary aim for the manifestation of the Bridegroom is the salvation of His bride. He said,

> But our Lord disparage Himself so that He would be unrecognizable (Jn 1:1-7; Phil 2:6) to the world until John revealed Him together with the Father and the Spirit. And as he was concealed among the people and none knew who He was; yes he was announced everyday along the river Jordan, but the Hebrews were not convinced of Him; and the news about Him spread among the crowds but they did not know from where He was or who He was, then, Christ, the Bridegroom, came to the one who betroths, John, that He might also wash, like others in the waters that were prepared for the bride.[142]

Jacob says that, before the baptism of our Lord He veiled Himself from before the world. The same can be seen in the *Homily on the Baptism of Our Redeemer*, Mar Jacob says that, the baptism of the Bridegroom is a revelation of the Bridegroom to the bride. He was unknown to the Church until the time of baptism. Therefore, He came before the bride to reveal Himself to her. The voice of the Father and the Spirit in the form of dove gave testimony to the Bridegroom.[143]

Mar Jacob portrays the scenario of Christ's baptism dramatically. Before the arrival of the Bridegroom, the friend of the Bridegroom prepares the bride for the betrothal and teaches her the prophecy regarding the arrival of the Bridegroom.[144] This is a wonderful attestation from the part of the friend of the Bridegroom. When the Bridegroom approached John to be baptized by the hands of His friend, he said:

> I attested before her that I am not worthy, not even for your sandals;
> and how shall I venture to place my hands upon your head?

[139] Bedjan, *HS* V, 449.7-8; ET. *FH* V, 143.33-34.

[140] Bedjan, *HS* V, 451.15-20; ET. *FH* V, 145.83-86.

[141] Bedjan, *HS* I, 186.11-20; ET. *FH* VI, 180.391-181.400.

[142] Rilliet, *SHF*, 556.7-12; ET. *FH* VII, 193-194.14.

[143] Bedjan, *HS* I, 184.16-186.20; ET. *FH* VI, 179.335-181.400.

[144] Bedjan, *HS* I, 175.11-176.10; ET. *FH* VI, 170.161-171.180.

> In your name I have been baptizing her so that she shall be adorned by you;
> and, O Holy One, in whose name shall I baptize you? I do not know….[145]

For the second time John told his disciples: "This is the Lamb who presented Himself to become a sacrifice. This One carries away the sin of the world in His being sacrificed."[146] This attestation abased the darkness in the mind of the bride:

> O Church, from the beginning, I betrothed you to this Bridegroom;
> in hope of this One I have held you from the time I came.
> This is the Lamb who presented Himself to become a sacrifice.
> This One carries away the sin of the world in His being sacrificed.
> Behold, for a long time I had assure you about this One.
> In the name of this One I have been keeping you waiting for Him.
> For this One I guarded you with watchful care like a faithful servant.
> Thank Him on account of me for I had not left you behind to be captivated by me…
> The church learned from John as well as from David and she became assured that He is the Bridegroom to who she is betrothed.[147]

The final attestation comes from the other two Persons of the Holy Trinity: the heavenly Father and the Holy Spirit. They attested before the bride and before the friends of the Bridegroom at Jordan[148] and at the heights of Tabor.[149]

> He rent the sky and raised His voice forcefully:
> "behold, this is my Son; this truly my beloved."
> The Spirit floated from the Father in a great wonder and flew down,
> descended, abode upon and rested upon His Beloved….
> The Spirit became a finger of the Father and with it He showed
> "This is my Son, you should not be in doubt about His advent"…
> The Spirit descended to rest upon Him in a holy manner
> not because holiness was insufficient in Him, and it had to be made perfect in Him
> The Law too of its own accord summons two witnesses
> because someone alone would not be accepted, even when he is true.
> The Father and the Spirit together bore witness to the Only-Begotten
> so that legally they might give what is due to the same True One.
> The voice of the Father and the Holy Spirit descended simultaneously
> so that no one should reject their testimony when she appeared.[150]

---

[145] Bedjan, *HS* I, 182.1ff; ET. *FH* VI, 177.297ff.

[146] Bedjan, *HS* I, 175.15-16; ET. *FH* VI, 170.165-166.

[147] Bedjan, *HS* I, 175.13-176.8; ET. *FH* VI, 170.163-171.178.

[148] Bedjan, *HS* I, 184.16-185.20; ET. *FH* VI, 179.355-180-380.

[149] Bedjan, *HS* II, 372.9-373.12; ET. *FH* VIII, 228.529-229.552.

[150] Bedjan, *HS* I, 185.8-186.18; ET. *FH* VI, 179.367-181.396.

This section discussed the seven-fold attestation of the Bridegroom. Through these attestations Mar Jacob assures his Church that He is truly the Savior of the world in whom all prophecies are fulfilled.

4.3.5. Bridegroom: The Redeemer

The 'Redeemer Bridegroom' is another strong imagery of the heavenly Bridegroom in Mar Jacob's homilies. Through this imagery of the redeemer or liberator Christ, Mar Jacob delineates the redemption of the bride from the clutches of idolatry and sin. The Old Testament provides a redeemer image to Yahweh (Ex 6:6). The Old Testament describes the fall of Israel, punishment of Yahweh, repentance of Israel, penitence of Yahweh and redemption of the People from their enemies. Isaiah 54 depicts Yahwẹh as the creator, betrothed and the redeemer of Israel. Israel rejected her husband and committed adultery with other gods. Therefore, the prophet instructs them that your husband Yahweh is your only redeemer. Holy one of Israel your redeemer (Isa 54:5). The New Testament proclaims Jesus as the redeemer of the Church and this redeemer will come from the house of David (Isa 11:10; Mt 1:6; Act 13:22).[151]

This part discusses the term '*praq*'. In the *peal* form it means: to remove, to liberate (Ex 2:17), to release, to save (Jer 15:20; 30:10; Ps 106:10), to redeem (Ex 13:15; Num 18:16), etc. In *pael* form it is, to take away, to tear apart, to chatter, to borrow money to pay off, etc. In *aphel* form it is, to command to depart, to remove, to depart, etc., term *porooqoyo* means saving, salvation, loosening, deliverance, etc. *purqono* is salvation, price of redemption, etc. St. Luke says about the savior is born in the city of David (Lk 2:11); the residence of the city of Samaria says: Now we believe … this is indeed Christ, the Savior of the world (Jn 4:42); the savior who brought forgiveness for sin (Acts 5:31); promised Savior (Acts 13:23); Lord Jesus Christ the Savior (Phil 3:20; 1 Tim 1:1); abolisher of death 2 Tim 1:10), etc.

Mar Jacob considers redemption not as an event that starts with Christ's Incarnation. But the planning of redemption has begun prior to creation. Nonetheless, a visible train of the redemption starts from the birth and ends with the ascension of Christ but not in a single point of His life. Christ is the Redeemer of the lost sheep; He said I came in search of the lost sheep of Israel (Mt 10:6; 15:24). Therefore, Christ is pictured as the good shepherd who came forth to find out and redeem the lost sheep and the One who gave his life for the sheep. Christ Himself claims that He is the good shepherd who gives His life for the sheep (Jn 10: 11).[152] The lost sheep were under captivity. Mar Jacob has seen different captivities like ignorance of darkness, idolatry, etc., the advent of the Bridegroom itself is a part of God's plan of redemption.

[151] Bedjan, *SMS*, 781.16-17; ET. *FH* II, 101.139-140.

[152] Bedjan, *SMS*, 762.19-763.20; ET. *FH* I, 82.897-918.

Therefore, the Father sent his Only Begotten, the Bridegroom and the Light of the world, to the world to redeem the bride from eternal perdition.

> The King wished to send his Son to rehabilitate the earth,
> which the evil one had led away captive with rows of idols,
> that he had brought along and (so) subjugated it.
> His ambassadors resounded to inform the earth before His advent,
> so that the Son of the virgin should be announced by His messengers.
> The ambassadors made an assault on the persecutor but he was not terrified.
> They shot at him arrows but he did not move away from the captives.
> The Merciful One saw that the world was wearied and the evil one had got
> the upper hand,
> and He sent His Son to snatch the prey away from the captor.[153]

The above passage explains the reason for the Incarnation of the Son of God. The King (Father) wished to redeem His people by sending His Only Son. In order to prepare His way He sent prophets but the bride did not give heed to them. Finally, He sent His Only Begotten. The Father chose Mary as an entrance of His Son: "Mary became the head of the way; By which He went down to become dead Himself; While for us the font is the head; Of the way which raises me up to heaven."[154] When he came to the world He trod the idols under His foot: "Today God has descended and unmasked the idols. And He has removed from them the name of gods and has despised them."[155] Therefore, the Sorrowful woman (the Church) exulted and assumed consolation because her bridegroom came to gather her from among the idols for the marriage feast. The woman who was enslaved to idolatry and the maid-servant of the demons obtained freedom, because the Lord, the Mighty One, broke the fetters of her imprisonment and put to flight the demons.[156] Thus, the bride saw the light of freedom right from the advent of the Bridegroom.

Another staging post of the Bridegroom is His baptism; Mar Jacob teaches that through His baptism, the bridegroom, unleashed the sin of the world. John preached the baptism for the remission of sin (Mt 3:2). The redemption through the baptism is the fundamental faith of the Church. Mar Jacob illustrates the redemption through water:

> Go Royal Son, redeem the captives, for behold, they are looking for you.
> You need to take no armor for yourself from the water...
> Behold, the captivity passed beyond the inhabited land; why are you waiting?
> Go forward, turn back the captivity from the stumbling blocks through which

[153] Bedjan, *SMS,* 725.19-726.3; ET. *FH* I, 47.121-128.

[154] Epiphany Hymn: Anonymous Author, ET. Brock, *The Treasure House of Mysteries,* 254.

[155] Bedjan, *SMS*, 771.1-2; ET. *FH* I, 90.1069-170.

[156] Bedjan, *SMS*, 769.15-770.3; ET. *FH* I, 88.1033-1050.

it has gone out.
Behold, the captors have plundered the region, hasten your course (of action);
proceed forth, go, and make the captivity return because it had gone out
of your dominion.
There is no addition in baptism with regard to yourself,
and for what (purpose) then are you endeavoring to descend and wash?[157]

See another argument of Mar Jacob regarding the redemption through the baptism of the Bridegroom. The people were under the captivity of sin and redemption was possible only through the baptism of the Bridegroom. Unless He is baptized and defeat Satan, who imprisoned the bride, redemption would not possible. He formed this argument in the form of a conversation between Christ and John the Baptist. When John hesitated to baptize his Lord, the Bridegroom replied, He is not lacking anything but only through this baptism His aim of Incarnation would be possible. The reason for the baptism is the redemption of Adam and his sons from the slavery of Satan. He states:

Our Lord says: I am not lacking but in one thing,
the recovery of Adam who was lost from me is being sought by me.
Allow me to descend to seek Adam, the fair image,
and when I shall find him the whole of my desire shall be fulfilled...
The recovery of him, that alone is lacking with me:
to regain Adam who was willing to perish at the hands of the evil one.
In this recovery my desire will come to perfection,
because Adam is needed by to enter into his inheritance.[158]

Thus the main aim and function of the Son of God is to bring Adam back into his inheritance. And through the washing of the Bridegroom three things are fulfilled: the purification of the cosmic waters, installing the robe of glory, and handing over the priesthood to His apostles, which provided the right of forgiveness of sin.[159] This is another realm of the Bridegroom's baptism by which He strengthened His bride against the sin of her children. Aphrahat says about the handing over the priesthood through baptism.[160]

---

[157] Bedjan, *HS* I, 179.13-14, 180.4-9; ET. *FH* VI, 174.247-248, 259-175.264.

[158] Bedjan, *HS* I, 177.16-19; ET. *FH* VI, 172.207-210.

[159] It should be noted that the fathers had the awareness of Jesus Christ's bestowal of the right to the forgiveness of sin to His disciples at two other occasions (Mt 18:18; Jn 20:21).

[160] This is the reason that called Him to come for baptism; so that the dominion of the priests should be concluded in Him and it should proceed from Him. The father gave the deposit to Moses on the mountain (Ex 29:9; 40:15) and sent His Son who received it from John in the water. It was handed down by the tribe of Levi, (Num 16:10) and Lion's Whelp (Gen 49:9) of the house of Judah arose and carried it from him [John] (Parisot, *Demo* I, 964; McVey "Prose Homily on Our Lord," 53, 54; cf. E. J. Duncan, *Baptism in the Demonstrations of Aphraates,* 105; Murray, *Symbols of Church and Kingdom,* 178-181; Brock, "Baptismal Themes," 329).

The baptism of the Bridegroom redeemed the bride in a three-fold way. This enabled the Church to continue the redemption of her children through the rite of baptism. The baptismal rite of the West Syriac tradition, which is in use in the Malankara Orthodox Church says: "And give him Your divine breath which Your Only Begotten Son has breathed on His holy apostles. Remove all remnants of idolatry from his mind by preparing him for the reception of the Holy Spirit, so that he may be made worthy of the baptism of new birth."[161]

The third staging post is Golgotha. Usually, the marshals of the world use arms and ammunition of the world to redeem the detainees from captivity. But here, the Bridegroom, the redeemer, appeared in an unconventional manner. Usually, the redeemer should be a king or a warrior. Here the redeemer, though He is King, came down like a feeble and neglected one born in a manger and appeared in swaddling clothes.[162] This redeemer came to redeem the flock as a pauper and a persecuted One. He does not have war cloths, lance or sword, adorned horse, or two-horse chariot with Him to defeat His enemy and redeem His flock.[163] Unlike other redeemers, this Bridegroom, the redeemer, sacrificed His body to redeem His bride.[164] In the *Homily on Transfiguration* Mar Jacob finds a pre-planning of this sacrifice. He said, in the heights of the mount (exalted speech) the story of the crucifixion was discussed at length before the disciples. The prophets praised the Son and marveled at His humility and they prostrated before Him. They said to Him that:

> Death is proper for you, for you employ it for redemption,
> and your slaughter is desirable because the sin of Adam is slaughtered in it.
> The road of suffering is right for you to walk on (it),
> so that you may take up all the passion of Adam when you suffer.[165]

With the suffering He betrothed the Church and He redeemed her with the sword.[166] Unlike other redeemers this redeemer carried valiantly the vast iniquity of all nations in His Passion on one of His sides:

> The Resurrection of our Lord is glorious, both magnificent and full of wonder,
> because He trod upon death as upon sleep and rose up victorious.
> He carried the iniquity of the world and slept like Ezekiel;
> He died to sin and rose up from the tomb without corruption. All debts of
> all peoples everywhere,
> the Mighty One carried and remained on the Cross but He did not become weak.

[161] *Koodashakramangal*, 17, 19.

[162] Bedjan, *SMS*, 758.18-759.16; ET. *FH* I, 78.815-834.

[163] Bedjan, *SMS*, 763.13-17; ET. *FH* I, 82.911-914.

[164] Bedjan, *HS*, 175.11, 16; ET. *FH* VI, 170.165-166.

[165] Bedjan, *HS* II. 365.17-366.2; ET. *FH* VIII, 222.389-392.

[166] Bedjan, *SMS*, 822.12; ET. *FH* XVI, 344.289.

The whole iniquity of the whole world in every place,
He carried in His death and was not corrupted when He rose up.
The sins of the peoples took flesh in Him and He immolated them.
Iniquity died in Him and he rose up with power but iniquity did not rise up.
He had carried the burden of debts and became wearied as Ezekiel.
Then He had been sealed up for three days as He carried them.
The Mighty One carried the iniquity of the earth which was greater than mountains,
and the sufferings dragged Him along but He did not lay it aside until He had brought it to an end.
The Father ordained for Him three days to remain in *Sheol*
so that in their number the iniquity of the world should be consumed.
The Omniscient One weighed the sins of the world and the death of His Son;
and set a limit that by how much duration they would be destroyed.
For all generations, the redeemer died for three days;
and the iniquity of all He carried off by His death and set them free.[167]

Throughout the above passage Mar Jacob repeatedly mentions the Bridegroom's act of taking away the sins of the world. He took away the sins of the people by His suffering, crucifixion, and the descent into the *Sheol*. Through this act the Son of God removed the sins of the world and redeemed it from the bondage of Satan. The liturgical texts frequently remind this fact:

… the Church, the betrothed of Christ,
Whom he redeemed from the curse with his blood[168]
O Church, betrothed of Christ who redeemed you with his blood from error
and gave you as a living food his body
which evil men sacrificed on Golgotha.
In your hands he made you hold the cup of salvation;
the precious blood that flowed from his side at the blow of the lance.
Listen and attend to the voice of your Redeemer with cries full of thanks praise to you.[169]

This section discussed the bridegroom's three-fold way of redemption activities: the advent, the baptism and the suffering and death. Through these activities the Bridegroom redeemed the bride from sin and death and made her as the bride of the eternal Bridegroom

4.3.6. Bridegroom: The Sanctifier

Since the bride could not be one with the Bridegroom the pure One without sanctification, before the betrothal, she has to be redeemed and sanctified.

[167] Bedjan, *HS* II, 628.21-629.17; ET. *FH* XIV, 311.100-312.118.

[168] *Mosul Penkitho* II, 50.

[169] *Chaldean Breviary* III, 431.

Therefore, the sanctification of the bride, who was in the filth of sinfulness, was one of the missions of the heavenly Bridegroom. St Paul says: "Husbands, love your wives, just as Christ loved the Church and gave himself up for her, in order to make her holy by cleansing her with the washing of water by the word, so as to present the church to himself in splendor, without a spot or wrinkle or anything of the kind—yes, so that she may be holy and without blemish" (Eph 5:25-27). Sanctification through Christ is an important theme of Paul (1Cor 1:2, 30; 6:11; 1Thes 5:23). Husband can be sanctified through the faith of the wife or sanctification of a wife through the faith of her husband (1Cor 7:14). The author of Hebrews says: "For if the blood of goats and bulls, with the sprinkling of ashes of a heifer, sanctifies those who have been defiled so that their flesh is purified, how much more will the blood of Christ, who through the eternal Spirit offered himself without blemish to God, purify our conscience from dead works to worship the living God!" (Heb 9:13-14).

Word Study: The term which is used for sanctify is the root *qdš* which means pure, holy, a holy one etc. Adverb is *qadeešoit* which means 'with holy.' A derivative *qadeešooto* used both as adjective and adverb which means sanctity, holiness (Jer 2:3) and sanctification or consecration (Gen 2:3; Ex 29:13). Another meaning which is relevant to the present theme is 'to join in marriage.'[170] In the early Church martyrs and other holy men and women are known by *qadeeše* or *qadeešto*. This term is also used to differentiate between married saints and unmarried saints.[171] The most important meaning is related to the sacrament of the Church. The sacraments are known in the Syriac tradition either *rozo* means 'mystery' which is equal to the Greek *mysterion* (μυστριον) or in Syriac *qoodošo*, as a verb which means sanctification or consecration of something and as a noun, a sacrament. Eucharist and other sacraments are known as sacraments of the Church.[172]

Jesus "the sanctifier of the world" is a prominent and cardinal faith of the Church.[173] Mar Jacob proclaims this aspect in his homilies. According to him, one of the main reasons for the malignancy or corruption of the bride is idolatry. And, in the Old Testament, idolatry is symbolically interpreted as adultery. Through the fumes of the sacrifice before the idols the body of the bride was blackened. Without sanctification she cannot approach Him because He is holy. When Mar Jacob discusses about the baptism of Jesus He uses

[170] Sokoloff, *Syriac Lexicon,* 1320; Smith, *Syriac Dictionary,* 490.

[171] Abou Zayd, *Ihidayutha,* 120; cf. Brock, *The Luminous Eye,* 136; cf. Baker, "Syriac and the Origin of Monasticism," 348.

[172] Sokoloff, *Syriac Lexicon,* 1325.

[173] One of the prayers of the West Syriac Church calls Jesus: "O Lord, the One who has arrived for baptism for the absolution of our sins and the One who absolves all; and the One who came to the baptism for our sanctification and sanctifies all…" (*Promiyon* I, 187).

this aspect very often in his homilies.[174] For the marriage union requires the purification of the bride;[175] because God says; "Be holy, for I am holy" (Lev 11:44; 1Pet 1:16). The expedient the Bridegroom has taken for the purification of the bride is baptism. In Mar Jacob's opinion when the Bridegroom intended to wash his bride he purified the source of water itself, because it was poisoned by the sin of Adam.[176] As the next measure He betrothed her by His own baptism: "The Bridegroom alighted from His Father's house to prepare the wedding feast for the Bride. In the womb of the font did He crown her and make her resplendent and pure."[177] In yet another occasion he says:

> He sent her down first to the tested waters as He betrothed her,
> in order to purge away fornication from her by sanctification.
> That smell of the holocausts sacrificed was concentrated in her,
> but He caused to pass unto her the wholesome waters to make her body fragrant.
> She was made corrupt by the foulness of the oblations.
> He besprinkled sanctity upon her so that she might be cleansed by it from
> defilement.[178]

Another recourse, in his opinion, to clean His bride permanently, he removed the temples of idols, which is the center of idolatry, from the nations and planted churches:

> The diligent Son of God uprooted and cast down the temples of the demons,
> and lo, He planted churches at the ends of the world.
> He uprooted the thorny tangle of idolatry from every quarter,
> and planted cedars to give shade to the world.
> He built up the creation with gold and precious stones,
> He made the world into a king's place full of lovely things,
> and set cross therein like a pearl column[179]
> He burned incense to sweeten the earth with a sweet fragrance,
> from a root of that Virgin Soil gave the world.
> The smoke of the high places, which had smothered all creation with its
> stench He passed from the world.
> The air that was troubled by the fumes of sacrificial victims,

[174] Bedjan, *HS* II, 366.19-20; ET. *FH* VIII, 223.409-410.

[175] *Koodashkramangal*, 67.

[176] Supra 3.7.3.1.

[177] Epiphany Hymn: Anonymous Author, ET. Brock, *The Treasure House of Mysteries,* 254-255.

[178] Bedjan, *HS* I, 168.2-7; ET. *FH* VI, 162.9-163.14.

[179] Homily *On Serpent of Brass* tells cross as the symbol of salvation. Those who look upon it will be rescued from the afflictions like those who were rescued who looked upon the serpent that erected in the wilderness (Bedjan, *HS* I, 55.9-57.21; ET. "On the Serpent of Brass," *TV* 6(1990), 46.131-48.186).

> which ascended through it to polluted demons, is become clear and pure and sweet.
> The head of the Son of God was lifted up on Golgotha
> and all corrupted world saw it and was restored.[180]

The Fathers in several occasions used the allegorical interpretation of Isaiah 5:2ff, which tells the story of the farmer who sow good vine but it produced bad vine.[181] This is an allegory which the prophet used to tell about the infidelity of Israel. The same is used here in an opposite way that by removing the temples of gentiles the Lord planted the churches in the land of nations. Again, idolatry was compared to thorns in liturgical texts and the confessors and martyrs are compared to the oxen who removed idols and unfaithfulness from among the nations.[182]

The Scripture says sanctification may acquire through the faith of the spouse. St. Paul writes that the faith of a person could save the soul of another person (1Cor 7:14; 15:29). Mar Jacob sees a 'type' of Jesus who sanctified the Church in patriarch Jacob and said, if through Jacob his wife Rachel, who is from among the idols, can be sanctified how much more through the innocent blood of the Bridegroom Christ the nations could be sanctified?

> If then Rachel, for Jacob's sake, was sanctified,
> how much more would the Church of the nations be purified through
> the Lord of Jacob?
> A pagan's daughters were sanctified through their righteous husband
> showing how the Son sanctified the assemblies of the nations.[183]

The same question is asked when he compares Ruben's sanctification through the sacrifice of Moses. If the sacrifice of Moses can give life to sinful Ruben how much more benefited the faithful departed through Your living sacrifice?[184] In another prayer of the Church renders:

> Glory to the heavenly bridegroom who had chosen for himself the Church, daughter of the gentiles and purified her with his innocent blood from all defects and defilements and betrothed to Himself the earthly Church, becoming her bridegroom, and saved her from the servitude of impure demons and set her free from all her debts and sins.[185]

The purification from sins is an important aspect of Christian life and salvation. In conclusion, Mar Jacob following the tradition of the Church says

---

[180] Bedjan, *HS* III, 413.5-21; ET. "The Parable of the Leaven," *TV* 3(1989), 47.29-44.

[181] *Pampakuda Penkitho,* III, 362.

[182] *Pampakuda Penkitho,* III, 362.

[183] Bedjan, *HS* III, 209.13-18; ET. "On Our Lord and Jacob," *TV* 4.4(1993), 52.29-32.

[184] *Vishuddha Qurbanakramam*, 219.

[185] *Koodashkramangal*, 61, 63.

that the Bridegroom, before the betrothal, washed and purified His Church through baptism. Secondly, He effaced all the temples of the gentiles and erected Churches in the four quarters of the world.

4.3.7. Eternal Bridegroom

Another characteristic feature of the Bridegroom is that, He is eternal. In many of his homilies Mar Jacob portrays Christ the Bridegroom as eternal, without beginning and end, and the One Who has no death or the One Whom cannot be conquered by death. Not only He has no death but He killed the death by the killing of His body. In one of his homilies he describes Christ's admonition to Peter when he attempted to withdraw Him from the upcoming passion and death, Mar Jacob writes:

> Do you not think that, if I die, my death will be corresponding to my (status)?
> When I die, the bars of *Sheol* will not prevail me
> and death will not be able to look me in the face, when I exit;
> I will not see destruction there among the departed,
> and death will have no authority to shut the gate in my face.
> They would not say to me, "If you are dust, the you must return to it,"
> and the worm and maggot would not crush me as is their custom.
> I will not be conquered by destruction among the departed,
> and death would not bind me in its den like the rest.
> *Sheol* the devourer would not confine me, when I have gone down to it,
> and the worm would not stick its tooth in me for destruction.
> I will not perish from my friends, like an (ordinary) human being..."[186]

On his homily *On the Reposed* Mar Jacob explains that the bridegroom is the source of eternity. He elucidates it with the example of Judas Maccabeus and says:

> Judas (Maccabeus) offered the blood of animals to the Lord and reconciled Him to the dead, and made atonement for them that were defiled: the Church today with no perishable sacrifices makes atonement for the dead, but with the blood of the Immortal. And if that common sacrifice of Judas made atonement, how much more rather shall that great slaying of the Son of God cleanse all.[187]

In another homily Mar Jacob sees Jesus as the fullness of all. Through Him everything happens and begins and ends and his "crown is eternal and is not changed."[188] It invokes Jesus, Who is the sum of all consummations.

---

[186] Bedjan, *HS* I, 502.14-503.5; ET. McCollum, "Homily on Peter," in *MHMJS*, Fasc. 22, 52.400-56.448.

[187] Bedjan, *HS* 544.19-545.5; ET. "Memorial of the Departed and on the Eucharistic Loaf," 268; cf. Bedjan, *HS* I, 544.1-545.5; ET. "On the Reposed," *TV* 5(1990), 49.165-188.

[188] Bedjan, *HS* I, 179.15; ET. *FH* VI, 174.249.

> He beginneth and He completeth all created things,
> all things made partake of Him, and return unto Him.
> He is the cause of all ages, and in Him they have their being,
> all seasons revolve upon Him and are for Him.
> He contains the height and the depth and every region...
> He orders the succession and the passage of the ages even from eternity.[189]

Mar Jacob is indebted to his predecessors in this regard. The eternal Bridegroom has a connotation of an eschatological Bridegroom; who lives forever and related to the eternal life in the eternal kingdom. Some ascetical works of the early Church and the Gnostic teachings of the formative centuries of the Christian Church strongly recommend dualistic ideology; contradictive and strictly opposite of this world and the world to come; and this world and that world. They taught this world is temporal and passing but the world to come is eternal and real. They strongly opposed marriage in this world and said that, marriage in this world is temporal and corrupted so faithful must avoid the marriage and bridal chamber of this world and wait for a life with the eternal bridegroom in the pure and eternal bridal chamber. Some other Biblical passages have also influenced this thought: "It is these who have not defiled themselves with women, for they are virgins; these follow the Lamb wherever he goes" (Rev 14:4). And Paul said, "I feel a divine jealously for you, for I promised you in marriage to one husband, to present you as a chaste virgin to Christ" (2Cor 11:2).

In the third and fourth century Syriac writings, the theme of "to be virgin for the sake of the eternal bridegroom" is repeatedly preached. *Odes of Solomon, The Book of Steps, Acts of Judas Thomas, Gospel of Philip, Aphrahat, Ephrem*, etc., discuss this theme widely and persuaded their audience to take an oath of virginity.[190] In this understanding they urged for the renunciation of the earthly marriage and to be ready for the heavenly eternal marriage. They said the earthly marriage bed is defiled and corrupted.[191] The early Christian ascetical work, *Acts of Thomas,* distinguishes these temporal and eternal realities:

> That was the bridal chamber which was taken down, this is a bridal-chamber which remaineth forever. That was bed which was covered with goodly clothes that decay; this is a bed which is covered with love and faith and truth. Thou art a bridegroom who passeth away and is changed; Jesus is the true bridegroom who endureth forever, and never dieth, and is never subject to corruption. That

---

[189] Bedjan, *HS* II, 384.17-21; ET. "Homily on Ten Virgins," *TV* 4.1(1992), 48.189-199.

[190] *AAA,* 132; cf. Parisot, *Demo* VI.19, 309.21-312.5; ET. Valavanolickal, *Demonstrations* I, 59-160.

[191] *AAA,* 109-111.

> marriage gift was money and clothes, which decay and pass away; this marriage-gift is living words, which never pass away.[192]

They encouraged to abstain from worldly marriage and encouraged spiritual marriage with Christ. In the Syriac tradition the one who abandoned worldly marriage were called as *ihidoe* single or solitary and *b'tulto* virgin. Another term which is used to call those who avoided the marriage of the world and engaged in the spiritual life is *bar qyomo* son of covenant or *bart qyomo* daughter of covenant. They used to be virgins for the sake of eternal life with the eternal Bridegroom. Aphrahat uses the term *qyomo* (covenant) to denote relation between God and monks of his times through the marriage imagery and he called the monks as *atto d'qyomo* (wife of covenant).[193] Nedungatt says that Aphrahat uses the term *qyomo* 35 times in relation with God and His people: patriarchs, people of Israel. He uses the Greek loan word *diyateeqe* (διαθηκη, testament) with the same meaning but especially in relation with Abrahamite and Mosaic covenants. He suggests that these words could be interchangeable.[194] Aphrahat uses this term two times with the intension of Church as the *qyomo* of God.[195]

> Let us keep a watch for the time of the Glorious Bridegroom that we will enter with him into the bridal chamber (Mt 25:10). Let us make ready oil for our lamps to greet him in happiness (Mt 25:4-7). Let us prepare provisions for our dwelling for the way is narrow (Mt 7:14). Let us throw out from us all that is unclean, so that we can wear the clothing of the wedding feast (Mt 22:11-12).[196]

Against the ephemeral earthly marriage chamber, the heavenly bridal chamber is eternal, not subject to divorce, pure, radiant, and free from blemish. Mar Ephrem said:

> The virgin who rejected the marriage crown that fades now has the radiant marriage chamber that cherishes the children of light, shining out because she rejected the works of darkness. To her who was alone in a lonely house the wedding feast now grants tranquility: here angels rejoice, prophets delight, and apostles add splendor.[197]

Thus, through these exhortations they used to teach their audience that marriage in this world is passing and bridegroom of this world will pass away,

---

[192] *AAA,* 132.

[193] Parisot, *Demo* XIV.19. 617.25; ET. Valavanolickal, *Aphrahat* II, 68.

[194] Nedungatt, "The Covenanters of the Early Syriac Speaking Church," 195.

[195] Parisot, *Demo* VII.20. 345.6-26; ET. Valavanolickal, *Aphrahat* I, 175-176.

[196] Parisot, *Demo* VI.1, 240.6-12; ET. Valavanolickal, *Aphrahat* I, 122-123.

[197] *HPar* VII.15; ET. Brock, *Hymn on Paradise*, 124.

but on the other hand, the marriage with Jesus Christ, the eternal Bridegroom, is everlasting.

Thus above the section affirms that the Bridegroom of the Church is eternal and controller of all. There was a strong influence of Gnosticism in the early Church, which taught that the bridal chamber of this world is passing, therefore one should wait for the eternal Bridegroom and bridal chamber. But more than that they believed in the imminent parousia and waited for the heavenly Bridegroom by abstaining from the earthly marriage, and bridal chamber.

4.3.8. Radiant Bridegroom

The Biblical imagery of God as Light is another mark of dualistic influence of the early Church in the making of theological interpretation. Ancient West Asia and Hellenistic neighborhood of the formative period of Christianity were under the strong influence of various philosophies. It is obvious that the influence of these philosophical ideologies were evident in the theological formation of the early Church.[198] Dualism is one of such ideologies; the basic principle of this thinking is that the world is an arena and in it two opposite forces are fighting each other. Zoroastrian theology teaches this as the fight between good and evil.[199] From this background Christian and other teachings used to explain their theologies or ideologies in a contrasting methodology such as good and evil, day and night, light and darkness, body and soul, etc. Here, the Christian teachers found light as a representative of God and darkness as evil.

The Bible has enormous citations of Jesus as the light of the world.[200] Jesus is "the dawn from on high" that will "give light to those who sin in darkness and in the shadow of death" (Lk 1:79; Isa 9:1). He is a light for revelation to the Gentiles and for glory to your people Israel (Lk 2:32). Jesus said: "I am the light of the world. Whoever follows me will never walk in darkness but will have the light of life" (Jn 8:12); "He is light in Him there is no darkness" (1Jn 1:5), etc.

Mar Jacob and other Syriac fathers also identified Jesus with the Light. The nature of God is light. Moses was illumined by the light God because He is the light of whole world (Jn 1:9).[201] Mar Jacob calls Jesus as: Flash

---

[198] Micinery, "Dualism," 915.

[199] Gnoli, "Zoroastrianism," 582.

[200] Lewis, "Light and Darkness," 662-664.

[201] Bedjan, *HS* II, 356.6, 357.1; ET, *FH* VIII, 213.184, 200.

Light,[202] the Sun,[203] the Sun of Righteousness.[204] He: "A Flash Light has shone forth suddenly upon the whole world, and the earth has been enlightened but the whole idolatry has grown dark."[205] The essence of the Son is light.[206] He describes the greatness of the Sun who had identified the nature of man and betrothed the daughter of nations but never lost the essence of His divinity: "The Flash of Light descended but did not cut off His root from His emissary."[207]

On the other hand Satan and his works are characterized as darkness and the father of darkness. See the following example when Mar Jacob says about Judas, the betrayer of his Master: "The darkness came forward and kissed the light."[208] He (Judas) said "peace, master (Mt 26:49), but there was no peace in him, and Jesus was not his master, because he had not taught Judas to be deceitful. He was under another master now, the father of darkness, shadow of death.[209]

Mar Jacob describes the Bridegroom, the Light, as a transforming agent who transforms the darkness of sin and idolatry from the face of the world and returns the creation into its Creator. The salient feature of the light is to eradicate the darkness (Mt 4: 16; Jn 1:5; 8:12); darkness is the symbols of

---

[202] Bedjan, *SMS*, 778.9-10; ET. *FH* II, 98.67-68.

[203] Bedjan, *SMS*, 746.8; ET. *FH* I, 67.553.

[204] Bedjan, *HS* II, 356.14.

[205] Bedjan, *SMS*, 778.9-10; ET. *FH* II, 98.68.

[206] First of all, the light of the Son shone before the disciples,
and then the Father too showed the cloud of light.
If the cloud of light appeared first,
it might have been considered that the Son of God had shone forth from it.
And because of this the Father delayed the light of cloud which He brought,
so that it might be made clear that the Son has light from Himself (Bedjan, *HS* II, 373.17-374.2; ET. *FH* VIII, 229.557-562). The third century *Odes of Solomon says*: "He is my sun, and his rays have lifted me up and his light has dispelled all darkness from my face" (Charlesworth, *Odes of Solomon*, 15. 2-3; 11.13) cf. "The daughter of the dark betroths the Sun of righteousness; and He poured out on her face, His fair grace and she dressed in light," (Narsai, "Dedication of the Church," 2-4). God's essential nature is ineffable, and unapproachable fire like the sun and man is like straw before fire. Ephrem in a long description delineates the characters of Sun (Jesus) from above. By describing the experiences of Paul, Daniel, and Moses, Mar Ephrem visualizes the nature of radiance of the Son. By the excellence of the Son's light Paul lost his eye sight (McVey, "Homily on Our Lord," 301). Through the glory of the angel's view Daniel felt "melted and flowed away from every side" (Dan 10:8) (McVey, "Homily on Our Lord," 302). God prevented Moses from seeing the splendor of Him; because frail eyes would not have been able to endure the overwhelming flood of its brilliance" (McVey, "Homily on Our Lord," 304).

[207] Bedjan, *SMS*, 740.13; ET. *FH* I, 61.432.

[208] Bedjan *HS* II, 507.15.

[209] Bedjan, *HS* V, 552.11.

sin (Jn 3:19), ignorance (Rom 1:21; Eph 4:18), etc.[210] Therefore, through the arrival of the Sun all darkness of sin, ignorance, and idolatry were expunged. The Bridegroom came to the world to efface the darkness of idolatry and sin from the face of the world; and enlighten and purify it; and to betroth it. In another sense the aim of the betrothal is to enlighten the bride by the Bridegroom. The prophecy declares the advent of Jesus as the rising of Light in the land of darkness (Isa 9:2; Mt 4:16). When Jesus dawned in the darkness the world saw the light and was enlightened by the Light of Jesus the world became the land of living from the land of death.[211]

Sin darkens the soul[212] but Jesus, the spotless and pure Bridegroom, the Light, eradicates the sin of the world. When the Light of God rose in this world He banished the sin of darkness from the world: If the Sun has been here, we would not be in darkness.[213] Christ illuminates the world held in darkness of sin. The light of Jesus, the true Sun, rose there and enlightened them, and the dark shadow of death was dispelled.[214]

> The son of God dawned upon the world like the day,
> and the darkness vanished whereby all creation had been stifled.
> The great Sun of Righteousness showed Himself,
> and put to flight the gloomy shadows from every quarter.[215]
> Your lightning illumined the earth and it saw the glorious Light;
> The earth was troubled by darkness until you came…
> This is the One whose name, I had told you, is Day-Star,
> behold, he has shone forth and extremities were enlightened by his rays.[216]

Regarding the abolition of sin through the suffering of Jesus, one of the prayers in the West Syriac liturgy says:

> The Sun shone upon the land of darkness and enlightened the creation with its splendor. He sent forth His rays upon the universe and dispelled darkness from it. The Lord of the creatures trampled upon the earth and with the power of His footsteps, He removed thorns. The clouds of error that covered the earth fled and the earth rejoiced with the light of His knowledge.[217]

---

[210] Kollamparampil, *Salvation in Christ,* 331.

[211] Bedjan, LP; 33-34; ET. "Homily on the Blessed Virgin Mary," *TV* 5.1(1993), 8.

[212] Bedjan, *HS* I, 313.19; ET. "On the Publican and the Pharisee," *TV* 9(1991), 30.300; Bedjan, *HS* II, 412.3.-413.21; ET. Johnson, "The Sinful Woman: A *Memra* by Jacob of Serugh," *Sobornost*, 24.1(2002), 68-69.

[213] Bedjan, *HS* II, 547.11-18.

[214] Bedjan, *HS* III, 471.8-9.

[215] Bedjan, *HS* III, 321.1-4; ET. "Why Our Lord Abode upon the Earth for Thirty Years," *TV* 4(1990), 37.1-4.

[216] Bedjan, *HS* I, 188.17-189.1; ET. *FH* VI, 182.437-183.444.

[217] *Kashtanubhavazhcha Namaskaram,* 26.

In another place Mar Jacob described Jesus as the Sun and the Law as torch. Jesus is the launcher of new law and the old is no more needed. The Sun, Christ, is described as the fulfillment of the Law, the torch that means, the Son of God is established a new sacrifice through His own sacrifice and the sacrifice of the old Law is no more necessary.

> It is night for you and you do not perceive
> that the sun has risen from Golgotha, giving light to all creation.
> Up till the cross the entire world was as it were in night,
> though the law was like a torch in the dark,
> and the whole earth sought out the light of that land
> just as the eye searches out for a lamp in the dark.
> By day neither torch not lamp are needed
> by the eye, since there is the sun which illuminates all.
> The Hebrew resembles the man who closes his door,
> and with his lamp lit, he is not aware that the sun is up;
> he does not open his door to see creation filled with light
> and to be illumined by the sun along with many others, without any need for a lamp;
> the windows of his soul are closed to understanding
> and so he looks for a small lamp in the middle of the day.
> O Jew, the sun has risen out on the height,
> and the earth, sea, world and air filled with it;
> open your door and receive light from the day
> and put away your lamp which was only needed by night.
> Why are you become a laughing stock in the world that is filled with light,
> you alone being far from the daylight, despite its being with you?
> The time for lamps and torches is at an end,
> for the sun's rising has removed and put them all away.
> Moses' Lord has come into the world in bodily form,
> and, instead of Moses, it is he who informs the world.
> While it was night the prophets set up a torch on earth
> to show the way by which the world might reach daylight,
> but when the great sun of righteousness arrived
> he removed them from a service for which they were no longer fitted;
> he had established them, not for daytime, but for the night,
> and when night ended, he honored them in their proper places.
> For the daytime the sun is needed, with its strong light
> which drives darkness from every corner.
> Moses is now honored for his service,
> for the Son of God took the towel, ready to serve.
> O Hebrew, put away your lamp that provides your light,
> for the daylight is spread over the mountains at his great epiphany.[218]

[218] Bedjan, *HS* III, 303.2-304.15; ET. Brock, "On the Veil of Moses," in *Studies in Syriac Spirituality,* 86.411-87.446.

This is a wonderful exposition of Mar Jacob against the Jews who do not believe in Jesus Christ. He compared Jesus with the great Sun of Righteousness (Mal 4:2) and the Law as torch. The torch is needed only at the time of darkness or at night but in daytime the torch is an unnecessary thing. Christ is the Sun dawned, who abolished the darkness from the world and there is no need of Law, which is only a torch that helps men to find things in the darkness. Since the sun is up there is no need of torch now.

Light as the instructor: The term *nhar* has a meaning 'to instruct.' Therefore, the light can eliminate the sloth of the world and educate and open its eyes "Let your light rise upon my weakness, and I will be enlightened by you."[219] In the *Homily on Ten Virgin* Mar Jacob points out that slothfulness is the reason for the failure of the foolish virgins. Instead of diligence and wakefulness by keeping the oil they became sloth by forgetting to get the oil beforehand. He writes:

> They themselves disregarded the preparation of the lamps,
> wherefore they acquired the name of "foolish" in the scripture.
> Of their own choosing, their lamps grew dark,
> and for this reason the Bridegroom abhorred them, for it is light that He loveth.
> In their sloth, and the laxity of their way of life,
> they did not show diligence and take oil in their vessels.
> It is not that the Bridegroom hates men, that He rejected them,
> it was themselves who were not earnest for that banquet, which is full of light.
> Forgetfulness entered and took complete hold of their minds,
> and they attended not to the way of the Bridegroom while they were yet awake.
> It lay within their will, to take oil for their lamps,
> who is to be reproached that they took it not, but they themselves?[220]

The Light removes darkness of sins from the mind of men. Because, "The Word is light and if it rises up in the dark souls they will shine for it is like the day."[221] "If anyone becomes a son of the bridal chamber, he will receive the light."[222] In his homily *On the Ten Virgins* Mar Jacob says that the wise virgins are those who shine their light with oil. The character of the betrothed is to keep vigil like the one who lives in the light and do the works of the day (Rom 13:12). On the other hand the wicked are those who stay in the darkness:

> He called the company of the just "wise virgins"
> who in their bodies preserved a treasure that is full of light.

---

[219] *Jacob of Serugh's Homily on the Dormition,* 408-409.

[220] Bedjan, *HS* II, 381.4-14; ET, "Homily on the Ten Virgins," *TV* 4.1(1992), 43.115-45.126.

[221] Bedjan, *HS* II, 198.3-4; ET. "Jacob of Sarugh's Homily on Malkisedeq," 54.17-18.

[222] Isenberg, *Gospel of Philip* 85.5-10, 151.

But sinners and the workers of iniquity He called "foolish virgins."
For they preserved not the beauty of their persons by the way of life.[223]

The following lines from the same homily narrate that righteousness and good works represent light and wickedness is dark and night. The righteous will be received and the unrighteous will be thrown into the darkness.

His face shall shine like a lamp with fine oil,
but he that is bare of justice and righteousness…
Those who in their doings shone like the day
go forth to meet Him glittering, blazing with light, resplendent.
But those whose deeds were darkened by their sins
stand in stupefaction like shadows, without any light.
The just are like unto clouds and gross darkness.
These rise up like days, with stately light,
those who resemble nights, with veil darkness.
The wicked are ashamed of themselves for being darkened,
scourged of their conscience on account of their deeds.
They stand in terror at the laying-bare of their works,
for they see the Bridegroom wroth with them, and the wretches stagger.[224]

Light gives life and hope to the dead ones in *Sheol*, which is a dark place; the appearance of Christ scattered the somber shadows of death, enlightened the eyes of the dead. [225] Christ devastated the city of *Sheol*, shattering its bars and gates and overturning its high walls, one collapsing on top of the other; and then he took out all its treasures. The words of the prophet were fulfilled, "Fallen, fallen is Babel" (Isa 21: 6, 9; Rev 14: 8).[226] This section examined various natures of Light and how it works in human beings who are in darkness and how it transforms them by illuminating their hearts and how it gives hope to those who were in the dark place of *Sheol*.

---

[223] Bedjan, *HS* II, 387.8-11; ET. "Homily on Ten Virgins," *TV* 4.1(1992), 50.243-246.

[224] Bedjan, *HS* II, 390.1-10; ET. "Homily on Ten Virgins," *TV* 4.1(1992), 53.292-306. Cf.
The Firstborn wrapped himself in a body, as veil to hide his glory;
the immortal bride shine out in that robe.
Let the guests in their robes resemble him in his;
let your bodies, which are your clothing, shine out,
for they bound in fetters the man whose body was stained.
O whiten my stains at your banquet with your radiance (*CNis.* XLIII.21).

[225] Bedjan, *HS* III, 561.17-18.

[226] Bedjan, *HS* III, 595.3-9.

4.3.9. Royal Bridegroom

Mar Jacob, sometimes, used to call Christ a Royal Bridegroom. The prophets prophesied Davidic Kingship of the Bridegroom (Isa 9:7; 22:22).[227] Messiah was always portrayed with His royalty and nobility.[228] Also often Mar Jacob uses this term to distinguish the Bridegroom Messiah from His 'types'. Some occasions he calls them as the ambassadors of the Royal Bridegroom.[229] However, it could be deduced that Mar Jacob uses this phrase to highlight the heavenly authority of the Bridegroom over the earthly bride.

Creating a great setting at Jordan where the betrothal had taken place Mar Jacob says: "The Royal Son (*bar malkooto*) wished to betroth the afflicted one (the Church) and He sent her to go to the fountain to wash away her dust."[230] The Church became resplendent after the reception of baptism from John the Baptist. Mar Jacob writes: "He called the girl and she presented herself to be adorned; because, she had learned that it was the Royal Bridegroom (*ḥatno malko*) who would be coming to her."[231] "When the entire wedding feast looked for the Bridegroom, where He might be, (then) the Royal Son (*bar malko*) came out from among the crowds to come to the river."[232] "The Church, the bride of Light, marveled at the Royal Bridegroom (*ḥatno malko*), because, through His washing the height and the depth were reconciled."[233] These are the perfect examples of Mar Jacob's portrayal of the Bridegroom. He wanted to show the loftiness of the stature of the Bridegroom to the bride. While instructing her he said:

> The sandals of your betrothed are exalted above my head. As I extended my hands I am not adequate. The beauty of His stature is well above my head, for, He is so much higher than I, as the height is above the abyss, as the heaven above the earth, as the Word above the voice, as the Spirit above the prophet and as God above man.[234]

Not only the human beings but nature also recognizes the presence of the Royal Bridegroom. Mar Jacob delineates the changes that occurred in nature. When he arrived for the baptism the river kindled with fire and overflowed. "Waters saw you and they feared you as the Lord. The breath of your energy

---

227 *CHer.*XXV.2, 5, 169.

228 Bedjan, *SMS,* 759.19-20; 760.9-762.18; ET. *FH* I, 79.839-840, 849-81.896.

229 Bedjan, *HS* III, 212.12; ET. "On Our Lord and Jacob," *TV* 4.4(1993), 55.92.

230 Bedjan, *HS* I, 167.2-3; ET. *FH* VI, 163.3-4.

231 Bedjan, *HS* I, 169.1-2; ET. *FH* VI, 164.29-30.

232 Bedjan, *HS* I, 174.5-6; ET. *FH* VI, 169.135-136.

233 Bedjan, *HS* I, 187.1-2; ET. *FH* VI, 181.401-402.

234 Rilliet, *SHF*, 554.17-22; ET. *FH* VII, 193.11.

heated them while you were descending."[235] "The Royal Son[236] came out from the crowds to come to the river; and when He was far off, the baptismal water became fervent in response to Him; and the river overflowed and silently proclaimed Him."[237]

All these show the high profile and the humility of the Bridegroom. He is the King of kings, Lord of angels; heaven and earth obey His commandments. The heavenly and earthly will shiver upon hearing His name. Though He is a King who resides in the upper above, He came into our feebleness and identified with us and saved us by the death of His body.

4.3.10. The Bridegroom: Fire Clothed in a Body

Mar Jacob often compared the Divinity of Jesus Christ with Fire and Light.[238] When Mar Jacob says about the Incarnated Jesus Christ, he pictured Him as "Fire clothed in a human body." The prophecy called Him 'Burning Coal' (Isa 6:6). By the use of this qualification the fathers intended to indicate the nature of God and the inapproachability of human being to the Divine power.

Mar Jacob often calls Christ the Bridegroom as unapproachable "Coal of Fire."[239] (Sometimes he calls angels as pure fire).[240] Yet, because of the love for His creation He came down and took the form of His creation by hiding his inflammable nature under the clothing humanity. This explanation is vividly spoken in his homilies. The Lord came down to earth to restore his image that had been corrupted.[241] He exclaims! Cloth carries the burning coal without consuming in it.[242] He is clothed in flame,[243] girded in swaddling clothes, yet incomprehensible. Reclined on the throne and laid in the manger, yet uninvestigatable.[244] Even the heavenly hosts, watchers, seraphs, ranks, legions, and choirs tremble and fear to approach the Son of God because of His fiery nature.[245] In short the essential nature of the divinity is inapproachability. He says:

---

[235] Bedjan, *HS* I, 188.17-19; ET. *FH* VI, 182.439-440.

[236] Bedjan, *HS* I, 167.2; ET. *FH VI*, 162.3.

[237] Bedjan, *HS* I, 174.6-8; ET. *FH VI*, 169.36-39.

[238] Supra, 4.2.8.

[239] Bedjan, *SMS,* 806.10; ET. *FH* III, 126.334; Bedjan, *SMS*, 764.20; ET. *FH* I, 83.939.

[240] Bedjan, *SMS*, 765.1; ET. *FH* I, 83.941; Bedjan, *HS* V, 334.10; ET. "Homily on Samson," *TV* 11(1992), 54.67.

[241] Bedjan, *SMS*, 725.2; ET. *FH* I, 46.104.

[242] Bedjan, SMS, 760.15; ET. *FH* I, 80.855.

[243] Bedjan, *SMS,* 760.15; ET. *FH* I, 80.855; Bedjan, *HS* V, 448.11; ET. *FH* V, 141.15.

[244] Bedjan, *SMS,* 760.15; ET. *FH* I, 80.855-856. See more in Bedjan, *SMS*, 793.3ff.; ET. *FH* III, 113.55ff. The whole homily says about the glory of the Son of God.

[245] Bedjan, *HS* I, 189.16-17; ET. *FH* VI, 183.455-456.

Lord, I pray, I am not fit to approach you.
The husk is too feeble to set its hand upon the Flame (*goozlto*).
How can a straw lay hold of the Flame (*šalhebeeto*)?
Or a dry stick set its hand upon the Coal of Fire (*gmurto*)?
Fervent heat of your energy had kindled itself in the river and behold it has set it on fire (*mauqed*)
and how is it that you will not burn (*maḥrok*) up the hands of flesh?[246]

Fire used to purify things from impurity. Furnace is a crucible which re-form the things. Therefore, Christ the heavenly Bridegroom became a burning coal in the furnace of baptism and re-formed the distorted sinful figure of human being and made them as His betrothed. This is a repeatedly used theme in Mar Jacob.

O Living Fire (*nuro ḥaito*), who hast sent Thy Fire on all the world,
may the fire that purifies all sins be kindled also in me.
Refine me with Thy fire, the purger-away the iniquity, to cleanse me,
that I burn not in that fire of the End, for it terrifies me.
Thou camest to send fire on the world, and behold, it has come down
upon those of the sons of men that hearken to Thy word, for it too is fire.[247]

Christ's fire was kindled in the waves [of the Jordan] before He even went down,
and the river danced at the great heat of the flame…
The water did not get hot in order to sanctify Him.
Rather, it embraced Him in order that its own womb might be sanctified.[248]

The waters were inflamed by the lightning of flames
because the Living Fire had come for the baptism to be washed by them.
It sets the ages on fire and casts its flame into the fountain
and the glow from it kindled the river in holiness.[249]

In the liturgy of the Church the 'Coal of Fire' represents the Eucharist. In a song which is attributed to Mar Jacob sings: "the fiery ones who tremble even to look at Him; the earthly ones celebrate Him in their hands."[250] In short, the Syriac fathers see Jesus Christ as an unapproachable fire. The divinity and holiness make Him power of fire. But this fire came down to earth, dwelt in the womb of the virgin, lived among the sinners, suffered by the hands of the wicked, and died for the sake of the sinful Church; yet the womb was not

---

[246] Bedjan, *HS* I, 179.5-12; ET. *FH* VI, 174.239-244.

[247] Bedjan, *HS* III, 412.6-13; ET. "The Parable on the Leaven," *TV* 3(1989), 46.9-14. See Lk 12:49 and compare with Malachi 3:2.

[248] Bedjan, *HS* I, 174.11-16; ET. *FH* VI, 169.141-146.

[249] Bedjan, *HS* I, 183.17-20; ET. *FH* VI, 178.335-338.

[250] *Vishuddha Qurbanakramam,* 213.

consumed,[251] the sinners not harmed, the hands that lifted against Him did not burn[252] but seeing the nakedness of the Son of the Righteousness, the sun closed its eyes.[253]

4.3.11. Bridegroom Sacrificed Himself for His Bride

This part of the study elaborates the sacrificial aspect of the Bridegroom. Through the prophecies the prophets proclaimed the sacrifice of the Bridegroom in a distant time. Isaiah prophesied, "He was oppressed and he was afflicted, yet he did not open his mouth; like a lamb that is led to the slaughter, and like a sheep that before its shearers is silent" (Isa 53:7). David told: "Many bulls have compassed me: strong bulls of Bashan have beset me round. They gaped upon me with their mouths, as a ravening and a roaring lion… For dogs have compassed me: the assembly of the wicked has enclosed me: they pierced my hands and my feet. I may tell all my bones: they look and stare upon me. They part my garments among them, and cast lots upon my vesture" (Ps 22:12-18). These prophesies were fulfilled with the sacrifice of the Bridegroom on the top of Golgotha; and this sacrifice was living sacrifice for His bride.

"O' Bridegroom who became a prey to death, today, the Church who is saved through the cross rejoices in you."[254] This is a prayer of the West Syriac Church tradition; and more prayers bear this meaning could be seen at least once in a cycle of prayers. This is imparted from the rich tradition of the Church as a whole who are thankful to her Lord who died for her on the cross and by His death He killed the authority of death and gave life to her children. The Bridegroom offered His life for the salvation of His bride; how marvelous and wonderful is the divine love! The Bridegroom taught His disciples that: "No one has greater love than this, to lay down one's life for one's friends" (Jn 15:13).

While describes about the deep love of the Bridegroom Mar Jacob portrays that the priest, the Bridegroom, became a sacrifice on behalf of sinners, the bride.[255] This love cannot be interpreted by human understanding.[256] The

---

[251] Mar Jacob and other fathers of the Church see a type of this at the burning bush incident (Ex 3:2). Cf. *Promiyon* I, 34.

[252] *Kashtanubhavazhcha Namaskaram*, 41.

[253] Rilliet, *SHF* IV, 608.12-13; ET. *FH* XI, 276.45.

[254] *Promiyon* IV, 21.

[255] Bedjan, SMS, 725.10; ET. *FH* I, 46.112.

[256] Mar Narsai states:

> Love of the bridegroom cannot be explained by words;
> and the love of the bride cannot be written by the books.
> The love of the bridegroom towards the bride is his erection of the wood;
> and love of the bride urged her to seek after the crucified bridegroom,
> who is the bridegroom that for the sake of the bride endured the cross?

love expressed on the cross is unfathomable and beyond the imagination of ordinary human being. The one who hears the story will accept that this is the demonstration of the greatest love. It may be seen in several epics that people fought each other or enter into a contest to marry a woman and the champion gets the woman as his wife.[257] However, here, the Bridegroom became a victim and gave Himself to the hands of His crucifiers to kill Him. This is a victory; a victory over Satan and Death. If He is not killed He cannot overwhelm Satan and would not be able to free His bride from the bondage of Satan. Until His death Satan thought that He will not give Himself unto death because He has no death. In order to prevent Him from the death Satan made several plots,[258] but the Bridegroom overcame all. This is a unique marriage nobody will dare to replicate. Mar Jacob and other fathers of the Church extol the love of the Bridegroom and said:

> What bridegroom died for his bride apart from our Lord?
> What bride sought out a slain man to be her husband?[259]

Immortality or eternal life with the eternal Bridegroom is the greatest goal of a human soul. Through Incarnation and death the Bridegroom brought down His exalted self to that of human nature, which is mortal. When His

---

> If not Christ, whose great love cannot be explained? (Narsai, Dedication of the Church, 29-30).

[257] In Samson's episode he fought against the Philistines to get Delilah. In Indian tradition Ramayana says about Lord Ram's contest in getting Sita as his wife.

[258] Bedjan, *HS* I, 490.11-495.16; ET. McCollum, "Homily on Peter," in *MHMJS*, Fasc. 22, 22.159-34.260.

[259] Bedjan, *HS* III, 290.11-12; ET. Brock, "On the Veil of Moses," in *Studies in Syriac Spirituality*, 78.141-142.

> What bridegroom is there who has endured the cross for the bride
> apart from Christ whose great love is ineffable?
> What bride is there who has loved a bridegroom suspended on the wood
> apart from the Church, whose tale is exalted above telling?
> For his death did the Church love him and attach herself to him.
> The slain Bridegroom and the redeemed bride cleaved to one another
> and all generations and races take pleasure at their wedding feast. (Narsai, II, 158).
> What Bridegroom has ever died for a bride, apart from Christ?
> What bride has sought to belong to a slain man
> apart only from the Church who was betrothed to the Crucifier?
> Who has made his blood flow for his betrothed in scripture
> apart from the Only-Begotten from the Father?
> Who, at death, wrote and sealed the marriage document for the daughter of light?
> Where have you ever seen a marriage feast?
> Where the Bridegroom was made the food for the guests?
> Instead of a variety of tasty wines
> He mixed the cup from his side…? (*Mosul Penkitho* VII, 109).

human body tasted death the Immortal One killed the death which imprisoned humanity from the time of their leader of the clan and liberated them from *Sheol*.[260] When the Bridegroom apportioned His body and blood to the Church, the Children of the Church got the opportunity to be united to His divinity; and therefore, to be part of His immortality. All these happened because of self-abased Son and through His sacrifice on the cross. In the Syriac tradition the cross is pictured as the sign of victory as well as a bridge that connects earth and heaven. It is laid across upon the fiery sea. A person who dies from this world have to cross the fiery sea and for this journey the cross is a bridge that keep him from the flames of the death.

The funeral rite of the West Syriac Church used in the Malankara Orthodox Church describes: "My Lord, the Lord of the creation, I became in Your likeness. I may not become the food of fiery *Gehanno*... The armor of His cross that you have girded on will help you to pass over the place of danger."[261] Another hymn sings: "May the Cross of our Lord become a bridge (*gšro*) for you; that you may cross over the place of danger."[262]

> The Son's cross became a bridge
> to the place of life whereby the Peoples
> who have faith and do believe might cross over,
> since it was on our behalf that He tasted death.[263]

Today the Church praise and worship Christ the Bridegroom, who humbled Himself for her sake. He endured sufferings on the cross and killed the killer death in order to restore us into Paradise.[264] Thus, Mar Jacob being part of this great tradition and acclaims the glorious sacrifice of the Bridegroom for the redemption of His betrothed.

4.3.12. Bridegroom Removed the Lance by Receiving the Lance

The Bridegroom removed the revolving lance which protected the gates of Eden, is a well discussed theme in Syriac theology. All of the early Syriac writers understood the significance of this incident.[265] The basis of this profound theological argument lies in two biblical references: John 19:34 and Genesis 3:24. The story starts from the Garden of Eden at the creation of man.

---

[260] Bedjan, *HS* II, 626.2-627.7; ET. *FH* XIV, 309.39-310.64.

[261] *Savasamskarakramam*, 46. Mar Jacob compares the water and blood which flown from the side of Christ (Church and baptism) as a bridge (Bedjan, *HS* III, 299.11; ET. Brock, "On the Veil of Moses," in *Studies in Syriac Spirituality*, 84.332).

[262] *Savasamskarakaramam,* 101.

[263] Brock, "Syriac Poetry on Biblical Themes" 68.

[264] *Kashtanubhavazhcha Namaskaram*, 44.

[265] Murray, "The Lance which Re-opened Paradise: A Mysterious Reading in the Early Syriac Fathers", 224-234.

The second creation narrative tells that God created Adam and Eve (Gen 2:7, 21-22) and later He planted a garden at the east of Eden (Gen 2:8) and placed them in the garden to keep it (Gen 2:15). But they transgressed the Law of God by eating the forbidden fruit and God drove them out of the garden and placed a Cherubim at the eastern part of the garden with a flaming sword which turned every way thus preventing the way to the tree of life (Gen 3:24).

Mar Jacob writes: He made me (Adam) a guardian of paradise (Gen 2:15). But I failed to guard it and so I am despised, for I stole the very fruit which has now killed me.[266] God placed an angel with a revolving sword (*ruhmo*) at the gates of Eden to prevent man enter in it (Gen 3:24).[267] He again writes that though God expelled them out of the garden, He did not wish the creation in His own Image to be perished and therefore, He planned to send His Only Son to redeem them from the fall. He told His Son: "Go, descend, and accept the lance and the nails those are reserved for you, because that also is the very purpose of your way."[268] According to the command of the Father, the Son, the Bridegroom, came to the world for passion and death. He received the Cross

---

[266] Brock, "Jacob of Serugh A Poem on Soul," 42.*nun.* For because he ate of the Tree of Knowledge, he was kept back from the fruits of the Tree of Life, so that he should not eat from it and live forever. And by this we know that because if the transgression of the human being against the commandment at the misleading of the Evil One, and presumptuously taking on for himself the exalted position in order to become an equal with his Maker by means of the discernment of knowledge that he received, there came into being a fence between him and the Tree of Life, seeing that, because of the cunning of the Evil One, he had been withheld from its fruits. And the Tree was fenced in by the command of the Great One by the strong and revolving flame of sword. Further more in the case of that human being, because he had awareness and knowledge, he was capable of going to that tree, yet his feeble state was not able to cross over the fence. (Parisot, *Demo* XXII.3, 5.14-8.5; ET. Valavanolickal, *Demonstrations* II, 257. Valavanolickal has a different translation regarding the sword: "awesome sword and revolving flame").

[267] Mar Ephrem has another interesting interpretation on the expulsion of Adam from the Garden, he writes, "The Lord God drove them out, [Moses] said, from the garden of delight, and at the eastern side of the garden of delight [God] fenced it in with the sharp point of the sword and with a fiery sword circling round about (Gen 3:24)." Here, Mar Ephrem added one more thing other than from the Genesis account that God fenced Adam and Eve on the eastern side of the garden. He got this from the Hebrews; in LXX it said "opposite" of the garden. Ephrem says several reasons for preventing Adam from eating from the Tree of Life: may be because he, the servant, may not become equal to God, his Master. Or prevent Adam from the discernment of good and bad. Or more than that Adam had evil in his mind and therefore, he needs chastisement; or to show him the power and glory of the Tree. Or to initiate Adam to long for which he had lost. Another interesting interpretation regarding the verse: Perhaps he will put forth his hand to take the fruit from the tree of life, and eat and live forever, (Gen 3:22) not that God detested Adam but because of His mercy that after eating the fruit he may live forever and suffer forever. Otherwise he would be dead as God said to him, Unto dust you shall be returned (Gen3:19) and escape from the eternal sufferings (Mathews, *Arm Comm. on Gen.,* 36-37).

[268] Bedjan, *HS* II, 369.8-9; ET. *FH* VIII, 225.463-464.

and died for the sake of His bride. When the soldier pieced the right side of Jesus with his lance blood and water flowed from there (Jn 19:34). This was the fulfillment of prophecy (Ps 34:20; Zach 12:10). Mar Jacob comments on this:

> As the Bride of Light was entering, the Bridegroom was wounded
> those who struck him did not know who it was who was struck.
> He received (*qabel*) in his side the sword, and seized (*šqal*) it from the guard;
> He let him go off (*nepuq*), and opened (*ptaḥ*) up the door for all to enter.
> The Lord of the Garden was struck (*bl'*) with the sword as he opened it up
> it having been carefully guarded over since Adam.[269]

The Bridegroom who has no death, through His death and as He received lance on His side has removed the revolving sword[270] from the gate and therefore the bride received a free entrance to His bridal chamber (Garden).

> With the Cross opened (*ptaḥ*) the door of the garden, the beautiful bridal
> chamber (*gnoono p`ayo*);
> and He brought in and set in it the lovely bridegrooms who had been expelled.
> He received in His side the blade of the lance (*ḥarbo drumḥo*) of that guard;
> and dismissed it to set it aside so that it would (no longer) drive away those
> of the household of Adam.[271]

Now the Bridegroom invites the bride to enter into the bridal chamber of light. The Bridegroom bruised the head of the serpent (Gen 3:15) and removed the sword of Cherub and thus your way is free now. Mar Jacob and other Syriac writers vividly painted this incident and its aftermath in their writings.

> The serpent is slain, the accursed one is crushed
> broken is the sword of the guardian cherub (Gen 3:24).
> O daughter of Light, come and enter into paradise.[272]

> Our Lord was pleased to be likened to a gardener,
> for it is He who opened the gate of Paradise for people to enter in;
> it was He who broke the cherub's sword,

---

[269] Bedjan, *HS* II, 588.8-13; cf. Brock, "The Wedding Feast on Golgotha," 125.

[270] In another occasion Mar Jacob says that even from the birth of the Son of God the sword was removed from the gate of the Garden, "because the Tree of Life is not more to be guarded: for, behold its Fruit is put in the manger in order to be the nourishment for the human beings." (Rilliet, *SHF* I, 542.14; ET. *FH* IV, 133.14).

[271] Bedjan, *SMS*, 813.1-4; ET. *FH* XVI, 335.91-94.

[272] Brock, "Jacob of Serugh A Poem on Soul," 43. *Qoph.*

and thus the banished Adam entered into his inheritance.
Rightly did he resemble a gardener at His resurrection.[273]

Genesis 3:24 of Hebrew bible, Hebrew Targum and Peshitta use the term *harbo*, means 'sword,' but John 19:34, Aphrahat, Ephrem, and Jacob of Serugh use *rumho*, means 'lance,' but Peshitta uses *lookoyto,* means 'spear.' Commenting on this Mar Ephrem writes "By the side pierced by the 'lance' I have entered the garden barred by the 'lance.' Let us enter by the wounded side, since we were despoiled by the counsel of the rib drawn out."[274] Jacob of Serugh uses both the terms '*harbo'* (sword) and '*rumho*,' (lance) however, he uses the latter one frequently. "Lance of justice passed through the belly of him; who despised Him Who made the lance of paradise pass away."[275]

In the great tradition, he teaches that the lance which was placed at the gates of Eden preventing the entrance of Adam and his children into the Garden is lifted up by the lance which pierced the side of the Bridegroom and saved the bride and betrothed her.

4.3.13. Bridegroom Offered His Blood as Bride-Price

Bride-price was a custom practiced in the Semitic culture of the time (It is practiced among the Arabs even today). The *Ras Shamra* text describes: "and I will pay her bride-price to her father" (77:19).[276] *Nuzi* texts reveal a bride price

---

[273] Jacob of Serugh, Hymn on Resurrection, ET. Brock, *The Treasure House of Mysteries,* 264.15.

Blessed is the compassionate One who saw, next to Paradise,
the lance that barred the way
to the tree of Life. He came to take up.
The body that would be struck so that by the opening in His side
He might break through the way in to paradise (*HNat* VIII.4, 59, ET, McVey, Ephrem the Syrian, 119-120; Murray, "Lance Reopen," 225; Murray, *Symbols of Church,* 126).
The lance of Phinehas filled me with fear,
because of that (sword) he routed out the plague.
The lance guarded the Tree of Life
made me joyful also sorrowful; because it prevented Adam from the (Tree of) Life
and prevented plague from the People. Yet the lance wounded Jesus
I became sad by it. He was wounded; and I wept.
Water and blood went forth from Him,
it washed Adam and (received) life and returned to Paradise (*CNis.,* XXXIX.7, 24-25; cf. Murray, "The lance which Re-opened Paradise," 225).
Blessed is He who was pierced and
so removed the sword from the entry to Paradise (*HPar* 5; ET. Brock, *Hymns on Paradise,* 85).

[274] McCarthy, *Commentary on Diatessaron,* 322.

[275] *CJul*, III:14, 84; ET. McVey, *Ephrem the Syrian,* 247.

[276] *Ras Shamra Parallels*, 72.

terḫatu which the bridegroom gives to the bride's father. This gives a kind of authority over the bride. This price may be returned to the bridegroom if the wife died without having children.[277] At the same time, the Jewish tradition also hold the same custom. Several Old Testament references underline the payment of the bride-price in ancient Israel. The Deuteronomic Code says that a man can take a virgin by paying the bride-price: "He will verily take her to wife by paying the bride price" (Ex 22:15). The prophecy of Hosea says: "I acquired her for fifteen shekels of silver and a homer and a letch of barley" (Hos 3:2). Redemption of the first-borns of Israel can be seen in Numbers 3: 49-51. The redemption through the blood of the Only Begotten is described in several passages of the New Testament. St. Paul when he discusses about keeping the bodily purity, he says: "You are not your own? For you are bought with a price" (1Cor 7: 19-20). Apostle Peter says; "You are not redeemed with corruptible things but with the precious blood of Christ" (1Pet 1: 18-19). The author of the Book of Revelations tells of the uncountable members of the Church who have whitened their robe in the blood of the Lamb (Rev 7:14). All these add to the background of Jacob and other Christian Fathers' cognizance of redemption through the blood and blood as the bride-price in the salvation history of the Church.

Making use of the above social as well as scriptural traditions the Fathers introduced bride-price in the marriage imagery in tune with the scriptural and social traditions. Mar Jacob elucidates redemption of the bride through the bride-price. The Bridegroom paid a bride-price to the master of the bride, death, because she was under the slavery of death. Adam wrote a bond to Satan when he became a slave of sin. Through the death of Christ on Golgotha He had written-off the bond by paying His blood as a price to the captor. Mar Jacob calls it as an unusual betrothal: "Who from the beginning ever gave his blood as the bride price? Apart from the crucified one, who sealed the marriage with his wounds?"[278] Now she is free from the slavery of sin and death.

> On Your cross You put a seal on my dowry
> and by your sufferings You have freed me;
> A Bridal Chamber on high have You set up for me
> and invited me that I should be Yours.[279]

In another homily Mar Jacob writes:

> You poured for me Your precious blood and with it You bought me (*zbantone*), posses me since You have bought me (*zbantone*), and enable me to posses

[277] Marsman, *Women in Ugarit and Israel,* 89.

[278] Bedjan, *HS* III, 290.16-17; ET. Brock, "On the Veil of Moses," in *Studies in Syriac Spirituality*, 78.143-144.

[279] Anonymous Marriage Hymn, ET. Brock, *The Treasure House of Mysteries,* 280.3.

Your word that I may recite Your story.
I with price (*ṭimo*) (am bought) and You my Lord were freely sold,
what does the world have to give and then to buy You?
What would Your hidden Father have received for His Beloved,
if He had given You with a great price on account of us?
It is pleasing to Him that He gave You freely to mankind,
since if You had to be bought for a great price, no one would have bought You.
Who would have had something to give as Your price, Son of God,
or what was there to him who would buy You to be exchanged for it?[280]

Mar Jacob says that the Church of nations is redeemed by [His] killing and blood was the ransom money; and her beloved ones dwell under the wings of the cross of light. Thus, through the death on the cross He betrothed nations and paid a dowry by the blood flown from the wound on His right side. And through the betrothal the captured was liberated from the captivity of death and she became the bride of the eternal King and opened the way to the bridal chamber of the Bridegroom. This is wonderful and such a sacrifice of a Bridegroom was never seen; even from the beginning of the world.[281] "Never before has any man given to his betrothed his own body and blood."[282] Therefore, the Church praises Him for his generosity and says: "Have mercy on us O Christ our God, who endured passion and death for the sake of Adam, and removed condemnation from us."[283]

The homilies of Mar Jacob finds several 'types' in the Old Testament for Church's redemption by Christ. One of them is the patriarch Jacob's courageous act of redemption of his two wives from the land of idolatry. Mar Jacob compares Messiah's blood with that of the tears of Jacob which he poured at his symbolic betrothal of Rachel at the well:

Jacob gave Rachel tears when he espoused her,
and our Lord sprinkled the Church with His blood when He redeemed Her.
So these tears were a foreshadowing (*ṭelonoe*) of that Blood
for except through suffering, they spring not from pupils.
The righteous Jacob's weeping was therefore a shadow
of the great passion whereby the Church of the nations was redeemed.[284]

Had patriarch Jacob's kiss of Rachel at the well was a usual one out of lust, he would not have poured tears. It was out of love and since he poured

[280] Bedjan, *SMS*, 686.7-18; ET. Puthuparampil, "On Perpetual Virginity," in *Marilogical Thought of Mar Jacob of Serugh*, i.15-ii.24.

[281] Bedjan, *HS* III, 290.12-13; ET. Brock, "On the Veil of Moses," in *Studies in Syriac Spirituality*,78.141.

[282] *Chaldean Breviary* III, 397= *Hudra* III, 569.

[283] *Kashtanubhavazhcha Namaskaram*, 77.

[284] Bedjan, *HS* III, 212.13-18; ET. "On Our Lord and Jacob," *TV* 4.4(1993), 55.93-98.

tears it typified the suffering of the Only Begotten and because he was the 'type' of the Son. About the redeeming effects of the blood of the Son, Mar Jacob, in his *Homily on the Reposed,* argues that, if the animal sacrifice of Judah Maccabeus can bring atonement to the dead souls in the battle how much more life could be brought through the blood of the Only Begotten. [285]

It is evident that the Bridegroom redeemed His betrothed through His sacrifice. No other bridegroom in the world betrothed his bride with his own blood as a bride-price. Christ, the heavenly Bridegroom is the only exception in this regard. He redeemed the bride by paying His own blood as a price for Satan who enslaved her.

4.3.14. Bridegroom Descended into the *Sheol*

Since the concept of *Sheol* has been discussed already in the first chapter this part would not concentrate on that; but analyze the effect of Christ's descent into the *Sheol*. Descend to the nether world (*Sheol*) is not new to the Mesopotamian Church. In the Sumerian myth of Inanna,[286] describes Inanna's descend into the nether world. Though it speaks of a different story the pattern is same as that of Christ's descent into the *Sheol*. Like Christ she remained in the nether world for three days. As against Christ, who visited *Sheol* after His death on the cross, Inanna died at nether world. If Christ broke the bars of *Sheol* to enter and exit, Inanna enters with the permission of the gate keeper and returned to her land by the power of her father god.[287] The Gospel of Nicodemus[288] describes the descent of Jesus Christ into the *Sheol* and the deliverance of the departed from the time of Adam to the time of Jesus. The gospel very dramatically portrays the incident as a narration by Charinus and Lenthius, the sons of Peter, from chapters XIII to XXII.[289]

---

[285] Bedjan, *HS* I, 544.1-545.5; ET. "On the Reposed," *TV* 5(1990), 48.165, 49.188.

[286] Inanna is the Sumerian and Istar is the Akkadian name of the goddess of love, sex, and war. Nanaya was more or less only another hypostasis of Inanna and was worshipped in the temples of Inanna in Uruk in the Ur III period and in Babylon and Kiss in the Old Babylonian period. Heimpel, "A Catalog of Near Eastern Venus Deities," cited (Lapinkivi, Pirjo., "The Sumerian Sacred Marriage and Its Aftermath in Later Sources," 8).

[287] *Sacred Texts,* "Inanna's Descent to the Nether World," XX,

[288] *Gospel of Nicodemus*, Online text http://www.sacred-texts.com/bib/lbob/lbob10.htm, Retrieved on 19/11/ 2013.

[289] When we were placed with our fathers in the depth of hell, in the blackness of darkness, all on a sudden there appeared the color of the sun like gold, and a substantial purple-colored light enlightening the place (Isa 9:2). Presently upon this, Adam, the father of all mankind, with all the patriarchs and prophets, rejoiced and said: That light is the author of everlasting light, who hath promised to translate us to everlasting light (XIII:3-4). They continue, John the Baptist appeared in the *Sheol* and announced the coming of the Bridegroom to Adam and others from all generations who are gathered there (XIII:14). When Satan heard the news he had a discussion with the prince of the hell and they tried to prevent Jesus from entering hell and the expected

A good account of Mar Jacob's vision on Christ's descent into the *Sheol* is portrayed in the *Homily on Simon Peter.*[290] According to Mar Jacob, Peter's hesitation to the sacrificial death of Christ was a plot of Satan. Satan had tried to stop Him by tempting Him through Peter not to suffer and die, but Christ was not stopped; but He overcame it by saying: "Get behind me, Satan. Do not lead me away from the path that goes to Golgotha; the Father sent me to be a sacrifice for sinners. For by my death I will release the prisoners of *Sheol* from darkness."[291] Jesus said; I will die in order to give life to the dead in *Sheol*. Life is in me when I go to *Sheol*, I will give life to the dead there.[292] Jesus instructs Peter by saying: You have not thought that the Son of God, who enters *Sheol*, will pull down, wreck it, lay it bare, and then return to His place.[293] When I die, the bars of *Sheol* will not prevail upon me, and death will not be able to look at my face, when I exit.[294] Long ago, a way through the sea was opened,

---

deliverance of their prisoners. During their discussion they heard the sound of the prophecy of David: Lift up your gates, O you princes; and be you lift up, O everlasting gates, and the King of Glory shall come in (Ps 24:7). Against this the prince of hell commanded his men to keep the doors of the hell shut intact lest Jesus come in and release the prisoners (XVI:4). But, in the form of a man, Jesus entered into the *Sheol* by trampling the death and breaking the bars of *Sheol* (XVI: 18-19). He broke down the prison from top to bottom and released the prisoners from their cells (XVIII: 4). Then Jesus stretched his hand to Adam, and said, "come to me, all you saints, who were created in my image, who were condemned by the tree of the forbidden fruit, and by the devil and death. Live now by the wood of my cross; I have overcome the devil, the prince of this world, and death is defeated" (XIX: 1-2). Then taking hold of Adam by his right hand, he ascended from hell, and all the saints of God followed him (XIX: 12). Then He handed over to Michael the archangel and he led them to Paradise (XX:1). This is one of the detailed descriptions of Jesus' act of deliverance of the departed from the prison of *Sheol* and this was the understanding of the early Church on the descent of Jesus in to the *Sheol*. There is only one biblical reference which reflects about the descent of Jesus into the nether world. Peter said, "For this reason gospel was preached among the dead" (1Pet 4:8). But the above description of the *Gospel of Nicodemus* and the liturgical tradition of the Church witness the impact and importance of the tradition in the early Church.

[290] Also see Bedjan, *HS* III, 419.13-420.20; ET, "The Parable of the Leaven," *TV* 3(1989), 52.161-53.188.

[291] Bedjan, *HS* I, 496.18-497.3; ET. McCollum, "Homily on Peter," in *MHMJS*, Fasc. 22, 38.284-288

[292] Bedjan, *HS* I, 502.1-2; ET. McCollum, "Homily on Peter," in *MHMJS*, Fasc. 22, 50.385-386.

[293] Bedjan, *HS* I, 503.16-17; ET. McCollum, "Homily on Peter," in *MHMJS*, Fasc. 22, 54.423-424.

[294] Bedjan, *HS* I, 502.16-17; ET. McCollum, "Homily on Peter," in *MHMJS*, Fasc. 22, 52.401.

and tribes passed through; now, ravenous *Sheol* is breached, and the nations stream out.[295]

Mar Jacob portrays the scenario of Christ's arrival at the gates of *Sheol*: Christ appeared before the gates of *Sheol* and Satan was protecting its gates by trying to stop the passage. Satan attempted to bar the gates and reinforce their stronghold. Christ demanded to let him in: "Lift up, your heads, O gates! and be lifted up, O ancient doors, that the King of glory may come in" (Ps 24:7). Satan replies, "Who is this king of glory?"[296] He returned the answer quickly: "Lord strong and mighty, the Lord mighty in battle." In reply Satan argued he has a bond of him (Adam) with him. "Because he failed in what he was supposed to do, he was guilty before God" and signed a bond, a promissory note, to death. Serpent and Eve also receive credit for writing this bond.[297] Then straightway the gates of brass were shattered,[298] the bars of iron were ground to powder,[299] and the dead were loosed from their chains.[300] The Son of God threw down the throne and crown of death, bound the tyrant captor and received the crown of victory.[301] By His death put death to death.[302] The King of Glory entered the realm of the dead, *Sheol*, and retrieved his bounty, Adam and Eve. He descended alone but He ascended with many.[303] The following arguments the power and immortality of Jesus:

> I was pleased to be conceived in a womb, born in a manger,
> and baptized in a river, it is (now only) the cross preventing Adam from living.
> Why should it be far from me to die and bring to life (*aḥe*) the dead of *Sheol*,
> for there they are looking for me to go in and release their bonds?...
> The image (*ṣalmo*) of the Father is swallowed (*ṭeb`*) up in mud: Look I am going down

---

[295] Amar, *A Metrical Homily on Holy Mar Ephrem*, 39.55. Here, Mar Jacob compares with the Passover from Egypt; both the Passover and Christ's act of salvation of the souls from the bondage of *Sheol* are holding the same form of liberation from the bondage.

[296] Satan showed Christ the signature of Eve and Adam and said:
> "Take note: Your parents signed and sealed this. Read and understand.
> a bond Adam wrote me in Eden, because he succumbed to sin;
> He could not repay, so he pledged his sons as interest (pledge).
> From the beginning, I have possessed authority over man;
> not in secret were they enrolled and enslaved as debtors." (Narsai, *Hymn on Resurrection*, 138.49-140.54).

[297] Bedjan, *HS* V, 809.3-6.

[298] *CNis* XXXVIII.7, 21.

[299] Bedjan, *HS* II, 612.10; ET. *FH* XIII, 294.26.

[300] Bedjan *HS* II, 632.1-2; ET. *FH* XIV, 314.163-164.

[301] Bedjan *HS* II, 633.11-18; ET. *FH* XIV, 315.193-316.200.

[302] Bedjan, *HS* III, 596.14.

[303] Bedjan, *HS* II, 613.20; ET. *FH* XIII, 296.56.

to draw it up in person, and unless I retrieve it, I will not ascend (*solqo*).
From paradise to the grave the serpent has cast (*šdi*) Adam
and for this reason I have come, to go in and bring him out from destruction…
and that Adam should be consumed there in *Sheol*, where he is.
If you hold me back from death, you hate life,
for unless I die, there will be no life available for Adam.
Captives are imprisoned in the dens of the grave, so I am going
to bring back. Why would you hold me back from their salvation?
The rulers of *Sheol* have plundered my possessions. Flee from my presence!
I am going to bring back my plundered possession from thieves!
The sons of destruction have bound Adam in the darkness;
let me go, and I will go in to release those who are bound, and then I will return.[304]

I have a path (*`urḥo*) from Golgotha to the depths of *Sheol*,
and it is trodden (*metdrš*) only through the sufferings of crucifixion.
For three days expect me here, until I come,
for it is not a journey for men, when I come.
Let me go and hold a vigil for the dead for three days,
and I will open (*`eptaḥ*) the gates of *Sheol* that had been closed.
I have travel (*masyoono*) two days' journey on the road of death,
and I will come on the third; do not be sad.
It is easy for me to die, and easy to live; I have the authority
to go and come when I want, and no one stops me.
The gates of *sheol* are not shut (*metthdin*) to me, when I will have entered it;
it will go down with a fall and the dead imprisoned in it will rise (*qoimeen*).[305]

Mar Jacob finds a 'type' in the Old Testament for demolition of the walls of *Sheol* by Jesus. He said, Joshua's demolition of the walls of Jericho is a 'type' of Jesus' breaking of the bars of *Sheol*. He said, Instead of Moses, God appointed Joshua for the destruction of the wall of Jericho; because, Joshua bears the name of Jesus.[306] Victory of Samson over the Philistine is also depicted as a 'type' of Jesus' victory at *Sheol*. Jacob compared Delilah as the 'type' of *Sheol*.[307] The tradition of Jesus' descent into Hades is deeply woven to Easter tradition of the ancient Church. Here, Mar Jacob reminds the story of Jonah who in belly of a fish for three days:

Jonah descended (*nḥet*) so that he might portray (*nṣoor*) the type (*ṭupso*) of the Son of God

[304] Bedjan, *HS* I, 497.10-498.16; ET. McCollum, "Homily on Peter," in *MHMJS*, Fasc. 22, 38.295-42.320.

[305] Bedjan, *HS* I, 504.3-14; ET. McCollum, "Homily on Peter," in *MHMJS*, Fasc. 22, 56.431-442.

[306] Bedjan, *HS* III, 300.14; ET. Brock, "On the Veil of Moses," in *Studies in Syriac Spirituality*, 84.357.

[307] Bedjan, *HS* V, 346.10-11; ET. "A Homily on Samson," *TV* 11(1992), 64.316.

> and become a sign (*`oto*) of the murder of the Son among the floods.
> The symbol (*`rozo*) called to him, "Descend (*ḥoot*), touch the depths because your Lord will be come
> and descend (*nohet*) and touch the depths of *Sheol* and empty it.
> Descend (*ḥut*) to the deepest part and become the type of that Son of the Living One,
> who descend (*nohet*) to the whirlpool of the dead like a diver.
> Come (*to*), become in to the sea of dead a living one without precedent,
> because that one who makes everything live also dies that he might resurrect all.
> He dived (*amad*) and descended (*a'ttaḥto*) and prepared a path in the heart of the earth,
> because your Lord who comes will descend (*noḥet*) to the lowest position of the earth.
> May the sea bury you and became a buries one who is incorruptible (*methablo*),
> for it will be achieved in the tomb of your Lord when he descends (*noḥet*) to it.
> Be dead while you are alive and being destroyed you will not be destroyed,
> for destruction will approach your Lord who also does not die.
> Become an explorer and investigate the depths of the great sea,
> for your Lord will touch the lake of the dead when he descends to it.
> Portray for us the type of the living dead one who is incorruptible,
> for this sign is not visible except in your Lord.[308]

Mar Ephrem taught:

> Our Lord humiliated *Sheol* and Error;
> he utterly defeated death and Satan.
> For our Lord split apart Error, which was in *Sheol*.
> In order to teach what is hidden through what is revealed.[309]

> Our Lord torn asunder (the forces of) error in *Sheol*,
> so as to teach through the visible, what was hidden.
> For as he visibly torn asunder *sheol*,
> so he burst open Error in hidden fashion.
> Many saw the graves ripped open,
> they did not see that Satan was defeated.
> By what is close at hand he demonstrated?
> what is hidden (and) far away?[310]

Against the teachings of the Gospel of Nicodemus Mar Jacob says that the captives were not aware of the arrival of the Bridegroom. Meanwhile, in the Gospel of Nicodemus the Bridegroom's arrival was published by John the Baptist prior to His arrival. He said:

---

308 Bedjan, *HS* IV, 413.16-414.12.

309 *Hymns on the Unleavened Bread,* IV, 2-3.

310 *Hymn on the Unleavened Bread,* IV. 3-7.

> Behold, the Redeemer has come to the captives but they were not aware of Him…
> Behold, the Mighty One who liberates the prisoners.
> Behold the Mighty One who by His power causes the captivity to return,
> And when He will be pierced by the persecutors, He will conquer them all.[311]

The Church is thankful to her Bridegroom; and today the Church celebrates the Bridegroom's victory over the captives of the mankind and praises her Bridegroom. She teaches her children the victory of the Bridegroom and praises Him: God descended into *Sheol* and broke the bars of hell. Death trembled as it heard His voice and He emptied its treasures. Adam rose up, knelt down and worshipped before Him and all the mysteries that the prophets prophesied about him (were fulfilled). Adam told Him, forgive me my faults, O Son of God, lest I might be frightened how I have sinned. May Your mercies be upon me.[312] "Today the Lord of Adam, by His love, descended to *Sheol* towards him, and by His power pulled down the *Sheol* with its high walls. His light dawned in its inner chambers and He raised those who were in the tombs."[313]

4.4. The Friends of the Bridegroom

In the Jewish community, the friends of the bride and bridegroom had an important role in a marriage. There were two specially chosen groups of 'friends,' in the wedding of Judean community, one group for the bridegroom, and the other for the bride. They conducted all the preliminary inquiries, made the bargain on the dowry, arranged the betrothal, and finally lead the betrothed couple to the bridal chamber, where the bridal bed was. They were responsible for the legality of the whole proceedings and were guarantors of the bride's virginity and chastity. The Bible speaks about the sons or children of the bridal chamber (Mt 9:15; Mk 2:18-28) and friends of the Bridegroom (Lk 14:7-11). The children of the bridal chamber, which is seen in the Bible, are different from the friends of the bridegroom. In the first century the former group was the bridegroom's bachelor friends. In the afternoon before the wedding the bridegroom used to leave his house, which is then occupied by the bride and her attendants; meanwhile he sits among his companions and they are the 'sons of the bridal chamber.' At a signal from the bridegroom's family he and his companions move slowly and ceremonially towards his home, where the bride was awaiting him for the bridal feast to be held. Chavess says, St. Peter, the Galilean, dictating St. Mark's Gospel knows only the invited guests, the 'sons

---

311 Bedjan, *SMS,* 763.3-8; ET. *FH* I, 82.901-906.

312 *Kashtanubhavazhcha Namaskaram*, 241.

313 *Kashtanubhavazhcha Namaskaram,* 240.

of the bridal chamber,' while St. John Baptist, the Judean, was acquainted with the office of 'friend of the bridegroom.'[314]

In the Gospel texts the friends of the bridal chamber (Mk 2: 19) are portrayed as those who rejoice with the bridegroom. In the homilies Mar Jacob portrayed several persons as friends of the bridegroom. In a faint sense he used the term friend of the bridegroom to denote those who serves the bridegroom or prepare something for him (here to prepare the bride for wedding), and those who suffer for the bridegroom. In the first group, it is to be assumed, Mar Jacob places John the Baptist, the apostles, and Moses as the friends of the Bridegroom. The second category is separated for the Martyrs who suffer for the Bridegroom. In the *Homily on the Descent of the Most High on Sinai and Mystery of the Church* he calls Moses as the friend of the Bridegroom. Here Moses acts as a middle man between the Bridegroom and the bride.[315] In the *Homilies on the Baptism of our Lord and Redeemer,* and *Epiphany of our Redeemer* Mar Jacob brings John the Baptist as the friend of the Bridegroom.[316] John the Baptist is portrayed as a man who knew all the mysteries of the Bridegroom in details. He knows the Son of God will come for the baptism and knows about the manifestation of the Holy Spirit in the manner of a dove and mighty voice of the Father.[317] Here, the duty of the Baptist is to prepare the bride before the arrival of the Bridegroom for the wedding. [318] He educated the bride about the Bridegroom through his preaching. But when the bride eagerly approached John, he revealed that I am not the Bridegroom and only a friend of Him. [319] He prepared the bride by the washing of her and adorned her with purity[320] to receive the holy Bridegroom. He said, "To bind the bride with the beauty of the Bridegroom, and kindle her with love for Him, to inflame in her passion for Him, to adorn her for union with Him and to confirm her in His covenant, he infused earnestly into her ears the grandeur of her Lord as well as his own smallness."[321] Mar Jacob calls young martyrs as the friends of the bridegroom and their feast days are considered as the marriage feast.[322]

[314] Chavesse, *The Bride of Christ*, 53-55.

[315] Bedjan, *HS* I, 8.15-16.

[316] Bedjan, *HS* I, 168.10-169.1; ET. *FH* VI, 163.16-164.30.

[317] Bedjan, *HS* I, 172.5-11; ET. *FH* VI, 167.95-100.

[318] Bedjan, *HS* I, 173.2; ET. *FH* VI, 168.111.

[319] Bedjan, *HS* I, 170.20-21; ET. *FH* VI, 166.69-70.

[320] Rilliet, *SHF* II, 556.10-13; ET. *FH* VII, 193.14.

[321] Rilliet, *SHF* II, 554.16-20; ET. *FH* VII, 192.10.

[322] Bedjan, *HS* III, 710.6-7; ET. "A Homily on Stephen," *TV* 7(1990), 43.6-7.

Conclusion

The discussion was on Mar Jacob's depiction of the salvific works of Jesus Christ through the marriage imagery. In this imagery Mar Jacob portrayed Jesus as the true Bridegroom of the Church. According to him the dispensation of the Bridegroom was the plan of the Father even before the creation of the world. He betrothed the Church to His Only Begotten at the creation and therefore, though He created human beings in His Image He drove out Adam and Eve from Paradise after their fall. But, He was compassionate to the creation He educated the first Bride, Israel, through prophesies for the coming of the real Bridegroom to save her from the slavery of sin and death. According to him almost all incidents and the 'just men' of the Old Testament are the images of the marriage or Bridegroom respectively. But the Nation was unfaithful and betrayed the Bridegroom and committed adultery through the worship of other gods.

In the fullness of time the real Bridegroom came down to earth and saved the Church through various salvific works. Mar Jacob found them as staging posts: the birth, baptism, suffering, and descent into the *Sheol*. Each of the staging posts was unique in the process of salvation. According to him each event was an event of a betrothal. The Bridegroom loved His bride and abased His image and descended to the earth in the form of the sinful bride. He lived among them as one of them and taught the mysteries of the Kingdom of God. Finally, He gave Himself for slaughter and made sure the entrance of the bride into the bridal chamber by removing the lance of the Cherubim from the gate of Eden. Then He went to *Sheol*, where the dead were imprisoned by the evil one from the time of Adam and destroyed the fortress of evil and liberated the bride from the slavery of the evil. Not only that, but the Bridegroom entrusted her with various instruments for salvation, such as baptism and Eucharist, to heal the bride from corruption. Through these acts the eternal Bridegroom restored the Image of His bride and made her the perfect bride for the eternal bridal chamber.

Chapter 5

Church as the Bride of Christ

Introduction

This chapter focuses on Mar Jacob's vision of the Church as the Bride of Christ. It comprises an introduction about the Church; analyzing the Church as the bride of Christ; its Old Testament form and relation to Christ; the cause and modalities for election of new Israel or the Church from the nations and it ends with the various charachteristics of the Church.

The term 'Church' is derived from the Middle Dutch *kerke*, Dutch *Kerk*, and German *kirche*, which might have been originated from Greek *kyriake* means 'Lord's.' In the New Testament the term for church is εκκλησια (eklesia). This term is etymologically derived from two words έχ (out) and καλεω (to call) thus "those who are called out"[1] or "call and separate." An undertone 'election' is linked with the idea of Church (1Thess 1:4; Deut 14:2). The original meaning is absent in the Bible. This Christian term is derived from the Septuagint, which introduced it as translation of the Old Testament *q^e^hal Yahweh* means "the assembly of the people of God." This term is also used in parallel with synagogue.[2] In the Old Testament there are several references for 'assembly of God'; and it uses *q^e^uhal* to denote this term. The Syriac Curetonian (3rd Cent.), the Peshitta (beginning of 5th Cent.), and Syriac Philoxenian (beginning of the 6th Cent.) use *idto* for *eklesia* (εκκλησια) as Christian Church and *knušto* for Jewish synagogue. The Syriac Sinatica (3rd Cent.) has *knušto* for both.[3] The term for 'bride' in Syriac Peshitta is *kalto* , (Isa 49:18; 61:10; 62:5; Jer 2:32; 7:34; 16:9; 25:10; 33:11; Joel 2:16; Jn 3:29;

[1] Roloff, "εκκλησια," 411.

[2] Schimdst, "εκκλησια," 529.

[3] Lagarde, *Bible Syriac*, (1892); Cited, Schimdst, "εκκλησια," 525.

Rev 18:23; 21:9; 22:17)}. The root of the word is *kal* which means perfect; the *pael* form is *kalal* which means crown; *ethpael* form *eskalal* has the meaning of martyrdom.

The only direct reference to the Church as the bride of Christ in the New Testament is in Ephesians 5:32, where St Paul says: "This is a great mystery, and I am applying it to the Christ and the Church." The Book of Revelation says about Jerusalem as the 'adorned bride' (Rev 21:2). The personification of Israel as the bride of Yahweh is one of the most effective imageries in the Old Testament. The direct examples of bride imagery in relation with Yahweh as the Bridegroom found in the books of later prophets; where Israel is portrayed as the adulterous wife who worships the gods of the gentiles. It is more evident in the Book of Hosea where Yahweh asked the prophet to take the adulterous woman Gomer as his wife to show the people of Israel how much He loves them. The symbolic action of Hosea shows the degree of His love towards his people in spite of their infidelity. Yahweh spoke through prophet Jeremiah: "I have loved you with an everlasting love: therefore, I have continued my faithfulness to you" (Jer 31:3). By this act of marriage God reveals His transcending love towards the sons of Adam who transgressed from the way of God. Another close and clear example of the imagery is seen in the Book of Ezekiel chapter 16; where Jerusalem was portrayed as the wife of Yahweh. When He found her orphan and wounded, He healed her and made a covenant with her and purified, adorned her with new dress and ornaments. But she again became a harlot and broke the covenant. This is a fine type of Jacob's bride imagery with all its wings and beauty.

The Jewish mystics believe that the soul or the intellect of the earthly mystic as the bride of God. The Kabala school, the theosophical Kabbalah, believes in the marriage between the earthly *Saddiq,* righteous man, and the divine *Shekhinah* as the wife. This union brings divine power to the lower world. According to *Zohar*[4] (I 49a, III 74b), the marriage of *Shekhinah* and her brother-consort *Tiferet*, the King, was originally celebrated in the temple of Jerusalem. Their marriage took place either daily, weekly, or annually.[5] After

---

[4] Zohar is set of commentaries on Thorah. According to Gershom Scholem, most of the Zohar was written in an exalted style of Aramaic language. The Zohar is first appeared in Spain in thirteenth century and was published by a Jewish writer called Moses ben Shem-Tov de Leon. He ascribed this work to a rabbi of the second century, Simeon ben Yohai. The Jewish hagiography says that during the time of Roman persecution, Rabbi Simeon hid in a cave for thirteen years by studying Torah with his son Eliazar. During this time he wrote Zohar by inspiration of God.

[5] Lapinkivi, "The Sumerian Sacred Marriage and its Aftermath," 31.

Zohar says after the destruction of temple, the Shekhinah was exiled, and God was separated from his wife. In its original Talmudic formulation, the concept of the exile of Shekhinah simply meant that, when the temple of Jerusalem was destroyed and the people of

destruction of temple, the *Shekhinah* was exiled, and God was separated from his wife.[6] Gnostics believe that human soul as the bride of God, or rather as brides of their angelic counterparts in the pleroma.[7] In the *Exegesis on the Soul,* soul is counted as feminine and transgressed soul as a prostitute. When it repents and turn back to the Father he will accept her. It says the soul has womb and other internal organs.[8] In the early Church, Clement of Rome exhorts the same idea very powerfully to his Church and says:

> So, then, brethren, if we do the will of our Father God, we shall be members of the first Church, the spiritual,— that which was created before sun and moon; but if we shall not do the will of the Lord, we shall come under the Scripture which says, My house became a den of robbers (Jer 7:11). So, then, let us elect to belong to the Church of life; that we may be saved. I think not that you are ignorant that the living Church is the body of Christ (for the Scripture, says, God created man male and female; Gen 1:27; cf. Eph 5:22-23 the male is Christ, the female the Church) and that the Books and the Apostles teach that the Church is not of the present, but from the beginning. For it was spiritual, as was also our Jesus, and was made manifest at the end of the days in order to save you.[9]

The Gnostics allude that the creation of man and woman (Adam and Eve) as the Church. The Western Valentinian Gnostic of Heracleon also had the same idea about the pre-existence of the Church.[10] In a note on Ophites Irenaeus also shows their concept of pre-existence of the Church. The Father was identified with the First Man, who begets the Second Man and the Holy Spirit. These in

---

Israel were exiled, the Shekhinah, God's presence on earth, went into exile with them. In the Kabbalah, the exile of the Shekhinah came to mean that a part of God was exiled from God-that is, the masculine and feminine principles in the Godhead were separated from each other. This disharmony of Godhead can be restored by the Kabbalistic performance of the commandments, such as performance of human sexual intercourse on Sabbath night. This pure sexual relations reflect the mysterious marriage of the male and female aspects of the Godhead and influence it by inducing a state of harmony above. When a pious earthly couple performs sexual intercourse on the Sabbath night, this act causes the heavenly King (the Sefirah of Tiferet) to fertilize the Shekhinah, who thereupon gives birth to human souls and to angels (Zohar I 12b). Note further that, according to the Zohar (I 49b-50a, 66b), although righteous men have intercourse with their wives on the Sabbath night, they live in celibacy and devote themselves to holy works for the rest of the week. Therefore, whenever these men are away from wives, the *Shekhinah* couples with these men, and thus they are never deprived of the male-female unity. But the teachings of sacred relationship with divine will be different according to the schools. For example, to the school of Hasidim the righteous man has two natures. When they ascend they consider them as female and when they descend they will be male.

[6] Lapinkivi, "The Sumerian Sacred Marriage and its Aftermath," 31.

[7] Lapinkivi, "The Sumerian Sacred Marriage and its Aftermath," 31.

[8] *Exegesis on the Soul.* 119-122.

[9] II Clement, XIV, 1-2.

[10] *Fragments of Heracleon*; cf. Pagels, "Pursuing the Spiritual Eve," 202.

their turn beget Christ and the true holy Church, which is an incorruptible eon.[11] Daniélou Jean says that, "Both in II Clement, therefore, and in the Valentinian speculations is to be found a doctrine of the pre-existent Church characterized by the representation of the Church as the bride of Christ."[12] By giving various analyses of the Jewish and other texts of the pre-Christian time he concludes that, though there are Gnostic factors in it, the pre-existence of the Church is a Jewish Christian Apocalyptic concept in nature and origin.[13]

5.1. Birth of the Bride

In Mar Jacob's homilies the birth of the Church is a complex idea. He finds many wombs for the birth of this conceptual reality, the Church. He envisions this with a spiritual eye. The New Testament presents the formation of the Church by the baptism of many on the day of Pentecost. If the Church is primarily a community of the followers of Christ,[14] then, the Church is born before the Pentecost event because many men and women followed and accompanied Jesus from the outset of His public ministry. Again, if the Church is a sacramental body it might be born at the baptism of Christ (Mt 315-17) or at the Eucharistic celebration in the upper room (Mt 26:26-29). Another prominent idea of the pre-existent Church, which is discussed earlier, needs consideration here. An absolute origin of the Church on the basis of biblical evidences is a matter of debate. Mar Jacob founds many birth of the bride, and they are not contradictory but complementary. The following is a discussion on the birth of the Church in this background.

Mar Jacob portrays the birth of the Church through various angles. The basic concept behind his imagination is the salvation or sanctification of the human being, because he believes that the Church has a prominent role in the salvation of the world.[15] Again he brings another concept that, the Church, the new bride, has replaced Israel, the old bride. By the birth of the new Church God established a new way for salvation; the old bride is replaced by the new (2Cor 5:19).[16] And through this new creation He reconciled to the earthly and He established peace between those of above and those of below (Eph 2:13-16).[17] It is inferred that, the term 'Church' signifies as a worshipping community. It has two realms: a community realm as well as an individual realm. That means the Church is a community of believers and individual

[11] Irenaeus, *Against Heresies*, 1:30

[12] Daniélou, "The Development of Christian Doctrine," 302.

[13] Daniélou, *Theology of the Jewish Christianity*, 311.

[14] Collins, "Church, Idea of the," 645.

[15] Infra 5.3.1.

[16] Bedjan, *SMS,* 770.20-21; ET. *FH* I, 89.1066-1067.

[17] Bedjan, *SMS,* 770.14-15, 789.7-8; *FH* I, 89.1061-1062; *FH* II, 107.295-296.

believer as well.[18] In another sense the birth of a spiritual being, regeneration through the baptism or regeneration through the Eucharistic communion, is the birth of the Church; hence an individual, is not Church, but as an integral part of the same body, the Church.

5.1.1. Three Wombs

Regarding the origin of the Church, Mar Jacob sees three births from three wombs; as if the Church is born like a baby from the womb of a mother. He personifies the Church with all human faculties with different stages such as infant, youth, bride and mother, and begetting children. All these three births (stages) are in relation to the Incarnation and the saving activity of Jesus Christ, because the function of the Church is to save souls for Christ. The three wombs are: the womb of Jordan, the Womb of Golgotha, and the womb of *Sheol*. As a womb plays a significant role in the making of human being, these wombs also play significant roles in the birth of the Church. These wombs are the three staging posts in the life of Jesus to save the world. Mar Ephrem in his *Homily on Our Lord* says: "The Father begot Him, and through Him He made all creation. Flesh begot Him, and His flesh He put passions to death. Baptism begot Him, that through Him it might make (our) stains white. *Sheol* begot Him to have her treasuries despoiled by Him."[19] The three terms Mar Jacob uses for womb are and (*mrb'o, karso,* and *'ubo*). See the usage of these three terms in the following lines:

> The baptismal womb is not narrower than the belly
> and the water of the river is not darker than the womb.[20]
> If you had withheld me from dwelling in the bosom of Mary
> I would also have passed over myself from the womb of baptism.[21]

5.1.1.1. Womb of Jordan

Mar Jacob visualizes the river Jordan as a spiritual womb begets the spiritual beings. By begetting the spiritual beings he purports the regeneration of a human being into a 'new creation' (2Cor 5:17) by removing his/her 'old man' (Rom 6:4). When he says about this, especially in the *Homily of the Baptism*

[18] In many of the references Mar Jacob uses the term individual believer as Church. For example, at the baptism of individuals was compared to the baptism of the Church of the nations (Bedjan, *HS* I, 167.2-14; ET. *FH* VI, 162.2-163.14; Bedjan, *HS* III, 290.3-4; ET. Brock, "On the Veil of Moses," in *Studies in Syriac Spirituality*, 78.133-134). Also, when deals about the salvation through the cross he uses the same (Jacob of Serugh, Hymn on Resurrection, ET. Brock, *The Treasure House of Mysteries,* 264).

[19] McVey, *Homily on Our Lord,* 277.

[20] Bedjan, *HS* I, 178.5-6; ET. *FH* VI, 173.217-218.

[21] Bedjan, *HS* I, 178. 19-20; ET. *FH* VI, 173.131-132.

of Our Redeemer, he conceives Church as a pre-existent one[22] and the bride of Christ who begets spiritual children through the womb of baptism.[23] In order to beget the spiritual children from the womb of Jordan the Bridegroom purifies the womb by His descent. Delineating the baptism of Christ at the river Jordan Mar Jacob dramatically illustrates the scene and portrays the reactions and the changes of the water.[24] The water recognizes the proximity of the Bridegroom and leaps in exultation by realizing that the Bridegroom is going to enter into its womb. This reminds the leap of John the Baptist in Elizabeth's womb (Lk 1:41). This part will only discuss what is pertinent to the situation as many aspects are discussed earlier.

"The comely woman stood looking for the Bridegroom, when He would come, in order to enter with Him into the womb (*'ubo*) of the waters to be sanctified."[25] This passage reminds the Church's desire to be born again. "The betrothed made the daughter of the day enter a new womb, and the testing waters of baptism were in labor and gave rebirth to her."[26] Here, Mar Jacob describes the Church as a community of people who eagerly waited for the baptism in the waters of Jordan. He observes that the river Jordan was a tomb, but by His descent the Bridegroom transformed it as a womb which begets spiritual children.[27] By His descent he purified the waters of the earth so that it became life-giving waters.[28] Secondly, He crushed the head of the serpent who had been swallowing the children of God.[29] Thirdly, He instituted the baptism for the remission of sin and installed the robe of glory in the waters of Jordan.[30] Those who enter in this womb will become resplendent by cleansing their filth and receive the lost glory.

As it was said, the changes in the water of Jordan, prior to the arrival of the Bridegroom, are noteworthy. Knowing His proximity, the womb of Jordan overflowed and silently proclaimed Him. The Holy Spirit came out by itself and stood above the water and the heat of His power kindled the waters. Through these acts the baptismal water earnestly desired Him who had

---

22 Bedjan, *HS* I, 169.1-171.3; ET. *FH* VI, 164.29-166.74.

23 Bedjan, *HS* I, 181.10-15; ET. *FH* VI, 176.285-290.

24 Bedjan, *HS* I, 174.6-19; ET. *FH* VI, 169.135-170.150.

25 Bedjan, *HS* I, 171.16-17; ET, *FH* VI, 166.85-86.

26 Bedjan, *HS* III, 290.3-4; ET. Brock, "On the Veil of Moses," in *Studies in Syriac Spirituality*, 78.133-134.

27 Bedjan, *HS* I, 181.10-11; ET. *FH* VI, 176.285-286; cf. Brock, *Holy Spirit in the Syriac Baptismal Tradition,* 104.

28 Bedjan, *HS* I, 180.9-20, 184.15; ET. *FH* VI, 175.265-274, 179.354; Rilliet, *SHF* II, 564.13-21; ET. *FH* VII, 199.32. See more in 3.5.3.1.

29 Rilliet, *SHF* I, 542.8; 540.7; ET. *FH* IV, 132.8.

30 Bedjan, *HS* I, 168.14-17, 177.11-20; ET. *FH* VI, 163.15-16, 172.201-212.

come to it like that horn of anointing in response to David (1Sam 16:1-13). The transformation of Jordan was not sanctifying Christ but to embrace Him so that its womb might be sanctified by Him.[31] Through these acts the water of Jordan became a womb that begets the spiritual children. The womb of Jordan[32] regenerates the 'old man'[33] into a 'new creation' in Christ (Rom 6:4; 2Cor 5:17).[34] Like the womb of a mother, the baptismal font of the church is a symbol of the womb of Jordan which begets children of the Church. In the West Syriac tradition, the baptismal font is known as the womb of the Church.[35] The Church with its priesthood begets spiritual children through baptism.

Eve is the archetypal mother (Gen 3:20), but Jordan became the new Eve, which begets all the living. He says: "Eve in the prophecy is the mother of all that lives, and what, if not baptism, is the mother of all life?"[36] Through the sin of the first mother the immortal became mortal.[37] Christ the Bridegroom begot a new mother, the baptism, to bring back lost immortality. If Eve, the first mother, bore mortal children, baptism gives birth to spiritual beings that live forever.[38] Here Mar Jacob sees the Church as an individual being, which means each individual represents the whole Church. In one of the prayers of the Church describes the following:

> Instead of Eve who produced children who were mortal and corruptible, may this womb of water produce children who are heavenly, spiritual and immortal; and as the Holy Spirit hovered over the water at the establishment of created things, do you, O Lord, be present in this baptismal water, which is the spiritual womb that gives birth to spiritual beings; and may it produce, instead of the Adam made of dust, the heavenly Adam, and may those who are baptized in it receive in you the lasting changes that will not be made ineffective: instead of corporeally, spiritually, instead of visibleness, communion with the invisible; and instead of the weak soul, your Holy Spirit.[39]

---

[31] Bedjan, *HS* I, 173.18-174.14; ET. *FH* VI, 169.129-145.

[32] Bedjan, *HS* I, 178.5; ET. *FH* VI, 173.218.

[33] Bedjan, *HS* II, 613.15-19; ET. *FH* XIII, 296.51-56.

[34] *HVir,* VII.7, 27.13-18; ET. McVey, *Ephrem the Syrian,* 294.

[35] *HVir* VII.7-8, 27.13-25; ET. McVey, *Ephrem the Syrian,* 294.

[36] Bedjan, *HS* III, 299.18-19; ET. Brock, "On the Veil of Moses," in *Studies in Syriac Spirituality*, 84.341-342.

[37] In Syriac Church Fathers' opinion God created Adam as a living creature between mortal and immortal. So that he can be immortal or mortal. But through the transgression he became mortal. On the other hand Aphrahat is one step ahead of this and he says that when God breathed on Adam he became immortal (Parisot, *Demo* VI. 293.5-9).

[38] Bedjan, *HS* III, 299.17-20; ET. Brock, "On the Veil of Moses," in *Studies in Syriac Spirituality*, 84.340-343.

[39] *Maronite Baptismal Service Attributed to Jacob of Serugh*, 339-340; cited Brock, *Holy Spirit in Syriac Baptismal Themes*, 104.

Mar Jacob reminds this duty of the Church and calls it, "the mother who daily gives birth to immortals."[40] In short, the baptismal font which represents the river Jordan, the spiritual womb of the Church, is the mother of all living and it initiates spiritual beings every day.[41]

Through the baptism Christ handed down the priesthood to His disciples and to the Church.[42] From there the Church through its priesthood undertook the glorious role of the Bridegroom, the eternal High Priest, and continues it on behalf of Him; St. Ephrem says:

> Since they have baptism, another womb.
> [Baptism] giving birth rejuvenates the old just as the river rejuvenated Naman.
> O to the womb that gives birth to royal sons every day without birth pangs.
> Priesthood is a servant to this womb in her giving birth.[43]

Since the Church is awarded this privilege of regeneration, the baptismal prayer of the West Syriac Church used in Indian Orthodox Church says:

> Mix O Lord God, in this water by the supplication of our feebleness, the power and operation of your Holy Spirit, so that this may be a spiritual womb and a furnace which forms immortality. And grant to your servant who is being baptized in it, that it may be an incorruptible and spiritual vestment to him, and remission from the bondage of sins by your good will and love of mankind of your only begotten Son, and through the operation of your Holy Spirit now and always forever.[44]

The power that made the water of Jordan into the water of redemption makes the water in the font of baptism, which is kept in the Church, into life-giving water, water of rebirth, and water that produces immortality. Thus, through the baptismal water the Church begets children of immortality. The fathers of the Church, including Mar Jacob, calls this water as a furnace that recasts the mortal children into the immortal image of God and adorns them with the robe of glory.[45] Theodore of Mopsusetia writes, "… Holy Spirit's grace to descend upon the water, [to] render it capable of engendering this [new] mysterious birth and turn it into a womb for a sacramental birth."[46]

By attributing Jordan as the spiritual womb that begets the Church, Mar Jacob highlights the corruption of the old nature of human beings; Christ's purification of the universal waters; recovery of the humanity through the

---

[40] Bedjan, *HS* I, 194.13.

[41] All baptismal fonts kept in the church is a replica of the baptismal font of Jordan.

[42] Bedjan, *HS* I, 192.4-5; ET, *FH* VI, 185.507-508.

[43] *HVir,* VII.7, XXVII:13-17; ET. McVey, *Ephrem the Syrian,* 294.

[44] *Koodashakramangal*, 32.

[45] Bedjan, *HS* I, 181.6-7.

[46] Theodore of Mopsustia, *Catechetical Homily* XIV.9.

institution of baptism and its continuity in the Church through the priesthood. All these acts enable the Church to beget spiritual Children in this world. Ecologically speaking the act of Jesus' purification of water gives a hope to the human race. Earth, water, and the air, the most essential units of human existence, are under the threat. The ruthless exploitation of these elements resulted in the loss of a harmonious co-existence of nature. It affected climate and biodiversity which generated deceases. The purification act of Jesus gives a hope and a paradigm in the cause of nature.

Water is the most abused natural element in the world. High usage of pesticides and fertilizers, plastic and dumping of other human waste made the water of the earth a tomb. The water lost oxygen and its life-giving elements and became poisonous which caused the abolition of bio-diversity in the water. Over use of water caused the decline of the ground water level, which causes the desertification of the fertile land. Therefore, this paradigm example will be a motivation to humanity to nurture a culture which honors the creation of God. Without a proper and healthy environment a plant cannot sprout out and grow healthy. Also, the social atmosphere is corrupted as a result humanity is also corrupted. For a just and empowered world this corruption should be abolished. Just as Christ washed away the sins of the world through the baptism a conversion and sanctification of human beings are necessary. For this purpose, the womb of baptism is a new model.

5.1.1.2. Womb of Golgotha

The birth of the Church from the side of Jesus Christ at Golgotha is another beautiful interpretation. John 19:34 is the foundation of this imagery; it says: one of soldiers pierced Jesus' side with a spear; and there came forth blood and water. Mar Jacob and other Church Fathers, especially those who are from the Syriac background, have seen multiple meanings here. The synchronic vision of the Syriac tradition makes it possible.[47] In the present context, Mar Jacob says that, the blood and water which flowed from the side of Christ resulted in the birth of a new child, the Church. He compares this verse with that of Gen 2:21-22 which narrates the creation of Eve from the side of first Adam. Like first Eve, the mother of all living, was created from the side of first Adam while the second Eve, the Church who is the mother of spiritual ones, is created from the side of Second Adam. Mar Jacob says: Christ came and opened (*ptaḥ*) up baptism on His cross so that it might be a mother of life in the place of Eve.[48]

> The groom's side has been pierced (*tri'*), and from it the bride has came out,
> fulfilling the type (*ṣoorto*) provided by Adam and Eve.
> For from the beginning he knew (*yod'*) and depicted (*ršem*)

---

[47] Supra 3.2.

[48] Bedjan, *HS* I, 162.3.

> the house of Adam in the likeness (*dmooto*) of the image (*ṣoorto*) of his Only-begotten.
> He slept (*dmek*) on the cross as Adam had slept (*dmek*) his deep sleep,
> His side was pierced (*tar'o*) and from it came forth the Daughter of Light.
> Water and blood as an image (*ṣoorto*) of the divine children,
> to be heirs (*yorto*) to the Father who loves his only Begotten.
> Eve in prophecy is the mother of all that lives-
> And what, if not baptism, is the mother of life (a*`mo dkul ḥaye*)?...
> Adam's side gave birth to a woman who gives birth to mortals,
> while our Lord's to the Church who gives birth to immortals[49]

See another homily of Mar Jacob which gives the same interpretation:

> Also Adam slept, then his side was opened (*`ettr'at*),
> and Eve came out, to become the mother of the whole world.
> This became the image (*ṣalmo*) for the sleep of death in crucifixion
> and for that side, which gave also the baptism.
> Adam was sleeping and giving a mother to the world,
> our savior died and from Him flows baptism.
> If the side gave birth to Eve as it is written,
> also the virgin gave birth to the Son as it is pictured.[50]

See another homily from Mar Jacob which gives the same interpretation:

> Christ slept (*dmek*) on the cross, and baptism came forth from him.
> The bridegroom slept (*dmek*), and his side was pierced (*`ettar'at*) in his sleep,
> he gave birth to the bride, as happened with eve, in Adam His type (*ṭupso*).
> The stillness of the sleep of death fell upon him on the Cross
> and from Him came forth the Mother who gives birth to all spiritual beings.
> The Lord of Adam produced the New Eve in his sleep,
> to serve as mother of the children of Adam, in Eve's place.
> Water and blood for the fashioning of spiritual children,
> flowed from the side of the Living One who died in order to bring life to Adam.[51]

These interpretations substantiate Mar Jacob's argument of the birth of the Church from the side of Christ on the Cross. Chavasse quotes the same interpretation: "As Adam was a figure of Christ, Adam's sleep shadowed out the death of Christ, who was to sleep a mortal slumber, that from the wound inflicted in his side might in like manner (as Eve was formed) be typified the Church, the true Mother of the living (*De Anima,* Ch. Xliii)."[52] Deep sleep and

---

[49] Bedjan, *HS* III, 299.11-300.2.

[50] Bedjan, *HS* III, 320.12-19; ET. Konat "On the Mysteries, Types, and Figures of Christ," *Le Museon* 118(2005), 85.317-324.

[51] Bedjan, *HS* II, 589.8-17.

[52] Cited Chavasse, *The Bride of Christ,* 131.

wound on the side could be parallel to the event of Genesis 3:24. Just like Eve was created from the side of Adam a new child was created from the side of Christ.

In the scripture, both water and blood represent life; it offers 'living water' or 'water of life' (Jn 4:14; 7:38; Rev 21:1, 6; 22:17; Jer 2:13) and blood as life (Lev 17:11; Gen 9:4; Acts 15:20; Jn 6:53). The blood and water are two important life-giving factors in the primary level and represent two sacraments in the spiritual level; the Eucharist and the baptism. The blood represents Eucharist and the water represents baptism that gives life to the faithful. From the time of Moses onwards blood was an offering for redemption. The Old Testament tells that the sacrifices were offered through the blood of mute animals (Ex 12:5; Lev 1:10; Isa 44:22) but in the New Testament redemption given through the blood of Christ. With His atoning blood Christ bought and redeemed humanity[53] (Acts 20:28; 1Pet 1:10; Eph 1:7; Col 1:14; Heb 9:12-14; 1Jn 2:2). Again, baptism or redemption through the water is another strong tradition in the Bible (Jn 3:5; 1Cor 10:1). Therefore, Mar Jacob uses both of these concepts in these lines:

> Christ came and opened up baptism by his cross,
> so that, instead of Eve, it might be the mother of living in the world.
> Water and blood for the fashioning of spiritual children,
> flowed forth from Him, and baptism became the mother of living.
> No previous baptism ever gave the Holy Spirit,
> only the baptism which was opened up by the Son of God on the cross;
> It gives birth to children spiritually with the water and blood.[54]

Ephrem in his *Commentary on Diatessaron* says:

> There came forth blood and water: that is, his Church, which is built on his 'side'. Just as in the case of Adam, his wife was taken from his side. Adam's wife is his 'rib,' so our Lord's "blood" is his Church. From Adam's rib issued death, from out Lord's rib life.[55]

Both, Mar Ephrem and Mar Jacob affirm the place of Golgotha in the begetting of the Church. By creating spiritual children from blood and water the Bridegroom makes the world fruitful.[56] Moses struck the rock with his staff, and water flowed from it which quenched the thirst of the people of Israel. On the cross, the soldier pierced the side of the Bridegroom with a

---

[53] Bedjan, *SMS,* 686.7-16; ET. Puthuparampil, "On the Perpetual Virginity," in *Mariological Thought of Mar Jacob of Serugh*, i.15-ii.24.

[54] Bedjan, *HS* I, 162.3-9.

[55] McCarthy, *CommDiat,* XXI.11, 323.

[56] Bedjan, *HS* I, 162.5-6; *HS* II, 589.8-17; *HS* III, 120.3-124.3.

lance and from there flowed water which gives life to all.[57] He compares the water with a well: The lance dug out a new well[58] (*bire hadto*) which became a Gihon, a fountain of Eden sending rivers of life to the whole world.[59]

Mar Jacob compares the creation of Eve and of the Church. Eve was not made out of the earth but from the flesh and blood of Adam. Mixing in marital relations of the watery seed of Adam and the flow of the blood of Eve, the human race arose.[60] They (Adam and Eve) were fruitful and filled the earth. Adam is the fountainhead and Eve the fountain from which the rivers of men flowed.[61] The Bridegroom, the second Adam, through His death conferred a new life to the bride. By the touch of the water and blood which has flowed from the side of Christ the dead ones, who slept in the *Sheol*, resurrected. [62] The water and the blood from the side of Christ represent Adam and Eve. The blood and water (the Eucharist) give life to the dead in sin and it is the birth of the Church.

Mar Ephrem says that the Church was born from the pierced side of the Son of God on Golgotha. In his commentary on Jn 19:34 he describes that, through receiving the sword on the side, the Son of God removed the sword/lance that was revolving at the gate of Eden. The water came from the side quenched the fire of the first Adam[63] and the water and blood flowed from the side of Christ gave birth to the Church, the New Israel. There came forth blood and water, that is his Church; which built on his side: just as in the case of Adam, his wife was taken from his side, Adam's wife being his rib, so for our Lord's blood is His Church. Adam's rib caused the birth of death and from our Lord's rib cause the birth of life.[64] Though Ephrem uses this imagery to show the birth of the Church, in this context, he is not depicting the Church as the bride of Christ. Mar Jacob, however, by explaining the same context describes Church as the bride of Christ. He says that, the Church is the true bride. Ephrem uses the biblical order "blood and water" on the other hand Mar Jacob uses in a reverse order "water and blōod" to interpret the theme. Mar Jacob has a detailed view, he says: Eve is the mother of all living (Gen 3:20) who are subjected to sin and death, the Church is the mother of all spiritual beings who are called to share the holiness of the heavenly Father. He sees the water and blood from the side of Christ as the signs of the sacraments of

[57] Bedjan, *HS* II, 336.3-6, 588.20-589.7.

[58] Bedjan, *HS* I, 445.5.

[59] Bedjan, *HS* II, 302.14-15,

[60] Bedjan, *HS* III, 122.5ff.

[61] Bedjan, *HS* III, 123.13-16.

[62] Infra 5.1.1.3.

[63] McCarthy, *CommDiat*, XXI.10, 322.

[64] McCarthy, *CommDiat,* XXI.10, 322; cf. Brock, "The Mysteries in the Hidden Side," 462.

baptism and Eucharist respectively. Through the baptism and Eucharist, the children of the Church share eternal life.

The Western Church also teaches that the Church was born from the side of Christ. "For it was from the side of Christ as he slept the sleep of death upon the cross that there came forth the wondrous sacrament of the whole Church."[65] Here it considers not only the birth of the Church but it refers that the Church itself is a sacrament. Louis Bouyer offers a threefold birth of both Christ and Church: Christ born in the eternity as the first born of all creation, in the fullness of time he was born from the virgin, and in beyond time he is born in us mystically through baptism. Symmetrically and properly speaking, the birth of the Church, in which her personal being in our persons' ascending to their supernatural perfection, is not only unveiled but actually came about in our world, and is preeminently the consummation of her unity with Christ and in Him, in the wedding of the Lamb at the time of the Parousia.[66]

As it was seen in the case of the womb of Jordan, here also Mar Jacob's main concern is the salvation of the souls. In this imagery he envisions two sacramental aspects: baptism and Eucharist. Both are necessary for the salvation of the soul. For Jesus said, without regeneration through water and Spirit (Jn 3:5) and communion of His body and blood (Jn 6:53-54) no one can enter into the eternal world. The flow of water and blood from the side of the Bridegroom is a means for salvation, which is the mother Church.

This section discussed the birth of the Church from the wound of Christ. Though the suffering of Christ, the Bridegroom, a positive effect was generated. His suffering brought forth a new life. In the present age many people are wounded in many ways: illnesses, exploitation of the powerful, wars, communalism, terrorism, etc. Every person who suffers by pain, agony, and despair, through his/her sufferings must bring life and hope to the world. The holy persons through their sufferings inspired the world. The blood of holy martyrs of the Church was the seed of the Church.[67] The present era also needs such persons; they could enlighten many who live in despondency into new life.

5.1.1.3. Womb of Tomb

Mar Jacob sees the tomb or *Sheol* as another womb from which the Church has taken flesh. He says: Human being had fallen from the rank of adopted

[65] *Sacrosanctum Concilium* 5,138, and the prayer after the second reading of the Holy Saturday in the Roman Missal preceding the reform of the Holy Week. Cited in Valenziano, "Liturgy and Symbolism," 41.

[66] Bouyer, *The Church of God: Body of Christ and the Temple of Spirit*, 286.

[67] Tertullian, *Apology* 50.

sons.[68] They became strangers to the house of their Father and were driven out from Eden, the divine abode. They became dust and the food of dragon.[69] *Sheol* and the abyss of dead became their abode.[70] Therefore, even Adam, Noah, Melchizedek, Abraham, Isaac, Jacob, Joseph, Moses, Joshua, Samuel, David, Isaiah, and others were not exception[71] from this ordeal and they rested in the *Sheol* expecting the arrival of the Son of God.[72] And the Bridegroom descended into the *Sheol* and released the slaves from their states. Mar Jacob describes how the *Sheol* was defeated: By the eternal mercy of God the Son became man, however, unlike sons of Adam He had no stain of sin. Since the death comes through sin, it had no gate through which to enter in and seize Him, because He was untainted. Therefore, death was not natural to Him, but He willingly accepted it because He wanted to descend into the *Sheol* to liberate the sons of Adam.[73] The Bridegroom died[74] and entered into *Sheol,* where the dead were imprisoned. He says "the Father ordained for Him three days to remain in *Sheol*."[75] And the bitter death swallowed Christ as a regular prey. Meanwhile, this living dead man was a fatal poison.[76] Death could not hold Him in his stomach, because He is living and has no death. Death ate Him as normal food, but was unable to hold the food and the Son of God triumphed pinning the very death to death.[77] Mar Jacob continues: The Mighty One rested in the *Sheol* but rose up and shattered the gates of *Sheol* and released those who were bounded there.[78] "He fixed the nail of life in the *Sheol* so that, its gates

---

[68] Rom 8:15; Gal 4:5; cf. Rilliet, *SHF* I, 540:13-14; ET. *FH* IV, 131.7; *SHF* III, 570:20; ET. *FH* IX, 236.8.

[69] Rev 12:9; cf. Bedjan, *HS* II, 142.15; *HS* III, 157.9; *HS* IV, 262.14. In his *Homily on Ephrem* Mar Jacob compares Pharaoh with dragon: "It crushed Pharaoh, the great snake, in the great sea; and it battered his wicked brood in the tide. Among the waves of the sea it drowned that deadly serpent; while the synagogue, (like) a dove, escaped and fled from between its teeth." (Amar, "A Metrical Homily on Holy Mar Ephrem," 43).

[70] Rilliet, *SHF* I, 540.7; ET. *FH* IV, 131-132.7.

[71] Rilliet, *SHF* V, 612.5; ET. *FH* XII, 281.5.

[72] Bedjan, *HS* V, 465.2-20; ET *FH* V, 157.373-158.389.

[73] Olingder, *Bp.* 7, 34.22f.

[74] The water from the side of the Bridegroom shows that He was really dead but at the same time, the blood shows that He had life in Him, because blood is a sign of life. Therefore, through this Mar Jacob indicate that Christ, while being truly dead, kept His life within Him. If He had not died He could not enter into the Sheol and liberate the prisoners from there, but the divinity did not leave from Him because He is true God who has no death (Bedjan, *HS* II, 589.18-590:19).

[75] Bedjan, *HS* II, 629.14; ET. *FH* XIV, 312.113.

[76] Bedjan, *HS* III, 615.9.

[77] Bedjan, *HS* III, 596.16ff.

[78] Bedjan, *HS* II, 616.9-10; ET. *FH* XIII, 298.105-106; *HS* I, 502.16-17; II, 632.20; V, 571.21-22. The phrase "*gates of Sheol*" which used Jesus' reply to Peters' confession (Mt 16-

might be shaken everyday at its fall."[79]At His resurrection a great earthquake shook the mountains and burst open the hard rocks. Graves were split open; birth pangs struck the earth, and the dead came forth.[80] The bars of *Sheol* did not withstand in His presence.[81] Death was defeated[82] and those who were imprisoned in *Sheol* were released and came out to life through the broken walls of *Sheol.*[83] This was the moment of the birth of Church. Mar Jacob says: "The mighty One descended alone but ascended with many."[84]

> On this day Light has shown forth amidst darkness
> and the resurrection stood holding the beginning of the new world.
> Today Life began to tread under the foot the region of death
> and set up mile-stones on the fearful road so that it should not fail again.
> This is the feast in which the walls of *Sheol* were uprooted;
> because the slaughtered King entered into it [*Sheol*] and subjugated it and opened a passage through them [the walls of *Sheol*].[85]

> He visited us in *Sheol* to deliver (*napşo*) us from perdition.
> He became the way for us and drew us along and went out of darkness.
> By His resurrection He subdued (*kbaš*) the regions that were fearful,
> and made to return the captives of all peoples who had been led away…
> He effaced consolation for Eve and Adam because He visited them
> and by His resurrection He made them return to the house of the kingdom.[86]

> They saw that the birth pangs had struck *Sheol* and it gave birth to life
> and they accepted upon themselves to become advocates of the Truth of the new world.
> They returned from the tomb with confidence to their companions
> while the proclamation about His victory was resounding within them.[87]

18) received special attention to modern scholars. Many early Syriac fathers used 'bars' instead of 'gates.' Brock made a special study on this usage on this subject (See more at; Brock, "The Gates/Bars of Sheol Revisited," 7-23).

[79] Bedjan, *HS* II, 621.10; ET. *FH* XIII, 303.207-208.

[80] Bedjan, *HS* 1, 455.1; II, 189.1ff, 584.3-11; V, 656.10, 803.8-10.

[81] Bedjan, *SH* II, 612.10; ET. *FH* XIII, 294.26.

[82] Bedjan, *HS* II, 613.6; ET. *FH* XIII, 295.42.

[83] Bedjan, *HS* II, 613.3-4; ET. *FH* XIII, 295.39-40; *HS* II, 624.5-12; ET. *FH* XIV, 307.5-308.12; cf. *Odes*, 11.12.

[84] Bedjan, *HS* II, 613.19; ET. *FH* XIII, 296.56.

[85] Bedjan, *HS* II, 612.1-6.

[86] Bedjan, *HS* II, 633.11-18; ET. *FH* XIV, 315.193-316.198.

[87] Bedjan, *HS* II, 623.2-5; ET. *FH* XIII, 304.241-244.

An interpretation of the Syriac Church regarding the resurrection of Adam and his children is seen in Mar Jacob's homilies. He compares the resurrection experience of the dead with the sprouting of a seed by the touch of water. Jesus sowed the seed of life and the water flowed down from the cross irrigated and made it sprout. He says: the water which flowed from the side of the Bridegroom became a fountain and the dead drank from it and they received life. Also, the same water washed away the dust of their captivity.[88] The Bridegroom, through His resurrection, sowed the seeds of life in the land of death and uprooted the walls of *Sheol*. Like the parable of the mustard seed (Lk 13:18-19) Jesus was buried as a small seed in the land of the dead where He sprouted and became strong and became a tree of new life.[89] He says that resurrection flows from Christ's body to the whole earth, dropping like dew on the bodies of the dead, making them sprout to life like seeds.[90]

Mar Jacob teaches another faith of the early Church that the resurrection of the dead was a hope of the Israel. According to this tradition, the Messiah will come and the dead will be released from the darkness of *Sheol*. Therefore, Simeon pleaded to baby Jesus that: "Send Simeon, and set me in the deposit among the dead until you come and take me on the day of resurrection."[91] Also, the tradition says that the men of God preached the good hope among the dead who are in despondency. They proclaimed the advent of the Messiah and the redemption of the desolate ones in the darkness of *Sheol.*[92] The Bridegroom gave life to the bride from the womb of tomb. This event also gives hope to the suffering.

5.2. Old Testament Types of Church the Bride

Mar Jacob found the two Old Testament figures: Rachel, and Tamar, as the images of the Church. Mar Jacob counts Ruth also in their row.[93] It is significant to note that these women were from nations and not from the Nation, but they

---

[88] Bedjan, *HS* IV, 638.5-12.

[89] Bedjan, *HS* IV, 638.5-12, 648.6-21; *The Cave of Treasures* says when the blood and water reached at the mouth of Adam he was delivered from sheol. "The Blood and water (from the pierced side of Christ) came down into the mouth of Adam (buried, according to early tradition, immediately beneath the cross), and Adam was delivered and put on the robe of glory (in other words, was baptized), and Christ wrote the edict of his return with his own blood, dispatching it (to the Cherub guarding paradise) by the hands of the thief (Budge, *The Book of the Cave of Treasures,* Cited by Brock, "Mysteries Hidden in the Side of Christ," 463).

[90] Bedjan, *HS* I, 425.12; *HS* II, 93:3-6, 295:22; *HS* III, 429:12-16, 430:2-3, 531:17-18; *HS* IV, 686:5-6; *HS* V, 452:17-453:2.

[91] Bedjan, *HS* V, 452.13-14; ET. *FH* V, 146.103-104.

[92] Bedjan, *HS* V, 463.11-22; ET. *FH* V, 155-156.329-340.

[93] Brock, *Jacob of Serugh's Homily on Tamar (Gen 38),* 283.90-95, 283.115-284.122.

became the root or integral part of the Nation. Thus they have significant role in the genealogy of the Israelites.

5.2.1. Rachel: A Type of Church

> The Church, though rejected, was loved by reason of her beauty,
> thus resembling Rachel, who was passed over, though she was fair.[94]

The above lines convey Mar Jacob's typological interpretation on the Church and Rachel. The Church was from the Nation and from nations. God chose the Nation for the salvation of humanity. But the position or destiny of the nations were ambiguous to Mar Jacob. The only reference to them is that, they were in sin. But from the pre-existent nature of the Church and the depiction of the proto types of the Church in various figures of the Old Testament it could be assumed that they were under the salvation plan of God. The figure of Rachel tells the same concern; it tells the story of the Church from the Nation and nations. Though the Church from nations was in sin, her beauty enkindled God, therefore, He wished to retrieve her from her old nature. (The nature of the Church's beauty will be discussed later). Mar Jacob finds 'type' of the Church in Leah and Rachel, the wives of patriarch Jacob. Leah was tender eyed and she has represented the Church from the Nation but Rachel was beautiful[95] (Gen 29:17) and she has represented the Church from nations. Jacob at his first sight felt love with Rachel and he kissed her. In order to marry her he served her father for seven years. But Laban deceived him; instead of Rachel Laban gave him Leah.[96] However, Jacob was determined and he served his father-in-law for another seven years (Mar Jacob, in another homily, says that Jacob served Laban for twenty years though the source is unknown)[97] to get Rachel.[98] Finally, he married her and returned to his father's house at Canaan.

Mar Jacob portrays Rachel as an Old Testament 'type' of Church who engenders very similitude in the New Testament Church. Like the Son of God betrothed the Church of nations,[99] Jacob betrothed a bride from the daughters of a pagan. Her sister Leah was the first wife of Jacob, but she was not fair and her eyes were ugly. Mar Jacob compared the eyes of Leah with the disobedient

---

[94] Bedjan, *HS* III, 223.8-9; ET. "On Our Lord and Jacob," *TV* 4.4(1993), 64.323-324.

[95] Bedjan, *HS* III, 220.2; ET. "On Our Lord and Jacob," *TV* 4.4(1993), 61.253.

[96] Bedjan, *HS* III, 216.1-21; ET. "On Our Lord and Jacob," *TV* 4.4(1993), 57.165-58.185.

[97] Bedjan, *HS* III, 331.17; ET. "Why Our Lord Abode on Earth for Thirty Years," *TV* 4(1990), 46.210.

[98] Bedjan, *HS* III, 218.13-14; ET. "On Our Lord and Jacob," *TV* 4.4(1993), 60.221-222.

[99] See more discussion at 5.3.9.

Israel. However, Rachel was very beautiful because she was obedient and faithful. He says that the mystery of the Church lay on her face.[100]

> How lightly esteemed is the tale of Leah, whose eyes were without beauty?
> Why then is it told, except for the type (*rozo*) that was brought to pass in her?
> How glorious is her sister Rachel in the readings!
> The beauty of the Church was hide in her, wherefore great is her glory.[101]
> The great Jacob wearied himself behind the flocks
> for twenty years because of Rachel, the daughter of the Haranites.
> And the Messiah came and showed His love by adding ten more,
> when because of the Church He abased Himself for thirty years.[102]

Mar Jacob in his homily *On Our Lord and Jacob and Church and Rachel* very beautifully portrayed and compared Rachel and the Church. He starts it from Jacob's first meeting with Rachel at the well. A parallel picture is visible in the *Homily on the Baptism of Our Redeemer* which depicts the emotions of the Church, the bride of Christ. Many similarities are visible between these homilies in the depiction of the Church and Rachel and Christ and Jacob relationships. When Jacob, the 'type' of Christ the Bridegroom, arrived at the well, Rachel, the 'type' of the Church, and her sheep were eagerly waiting for somebody to lift away the stone on the top of the well. The well was filled with mysteries rather than water.[103] When Christ, the Bridegroom, arrived for the baptism from the hands of the Baptist, the Church was enthusiastically waiting for the Bridegroom to inaugurate baptism.[104]

Mar Jacob compares the weight of the stone lid on the well with the heaviness of the sins. Just as the shepherds could not remove the stone, but only Jacob, only Son of God could remove the sins of the world. But when Jacob, the 'type' of Christ, saw the beauty of Rachel and her thirsty flock the mystery came upon him and multiplied his strength and removed the rock.[105] On the other hand, the beauty of the Church compelled the Bridegroom to baptism. When He saw the beauty of the Church; though He has no necessity to be baptized He descended into the water for baptism and quenched the thirst

---

[100] Bedjan, *HS* III, 223.13-14; ET. "On Our Lord and Jacob," *TV* 4.4(1993), 64.13-14.

[101] Bedjan, *HS* III, 209.19-210.1; ET. "On Our Lord and Jacob," *TV* 4.4(1993), 53.35-38.

[102] Bedjan *HS* III, 331.17-332.2; ET. "Why Our Lord Abode on Earth for Thirty Years," *TV* 4(1990), 46.209-212.

[103] Bedjan, *HS* III, 210.13-211.17; ET. "On Our Lord and Jacob," *TV* 4.4(1993), 53.47-54.76. In Eastern Church's tradition as a whole the sacraments are known as mysteries. ܐ̈ܪܙܐ in Syriac and μηστιριον in Greek tradition. Mar Jacob uses the same term here. Thus, by telling mystery was filled in the well, he prefigures the symbol of baptism in the well of Jacob.

[104] Bedjan, *HS* I, 171.20-21; ET. *FH* VI, 167.89-90.

[105] Bedjan, *HS* III, 210.19; ET. "On Our Lord and Jacob," *TV* 4.4(1993), 53.56.

of the Church.[106] For the sake of Rachel, Jacob served Laban (fourteen years); in order to betroth the Church our Lord served thirty years in this world. Rachel was taken with tears and the Church was espoused with the passion of her betrothed.[107] The Church was redeemed by Jesus Christ from sin and death. By the betrothal Rachel was redeemed from among the idols. He is seeing a 'type' of Church in Rachel. When Jacob lifted the stone from the mouth of the well to facilitate water for Rachel and her flocks is typified as Son of God who lifted away the sins of the Church by His redeeming activities of baptism and crucifixion. Like Rachel and her flocks were able to drink from the well through the intervention of Jacob; the Church was able to drink the cup of salvation through Jesus Christ. Thus, Rachel represents the Church from the nations. More than that, Rachel despised her father's house gods by putting them as a seat (Gen 31:34)[108] and the bride from the nations cast away the idols and worshipped the true God. Mar Ephrem also comments on this and says, "now Jacob loved Rachel greatly, since she loved his God and despised her father's images: for not only by stealing them did she dishonor them as something totally useless, but she even made them into a seat for menstruation when her father's servants searched for them."[109] Ephrem says Leah is the prototype of the earlier nation; Rachel is the prototype of the Church.[110] Justin Martyr said, "However, Leah is your people and the synagogue, but Rachel is our Church."[111]

5.2.2. Tamar: A Type of Church

Mar Jacob portrays Tamar, who had found a place in the genealogy of the Son of God (Mt 1:3), as a 'type' of the Church. The story of Tamar is depicted in Genesis 38. According to Botha, this must be a later addition to the text. Because, he substantiates that, the story falls in the middle of the story of Joseph.[112] Both Jewish and Christian traditions laud and praise Tamar. *Midrash ha-Gadhol* affirms that, "Neither has Tamar incited fornication, nor has Judah sought to fornicate: it is from me that the matter originates, since the King Messiah will arise from Judah."[113] Mar Ephrem says that Tamar strongly

---

[106] Bedjan, *HS* I, 193.5-8; ET. *FH* VI, 186.529-532.

[107] Bedjan, *HS* III, 211.22-212.10; ET. "On Our Lord and Jacob," *TV* 4.4(1993), 54.27-55.90.

[108] Rilliet, *SHF* IV, 596.8-9.

[109] Mathews, *GenComm,* XXIX. 4, 179.

[110] McCarthy, *CommDiat.* III.17, 81.

[111] Justin, *Dial.* 134.6.

[112] Botha, "Ephrem the Syrian's Treatment of Tamar," 16. See the story of Tamar described at 2.1.7.

[113] Brock, *The Treasure House of Mysteries.* 85.

believed that the Messiah will come from Judah; therefore she dressed like a prostitute and it is for our sake she became a prostitute.[114] He states Tamar's adultery was chaste and because of this the Church is saved.[115]

According to Mar Jacob, the story of Tamar tells the story of a holy prostitute. Mar Jacob asks the question why Moses, who drove away all prostitutes from his people, extols this one? And he finds answer and says: "Though her way was ugly, her intention was right and her faith was beautiful."[116] Mar Jacob says that Tamar had divinely known the importance of the seed of Abraham[117] and she yearningly desired for that. He says: "Tamar's intention and prayer made her a holy woman. Tamar very earnestly looked for a seed from the root of Judah."[118] Her two husbands were killed because of their inequities and her father-in-law, Judah, also was unfair with her. Even though she was in a desperate situation, she was looking for a chance to achieve her goal. Therefore, she put-on the dress of a prostitute and ensnared Judah and snatched what she wanted from him.[119] He writes: "This woman openly became a wanton-hearted prostitute; she went out and sat by the crossroads to ensnare a man. It was for You, O Son of God, that she was gazing out You to come to her."[120] According to her wish she conceived from Judah.[121] But when Judah knew that his daughter-in-law became pregnant he ordered to kill her. But she produced three pledges (the ring, the staff, and scarf) to the executioners and told them to show these to their master and say that the owner of these things is responsible for her pregnancy.[122] They brought to Judah and Judah became ashamed and acknowledged openly that "she is more innocent than I; let her not be abused."[123]

Both the Church and Tamar earnestly waited for the Savior; and Tamar trod the way resembling the Church's way before her.[124] Tamar was brought from the nations and the Church was also brought out from among nations. Tamar was deprived for a long time and the Church also was deprived for long

---

[114] *HVir.* XXII.19-21, 80; ET. McVey, *Ephrem the Syrian,* 359-360.

[115] *HNat.* IX.10, 65; ET. McVey, *Ephrem the Syrian,* 126.

[116] Brock, *Jacob of Serugh's Verse Homily on Tamar (Gen 38),* 296.150-155.

[117] Brock, *Jacob of Serugh's Verse Homily on Tamar (Gen 38),* 295.67.

[118] See, the King was hidden in Judah; Tamar stole Him from his loins
Today there has shone out the splendor of the beauty
Whose hidden from she loved, (*HNat*, I.12, 2; ET. McVey, *Ephrem the Syrian,* 65).

[119] Brock, *Jacob of Serugh's Verse Homily on Tamar (Gen 38),* 299.271.

[120] Brock, *Jacob of Serugh's Verse Homily on Tamar (Gen 38)*, 296.127-128.

[121] Brock, *Jacob of Serugh's Verse Homily on Tamar (Gen 38),* 300.294.

[122] Brock, *Jacob of Serugh's Verse Homily on Tamar (Gen 38),* 301.340.

[123] Brock, *Jacob of Serugh's Verse Homily on Tamar (Gen 38),* 301.360.

[124] Brock, *Jacob of Serugh's Verse Homily on Tamar (Gen 38),* 301.373-374.

time. Tamar held three pledges for her deliverance from death; the Church also has three pledges for the deliverance of her children, faith, baptism, and the Cross of Light, these will deliver her children from the heat of *Gehenna.*[125]

Mar Jacob brings out three women in the history of Israel who were conscious about the importance of the seed of Judah: they are Rachel, Leah, and Ruth. All three of them were chaste women but they acted like wanton and prostitutes and impudently asked for the seed of Abraham;[126] they were aware of the wealth hidden in Abraham's seed. Therefore, Tamar and Ruth snatched the seed even without the will of their husbands; they actually plundered the wealth that they desired.[127] Moreover, this was a divine plan and the mistress of mysteries (Holy Spirit) invited them to be part of the plan which was eternally decided by the Father.[128] Otherwise, these chaste women, who lived in modesty and nobility, would not act like harlots in impudent ways. To them the deed which they did was not harlotry, but love for the blessed seed which was hidden in the descendents of Abraham.[129] Mar Jacob states:

> These women, while running after men,
> were yearning for the Son of God's great Epiphany.
> And they struggled for the seed of the house of Abraham,
> since they had learnt in it the peoples of the earth would be blessed.
> It was not harlotry in the case of these sincere women;
> but love for the blessed seed of that incited them.[130]

The Churches from the Syriac tradition extol and remember Tamar's name for her heroic acts. Especially, they see importance to Tamar's three witnesses that rescued her from punishment. Today, the Church considers them as 'type' of sacraments of pledge that rescue the believer from eternal perdition. A prayer from the East Syriac Church says: "For as by a ring truth of Judah towards Tamar was brought light, and by a ring the rule over Egypt was given to Joseph… This is the ring wherewith the holy Church is espoused to the heavenly Bridegroom, and the body and the blood of Christ is received for the forgiveness of sins…"[131] *The Order of the Holy Matrimony* of the West Syriac tradition describes the signet rescued Tamar from being slain.[132] To show the importance of the Holy Trinity the same liturgy sings: "Tamar became

---

[125] Brock, *Jacob of Serugh's Verse Homily on Tamar (Gen 38),* 301.375-379.

[126] Brock, *Jacob of Serugh's Verse Homily on Tamar (Gen 38),* 295.75-85, 90-95.

[127] Brock, *Jacob of Serugh's Verse Homily on Tamar (Gen 38),* 295.85-88, 90-96.

[128] Brock, *Jacob of Serugh's Verse Homily on Tamar (Gen 38),* 295.99.

[129] Brock, *Jacob of Serugh's Verse Homily on Tamar (Gen 38),* 282.67-70, 295.111-112.

[130] Brock, *Jacob of Serugh's Verse Homily on Tamar (Gen 38)*, 283.107-112.

[131] Badger, *The Nestorians and their Rituals* II, 252.

[132] *Koodashakramangal,* 59.

splendid through three and David became splendid with three. The faithful and holy Church is glorifying the Trinity with songs of praise."[133] Thus, Tamar has an unequal reputation in the Church as a bold woman who by her faith and prayer became the grandmother of Jesus Christ the bridegroom.

These examples of women in the Old Testament expound the importance of women in the Church as well as their piety in the making of the Church. Even in a patriarchal social background these women achieve their goals and stand up along with heroic men. They are role models to the marginalized women folk of the Church. The women have a pertinent role in the Church in the present day to keep the faith and practices continued and undistorted as it was in the early Church. It also shows the importance of sacraments in the modern world. Just like the belongings of Judah saved Tamar from death the sacraments save the faithful from eternal damnation.

5.3. Various Aspects of Bride Imagery in Mar Jacob's Homilies

When the Church is considered the prospective bride of the Son of God, the heavenly Bridegroom, Mar Jacob attributes several qualifications and dimensions to the Church and they are looked into in this session. The whole perception is based on two aspects: Bride a means or medium of salvation and the selection of nations as Church, the bride, in lieu of the Nation, Israel.

5.3.1. Bride: A Medium of Salvation

The 'bride' imagery of the bible is a symbol of divine protection and eternal salvation. The Scripture says that whoever believe in the Bridegroom will be saved (Jn 3:36). Sons of the bridal chamber, as long as the bridegroom is with them, do not want to fast or worry about the world's troubles (Mt 9:15; Mk 2:18). Those who are ready to receive the Bridegroom will enter with Him in the lighted chambers where the Bridegroom abides (Mt 25:1-10) and they will become one (Eph 5:32). The bride is predestined for a life with the Bridegroom at the eternal bridal chamber. Therefore, the image of the bride, as an individual, is a symbol and, as a community (Church), is a medium of salvation. The Old Testament covenants also remind the same divine protection of the Bridegroom Yahweh. Through the election and covenantal relationship with Israel Yahweh chose her as a medium of salvation for the people of God.

According to Mar Jacob the Church and a believer are not two identities. He uses both as two sides of a coin; or a believer is a microcosm of the greater Church. According to him the creation of 'man and wife' in itself is a symbol of the divine protection. Though it could be seen in different places of this study this paragraph delineates the whole salvation process through the Church in brief. The 'man' and 'wife' in the Genesis account (Gen 3:24) represents God

[133] *Koodashakramangal,* 70.

and the Church.[134] Therefore, the abstraction of Church is imbedded in the Bible from the beginning and is symbolically and mysteriously delineated throughout the Old Testament.[135] The Old Testament Israel, which elected as the people of God, is a prototype of the Church. The Bridegroom is a forgiving figure. He redeemed Israel from the slavery of Egypt[136] and later redeemed the Church from the slavery of idols.[137] He washed the bride and instituted priesthood and baptism in the Church for the renewal of the bride.[138] He parted His body and blood for the salvation of the bride and for eternal communion with her.[139] He opened the gates of Paradise by receiving the lance on His side to confirm the entrance of the bride into salvation.[140] He removed the idols from the nations and established Churches in the four quarters of the world and cross for her protection and sacraments for her salvation.[141] Those who renounce their old nature of idolatry and enter the community of thr Church will be saved. In view of the above, the Church in the world is a medium of salvation.

5.3.2. Bride from Nation and Nations

The notion of Church from the Nation and nations is one of the well developed ecclesiological themes in the theology. In another sense the Church's foundation is laid on two grounds: from the Nation and from the nations. The Church believes that New Testament is the culmination and fulfillment of the Old Testament prophecy and the Church is the New Israel. The Old Testament tells the story through the election of Abraham. God has chosen a special race for the salvation of the world. Salvation to the world through the descendants of Abraham is the basic concept of the Old Testament. Yahweh betrothed His bride through various covenants and finally consecrated her on the top of Mount Sinai. But, Israel, the betrothed one, rejected her Bridegroom, who delivered her from Egypt, and made relation with other gods. When the real Bridegroom came to earth to redeem her from her sins she not only rejected the Bridegroom but she killed Him (Mt 21:38). Now the Bridegroom selected another bride from the nations, which is the Church. But the Jews did

---

[134] Bedjan, *HS* III, 288.20-21; ET. Brock, "On the Veil of Moses," in *Studies in Syriac Spirituality*, 77.108-109.

[135] Bedjan, *HS* III, 211.11; ET. "On Our Lord and Jacob," *TV* 4.4(1993), 54.69; cf. Bedjan, *HS* V, 335.1-8; ET. "A Homily on Samson," *TV* 11(1992), 55.79-86.

[136] Amar, "A Metrical Homily on Holy Mar Ephrem," 36.49-38.61; Bedjan, *HS* I, 7.4-11.

[137] Bedjan, *HS* II, 237.3-10.

[138] Bedjan, *HS* I, 192.4-5; ET, *FH* VI, 185.507-508.

[139] Bedjan, *HS* III, 647.2-3.

[140] Bedjan, *SMS,* 813.1-2; ET. *FH* XVI, 335.91-92.

[141] Bedjan, *HS* III, 413.5-20; ET. "The Parable of the Leaven," *TV* 3(1989), 47.29-44.

not accept the argument of the Church that God elected another bride from nations. Against the Jewish argument of salvation through the Nation the Fathers make counter argument that, Abraham was not only the father of Israel but of all nations. Aphrahat says that God extended salvation through Abraham to all nations and not for the Jews only.[142] Jacob's returns from Laban's place with two wives represent our Savior.[143] Ephrem says that when Jacob blessed Manasseh and Ephraim by the crossed hands represent the Churches of two nations.[144] From this foundation Mar Jacob built his teachings.

Mar Jacob finds many 'types' in the Old Testament which represent both the Church from the Nation and from nations. Jordan is the meeting point of these two streams; he says that the arrival of our Lord to Jordan is the true boundary between the two.[145] The two wives of Jacob, the great patriarch; Leah and Rachel represent the Church from the Nation and from nations. He writes: "The Nation and the nations were signified Leah and Rachel; The Synagogue and the Church were heralded in the two sisters."[146] The beautiful Rachel represents the nations and Leah, who with tender eye, represents the Nation. He says regarding the betrothal of Christ from the nations: "He set his face to come to espouse the Church of nations, and in divers times He was revealed in allegories."[147] Another illustration about this pair is:

> Now, for the Church's sake, God served mankind
> through revelations and mighty works of the manhood.
> And because the daughter of the nation (*ame*) was the elder, though ill-favored
> she was given to the Lord, like Leah, the elder,
> For this nation (*amo*) was, indeed, God's first-born (*bukro*)
> and though the daughter of the nations (*amme*) was beautiful, she was left aside.
> It was not fair that the younger should go in before the elder,
> and so Laban bore witness that instead of Rachel, he gave Leah.[148]

---

[142] When God blessed Abraham and set him as the head for all who have faith, who are righteous and just, it was not for only one nation that God made him father, but for many nations, as he said to him: The name shall not be call Abram, but Abraham shall be thy name, because I have made thee father for a multitude of nations (Gen 17:5) (Parisot, *Demo,* XI. 1; 468.5-8; ET. Valavanolickal, *Demonstrations* II, 2).

[143] Parisot, *Demo,* IV.6, 149.12-16; ET. Valavanolickal, *Demonstrations* I, 81.

[144] Here too the cross is clearly symbolized to depict that mystery with which Israel the firstborn departed, just as Manasseh the firstborn, and the peoples increase in the manner of Ephraim the younger (*CommGen,* 110; ET, Mathews, *CommGen,*199).

[145] Rilliet, *SHF* II, 552.3-9; ET. *FH* VII, 190.4.

[146] Bedjan, *HS* III, 219.7-8; ET. "On Our Lord and Jacob," *TV* 4.4(1993), 60.237-238.

[147] Bedjan, *HS* III, 208.5-6; ET. "On Our Lord and Jacob," *TV* 4.4(1993), 51.5-6.

[148] Bedjan, *HS* III, 220.12-19; ET. "On Our Lord and Jacob," *TV* 4.4(1993), 61.263-62.272.

Mar Jacob's contemplation is clear in these lines. Though, through their disobedience, the nation's beauty has turned to ugliness, but being the first born, God received them to the row of the saved. Beyond that, although she was lame she entered the bridal chamber being the firstborn due to the covenant with Abraham before the beautiful nations.[149] Aphrahat and Ephrem bring another type comparing David's marriage with the daughters of two kings to explain the dual origin of the Church corresponding to Israel and nations.[150]

Mar Jacob in his homily *A Metrical Homily on Holy Mar Ephrem* compares Prophet Moses and Mar Ephrem, in which he compares women of Israel with women from the Church of Syria: As Moses taught women of Israel not to refrain from the praise of God, Ephrem instructs women to praise God. He compares the deliverance of Israel from Egypt with that of the deliverance of nations through Jesus Christ. The daughters of Hebrew saw the deliverance through the sea and at the inspiration of Moses they praised God; Ephrem taught the women of the nations their deliverance through Jesus Christ and they praised the deliverer.

> The daughters of the Hebrews saw the deliverance, and clapped (their) hands
> to give praise at the command of Moses to the One who delivered them.
> Chosen Ephrem (did) the same with his teaching;
> by the daughters of the nations, behold, (our) great Deliverer is praised.
> Greater is this glory than that which was there,
> just as the deliverance which here is greater than that one.
> With that deliverance, the sea parted before the daughter of Jacob;

---

[149] In another homily Mar Jacob portrays Leah and Rachel as two women who were desired for the seed of Abraham:

> Leah and Rachel, straightforward women of integrity,
> were contending over Him in the land of Aram.
> They had heard that in the seed of the House of Abraham
> all the peoples were going to be blessed and fire fell upon their minds!
> For this reason there befell a dispute between the two of them,
> and, as if over some treasure, they fought over a righteous man.
> They performed an action that was most hateful to chaste women:
> one desired, and one asked, impudently;
> they acted without restraint, showing no shame, because they were aware
> of what wealth was concealed in the godly man.
> Rachel, importunate and like a prostitute, demanded of him,
> saying, "Give me children, otherwise I will die."
> Leah, like someone infatuated and loving adultery, hired him,
> and she was not ashamed to plunder the wealth that she so desired.
> It was not with the lust of adulterous women that they were fired,
> but it was for the seed of their weighty man that they longed (Brock, *Jacob of Serugh's Homily on Tamar (Gen 38),* 282.75-283.90).

[150] Parisot, *Demo,* XXI.13, 965.3; ET. Valavanolickal, *Demonstrations* II, 216); cf. Murray, *Symbols of Church and the Kingdom,* 136.

with this (deliverance) of ours, tombs burst open by the hands of our Lord.
Long ago, King Pharaoh drowned because he was obstinate,
now, death is swallowed up by life, and behold, (death) is in disarray.
There, a staff built a wall in the seas that had been breached,
now the cross on solid rock wrought wonders.
Long ago, a way through the sea was opened, and the tribes passed through;
now ravenous *Sheol* is breached, and the nations stream out.
That deliverance caused the living of Egypt to die;
but this (deliverance) of ours raised the dead from (their) tombs.
Long ago, the tides that had fled from the staff flowed back;
while here, the cross has pulled down the idols that were numerous.
Long ago, a boastful bride came up out of the sea,
while Hebrew women played tambourines to give praise.
And now, with the redeemed church bathed in baptism,
our sisters play the melodies of Ephrem to make a joyful sound.[151]

Here, Mar Jacob comments on the intervention of God in the historical times and compares His saving acts in two different occasions among the Israelites. The first one is exclusively for the redemption of daughters of Jacob from the slavery of Egypt and the second one is for the salvation of the whole world through the establishment of the Church. Here, 'the whole world' will include both Israel and nations; the Church from Nation and nations. Origen commenting on Ephesians says the salvation was predestined to the whole world from its beginning.[152]

The Fathers of the Church, especially Mar Jacob, have the opinion that the Church is brought out of the whole world; inclusive of the Nation. Earlier it was considered that salvation is only through the Nation or Israel. But it is extended to the all nations in the time of New Testament bring under umbrella of One Church.

5.3.3. Israel as Bride

Since this aspect has been analyzed earlier[153] only relevant unexplored areas are looked into here. Mar Jacob visions interconnectedness between Yahweh and Israel even from the creation itself.[154] Mar Jacob, when he admonishes

---

[151] Amar, "A Metrical Homily on Holy Mar Ephrem," 37.49-39:59.

[152] For You must not think that she is called the Bride or the Church only from the time, when the Savior come in the flesh: she is called from the beginning of human race and from the very foundation of the world. In fact, if I look for the origin of this profound mystery under Paul's guidance, even "before" the foundation of the world… "as He chose us in Christ before the foundation of the world, that we should be holy and unspotted in his sight, predestinating us in charity unto the adoption of sons (*Eph.* 1.4; in *Cant. Liber* II, GCS 33, 157; cited Desimone, *Bride and Bridegroom,* 40).

[153] Supra 3.4.1.

[154] Supra, 3.5.1.

Jews on their betrayal of Christ, portrays the Nation as the bride who rejected her heavenly Bridegroom. Israel is depicted as the one who was chosen by the Father for the redemption of the world but went astray. Finally she rejected and killed the true Bridegroom, Christ.

Mar Jacob says: "Moses then gloriously depicted the bride of light who sang praise, once delivered from persecutors."[155] He calls the liberated Israel from the bondage of Egypt as the "daughter of Jacob,"[156] the boastful bride who came up out of sea,[157]and as an innocent dove.[158] But, after the incident of worship of the molten calf under the leadership of Aaron (Ex 32:6), he calls Israel as an adulterous bride.[159] He vividly portrayed the betrothal of Israel in three homilies.[160] In these homilies he depicts the Sinai covenant as betrothal of Yahweh with Israel. One of the prayers of the West Syriac Church says: "From Egypt, You had redeemed the daughter of the Hebrews to be Your bride. But she forsook You and associated with the strange calf. Since she had forsaken You, rejected her, and come to our clan and I exist in Your name."[161] Still, Yahweh was sympathetic and mercifully forgave her infidelity. In his "Hymn on Resurrection" Mar Ephrem also depicts the betrothal at Mount Sinai:

> A chaste wedding feast took place in the wilderness,
> With bridal chamber set on Mount Sinai
> The Holy One descended and took in betrothal
> The daughter of Abraham His beloved friend.[162]

In his writings Mar Jacob portrayed Israel as the bride of Yahweh. But she rejected her Bridegroom and went for others. The following is a discussion of various characteristics of the bride.

---

[155] Bedjan, *HS* III, 294.11-12; ET. Brock, "On the Veil of Moses," in *Studies in Syriac Spirituality*, 81.227-228.

[156] Bedjan, *HS* I, 13.7-16; Amar, "A metrical Homily on Holy Mar Ephrem," 37.52.

[157] Amar, "A Metrical Homily on Holy Mar Ephrem," 39.58.

[158] Amar, "A Metrical Homily on Holy Mar Ephrem," 43.73.

[159] Rilliet, *SHF* IV, 596.1-2; Bedjan, *HS* I, 449.3; Bedjan, *SMS,* 778:18.

[160] "On the Descent of the Most High on Mount Sinai and the Mysteries of the Church," *HS* I, 3-38,

(no 2), "On the Consecration of the Church and Prophet Moses," *HS* I, 38-48, (no 3), "On the

Consecration of the Church," *HS* IV, 767-789.

[161] *Kashtanubhavazhcha Namaskaram,* 145.

[162] *Resur* III.2, 85; ET. Brock, *The Luminous Eye,* 117.

5.3.4. Israel: The Veiled Bride

Just as the Bridegroom was hidden in the Old Testament[163] Mar Jacob and other Fathers of the Church believed that the bride, Church, was also hidden in the prophecies. They described Israel as the shadow or a prototype of the New Testament Church, and she was veiled under the prophecy. In order to prove this pre-existence of the Church they adopted the prevalent custom, 'veiling', of the Semitic culture. Veiling the woman was a common custom in the Semitic culture (Gen 38:14). Veiling was considered as a symbol of chastity and modesty.[164] In Jewish tradition the betrothed girl should cover her face from men until her marriage. But she can unveil her face before her husband.[165] The author of *Acts of Thomas* brings this cultural peculiarity to the readers. When the bride appears in the bridal chamber she puts her veil on her face.[166] But when the father of the bride arrived in the early morning he sees that bride and the bridegroom are sitting opposite to each other and the veil of the bride was taken off and she does not feel shame.[167]

Mar Jacob also portrays the same when he says about the bride, Israel: "The words of the prophecy had all been like betrothed girls, hidden by a veil from the onlookers. But now the groom has come and uncovered her face, and made her shine (*nahar*). No longer do the betrothed require that veil."[168] The readers can observe that enlightenment occurred in both occasions. The root (light) is used in the *Veil of Moses.* In the *Acts of Thomas,* Jesus appeared to the bridegroom and to the bride in the wedding night and taught them the corruptibility of the marriage bed of this world. Having enlightened, finally, they rejected the wedding of this world and persuaded for the everlasting bridal chamber of the world to come with the eternal Bridegroom. In the case of Israel also Yahweh teaches and prepares His bride through the prophets for the marriage feast.[169] In fact the role of the bridegroom is to teach or enlighten the bride. Thus through the custom of veiling the fathers express their conviction of the pre-existence of the Church in Israel.

Why did God put a veil on the face of Israel is a good question to ask. Mar Jacob has his own answer for this question. He says that God out of His love put a veil on the face of the bride because she was ugly looking.[170] The

---

[163] Supra 4.2.1.

[164] Bedjan, *HS* III, 216.12-13; ET. "On Our Lord and Jacob," *TV* 4.4(1993), 58.175.

[165] Adams, *Experiencing World History,* 72.

[166] *AAA*, 71.

[167] *AAA*, I.13.

[168] Bedjan, *HS* III, 299.9; ET. Brock, "On the Veil of Moses," in *Studies in Syriac Spirituality*, 83.327-328.

[169] Bedjan, *HS* I, 449.19-20; ET. *FH* X, 252.99-100.

[170] Bedjan, *HS* III, 219.20-220.1; ET. "On our Lord and Jacob," *TV* 4.4(1993), 61.250-252.

'ugliness' which Mar Jacob mentions is regarding Israelites' worship of the golden calf or idol worship. When Moses was with Yahweh on the top of Mount Sinai, in the valley, the people under the leadership of Aaron, worshipped the golden calf (Ex 32:1-7), which made her ugly. But the greatness of Moses covered this ugliness. He says: "

> The daughter of the Hebrews stood veiled (*mḥapyo*) before Adonai,
> her ugliness (*soonoyoh*) concealed by Moses' brightness, and she was not known.
> She was thought by the onlookers to be great Church,
> and so she sought for a covering (*taḥpeeto*), lest she be found out.[171]

The next lines elaborate the reasons for the veiling of the Nation. She was in her appearance more hateful than Leah. The Nation was blind; though Leah had tender eyes she had vision. To call a molten calf Lord she lost the power of discernment. The lack of discernment on the part of the Nation is her blindness. On the other hand, Leah has the discernment and like an infatuated one entered the bridal chamber in the shade of darkness.[172] Even in this hateful condition, Yahweh from the depth of His eternal love, and not because of her beauty, chose the Nation as His Bride. In spite of the ugliness since she was the first born of God. He veiled it from the onlookers and married her:

> Her light was taken away, for her eyes were not even soft (Gen 29:17).
> She looked at the calf and called it Lord because she was blind,
> for she had no sight that discerns the truth.
> She, then, who was bereft of light, went in first,
> while the comely Church, in Rachel's likeness, was left aside.
> She was veiled (*mḥapyo*) by Moses and no man knew that she was blind (*sameeto*);
> and in her covering (*teḥpeeto*) she seemed to be beautiful.
> She who was well favored was hid among the nations and unknown
> While she who was entirely without beauty was veiled and entered the house of God.[173]

Mar Jacob has the opinion that God veiled the bride from the Nation out of His love and betrothed her. Christ extended the same love towards the Church when He had taken her from among the idols and betrothed her.

5.3.5. Prophets: The Teachers of the Bride

In the Old Testament the prophets repeatedly ask Israel to return to the covenants and to her real Bridegroom Yahweh (Lev 19:4; Deut 3:30; 30:2; Isa 31:6; 44:25; 55:7; Jer 3:1,7, 14; 4:1; 18:11; 24:7; 31:18; 36:3; Hos 3:5; 6:1; 12:6; 14:1). Whenever the Nation went astray and embraced the paramours

---

[171] Bedjan, *HS* III, 219.20-220.1; ET. "On our Lord and Jacob," *TV* 4.4(1993), 61.249-250.

[172] Brock, *Jacob of Serugh's Homily on Tamar* (*Gen 38*), 283.87-90.

[173] Bedjan, *HS* III, 220.3-11; ET. "On Our Lord and Jacob," *TV* 4.4(1993), 61.254-262.

the prophets intercepted and warned them. Prophet Hosea is the greatest among them who was explicitly asked to teach Israel about her adulterous nature through the symbolic act of his own life.[174] Through this example God used the prophet to teach the people about His unmerited love. Jeremiah also curses the infidelity, and faithlessness of Israel (Jer 3:1). These prophets were great teachers against the Phoenician and Canaanite fertility cults and they constantly asked the people of Israel to return to the God of Israel.

Mar Jacob considers these prophets instructors of the people of Israel.[175] People were in the darkness of idolatry and sin. At the time of Moses, the voice of idolatry was powerful. The earth was full of assemblies of empty feasts. Lord bestowed the Law, as a medicinal herb to battle the immense wound of the impiety.[176] Therefore, God sent prophets as His ambassadors to instruct and chastise the People of Israel. But the Nation did not listen to them.[177] They gave laws and commandments to enlighten the people. He called mankind towards Him by all means. He says:

> In times primeval, the world was in darkness (*ḥeško*); away from knowledge.
> It was the night of idolatry (*lileo dptkrwto*) over the whole universe.
> The sculpted idols in the whole world were as obstacles (*tql*),
> but because it was night, one endeavored not to see them.
> And the Law descended from Sinai
> to be in the world, as a lamp in the night, where it would advance strongly
> as a column of fire *amoodo dnooro*) in the midst of a camp.
> The Law of God found itself in the world
> for that person stumbled neither against idols nor carved stones.
> Moses, in the night, carried the light, and made it apparent.[178]

But the efforts went in vain. "Prophets were beating at her high gates and awakening her, but she was sleeping with her many beloved companions."[179] However, by the time of the Church, she was eager to hear from the prophets and was willing to learn about the true Bridegroom and prepares to abandon their unfaithfulness. Therefore, she invoked the prophets to teach her. Mar Jacob states:

> She invoked Isaiah to learn from him about John;

---

[174] Schillebeeckx said about this: "God's activity within the covenant provided the model for his own married life, as a prophetic message to be passed on to God's people" (Schillebeeckx, *Marriage: Human Reality and Saving Mystery,* 40).

[175] Bedjan, *HS* I, 49.10-50.8; ET. "On the Serpent of Brass," 41.10-42.24.

[176] Albert, *HCJ,* 90.70-75; cf. Benin, "Command, Covenants, and Jews," 146.

[177] Bedjan, *SMS,* 725.23-726.1; ET. *FH* I, 47.125-126.

[178] Albert, *HCJ* VII, 210.445-457; cf. Benin, "Command Covenants, and Jews," 147.

[179] Bedjan, *HS* I, 449.19-20; ET. *FH* X, 252.99-100.

"who is this one who announces to me the kingdom of high"?
Come, O Prophet, come explain to me about the herald,
because I need to learn the truths from you
I am accepting your word because it is for my sake;
for, behold, I have heard the speech of your discourse since a long time back.
You assured me about conversion in your prophecy;
"Come, see, may be the time has come that I may enter into it..."
Isaiah approached to teach the Church about John the Baptist.
Since he is a son of the mystery of the Bridegroom, your Lord, accept his words.
This is the voice that cries in the wilderness before the Son of the King;
"Prepare, O you prepare, the way for the Lord in faith.
God descended, and be purified, do not excuse yourself from the herald.
He makes smooth the steep place so as to set in order the way for the King
She invoked Isaiah to learn from him about John;
who is coming."[180]

Now she took John as a friend of the Bridegroom and listened to the mysteries of the Bridegroom. John prepared the bride pure for the pure Bridegroom. In order to purge her, he reminded the prophecy of David, "forget your people and cling to your husband" (Ps 45:10). The bride was enlightened by the voice of John and cleansed her mind from adulterous thoughts. Mar Jacob states:

Behold, David, the singer of the Spirit, approached singing to her:
"Hear, my daughter and look and give heed to the glorious things.
Forget your people and those of your father's house because they are wavering..."
The church learned from (*ilep*) John as well as from David
and she became assured that He is the Bridegroom to whom she is betrothed.[181]

Mar Jacob, when he was describing the scene on the shore of Jordan, writes, when John finished the teaching on the Bridegroom the bride yearns for the Bridegroom. She saw several men there, but waited for a confirmation from the Baptist to receive the Bridegroom.[182] Mar Jacob called the Church a chaste woman who is looking for the Bridegroom.[183] God sent the prophets as teachers to educate the bride but no avail. Unlike the old bride Israel, the Church was obedient to the prophets and received the Bridegroom as her beloved.

5.3.6. Corrupt and Adulterous Bride

The virginity of the bride is an important concern in the Jewish tradition. During the marriage they often demonstrated it in public (Deut 22:15-16).

[180] Bedjan, *HS* I, 169.2-170.7; ET. *FH* VI, 164.31-165.55.

[181] Bedjan, *HS* I, 176.1-8; ET. *FH* VI, 171.172-178.

[182] Bedjan, *HS* I, 173.6-7; ET. *FH* VI, 168.115-116.

[183] Bedjan, *HS* I, 171.16; ET. *FH* VI, 167.86.

Although, in biblical times, polygamy was common among the upper classes (Judg 8:30; 2Sam 5:13; 1Kings 11:1-8) the biblical concept of marriage is essentially monogamous (Gen 2:24). Many references to marriage in the wisdom literature seem to assert monogamy (Ps 128; Prov 12:4; 18:22; 19:14; 31:1031; Sir 25:1).[184] In the Old Testament, Israel was portrayed as an adulterous wife because of her infidelity towards her Bridegroom, Yahweh. Yet He loved her and protected her.

Mar Jacob portrays Israel as an adulteress. In one occasion Mar Jacob laments that the Bridegroom arrived but the bride is not ready. She is in slumber. Mar Jacob describes the prophetic call: Prophet Zechariah cries out "behold, your king has come" (Zech 9:9). Isaiah cried out: Awake, awake and put-on the power of the arm of the Lord (Isa 51:9). But the bride remained in sluggishness and heavy sleep with love of idols and an adulterous mind.[185] "She had embraced (*apaq*) the calf (Ex 32:1-6), her corruptor (*mšḥṭno*), she carried the tent of Malcum (Acts 7:43), she slept with the star [Saturn] (Amos 5:26), she kissed the four-faced idol {2Chron 33:7 (peshitha)}, she took herself to wicked folly with the idols of Jeroboam (2Chron 13:8)."[186] The following is a detailed analysis of the adulterous nature of Israel:

> Truth is her adversary and falsehood is the light of her countenance;...
> She loves to commit adultery, and since you are holy, she flees from you;
> she loves idols, and since you are God, she hates to see you.
> At the table of Baal the daughter of Hebrews grew fat,
> and she forgot (*ṭ'o*) your Father and does not receive you because she is polluted.
> She rejects (*ṭlam*) and kills because this is her work and the labor of her hands;
> she loves darkness and because you are light, she shuns you.[187]
> She was marred and become grieved that the Bridegroom had come...
> She became tied (*sbk*) up with the shameful four-faced idols
> and she was not able to open the gates to the King who had come.
> She was anxious to serve her small idols
> but for the service of praise to her Lord she was not solicitous.
> She adorned (*sgd*) the totem pole and for Tammuz she made lamentation;
> She loved Malcom and offered (*dbḥ*) up sacrifices to Baal her companion.
> She openly worshipped Saturn and Chemosh and Ashima,
> and to the gods of all gentiles she made feasts.
> She was addicted to the Egyptian idols
> and she was not able to sing praise together with the disciples...[188]

---

184 Raymond, "Marriage," 563.

185 Rilliet, *SHF* IV, 596.13-25; ET. *FH* XI, 268.21.

186 Rilliet, *SHF* IV, 596.3-6; ET. *FH* XI, 269.23.

187 Bedjan, *HS* II, 368.18-369.7; ET. *FH* VIII, 225.451-462.

188 Bedjan, *HS* I, 449.1-14; ET. *FH* X, 251.81-252.94.

The miserable bride was intoxicated with the lust of idols. She rejected the Royal Bridegroom and became adulterous.[189] When the real Bridegroom, who betrothed her on Sinai,[190] arrived to marry her, the adulterous wife doubted His identity.[191] Mar Jacob continues; she was not able to identify Him because she has several men.[192] Mar Ephrem also has the same opinion in this regard.[193]

Through this concept adulterous bride Mar Jacob conjures up the unfaithful Israel who rebuffed the heavenly Bridegroom who really saved her from the tribulations of Egypt and guided her through the desert to the land of Canaan. Israel worshiped other gods and offered sacrifice to their idols. This was serious crime and transgression of the commandments. The reason for rejecting the bride 'Israel was their deprivation.

5.3.7. The Bride Divorced the Bridegroom

God Almighty never wished to let His creation into destruction, therefore, He, through the covenant betrothed His people like a bride. He seized her from their enemies and made her as His own. He liberated her from Egypt and gave enormous livelihood in a splendid place and gave laws and commanded to be faithful. But against His ordinance she rejected and divorced Him against the covenantal law.

The Old Testament has two views first it permits divorce with a divorce note and it is held by Torah and in the other view, marriage is a divine covenant and is against divorce without valid reason. According to the earliest concept in this regard man has the full right over his wife and he can divorce her at any time on proving adultery (Deut 20: 5-7). At the same time, woman has no authority over her husband (Judg 19:1-10). Later it is modified : "Suppose a man enters into marriage with a woman, but she does not please him because he finds something objectionable about her, and so he writes her a certificate of divorce, puts it in her hand, and sends her out of his house; she then leaves his house and goes off to become another man's wife." (Deut 24:1-2). So that, at the time of Jesus, the 'bill of divorce' was a practice among the Israelites (Mt 10:4; 1:19). In the due course prophets like Malachi argued that marriage cannot be dissolved without proper reason (Mal 2:14, Prov 2:17). In their

---

[189] Rilliet, *SHF* IV, 596.10-11, 598.9, 602.14; ET. *FH* XI, 269.24, 270.25, 273.35.

[190] Rilliet, *SHF* IV, 596.13; ET. *FH* XI, 269.24.

[191] Rilliet, *SHF* IV, 600.4; ET. *FH* XI, 271.30.

[192] Rilliet, *SHF* IV, 600.21-22; ET. *FH* XI, 272.32.

[193] Moses gave the waters of testing to the synagogue that had fornicated with the calf, so that the mark of the adulteresses would appear on it. This where the law comes from concerning women drinking the waters of testing, so that, in the mark which appeared on the adulteresses, the synagogue would recall its fornication with the calf, and with fear be on guard against another (fornication), and with regret remember the first one. So when they are passing judgment on themselves for straying from their God (McVey, *Homily on Our Lord*, 282-283).

vision marriage is a divine institution, so that, it is indissoluble. Therefore, the reformed prophets like Ezra, Nehemiah, Malachi, etc. repudiated divorce. Jesus was also against divorce (Mt 19:6-9). He said, once two persons enter into the wedlock they will become one body and it is a perfect union nobody can dissolve it. He found the basis of His argument from Genesis 2:24 "Therefore, man shall leaves…"

Obviously, Mar Jacob follows Jesus and prophets; repeats the unfaithfulness of Israel as well as her rejection of her betrothed. Here, against the dominant husbands, bride is the villainess. The prophets through their prophecies educated the bride in several means; forget your people (Ps 45:10)[194] and awake from among the idols.[195] But the bride did not give heed to their call. She rejected the call of the prophets. She ignored the rules of her real Bridegroom, and unwilling to repent and return to Him and live a life which is pleasing to Him (Hos 14:1). Nonetheless, the Bridegroom loved the bride, who was defiled among the Egyptians, and redeemed her from the slavery. In spite of it, the bride loved the idols, despised the Holy One, and openly renounced Him. The more He increased favors to her, and more she adhered to the calf.[196] Israel continuously rejected her true Bridegroom and committed adultery with her lovers. Yet, the Bridegroom did not give the bill of divorce (Isa 50:1). Mar Jacob portrays the cry of Moses regarding the ingratitude of the daughter of the Hebrews:

> O Lord, her (people Israel) mouth is a sea that full of false spirits and all sorts of abuses like rough storms. They forget everything that You did for her in the wilderness. When You with Your father sent me from Mount Sinai with a staff, I performed miracles among them by Your power. I divided the sea, divided the rock, brought manna and quail for their luxurious life in the wilderness. But she forgot all these favors and abused and rejected me. She became crazy and committed adultery by loving forged images and became slave before them. She killed Your priests and prophets.[197]

Here, Mar Jacob elucidates the bride's unfaithfulness and rejection to her Bridegroom through the Old Testament characters. But nowhere has the Bridegroom rejected His bride for her unfaithfulness. Finally the Bridegroom presented himself in person to save her but she receded. Mar Jacob writes:

> Prophets were beating (*ṭorp*) at her gates and awakening (*'er*) her,
> but she was sleeping (*mek*) with her many beloved companions.

---

[194] Bedjan, *HS* I, 176.4; ET. *FH* VI, 171.174.

[195] Bedjan, *SMS,* 769.21; ET. *FH* I, 88.1046; Rilliet, *SHF* IV, 594.14-25; ET. *FH* XI, 268.22.

[196] Bedjan, *HS* II, 369.2-7; ET. *FH* VIII, 225.456-457; cf. *Kashtanubhavazhcha Namaskaram*, 95.

[197] Bedjan, *HS* II, 366.2-21; ET. *FH* VIII, 222.393-223.412.

> Exult, daughter of Zion, but the comrade of claves did not exult,
> for she was grieved (*'oqo*) that the Heir of the Father had come to her.
> She knew Him, for He was unmasking (*prs*) her and she hated Him,
> then she was not pleased that He should be praised by the children…
> Isaiah call out, "Wake up, be stirred, and put on strength"
> And Zechariah called out, "Exult much and be glad because your King has come."…
> But the Hebrew nation was not willing to hear them,
> Nor Isaiah, nor Zechariah or the children either.[198]

Due to unfaithfulness, Mar Jacob concludes that, in the fullness of time the Bridegroom has arrived to marry, but the adulterous bride rejected Him and killed Him. Zechariah sung before the Hebrew nation with his spiritual harp: "Rejoice greatly, O daughter Zion! Shout aloud, O daughter Jerusalem! Lo, your king comes to you; triumphant and victorious is he, humble and riding on a donkey, on a colt, the foal of a donkey (Zech 9:9). But the scornful bride (*kalto bseerto*) did not dance and receive Him.[199] He came to His own and was not received by the lawless (Jn 1:10-11).[200] The Chief Shepherd stood by His flock, but they did not recognize Him.[201] Consequently, the Bridegroom selected a new bride: the Church. Many of the predecessors of Mar Jacob uphold this hypothesis.[202]

Mar Jacob uses the term 'divorce' to exemplify the unfaithfulness of the bride: "She desired to give a letter of divorce (*doollo*) to the Bridegroom, to separate herself from His company [of marriage]."[203] In another homily Mar Jacob states: "When a betrothed woman desires to separate herself from her betrothed, she throw His clothes to Him. Thus the synagogue too, because her

---

[198] Bedjan, *HS* I, 449.20-450.16; ET. *FH* X, 252.99-253.116.

[199] Bedjan, *HS* I, 448.12-20; ET. *FH* X, 251.71-78.

[200] Bedjan, *HS* III, 321.6; ET. "Why Our Lord Abode upon Earth for Thirty Years," *TV* 4(1990), 37.6.

[201] Bedjan, *SMS,* 763.4; ET. *FH* I, 82.903.

[202] Because of all the work of The Lord our God, The Lord has turned it from the Nation to the Church by means of us the Apostles, and He hath removed and forsaken the Nation, (as written in Isaiah, that He hath forsaken the people of the house of Jacob Is 2:6) and Jerusalem is forsaken; and Judah is fallen, and their tongues are iniquity, and they have obeyed not The Lord, (and He hath abandoned the vineyard Matt 23:38), and behold your house is left unto you desolate (*Didascalia*, 104-105). One of the prayers of the West Syriac Church says: "My beloved had a vineyard at the heart of the fertile land. He labored in it and built a fence around it and waited that I produces grapes. In return it produced wild grapes. (Therefore), he rooted it up and scattered it among the gentiles, and he betrothed the holy Church, and her children sing praise (to Him)" (*Kashtanubhavazhcha Namaskaram*, 15). Mar Ephrem says that the Bridegroom divorced the bride because of her unfaithfulness. They brought Him a donkey to ride when He entered Jerusalem to announce her destruction and the expulsion of her children (McVey, *Homily on Our Lord*, 278).

[203] Rilliet, *SHF* IV, 600.2; ET. *FH* XI, 271.

mind fled away from the Holy One…"[204] They realized how they had played the harlot and run after other gods, so they gave him a reed with which to write them a bill of divorce.[205] Though they dipped their hands in his blood they had chance to wash themselves in the waters of baptism.[206] Pilate had his baptism of hands only, later baptism for his whole body, but the bride did not confess.[207] The honor of being the elected one was lost and the Bridegroom elected the new bride, the Church. One of the prayers of the Church states: "In Judas, the congregation separated herself and left Him. (The Son) came and betrothed the loving daughter of the Gentiles and by His covenant, He brought her in."[208] In one the prayer song sung by Mar Jacob proclaims the song of the Church's lamentation:

> The halleluiahs and cries of 'holy' of those above
> and the glorious ministry of spiritual beings.
> You have abandoned and gone after wild animals.
> Alas! O soul, neighbor of the Luminous One,
> image of the Great One (Gen 1:26), how far has your fallen state reached!
> For now thorns are mingled for you in your bread (Gen 3:18-19).[209]

In this way the bride, the corrupt Israel rejected and divorced the Bridegroom. Mar Jacob taught against the Jews and condemned the acts of the bride. His words are very systematic and he brought out the description on the idolatry of Israel by the prophets. He argued that it was not the Bridegroom who divorced the bride but the bride herself divorced her Savior because of her adulterous attributes.

5.3.8. The Crucifier Bride

This section explains Mar Jacob's portrayal of Israel as the crucifier bride. The adulterous bride hated the Bridegroom and went after her lovers. Later, when the real Bridegroom arrived for marriage, she said, He is the heir; let us kill Him (Mk 12:7). The bride went mad, betrayed the Bridegroom and crucified Him. [210] According Mar Jacob the killing is not the first experience for her, even before this, she killed the righteous and innocent men (Mt 21:35; Rev18:23). Satan was proud about her as a dear friend of him. She will act

---

[204] Rilliet, *SHF* V, 622.17-19; ET. *FH* XII, 287.

[205] Bedjan, *HS* II, 547.6.

[206] Bedjan, *HS* II, 561.11-562.21.

[207] Bedjan, *HS* II, 560.1-561.10.

[208] *Kashtanubhavacha Namaskaram*, 145.

[209] Brock, "A Prayer Song by St Jacob of Serugh Recovered," 33, 35.

[210] Bedjan, *HS* II, 587.16; cf. Brock, "The Wedding Feast on Golgotha," 124.

whatever Satan proposes; she killed righteous and innocent men.[211] Mar Jacob calls Israel as the Daughter of Jezebel who knows how to kill innocent.[212] He comments that treachery and cunningness is an inherent nature of Hebrews.

Mar Jacob finds reason for the agitation of the bride: she agitated, because her treachery was revealed to her Bridegroom. She perceived that the Bridegroom will come and asks from her (Mt 21:38) to show Him the truth on the day of the marriage feast. Therefore, she was shaken by her deeds and knew that all the wiles of her misconduct would be unveiled by the Bridegroom.[213] In fact, she was in the snare of the Satan who misled her to the crucifixion of the Son of God. Satan made her heart hard and created envy and jealous in her.[214] She made false witness the Bridegroom and made Him stand in front of the judgment seat. Synagogue, sons of inequity (*bnai avole*)[215] and the sister of Jezebel,[216]gathered false witnesses (*sohade šookore*) and accused against the Bridegroom before Pilate. Jealousy became hot in them (Israel, the bride) and wrath burned in them, and their soul were heated up with a desire for slaughter as they were inflamed by anger so to shed innocent blood, they sought an accusation and they found it by means of cleverness of the ancient serpent.[217] Mar Jacob interprets that when the Jews put him on the scarlet (Mt 27:28) they uses the law of the Old Testament that, if any one touches the holy things he shall die (Num 4:15). Therefore, they put-on Him a part of the veil of the sanctuary and made sure of His death.[218] Mar Jacob says about the wicked deeds of the bride:

> Behold she attacks (*sobko*) you and reviles (*ḥasdo*) you and insults (*ṣar'o*) you
> and through blasphemy her mouth gives vent against your holiness.
> She hates (*sonyo*) and rejects (*ṭo'yo*) and forgets all your good deeds,
> and Zion mocks (*bezḥo*) you and shakes her head at you.

---

[211] Bedjan, *SMS,* 778.11-12; ET. *FH* I, 106.279-280. One of the prayers of Passion Week uses in the West Syriac Church says: The one who killed the prophets and drank their blood, what fault has Isaiah had done to you that he was swan asunder? Jeremiah was thrown into a pit of mud. Zachariah was killed near the altar. O murderous bride, your insanity was incomplete, until you killed the Son and His murder you have destroyed yourselves forever. (*Kashtanubhavazhcha Namaskaram,* 96).

[212] Bedjan, *HS* III, 714.19; ET. "A Homily on Stephen," *TV* 7(1990), 46.85.

[213] Rilliet, *SHF* 596.20-598.4; ET. *FH* XI, 270.25.

[214] Rilliet, *SHF* 616.2-3; ET. *FH* XII, 283.11.

[215] Rilliet, *SHF* V, 616.15.

[216] Rilliet, *SHF* V, 616.14-15; ET. *FH* XII, 283.13.

[217] Rilliet, *SHF* V, 618.16-19; ET. *FH* XII, 285.17.

[218] Rilliet, *SHF* V, 618.18-20; ET. *FH* XII, 285.17; cf. Bedjan, *HS* II, 544.2-3; *Crucif* IV: 3, 56. The interpretation the robe that Jews put on Jesus was the veil of the sanctuary is not taken from the biblical account. Mar Ephrem also discusses the same. Therefore, it should be a common tradition among the Syriac Christianity.

She constructs (*rakbo*) the cross and sharpens (*lotšo*) the spear and unsheathes (*šomto*) the swords.
She plaits a crown and mingles vinegar and mixes it with gall.
And she makes bonds and casts nails and mocks at you.
She crucifies and kills, thirsting for blood, and then it satisfies her.[219]

Israel, the bride made treachery against the Bridegroom and cried out to sentence Him death. She produced false witness (*sohde dšooqr*),[220] clothed in purple (*kalmees dargoono*),[221] and asked for Barabbas.[222] He was smitten, endured torture and pain, mounted on the cross and slept on it.[223] But the Bridegroom willingly suffered all these for the liberation of Adam.[224] Mar Jacob says: "It is not by compulsion that she led you off to suffer, but you yourself wished it."[225] Therefore, Mar Jacob interprets in a very florid language: "the Judge of judges Himself was standing before the judge to be judged as a culpable one. The grass seated on a throne before the Fire while He was standing. A feeble straw questions the Coal of Fire. The Flame embraces the column and the twig scourges it with whips…"[226] Otherwise, nobody can reach His side, because He is a flame of Fire who consumes all. The Church is thankful to her Bridegroom for the sufferings to liberate her from the bondage and sings praise to Him always:

> My beloved, where and when have You seen the bride who committed fornication inside the bridal chamber and suspended her bridegroom on the cross, except Zion, the one who crucified Him? She worshipped the calf and bull and suspended the Good One on the tree. Blessed is He Who had driven out the harlot and betrothed the church instead of her.[227]

In this way the bride became a crucifier of her Bridegroom. Through the killing of the Bridegroom, the adulterous bride made herself a destruction and she made a mockery of herself among the people and she was cast away from the bridal chamber of the Son of God. Mar Jacob says:

The bride went mad and crucified the Bridegroom thus angering the Father
Who entered (the sanctuary) and tore (*sadeeq*) her garments, driving (*trdoh*) her from his inheritance,

---

[219] Bedjan, *HS* II, 367.7-14; ET. *FH* VIII, 223.419-224.426.

[220] Rilliet, *SHF* V, 616.13; ET. *FH* XII, 283.13.

[221] Rilliet, *SHF* V, 622.21-22; ET. *FH* XII, 287.25.

[222] Rilliet, *SHF* V. 626.22-23; ET. *FH* XII, 290.32.

[223] Bedjan, *HS* II, 624.13-625.13; ET. *FH* XIV, 308.13-26.

[224] Rilliet, *SHF* V, 614.8-15; ET. *FH* XII, 282.9.

[225] Bedjan, *HS* II, 367.17; ET. *FH* VIII, 224.428.

[226] Rilliet, *SHF* V, 610.11-15; ET. *FH* XII, 280.2.

[227] *Kashtanubhavazhcha Namaskaram*, 64.

He uncovered her head because she had despised the head of the household.
He made her an object of scoffing among the synagogues for all the harm she had done.
With temple veil, as a covering for one betrothed, he had decked her out in modesty so that she might be chaste in her bridal chamber.
But when she caused him harm (*serḥat*) he tore (*ṣro*) off her veil and spat (*raq*) in her face;
He bared her head and made her an object of ignominy upon earth.
So now your House is left desolate, O Levites,
without any priesthood or sacrifices from now on.[228]

One of the prayers of the Church says about the unfaithfulness and betrayal of the bride and the election of the Church, the new bride, in the place of Israel, the old bride:

> As the bride whom I betrothed, has despised me, I shall betroth another for me, and I shall give her everything that I have. Though I have betrothed Zion, she has despised me and I have dispersed her among the gentiles, lest she might never gather together. Now I have betrothed the Church and (behold) from all quarters of the world, all gentiles are coming to honor her.[229]

This part discussed the unfaithfulness and cruelty of the bride against the Bridegroom. The bride out of her pride and through the deceit of the Satan betrayed the Bridegroom and went behind the paramours and further when the real Bridegroom arrived to save her, she crucified Him. Thus the prophecy was fulfilled (Isa 53:7; Ps 22:12, 18).

5.3.9. Bride from Nations

The same God who reprimanded the people of Israel from taking wives from among the nations (Gen 24:4; 27:46; 28:1,2; Num 12:1) and constituted it as idolatry and adultery says that many from East and West shall sit down with Abraham, Isaac, and Jacob in the Kingdom of God (Mt 8:11; Lk 13:29). In another parable He teaches that God will invite everybody to His kingdom to enjoy the wedding feast (Mt 22:10-15). Though contradictory to each other; still that is the truth. Therefore, as any other actions of Jesus Christ, the concept of inviting people from the nations, especially in the nuptial imagery, are iconoclastic and bold. It involves a liberation aspect as of the event of exorcism of the daughter of the Canaanite woman to whom Jesus told that "it is not good to give children's bread to dogs" (Mt 15:26).

Mar Jacob has the conviction that the Bridegroom took His bride from the Nation and from nations.[230] The Nation, by her free will, committed adultery

---

[228] Bedjan, *HS* II, 587.8-17; cf. Brock, "The Wedding Feast of Blood," 124.

[229] *Kashtanubhavazhcha Namaskaram*, 34; cf. Brock, "Syriac Poetry on Biblical Themes," 68.

[230] Bedjan, *HS* III, 217.17; ET. "On Our Lord and Jacob," *TV* 4.4(1993), 59.203.

by practicing idolatry. On the other hand nations, out of her ignorance, became adulterous through her idolatry. However, when nations came to know the true Bridegroom she did not go back to the adulterous nature. The Bridegroom made a new covenant at the upper room (Mt 26:26-28) to betroth nations. This covenant is the revision of the old covenant through which Yahweh betrothed the Nation as His bride.[231] Both covenants were made by the bloodshed of the lamb. The old covenant was made by the blood of animals but the new covenant was made by the blood of the real Lamb from heaven. The Nation was stubborn in her decision and divorced her Bridegroom by rejecting faith in Him. While nations put allegiance in the Bridegroom and embraced Him. Mar Narsai also comments on the unfaithfulness of the Nation.[232]

Regarding the earlier nature of nations Mar Jacob says: "When the *Just Prince*, came down to espouse to Himself the daughter of pagans (*bart ḥanpe*),"[233] she was among the idols[234] and was a bride to gods of the nations. But the Bridegroom lifted her from her whoredom and retained her virginity.

> The idols abused her and she was a bride to the gods.
> She committed adultery with the evil spirits and demons were for her (as) defiled friends.
> The daughter of Arameans (*bart armoee*) committed whoredom and was satisfied, committed adultery and was ashamed.
> And the Bridegroom lifted the harlot up from the street
> and sent her down to the waters and made her a virgin and behold she is with him.[235]

When the husband is alive and the wife engages in conjugal relation with another person, it is adultery. In the case of Israel it was true, because even though she was betrothed to Yahweh she committed conjugal union with idols. But, though there was no contract with Yahweh, Mar Jacob says that, nations' engagement with gods was adultery. A second notion, which arises from these lines, is that the gods were abusing nations. Then, it should be understood

---

231 When the King's Son perceived her wicked behavior
He came to look in betrothal the Church of the Nations,
For He had tested her love and loyalty
He mingled her with Himself, and was mingled with her (*Resur* III.7, 86; cf. Brock, *The Luminous Eye,* 119).

232 The synagogue went out because she hated the bridegroom, to whom she was betrothed;
And the church entered and became bride steadfast in her love
The synagogue crucified and the church of gentiles lived by his cross
And behold, she is made happy by his body and blood remitting debts. (Narsai, "Dedication of the Church," 167-168).

233 Bedjan, *HS* III, 209.8; ET. "On Our Lord and Jacob," *TV* 4.4(1993), 52.24.

234 Bedjan, *HS* III, 209.9; ET. "On Our Lord and Jacob," *TV* 4.4(1993), 52.25.

235 Bedjan, *HS* II, 237.3-10.

that nations were helpless and was trounced by the dominant gods. In this situation, the Savior Bridegroom came and liberated her (nations) from the slavery of the enemy and made her as His own bride. Still it would not be a satisfactory answer because Mar Jacob uses another term 'harlot' to denote nations. The problem is, in the normal case, a harlot would not be a victim, because she is doing the adultery by her own decision. If so, nations were not simply a victim but out of ignorance she committed adultery. Thus, the bride was an ignorant girl who was engaged in adultery, but the Bridegroom arrived and snatched her from ignorance, slavery of adultery, and sin. Mar Jacob prefigures this redemption of the Bridegroom in several Old Testament stories such as patriarch Jacob, Samson, etc. He sees Jacob's betrothal to Rachel as the pre-figuration of the event:[236]

> If then Rachel, for Jacob's sake, was sanctified,
> how much more the Church of the nations (*idto amme*) be purified through the Lord of Jacob?
> A pagan's daughter (*bnoteh dḥanpe*) were sanctified through their righteous husband,
> showing how the Son sanctified the assemblies of the nations (*knušto damme*)?
> For if Jacob had not borne the image of the Son,
> he would not have been famous in his deeds…
> How glorious is her sister Rachel in the readings!
> The beauty of the Church was hide in her, wherefore, great is her glory…
> He was a foreshadowing of our Lord in his deeds;
> for he came down, was betrothed, waxed rich, and ascended to his father.
> Consider how much Jacob, when he journeyed in poverty,
> resembled the Son, Whom emptied Himself and came down.[237]

Here, Mar Jacob compares Jacob and Jesus in their journey and mission. Mar Jacob covered long distance to betroth Rachel, who is his cousin. Not only that, though his father was rich he left all and served his uncle as a servant to receive Rachel. Jesus Christ also covered lot of distance to betroth the bride. Although He is rich, He took the form of a servant to redeem the bride, the Church. Both Rachel and the Church were beautiful.[238] Mar Jacob uses the words of Paul and says that, since her husband (Jacob) is holy she will also become holy. Paul says that, a non-believing husband would be saved by the faith of the wife (1Cor 7:14). Since the patriarch Jacob is holy and through him his wife also will become holy. In the same way, since the Bridegroom is holy His bride, though she was a harlot and lived among the idols, will become holy

[236] Bedjan, *HS* III, 208.1-5; ET, "On Our Lord and Jacob," *TV* 4.4(1993), 51.1-5.

[237] Bedjan, *HS* III, 209.15-210-9; ET. "On Our Lord and Jacob," *TV* 4.4(1993), 52.29-53.41.

[238] Infra, 5.3.11.

through her Bridegroom. The same can be seen in the Book Deuteronomy; where Moses made sacrifice for Ruben, who blemished the bed of his father (Deut 33:6) and saved him. In his *Homily on Samson* Mar Jacob interprets Samson's journey to marry the Philistine woman as resembling Christ's journey to marry the Church:

> He went down to their country for a woman that he desired to marry,
> and a mystery encountered him that was yet manifest and clear.
> To espouse a wife, he went down to the country of the Philistines…
> Whom does Samson resemble if not our Lord, who came to espouse,
> the Church of the nations (*idto amme*), and death met Him like a mighty foe.
> Samson went down to take wife that daughter of the uncircumcised (*bart urle*),
> hereby depicting our Lord, Who betrothed with His Gospel the daughter of the Pagans (*barto dḥanpe*).[239]
> And against our Lord, whom came to espouse the daughter of Arameans.[240]

Mar Jacob says Samson went to the land of Philistines without armor and tore his enemies with armor of mysteries.[241] He went to espouse a woman who depicts a figure of the Church of the light and this daughter of the nations was prefigured in the daughter of the pagans.[242] In the same way the Son of God came to earth to espouse the Church of the nations.[243] In another homily he says:

> Samson stooped down and took the daughter of the Gentiles (*bart urle*),
> and pictured our Lord who betrothed the daughter the heathen (*bart ḥanpe*) in His Gospel.
> The Son of God moved from His home and came to our earth,
> to betroth the Church of the Gentiles (*idto damme*), like we said.[244]

In the same homily Mar Jacob sees the widow of Zarephath prefigured the Church nations:

> Why a bowl and a horn are proclaimed in the house of the widow,
> but (because they are) the symbol of shew-bread and anointment.
> The Church of the Gentiles (*idto damme*) was seen in that widow,
> she (had) no husband, and the (Church had) neither Lord or God.

---

[239] Bedjan, *HS* V, 335.1-8; ET. "A Homily on Samson," *TV* 11(1992), 55.79-86.

[240] Bedjan, *HS* V, 335.14; ET. "A Homily on Samson," *TV* 11(1992), 55.91.

[241] Bedjan, *HS* V, 336.6; ET. "A Homily on Samson," *TV* 11(1992), 56.106.

[242] Bedjan, *HS* V, 336.10; ET. "A Homily on Samson," *TV* 11(1992), 56.109.

[243] Bedjan, *HS* V, 336.14-15; ET. "A Homily on Samson," *TV* 11(1992), 56.113-114.

[244] Bedjan, *HS* III, 316.14-16; ET. Konat "On the Mysteries, Types, and Figures of Christ," *Le Museon* 118(2005), 82.235-238.

That widow had no head who exists and leads her,
neither did the Church (have), one God who names her.[245]

According to him the pitcher of the widow symbolizes the body of Christ which is unending on the table of the Church and the horn prefigures baptism of the Church which gives life to the believers.[246] Aphrahat compared Asneth, the wife of Joseph, with the Church from gentiles: "Joseph married the daughter of an unclean priest, and Jesus brought himself the Church from the unclean gentiles."[247] Clement of Rome also explains the infidelity of Israel and the love of the nations.[248]

In a prayer of the West Syriac traditions states: "O Church, the daughter of gentiles, sing praise to the First-born of the Most High, who betrothed you on His cross and by His passion and death, gave life to you."[249] Thus, along with his predecessors Mar Jacob portrays the election of nation in the place of the Nation.

5.3.10. The Afflicted and Persecuted Bride

The Exodus account gives the suffocated and pathetic nature of the persecuted bride.[250] During the time of the exile the bride was persecuted physically and mentally and was under the torments of the Egyptians. The situation is repeated when the Israelites were taken into the Babylonian captivity. But, when Mar Jacob says that the Church was under the affliction, it should be understood that she was under intellectual or psychological exploitation rather than physical abuse; because she was more or less physically free but she was under the

---

[245] Bedjan, *HS* III, 314.3-8; ET. Konat "On the Mysteries, Types, and Figures of Christ," *Le Museon* 118(2005), 80.179-184.

[246] Bedjan, *HS* III, 314.9-12; ET. Konat "On the Mysteries, Types, and Figures of Christ," *Le Museon* 118(2005), 80.185-188.

[247] Parisot, *Demo,* XXI, 957:3-5: Valavanolickal, *Demonstrations* II, cf. Murray, *Symbols of Church and the Kingdom,* 136.

[248] Thou hast inherited the covenant of Israel, speaking to those called from among the nations that were once barren, being formerly destitute of this husband, who is the Word,--desolate formerly,--of the bridegroom. "Now the just shall live by faith," which is according to the covenant and the commandments; since these, which are two in name and time, given in accordance with the [divine] economy--being in power one--the old and the new, are dispensed through the Son by one God. As the apostle also says in the Epistle to the Romans, "For therein is the righteousness of God revealed from faith to faith," teaching the one salvation which from prophecy to the Gospel is perfected by one and the same Lord. (Clement of Rome, *Stromata,* II.4).

[249] *Kashtanubhavazhcha Namaskaram*, 52.

[250] Amar, *A Metrical Homily on Holy Mar Ephrem,* 36.46-53; Bedjan, *HS* II, 367.1-4; ET. *FH* VIII, 223.413-416. Mar Narsai says: "One who is exiled, broken, and wearied is set free; She became the wife of the Son of Height, dwelling in the height. (Narsai, "Dedication of the church," 7).

captivity of indoctrination of the evil spirits. Therefore, the challenge was in a psychological level which compelled her to worship the gods of the nations.

The observation of the afflicted bride is well-built in the homilies of Mar Jacob. The bride was under the slavery of the idols and therefore, she was oppressed and marginalized. The idols of the nations seized her under their treachery and indoctrinated their percepts in her. She was ignorant about the real Bridegroom. When, by His eternal mercy, the Bridegroom arrived, He taught her gospel and redeemed her from ignorance and slavery. The education and preparation of the bride has gone through various staging posts. Every staging post has its own importance in the process of liberation. The nativity of the Bridegroom itself marked the liberation of the persecuted bride. Mar Jacob explains the rescue operations of the Bridegroom in the nativity homily:

> On this day the sorrowful (*kmerooto*) woman who had been repudiated has exulted,
> because, the Bridegroom has come and collected and gathered her from among the idols.
> On this day the lamenting (*mmakakto*) woman has exulted,
> because, there was the marriage feast at which she has been comforted from her distresses (*'oqotoh*).
> Today freedom has come for the enslaved woman (*mša'badto*),
> who had been bound to minister to idolatry.
> Today the one who was persecuted (*rdap*) for a long time has been released,
> because, the Mighty One stood up and broke the fetters of her imprisonment.
> Today the maid servant of the demons has obtained freedom,
> because, the great Lord has put them to flight and led out what belongs to Him.
> Today the imprisoned (*ḥbeešto*) has gone out of darkness,
> because, the Light has shone out and shattered the gates of the house of darkness.[251]

In these lines Mar Jacob shows the bride from nations as a salve who was compelled to minister the idols of the nations. The reason for the slavery is, he implicates that, the darkness. When the Light came in, the darkness went away. Through the term darkness he must mean ignorance or impoverishment due the improper education. This should be considered in the light of Mar Jacob's assertion of prophets as the instructors of the Nation to educate the bride from her depravity. But the presence of such educators was not mentioned in the case of nations. Another possible meaning of darkness or the term darkness represents wickedness of the nations. However, since Mar Jacob uses maidservant, there is a possible dominance for the first hypothesis. Nevertheless, in both cases she was under the ascendancy. Light is Jesus Christ, the Bridegroom. The dawn of Jesus Christ effaced the darkness from the mind of the bride. During His baptism the Bridegroom saw the persecuted (Church),

[251] Bedjan, *SMS,* 760.20-770.9; ET. *FH* I, 88.1045, 89.1055.

who was weak, desiccated and wearied, then He mixed waters and sent her to wash herself, and then betrothed.[252] "The Royal Son wished to betroth the afflicted (*ṭarpto*) one (the Church) and He sent her to go to the fountain to wash away her dust."[253] At Golgotha "It (Cross) summoned the serene one, the Church of nations that had been driven away, and gave peace to the afflicted (Church) which had been persecuted."[254] In short, the bride was a persecuted and afflicted one. But, when He arrived, the Bridegroom rescued her from the tortures of the idols and liberated her as His own bride.

5.3.11. Bride was Corrupted and Black but Beautiful

In the writings of the Syriac Church Fathers it can be observed that they always found the Church as beautiful. The most frequent adjectives of the Church in the West Syriac Liturgy are, true, glorious, fragrant, beautiful, etc. Here the term 'beautiful' (*šapheerto*) required special attention. The term has another meaning 'to please.' Noah pleased God (Gen 6:9); She pleased Herod (Mt 14:6); we will please God by our confession (Jul 31:28). Another meaning of the term is 'to behave well.' Therefore, by using this term Mar Jacob may say that one who pleases God by his/her deeds. According to Mar Jacob Israel was unfaithful and grieved Yahweh but the Church was faithful and pleased Him. Rachel is an image of the Church and Leah is an image of Israel. He compares Rachel with Leah. Leah's eyes were not beautiful as Rachel's.[255]

In the Song of Songs the author says "I am black but beautiful" (Songs 1:5). Mar Jacob and other Fathers of the Church use this theme to distinguish between the former and later stages of the Church who was stained with idolatry but now she is pure. The reason for the blackness is the fume of sacrifice to the idols. But when the real Bridegroom arrived He washed her and made her pure and clean. In the *Homily on the Baptism of our Redeemer* Mar Jacob states that John the Baptist, the friend of the Bridegroom, cleansed the bride from filth and made her ready for marriage. John appeared in the desert, filled with all virtues, ornate with spiritual practices, exalted above the usual ways, despising possessions; while he despised and rejected love of the world, and the care (this life) that corrupts the soul it had deserted and had taken flight from him. He despised and trod gluttony under foot. He fastened, bound and chocked the

---

[252] Bedjan, *HS* I, 167.5-6; ET. *FH* VI, 162.5-6.

[253] Bedjan, *HS* I, 167.3-4; ET. *FH* VI, 162.3-4.

[254] Amar, *A Metrical Homily on Holy Mar Ephrem,* 47.94.
I was in captivity and distraught
Among the mountains and the hills, (Song 2:8, 4:6)
But He treated my wound with oil and with wine, (Lk 10:34)
And with the comfort He gave me I forgot all that had caused me to stumble (Epiphany Hymn: Anonymous Author, ET. Brock, *The Treasure House of Mysteries,* 254).

[255] Bedjan, *HS* III, 209.19-20; ET. "On Our Lord and Jacob," *TV* 4.4(1993), 53.35-38.

entire love of mammon. In him blazed chastity, and upon him was depicted purity and in his person shone virginity. He embraced total sanctity with love and he had neither defect in his beauty, not cause for scandal in his conduct and the virginity personified in him and he became a model to the Church.[256] According to this description virginity means the abstention of the worldly passion and possessions. In other words virginity is the pure love of Christ. Inspiring from the teaching of John, the Church from nations abandoned her gods and fornications that made her filthy, corrupt and therefore black. She embraced the true Bridegroom and therefore, she is bright now. After this kind of self preparation of the bride, in order to purify her, the Bridegroom made her enter into the water of purification. Mar Jacob says:

> He had regard for her beauty that was altered by the incense of idols (*ḥor beh bšooproh deštan hwo beṭre dṣalmo*);
> and He poured out rushing streams of the river upon her face to brighten her color (*nešpr gwnoh*).
> He sent her down first to the tested waters as He betrothed her,
> in order to purge (*mrq*) away fornication (*zanyooto*) from her by sanctification.
> That smell of the holocausts (*debḥto*) sacrificed was concentrated in her,
> but He caused to pass unto her the wholesome waters to make her body fragrant.
> She was made corrupt by the foulness of the oblations;
> He besprinkled sanctity upon her so that she might be cleansed by it from defilement.[257]

Also, Mar Jacob condemned false teachings as corruption that makes stains on human beings. While he is upholding the place of Mar Ephrem in the Church of Syria and his untiring fight against the false teachers like Mani, Marcion, Arius, and Sebellius he says that the false teachings stained the true faith of the Church.

---

[256] Rilliet, *SHF* II, 560.12-14; ET. *FH* VII, 196.22.

[257] Bedjan *HS* I, 167.7-168.7; ET. *FH* VI, 162.7-163.14. Narsai also wrote about this:

> One washing, full of life, had restored her
> He washed, purified and cleansed her face from vices
> In the living waters, he washed the impurity, of the contaminated
> And he poured out the holy oil upon her head and gladdened her face.
> In the oil and waters, he washed her body and purified her soul
> And he set up, a name for her, the Holy Church full of graces.
> He took off from her, he hated name with her faults
> And he dressed her grace and put the name, the chosen church (Narsai, "Dedication of the Church," 14-18).

Until the bride take bath and ascended from the water King David stood on the banks of the river; he took his harp and began to sing this forget your people and race of your fathers' house. The Holy Church, who became the queen and rich all on a sudden, the king desires your beauty (*Anduthaksa* = *Hudaro*, 185-187).

Heresies arose that error reared like thieves
to lay waste the truth of the proclamation.
The city of Addai from which uprooted foolish idols,
the evil one entered to renew paganism there.
(The evil one) Encircled it with heresies like traps on all sides,
to muzzle the mouth of the Church with silence by every means.
On the one side, he stirred up the ranks of the followers of Marcion,
on the other side, he marshaled the legions of Easterners.
He availed himself of partisans from the followers of Arius and Sabellius.
and set up ranks among the cunning assemblies of the followers of Bardaisan...[258]

The Bridegroom lifted the bride up from the street of harlotry and was taken her for Himself. Unlike the Nation, she was not virgin. She was married to the gods of the nations. But after the marriage at cross she retained her virginity:

That while he lifted up the harlot from the street and made her a virgin.
At the marriage, the virginity of the betrothal perishes;
however, the daughter of the gentiles received them from her marriage.
Until that day of her marriage feast, she is a harlot (*zneeto*)
and from her marriage and henceforth the virgin is a great wonder...
While the marriage, the Cross made her virgin and she stood firm.[259]

The retaining of the virginity of the bride at marriage on the Cross reflects another important aspect. It echoes the world's redemption through the Cross. Through the crucifixion of the Bridegroom the world receives the absolution from sin and redemptions from death. Therefore, though she was a wanton girl before the marriage, her sins are remitted after the salvific death of the Savior Bridegroom. This reflects the importance of repentance of the sinner.

For a faithful, the pure marriage with the heavenly Bridegroom is; to consecrate herself to Christ and delete all thoughts of wantonness from her. In one of his homilies Mar Jacob says that the Church is pure and holy and let her keep this purity:

This holy one is venerable and chaste and who has no blemish;
glorious, and pure, transparent, and clean in all our fashion.

---

[258] Amar, *A Metrical Homily on Holy Mar Ephrem,* 55.118-122.

[259] Bedjan, HS II, 238.17-239.3; cf. She who was perished and was perishing in the power of deception;

the seeker of all sought her and led, brought her to the place of life.
The honorable one betrothed a prostitute and a dishonored one;
and he made her chaste in his brightness and clothed her dishonor with the garment of glory.
The holy one chose the companion of evil spirits and maid-servant of devils
He sprinkled her with his love and washed away her great wickedness (Narsai, "Dedication of the Church," 11-13).

> Let she closely guarded and pure quiet and silent;
> innocent and vigilant and that of without stain.[260]

Regarding the removal of corruption after the marriage with the real Bridegroom the author of the *Acts of Thomas* rightly puts that after the marriage the corruption will be effaced and no more needed the veil of corruption. In a dialogue between the bride and her mother in the same book says:

> Truly my mother, I am in great love, and I am praying to my Lord that I may continue in this love which I have experienced this night, and may call for the incorruptible bridegroom who has revealed himself to me this night. I am not veiled, because the veil of corruption is taken away from me; and that I am not ashamed, because the deed of shame has been removed far from me; and I am not repentant, because the repentance which restores to life, abides in me. And I am cheerful and glorious, because, in the day of this transitory joy, I am not agitated by it; and that this deed of corruption is despised by me, and the spoils of this wedding feast that passes away, because I am invited to the true wedding feast; and that I have not had intercourse with a husband, the end whereof is bitter repentance, because I am betrothed to the true Husband.[261]

Regarding the incorruption of the bride the Church says in her prayers:

> How beautiful are you, O daughter of the gentiles and how fair to look upon. King Solomon sings your praises, O Holy Church, your lips drop honey; the fragrance of your garment is like roses in Nisan, and you are altogether beautiful and spotless… How beautiful are you, O daughter of gentiles, and how fair to look upon. You resemble the sun that dawn upon the whole world. There is the sign of the cross upon your forehead and your pure mouth sings praise…[262]

> He has given these riches to the daughter of the gentiles who loved her Savior. Tarshish and the islands came and worshipped her and the kings of Sheba and Seba offer gifts before her. He saw her lovely and He was pleased with her. From all the congregations, He had chosen her to be always beautiful before Him. On the palm of His hand, He established her, lest she might ever shake. With this cove, deprived of wrath and fury, the innocent, Pure, simple and the Fair One ascended and it became the image of the beloved Church.[263]

In many writings of the Church Fathers portray the Church as a comely woman who was black in her former days because of the idolatry. In one of the prayers of the feast of St. Thomas, the apostle of India says; the apostle came and

---

260 Bedjan, *HS* I, 9.17-20.

261 *AAA*, I.14, 71-72.

262 *Koodahskramangal*, 95-97.

263 *Kashtanubhavazhcha Namaskaram*, 146.

enlightened India, a country which was in darkness, with the knowledge of Christ.[264] See two other hymns which the Church sings:

> I have come up from the street full of idols (Song 3:2)
> and been baptized in the living water; (Song 4:15; Jn 4:10)
> In Fire and Spirit have I been made to shine,
> And I am joined to the glorious Bridegroom.[265]
> I was blackened in my sins,
> as a result of sacrificial burnt offerings.
> The daughter of Jerusalem has become jealous of me,
> for I am glorious now that I have been made to shine.
> Jesus is mine, and I am His
> He has desired me; He has clothed Himself in me, and I am clothed in Him.
> With the kisses of His mouth has He kissed me
> and brought me to His Bridal Chamber on high.[266]

Thus according to Mar Jacob and other Fathers of the Church the Church from nation was black and corrupted but after she became cleansed from the filth and embraced the real Bridegroom she became glorious and never went back to her earlier nature.

5.3.12. Church the Royal Bride

Mar Jacob, in many of his homilies, ornate the bride with the qualification of "royal." This regal character could be seen in the scripture also. He sees the adorned New Jerusalem as a new bride prepared for marriage with Lamb (Rev 19:7, 8, 21).[267] David calls her as the princes (*meškallat*).[268] Of course, Mar Jacob follows these traditions. More than that, her Bridegroom is the Royal King from the house of David, obviously, the bride will also get the same status of the Bridegroom. Apparently, her appearance also looks like a royal bride as resplendent and adorned with beauties. She is portrayed with the crown and other royal vestments. Mar Jacob says that, "He (the Father) built (*bno*) a great palace for the bride of light and depicted the bridegroom in various ways in her royal home."[269] The crux is that she is not a princess born but princess made by the grace of the Bridegroom. She was spilled with dirt but she was cleansed by the water of sanctification. Mar Jacob says: "The Church, the Royal bride (*kalat malko*), approached towards John, and he began washing,

---

[264] *Promiyon* IV.

[265] Epiphany Hymn: Anonymous Author, ET. Brock, *The Treasure House of Mysteries,* 254.

[266] Epiphany Hymn: Anonymous Author, ET. Brock, *The Treasure House of Mysteries,* 256.

[267] Bedjan *HS* I, 41.4.

[268] Bedjan *HS* I, 44.12-13.

[269] Bedjan, *HS* III, 287.20-21; ET. Brock, "On the Veil of Moses," in *Studies in Syriac Spirituality*, 77.87-88.

cleansing, polishing and sanctifying her.[270] The Church attributed this regal nature even to the regular bride too. The crowning custom, which followed in the matrimonial liturgy in the West Syriac and East Syriac Churches, the bride and the bridegroom are pictured as the king and queen of the family.[271]

Conclusion

This chapter elaborated the concept of Church and how the Church is a medium of salvation of the world. First of all, according to Mar Jacob, the Church is the progeny of God's love and grace to humanity. The Church is not an institution but it has a unique identity of believers. It has a history even from the creation of humanity or beyond it. It is a preexistent one. In the days of creation God said, "Therefore, man shall leave his father and mother and shall cling to his wife, and they shall be one" (Gen 2:24). The utterance of God is not limited on man and woman but beyond that to God and the Church. The prophets conveyed this mystery throughout the prophecy, but it was hidden under the veil. God revealed His love through various covenants and betrothed the Church. The Father sent His ambassadors to the world to educate the bride and cried out in their streets and on the gates. The bride did not listen and follow her Bridegroom and loved other gods and committed adultery. With the eternal mercy of the Father, the real Bridegroom descended and encountered but the bride divorced Him and killed Him. The Bridegroom selected another bride from the nations although lived among the idols, was black with the fume, and fetid smell of sacrifice. She was under the slavery of idols but He liberated her by the betrothal at Jordan through washing and at the cross and her purity regained. She loved Him and became a pure virgin.

---

[270] Bedjan, *HS* I, 170.8-9; ET. *FH* VI, 165.57-58.

[271] The crown is also representing the symbol of victory in the second coming of Jesus Christ.

Chapter 6

Eschatological Aspects in Mar Jacob's Interpretation of Bride Imagery

Introduction

Give thanks, Church, to the King's Son
who has betrothed you, to be his queen;
He has brought you into his bridal chamber,
making flow the blood from his side as a wedding gift
clothing you in the glorious Robe of Light that does not fade away.
And placing on your head the radiant crown of glory[1]

The hymn is a prayer of the East Syriac Church and this may be a right introduction to this chapter. The summery of this chapter is condensed in this small hymn. While the former chapters discussed the place of betrothal and marriage, how the Bridegroom acted as the Savior of the Church, the bride and how the Church became the bride of the eternal Bridegroom, this chapter discusses the culmination of this relationship and deals with eschatological nature of the theme. The present chapter describes the bridal chamber, the robe of glory, wedding feast, and finally the union between the Bride and the Bridegroom.

6.1. Historical and Eschatological Marriages

Christian faith itself is based on the eschatological fulfillment of the Christ event, basically on the theology of Second Coming, Day of Judgment, Kingdom of God, and the Hell or Gehenna.[2] The writings of the Church Fathers and the

[1] Chaldean Breviary, III, 430=Hudra III, 609.

[2] *Ktobo d-zlooto šheemto*, 214.

liturgy repeatedly refer to these concepts. This chapter is exclusively devoted on the eschatological aspects of the divine marriage and related festivities which is held in the heavenly bridal chamber focusing in the writings of Mar Jacob of Serugh. It brings out visualization of the divine marriage and its eschatological implications.

The important aspects of the wedding ceremony of the early Semitic culture can be gathered from the Bible and the early West Asian cultural background as well as the liturgical and patristic texts. The Old Testament does not throw much light on the order of marriage ceremony of that time. A few aspects of it are available in the narrations of the patriarchal, prophetical, as well as the Wisdom Literature of the Old Testament. Marriage was a grandeur ceremony in the Jewish culture. They celebrated it with all measures and merry makings. It is a community affair. There was a week-long celebrations conducted in the maid's house (Gen 29:27; Judg 14:12). All the relatives, friends and important individuals of the place were invited for the marriage feast (Gen 27:22). A procession was a central part of marriage feast; [3] in which both bride and bridegroom were received with great procession accompanied by music (Ps 78:63; 1Macc 9:39). The bride and bridegroom were adorned with magnificent dresses (Ps 45:9, 13; Rev 19:7-8). Mathew 22:11-12 shows the importance of the wedding garment to the invited guests. The documents of the Talmudic period offer ample evidences of the feasts and merrymaking of Jewish marriage ceremony. Dances, drinking different types of wine, and serving of rich food are integral part of the marriage. The bride was adorned with wedding garments, sometimes crown or long head dress or veil.

Mar Jacob portrays life with Christ in the Kingdom of God as an experience of the bridal chamber.[4] Here the faithful or the Church is presented as the bride and Christ as the Bridegroom. He compares the Kingdom of God as the bridal chamber. The Chamber is adorned with bright light and a place full of joy. There is no space for sorrow and worldly limitations. The bride and the Bridegroom will be in jubilant mood. They will be in white and spotless robe, which is also called the robe of glory. It will be like bright light. The bride will be adorned with various ornaments. Another important aspect of the bridal chamber is that there will be a wedding feast with sweet food and wine. In Mar Jacob's homilies it can be seen that the marriage and marriage feast took place in historical time as well as expecting an eschatological time. He portrayed the birth of Christ, His baptism, and His death as the earthly marriage feast. Whenever he says about the Golgotha event Mar Jacob pictured it as both a betrothal as well as a marriage of the Church with her Bridegroom Christ. In this marriage the Bridegroom presents the marriage feast in a different

[3] Posner, Raphael, "Marriage," *Encyclopedia Judaica,* Vol. 13, 565-566.

[4] Bedjan, *HS* II, 377.8-10; ET. "Homily on the Ten Virgins," *TV* 4.1(1992), 41.39-40.

way; he divided his body and blood as the marriage feast. Therefore, "Let the virgin Church who betrothed to you rejoice in you, my Lord, when she sings to you new praise with an exalted voice. Let the gatherings of the peoples and congregations rejoice in you because on your feast day, behold, they gladdened in you abundantly."[5] The following part will discuss the bridal chamber and other various aspects related to the eschatological marriage.

6.2. The Bridal Chamber

> A great tent (*maškan*) and the royal ranks were set out within it,
> and a chamber (*gnoono*) of light with children of light who delighted within in it.[6]

According to the Syriac theological understanding Life with the Bridegroom in the bridal chamber is the eschatological culmination or the goal of Christian life. Regarding the marriage feast and bridal chamber two facts are to be considered. First of all, the life with the Bridegroom Jesus Christ is a future reality. Secondly, the marriage feast and the union with the Bridegroom that have already happened in this world is a theme prevalent in the Christian circle including Mar Jacob.[7] The biblical passages of Mathew 25:1-10 and 22:11-12 are the biblical foundations of this magnificent imagery. According to Brock the concept of the bridal chamber might have originated in the Syriac Church with *Diatessaron*.[8]

As the other stages of the bride-bridegroom imagery, the concept of bridal chamber is also a well established one in Sumerian culture. Lapinkivi writes: Ur-Nammu, the founder of the Ur III dynasty (ca. 2112-2095 B.C.E.), alludes to the sacred marriage in Ur-Nammu (c. 73-76), which says that he was "lying down on the splendid bed in the delightful bedchamber in the Gipar."[9] Mar Ephrem witnesses that Bardaisan taught that the righteous souls will be elevated to "Bridal Chamber of Light."[10] *Acts of Thomas* widely uses this concept. In the Valentinian tradition the bridal chamber is understood as the final stage of marriage between Jesus and Sophia. This would only happen at

---

[5] Bedjan, *SMS*, 807.18-19; ET. *FH* III, 127.366-367.

[6] Bedjan, *HS* III, 13.21-14.1; ET. "First Day of Creation," 36.249-250. A similar interpretation can be seen in Mar Ephrem:

> A garden full of glory, a chaste bridal chamber,
> Did he give to that king fashioned from the dust,
> And sanctifying and separating him from the abode of wild animals,
> For glorious was Adam in all things… (*Hpar*. XIII.3; ET. Brock, *Hymns on Paradise*, 169).

[7] Kollamparampil, *Salvation in Christ*, 239-240.

[8] Brock, "The Bridal Chamber of the Light," 181.

[9] Lapinkivi, "The Sumerian Sacred Marriage and its Aftermath," 20.

[10] *Prose Refutation* II, 164; cited in Brock, "The Bridal Chamber of the Light," 182.

the eschatological life (*Val. Exp.* 39. 30-33).[11] In the Ptolemaic version, once the seed has had time to be perfected, Achamoth reenters the Pleroma and receives her bridegroom (τόν νθμφίον αύτῆς) as they are wedded (σθζθγία γένηται). They are announced as "Groom and Bride" (τοῦτο εἶναι νυμφίον καί νύμφην). The Pleroma in its entirety becomes their "bridal chamber (νυμφῶνα).[12] Another strong notion on the bridal chamber in Valentinian tradition which was written by Irenaeus is that it could be a ritual among them. He writes: "For some of them prepare a (bridal chamber, νυμφῶνα) and perform a sort of mystic rite (pronouncing certain expressions) with those who are being initiated, and affirm that it is a spiritual marriage (πνευματικόν γάμον φάσκουσιν εἶναι) which is celebrated by them, after the likeness of the conjunctions above."[13] Thus in Valentinian and other West Asian cultures the concept of bridal chamber had a prominent place. Commenting on the nuptial imagery in *The Acts of Thomas* Richard Valantasis exposes three different levels of understanding:

> Each of these characters presents a different understanding of the nuptial chamber, and each of these different interpretations are, in turn, related to different discourses. These interpretative reactions to the nuptial chamber displays differing interpretations according to the gender of the person, and each of these interpretations creates different meaning for the cultural phenomenon of the nuptial chamber by invoking different cultural systems for their understanding. Jesus presents the nuptial chamber as a means of constructing an immortal and impassible life, far distant from the cares and tribulations of physical marriage and child rearing, and from the distractions which these physical children provide. The Bride characterizes the nuptial chamber as a marriage to an impassible husband, modeled on the traditional understanding of social marriage, but transferred to a spiritual realm. The groom extols the bridal chamber as the means of union with a divinity.[14]

The Gospel of Philip portrays that the entrance into the bridal chamber is the restoration of salvation.[15]

By the notion the 'bridal chamber,' from the writings of Mar Jacob, inferred as the presence of God. But this presence may not be always an eschatological one. Also the Syriac Fathers often use the notion entering into the bridal chamber is equal to the entrance into the Kingdom of God or salvation. Again, salvation is frequently demonstrated as entrance into the primordial paradise. In his *Hymns on Paradise*, Mar Ephrem says that Paradise

[11] DeConick, "The Great Mystery of Marriage," 327.

[12] Irenaeus, *Against Heresies,* 1.7.1; cf. DeConick, "The Great Mystery of Marriage," 328.

[13] Irenaeus, *Against Heresies*, 1.21.3.

[14] Valantasis, "The Nuptial Chamber Revisited," 264.

[15] Isenberg, *Gospel of Philip*, 106.

is the seat of the *Shekinah* of God's presence.[16] Paradise is even depicted as an earthly and heavenly; imminent and transcendent. This kind of complex interpretation on salvation is rare in other traditions. Regarding the complexity of Ephraim's language Thomas Buchan says that it is a strategy. He said: "The seeming inconsistency of these two perspectives should not be taken as a shortcoming of Ephraim's thought, but seen as an intentionally deployed strategy to describe the simultaneous situation of paradise both in moral and spiritual relations to and in temporal and spatial distinction from the inhabited space."[17] The term 'inconsistency' which he used is a misunderstanding one and has a negative rendering; but it would be likely to use the term 'complexity' rather than 'inconsistency'. But the fathers of the Syriac tradition, such as Mar Ephrem and Mar Jacob intentionally uses this kind of interpretation, therefore, it is not inconsistency but consistently use the complex nature of salvation event, because salvation itself is beyond the human understanding and comprehension.

Mar Jacob portrays the bridal chamber primarily as an eschatological reality which situated in the heights:[18] "For without you I will not rise up on the last day. Weather to the bridal chamber or to Gehenna I will walk on you."[19] When he attribute bridal chamber as an eschatological one, he calls it as a synonym to the Kingdom of Heaven. In his letter to the monks of Mount Sinai he wrote:

> Now, you, O elect and holy ones, He has roused you for His glory by the sufferings of His crucifixion, for you have realized that God was crucified for your sake. Trembling has fallen upon you so that you might despise the world and abandon country and family, brothers and fathers, transient possessions and temporal leisure. Carrying His cross, you will follow Him in order to enter the glorious bridal chamber (*gnoono*) with Him.[20]

This explains an expectation of the faithful for a future bridal chamber of heaven and therefore, it is an eschatological one. The fourth chapter of this study discussed in detail that the Bridegroom is Light and dwelt in the lighted chamber.[21] Therefore, His eschatological bridal chamber is full of glory

[16] *HPar.* 1.8; 33-4, cf. Mathews, "Letter to Publius," 353.

[17] Buchan, "Paradise as the Landscape of Salvation in Ephrem the Syrian," 148.

[18] Bedjan, *SMS*, 766.8; ET. *FH* I, 84.965-966.

[19] Bedjan, *AMS* IV, 658.4-7; E.T. Harvey, "On Simeon the Stylite," in *Ascetic Behavior in Greco-Roman Antiquity*, 22.

[20] Olinder, *Ep*, 34.26-35.4; ET. Brock, "Jacob of Serugh, Letter VII, To the Monks of Sinai," 243.

[21] Supra 4.2.8.

and those who dwell in this chamber will be resplendent[22] with the glory of the Bridegroom. Also this bridal chamber is filled with all kinds of richness and happiness. There is neither groaning nor sorrow in it. The eternal joy and bliss are the characteristic features of this bridal chamber. From it sound the halleluiahs and cries of holy of the spiritual beings.[23] Those who, while they lived in this world, are upright in their deeds and illuminated their body and soul will enter into the bridal chamber with the Bridegroom.[24] In another occasion he says that the festivity will be overflowed in the lighted bridal chamber. The saints will be delighted with food and drink in the splendid chamber of the Bridegroom. They will recline on His breast and suckle life from Him. The Father makes them recline (*smq*), the Son will serve (*šameš*), and the Holy Spirit will perfect (*gmr*) all.[25] Regarding the lighted chamber He writes:

> Upon those foolish who inherited darkness in the stead of light!
> Alas, alas! For instead of the joyous light of the marriage banquet,
> they were tormented in darkness without the door.
> Instead of that great Nuptial Chamber (*qetoono*) of the bride, the daughter of the Light,
> the Bridegroom cast the darkened maidens into a place of gloom…
> Five leap for joy at the marriage in vast light,
> but five weep in a place filled with all afflictions[26]

Here Mar Jacob describes the difference between wise and foolish virgins and differences between paradise and hell. The foolish will be thrown into the darkness and the wise virgins will inherit the lighted chamber of the Bridegroom which is full of joy. In the bridal chamber there will be only two

---

[22] Brock, Jacob of Serugh: A Poem on the Soul, 41, *beth*; cf. The bridal chamber, he formed from the rays of his light, (which is) of his father and he called ages and generations for her marriage feast, (that) shed forth life (Narsai, "Dedication of the Church," 26).

[23] Brock, Jacob of Serugh: A Poem on the Soul, 41.*he*.

[24] Bedjan, *HS* II, 396.12-397.3; 400.4; ET. "Homily on the Ten Virgins," *TV* 4.1(1992), 58.429-430; 61.501-502; cf. I saw their bridal chamber, which not no one who has not a lamb may enter; I saw their joy, and I myself sat down in mourning, not possessing works worthy of that bridal chamber. I saw them clothed with the 'robe of light,' and I was grieved that I had prepared no virtuous raiment" (Mathews, "Letter to Publius," 349; cf. Brock, *The Luminous Eye,* 57).

[25] Bedjan, *HS* II, 396.19-397.7; ET. "Homily on the Ten Virgins," *TV* 4.1(1992), 58.443-444.

[26] Bedjan, *HS* II, 379.7-20; ET. "Homily on the Ten Virgins," *TV* 4.1(1992), 42; cf. All the pure virgins who are betrothed to Christ will have their lamps shining brightly, there as they enter, with the bridegroom to his bridal chamber. All those who are betrothed to Christ are far removed from the curse of Law, and they are delivered from the punishment of Eve's daughters… Instead of lamentation of Eve's daughters, these women will utter the bridegroom's songs. The wedding feast for Eve's daughters last seven days, but in the case of these women, their bridegroom never departs (Parisot, *Demo*. VI.6:7-22, 269; cf. Valavanolickal, *Demonstrations,* I, 141-142).

persons: the bride and the Bridegroom. The Bridegroom is well adorned and charming. He dresses like a prince and Bridegroom:

> I love Him because He is much more beautiful than all beauties.
> Compassion is poured out upon His lips when He speaks.
> In His appearance He is the most beautiful of men for the one who looks at Him.
> His garments are fragrant with the vapor of the incense like that of Aaron;
> and white and red that flowed from Him. Water and blood
> as the couch of perfumes are His cheeks to the one who perceives Him.
> He is wholly perfume, for His father was reconciled to the world through Him.[27]

On the other hand, the bride also will be in a jubilant mood. Mar Jacob calls the members of the Church as "Children of bridal chamber,"[28] "children of wedding feast"[29] (Mk 2: 18). The heavenly Bridegroom retrieved the bride from the slavery of sin, Satan, and death and thus the bride is jubilant now. She is now honored before the persecutors; her bent head is lifted up and her sorrow is washed away from her face.[30] Also, the long waited life with the heavenly Bridegroom in the celestial bridal chamber is fulfilled now. Before the marriage the bride was veiled, but after the marriage the veil is not needed.[31] "On the day of Wedding there is no veil for the betrothed woman."[32] After the marriage Paul entered and removed the veil from the face of the bride.[33] The Bridegroom uncovered the face of the bride after the marriage ceremony and she is free now.[34] Therefore, the bridal chamber is an eschatological Kingdom of God. It is pure, resplendent, and filled with eternal bliss where the Bridegroom and the bride will enjoy.

Mar Jacob also portrays bridal chamber (*gnoono*) as Primordial earthly reality. God made a bridal chamber of Eden and placed Adam and Eve as bridegroom and bride in it. He put on them with radiant garments and gave everything, even sea, land, and air to enjoy.

---

[27] Bedjan, *SMS,* 823.7-13; ET. *FH* XVI, 345.306-312.

[28] Brock, "Sleepers of Soul." 9, 23.

[29] Amar, "A Metrical Homily on Holy Mar Ephrem." 59.136.

[30] Bedjan, *SMS*, 767.8; ET. *FH* I, 86.990.

[31] Bedjan, *HS* III, 298.17-18; ET. Brock, "On the Veil of Moses," in *Studies in Syriac Spirituality*, 83.317-318.

[32] Bedjan, *HS* V, 315.6; ET. Harvey, "Jacob of Sarugh's Homily on Jephthah's Daughter," *MHMJS*, fasc. 16, 28.185.

[33] The great apostle uncovered its beauty and showed it to the world,
and so Moses' words, "the two shall be one," stood illuminated. (Bedjan, *HS* III, 291.13-14; ET. Brock, "On the Veil of Moses," in *Studies in Syriac Spirituality*, 79.163-164).

[34] Bedjan, *HS* III, 299.8; ET. Brock, "On the Veil of Moses," in *Studies in Syriac Spirituality*, 83.330.

> God made Adam a bridegroom in this great Bridal Chamber that He had decorated,
> He adorned Eve as a virgin bride, and gave her to Adam,
> providing, in her dowry, the sea, dry land and air.
> All the ages gathered for the great wedding feast He had made,
> the bridal couple were radiant in their crowns and their garments.
> He had covered them with glorious light and splendid radiance.
> He left them on their own among the trees with their fruits,
> having given them as a wedding present every kind of tree and fruit,
> the Garden rejoiced at the beloved bride and Groom.
> As for the Tree of Life, He had hidden it in Eden's great Bridal Chamber
> to be there for the bridal couple of light once they had been perfected. [35]

According to him Garden of Eden is a bridal chamber where Adam enjoyed life with God. But he was ousted from it through the sin. Mar Jacob asks the soul who drove away you from the Paradise: "In Paradise (full) of blessings you were resplendent as you reclined in glorious delights; who is it who has cast you down into the land of the curses? (Gen 1:3)."[36] In reply the soul says the serpent deceived and I transgressed the Law of God.[37] God drove away me from the glorious Paradise and closed its gate. But, through His sacrificial death, Jesus reopened the Eden to Adam and his Children. Thus he compares the primordial Paradise of Eden with eschatological Paradise. In his opinion the key of the eschatological bridal chamber is the cross. "With his cross He opened the door of the garden, the beautiful bridal chamber (*gnoono*)."[38]

Mar Jacob not only envisioned the bridal chamber as an eschatological and primordial, but also he depicts several places in the Christ's life like Nativity cave,[39] clouds of the Mount Tabor,[40] the tomb of Jesus,[41] the temple of Jerusalem,[42] Garden of Eden, which is full of banquet table with desirable food,[43] Mount Sinai,[44] Abraham's bosom,[45] as bridal chambers. As said in the beginning of this section most of these different bridal chambers in the homilies enjoy the physical presence of Jesus Christ. A real divine-human

---

[35] Alwan, *QHC* IV, 87.158-168; ET. Brock, "The Bridal Chamber of the Light," 185.

[36] Brock, "A Prayer Song By Jacob of Serugh Recovered", 32.2, 34.2.

[37] Brock, "Jacob of Serugh, *A Poem on Soul,*" 42. *heth*

[38] Bedjan, *SMS*, 813.1; ET. *FH* XVI, 335.91.

[39] Bedjan, SMS, 775.7; ET. *FH* II, 95.7; cf. Bedjan, *SMS*, 809.13; ET. *FH* XVI, 332.22.

[40] Bedjan, *HS* II, 374.7; ET. *FH* VIII, 229.566.

[41] Rilliet, *SHF* VI, 632.7.2; ET. *FH* XV, 321.7.

[42] Rilliet, *SHF* V, 596.3; 602.18; ET. *FH* XI, 269.22; 273.36.

[43] McVey, "Letter to Publius," 353.

[44] Bedjan, *HS* I, 20.6-11.

[45] Bedjan, *HS* I, 380.10-381.21.

encounter occurs in all these occasions. Therefore, it could be assumed that the bridal chamber is a place where divine-human interaction is possible. Thus, Mar Jacob portrayed such places in Jesus' Incarnation is called bridal chamber.

The first among the bridal chamber of Christ is the cave of Bethlehem where Jesus was born: "A breast is His sustenance, a cave His Bridal Chamber (*m'arto gnooneh*), and a manger His bed."[46] The purpose of making the cave as the bridal chamber is to lift up the bride to the Bridegroom's status: "Today, the cave became a bridal chamber for that celestial Bridegroom who wished to unite himself to the race of the earthly and uphold them as they ascend from the depth to the height."[47] Cave is also considered as the source of life and salvation: "Behold the castles are empty and desolate, without redemption, but the cave became full of hope and life for the whole world."[48] Mar Jacob sees the divine-human encounter in the cave. It is significant to note that the divine assimilation of the humanity in the cave. Through this assimilation of human form of the divine the humanity received a great hope of salvation. Moreover, the imminence of God sowed courage in the minds of humanity.

Mar Jacob often portrays cloud as a bridal chamber. *The Descent of the Most High on Mount Sinai and Mystery of the Church* he sees cloud that descended on the Mount Sinai is bridal chamber of Most High.[49] In his Homilies *On the Baptism of our Redeemer* and *On the Transfiguration of Our Lord* Mar Jacob describes 'cloud of light' as another 'type' for the bridal chamber.[50] He found the cloud that appeared on the Mount of Tabor (Mt 17:1-8; Mk 9:1-8; Lk 9:29-36) as a 'type' of the eschatological bridal chamber in the heaven. He says that the Father prepared a tabernacle of light for the Son that is the Church. In the Old Testament the cloud is portrayed as the presence of Yahweh and the meeting place of Yahweh and the people of God (Ex 13:21, 16:10, 19:9). The Book of Daniel foretells the Messianic arrival of Son of Man in the cloud (Dan 7:13; Mt 24:30, 26:64; Mk13:26, 14:62; Lk 21:27). The Fathers of the Church describe that the Bridegroom appears for his marriage feast on

---

[46] Bedjan, *SMS*, 775.7; ET. *FH* II, 95.7. See what Gospel of Philip says about the bridal chamber at Bethlehem: Indeed, one must utter a mystery. The Father of everything united with the virgin who came down, and a fire shone for him on that day. He appeared in the great bridal chamber. Therefore, his body came into being on that very day. It left the bridal chamber as one who came into being from the bridegroom and the bride. So Jesus established everything in it through these. It is fitting for each of the disciples to enter into his rest. (Isenberg, *Gospel of Philip* 71.5-15, 174).

[47] Rilliet, *SHF* I, 544.16; ET. *FH* IV, 134.19.

[48] Bedjan, *SMS*, 797.16-17; ET. *FH* III, 118.149-150.

[49] Bedjan, *HS* I, 19.16-17.

[50] Bedjan, *HS* II, 374.7; ET. *FH* VIII, 229.267.

a chariot of clouds.[51] Mar Jacob states that, the Father believes the Church in the cloud of Light.

> The Father made the cloud of light as the bridal chamber (*gnoono*) for His Son,
> so that Simon might not make the tabernacle as he had requested.
> One alone was made for the One, who is the Only-begotten,
> and He brought the other two nothing, and so Simon knew that the Son is the only One.
> The Father taught him through the single tabernacle (*mṭalto*) of light that He made,
> that one is the Church and one is the Cross that is ministered in it.[52]

This passage brings a tangle as it seems that the bridal chamber is likely to be the Church which the Father made for the Son. But on the other hand, the ambiance is very accurate for the nuptial bridal chamber with the presence of the Bridegroom in a heavenly light with the representatives of the Church from the Old and New Testaments. Mar Ephrem prefigures the cloud on the tabernacle as bridal chamber.[53] In the homily *On the Baptism of Our Redeemer* Mar Jacob calls the clouds of light as the bridal chamber of the Son:

> Clouds of light (*'nono dnuhro*) floated from the extremities and stood still there,
> to become a bridal chamber (*gnoono*) for the glorious Bridegroom to descend to be baptized.
> Dark clouds (*arplo*) issued forth, like veils (*šoošopo*) of the royal palace,
> so that when the Son of the King has been bathed, He could be received within them.
> The Father stretched out chosen garments (*mo'ne gb'o*) above the air;
> brightness and glory and flashes of astonishment as well as dark clouds.
> He surrounded the river with amazing colors that were not apprehensible.[54]

Here, the cloud formed like a palace of a king with different adornments and beam of light made it resplendent. The wedding garment and the brightness of glory added the pomp of the royal atmosphere. Therefore, the cloud of light, a meeting place in the Old Testament, has also became a meeting place between the Bridegroom and the bride with the escort of the light of the eternal bridal chamber. On both occasions, the baptism and at the transfiguration, the divine-human encounter happened. The first one elevated the human beings into a status of salvation through the cleansing and in the second occasion, the Bridegroom prepares the bride to the salvific encounter through His death. This is an occasion of the 'theophany' of the Bridegroom.

---

[51] Bedjan, *HS* IV, 589.15; cf. *HPar.* 1.5-7, 2; 6.23, 24.

[52] Bedjan, *HS* II, 374.7-12; ET. *FH* VIII, 229.567-572.

[53] Walters, *Hymn on Unleavened Bread,* 64.

[54] Bedjan, *HS* I, 184.21-185.6; ET. *FH* VI, 179.359-365.

The tomb (*qbr*) of Jesus is another place where Mar Jacob found a 'type' of the Bridal chamber.[55] The tomb is also a place of the strong presence of Jesus Christ. The tomb is considered as a dark place[56] but transformed into luminescence by the bright light of the Bridegroom and the presence of the fiery beings (angels):

> The angels came down from the heights above
> and stood beside the tomb in white raiment.
> The tomb became a beauteous Bridal Chamber,
> for the supernal being who came down and saw it.
> The guards were reproached by the angels' descent.
> The angels entered that tomb of wonder
> and looked in amazement at the Hero's couch;
> He had been laid here of His own will,
> yet the heavens are filled with His praises.
> Here the watchful One slept, while His ministers do not sleep.[57]
> The women disciples brought spices,
> fragrant herbs, to the tomb of the Fair One:
> the chaste women came with their fragrances together with the tears of their eyes.
> The chaste women came, carrying fragrant herbs
> as a wedding gift for the Bridal Chamber of the One who was slain.
> The Bridegroom came forth in glory
> from the tomb, and the guards were put to shame;
> but Mary did not realize that her Beloved had arisen.[58]
> Your tomb is like a marriage chamber
> and in it you, my son, are like the Bridegroom.
> The dead resemble the wedding guests,
> who are served in the presence of angels.[59]

These hymns reveal other features also. The chamber would be filled with fragrance and praises of the Bridegroom and it will be beautified with effulgent light, the presence of the heavenly beings as servants of the

[55] Rilliet, *SHF* VI, 632.17; ET. *FH* XV, 321.7; Bedjan, *HS* II, 612.14; ET. *FH* XIII, 295.30.

[56] Bedjan, *HS* II, 632.21; ET. *FH* XIV, 315.182.

[57] Brock, "Jacob of Serugh, Hymn on Resurrection," ET. *The Treasure House of Mysteries.* 262; cf. Tomb resembles a bridal chamber and in it You sleep like a bridegroom, O my Son! The dead resembles the friends of the bridegroom. They exalt the magnificence of the bridegroom (*Kashtanubhavazhcha Namaskaram*, 242).

[58] Brock, "Jacob of Serugh, Hymn on Resurrection," ET. *The Treasure House of Mysteries.* 261.

[59] Mathews, "Jacob of Serugh, Homily on Good Friday," 147; cf. Brock, *Bride of Light,* 40.20-24, 138.

Bridegroom; altogether the Bridegroom is the Hero of the chamber.[60] Another important aspect to note is the believers are only wedding guests and not bride; the bride is the Church.[61] That means, here Mar Jacob does not consider the individual believer as an entity of the Church.

This section was a discussion about the concept of bridal chamber in the writings of Mar Jacob. First of all the bridal chamber is a biblical concept where Jesus Christ is portrayed as an eschatological culmination of Christian life. Prior to the Christianized interpretation of the bridal chamber this concept was prevalent in Ancient West Asia. In the understanding of Mar Jacob the bridal chamber is a place where the Bridegroom and the bride meet and exchange their joy. This chamber is portrayed as a lighted chamber full of glory and filled with joy and happiness. It is also described as a chamber with a beautiful banquet. This may be either an eschatological one or a historical reality.

6.3. Robe of Glory

Robe of glory (*'estal šubaho*) is an acclaimed biblical theme in the Syriac theology. As the bridal chamber, the robe of glory also has an eschatological character. It is a requirement for the entrance into the bridal chamber. A believer can attain the robe of glory primarily through baptism[62] and it is usually known by the term 'putt-on' (*lbeš*). The Syriac Church Fathers use the phrases 'put-on humanity' (*lbooš nošutho*) or 'put-on the body' (*lbooš pagaro*), took the body (*'etgašam*), etc., to denote the Incarnation of Jesus Christ. According to the Syriac theology God created Adam in His image and likeness and adorned him with the garment of light (glory);[63] when he transgressed the Law of God

---

[60] The place is adorned, crowned with glory, for this is the festal day of the wedding feast; new is the bride chamber, Christ is the Bridegroom, the 'watchers' exulting, men are giving thanks. The altar is established, robed in truth, the priest is standing, he kindles the fire. He takes bread and gives the Body, he receives wine and distributes the Blood. The altar of stones supports our hope and the pure priest calls on the Spirit. The gathered people cries out 'Holy,' the king hears and makes mercy flow (Balai, *Hom.* 32:14-16; cited Murray, *Symbols of Church and Kingdom*, 272).

[61] The guests who have assembled for the marriage feast of the heavenly bridegroom, light the lambs of your souls and rejoice with Him (*Kashtanubhavazhcha Namaskaram,* 14).

[62] But Jacob portrays other occasions like birth of Christ and *Sheol* also provide robe of glory (It will be discussed later in this section).

[63] Brock, "Jacob of Serugh, *A Poem on the Soul,*" 41*dalath*; Ephrem says that, God gave Adam and Eve the garment of skin because they would be better than beasts (Mathews, *Commentary on Genesis,* 121). Jacob of Edessa also has the same opinion; he said: "Then they were treated with compassion by Grace lest they out naked from Paradise, and they were clothed in garment of skin so that they would be more honorable than the beasts (Cited in, Mathews, *Commentary on Genesis*, 35).

All creation was betrothed to God in the Blood of His Son.
For the lamps are those images of the Godhead

he was stripped off the glory of God and drove out from the Garden of Eden.[64] But, according to His eternal mercy, God sent His Only Begotten Son to re-clothe humanity with the robe of glory. He made this possible mainly through three salvific acts in His life: birth, baptism, and resurrection. Among them baptism has a major role. Through His baptism at the river Jordan He installed the robe in the spiritual water; whoever immerse in this spiritual water can attain this robe and it is a requirement for the entrance in the Kingdom of God.[65] In the writings of Mar Jacob and other Syriac Church Fathers like Mar Ephrem robe of glory and the wedding garment are used as synonyms.

The proto type of the idea of the robe of glory can be seen in Ancient Mesopotamia. David Freedman shows three occurrences of the use of the 'robe of splendor' in Akkadian literature: *Descent of Ishtar (Inanna):60-62*, *Gilgamesh Epic XI: 243* and Lambert, *BWL, 228, iii:13*.[66] The descent of Inanna describes the stripping of the 'garment of ladyship' (*ṣubāt bāšti*). The Gilgamesh Epic uses the same term:

> Therefore, take him, Urshanabi, and bring him to the washing place, and
> let him wash his filthy hair in water like a cultically clean person (ie. a priest).
> Let him cast off his skins and let the sea carry (them) away.
> Let his fair body be smooth.
> Let his headband be renewed;
> let him be clad in luxurious garment, his robe of splendor (*ṣubāt bāšti).*
> Until he gets to his city (var., his country),
> until he arrives at his destination,
> may his garment not be discolored, but always stay new.[67]

In Freedman's opinion *ṣubāt bāšti* is a prototype of the royal garment. In both the pre-Christian and the post-biblical literature the robe of glory is used to indicate dignity or royal nature. In the Christian tradition the concept of the 'robe of glory' or 'garment of glory' reminds the Genesis account 3: 7-10, 21; where Adam and Eve realized that they were naked.[68] Nudity symbolically

---

which were fashioned for the sons of men from the beginning.
The countenance of the sons of men are light,
which formed them, were formed in that image of Glory (Bedjan, *HS* II, 386.11-15; ET. "Homily on Ten Virgins," *TV* 4.1(1992), 49.226-230).

[64] Bedjan, *HS* II, 394.15-16; ET. "Homily on Ten Virgins," *TV* 4.1(1992), 56.87-88; Bedjan, *HS* I, 209.13-14.

[65] Brock, "Jacob of Serugh: A Poem on the Soul," 41-43); Sebastian Brock discusses the theme in detail in his "Clothing Metaphors as a Means of Theological Expression in Syriac Tradition."

[66] Freedman, "*ṣubāt bāšti*," 91.

[67] Gilgamesh Epic XI: 243; cited Freedman, "ṣubāt bāšti," 92.

[68] Parisot, *Demo*, XVII.7, 800:8-9;

represents sinfulness of man.[69] Regarding the biblical account of robe of glory in Genesis account Sebastian Brock explains the variant readings: "in Genesis 3:21 "and the Lord God made for Adam and his wife garments of skin and He clothed them." Although the Septuagint and Peshitta have made literal translations, Targum tradition says 'garments of glory,' while Midrash Genesis Rabba 20:12 tells 'Garment of light."[70]

The Scripture has enough evidence where glory is used for garment: Psalms 8:6 says adorned me glory and honor (ee*koro wšubaho athap*); clothed in honor (Dan 10:5)[71] (*lbooš ikoro*); clothed glory (*l'beš šubaho*) (Ps 132:16) and Enoch 62:15 say glory as clothing of the just ones. Peshitta translation of Hebrew 10:5 rendered "you clothed me in a body" (*pagaro den ʹalbešthon*). Shining (*Hedaro*) is uses in Proverbs 31:25; Isaiah 63:1; Psalms 104:1. In the transfiguration episode, the gospel writers explain the change of the body or clothe of Jesus Christ; they use the verb to indicate the changes: *zahar* (shining) (Mk 9:3); *nahar* (shine), *havar* (white) (Mt 17:2}; *havar* (white) (Lk 9:29). In the resurrection event the gospel writers use the raiment of the angel appeared in the tomb: *hevoro* (white) (Mk 16:5); *hevoro* (White) (Mt 28:3); *mabarqo* (lightening) (Lk 24:4).[72] Mathew 22:11-14 says about *lbooše mešthootho* (the wedding garment); and Revelations 3:5; 7:15 *lbooše hevore* (white garment). All these references in the Bible highlight splendor of the clothing of God Himself or righteous persons. The prophet proclaims the adornment of the righteous: "I will greatly rejoice in the LORD, my soul shall be joyful in my God; for he hath clothed me with the garments of salvation (*dmulbešene goowle dpurqono*), he hath covered me with the robe of righteousness, as a bridegroom decketh himself with ornaments (*ak hatno dmašper šamlo*), and as a bride adorn herself with her jewels (*wak kalto dsoqlo bhešaltoh*)." (Isa 61: 10) The phrase "all the glory of Adam" occurs three times in the *Dead Sea Scrolls*.[73] In the *Community Rule* IV, 22-23 of Qumran reads: "He (God) will instruct the upright with knowledge of the Most High, and teach the wisdom of the sons of heaven for the perfect of way. For those God has chosen for an everlasting covenant, and to them shall belong *all the Glory of Adam*."[74]

A similar type of interpretation on the garment of glory could be seen in the Jewish Targums, and Aramaic interpretations of the Hebrew Bible. The Targums, both Palestinian and Babylonian, read in Genesis 3:21 "and God

---

[69] Smith, "Garment of Shame," 220.

[70] Brock, "Clothing Metaphors," 14.

[71] Bedjan, *HS* II, 619.17; ET. *FH* XIII, 301.174.

[72] Rilliet, *SHF* VI, 636.9; ET. *FH* XV, 323.12.

[73] *IQS* IV, 23, CD, III, 20; cited Golitzin, "Recovering the Glory of Adam," 279.

[74] Tigchelaar, *The Dead Sea Scrolls Study Edition*, 1.78-79; cited, Golitzin, "Recovering the Glory of Adam," 279.

made to Adam and his wife garments of glory" in place of Masoretic text's "garments of skin." The Targums specify further by "garments of honor (to be worn) upon/for the skin of their flesh." The "garments of light" in R. Meir's Torah is very similar to the parallel phrase in all Targums, it only omits the reference to flesh.[75] Jewish *aggaidc* tradition uses the term *tselem* for the image of God. In rabbinic and Gnostic circles use the *tselem* imagery to characterize the human heart.[76] Jewish scholar Scholem observes that "this garment also becomes the soul's heavenly attire when it returns to Paradise after death."[77] Taking the examples from the Old Testament Rubin and Kosman says that, the dress connects two worlds: this and the world above.[78] Priestly vestments makes the wearer holy, "You shall make holy garment for your brother Aaron," that makes him get "respect and glory" (Ex 28:2, 4; 31: 10; 39:1, 41; 40:13; Lev 16:4, 32). Again, it symbolically connects the earthly and heavenly worlds. The representatives of God adorn their special garments. Aaron transfers his priestly garments to his son Eleazar (Num 20:25-28). The prophets also had their own specialty in wearing garments: Samuel's special coat (1Sam 15:27; 28:14) and Elijah's distinctive mantle (1Kings 19:13). The kings had their own regal dress (Est 6:8). A late Midrash that reflects the viewpoint of more ancient Midrash states: "For I was naked" (Gen 3:10). What was the garment of Adam? Skin of fingernail and cloud of Glory covered him. When he ate of the fruit of the tree, the fingernail skin fell off him, and he saw himself naked, while the Cloud of Glory departed from him.[79]

Clothing has manifold meaning in Syriac theology: Clothe the body, limbs,[80] clothe suffering,[81] cloud of fire clothed,[82] clothed by the Holy Spirit,[83] clothed power,[84] clothed glory.[85] All these 'clothing' imageries render adding of an external or foreign aspect to the existing one just like put-on a cloth on a body. Clothing of the robe of glory is also such a figurative interpretation. The Syriac theology teaches that Adam and Eve were created with the garment

[75] Reuling, *After Eden: Church Fathers and Rabbis on Genesis 3:16,* 253.

[76] Golitzin "Many Lamps are Lighted," 289.

[77] Gershom, *On the Mystical Shape of the Godhead,* 264.

[78] Rubin and Kosman, "The Clothing of Primordial Adam," 164.

[79] *Pesiqta in Human Society* (Warsaw ed., 1852) 14; with commentary by David Luria, 33b; Cited Rubin, Nissan and Admiel Kosman, "The Clothing of Primordial Adam," 171.

[80] Bedjan, *HS* V, 448.12; ET. *FH* V, 141.17; Bedjan, *SMS*, 733.9; ET. *FH* I, 55.283.

[81] Bedjan, *SMS*, 751.21; ET. *FH* I, 72.668.

[82] Bedjan, *HS* V, 448.12; ET. *FH* V, 141.15; cf. Bedjan, *SMS*, 753.19; ET. *FH* I, 73.711.

[83] Bedjan, *HS* V, 451.11; ET. *FH* V, 145.79.

[84] Bedjan, *HS* II, 622.20; ET. *FH* XIII, 304.239; cf. Bedjan, *SMS*, 822.4; ET. *FH* XVI, 344.281.

[85] Bedjan, *SMS*, 733.4; ET. *FH* I, 54.778.

of glory and they lost this garment through the sin and became the food for dragon and dust and their destiny is in the *Sheol*.[86] In the *Prayer Song of Soul* Mar Jacob asks to the soul "who stripped you of your beauty and mocked you"[87] (*man šlah šuparok w'ahel b'ki*) and the soul answered:

> The serpent laid snare against me and disgrace in me;
> he steel my clothes and I stood naked
> and with leaves he clothed me; I am despised.[88]

Adam's Sin caused the distorted image of humanity. But the sins of the individual are adding the spots with the existing ones. When they listen to the word of God, which is light,[89] obey it, repent and turn to the paths of God their souls will be enlightened and became glorious.[90] According to the Syriac Church Fathers Jesus Christ is the source or provider of the lost glory. They write that according to the eternal mercy of God the Father, He sent His Only Begotten to re-clothe His creation with the garment of glory which was stolen by the serpent. Therefore, instead of Eve He chose Mary, the second Eve, and the Son clothed humanity from her.[91] Mar Jacob sees that the dispensation of

---

[86] Rilliet, *SHF* I, 540:16-19; ET. *FH* IV, 132.7; cf. "You draw therefore near to the holy baptism and before all you take off your garments. As, in the beginning, when Adam was naked and was in nothing ashamed of himself, but after having broken the commandment and become mortal, he found himself in need of an outer covering." (Mingana, *Commentary of Theodore of Mopsuestia on the Lord's Prayer and on the Sacraments of Baptism and Eucharist*, 53).

[87] Brock, "Jacob of Serugh, *A Poem on Soul,*" 41.*alaeph.*

[88] Brock, "Jacob of Serugh, *A Poem on Soul,*" 42. *heth*; see a similar interpretation in, Bedjan, *HS* II, 394.16-21; ET. "Homily on the Ten Virgins, *TV* 4.1(1992), 56.390-394; With radiance and glory was Adam clothed at the beginning, before he sinned; the Evil one was envious, led Eve astray, and had Adam ejected from Paradise: he was then covered by fig leaves in place of the glory with which he had been clothed. This day did the Lord fashion Adam, today too did he drive him from Paradise; priest, pontiff and king did the Lord make Adam when he created him (Maronite Liturgy, cited, Brock, "Clothing Metaphors," 14 see fn. 14; cf Zohar 1. 36b).

[89] Bedjan, *HS* I, 299.1-4; ET. "Homily on the Publican and the Pharisee," *TV* 9(1991), 19.1-4.

[90] Bedjan, *HS* II, 413.3-6; ET. Johnson, "The Sinful Woman: A *Memra* by Jacob of Serugh," *Sobornost*, 24.1(2002), 69; The *Gospel of Thomas* writes: His disciples said to him: 'When will you appear to us? When shall we see you?'Jesus said: 'When you disrobe yourselves without being ashamed, when you take off your garments and lay them at your feet as small children do, and trample on them, then you will become the sons of the Living One, and you will have no fear Who can add to your age? He himself will give you your garment. His disciples say to him: when will you revealed to us and when shall we see you? He says: When you undress and are not ashamed (1:37). (Cited in Smith, "Garment of Shame," 218).

[91] Bedjan, *SMS,* 733.9-10; ET *FH* I, 55.283-284; cf.
The Firstborn wrapped himself in a body, as veil to hide his glory;
the immortal bride shines out in that robe.

the garment of glory is elated throughout the Incarnation of the Son of God, especially in three stages: the nativity, the baptism, and the visit of *Sheol*. Each stage of Christ's life was instrumental to the re-clothing of the robe of glory. The Son of God through His Incarnation brought the access of the robe of glory to the children of Adam. Since He clothed the human body humanity could cloth the eternal body of the Son. The Son, though He is not viable to sin, received the baptism of the sinners and installed the robe of glory for the sons of repentance.[92] Through His nakedness on the Cross He removed the nakedness of humanity. In the opinion of Sebastian Brock though they occurred in three different stages of profane time they are intimately linked with sacred time.[93]

Mar Jacob states that there is only one robe; the same robe is distributed to everyone; and it cannot be partitioned.[94] That means, the same robe that the Father wears is clothed by the Son and the same is clothed by all human beings. Therefore, the robe could be the holiness of the God and it could be attained through repentance, baptism (through which the faithful receives the remission of sin and purification), and the communion with the Son.[95] Mar

---

Let the guests in their robes resemble him in his;
let your bodies, which are your clothing, shine out,
for they bound in fetters the man whose body was stained.
O whiten my stains at your banquet with your radiance. (*CNis.* 43.21; ET; Brock, *The Luminous Eye*, 95).

Because the serpent had stolen the clothes
of Adam, that fair image,
the royal Son brought them back
to reclothe Adam in his adornment.
The serpent led Eve astray
and stole away from her crown,
but virgin's son trampled down the serpent
and from the baptismal water gave back to Eve her crown (Brock, Epiphany Hymn: Anonymous Author, ET. *The Treasure House of Mysteries*, 255-256).

[92] Bedjan, *HS* I, 298.3-21; ET, "On the Prodigal Son," *TV* 5.4(1994), 37.629-646.

[93] Brock, "Clothing Metaphors," 12.

[94] Bedjan, *HS* I, 298.3-9; ET, "On the Prodigal Son," *TV* 5.4(1994), 36.629-634.

[95] Let us take off and cast from us all filthiness so that we may put on the wedding garments (Parisot, *Demo* VI.1, 240.11-13; cf. Valavanolickal, *Demonstrations* I, 123); The *Gospel of Philip* writes: It is from water and fire that the soul and the spirit came into being. It is from water and fire and light that the son of the bridal chamber (came into being). The fire is the chrism, the light is the fire. I am not referring to that fire which has no form, but to the other fire whose form is white, which is bright and beautiful, and which gives beauty (Isenberg, *Gospel of Philip*.67.1-5, 140). From the writings of Mar Jacob Robe is the holiness of God and Jesus put this in the water at the time of His baptism (Bedjan, *HS* I, 168.7-8; ET. *FH* VI, 163.14-15). This is the common tradition of the Syriac Churches that Christ put the robe of glory under the water during his baptism and everyone who receive baptism from the church will receive this robe for

Jacob writes about the acquisition of the garment of glory through repentance[96] and baptism[97]; in his *Homily on the Prodigal Son* he writes:

> When the younger son came back from stumblings,
> they clothed him in that robe, which was the chief his father had.
> There was one robe for both the last and the first;
> for it was not rent asunder that each should take half.
> That chief robe was given to the younger son,
> and there was not some other that the elder son might put on.
> There is one faith and Baptism in God,
> and one is the garment which He bestows on them that are baptized in water.[98]

In the Bible and the Syriac liturgical tradition, shabby cloth is counted as a symbol of sin and fall; on the other hand white, wedding dress, festal dress is considered as the dress of holiness (Zech 3:3-5). Mar Jacob writes: "Embroidered cloth was put on like the high priests in the temple; fire and spirit wove you a fiery wedding garment."[99] In the homily *On Ten Virgins* he says that if righteous all creation can shine like the wise virgins,[100] because God created human with robe of glory. Their face will shine like light; he writes: "The countenance (*parsoopo*) of the sons of men is light, which, when He formed them, were formed in that image of Glory (*zalmo dšubḥo*), and they shine in the Kingdom, brighter than the sun."[101] For this reason, "He (Jesus) called the company of the just as virgins"[102] so that, Mar Jacob says, just men will be brighten like sun and enter into the bridal chamber of light. In another sense, those who keep away from the spots and filths of this world and preserve their bodies like a treasure house which is full of light could enter into the palace of the bridegroom.[103] But this cloth can be defiled through the evil deeds and could be expelled like foolish virgins.[104]

---

the protection of his/her soul. By blessing the water before the immersion of the candidate the priest says, "Lord, make this water to be a bath of re-birth, gift of adoption as sons, the garment of incorruptibility (*l'boošo d'lo methabalonooto*), the renewal of Your Holy Spirit (*Order of the Baptism*, 41-42; cf. *HPar*, ET. Brock, *Hymn on Paradise,* 66).

[96] Bedjan, *HS* II, 422.1-4; ET. Johnson, "The Sinful Woman: A *Memra* by Jacob of Serugh," *Sobornost*, 24.1(2002), 80.

[97] Bedjan, *HS* II, 414.1-415.12; ET. Johnson, "The Sinful Woman: A *Memra* by Jacob of Serugh," *Sobornost*, 24.1(2002), 70-72.

[98] Bedjan, *HS* I, 298.3-10; ET, "On the Prodigal Son," *TV* 5.4(1994), 36.429-436.

[99] Bedjan, *HS* I, 208.9-10.

[100] Bedjan, *HS* II, 386.19-20; ET. "Homily on the Ten Virgins," *TV* 4.1(1992), 49.233-234.

[101] Bedjan, *HS* II, 386.15-16; ET. "Homily on the Ten Virgins," *TV* 4.1(1992), 49.229-230.

[102] Bedjan, *HS* II, 387.8; ET. "Homily on the Ten Virgins," *TV* 4.1(1992), 50.243.

[103] Bedjan, *HS* II, 387.9; ET. "Homily on the Ten Virgins," *TV* 4.1(1992), 50.244.

[104] Bedjan, *HS* I, 209.9-10.

Mar Jacob portrayed Christ as light, and fire clothed one.[105] The biblical exposition of transfigured Christ is an example of the same. Also Mar Jacob uses garment of glory and garment of light as synonyms. Glory of God also was portrayed as light.[106] Thus, according to the imagination of Mar Jacob, the nature of the garment must be fiery light in white color (*ḥwar*).[107] And God's holiness also portrayed as fire. Thus the robe of glory might be the state of holiness or participation in the holiness of God. Above discussion described the origin, dispensation, and nature of the robe of glory. The following is a detailed analysis of Mar Jacob's interpretation on the robe of glory and its dispensation through various events of Jesus Christ.

6.3.1. Robe of Glory through the Birth of the Bridegroom

The nativity of Christ is the first staging post in which He dispensed the robe of glory to the Church. God has put-on the body of human being in order to give His nature to human beings. In the Garden of Eden, by his sin, the father (Adam) was stripped; and his stripping caused stripping of all his descendants. Now the daughter of Adam (Mary) is going to weave robe of glory to the father.[108] In his homily *On Nativity,* angel Gabriel says that Jesus Christ is going to bring back the lost garment and to re-clothe Adam:

> I am not stripping (*mašlaḥ*) you of glory, as happened in the garden;
> I have brought a cloak (so that) you can cover your forefather who was stripped bare.
> I am not weaving for you a garment of shame (*lboošo dḥesdo*) from leaves.
> I brought a garment of glory (*'esṭal šubḥo*) for Adam to be clothed in it.[109]

In another occasion Mar Jacob says that, when Jesus was wrapped in the swaddling cloth the cloth of shame with fig leaves was removed from humanity:

> Today, Adam has exchanged his leaves for the garment of light and by its glory, he put to shame the serpent who had smitten him and carried away his garment from him. Today, the Lord of Eden has been wrapped in swaddling clothes instead of with the leaves in order to exchange glory for the shame so that the earlier glory might be returned to Adam.[110]

Again from another nativity homily:

---

[105] Rilliet, *SHF* II, 564.11; ET. *FH* VII, 198.32.

[106] Bedjan *HS* II, 354.13-14; ET. *FH* VIII, 211.149-150.

[107] Bedjan, *HS* II, 355.8-357.10; ET. *FH* VIII, 212.165-214.208.

[108] Bedjan, *L P*, ET. "Homily on the Virgin Mary," *TV* 5.1(1993), 9.45-50.

[109] Bedjan *SMS*, 733.1-4; ET. *FH* I, 54.275-278.

[110] Rilliet, *SHF* I, 544.1-6; *FH* IV, 134.15,16.

> In this month that sheds the leaves from the trees
> the leaves of Adam have been exchanged for the garment of light (*lboos nuhro*).[111]
> In this month that comes to strip off all ornaments
> the nakedness of the leaders of our race has been clothed.[112]

These passages describe the fall of Adam, stripping of garment of glory and intervention of Son of God to re-clothe the garment of glory through His birth. Upon His robe of glory Jesus clothed the swaddling cloth of the world. Through this clothing the Son of God returned the robe of glory to human beings. Thus, the birth of Jesus Christ made pertinent the event and through which He received the nature and form of sinful human being. By this act He made a bridge between divine and human natures. He deleted the chasm between God and humanity.[113]

6.3.2. Robe of Glory through the Baptism of the Bridegroom

Mar Jacob opines that the Son is the authoritative person to distribute the robe of glory. He writes: "The Father prepared (*atad*) the robe, the Son wove (*zqr*) it, the Spirit cut (*gad*) it (off the loom), and you went down and put it on in divine fashion."[114] Therefore, the authority to disburse the robe of glory is vested with the Son of God only; no one else is authorized the same. He spreads this message in his homilies. He writes that, those who cleansed from their sins by the washing of John the Baptist remained stripped until the arrival of the Son of God for the baptism. When the Son was baptized in the river Jordan He placed the robe of glory in the baptismal water and only then they were able to adorn it.

> And when the marriage feast was made ready with all its preparations,
> yet the Bridegroom alone held Himself back from coming to visit His own.
> When the washing took place for the wedding guests and it [the washing] had cleansed them,
> yet they were not clothed in the garment of the Spirit from the water.
> And when all the peoples were standing stripped (*šaleeḥooto*)
> and were waiting for the Bridegroom to come and clothe (*nelbeš*) them.
> And when the impurity of the bride was washed away in the water and she came up,
> and everyone looked for the white garments that the Bridegroom would bring.
> And since the baptism was deficient of forgiveness,
> and no one had received the Spirit of Holiness from the waters.[115]

[111] Bedjan, *SMS*, 772.11-12; ET. *FH* I, 91.1101-1102.

[112] Bedjan, *SMS*, 772.15-16; ET. *FH* I, 91.1105-1106.

[113] See Koonammakal, "Ephrem's Imagery of Chasm," 175-183.

[114] Bedjan, *HS* I, 211.6.

[115] Bedjan, *HS* I, 173.15-174.4; ET. *FH* VI, 168.127-169.134.

The above passage propels that John's baptism was not of the Holy Spirit; he just cleansed the body and mind. The faithful stayed stripped until Jesus came and dispensed the garment of Spirit. The Bridegroom mingled the Spirit in the water, placed the robe of glory in it, and made the womb of water as a furnace which makes the robe.[116] Now, the faithful who immerse in the water can receive the white garment of Spirit.[117] This may be an argument against the Old Testament priesthood and affirmation of the New Testament priesthood. Because John is from the tribe of Levi and therefore, he is a Jewish priest; since Mar Jacob finds John's baptism is insufficient for the remission of sins he repudiates the Old Testament priesthood itself. Remission of sins through the baptism of Christ affirms the need of the New Testament priesthood which springs forth from the authority of Jesus Christ. Mar Jacob describes the institution of New Testament priesthood in the same homily asserting this view.[118]

Mar Jacob again claims that Christ is the source of the robe and baptism is a process to obtain the Robe of Glory. The following comments and dialogue between John and Jesus in the homilies Mar Jacob asserts the authority of Jesus Christ as the One Who baptizes people with the Holy Spirit and adorner of the robe of glory. "Christ put on the Church in the virgin's womb, and she put on him in the waters of baptism."[119] Again, "He (Christ) came to baptism; He went down and placed in the baptismal water the robe of glory, to be there

---

[116] Bedjan, *HS* I, 181.6-7; ET. *FH* VI, 176.281-282; cf.
Like the coin out of the lake
have I come up from the font;
with Fire and Spirit have I been forged.
I have entered the flock of the Son.
With garments of glory am I clothe,
with raiment of light am I wrapped.
From the water I have become a virgin,
and behold, angels are rejoicing at me (Brock, Epiphany Hymn: Anonymous Author, ET. *The Treasure House of Mysteries,* 257).

[117] See a similar interpretation from John Chrysostom: Therefore, as soon as you entered in, you put your garment which was an image of putting off the old man and his deeds… what a marvel! They [ie., the newly baptized] were naked before the gaze of all and did not become ashamed, because they were the image of the first created Adam who, in Paradise, was naked and not ashamed (Chrysostom, *Homily on Col. 6.4, PG LXII.*342).

[118] Bedjan, *HS* I, 191.14-15; ET. *FH* VI, 185.497-498.

[119] Bedjan, *HS* III, 288.9-10; cf.
Son of the Most High who came and dwelt in me,
Another birth, He bore me also
[in] a second birth. I put on the glory of Him
who put the body, the garment of His mother (*HNat.* XVI.11, 85; ET. McVey, *Ephrem the Syrian,* 150).

for Adam, who had lost it."[120] And "Christ wove garments of life for Adam in the baptismal water."[121] See the dialogue between John and Jesus, in which John asking to Jesus that since You are the Lord and provider of all how could I baptize You?

> To the bride of light who was betrothed to you I said this;
> "The bridegroom, your Lord, will baptize you with the Holy Spirit and fire."
> Behold, she is looking to you that you may baptize her as I taught her,
> and now how is it that she should approach to see that you are baptized by me?...
> In your name I have been baptizing her so that she shall be adorned by you
> and, O Holy One, in whose name shall I baptize you? I do not know[122]

Subsequently Mar Jacob says that John the Baptist, the carrier of adornment, brought and "opened the trunk of the Spirit over the waters and brought out the garments to clothe the church in sanctity."[123] This seems contradictory; he argues that the baptism of John is insufficient and he brought Spirit and cleansed the people who took baptism from him. But the rest of the homily describes the role of the Bridegroom as the provider of the robe and John the Baptist's effort to clean the bride from the filth by his teachings and cleansing her body.[124] Regarding the robe of glory Sebastian Brock claims that, Baptism ensures the robe of glory and therefore entrance into Paradise, which is the bridal chamber. But it is not the primordial paradise but eschatological paradise. At baptism the robe of glory is regained in potential, but not fully in reality, for this will happen only at the end, during the second coming.[125]

6.3.3. Robe of Glory through the Death and Resurrection of the Bridegroom

Baptism is mainly aimed for people who live in the physical world from the time of Jesus Christ. Jesus was not only the Savior of the living but He is also the Savior of the dead from the time of Adam. The dead ones prior to baptism of Jesus was not able to baptize in the water and put-on the robe, therefore, Jesus went to the *Sheol* where the dead were assembled and clothed them with the light of His glory. This will be discussed in the following section.

Christ, the Bridegroom is the first born from the dead. Through His death and resurrection the Bridegroom killed the death. Mar Jacob states: "From His resurrection life reigned over the mortals, and we have truly stripped off the

[120] Bedjan, *HS* III, 593.8-9.

[121] Bedjan, *HS* V, 681.19.

[122] Bedjan, *HS* I, 181.16-182.5; ET. *FH* VI, 176.291-177.300.

[123] Bedjan, *HS* I, 168.14-15; ET. *FH* VI, 163.20-21.

[124] Bedjan, *HS* I, 170.8-11; ET. *FH* VI, 165.57-60.

[125] Brock, "Clothing Metaphor," 13.

old order (*'ateeqooto*) by His death."[126] By referring the 'old order' here he meant the dominance of death and the evil one over human beings. Therefore, by His death the Bridegroom overcomes the evil one and removed the cloth of destruction and re-clothed humanity with the robe of life. In one of his homilies Mar Jacob reproduces Jesus' words to the repentant thief and says: "I will clothe you with the robe of light in the bridal chamber on high."[127] The Scripture lacks any reference except "today you will be with me in Paradise" (Lk 23:43). By His death Christ defeated the evil one and took away power from him. As a result the sinful human beings received the robe of salvation. The two robes referred here are the robe of death and the robe of life; thus robe may be state, status, or possibility of life.

Mar Jacob points out that the bridal chamber has its own clothes. The clothing of the bridal chamber is worthier than that of this world. The sons of resurrection who are eligible for the bridal chamber will secure the garment of glory;[128] because without the garment of glory no one could enter into the bridal chamber; but they will be thrown out from the bridal chamber (Mt 22:11-13). People of this world put-on the garments of this world: they use linen and wool; the children of the bridal chamber do not want the clothes of this world. Jesus Christ, when He embodied the human nature, He put-on the garments of linen and wool but when He resurrected from the dead He put-off the clothes of this world and put-on the dress of His Father's house (*bet abooh*).[129] After the resurrection, the apostles and the women followers found the garment of linen by which His body was covered and the head band were placed at the side of His tomb (Jn 20:7). The garment of this world (*lbooše darao*) decays but the garment of glory does not wear out.[130] Mar Jacob sees the garment of this world as the symbol of old nature. Jesus Christ put-on the garment of this world by His birth and at resurrection He put-off this garment and clothed in

---

[126] Bedjan, *HS* II, 613.17-18; ET. *FH* XIII, 296.53-54. See Cyril of Jerusalem's comment on putting-on the cloth on the cross. Stripped of your garments you were naked and thus resembled Christ on the cross. There, by His nakedness, Christ despoiled the Principalities and Powers and, by means of wood, dragged them after him in his triumphal procession (Col 2:15). Now, since the hostile powers were hiding in your members, you could no longer be allowed to wear shabby clothes. I am speaking, of the course, not of the garment men see but of the old self that is being corrupted by the lusts that lead astray (Eph 4:22). May the soul that has stripped off that garment once and for all not put it on again! Let it say, rather, as the spouse of Christ says in the Song of Songs: "I was stripped off my tunic, how shall I put it on again? (Song 5:3). What a marvelous thing! You were naked in the sight of all, yet you did not blush. In very truth, you were an image of the first man, Adam, who in the garden was likewise naked and did not blush (Cyril of Jerusalem, *Cat.* 20:2, cf. Deiss, *Springtime of the Liturgy*, 279).

[127] Bedjan, *HS* V, 669.1.

[128] Bedjan, *HS* II, 619.17-620:7; ET. *FH* XIII, 301.175-184.

[129] Bedjan, *HS* II, 620.13-17; ET. *FH* XIII, 302.190-194.

[130] Bedjan, *HS* II, 620.1-6; ET. *FH* XIII, 301.179-184.

the new robe of light. He writes that He left the garment of the dead in *Sheol* and clothed Himself in the garment of glory (*šubḥo lbeš*).[131] The resurrected body resembles the body of Adam and Eve prior to the fall which does not need a garment of this world. Therefore, Mar Jacob often portrayed the resurrected Christ as the Luminous One.[132] After the resurrection He clothed Himself the garment of glory and descended into the *Sheol*: The Lion's whelp by His might destroyed the old order of slavery to death and captivity in *Sheol*. The Bridegroom descended into the *Sheol* where the dead assembled. He defeated the king of *Sheol* and shattered its walls.[133] In *Sheol* He shared His garment of light with the dead who assembled there. "By His voice, the Son raises the dead from their tombs and clothed them with the garment of glory on the day of resurrection."[134] In the *Hymn on Soul* Mar Jacob says about the salvific acts of Jesus on the cross and the clothing of the robe of glory:

> Your greatness and your beauty which were lost
> all this you have now found on the height of Golgotha.
> Arise, clothe yourself, and return to your inheritance;
> strip off your rags and the leaves that cover your nakedness;
> take and put on the glorious robe.
> Enter into Eden which is opened up and awaits you
> that garment, which the serpent stole from you.
> The king's son has brought and given to you.
> Praise be to him who has returned to your father's house.[135]

In the nativity of the Bridegroom Mar Jacob writes that He clothed humanity from the womb.[136] On the resurrection of the Bridegroom, Mar Jacob states that, He shed off from himself the garment of dead and clothed Himself in the garment of glory from the house of His Father.[137] In the former he says glorious robe is covered by the earthly robe. But in the latter he opines that robe of dust left in the tomb and garbed with the robe of glory which cannot be worn out. These are contradictory to each other; because he says that the Bridegroom has glorious garb in Himself and at the same time he says that when He resurrected He took glorious garment from His father's house. Here, the problem is, if He has the robe of glory in His nature what is the need to

[131] Bedjan, *HS* II, 619.15-18; ET. *FH* XIII, 301.173-176.

[132] Supra, 4.3.8.

[133] Bedjan, *HS* II, 612.1-10; ET. *FH* XIII, 294.17-26.

[134] *Kashtanubhavazhcha Namaskaram*, 245.

[135] Brock, "Jacob of Serugh A Poem on the Soul," 43. 20-23; cf. Brock, "A Prayer Song by St Jacob of Serugh Recovered," 33, 37.

[136] Bedjan, *SMS*, 733.9-12; 760.5-6; 763.13-18; ET. *FH* I, 55.283-286, 79.845-846, 82.911-918.

[137] Bedjan, *HS* II, 620.12-13; ET. *FH* XIII, 302.185-186.

re-clothed in the robe of glory from His Father's house? If He has the robe in Himself, He just wanted to shed the acquired dress from the earthly womb. Therefore, Mar Jacob's interpretation is very complex and complicated to explain the nature of robe. This kind of interpretation is visible throughout his homilies. Otherwise, he is not a systematic interpreter of the scripture but he sees everything with spiritual eyes.

The death of Christ brought back the lost glory to the humanity. He was the first born from the dead and the guide to the earth-born. Through this the stripped ones (human beings) left the garment of skin and leaves and adorned with the robe of glory, which allowed their entry into their original house, the Paradise. He re-clothed humankind in three fold way: by His birth, baptism and His resurrection. Through the birth He received the earthly robe and thus He opened the way of humanity to be re-clothed in the robe of the heights. In the baptism He placed the robe in the baptismal womb; for those who enter into the baptismal font could attain the garment of glory. At the resurrection, He removed the old garment of linen and wore the cloth of light and shared it with the dead. Unlike in the baptism, the process of clothing is not mentioned in the homilies. By the notion clothing the robe of glory it is to be presumed as acquiring the holiness by the sanctification of the human soul. *Sheol* witnessed the culmination of Jesus' sacrificial deliverance on Golgotha. Through the death He removed the authority of death and through the shedding of water and blood from His side He baptized the dead and established the Holy Communion with God.[138] Both in baptism and in resurrection the souls received the cloth of holiness, which is the Robe of Glory. Another main thrust of the concept of robe of glory is that it segregates the two realms of human existence: the sinful state where they need garment of this world and the luminous state where holiness clothed on their body.

6.3.4. Robe of Glory is an Armor for the Faithful

Mar Jacob portrayed the robe of glory as an entry pass to the bridal chamber and also as a shield to protect from evil spirit.

> I descended to the fountain not to take up a shield for myself
> but to forge mighty armor (*aḥšool zaino rabo*) for warriors.
> I am anxious to cleanse humanity in the contest of battle
> so that everyone who comes to fight (*taktooš*) should fight (*qreb*) like me.
> I am instituting baptism as an armory (*bet zanyo*);
> unless man has entered and clothed himself from it, he will not fight.
> If I pass over and do not get baptized as you would withhold me
> no one will be able to take up the armor from the waters…

[138] Bedjan, *HS* III, 613.15-615.5; ET. *FH* XIII, 296.51-297.82.

> And if they do not equip themselves with my power (*ḥ'lo deel*) from the waters they will not encounter the great battle as diligent ones (*kašeere*).[139]

In the argument between John and Jesus on the former's hesitation to baptize the latter Jesus says that without He being baptized nobody would be saved as He has to descend in the water to place the robe of glory and hence He (Jesus) has to undergo baptism by John for salvation of humanity. However, there is no reference regarding the function of the robe of glory or how the robe of glory saves the person from his/her enemy. The robe of glory in general meant as the symbol of holiness and a requirement for the entrance into the bridal chamber. Most probably the robe is the Holy Spirit.[140] John the Baptist, the friend of the Bridegroom, makes the bride ready for the marriage with the ornaments of repentance (*ṣebte dtyobooto*), and washing in water,[141] but not with Spirit.[142] However, she is waiting for the garment of Spirit (*naḥto droọḥo*) from the water, which only the Bridegroom could bring.[143] The same homily gives reference about the *roošmo* of the cross on the forehead;[144] this would be about the post baptismal anointing in the West Syriac tradition, where, the priest anoints the candidate with the holy Myron that represents Holy Spirit.[145]

---

[139] Bedjan, *HS* I, 180.12-181.6; ET. *FH* VI, 175.267-280; cf. Whoever has put-on armor from the baptismal water, let him not take of his armor lest he find himself defeated. Parisot, *Demo*, VI.1, 252:17-20; ET. Valavanolickal, *Demonstrations* I, 132.

[140] Bedjan, *HS* I, 181.16; ET. *FH* VI, 176.294; cf.
The son of the King ascended to His Father in order to send
the armor of the Spirit form his Father to his servants.
Before his ascension, while being elevated, he gathered them
and breathed upon them so that they might receive the Spirit from him…
He clothed them with the power of the Spirit before he ascended,
and sent to them all the armor after He had ascended (Bedjan, *HS* II, 676.17-677.4; ET. *FH* XVII, 360.135-142).
The Spirit with sound and fire in appearance have commingled
And for the disciples it cast the armor and clothed them (Bedjan, *HS* II, 677.11-12; ET. *FH* XVII, 360.149-150; Bedjan, *HS* II, 687.11; ET. *FH* XVII, 368.355).

[141] Bedjan, *HS* I, 173.14-15; ET. *FH* VI, 168125-126.

[142] Bedjan, *HS* I, 173.10; ET. *FH* VI, 169.128.

[143] Bedjan, *HS* I, 173.17-174.3; ET. *FH* VI, 169.132.

[144] Bedjan, *HS* I, 181.7; ET. *FH* VI, 176.282. Cross is depicted as a symbol of protection from the enemies.

[145] O Lord, Let your servant who has been counted among your worshippers through the faith in baptism, receive this holy seal and sign in your name. So that being spiritually filled with all the sweet odor by this Myron, he may not be seized by the hostile powers and rulers of darkness, but walking in your light let him be a son of light and following you he may come to you (*Koodashakramangal,* 47-50); You have clothed her with the garment of glory and betrothed her with water and Spirit. You have made her Your bride and trampled mightily upon the head of the enemy (*Koodashakramangal*, 65).

Therefore, the robe would be the Holy Spirit, who protects the faithful from dangers.

Through the baptism one acquires armor, which is a white garment that guards against the evil. Mar Jacob said, even after the baptism of John the Baptist, the bride was stripped. He mixed the splendor of His holiness with the waters. He makes humanity enter into the furnace of water to recast into His own Image. Thus, baptism and the robe of glory is an institution which retain the Image of God to the lost humanity. This Image is an armor to the one who baptize and without which no one can enter the bridal chamber. Thus according to Mar Jacob Christ is the provider of the robe of glory. Robe is the armor against the evil forces and a pledge to the entrance into the bridal chamber. Robe is a garment of holiness and the communion with the Holy Spirit provides this precious garment.

6.3.5. Different Ornaments of Bride

Mar Jacob mentions the ornaments adorned by the bride. In the Old Testament it is narrated that in the royal weddings the bride undergoes different orders of purification. (Esth 2:3). The Book of Revelations points Jerusalem as the adorned bride (Rev 21:2). Mar Jacob gives a different meaning to the ornamentation of the bride. Foremost and greatest of all the ornaments is the repentance of the bride.[146] The suffering for the Bridegroom is also portrayed as the ornament of the bride. Whereas, he portrayed the liberated bride from the slavery of Egypt as the adorned bride.[147] In the homily *On the Baptism of Our Redeemer* Mar Jacob depicts the adorned bride who is ready for the betrothal; John the Baptist enters and makes the bride ready for betrothal by washing her bodily blemishes and by his exhortation cleansing her faulty thoughts from her mind.[148] In his homily of *Repentance and Fasting* he brings a host of Semitic bridal ornaments and compares them with divine ornaments. Houses will decorate with colorful clothes, bride and bridegroom are adorned with bright bridal dress and beautiful golden ornaments, the guest wore woolen garments, incenses are burned for sweet aroma, wine is served at the feast. But in the bridal chamber of repentance they wore sack clothes instead of

[146] In the book of *Joseph and Asneth* says ornaments as repentance μετανοια: For penitence is the most high's daughter and she entreats the Most High on your behalf every hour, and on behalf of all who repent; for he is the father of penitence and she the mother of virgins and every hour she petitions him for those who repent, for she has prepared a heavenly bridal chamber for those who love her and she will look after them forever. And penitence is herself a virgin, very beautiful and pure and chaste and gentle, and God Most High loves her, and all his angels do her reverence (*Joseph and Asneth*, (short text) 15.7-8; Cited Nir, *Joseph and Asneth: A Christian Book*, 78).

[147] Bedjan, *HS* I, 13.11-14.

[148] Bedjan, *HS* I, 173.14-15; ET. *FH* VI, 168.125-126.

bright and woolen clothes, tears instead of wine, ashes instead of incense and everywhere filled with black clothes and mourning.[149] Therefore, repentance is considered as the greatest among the ornaments. In one of the hymns sung in the West Syriac Church, attributed to Mar Jacob, says: "When the sinner's face soaked with tears and when his mouth became silent because of weeping he will be honored with love. The tears of repentance of a sinner is precious than invaluable gems (*ak nooṭpoto dmardyon temr`w da`no dtobo*).[150]

Another important aspect which Mar Jacob considers as the ornament of the bride is purity. The bride's chastity is very important in this concept. The bride should be the bride of one husband her thoughts and deeds should be on Him. In his homily *On Ten Virgins* Mar Jacob says:

> The wise maiden who took oil in their vessels,
> they are the just (*ke`no*), who were diligent in righteousness (*zadeeqooto*).
> The vessels are the bodies of men,
> wherein they store oil to be for the brightness (*nuhro*) of their persons.
> He calleth 'oil' the soul's love (*ḥoobo*) and purity (*šapeeroto*),
> wherein is gathered the entire course of virtues.[151]

Another ornament is the suffering for the Bridegroom. This may also come under the aspect of chastity. A bride should suffer for her spouse. Paul exhorts that he will suffer even death for the love of Christ (Rom 8:35-39). Mar Jacob rewrites Paul's remarks on his sufferings for the Bridegroom Christ: became prisoner, servant of crucifixion, hungered, thirst, fasted, bore marks of Christ on his body. He describes wounds as necklace, he considered cross like a jewel, scars as ornaments and he considered all these are gems on his crown on the day of resurrection.[152] Therefore, the suffering for the love of the Bridegroom is considered as ornaments. A bride must overcome the temptations of the world to keep her chastity. Regarding the true bride of Chris Mar Jacob writes:

> Behold! She is being carried magnificently (*metg`ayo*), with the chastity
> (*btooloto*) that the bridegroom gave her.
> and with white clothes she dressed up (*lbeš`t*) from inside the waters.
> By His cross of the light that is hung by her neck like a necklace (*hmneeko*)
> and the ornaments (*ḥešlto*) of the Son's sufferings that are being set on fire for her.[153]

In another homily Mar Jacob describes various ornaments of bride: "Here are the ornaments of His percepts upon your ears, the dowry of His laws in

---

[149] Bedjan, *HS* IV, 455.1-14; ET. Bchery, "Repentance and Fasting," 5.

[150] *Ktobo d-zlooto šheemto*, 136-137.

[151] Bedjan, *HS* II, 387.2-7; ET. "Homily on the Ten Virgins," *TV* 4.1(1992), 49.237-242.

[152] Bedjan, *HS* II, 749.2-750.6; ET. "On Paul the Apostle," *TV* 10(1991), 58.31-59.54.

[153] Bedjan, *HS* II, 237.20-238.2.

your hands, the necklace of priesthood around your neck, the garment of His ministry upon your body!"[154] The precepts, laws, priesthood, and ministry are portrayed as ornaments. In fact all these factors are used for the well being and purification of the people of Israel. All these ethical components are addressed for a just family and society which again are the qualification for remaining pure as bride. Thus, it could be inferred that the purified soul is the greatest ornament. The symbol of purity is referred as bright light:

> For the daughter of light the Father set the signet ring of light (*'ezqoto nuhro*)
> and He betrothed her to His Son because the Bridegroom as well is wholly light.[155]
> You were clothed in rays of light (*zleeqo dnuhro lbeešo hweet*)
> you were sealed (*ṭbee`o*) with the king's own necklace (*hmneeko*);
> who is it who has given leaves (to cover) your nakedness (*pursoyo*).[156]

Mar Jacob opines that the ornaments are obtainable at two points: from the baptismal font and from Golgotha. When the Bridegroom came to betroth the bride, she was an adorned one; because the servant of the Bridegroom taught her and cleansed her before presenting her to the Bridegroom for betrothal.[157] He states: "When the bride made perfect with the ornaments of repentance, she was cleansed and came out of the waters of baptism."[158] Mar Ephrem sees baptism as a coronation: "You to be baptized, who have found the kingdom in the very bosom of Baptism, step down, put on the *iheedoyo* who is the Lord of the Kingdom. Blessed are you who have been crowned."[159] The *Odes of Solomon* depicts Christ Himself as the crown of the faithful. And the author connects this crown with floral garland.[160] The crown is considered as the crown of immortality.[161]

Another place of taking the ornament is at the cross. Cross itself is depicted as ornament. Mar Jacob writes that the nails which the Jews nailed Jesus on the Cross became the wedding ring: "The royal ring was forged with

---

[154] Rilliet, *SHF*, 596.19-21; ET. *FH* XI, 269-270.24.

[155] Bedjan, *HS* II, 374.17-18; ET. *FH* VIII, 230.577-578.

[156] Brock, "Jacob of Serugh: A Poem on Soul," 43.

[157] Bedjan, *HS* I, 169.1-2; ET. *FH* VI, 164.29-30.

[158] Bedjan, *HS* I, 173.14-15; ET. *FH* VI, 168.125-126; cf. Brock, *Bride of Light,* 30.

[159] *Epiph.* XIII.14, 53-54; cf. Our brother, sing glory to the Son of the Almighty, who has fashioned for you a crown which kings would envy. Your garments, O our brother, have the brightness of snow and your brightness is more pleasing than the river Jordan. You ascended like an angel, O our beloved, from baptism by the power of the Holy Spirit. Behold, an unfading crown is placed on your head, and today you have put on the glory of Adam's race. You received, O our brother, the bliss of the heavenly ones, watch, lest the Evil on snatch it from you (*Koodashakramangal*, 53).

[160] Charlesworth, *Odes of Solomon,* 20. 7-8.

[161] *AAA*, 220.

the nail of his hands and the betrothal was given with his holy blood."[162] In another occasion he compared the Eucharist with the wedding ring: "And with one ring (*ʹezqoto*) are the treasures of the House of God sealed (*ṭbʿ*)."[163] Again, "He placed the crown of light upon her head, which is glorified. He broke his body for her and he mixed his blood for her and gladdened her heart."[164]

6.4. The Wedding Feast

In all cultures wedding feast is an important custom. In ancient West Asia the decision of a man and a woman was not enough to be a couple. The 27th law of Ršnunna declares: "If a man marries the daughter of another man without the consent of her father or mother, and moreover does not conclude the nuptial feast and the contract for her father and mother, should she reside in his house for even one full year, she is not a wife."[165] Also, meal has an important place in the religious history of Israelites.[166] To them almost all meals represented the Messianic banquet feast or eschatological banquet with Messiah. The adaptation of this Messianic banquet in the religious spectrum of Israelites can be traced to several mythological heritages. Smith rightly says that, "The messianic banquet in Jewish and early Christian literature is almost entirely a mythological/literary motif."[167] He uses two scales to expound the background of the messianic banquet feast: the motif of sacred food in the early West Asia that impart divine blessings of immortality and this would be turned into the concept of eternal life in the eschatological life. The other motif of the banquet feast, he considers, is a thanksgiving meal after the victory of a great battle.[168]

The allusion of a sacred banquet is described in the prophecy of Isaiah: "On this mountain the Lord of hosts will make for all peoples a feast of rich food, a feast of well-aged wines strained clear. And he will destroy on this mountain the shroud that is cast over all peoples, the sheet that is spread over all nations; he will swallow up death for ever. Then the Lord God will wipe away the tears from all faces, and the disgrace of his people he will take away from all the earth, for the Lord has spoken" (Isa 25:6-8). 1 Enoch 62: 12-14 says: "the righteous and elect ones… shall eat and rest and rise with that Son of Man forever and ever". This will happen "in the day" when the Lord shall triumph over the kings and other rulers of the earth. This is a banquet at which there will be lavish provisions of food and wine, as is appropriate to a festive

[162] Brock, "The Wedding Feast on Golgotha" 124-125.

[163] Bedjan, *HS* I, 298.12; ET, "On the Prodigal Son," *TV* 5.4(1994), 37.638.

[164] Narsai, "Dedication of the Church," ܫܠܡ:12-13.

[165] Cited Carr and Conway, "Constructions of Gender and Bodies," 278.

[166] Lieber, "I Set a Table Before You," 66.

[167] Smith, "Messianic Banquet Reconsidered," 65.

[168] Smith, "Messianic Banquet Reconsidered," 65.

meal (Joel 2:24-26; 4Ezra 9: 19). In ritualized messianic banquet where the messiah is said to be present was a regular part of Qumran community life. This is the order of the session of the "Men of the Name who are invited to the Feast" for the communal council when God sends the Messiah to be with them: The Priest shall enter at the head of all the congregation of Israel and all the fathers of the Aaronids... and they shall sit before him each according to his rank. Next the Messiah of Israel shall enter, and the heads of thousands of Israel shall sit before him each according to his rank... When they solemnly meet together at a table of communion or to drink the wine... the Messiah of Israel shall stretch out his hand to the bread. Next all the congregation of the community shall give thanks and partake, each according to his rank" (1QSa ii. 11-18.20).[169]

Many of the Jewish feasts include a meal, which is a symbol of joy; moreover it has an eschatological character. Jewish tradition has lots of communion meals according to the occasion. Even the festival meal of Jesus with his disciples is part of a long series of communion meal which began at Mount Sinai (Ex 24:11).[170] The final link in that long chain will be the eternal banquet. But the Old Testament hardly gives the details of the marriage ceremony; but simply 'taking' of a woman. "When a man taketh a wife," (Deut 20:7; 22:13); "and there went a man of the house Levi and he took a daughter of Levi," (Ex 2:1). However, from the story of Jacob and Lea it is obvious that some sort of celebrations took place; "And Laban gathered all the people of the place and made feast" (Gen 29:22) and later, when Jacob complained that he had been cheated and demanded Rachel, the daughter for whom he worked hard, he was told, "Wait until bridal week of this one is over and we will give that one too" (Gen 29:27). But no details of bridal feasts are recorded. But the New Testament gives several references to messianic banquet feasts (Mk 2:18-20; Mt 9:14-15; Lk 5:33-35; Mt 22:1-14; 25:1-13; Jn 3:22-30; 2:1-11).

Mar Jacob finds several wedding feasts in the public ministry of Jesus, in the personal relationship of the faithful with Christ, and the eschatological wedding feast with the Bridegroom. In the public ministry of Jesus Mar Jacob finds the wedding feast at the time of birth, at baptism, and suffering on Golgotha. Some of the occasions in the life of the faithful ones such as repentance and martyrdom are counted as wedding feasts. He uses many

---

[169] Cross, *Ancient Library*, 87-89.

[170] Deiss, *Springtime of the Liturgy*, 23. Philo sees this as a meal of immortality (Marcus, *Questions and Answers on Exodus*, 82).

words to indicate the wedding feast: (*hloolo*)[171] (*meštooto*) [172] (šoroōto), [173] (*smaq hašmeeto*),[174] etc. But most often he uses the first two words in terms with the wedding feast of the heavenly Bridegroom. In some occasions *šoruto* is used to indicate the regular wedding feast. For example when he writes about the wedding feasts of Nineveh he uses *šoruto*.[175] At some occasions he uses *šorooto* to refer to Eucharist.[176] In short, Mar Jacob uses all these terms interchangeably.

The marriage feast of heavenly Bridegroom and the earthly bride is always portrayed in the salvific settings. That means, the various staging posts in the life of Jesus Christ which saved humanity is considered as betrothal and marriage feast. Marriage feast may not be always with food and drink, but a joyous occasion like birth and baptism of Jesus Christ. On the other hand when it deals with Eucharist and Eschatological it indicates a marriage feast with food and drink.

6.4.1. Wedding Feast at Jordan

Mar Jacob finds several marriage feasts in the history of redemption through Jesus Christ, the Bridegroom. Baptism of Jesus is one of such occasions. He opens his homily on the *Baptism of Our Redeemer* with such a comment: "Christ the Bridegroom prepared the marriage feast (*hloolo*) for the Church of the nations and the world became aware of the wedding feast (*meštooto*) He had furnished for her."[177] This is a joyous occasion of the betrothal of Christ and the Church and not a literal or metaphorical banquet feast. It is a festive occasion of purification and adornment. Many occurrences of these terms could be seen in the same homily. One such occurrences is about the repentance of the bride.[178] In another occurrence says: "when the entire wedding feast (*meštooto*) looked for the Bridegroom."[179] Thus it might be about the gathering and not about the feast.

---

[171] Bedjan, *SMS*, 770.1; ET. *FH* I, 88.1048; Bedjan, *HS* I, 167.1, 173.16, 185.7, ET. *FH* VI, 162.1, 168.127, 179.366; Bedjan, *HS* II, 619.13; ET. *FH* XIII, 301.171; Bedjan, *HS* III, 663.13, 647.2, 710:1; ET. "A Homily on Stephen," *TV* 7(1990), 43.1.

[172] Bedjan, *SMS*, 774.13; ET. *FH* I, 93.144; Bedjan, *HS* I, 167.2, 187.7; ET. *FH* VI, 162.2, 181.408; Bedjan, *HS* III, 663.10.

[173] Bedjan, *HS* II, 229.12; Bedjan, *HS* III, 290.16; ET. Brock, "On the Veil of Moses," in *Studies in Syriac Spirituality*, 78.145.

[174] Bedjan, *HS* I, 298.14-16.

[175] Bedjan, *HS* IV, 454.11-14; ET. Bcheiry, "Repentance and Fasting," 5.

[176] Bedjan, *HS* II, 229.12.

[177] Bedjan, *HS* I, 167.1-2; ET. *FH* VI, 162.1-2.

[178] Bedjan, *HS* I, 173.16-17; ET. *FH* VI, 168.127. (See more 6.4.3)

[179] Bedjan, *HS* I, 174.5; ET. *FH* VI, 169.135.

He portrays the baptism of the Bridegroom as marriage feast (*hloolo*).[180] Invited David to sing the song appropriate to the wedding feast:
She sent for and called the Harp of the Spirit, David,
to come to sing the songs those are suitable for the marriage feast (*hloolo*).
"Come, son of Jesse and bring with you your hymns,
so that today, on the marriage feast (*meštooto*) of your Lord and your son we may rejoice.[181]

All scenario of the wedding feast is magnificently described; heaven and earth, all nature, and those who gathered are in a mood of exultation and merrymaking at the arrival of the Bridegroom. Heaven poured out thunder and lightning; water in the river, pools, steams, and waters of ocean exulted, warmed up, and the odor of fragrance, watchers of heaven sing praises with trembling, the heavenly hosts marveled at the descent of the Bridegroom.[182] In this manner Mar Jacob portrays the baptism of Jesus Christ as a wedding feast.

6.4.2. Bridegroom's Body/Eucharist as Feast

Mar Jacob interprets the death of Jesus Christ as a wedding feast. He writes: "The Lord of the feast hung nakedly on the cross, and cast his blood on every one who came to be a guest."[183] Just like the birth and baptism of Jesus Christ the death and resurrection is also a major milestone or a staging post through which Christ redeemed the world. Unlike the other two occasion death of Christ was a real wedding feast. In this wedding banquet He served His own body and blood as wedding meal. By dividing His body and pouring His blood on the cross He fulfilled what was said at the upper room. Mar Jacob states: "King's Son made a wedding feast (*hloolo*) of blood at Golgotha and He betrothed the daughter of gentiles there that may be for you."[184] This is an unusual wedding; he says that never before or ever after a bridegroom gave his body and blood as wedding feast:

---

[180] Bedjan, *HS* I, 185.7; ET. *FH* VI, 179.366.

[181] Bedjan, *HS* I, 187.5-8; ET. *FH* VI, 181. 405-408. Singing spiritual hymns and other songs are an essential part of the wedding settings in the ancient Semitic culture. The *Acts of Thomas* portrays such a hymn. *Remban pattu*, which sung during the marriage night of ancient Syrian Christians in India is another example of this kind of culture. *Knanaya* community lives in India still following this cultural practice.

[182] Bedjan, *HS* I, 188.1-189.21; ET. *FH* VI, 182.421-183.462.

[183] Cureton, "An Oration on Shamuna and Guria, Composed by Mar Jacob," 105.

[184] Bedjan, *HS* II, 587.18-19; cf. The bride whom I betrothed hated me and in her place, I have betrothed another. I have prepared a great banquet for her. Instead of lambs and calves, I have slain a fattened ox and placed it before her at the marriage feast- I have sacrificed my Only-Begotten Son. Behold, she holds him and divides for the atonement of all her children (*Kashtanubavazhcha Namaskaram,* 15).

Who has ever seen a corpse placed in the midst of the wedding feast (*meštooto*),
with the bride embracing it, waiting to comforted by it?
At what wedding, apart from this, did they break
the body of the bridegroom for the guests in place of other food?[185]

Commenting on its sacrificial aspect Mar Jacob states that if I have wings to fly I will proclaim this all over the world and everyone will move on when they hear it:

Would that I were an eagle, my Son,
that I might fly to the four quarters of the earth
to invite and bring in all the nations
to the great wedding feast of your death.
Who is it who has been moved by envy against you, my sweet one?[186]

Mar Jacob finds its sacramental importance which is a precious gift for the Church. By His mercy the Bridegroom divided His body and poured His blood for the eternal life of His bride.[187] And the Church, in response to the exhortation of her Bridegroom everyday repeats the same on her table. In the following passages in which Mar Jacob beautifully narrates the wedding feast on Golgotha:

The bride closes the door and consumes the Bridegroom who betrothed her…
Who has ever beheld a Bridegroom sacrificed at the very wedding feast (*meštooteh*)
or brides consuming their betrothed?
A novel action has the Son of God performed in the world,
one that has never before been done by any but he:
His own body and blood has he laid out for the guests at the wedding feast (*hloolo*),
so that they might eat of him and live in him without end.
She eats and drinks our Lord in the banquet chamber
blessed are you who gave his body and blood.[188]

---

[185] Bedjan, *HS* III, 290.16-19; ET. Brock, "On the Veil of Moses," in *Studies in Syriac Spirituality*, 78.145-148.

[186] Brock, *Bride of Light,* 40.3-6, 137. cf. Mathews, "Jacob of Serugh, Homily on Good Friday," 147.

[187] This running of mortality immediately comes to an end.
Her beauty shines to him in the exalted place without mortals.
Here she rejoices in the body and blood of the bridegroom, her Lord,
and there she greatly rejoices in his fair brightness clothed in fire (Narsai, "Dedication of the church," 136-137).

[188] Bedjan, *HS* III, 663.8-17; Cf. Brock, "The Wedding Feast of Blood…" 13.
cf. Who has ever seen a Bridegroom
sacrificed at his own wedding feast,
or a bride exulting at the slaying of her betrothed?
Who has given for her his own body as food,
while she mixed a bowl of his blood for her Beloved.

The bride of Light called us today, let us enjoy with her.
She killed the bridegroom and behold divides it on the table.
Come enjoy with us from her heavenly meal (*šorooto*)...
That I shall show her that, the Bridegroom is food and drink.
Now the generations of the world with us has not understood.
The bride commanded that everyone in the generation of the bridegroom shall sing.[189]
He died on the cross and gave his body to the bride made glorious
and she plucks and eats it every day at his table.
He opened up his side and mixed his cup with holy blood.
He gave it her to drink that she might forget her many idols.[190]

Three things are happening here: the sacrifice of the Bridegroom on the cross, the participation in the wedding banquet in this world, and the participation of the eschatological banquet. Therefore, the Eucharistic meal is a perfect one in all aspects. Through the participation of the earthly wedding feast, Eucharist, the Church not only participates in the sacrifice and body of the Bridegroom but it is a prefiguration of the bridal chamber in the heights. Usually the death of the bridegroom brought pain and sorrow to the earthly bride but here it is a joyous occasion for her: "The bride of the King (Church) made a wedding feast (*hloolo*) for the partakers of her communion and she beseeches with them that she may rejoice today very much."[191] Though there would be a wedding feast after the wedding a bridegroom never ever divided his own body as wedding feast. But this Bridegroom gave His own body and blood as wedding feast. The regular wedding feasts prolong for one week (Gen 29:27; Judg 14:12)[192] but here it is a perpetual and an unending one. After

---

As she carried his cross in escort,
marking with it her children who had been redeemed?
Blessed is he who redeemed her at his resurrection (*Mosul Penkitho*, VII, 259).
Who has ever seen a Bridegroom
sacrifice himself at his own wedding feast
and give his body to his betrothed.
Who takes delight in his blood? (*Pampakuda Penkitho*, 1, 13-14).

[189] Bedjan, *HS* II, 229.10-17; cf. "My Lord and God had prepared a feast for me," cries out the believing Church. "Strangers cannot draw near to the fattened Bull sacrificed on my (altar); the thus He has commanded me saying, let anyone who comes towards you not enter and learn the hidden mysteries in us, unless I have given him birth from water (*Anduthaksa* II, 69).

[190] Bedjan, *HS* III, 291.1-4; ET. Brock, "On the Veil of Moses," in *Studies in Syriac Spirituality*, 78.151-154.

[191] Bedjan, *HS* III, 647.2-3; cf. Harak, "The Syriac Orthodox Celebration," 92.

[192] All the pure virgins who are betrothed to Christ will have their lamps shining brightly, there as they enter, with the bridegroom to bridal chamber. All those who are betrothed to Christ are far removed from the curse of Law, and they are delivered from the punishment of Eve's daughters...Instead if lamentation if Eve's daughters, these women will utter the

the wedding she has only one husband and she has a permanent relation with him by eating his body and drinking his blood.[193] Mar Jacob indicates that the meeting of Moses and the elders with Yahweh (Ex 24: 9-11) is a 'type' of this great wedding feast: "It was the same to the elders of Israel, when they were invited to Mount Sinai for a banquet without bread and there burst out a delightful drink which was not of wine."[194] Through these interpretations Mar Jacob portrays the wedding feast on Golgotha what the Bridegroom has done for the Church, the bride. This was amazing and the food of the bridal chamber absolved the sins of the bride and made her entrance to the heavenly bridal chamber possible.

6.4.3. Repentance and Martyrdom as Bridal Feast

Mar Jacob portrays the personal experiences like repentance from sin and confession of faith as a marriage feast. The former one is the fulfillment of salvation which the Bridegroom brought forth through His Incarnation. Repentance is a return of the bride from the adulteress nature to the nature of chastity and to the real Bridegroom.[195] Mar Jacob portrays this experience through different homilies like *On the Forty Days' Fasting*,[196] *On Jonah and Nineveh*,[197] *On Zakai the Tax Collector*,[198] and *On the Prodigal Son*.[199] In these homilies he finds repentance as a great feast. The confession of faith against death is another great feast. Here the blood of the martyrs is considered as feast. Homilies *St. Stephen*,[200] *On Paul the Apostle*,[201] *On Sergius*,[202] *On Habib the Martyr*,[203] and *Guria and Shamuna*[204] interprets the Martyrdom as wedding feast. The following are some passages which Mar Jacob writes about the repentance and marriage feast:

---

bridegroom's songs. The wedding feast for Eve's daughters last seven days, but in the case of these women, their bridegroom never departs (Parisot, *Demo,* VI.6, 269.7-12; ET. Valavanolical, *Demonstrations,* I, 141).

[193] Bedjan, *HS* III, 291.4; ET. Brock, "On the Veil of Moses," in *Studies in Syriac Spirituality*, 78.154.

[194] Rilliet, *SHF* III, 582.23-25; ET. *FH* IX, 244.40; cf. *HPar.* 22:29.

[195] Bedjan, *HS* I, 290.2; ET, "On the Prodigal Son," *TV* 5.4(1994), 29.460.

[196] Rilliet, *SHF* III, 568-585.

[197] Bedjan, *HS* IV, 368-490.

[198] Bedjan, *HS* I, 344-364.

[199] Bedjan, *HS* I, 267-299.

[200] Bedjan, *HS* III, 710-723.

[201] Bedjan, *HS* II, 747-769.

[202] Bedjan, *AMS* VI, 650-661.

[203] Bedjan, *AMS* I, 160-172.

[204] Bedjan, *AMS* I, 131-143; ET. *ANF* Vol. VIII, 708-720.

Nineveh made a banquet (*šorooto*) to her angry Lord
for he may enter and rest on her table and to be pleased in her.
She adorned her house with clothes of free men and women
and wet the market with tears which flowed from her eyes.[205]

Christ made there a great act in that feast (*šorooto*)
he did not go there for eating bread, because he was not hungry.
He (Christ) has made there a great feast (*hloolo*) for repentance
in the house of tax collector and he has invited all sinners.
It was a wedding feast (*meštooto*) which righteousness can be bought through it
and our Lord went here to rejoice with repentant ones.[206]

One is that Sacrifice whereby all sinners find pardon;
and with one ring the treasures of the House of God sealed.
The Son of God is the Friend of repentance;
come, sinners, recline at His Banquet (*smaq*) that He might make you glad![207]

Here Mar Jacob simultaneously uses the terms *šorooto, hloolo, meštooto,* and *smaq* to indicate the term wedding banquet. In the regular marriage feast and the eschatological marriage feasts, the bride adorned bright bridal woolen dresses, sweetened their feasts with wine and smelled with incense, and the bride was adorned with jewelry.[208] But in the feast of repentance they wore sack cloths as a symbol of repentance. Against the eschatological wedding feast in the banquet of repentance the Bridegroom invites the sinners who do not have the bridal clothe and adorn them with wedding garment. Those who enter into the banquet of repentance find life and are entitled to sit at the eschatological banquet feast (*smaq*) of the Son.[209]

Secondly, martyrdom is considered as a great marriage feast of light. The martyrs were not frightened with their suffering; Mar Jacob says they are betrothed to the sacrifice of suffering and torture.[210] He writes that the martyrs have indulged with the crucifixion's wine in their heart.[211] The Church is delighted about the martyrdom of her children. When Habib, the martyr, was taken to slaughter, Mar Jacob writes: "The Church with him went out, like a bride full of light; and her face was beaming at the beloved martyr joined to her."[212] The Church participates in the sufferings of the martyr by

[205] Bedjan, *HS* IV, 454.11-14; ET. Bcheiry, "Repentance and Fasting," 5.

[206] Bedjan, *HS* I, 360.17-361:2; ET. "Jacob of Serugh's Memro on Zakai," 93.

[207] Bedjan, *HS* I, 298.14-16; ET. ET, "On the Prodigal Son," *TV* 5.4(1994), 36.637-37.642.

[208] Bedjan, *HS* IV, 455.5-10; cf. Bcheiry, "Repentance and Fasting", 5.

[209] Bedjan, *HS* I, 298.16, 299:1; ET, "On the Prodigal Son," *TV* 5.4(1994), 37.642.

[210] Cureton, "Oration on Habib the Martyr, Composed by Mar Jacob," 91.

[211] Cureton, "Oration on Habib the Martyr, Composed by Mar Jacob," 91.

[212] Cureton, "Oration on Habib the Martyr, Composed by Mar Jacob," 94.

adorning white garment like bridegroom.[213] Mar Jacob describes the attitude of the mother of Habib, the martyr: "His mother, then, for it was her son's marriage feast, in garments nobler than her wont, adorned herself; since sordid raiment suits not the banquet hall, all tastefully she clad herself in white."[214] He considers the martyrdom of St. Stephen as the Spiritual marriage feast. "The first born of the martyrs has called me to his spiritual marriage feast (*hlooleh*)."[215]

Mar Jacob envisages the repentance and martyrdom of saints as marriage feast. These are personal experience and conviction of individual believer to closely associate with Christ the Bridegroom just as an unchaste woman repents and returns to her husband. As a faithful wife loves only to her husband, a true believer of Jesus Christ could not adore and worship other gods. For the ardent love for her Bridegroom the martyr spares his/her own life for true love.

The spiritual wedding and wedding feast has two faces: a present reality and a forth-coming reality. The wedding banquets which delineated earlier are concerning the present reality or happening in the present world. But they have an eschatological culmination or fulfillment. Otherwise, the spiritual marriage and marriage feast has an eschatological reality. The most popular interpretation in the bible in this regard is the parable of the ten virgins. Portraying this parable Mar Jacob writes:

> The Kingdom of the Heavens therefore is like unto ten virgins
> who took their lamps, and went forth all,
> to meet the Bridegroom and the Bride who were coming,
> that they might enter with Him into the great marriage feast (*meštooto*) that
> He made.[216]

The feasts and festivities of this world are short and its merrymaking is cursory. But the feast of the upper world or the eschatological bridal chamber is unending and forever. Mar Jacob states: "He arranged his body and his blood at the wedding feast before those who are reclining/guests that they may eat with him and live with him without end."[217]

6.5. Union Between Bridegroom and the Bride

The final aspect of the eschatological hope of a believer is the union with the Almighty God. This is a fundamental hope of the Church, especially in the Syriac and the Byzantine Churches define salvation as union with the

---

[213] Cureton, "Oration on Habib the Martyr, Composed by Mar Jacob," 95.

[214] Cureton, "Oration on Habib the Martyr, Composed by Mar Jacob," 94.

[215] Bedjan, HS III, 710.1-2; ET. "A Homily on Stephen," TV 7(1990), 43.1-2.

[216] Bedjan, *HS* II, 377.10-14; ET. "Homily on the Ten Virgins," *TV* 4.1(1992), 41.39-42.

[217] Bedjan, *HS*, III. 663.14-15; cf. Harak, "The Syriac Orthodox Celebration," 92.

Almighty God. The Syriac Churches explain this union with the example of conjugal union between husband and wife. The following section discusses the thoughts of this union in the teachings of Mar Jacob of Serugh. Before that it enquires on how the West Asian counterparts of the time taught about it.

Valentinian Gnostics believed in the union between the Supreme Being, god, and lower beings, the human souls. They taught that their souls (that is, the souls of the pneumatics) were brides of angels. They saw the entrance into the world beyond as a wedding feast: at the same time the Mother Sophia (the last *aeon* in the *Pleroma*) receives her bridegroom brother, Christ, and the pneumatics also receive their bridegrooms, the angels. After this, they enter the bridal chamber within the *pleroma* border to receive a vision of the Father, and become spiritual *aeons*, entering into the spiritual and eternal marriage or union. This eschatological act, which takes place after death, is the real means of liberating the spirit, the soul, the understanding, or the self. It is at this time that the divine particles of light are separated from the physical body, which belongs to the realm of darkness.[218] Thus, the bodily form of evil will disappear and the divine form will enter into a union with the Supreme Being.

The rabbinic consensus concerning the creation of Man is that, God originally created man as a single person in his own image and afterward divided him into two complementary parts - male and female. The reunion of man and woman into one flesh constitutes a permanent blending which restores the original wholeness of Man and brings peace and satisfaction.[219] Rabbi Abulafia suggests that the union between a man's soul or intellect with God is the "pleasure of the bridegroom and bride."[220] As a representative of Hellenistic Judaism, Philo considered the creation of woman to be an intrusion into the life of solitude, meditation, and communion with God enjoyed by the first Man.[221] These backdrops paved way to a Christianized understanding of human's union with the Almighty God. In this understanding the Syriac Church interprets it as a communion with God and not a metaphysical union.

The paradigm model for union between God and human is the unity between the Father and the Son.[222] "Father, just as You are in me and I am in You. May they also be in us so that the world may believe that you have sent me" (Jn 17:21). This is a mystical or metaphysical union. But the man

---

[218] Lapinkivi, "Sumerian Sacred Marriage and its Aftermath in Later Sources," 30. He said, many Gnostics believe that redemption is happens when it begins with gnosis rather than through the death.

[219] Batey, *New Testament Nuptial Imagery,* 32.

[220] *'Or ha Sekhel*, MS Vatican, 233, fol. 115; cited Lapinkivi, "Sumerian Sacred Marriage and its Aftermath in Later Sources," 31.

[221] *De Opificio Mundi* LIII; cited Batey, *New Testament Nuptial Imagery,* 32.

[222] Bedjan, *SMS*, 824.21; ET. *FH* XVI, 346.339.

Jesus Himself is the solid and perfect example of union between God and man. The eternal Word of the Father, born in Virgin Mary, one of the daughters of Eve, has become of one race and family with us (Heb 2:11). Against the logical reality, the Word of God united with our sinful nature and became one among us in body and spirit. If God can make possible the unity with human, humanity can also unite with God in the same manner. In fact the union is already happened through the incarnation. The following passages of scripture proclaim the union between divinity hand humanity (Jn 14:23; 1Cor 6:15, 17; Eph 5:30; 2Pet 1:4; Gal 2:18, 20; 3:27).

In Louis Boyer's opinion there are two inseparable aspects regarding the union of the Church with Christ. In the first aspect, Church or individual believer unites with Christ through the Word of God; "the word became flesh and dwelt among us" (Jn 1:14). Through the Word of God Christ not only presented in the Church but presented to the world through the Church; because, the Word is none other than Christ himself. The second aspect is a reversal of the first; the Church come together and assembles saved mankind in herself in order to be united to Christ by freely corresponding to the divine initiatives which are brought to her apostolic ministry.[223] The Eucharistic union between Christ and the Church is a model for the second union.

In the worldly sphere a union between husband and wife is cognate to the conjugal union. But in the case of union between Christ the Bridegroom and Church the bride is in an exalted realm of understanding and it has a spiritual meaning. This union is neither according to the desire of flesh nor according to the temporal satisfaction, but this is an eternal and life-giving union. This union is made possible through the sacrifice of the Bridegroom. Unlike the animal sacrifice the Bridegroom has offered himself for voluntary sacrifice for a union with the bride. Christ, the Bridegroom, accepts being the sacrificial offering. Out of love, He gives His own life to His bride and invites her to participate in His offertory, the Eucharist. In this particular sacrifice the act of sacrifice is a prolonged one; a length of thirty-three years in the historical time and in mystically it has a history of creation itself. That means, every moment of Christ's life in this world is a part of sacrifice. And the decision to take the flesh, which occurred at the creation of humanity, itself is identification and a type of union. Thus, firstly, the very birth of the Bridegroom is a process of union. Secondly, when the Bridegroom identified the bride in order to cleanse her and though He was clean He took baptism. This is portrayed as another union. Finally, as the summit of all other unions He united to the bride through the Eucharist. Through these three modes, after the resurrection of the Bridegroom, in the Church, human beings by their free will initiate the mystical union with Jesus Christ. The Syriac Fathers, in all Incarnational acts,

[223] Bouyer, *The Church of God*, 493-494.

envision a process of union. The following part will discuss how Mar Jacob and other Fathers saw this event.

6.5.1. Union at Creation

Mar Jacob finds several incidents of the Old Testament that typify the union of the Son and His bride, the Church. He compares the union between the Old and New Testaments, Prophecy and Gospel, Prophets and the Apostles,[224] Son's glory and the Father's Light with that of the union between the Only-Begotten Son and the Church.[225] All these unions happened in historical time at the salvific acts of Jesus Christ. Mar Jacob interprets these unions as the betrothal between the Son of God and the Church. "His Father portrayed the bride of light in the cloud of light, for she is the only one whom the symbols betrothed affectionately to the One."[226]

One of the major occurrences in this line is the prophecy of Moses 'the two shall be one' (Gen 2:24). He actually saw Christ and the Church and indicated Christ as the Bridegroom and the Church as the bride. But, the Jewish people were not competent to comprehend this mystery, he put it simply as man and woman.[227] Mar Jacob portrays Moses as an artist who drew a picture and covered it with a veil.[228] A few lines later he again brought the same:

> And so he painted a picture inside the chamber of the royal bridegroom;
> he called them 'man and woman', although he knew the truth,
> that the one was Christ and the other the Church, both being veiled,
> and he announced them as 'man and his wife' simply as a device.[229]

But after the wedding was over, Paul entered and removed the veil of Moses and proclaimed that 'man' is Christ and the 'woman' is the Church.[230] Thus though the union had happened already, and even Christ the Bridegroom explained the duty of the Bridegroom to his groomsmen during his ministry, it was revealed in its full depth through Paul only. He announced that "I am going to tell a mystery that the "man and wife" is Christ and the Church (Eph 5:22-32). Thus Paul announced this mystery to the world which was concealed for a long period. In the same homily Mar Jacob says that, in many

---

224 Bedjan, *HS* II, 372.15-373.10; ET. *FH* VIII, 228.535- 229.552.

225 Bedjan, *HS* II, 373.13-21; ET. *FH* VIII, 229.555-560.

226 Bedjan, *HS* II, 374.15-16; ET. *FH* VIII, 230.575-576.

227 Supra, 4.3.1. cf. 5.3.4

228 Bedjan, *HS* III, 287.19-288-4; ET. Brock, "On the Veil of Moses," in *Studies in Syriac Spirituality*, 77.87-92.

229 Bedjan, *HS* III, 288.20-21; ET. Brock, "On the Veil of Moses," in *Studies in Syriac Spirituality*, 77.107-110.

230 Bedjan, *HS* III, 289.3-6; ET. Brock, "On the Veil of Moses," in *Studies in Syriac Spirituality*, 77.113-115.

incidents Prophet Moses with his exalted eyes saw the betrothal of Christ and the Church.[231]

6.5.2. Union through the Birth of the Bridegroom

The Church's union with Christ the Bridegroom is ultimately an eschatological one. But as Christ said in his ministry that Kingdom of God is within you (Lk 17:20-21), the eschatological union is already started in this world. According to Mar Jacob the union occurred in three-fold ways: at the virgin's womb, at the womb of waters of Jordan, and at the womb of *Sheol*. "He (Bridegroom) came down to the depth and raised up the lowly maid to the height for they are one, and where he is, there is she with him."[232] When the Bridegroom entered and dwelt in the womb of Mary He was united with the bride in her nature.[233] Through the birth of the Bridegroom sons of Adam acquired the divinity.[234] Through His birth the reentry into the Garden of Eden was made possible.[235] His birth reconciled and united the heavenly and the earthly.[236] When He entered into the womb of *Sheol* the Bridegroom gave His own body for ingestion and became one with her.[237]

6.5.3. Union through the Water

Mar Jacob sees another union through the baptism of Jesus Christ. Through the birth He united with the human beings and through the baptism she put on Him and united with Him by the betrothal (Mar Jacob finds baptism as betrothal). He writes: "He (Bridegroom) rested in the water and invited her: she went down clothed herself in him and ascended."[238] This union was prophesied by Moses in his great prophesies.[239] When the Bridegroom entered and immersed

---

[231] Bedjan, *HS* III, 288.10-11; ET. Brock, "On the Veil of Moses," in *Studies in Syriac Spirituality*, 77.95-98.

[232] Bedjan, *HS* III, 289.19; ET. Brock, "On the Veil of Moses," in *Studies in Syriac Spirituality*,78.127-128.

[233] Bedjan *HS* III, 288.9; ET. Brock, "On the Veil of Moses," in *Studies in Syriac Spirituality*, 77.97.

[234] Bedjan, *SMS*, 767.5-6; ET. *FH* I, 86.987-988.

[235] Bedjan, *SMS,* 767.9-10; 770.16-17; ET. *FH* I, 86.991-992, 89.1063-1064.

[236] Bedjan, *SMS*, 767.13-14; 770.14-15; ET. *FH* I, 86.995, 89.1061-1062.

[237] By the womb of *Sheol* here intends the sacrificial death of Jesus Christ on the Cross. Bedjan, *HS* II, 238.3-10.

[238] Bedjan, *HS* III, 290.7; ET. Brock, "On the Veil of Moses," in *Studies in Syriac Spirituality*, 78.135.

[239] Bedjan, *HS* III, 288.9-10; ET. Brock, "On the Veil of Moses," in *Studies in Syriac Spirituality*, 77.100-101.

in the womb of Jordan He united (*ḥlaṭ*) with the bride and made her chaste.[240] This union has two steps: the sanctification of the bride and the actual union. The main aim of the Incarnation of the Bridegroom itself is the purification of the bride because she was impure.[241] The baptism of the bride is a communion in the holiness of the Bridegroom which He kept in the water for His bride.

6.5.4. Union through the Eucharist

The Eucharist is another occasion where the Bridegroom and the bride meet together: "in the Eucharist she received Him."[242] This is at the same time ontological as well as a mystical union. The physical participation in the body and blood of Jesus Christ enables the ontological union and at the same time it mystically unites the believer in Christ.

The great sacrifice of the Bridegroom was conducive to this great union. The Bridegroom gave up His life and offered His own body and blood as a sacrifice in order to fulfill this union. The death of the spouse enabled an eternal union between them. This is an unusual thing. Usually the death of the spouse takes apart the other one. It is reversed here. Mar Jacob comments: Wives are separated from their husbands by death but this bride is joined (*ḥlaṭ*) to her beloved by death.[243] His death opened a way to meet each other (Bridegroom and the bride) often in the form of Eucharist.[244] "She anointed (*mšḥ*) him with oil, she put him on (*lbeš*) in the water, she consumed (*`ekl*) him in the bread she drank him in the Wine, so that the world might know that the two of them are one."[245] This is a fulfillment of the prophecy of Moses: "In the Eucharist she received him, and so Moses' words that the two shall be one were established."[246] Mar Jacob offers a very detailed description on the

---

240 Bedjan, *HS* III, 290.9; ET. Brock, "On the Veil of Moses," in *Studies in Syriac Spirituality*, 78.138; Bedjan, *HS* III, 310.1-16; ET. Konat "On the Mysteries, Types, and Figures of Christ," *Le Museon* 118(2005), 77-78.

241 Supra 3.5.3.1.

242 Bedjan, *HS* III, 290.7; ET. Brock, "On the Veil of Moses," in *Studies in Syriac Spirituality*, 78.136.

243 Bedjan, *HS* III, 290.20; ET. Brock, "On the Veil of Moses," in *Studies in Syriac Spirituality*, 78.170; cf. If the woman had not separated from the man, she should not die with the man. His separation became the beginning of death. Because of this, Christ came to repair the separation, which was from the beginning, and again unite the two, and to give life to those who died as a result of the separation, and unite them (Isenberg, *Gospel of Philip* 70.10-15, 141).

244 "In the upper chamber she saw her Lord break His body; and from Him she learned to do daily as He appointed to her" (Connolly, On the Memorial of the Departed and on the Eucharistic Loaf," 264).

245 Bedjan *HS* III, 291.5-6; ET. Brock, "On the Veil of Moses," in *Studies in Syriac Spirituality*, 79.155-156.

246 Bedjan, *HS* III, 290.6; ET. Brock, "On the Veil of Moses," in *Studies in Syriac Spirituality*, 78.135.

union of the Bridegroom and the bride through the Eucharist. He finds the real presence of the Bridegroom in the Eucharist and when the bride, who died through the sin, consume the Eucharist of the Bridegroom she imparts His life. Thus through the communion (*šautopooto*) the bride acquires the life of the Bridegroom and became one:

> And by the spring of the blood and the water that proceed from Him
> she entered it and sits as if upon the Gihon that filled with life.
> As she eats from Him because he agreed to be the food
> and she drinks from him because he desired to be the drink.
> She breaks His body and brings and put in the mouth of her children
> and she mixes his blood and they drink all their life from it.
> She tears it in pieces and puts every day upon her table
> and she distributes it to the people and the world that they will live from it.[247]

Elsewhere he remarks in a homily that the bride "reclining on His breast, they suckle life from His essence (*itooto*)."[248] Here, Mar Jacob tells about an essential hypostatic union but the question of how man could be one with God in essence is remaining. Or how the Creator and the creation would be one in essence is a question.

Conclusion

The bridal chamber gives a hope in the life of those who are in distress and in agony. The newly wedded bride and the bridegroom of this world, though they have anxieties, enter into the bridal chamber with new hope and expectations. They begin a new life with new resolutions. The bride of the eternal Bridegroom also looks at the eschatological bridal chamber with new hope. The bridal chamber is an answer to the loneliness and insecurity of this world. The companionship of God provides a renewed energy to the faithful. Just like a bride can remove her veil in the Bridal chamber the veil of burden could be unloaded in this habitation.

The robe of glory is portrayed as a bright light and an aspect of purity is highlighted in it. Light could not accommodate the impurity. The nature of God is purity and incorruptibility and His raiment is portrayed as effulgent light. Corruptibility is an existential factor of this world and this corruptibility caused the stripping of the robe of glory. One of the main reasons for the

---

[247] Bedjan, *HS* II, 238.3-10; cf. I ran to all your limbs, and from them all I received every kind of gift. Through the side I pierced with the sword I entered the garden fenced in with the sword. Let us enter in through that side which was pierced, since we were stripped naked by the counsel of the rib that was extracted. The fire that burnt in Adam, burnt him in that rib of his. For this reason the side of the second Adam has been pierced, and from it comes a flow of water to quench the fire of the First Adam (*Commentary on Diatessaron.* ET. McCarthy, XXI.10, 322).

[248] Bedjan, *HS* II, 397.4; ET. "Homily on Ten Virgins," *TV* 4.1(1992), 58.441.

corruptibility is ignorance or absence of right knowledge. Proper education and enlightenment of the society is the remedy. This enlightenment often turns a person to repentance. The enlightened son of the rich man returned to his father's house. Zakai the tax collector and the sinful woman are good examples of this enlightenment and repentance. Enlightenment helps to transform the social order existing in the society. When people attain moral strength the society also receive its effect. Therefore spiritual health of a person while serving himself, serves the community.

Mar Jacob portrays the wedding feast as a joyous occasion. The reason for the joy is the divine intervention in human history or life situation. The divine intervention in human life would be able to change the life situation of humanity. In the present world people are seeking happiness. What they are seeking is material happiness. Even if being successful, in the end the joy and happiness they strived for and yearned is found transient. But the joy obtained through the intervention of divine is perpetual and permanent. The joy that was given by the Bridegroom in the life of the bride is perpetual and it transforms the life of bride. Unlike the Jews who indulged in the manna and quail in the desert the modern world should seek the eternal banquet which the Bridegroom offered (Jn 6:48-51).

The absence of cohesion of ideologies and conclusions is one of the major predicaments facing the modern society at large. This has been percolated into families, communities, religions, churches, societies, and nations, from micro to macro level. It's after effect is disaster in the respective grounds starting from family to nations. The absence of empathy, respect of other ideologies, lack of understanding and refusal to know others, exploitation of nature, living for the present ignoring the future generations and above all self love in all its variations and dimensions are some of the major causes of the present day tragedy. The union between the Bridegroom and the bride is a paradigm model for the unification of the world. In the opinion of Mar Jacob main hindrance before the heavenly Bridegroom for the union was the wickedness of the bride. But He overcame the tension between the Him and the bride and purified the heart of the bride and made her His own. The main hindrance before the world is also the wickedness in the mind of the people. The Bridegroom purged the bride in three stages: through the Incarnation He emptied Himself, through His baptism at Jordan, He shared His riches with the poor bride, and by His sacrifice He offered Himself to His betrothed. These stages are archetypal to be exercised by the people of God to purify the world, taking as a mission of the Master. People of God should empty their selves and should come to the feet of the wicked men, leaving their ego and love the wicked world just as Christ has walked along with the publicans and sinners and as the stewards of the Master should walk along with the wicked in their mind and educate them to change their minds. Just like the Bridegroom, through His baptism, shared

His riches with the pauper the people of God should be able to share their riches both sacred and profane; that means, their holiness and wealth with the poor and needy and care for them like their own. Thirdly, sacrifice is necessary to retain the world. The Bridegroom gave His own life and parted His body and blood as feast and for the salvation of sinners. When the people of God are willing to share their life with the wicked the harvest will ripen. This is not a Utopian idea. Many leaders of the world like Mahatma Gandhi, Martin Luther King, and Nelson Mandela showed their prowess to the world. Violence and retribution cannot conquer enemies, but unconditional love and nonviolence could help retain the enemy as a friend.

Chapter 7

Relevance of the Bride-Bridegroom Imagery in the Present World

Introduction

God created human being in His own Image and Likeness. It was the fall of humanity that distorted this Image and interrupted God-human-nature relationship. Notwithstanding God did not discard His creation but loved them and intervened in the history and reinstated the God-human-nature relationship. The Scripture vividly explicates the whole story by way of the imagery of 'bride-bridegroom'. The initial chapters of this study discuss the various implications of this imagery, with special reference to Mar Jacob of Serugh. This chapter discusses the relevance of the imagery in the contemporary human interactions from a Christian perspective in the background of Christian family moral values and ethics.

When He created human beings He created them male and female or as a family. 'Ideal family' is a model concept and is a foundation of the social structure for many reasons. The concept of 'ideal family' emphasized here is conceived from a traditional angle and has connotations according to social ethics, culture, and traditions and is construed on one man one woman relationship and as a single unit consisting of father, mother, and children and occasionally grandparent(s). However, this traditional family system suffered a functional loss.[1] This functional loss in married life has resulted in married couples being faced with an unknown future[2] which is against the very purpose of creation itself. This chapter is an attempt to bring the spousal imagery in

[1] Schillebeeckx, *Marriage Human Reality and Saving Mystery*, "Introduction," xvii.

[2] Schillebeeckx, *Marriage Human Reality and Saving Mystery*, "Introduction," xviii.

the everyday life of a family. It would suggest to him/her to recognize, respect, and respond to the call of the Bridegroom.

7.1. Ecclesiological Relevance of Marriage Imagery

Christ Centered Ecclesiology: The foundation of the ecclesiology is based on the Apostolic Church, where the apostles came together for worship and prayer: "And they continued steadfastly in the apostles' doctrine and fellowship, and in breaking of bread, and in prayers" (Acts 2:42). The four elements in this verse, which requisite for ecclesial assembly are: (1) The leadership of the apostles or apostolic authority; (2), the apostolic teachings based on the teaching of Jesus Christ; (3), fellowship among the congregation of the faithful by breaking the bread; and (4), praise and thanksgiving. All these four elements are still relevant and practiced in the apostolic Churches. In alluding the bride-bridegroom relationship with apostolic foundation of the Church, the imagery assumes importance. The apostolic community assembles in the name of Jesus Christ, the Bridegroom and the True Shepherd. Like the bridegroom is the head of the family Jesus is the Head of the Church. The word of the head of the family is its gospel and the Word of God is the canon of the Church. The Bridegroom continues communication with the bride, the Church, through love talk (Song 2:10; Hos 2:14). The bedrock of family is the partnership achieved primarily from sincere and open communication. Fellowship is maintained through the Holy Communion or bridal feast. In the spousal imagery the Bridegroom presented His own body as the wedding feast.[3] On the same line, in the family life the love arises out of living for each other, a sacrificial life for the sake of partner. The bride honors the Bridegroom through her praise and prayers. Mutual honor and respect are the hallmark of a well-ground family. Therefore, the concept of ecclesiology of the apostolic Church is in agreement with the idea of an ideal Christian family.

Kingdom of God Ecclesiology: The Church and the nuptial imagery represent a transcendental union. The Apostles are considered as the Icons of Christ because He entrusted them to continue His mission, which is received from the Father. The visible presence of Jesus Christ in this world is His apostles. When the congregation assembles under the apostolic leadership, Christ will be present in the assembly. Secondly, when the congregation joins with the apostolic teaching they are joining to the body of Christ. Thirdly, a physical union happens in the congregation of the faithful through the fellowship and through the Eucharist. In this they are consuming the same Word, the body of Christ, from the same paten and chalice. Apart from the spiritual aspect through this communion a social phenomenon of mutual sharing is also taking place. When the community shares the Holy Communion from the same chalice

[3] Bedjan, *HS* II, 587.18-19; see more supra 6.4.2.

each one joins together as a part of the same Body and Blood. This leads to consensus of sharing; sharing the needs of each other. They are praising God in one accord. This shows the unity of the bride and the bridegroom. The visual imagery of 'bride-bridegroom' of the Church and Christ union is corresponding to the union between the bride and the Bridegroom. This assembly emits the fragrance of union with God. Pathil rightly says that "The Church is primarily a mystery, a spiritual reality, the body of Christ, the People of God, the communion with God in Jesus Christ, which transcends all space and time."[4] Likewise a Christian family could transcend their family life creating a visible Kingdom of God.

Communion Ecclesiology: Christian marriage reflects and enhances a communion ecclesiology. According to the New Testament, marriage is not merely an intra-personal endeavor but an inter-personal relationship. Through the marriage the couples join to a larger community of believers because the Church is a body that comprises all faithful in Christ. The couples ought to be conscious that they are not alone but a part of a greater and larger community. They are the part of the body of Christ. Here, the union occurs through bride's participation in the body and blood of her Bridegroom.[5] However, the prerequisite for this profound union is: just as the Bridegroom is pure the bride should be clean from all spots and blemishes of this world.[6] Equality in status and purity is required because union gets completed only when two are brought equal to status. Therefore, the Church reminds her faithful that "the Holies for the holy ones."[7] One must be pure in order to become a part of the large community of bride, the Church. Further in the greater and wider community or in communion ecclesiology the couple needs to live within the Eucharistic communion and in the continuing life of the Church. It is an extension of Christ's self-giving love and not a realm of private possessions, but shared in the worship and works of the Church.[8] Therefore, Pannenburg rightly says "Only if the community of the Church is based solely on the lordship of God and of Christ can the Church be the symbol and instrument of the unity of mankind."[9]

In this age of alienation, diversity, and anxiety the concept of marriage chamber receives an important role for pacification, cohesion, and solidarity. Marriage bridges and bridal chamber unites; which means, marriage is an act

---

[4] Pathil, *Theology of the Church New Horizons,* 12.

[5] Bedjan, *HS* III, 290.6; ET. Brock, "On the Veil of Moses," in *Studies in Syriac Spirituality*, 78.135; Supra 6.5.4.

[6] Bedjan, *HS* I, 168.2-7; ET. *FH* VI, 162.9-163.14.

[7] *Ktobo dtakso dqurobo*, 77.

[8] McCarthy, "Becoming One Flesh: Marriage, Remarriage, and Sex," 281-283.

[9] Pannenberg, *The Church*, 20.

of bridging two persons and their union. The bridal chamber offers a place where the Bridegroom and the bride come together. The concept of marriage provides a paradigm model for unity: a unification of individuals and nations in Christ. The author of the Book of Revelation says that kingdom of God is a place of rest where there is no pain or agony, tears or sorrow or death (Rev 21:2-4). Thus, bridal chamber offers a place full of peace to those who are in pain and in agony in this busy and competitive life. The Church is a place and a platform for the bride to come together and rest in the bosom of the Bridegroom. The Church is a place where divine-human interaction is taking place. All the bridal chambers in Christ's life such as cave of birth, baptismal font, cloud of light, the tomb of Christ, etc.,[10] are meeting in the Church. Altar is portrayed as the cave and tomb of Christ; baptismal font is kept in the church for the rebirth of the bride. Altar or Holy of holies is filled with the cloud of light where the presence of the Bridegroom descent and indwells.[11]

Mission Ecclesiology: Mission ecclesiology is another paradigm model that the bride imagery offers. Advancement of science and technology has transformed the world with more information and knowledge and thus creating a new world order. Time and space shrank and world became a global village. The barriers among nation are removed and all affairs like economy, trade, technology and culture are brought under one umbrella. The impact of this newly emerged trend of globalization can be observed in all activities and pursuits irrespective of local or national perspectives. The new scenario of the world order has its impact in every way of existence, socially, culturally and economically. New definition is given to social ethics and human relations and this has been extrapolated to family relations also. Change in the society in time progress in life is inevitable. The shift from the agrarian to industrial society was slow and gradual. But the shift in the electronic and communication era has left little space to comprehend and adjust. Social values built upon the religion are questioned or ignored. At the same time no alternative is created to hold on. This void has created a situation of dilemma for the society. In the present day context, as far as the family is concerned, the 'bride-bridegroom imagery' imparts greater implications. Both the present day society and the bride are pluralistic nature. Bride from the nations is religiously, culturally, economically, and linguistically different sometimes diametrically opposite. In a pluralistic country like India the 'bride from the nations' imagery concept offers much scope and insight for mission ecclesiology. It is the duty of the Church to preach the good news of Christ to those who are ignorant about Christ. Christian communities, like traditional Syrian Christians community, are reluctant in witnessing the gospel and prefer to be a class in themselves.

[10] Supra 6.2.

[11] Bedjan, *HS* I, 20.5-8.

Time has reached to invite others into the flock of Christ. A wider ecumenical opening of the Church is necessary to incorporate others into the community of believers. The marriage imagery invites the Church leaders to compromise in practical realms and to widen the boundaries of the Church. If the heavenly Bridegroom had not emptied Himself and loved the hateful adulteress nations there would not have been a Church today. In this imagery the Bridegroom not only suffered for the bride but He paid ransom for her. He paid this ransom for all, irrespective of the ethnic backgrounds (Rev 5:9-10). In the current situation the Church should leave from its comfort zones and go out in search of the lost ones. In order to gain these lost ones Church should give up the narrow outlook and selfishness, and rather love and help others mentally, physically, psychologically, and financially and save herself from the disgraceful situation. Therefore, the selection of the nations is a paradigm for a current ecclesiology.

Ecclesiology of Caring and Nurturing: Ecclesiology of affection is another model that the spousal imagery portrays. Two Greek terms are integrally related to the Church: *ekklesia and kyrios*. The former means the assembly and the latter means Lord. The Church is the assembly of our Lord, *Quhal Yahweh* (Deut 4:10; 31:30 Josh 8:35).[12] Jesus said to Peter that: "Blessed are you, Simon Peter… an on this rock I will build my Church (*ekklesia*), gates of hades will not prevail against it" (Mt 16:18). When Jesus says, "my church;" He affirms that the Church is His own and no power could overwhelm her because He is her protector. Nobody can define the Church without Jesus Christ. Therefore, the Church is an assembly that is integrally related to the Lord. The bride-bridegroom imagery is the right symbol for this kind of relationships. The members of the Church should have this understanding that they are the private possessions of their Lord. Paul reminds us that we are His inheritance (Eph 1:18). Any kind of unfaithfulness would not be tolerated. Mar Jacob is very punctilious in this kind of interpretation and he uses the bride-bridegroom imagery to show the bond between Christ and His people. Through this he shows the integrity and love between the Church and Christ. This affection, love, and integrity to their Lord generated martyrs in the early Church. The believer-Christ relationship has deteriorated alarmingly in the present day. Affection, love, and faithfulness have hit to its lower ebb in the Church. Reintroducing this imagery in the modern world would be an impetus to bring back the zeal of the early Church to her Lord.

In the present scenario, especially in the West where emerged Christianity into major world religion it is post Christianity. Huge churches are deserted and often being converted into other religion's temples or shopping centers. The successors of the former missionaries have become irreligious or lost in their zeal in God or religion. Once they passionately loved God but now standoffish

[12] Rodriguez, "Theological Method for Ecclesiology," 153.

their love to their God; a kind of apathy happened in their life because of the influence of the new thought and modern life style based on materialism. They moved away from their love of God to pleasures of modern lifestyle and they are divorcing the real One for the sake of their fantasies. This lost love should be regained. The awareness of the love of Christ and the loving Christ would make a change in the attitude of the unfaithful. Bride-bridegroom imagery is obviously a right pedagogical tool in this regard. Through this imagery Mar Jacob offers the depth of God's love towards His people. He says even the creation itself is an epiphany of God's love. Moreover, because of His love towards humanity God descended to the earth to create and save human beings. Thus, the awareness of the loving God will make changes in the heart of humanity.

Ecclesiology of *Koinonia*: In the apostolic Church the believers gathered under the leadership of the apostles for worship and broke the bread. Thus, *Koinonia* (*šauthoputho*) was another salient feature of the apostolic Church. Bride imagery puts forward a strong experience of *koinonia.* Without a strong *koinonia* a family cannot exist. A family sitting together around the dining table shows the glory of its relationships and zenith of its unity. A bride along with her husband and children is a parameter of the family's integrity. Thus this imagery is very relevant in the social as well as religious realm of life. The Church as a wider family that eats together from the Lord's Table is a symbol of this familial unity.[13] Mar Jacob very effectively analyzed this mealtime unity in his homilies. Jesus brought together the disciples around a table and shared His own body and blood for the salvation and the unity of His bride, the Church. It is a sacrificial symbol of the unity and the salvation of the Church. The self emptying and the self sacrificial love Christ is par excellence which no human can ever march. Therefore this is a perfect model implementation in the family, in the parish church, in the local community, or in other groups where people come together the leader could follow this pattern. Leaving the ego-centric train behind one could follow the great Master by imitating His sacrificial model and His care for the others. Jesus the Bridegroom humbled Himself and washed the legs of His disciples. Also He broke His body and offered His blood as a ransom to His Bride. This sacrificial mentality should inspire leaders of the community. In the disintegrated families of this day the sacrificial meal of forgiveness is helpful to the union of family which is united by God Himself.

Multinational companies follow this example of *koinonia* for their success in business. They often conduct get-togethers at various levels to improve the

[13] Lieber quoting Nancy Jay says "Communion sacrifice unites worshipers in one moral community and at the same time differentiates that community from the rest of the world." (Lieber, "I Set a Table Before You," 66).

quality and efficiency of their staff. From my personal experience I can say that the meal I prepared and served for the managing and building committees of one of my parish churches was conducive to successful completion of the church building construction. Just like Jesus saved the Church through the *koinonia* a leader could save and increase the well-being of his/her community through the *koinonia.* In today's the most modern 'no-time family' the sacrificial love of the Bridegroom and mealtime *koinonia* will heal the disunity among the members of the family. Therefore, it is relevant in the family also. This *koinonia* will give the congregation of the faithful an awareness of a bodily unity. Mar Jacob of Serugh was very much concerned about this unity among the church members so that he often repeated the prophecy: "Therefore man shall leave his father and mother and cleave to his wife and they shall be one flesh" (Gen 2:24).

7.2. Soteriological Relevance of Marriage Imagery

Redemption of the bride is a prominent theme in the marriage imagery. Powathil says, "The title bride reminds us of the two aspects of the Church: the mystical aspect of her union with Christ and then her soteriological role in relation to Christ the Bridegroom."[14] St. Paul reminds in his letter to Romans that, the creation is crying for salvation (Rom 8:22). The bride-bridegroom imagery is a hope for this anticipated redemption of the creation, because, it says about the story of redemption of the bride who was in captivity. In this world the whole creation is groaning for liberation because it is under captivity in many respects: war and terrorism, natural calamities, economic depression, diseases, domestic violence, climatic variations, etc. The bridal imagery offers salvation to the creation, because the intention of the marriage is salvation of the bride.[15] The creation account of Genesis shows a harmonious coexistence of nature-animal-human world. If the creation goes back to the pre-fallen state it could achieve real peace and liberation. In the early Church spiritual marriage was considered as a way to the kingdom of God. The conjugal life and love, which is founded at the time of God's creation, will elevate the spouses into the eternal bridal chamber. Therefore, Basil the great says, "If anyone rushes into marriage by law, the whole inhabited earth is opened to him; but if his zeal is the result of passion, it will only serve the more to exclude him, 'that everyone should know enough to keep his vessel in sanctities and honor, not in the lust of concupiscence (1Thess 4:4-5)."[16] Therefore, 'Marriage by law' of course was a system that God initiated to find a right companion to man (Gen 2:18).

[14] Powathil, *Church as the Mystery of Communion: A Tribute to the Ecclesial Vision of Father Placid Podipara*, 177.

[15] Bedjan, *SMS*, 769.14-770.21; ET. *FH* I, 88.1039-89.1068.

[16] *Pedalion*, 844.

Though this companionship was carnal, it was meant to bring divine love since the lust belongs to fallen state. The Bridegroom's love on the cross reveals the divine love.[17] This love reminds the spouses how it renders their own salvation as well as their immediate neighbors. According to this imagery the Church is the tangible expression of God's eternal plan of salvation.[18] Without Church there is no salvation or in other words without becoming a true bride salvation is impossible. Christ is the source of salvation and the Church is the medium of salvation. Family occupies a prominent place in the Church; therefore, the family may serve as a channel for bringing salvation to the world. It is a great task and vocation of the Church to create unity and integrity in the family and therefore, in the divided wounded society.

The already and not-yet tension of eschatological hope is visible in this imagery. That means, both the eschatological fulfillment and the presence of the Kingdom of God in the present world (Lk 17:21) is visible in the spousal imagery. This imagery teaches that a Christian family should be a miniature of the Kingdom of God. The essential nature of the Kingdom of God is righteousness, peace and joy (Rom 14:17).[19] The righteous people love and care for others. When there is mutual love and care among each other in the family, joy and peace prevail. Jesus Christ cared for and loved the world by giving Himself. Therefore, Bridegroom's nature of selfless love or sacramental love must be a force for the husband's and the wife's mutual fidelity. Participation in the sacraments, especially in the Holy Eucharist, should initiate the spouses to share the sacramental love between them and among the community that they live in. A good example of this love from the ordinary life which was nurtured through the Christian sacramental life is portrayed in the Florence Caffrey Bourg's *Where Two or Three are Gathered: Christian Families as Domestic Churches*. She shares one of her house hold experiences: "If I hadn't heard that Gospel and participated in Holy Thursday liturgy in the years past, I wouldn't have had the necessary reference point to understand what it meant to wash the vomit of my son's feet. But if hadn't washed the vomit of my son's feet, I wouldn't have had the necessary reference point to appreciate all those Holy Thursday Eucharist I had participated in before."[20] Therefore, Christ, the Bridegroom taught the real love and care and the faithful can experience this through the sacramental life in the great house of the Church. This love and care lead a person's salvation both in this world and the world to come. By

---

[17] Bedjan, *HS* III, 290.11-12; ET. Brock, "On the Veil of Moses," in *Studies in Syriac Spirituality*, 78.141-142.

[18] Rose, *The Church as the Mystery and Communion*, 381.

[19] Bedjan, *HS* II, 379.9; ET. "Homily on the Ten Virgins," *TV* 4.1(1992), 42.79.

[20] Bourg, *Where Two or Three are Gathered: Christian Families as Domestic Churches*, 133-134.

love and care in this world a suffering person could finds comfort and solace in his life. On the other hand, following the way of God, they will lead a person to eternal Kingdom of God.

In the matrimonial rite of the Church of the East while the priest joins the hands of the bride and the bridegroom says: "this bridegroom has engaged to hold this bride as his own self in everything meet and proper appertaining to the nature of body and soul, in youth and in age, in health and in sickness, in joy and in sorrow, that the saying of the Gospel may fulfilled: A man shall leave his father and mother…"[21] This oath explains the visible meaning of Christ's love. Thus, the redemption should come from the basic unit of the society, the family. A model family is a blessing to many. One of the missions of the family life is to bring others to the Kingdom of God.

The marriage imagery reminds the faithful to prepare themselves to receive the Bridegroom or be ready for the salvation.[22] In the early Jewish marriage custom there was certain period of preparation for marriage between the betrothal and actual marriage. During this period the bride prepares herself for the marriage; particularly in three matters: She should prove herself pure and virgin for which she stays back for nine months after betrothal to ensure that she is virgin.[23] The bride sanctifies herself to examine everything in her life to keep ready for the covenant. The bride makes her wedding garment by herself and appears on the wedding day in this garment. Moreover, in the Jewish marriage custom the day of the wedding is not disclosed to the bride and to the bridegroom but makes known only immediately before the marriage function. This has a resemblance to the arrival of the Bridegroom in the imagery of Ten Virgins (Mt 25:6). St. Paul also gives such a notion: the Lord shall come from heaven with shout and voice of archangel and with the trumpet of God… so we shall always be with God (1Thess 4:16-17). In order to meet and greet the Bridegroom we need to keep our virginity and put-on bridal garment. Therefore, this life is a preparation for the coming world. The marriage imagery calls for the preparation as true and pure virgins of Lamb.

7.3. Eschatological Relevance of Marriage Imagery

Marriage life is a preparation to the next world: The opening prayer of the West Syriac Marriage rite, uses in the M O S C, reminds the faithful that the wedding and the family life in this world is a preparation of the life in the other world with the heavenly Bridegroom.[24] Other prayers also have this eschatological color. These prayers intones that the earthly marriage is a

---

[21] Badger, *Nestorians and their Rituals*, 245.

[22] Bedjan, *HS* I, 167.1-168.9; ET. *FH* VI, 162.1-163.15.

[23] Fruchtenbaum, *The Jewish Wedding System and the Bride of Messiah*, 3-4.

[24] *Koodashakramangal*, 57.

preparation for the one to come. As William Robers sums up that through the love for one another along with the time spent in translating their Christian discipleship into their married life will make them "the new creation"[25] (Rev 21:1-2).

Mar Jacob's eschatological idea is based on the biblical portrayal of ten virgins' imagery (Mt 25:1-10). On the Day of Judgment the wise will enjoy with the Bridegroom and the foolish will mourn in the darkness.[26] In this parable Christ instructs the Church how to live in the time between his resurrection and his Second Coming as royal Son of God. The Church must not be deceived by false prophets/bridegrooms but she should be vigilant against them.[27] This imagery is a good moral principle to the modern world. The following discussion will be based on these aspects.

Marriage leads to holiness: One of main eschatological aspects of the nuptial imagery is its state of holiness.[28] This holiness is represented by light. In the New Testament Jesus calls Himself as 'light' (Jn 8:12) and His dwelling place is light. The one who enter with Him in this place should be an illumined soul. Illumination is purification of the soul from all follies of the world so as to know the Will of God and be keep away from sins.[29] Also Jesus, the True Bridegroom says that nobody can enter into the Kingdom of God without wedding garment or robe of glory (Mt 22: 11-13). Baptism offers the wedding garment and without becoming part of the Church through the baptism nobody could reach in the Kingdom of God.[30] Both the enlightenment and the wedding garment require purity of life and good works. This calls for the good work in the world to maintain peace and tranquility. Mar Jacob often compared 'oil in the lamp' with virtues or good works.[31] Absence of the virtues in the modern society has led to a chaotic situation of darkness. Crime, corruption, selfishness, exploitation of persons and nature, war and terrorism, natural disasters and climatic changes, etc. remind the vices of the foolish virgins. The faithful keep away from the follies and keep the oil of good works to create a Kingdom of God. These aspects bring an eschatological kingdom in the earth itself.

Foretaste of the eschatological Kingdom of God: The wedding banquet is the culmination of the wedding ceremony. The spousal imagery

---

[25] Roberts, "Theology of Christian Marriage," 49.

[26] Bedjan, *HS* II, 379.10; ET. "Homily on the Ten Virgins," *TV* 4.1(1992), 42.80.

[27] Matera, "Theologies of the Church in the New Testament," 4.

[28] Bedjan *HS* I, 167.7-168.7; ET. *FH* VI, 162.7-163.14.

[29] Bedjan, *HS* I, 284.9ff; ET, "On the Prodigal Son," *TV* 5.4(1994), 24.343ff.

[30] Bedjan, *HS* III, 593.8-9; Bedjan, *HS* V, 681.19.

[31] Bedjan *HS* I, 389.15-18; ET. "Homily on the Ten Virgins," *TV* 4.1(1992), 51.291-53.294.

portrays the importance of wedding banquet.[32] But it is a life in the presence of Heavenly Bridegroom. The Scripture portrays the life with the Bridegroom as a transformed life from the worldly sufferings. The Church creates this blissful atmosphere during the Eucharistic celebration.[33] It is the foretaste of the eschatological union between the Bridegroom and the bride. Creating a pleasant and peaceful situation in this world is the demand of the present time. Therefore, this imagery recreates a model of eschatological life and creates peace and bliss in the minds of the participants.

Faithfulness secure peace and happiness: Another important aspect of the imagery is the holiness of the bridal chamber of this world. It teaches and calls for a pure and unsoiled bridal chamber; that means, the bride and the bridegroom should be faithful to one another (Heb 13:4). Moral values of society have decayed. Man and woman have developed separate identity which challenges the very concept of one soul and two bodies. Individual happiness gives way to united happiness. Licentiousness and debauchery creep in to destroy marital relationships. Carnal pleasures found in bi-sexual relationships, swinging couples, homosexuality, are few of the modes of aberrations inflicting the conjugal relation. The imagery calls for one husband and one wife relationship and all other forms are immoral.[34] Such immorality is a poison that infringes the family and further contaminates the community, with the children becoming the casualty. The unrest in the home generates feeling of insecurity among the kids. An unbalanced or disintegrated family produces behaviorally challenged kids to the world. They in turn create problems to the community. But the nuptial imagery calls for a pure and unsoiled bridal chamber of light. And this unsoiled life offers an eschatological experience with the Bridegroom in the present world itself in a pleasant manner as a foretaste.

7.4. Spirituality and the Relevance of Marriage Imagery

Transforming spirituality: Spirituality is a process of personal transformation in accordance with religious ideals and living according to the dictum of the religion being practiced. As a member of the Church every Christian is wedded to Christ. In a sound family both husband and wife will communicate each other. In this modern world, even if they are staying in faraway places, in most cases, the husband and wife will keep in touch at least once in a day via phone or through some other media. If we are wedded to Christ we should communicate with Him without any break (Col 1:9). Prayer is the right way

---

[32] Supra, 6.4.

[33] Meyendorff, *Marriage: An Orthodox Perspective*, 22-23.

[34] Bedjan, *HS* III, 333.9-13; ET. "Why Our Lord Abode upon the Earth for Thirty Years," *TV* 4(1990), 48.42-46.

of communication between bride and the Bridegroom. Not once in a week in the Church but always keep touch with Him. Otherwise our relationship with Christ will be badly affected. The 'bride-bridegroom' imagery demands such a need of communication which in turn makes a person holy.

Marriage imagery and devotion: Like Mary the virgin bride who produced herself before the Savior to become His abode so that He could come down and dwell in her, the Church might be presented herself as a bride without spot or wrinkle (1Cor 11:1; Eph 5:25-27). It is seen that the main attribute of bride is her virginity and chastity.[35] In the Christian spirituality, especially in the Syriac spiritual tradition this concept has an important place. One of the titles for the ascetics in Syriac tradition is 'bride.' In the monastic circle they called themselves as the pure virgins of heavenly Bridegroom or *barth qyomo/bnai qyomo*.[36] In order to get a place in the heavenly bridal chamber they avoided the bridal chamber of this world.[37] Moreover, they thought that marriage bed in this world is corrupt and it will spoil the souls.[38] Like the ascetics, seeking heavenly Bridegroom has relevance in present day. Exposure and opportunities are immense in modern world and human beings are succumbed to them to a great extent. Even the so-called spiritual people though they claim to have renounced worldly passions indulge in depravity. They embrace carnal passion, monetary benefits, maximum comforts forgetting their vows of a monastic vocation-chastity, poverty and obedience. The people who lead secular life seek and collect beyond their needs, live in extravaganza, exploiting others. These factors are detrimental to the spiritual life of the faithful. Absence of a strong model is the reason for running after pleasures of the world. Spousal imagery upholds seeking the Kingdom of God and working for the social justice. Spiritual marriage and seeking for the heavenly Bridegroom and the bridal chamber will be a good model for this complicated world.

Committed and holistic relationship: Commitment and self-emptying is needed in family. A current saying "a man weds an engineer and not a woman" illustrates the situation. It is not man and woman engaging in marriage but two professions – a doctor, engineer, agriculturist, businessman, and industrialist and so on. It is a reality at least among the St. Thomas

---

[35] Rilliet, *SHF* II, 560.12-14; ET. *FH* VII, 196.22.

[36] Nedungattu, "The Covenanters of the Early Syriac-Speaking Church", 193; Murray, "Exhortation to Candidates for Ascetical Vows at Baptism," 61; Griffith, "Asceticism in the Church of Syria" 229-230; Harvey, "Women's Service in Ancient Syriac Christianity," 231-232.

[37] Chrysostom says: "What is sweeter and more beautiful, more brilliant that virginity? Indeed, it sparkles more radiantly than the rays of sun. It removes us from all worldly while preparing us to look with pure eyes into the sun of justice" (*On Virginity* XI.1; cited in, Ford, *Women and Men in the Early Church*, 76).

[38] *AAA*, 132.

Christians who live in Kerala. People are searching their spouses from higher status; family and profession and not their personal values. The monetary aspects preferred rather than love between two souls; it could be called an 'industrial spirituality'. The society needs a 'spiritual philosophy' which leads the couples to a mutual divinization. The earlier one is the product of enlightenment of the materialistic culture, where money and worldly comfort is the yardstick. But the latter one was the typical nature of Eastern World that seeks for a spiritual elevation of a person. The Royal Bridegroom who married the poor and sinful bride[39] is an effective symbol to spiritual brightening up of the modern families of professionals. People are exhausted physically and psychologically due to stress factor in their work atmosphere. Most families undergo stress problems consequently affecting their personal relations. Early aging is another important problem prevalent in the twenty-first century. Most of these problems are due to the impact of new social environment created by scientific and social advancement and its adaptation in life atmosphere. Peace and tranquility in life are the need of the hour. The substitute is spirituality and holistic life. A model based on the bride-bridegroom imagery can open up the new horizon to address these impending issues.

Spiritually oriented life: A divinely inspired theology is the necessity of the time; because, due to the after effect of modernism, the literal interpretation of the scripture is dominating in the theological web. As a result, just like any other branches of science, theology became a branch of empirical science. This has made serious threats even to the basic faith of the Church. The scripture, which was formed in the community of the faithful for their daily devotion, became a tool of experiment against its fundamental characteristic feature of divine inspiration. In his homilies Mar Jacob repeatedly teaches that everything related divine as a mystery and beyond the human understanding.[40] The imagery offers a model of blind faith of bride in the Bridegroom; because, the Bridegroom loves the bride even up to His death and offered His body as food and blood as a ransom.

Spirituality and Security: Bridegroom or the head of the family, throughout the centuries, is considered as the protector of the family. In the spiritual level of understanding the bride-bridegroom imagery arouses a feeling of protection in the minds of the readers. This feeling is arising not from the modern single parenting cultural situation but from a traditional social set up of joint family system, where the head of the family acts as the protector of the entire family members. In this system the head of the family will look after physical, spiritual, and social needs of the whole family. Therefore, the members of the family look upon their chief as protector and

---

[39] Rilliet, *SHF* II. 558.14-17; FH VII, 195.19; Bedjan, *HS* I, 167.2-3; ET. *FH* VI, 163. 3-4.

[40] Bedjan, *HS* III, 587.9-12; 630.20-631.1.

guardian. Here, in the spiritual life, Christ the Bridegroom is a protector of His Church (members).[41] He is a spiritual resort, a good haven in their distress and agony, a person to put down their worries. He is a spiritual counselor and He invites those who are in weary and in burden towards Him (Mt 11:28).[42] In the monastic tradition of the Eastern Churches a spiritual father is necessary for each monk. He is supposed to confess before the spiritual father periodically. This is an opportunity to redress the worries and guilt feeling of the monk, to evaluate his spiritual life, and empower his spiritual life. The same could be applied to the common believer. Therefore, cultivating a culture of a spiritual and physical protector will enhance the spirituality of the world.

7.5. Liturgical Relevance of Marriage Imagery

Liturgy a pedagogical instrument: Liturgy is the locus of the Church and therefore the Church is known as the worshipping community.[43] In the West Syriac tradition the 'bride-bridegroom imagery' is well delineated in many liturgical rites; especially, it is vividly described in the *Penkitho* prayers of consecration of the church, epiphany, marriage rite, etc. The Church considered liturgy as the vehicle of theological expression. As a pedagogical instrument the Fathers of the Church and early Christian writers explained their theology in the light of the liturgical context. Moreover, liturgy is the re-enactment of Christ's saving activities. Therefore, liturgical relevance is a matter of importance in this particular imagery.

Worship keeps the Bridegroom and the bride intact: Prayer and worship are the media to keep an intimate relationship with God. The main reason for the rejection of Israel, the first bride, was her idol worship. Mar Jacob calls her as adulterous. When person worships other gods s/he will become an adulterous person. When s/he does not pray to God her/his mind will be away from God. Therefore, the liturgy has an important role in making a soul loving and keeping an integral relation with Christ the Bridegroom. Sociologically speaking family is the basic unit of society. A worshipping family makes the first ecclesial unit in the Church. While social ethics of the families makes a society the liturgy makes the families a micro Church. As a part of the large worshipping community, the family translates faith into individual believer's mind through worship. The second Vatican Council by explaining the sharing values of the family life defines family as domestic church:

> From the wedlock of Christians there comes the family, in which new citizens of human society are born, who by the grace of the Holy Spirit received in baptism are made children of God, thus perpetuating the people of God through the

[41] Bedjan, *SMS,* 725.19-726.3; ET. *FH* I, 47.121-128.

[42] Bedjan, *HS* III, 418.9-419.14; ET. "The Parable of the Leaven," 51.135-52.160.

[43] Jungmann, *The Early Liturgy to the Time of Gregory the Great*, 12.

> centuries. The family is, so to speak, the domestic church. In it parents should, by their word and example, be the first preachers of the faith to their children; they should encourage them in the vocation which is proper to each of them, fostering with special care vocation to a sacred state.[44]

Therefore, a worshipping family holds an intimate relationship with God. Eucharist is the core of Christian worship. Mar Jacob portrays Eucharist as the bridal feast; therefore, every liturgy is a nuptial experience with the eternal Bridegroom.[45] Nearness with the Bridegroom, Christ, enhances the relationship between divine-human relationships and helps and nurtures the human-human relationship.

In the liturgical realm Eucharist is one of the perfect examples of the effective marriage union. In the 'bride-bridegroom imagery' Mar Jacob proposes that Christ, the Bridegroom, offered His own body and blood as a wedding banquet and through this act the Church united to her Bridegroom bodily.[46] The Church in response reenacts this great mystery everyday in order to remember and keep the bond with her Bridegroom.[47] Owen Cummings reminds the same: "the Church is imaged as a bride prepared for marriage to her husband. Christ crucified is the husband of the Church, and Lady Church's dowry is his body and blood. Every time the Eucharist is celebrated, this event is remembered by the Father as the dowry of the Lady Church."[48] Altar is compared as the bridal chamber of Christ the Bridegroom and the Church, the bride.[49] Therefore, Eucharist is one of the best pedagogical instruments to teach the love of Christ.

Liturgy makes person holy: Through the baptism and repentance one is able to experience the soteriological life in this world itself. The bride-bridegroom imagery reminds these liturgical experiences.[50] The first qualification of a girl to become bride of Christ is that she must be pure from impurities. Baptism is one of the ritualistic purification that is offered in the imagery. Through this bath the bride will be purified from her earlier impurities.[51] The Jewish and Babylonian culture also had followed this ritualistic purification. According to the Book of Esther the bride should be purified in the Myrrh bath for six months. This bath will clear all her old scars and impurities and makes her to the status of king's wife. Repentance

[44] *Lumen gentium*, 11.

[45] Bedjan, *HS* II, 587.18-19; Supra, 6.4.2.

[46] Bedjan, *HS* III, 290.16-19; ET. "On the Veil of Moses," 78.145-148.

[47] Bedjan, *HS* I, 538.9-10; ET. "On the Reposed," *TV* 5(1990), 43.57-44.58.

[48] Cummings, "Mystical Women and the Eucharist," 12.

[49] Long, *The Eucharistic Theology of the American Holy Fairs*, 11.

[50] Bedjan, *HS* I, 289.17-291.10; ET, "On the Prodigal Son," *TV* 5.4(1994), 29.455-468.

[51] Bedjan *HS* I, 167.7-168.7; ET. *FH* VI, 162.7-163.14; Supra, 3.5.3.

is another means for the salvation of souls.[52] Marriage imagery reminds the need of repentance from the sins (it dramatically calls adultery). In the Song of Songs and in Hosea the brides are going to wilderness in order to be ready for the marriage (Songs 2:8-8:5; Hos 2:14). Jephthah's daughter went for lamentation for two months before her marriage feast[53] (Judg 11:37).

Jesus went to wilderness before he begins his public ministry (Mt 4:1ff) and Paul went to the desert between his conversion and ministry (Gal 1:17). These are instances to show the importance of preparation for the marriage feast. The early Christian tradition also considered wilderness experience as a preparation to receive the eternal Bridegroom. The desert fathers and mothers avoided their earthly bridal chamber and went to the wilderness and mortified their worldly passions and pleased their eternal Bridegroom. In fasting and prayer the ordinary members of the Church are doing the same. Through these exercises they are pleasing the eternal Bridegroom. The same is expected from the bride of Christ. She must be pure just as her Bridegroom is pure. This is a call for each one who believes in Christ. Make ourselves pure and ready to receive the Bridegroom. Through the spousal imagery the Church reminds its faithful to be ready to receive the heavenly Bridegroom. Baptism and repentance are the two liturgical rites that make a faithful pure in spirit.

Forgiveness is another virtue in Christian life. The marriage imagery which Mar Jacob portrays upholds the Bridegroom's forgiveness to the bride, the nations, who slept in adultery. Though she was blackened with the smoke of holocausts He washed her and made beautiful and betrothed her as His life partner.[54] This incident calls the faithful to forgive each other. Forgiveness will heal many of the wounds which may cause great catastrophes in the human history. The Sacrament of forgiveness is considered as the second baptism in the Church. This shows the importance of this great mystery. The bride-bridegroom imagery seriously upholds the sacrament of confession.

Sacramental life and marriage imagery: When interpreting the family life from an Orthodox perspective, McGuckin says, "… it is God who bonds a man and a woman in a mystical union that grows out of the union of flesh. It is not the man and woman who make the marriage between them, therefore (as it is in many aspects of western Christian liturgical reflection), but God who makes the marriage into a living mystery out of the raw material of human affectivity."[55] The sacramentality of marriage makes transforming effects on the bride and bridegroom and then to the entire family. The marriage rite of the

---

[52] Bedjan, *HS* I, 296.1-2; ET, "On the Prodigal Son," *TV* 5.4(1994), 34.587-588.

[53] Mar Jacob called the execution of Jephthah's daughter as wedding feast. He called her as "bride of blood." Bedjan, *HS* V, 315.7. cf. Harvey, "Bride of Blood, Bride of Light," 189-190.

[54] Bedjan *HS* I, 167.7-168.7; ET. *FH* VI, 162.7-163.14; Supra, 5.3.11.

[55] McGuckin, "The "Great Mystery" of Marital Communion," Introduction, xvi.

West Syriac Church, which MOSC uses, vividly expresses the sacramentality of family life. It praises the divine intervention in the lives of the patriarchs especially through their marriage.[56] This sacramentality may be viewed in Jesus' blessing of the wedding of Cana.[57] Mar Jacob reminds the Church that God instituted and blessed the marriage between Adam and Eve. According to Mar Jacob the marriage is essentially a God given gift. The sacramental aspect of marriage suggests that God Himself is the author of marriage. The sanctifying grace of marriage is reaffirmed in the writings of Mar Jacob and the liturgy of the Church. The spouses' awareness of this sacramentality of marriage will help them to build a sound family. It will remind them about their call and vocation through the marriage life. Covenantal agreement shows the sacramentality of marriage.

7.6. Anthropological Relevance of Marriage Imagery

Importance of body and soul: Many heretical groups in the early centuries classified body as secondary to soul.[58] This dualistic thought would be seen even in the modernism also. They considered body as the lower principle and the soul as the higher principle; therefore, Descartes called the body as machine and soul as ghost in the machine.[59] Against such dualistic thought Mar Jacob often reaffirmed the divine nature of human body. In this understanding bride's body was created from the image of the Bridegroom's body, therefore, it is holy. Just like any other orthodox teachers, he accepted the place of body in the salvation or he never diminished the value of body. Both body and soul has its own importance and the bride is the partaker of the divine nature (2Pet 1:4).

Divinity of body: Mar Jacob portray individual members as bride and the bridal chamber of the heavenly Bridegroom simultaneously.[60] Through this they found a transcendent body of the faithful. As a part of the Church an individual soul is the bride of the Bridegroom; when the same individual soul consumes the body and the blood of the Bridegroom he will become the bridal chamber, because the Bridegroom is dwelling in his/her body. In one of the prayers of the MOSC the believers pray "make me your holy habitation."[61] When he participates in the body of Christ his human body will become a transcendent body of Christ. Therefore, a Christological anthropology is visible in the Bridegroom imagery. The Bridegroom is beyond the human conception

[56] *Koodashakramangal*, 88.

[57] *Koodashakramangal*, 100.

[58] Wilson, *Our Father Abraham*, 168.

[59] Dicker, *Descaretes: An Analytical and Historical Introduction*, 87ff; cf. Rozemond, *Descartes' Dualism*, 70ff; cf. Baker, *Descartes' Dualism*, 17-20.

[60] Supra, 5.1.

[61] *Prarthanakramam*, 317.

but now lowered His Image to the bride's own image in order to elevate her image into His own Image. It really honors the body of the bride and this will lead the bride to increase self esteem and self-awareness.

Through the marriage imagery the conjugal love gets a new meaning; marriage is not simply for carnal gratification but it is a means of purification and deification of the human soul. When Christ betrothed the Church at Jordan and at Golgotha the bride was purified and deified.[62] Through the baptism the bride washed away the follies of the world and through the participation in the body of Christ she was identified with the body of Christ. Through both these events the bride is attaining a metaphysical change within her or attaining a transcendental nature. Therefore, through the conjugal love the spouse should be purified. Kelly rightly says "conjugal love is the virtue by which man and wife wish to communicate to each other the benefits proper to marriage."[63]

7.7. Feminine Relevance of Marriage Imagery

Women and earth are the two principal reproductive members of the universe that have been rejected and marginalized, for millennia, by the patriarchal society. Bible also was not away from this trait. Ancient Hebrew society was patriarchal in nature. Therefore, the scripture is written in the language of male where female were treated as secondary. Twentieth century witnessed a revolt against this male dominant culture and scripture. As a result of male chauvinism many feminist theologians and feminist theological interpretations were popped up. They fought against the male hegemony and stood for the equal right for woman. They found that women played an important role in the salvation history both in the Old Testament and in the New Testament.

Egalitarian concept of nuptial imagery: Some critics believe that the spousal imagery is against women identity and it will increase gender inequality in the society.[64] Susan Ross says, "The relationship of bridegroom and bride is not an egalitarian relationship. This metaphor was used precisely because men and women were not equal."[65] But, instead of this kind of pondering, the bride imagery should be treated as a privilege; because in the eyes of God there is no distinction between man and woman. Both are created in His own Image and both are the part of the Church. We must look upon this Imagery in a vertical dimension, i.e., our relation with the God and not with the dominating husband and wife relation in the primitive life. Through this our identity is

---

[62] Bedjan, *HS* I, 183.9-184.15; ET. *FH* VI, 178.327-179.354; Bedjan, *HS* I, 174.9-16; ET. *FH* VI, 169.139-144; Bedjan, *HS* II, 286.19-20; ET. "Homily on Ten Virgins," *TV* 4.1(1992), 49.233-234.Supra, 3.5.3.; 3.5.4.

[63] Kelly, *Contemporary Moral Theology*, 110.

[64] Chukwu, *The Church as the Extended Family of God*, 68.

[65] Susan, *Extravagant Affections*, 111.

being revealed. More than that in the bride-bridegroom imagery "the freedom of both the bride and the Bridegroom is fully safeguarded. In the body image the identity of the Church is somehow lost in the Head but being a bride she regains her identity as a person and her union demands a consent which come out of love obedience to Christ Himself."[66] The equality between male and female in relation to Christ-Church was well discussed even from the middle ages. Bernard of Clairvaux portrays this equality of sharing each other even up to the point of "eating one another."[67]

To a privileged position from an underprivileged position: In the imagery of "bride-bridegroom' the female participants are having an important place. Earlier she was ignored and darkened by the fumes of holocaust but now she is the center of the family and she shines as a resplendent one.[68] The election of the Church from the nations is a model for the salvation of the marginalized and under privileged community.[69] Just like women are marginalized from the mainline society the nations were sidelined from the mainstream of the society. Moreover, in a community where discrimination prevailed (Jn 4:9) the Bridegroom emancipated the bride from the slavery of sin and marginalization. Empowerment of women is a need of the twenty-first century. Therefore, the feminist role portrays in Mar Jacob's homilies will be an encouragement to the world to respect the need of women in the liberation and the salvation of the world. The part of Virgin Mary played in the nuptial imagery is an example in this regard. By giving birth to the Bridegroom a lady became an integral part of the salvation history.[70] Therefore, women folk should be an essential part in the salvation of the family and society. But their place is not below or above the male characters; but both of them are equal in status. On the other hand just as the Church is submissive to Christ, as a social character, the wife should obey the husband. Spouse should act as Christ and the Church. St John Chrysostom says that God created Adam and Eve for marriage before the fall. Husband and wife have different roles. Wife must obey her husband, considering her obedience a part of her duty to the Lord even if she is not inclined to obedience for her husband's sake. The husband, as he hopes to receive obedience, has the responsibility to treat his wife with loving care.[71] The role of woman in the salvation is important as men; it should be recognized. Both man and woman play different roles in family, but in order to maintain the equilibrium, woman should obey her husband.

---

[66] Arby, *The Beauty of Communion*, 141.

[67] Cited in Roch, "Bride and Mother," 427-429.

[68] Bedjan *HS* I, 167.7-168.7; ET. *FH* VI, 162.7-163.14.

[69] Bedjan, *SMS,* 760.20-770.9; ET. *FH* I, 88.1045, 89.1055.

[70] Bedjan, *LP*; ET. "Homily on the Blessed Virgin Mary," *TV* 5.1(1993), 27.501-502.

[71] *St. John Chrysostom on Marriage and Family Life*, 17.

Women are endorsed in the spousal imagery through the female figures in the Bible. The Church which is the means of salvation is feminine in gender and feminine characteristics are attributed in the imagery. This correctly puts the importance of female principle in the world. In the first creation story both male and female carry a single essence, the Image of God; in other words they are equal in essence. The union between the Bridegroom and the bride reaffirms the equality in Image; because two different images could not be mingled as one unit. Mar Jacob praises woman in his homilies. In the *Homily on Ephrem* he praises the women of Israel and women in the Church. He accepts women and gives a place for women in the Church during his time.[72] He lauded the stories of Tamar,[73] Rachel,[74] Virgin Mary,[75] sinful woman,[76] and other women[77] in the Scripture and their characters are compared with the bride. He portrayed all these women as women of discernment. They passionately desired a place in the divine economy of God and therefore, they became part of the salvation history. Womb is another feminist theme in Mar Jacob's homilies. The womb of Mary, the womb of waters (River Jordan), the womb of *Sheol*, etc., and all these wombs played significant roles in the history of salvation.[78] The concept of second Eve is another feminist thinking of Mar Jacob.[79] Male dominant community often curse the women folk for the fall at Eden. If the first Eve became a cause of fall the second Eve made the salvation through her obedience which points that women are capable to make change in the world and it has elevated womanhood. Just like Mary brought salvation to the world an ideal woman in the family can bring progress and salvation to the household. Therefore, the feminist role played in the salvation history is an encouraging factor to the women-fold in the modern Church and impetus to bring them in the work of God.

---

[72] The place of women in the early Church is well established. See in Amar (ed.), *A Homily on Holy Mar Ephrem*, 34.40-37.50.

[73] "Jacob of Serugh's Verse Homily on Tamar (Gen. 38)," ET. Brock, Sebastian, *Le Museon* 115.3-4 (2002): 279-315.

[74] Bedjan, *HS* III, 208-229 (no 75); ET. "On Our Lord and Jacob," *TV* 4.4(1993), 50-64.

[75] "On the Perpetual Virginity" = "On the Perpetual Virginity," SMS, 639-661 (no. 4); ET. Puthuparampil, James. *Mariological Thought of Mar Jacob of Serugh* (451–521), Appendix i-xxi; IT. C. Vona, "Sulla Santa Generatrice di Dio e Vergine perpetual Maria," Lt (Nova Series) 19(1953), 169-185.

[76] Bedjan, *HS* II, 402-427, (no 51); ET. Johnson, "The Sinful Woman: A *Memra* by Jacob of Serugh," *Sobornost*, 24.1(2002), 56-88.

[77] "On Jephtha's Daughter," *HS* V, 306-330, (no 159); ET. Susan A. Harvey, "Jacob of Sarugh's Homily on Jephthah's Daughter," Texts from Christian late antiquity 22. *MHMJS*, fascicule 16, 2010.

[78] Supra, 5.1.1.

[79] Bedjan, *LP*; "Homily on the Blessed Virgin Mary," *TV* 5.1(1993), 9.45.

7.8. Ecumenical Relevance of Marriage Imagery

Marriage a symbol of Divine unity and need of the day: The bride imagery is mainly focusing on the unity of bride and the bridegroom.[80] The union of the divided Church, the Church from the Nation and Church from nations, is one of the focal points of marriage imagery.[81] Therefore, the unity within the Church is an important matter of concern. Ecumenism is a need of the modern Christendom, especially when it is challenged by many religious and social issues. Fragmentation does not help the smooth existence of the Church. A paradigm model for wider and stronger relationship among Christian denominations could be seen in the marriage imagery. A strongly married couple can be a symbol of hope to the community because they care for each other and remain together even when it would be easier not to.[82] Again it says, "Marriage is a statement against the isolationism of the world. This union is to empower people to live more fully, to connect and act together."[83] Since human beings are created in the Image of God unity of the Trinity should be our model of unity; it is a strong model for a complete love one another.[84] Therefore, the marriage rite of MOSC chants that there is no space between the Trinity.[85]

Wider ecumenism: Another important reason for the call of ecumenism is, countries like pluralistic India, where Christianity is a minority religion, a platform of unity must be identified. This is a need of the time. The bride-bridegroom imagery is a very relevant one in this regard. It narrates a household, oikos, story of husband and wife. Earlier the bride was from the nation now the bride is taken from all nations but now joined not merely to flock but as dear one of the Heavenly Bridegroom. As Rachel, Tamar, and Ruth, who were from the foreign background, joined to the stock of Jacob and Jesse nations joined to the family of the great Church; which brings a clear ecumenical vision. It is a beacon to the modern Church to bring those who are away from God to the real communion with God. This should be a call of the Church. Both the vertical and the horizontal relationship is necessary (1 Jn 2:9-11). If one part of the body fails the impact is on entire body. If one takes his community as exclusive there would not be any existence beyond that community. Consideration to other denomination as part and parcel of the whole Church is what ecumenism calls for. Such ecumenism covers salvation for all creation.

---

80 Through the betrothal events Mar Jacob portrays the unity between Christ and the Church.

81 Supra, 5.3.2.

82 Rubio, *Family Ethics: Practices for Christians*, 24.

83 Empereur, *Liturgy that Does Justice*, 183.

84 Sheed, *Theology for Beginners*, 25.

85 *Koodashakramangal*, 98.

A Pro-union God: God always stands for the union. God made the union between man and woman because He saw that, it is not good for man to be alone (Gen 2:18). She is originally from the man and God took her from his side. Christ united the upper ones and the lower ones through His death (Eph 2:14).[86] He is our peace (Eph 1:14); He brought the nation and nations together.[87] Prior to all human effort, unity prevailed because Christians are Christians, because, of their "union" with Jesus Christ. This Christian unity, founded on and existing through Christ, is none other than that fellowship which we Christians repeatedly acknowledge in worship through…[88] The Bridegroom calls for worship through the participation in His body and blood. This itself is a means of unity among the faithful through the body of Christ, the Bridegroom.

7.9. Ecological Relevance of the Marriage Imagery

We are living in an ecological web of networking; any fault in any part of the network will affect the entire network. It is essential to prevent malwares that could attack the network to sustain the system from a shutdown. In order to maintain a robust network chain it should be careful to add any additions to the default programs. Our ecological chain is under serious threat and the virtual thoughts of bride-bridegroom imagery may be relevant preventive method to this badly affected threat.

The love of the Heavenly Bridegroom to the bride is a prominent theme of the spousal imagery. It teaches a relationship pattern. When it was disturbed, in order to bring back the old unity between the God-human and human-nature the Bridegroom offered Himself. By His love the Bridegroom reconciled and united the heaven and the earth and the heavenly and the earthly. This pattern of love should be a role model to the modern world too. Unity of creation is essential for the sustainability of the created world. The creation is a link in the chain and hence to ascertain our deeds are enhancing the unity and sustainability in this world. Well being of the world does not mean the well being of humanity but the entire nature as a whole. One of the five kinds of liberations that Moltmann suggests to attain peace in the universe is the liberation of the nature from exploitation: economic liberation from the exploitation; political liberation against human right violations; solidarity against the alienation of man from man; liberation of nature against the violent exploitation; and liberation from apathy in building up hope in the minds of human beings.[89] He says: "A human society deserving of the name cannot

---

[86] Bedjan, *SMS*, 789.8-9; ET. *FH* II, 107.295-296.

[87] Bedjan, *HS* III, 219.7-8; ET. "On Our Lord and Jacob," *TV* 4.4(1993), 60.237-238.

[88] Pannenberg, *The Church,* 24.

[89] Moltmann, *The Future of Creation: Collected Essays*, 110-112.

be built without peace with nature."[90] The relevance of the bride-bridegroom imagery lies here. According to His love the Bridegroom made peace in the world but He needed a reciprocal love to sustain this peace, without which the peace would not sustain. This is evident in the story of Israel, the first bride. When they ignored the real Bridegroom and committed idolatry, He elected another bride. If the bride loves anything or anybody other than her Bridegroom the relation strains becomes defunct. This applies to nature-human relationship also. If our love is with the electronic items we are creating e-waste. If our love is with cars we are creating more carbon-dioxide and toxic air. If we love more profit from our agriculture through the use of fertilizer and pesticides we are creating a toxic earth. All these are against the relationship pattern and the creation policy of the Bridegroom.

The nuptial imagery puts-forth many betrothal events such as betrothal at Golgotha, at manger, at Jordan, and at Golgotha. In all these events, according to Mar Jacob, the ecosystem actively involved. He dramatically created a marvelous scene during these betrothal events. Water, air, earth, fire, clouds, thunder, lightning, and birds are actively participating in the drama. This shows the participation of created beings along with the divine will. And this is a harmonious co-existence of the created beings. This example demands the modern world to be a balanced ecological system.

The imbalanced ecosystem is one of the major problems that face the modern world. In the present age the basic elements like, water, air, and earth are polluted at a large extent. The problem is as detrimental to humanity as the world at large. Deadly diseases and climatic change are emerging challenges to humanity. During the industrial revolution human beings were never concerned about the ecosystem. The profit maximization is the core objective of the capital economy. In the intention of profit making they seldom considered the nature which created environmental issues like climate change, imbalances in the ecosystem, pollution, etc. Restoration of the already distorted creation is a vital point in the Bride-Bridegroom imagery. Purification and the restoration of earth, water, and air is an essential immediate need of today. The solution should be made to reinstate the healthy relation between humanity and the created world immediately. The care and consideration of the Bridegroom to the oppressed bride in the Bridegroom imagery may help the restoration of the ecosystem. Among the natural elements water receives more importance in the marriage imagery. The imagery portrays that the Bridegroom purifies the water of Jordan by His descend. Though He had no need to immerse in the water for the sake of His bride He took baptism.[91] Again, the water of Jordan cleansed

---

[90] Moltmann, *The Future of Creation: Collected Essays*, 112.

[91] Rilliet, *SHF* II. 558.14-17; FH VII, 195.19.

the filths of the Church.[92] The water flowed from the side of the Bridegroom enliven Adam and his sons from death and perdition. Mar Jacob says that by the touch of the water that irrigated from the side of Christ made the dead ones sprout like seeds sprout by the touch of water.[93] These examples show that for a sustainable life, every created being needs to be clean and pure. In order to stay clean they need pure water. Just as the Bridegroom cleansed the water by His self-emptying act, the human world themselves must make sincere attempt to clean the impure water system. In order to restore the God created nature, just like the exuberant Bridegroom suffered for the restoration of the Image of humanity, human beings ought to suffer some sacrifice and to be compatible with the common ecosystem. Our technologies and the developments should be compatible to the ecosystem. Then only new lives will sprout into the world.

7.10. Social Relevance of Marriage Imagery

Bride-bridegroom imagery has a wider dimension of appeal to the society. This imagery is telling a love story; the love of God towards the human beings. Therefore, human beings are indebted to share the same love, which God shared to them, among themselves. As discussed above the major role of the imagery in the social realm is also love. In the Incarnation of Jesus Christ, the Bridegroom, the transcendent love personified in bodily form; on the other hand, in marriage the same love blooms its fruits as a union of two individuals into one organic personhood. Therefore, God's love is transmitting its transcending character into an imminent form through the faithful. But this conjugal love does not end with the couple, because it makes them capable of the gift by which they become cooperators with God in giving life to a new human person. According to the plan of God, since marriage and conjugal love are ordained to the procreation and education of children, marriage is the foundation of the wider community of the family. Thus, the couple, while giving themselves to one another, give not just themselves but also the reality of children, who are a living reflection of their love, a permanent sign of conjugal unity and a synthesis of their being a father and a mother.[94] Thus the couple has a wider responsibility.

The society raises several challenges against the faithful Christians. This study proposes that the spousal imagery will enable to withstand the challenges of the society. In the imagery the bride, the Church, is a representative of moral principles. In this imagery the Church is portrayed as chaste and pure. Cyprian

---

[92] Bedjan, *HS* IV, 702.17-19; Bedjan, *HS* I, 174.5-17; *FH* VI,169-170.135-145.

[93] Bedjan, *HS* IV, 638.5-12; Bedjan, *HS* IV, 638.5-12, 648.6-21; Bedjan, *HS* I, 425.12; *HS* II, 93:3-6, 295:22; *HS* III, 429:12-16, 430:2-3, 531:17-18; *HS* IV, 686:5-6; *HS* V, 452:17-453:2.

[94] Villar, "The Plan of God for Marriage and the Family Life: A Roman-Catholic Perspective," 84.

of Carthage reaffirms this statement: "The Bride of Christ cannot be made false to her Spouse: she is incorrupt and modest. She knows but one dwelling, she guards the sanctity of the nuptial chamber chastely and modestly."[95] St. John Chrysostom exhorts that either husband or wife are not their own but the other person's. He states: "wife has no power over her own body, but she is her husband's slave… As for you, husband, if a prostitute tries to seduce you, tell her that "my body is not my own, but my wife's."[96] This image of chastity and purity of the bride could be model for the modern family. Moreover, the biblical imagery shows the Church as a channel or vehicle of God's presence and grace.[97] In one way, the marriage administered through the Church should bring forth the love which is both God Himself and His grace. On the other hand, as an individual believer is a representative of the broader Church, the bride and the bridegroom should be the vehicle of God's presence and grace. Therefore, the individual church member is expected to have God's purity.

Some of the most important problems facing the modern society are the disintegration and the absence of committed family life. It is an end result of a degradation of the social values and faith in God. The religious marriage ceremony will help as a partial remedy for this grievous problem. Marriage in front of a community especially a socially respectable community will compel the couple to cope with the values of the community. As against the totally secluded life from the community socialization and mutual interaction within the community will enhance the couple to live together as a respected family even amidst minor problems between the couple. Empathy, sympathy, and compassion of the similarly affected and experienced persons will augment the persons to endure the problems in their lives. Moreover, interaction with the religious people will help to get consoled and to be encouraged to face the problems in their lives. In Jewish understanding a marriage which is legally conducted is a social as well as a religious act by which sanctification and the spouses are mutually obliged each other to stay away from divorce.[98] In the light of scriptural interpretation marriage is a type of covenantal relationship. In the marriage imagery a covenantal relationship between God and Church is evident. The primary mode of covenant is given in scripture as: "This day you have accepted God's commitment, and God has accepted yours" (Deut 16:17). Thus covenant is seen in scripture primarily as a personal relationship and mutual commitment.[99] In special reference to the marriage, covenant is based on the love of God towards the Church and therefore the basis of marriage

[95] Cyprian, "The Epistles of Cyprian," LXXV.2.

[96] Chrysostom, XIX. *On 1 Corinthians 7*, 26-27.

[97] Avis, *ReShaping Ecumenical Theology*, 143.

[98] Millgram, *Jewish Worship,* 326.

[99] Siegle, *Marriage According to the New Code of Canon Law*, 3-4.

covenant between man and woman must be on the basis of love and fidelity to each other. This fidelity creates a healthy family relationship. Bible and most of the Christian traditions support monogamy and are against the divorce. They considered marriage as a divine institution or a sacrament and it should not be annulled. Tertullian wonderfully observes the divinity of marriage life:

> That which joined together by the Church, strengthened by an offering, sealed by a blessing, announced by the angels and ratified by the Father... How wonderful the bond between two believers with a single hope, a single desire, a single observance, a single service! They are both brethren and both fellow-servants; there is no separation between them in spirit or flesh; in fact they are truly two in one flesh and where the flesh is one, one is the spirit.[100]

The bride-bridegroom imagery reemphasizes the unity between the bride and the Bridegroom. It says: "Therefore, man will leave his father and mother and cleave to his wife and they will become one flesh" (Gen 2:24). The sacramental unity in Christ-Church relationship is a paradigm of conjugal union of husband-wife relationship. God in His eternal love to humankind shares His own body for the salvation of His bride and the same spiritual love of God enables the spouses to share their body and soul in married life. Thus, marriage imagery may serve as a model against the disintegration of the modern family.

Social and natural justice is another concern of the marriage imagery. Many such attributions are described in the imagery: Nation took upper hand in the society and trampled the nations, who were also inheritors of the Kingdom of God, bridal chamber. Then Christ, the Bridegroom, came and liberated them from the marginalization to the mainline of the society. The generations from Adam were under the torture of the evil one in *Sheol*. Jesus, the liberator, came and dashed the walls of *Sheol* and released them from the captivity. He gave natural justice to the inmates of evil one. More than that, when He liberated Barabbas He liberated the sons of Adam. But, the modus operandi is different from other heroes of the world; in order to liberate Barabbas He gave Himself as a ransom. Therefore, to build up a just society the marriage imagery is a good example. In the Indian context, the dalit, tribal, economically backward, and the marginalized people from the mainline society should be liberated and empowered. The marriage imagery should be a model for retaining the above mentioned societies from their despairing conditions. It is the duty of the Church to bring them to the fraternity of the great-one-family of this big democratic country. Therefore, the spousal imagery is a call for social and natural justice.

[100] Tertullian, *The Second Book to His Wife,* 2.8.

Conclusion

This chapter discussed various implications of bride-bridegroom imagery in the context of modern world and society. This imagery is rich in many respects. Since this imagery is an example from the very human life itself and involves human life from its very beginning it is logical, appealing and simple to understand. The love of God towards the humanity is vividly portrayed through this imagery. When this love is transmitted into the society through the Church the society enjoys revelation of the Kingdom of God, where, there is no pain, hunger, or discrimination. The establishment of the Kingdom of God in the world is the very goal of creation itself. Therefore, nuptial imagery is relevant to the modern world.

General Conclusion

This research is an enquiry into the scope and dimensions of the biblical imagery "Bride and Bridegroom" based on Mar Jacob of Serugh who lavishly resorts to this imagery in his homilies. In the Syriac Orient the Church Fathers and the Liturgy used this biblical nuptial imagery as a pedagogical tool. On par with the concept of 'theosis' or 'deification' of the Byzantine Church they taught the salvation event through the 'betrothal and marriage with Christ.' This imagery portrays the salvific acts of the Redeemer Messiah on behalf of His beloved spouse, the Church. Perhaps, Jacob of Serugh (451-521 AD) might be the most celebrated Church Father, who used this imagery in its wider, length, and breadth. According to this imagery, there is only one God and He has a singular plan to save His creation from the perdition. Therefore, Christ initiated the Church as a medium for this salvation.

Mar Jacob was the bishop of Batnan in the West Syriac Church (519-521) in Serugh, in modern Turkey. He was known as the "flute of the Holy Spirit and harp of the believing Church." He is one of the greatest theologians of the early Church. For a long time he was *Cor-episcopo* and the *Malphono* of the West Syriac Church. He was a prodigy and his verse homilies are counted 760 besides prose homilies, dialogue poems, letters, etc. He was born in a period of serious Christological controversy in the Church which faced the first major division in the Christendom. In this controversy our author had clear vision on his theological understanding but he never become a controversial figure. Though he studied in the theological school of Edessa, which was pro-Antiochene, he followed the Alexandrian Christology. His inclination to the non-chalcedonian side is evident in some of his letters. However, more than the allegiance to any side in the Christological controversy or as a systematic theologian, he was a spiritual as well as a pastoral theologian who used poetry as a vehicle to spread the Word of God. In order to interpret the Scripture he developed a combination of Alexandrian and Ephremian methodology. Through this method of writings he received the attention of both the theological authors and the general public. This acceptance made the prolific author to attain a great position in the Church.

He wrote homilies on scriptural episodes and persons, of both the Testaments, on Church, liturgical themes, refutations against those who challenged the divinity of Christ, etc. However, always the focal point is on Christ and the Church. Every incident and person of the Old Testament pre-figures and proclaims Christ and His salvific acts.[1] Since this research is concentrated on Christ and His salvific acts through the Church, the discussion is on the role of the Church in the salvation of creation. His hermeneutical approach is very effective in digging out the spiritual meaning of the Scriptures. He is not a systematic interpreter of the Scripture. His interpretation is symbolic and typological, which may not be acceptable to the modern scientific interpreters. He prefers symbols and types to interpret the scripture rather than the literal or allegorical method. Symbols are the vehicles of deep meaning. Their meanings are not linier or static but their horizons are very wider and meanings are dynamic and cyclic with multivalence. Readers of different times and cultures could understand the meanings in their own ways and cultural backgrounds. Through the 'type' he professes the unity of the Scripture and the truth of the prophecy and the authenticity of the Christ event. Through these kinds of interpretation instills the deeper meanings of the Christ event into the minds of the faithful. He uses various rhetoric methods, such as paradox, acrostic, parallelism, dialogue, etc., to communicate his theology. The polyvalent nature of his interpretation helps him to bring Christ, Church or sacraments to any part of his homilies on any subject. The modern systematic theologians or ancient Greek or Latin theologians, who did the theologizing in systematic way, cannot enjoy this kind of freedom in their interpretations.

As it was described above, this research is focused on the salvific acts of Jesus Christ, the Bridegroom, on behalf of His bride, the Church. This theme is a dramatic presentation of Christ's own Words. In many instances Christ calls Himself as Bridegroom. Through the nuptial imagery of 'Ten Virgins' Christ portrays His second coming. Finally, St. Paul proclaims the bridegroom and the bride as mysteriously representing Christ and the Church. However, this imagery had its roots in the Semitic culture. The divine-human encounter through the marriage was well established in the Mesopotamian, Canaanite, and Hebrew backgrounds. Mar Jacob uses this imagery to teach the salvation history of the Church. From the above backgrounds Mar Jacob is mostly indebted to the Jewish literature and the Bible for the elaboration of this imagery.

Mar Jacob sees the important events in the life of Christ as betrothal. He calls Christ's birth, baptism, and the death on the cross as betrothal events.

---

[1] Bedjan, *HS* V, 331.1-332.9. ET. "A Homily on Samson," *TV* 11(1992), 51.1-52.24.

To some modern thinkers this would seem absurd. How could a man betroth a single woman in three different periods of his life? How could the effect of all these betrothals will be the same, the liberation of the bride? Here lies the importance of sacred or cyclic time sequence. His synchronic and cyclic vision of time enables him to connect these multiple actions in to a single act of betrothal. For a spiritual interpreter time and space would not be a barrier. Especially, the birth, baptism, and the sacrificial death of the Bridegroom are the three staging posts in the redemption process of the bride. Mar Jacob finds equal prominence to every act of the Incarnate Son for this deliverance. In these betrothal events the Bridegroom defeated the evil one and made possible the re-entry of the children of Adam and Eve into the Paradise. Through the birth the Bridegroom became identified with the bride, walked in her ways, and became approachable to her. With His baptism the Bridegroom cleansed the waters of the earth, retrieved Adam from the hands of evil one, and put the 'robe of glory', which was lost in the Garden of Eden, in the womb of baptismal waters. By His death the Bridegroom killed the death and sin. He received the lance on His side at Golgotha to remove the revolving lance of the Cherub from the gate of Eden.

As a spiritual and a typological interpreter Mar Jacob found the betrothal in the various accounts of the Old Testament, such as, creation, covenants with Noah, Abraham, and Moses, in the lives of Isaac, Jacob, Jephthah, Samson, liberation from Egypt, and more. He found the Genesis account "Therefore, a man shall leave his father and mother and cling to his wife, and they become one flesh" (Gen 2:24) as the foundation of this imagery. Mar Jacob believes that this prophecy is not just for Adam and Eve but it was a prophecy on Christ-Church relationship. They foreshadowed Christ and the Church respectively. God intervened in the history through different holy men including prophets and they educated and chastised them. In order to save humanity God made progressive covenants with Noah, Abraham, Moses and other figures of the Old Testament. The later prophets used the bride-bridegroom imagery to remind the covenantal relationship of Israelites to Yahweh. But they never gave heed to them. Mar Jacob portrays that these incidents and many men of the history were foreshadowing 'types' of the bridal imagery. According to him more than the historicity of the events they are prefigurations of Christ's saving activity.

In the fullness of time, Christ, the Bridegroom, arrived and redeemed the humanity, in a wider sense the whole creation, through the establishment of the Church. As described above, Mar Jacob portrays that the Bridegroom was hidden in the Old Testament and all just men of the Old Testament were the 'types' of the Bridegroom. This study explains that in Mar Jacob's interpretation, the figures of the Old Testament like Isaac, Jacob, Moses, Samson, etc., are the 'types' of the Bridegroom. This truth was foretold in the prophecies but Israel was not mature enough to grasp this hidden truth. Therefore, the Father veiled Him from her. But, the arrival of Christ, the Bridegroom, was the fulfillment of these prophesies and unveiled the Bridegroom.[2] During His public ministry He was attested by many that He is the real Bridegroom who was foretold in the prophesies and the One who came for the salvation of the world. He walked all the ways of Adam, and instructed the bride in order to sanctify her. Though He has no need to be baptized, in order to cleanse the bride, He was baptized by the hands of His servant John the Baptist. Even when He remains as Immortal God and Creator of all, He dwelt in the womb of a virgin, took form of His creation, lived as an obedient child, received scoff and stripes on His body from the hands of the sons of Adam and died as a mortal man. While He is eternal, King of kings, and rich, He became limited to an ordinary human being, and lived as a pauper. While He is luminous like fire and holy, He took human body and counted with sinners. He received lance on His side and therefore, the lance at the gate of Paradise was removed. He gave His body and blood as the bride money and food. Now the Bridegroom, by His death, defeated Satan, killed the death, and redeemed the bride from the bondage of slavery. He went to the *Sheol*, devastated its walls and emancipated the sons of Adam who were in the slavery of Satan.

As an obedient bride, who is the backbone of the family and behind all the success of a family, along with the Bridegroom, Christ, the bride, the Church, plays an important role in the salvation of human beings. Mar Jacob illustrates about two Churches: the Church from the Nation or synagogue and the Church from the nations. He calls Israel as bride. By finding the 'type's of Church in the Old Testament Mar Jacob tries to prove that the Church was a pre-existent one. He sees many 'types' of the Church in the Old Testament like, Rachel and Tamar. Moreover, he affirms that the 'woman' in Genesis 2:24 is really about the Church. In order to save the humanity God the Creator elected the Nation as His bride but the rebellious one disobeyed Him, and offered sacrifice to other gods. God sent prophets to teach and correct the bride but they never give heed to them. By serving other gods she became adulteress. Finally, instead of prophets, God sent His only Begotten, the real Bridegroom, but she not only rejected but killed Him. Therefore, the Bridegroom elected the Church from the nations as his bride. Notwithstanding the fact that she was blackened with the fumes of idolatry and therefore adulteress, she was enlightened and became faithful to her husband. She was born from the wombs of Jordan, the side, and Tomb of her Bridegroom. In Jordan she put-off her old nature and put-on the new and thus she became a new creation. On the cross the Church

[2] Bedjan, *HS* III, 289.4; ET. Brock, "On the Veil of Moses," in *Studies in Syriac Spirituality*, 77.113; cf. Bedjan, *HS* III, 287.13-14; ET. Brock, "On the Veil of Moses," in *Studies in Syriac Spirituality*, 76.81.

was born from this wound and from the water and blood that flowed from His side which cleansed the Church from her sins.[3] She became resplendent through the baptism and satiated by consuming the body and blood of her Bridegroom. Finally, the Bridegroom descended into the *Sheol* and smashed its fortress and liberated the captives from the time of Adam. Thus it was a birth of a new creation into the sheep fold Christ.

The marriage imagery not only contemplates the earthly saving activity of Christ but also ponders over an eschatological expectation. Mar Jacob portrayed it as the consummation of the betrothals of the bridal imagery. A blissful life with the Bridegroom is the ever cherished hope of the bride. The eschatological realm of the marriage imagery describes this life. The bridal chamber, robe of glory, and the wedding feast are discussed in this event. Just like any other betrothal event which is consummated with the marriage the betrothal of the Church with the heavenly Bridegroom would be fulfilled through the wedding feast at His second coming. At that time those who have the 'garment of glory' will enter the bridal chamber with the Bridegroom and enjoy the wedding banquet. He describes the bridal chamber as a luminous beautiful palace. Through the bridal chamber Mar Jacob intends to portray the heavenly abode. The requirement for the admission in the bridal chamber is the 'robe of glory' that was lost at the Garden of Eden. Baptism and Eucharist are the two covenantal realities that make a person clean and resplendent. The Bridegroom deposited this robe for the bride through His baptism at Jordan. Those who are baptized in the name of the Father, the Son and the Holy Spirit will obtain this robe from the water. Those who receive it should keep it clean until the Second Coming. Wedding feast is the crowning feature of the eschatological life with the Bridegroom. The participation in the Eucharist is a pre-taste of this eschatological wedding feast. Finally the marriage union or conjugal union is described. The marriage union is completed only through the conjugal life. The union happens through the participation in the body and blood of the Bridegroom. The first prophecy "Therefore, a man shall leave his father and mother and cling to his wife, and they become one flesh" (Gen 2:24), through the participation in the body and blood of the Bridegroom, brings in the realization.

The bride-bridegroom imagery focuses on several insights which will be helpful to the present day life of a Christian. The foundation of the imagery is the Genesis account of "Therefore, a man shall leave his father and mother and clings to his wife, and they become one flesh" (Gen 2:24). Therefore, the imagery speaks about a deep individual relationship between the Bridegroom and the bride. It is a personal, close, and an intimate relationship; there is nothing alien between them. Everything is revealed or known to the other

[3] This is one of his interpretations only. He interpreted the same as Eucharist, baptism, etc.

person; because they are one as parts of the same body (1Cor 12:14-24). Just like many limbs come together and are integrally related to each other and forms a single body husband and wife will become one body and one soul. As the Greek Church fathers explain the function of the Holy Trinity through the term *perichoresis*[4] which explains that every action of each Person of the Holy Trinity is with the knowledge of other two Persons, every small and single action of one of the spouses will be known to the other. One of the hymns of the West Syriac marriage rite explains that there is no gap between the persons of the Holy Trinity.[5] The same would be applicable to the husband and wife relationship. One member's suffering will be suffering of the other member; one member's joy is other member's joy too. This closer relationship of bride and the bridegroom in the imagery will enhance a person to improve his/her relationship to both the heavenly spouse (Christ) and earthly marriage partner. In other words this imagery will make an impact to create deeper relation to his/her God in spiritual life and to the spouse in family relationship. Therefore, more than a regular interpretation of the Church as a community a personal relationship with God will create more impact on the ordinary believer.

In the Ecclesiological understanding, the kerygma, communion, and mission of the Church demand an ecclesial unity with Christ and the Church. The Christ-Church relationship pattern in the nuptial imagery make awareness in the minds of the couples that they are not alone but they are integrally united to a larger community in holiness. The idea of the Church from nations would enhance the ecclesial life in the modern pluralistic society. Moreover, the imagery will engender a close affection to Christ in the mind of the believers.

The essential nature of the imagery itself is liberation or a life with Christ in eternal Kingdom. The soteriological expectations offered by the nuptial imagery offers a hope in the minds of the believers who are suffering in the busy and stressful world. It promotes harmonious and peaceful coexistence in the family and society in a deeper and meaningful manner. This imagery also demands the modern world to lead a quality life. The imagery brings the reader to an eschatological setting where everything is pure from defilement against the wider unfaithfulness in the modern family life. In the spiritual level this imagery offers committed closeness in the individual and social relationships. Also it advocates for a simple life while a good number of fellow human beings are in starvation.

All these show that the imagery of Bride-Bridegroom remains very relevant in the present busy social life where genuine intimate relationships and love are losing values. Without imitating the selfless love, which our Lord

---

[4] The Church fathers used this term to explain the unity of the Holy Trinity. See Prestige, *God in Patristic Thought,* 297-299.

[5] *Koodashakaramangal*, 98.

showed from the very beginning, peace cannot be achieved in the world. Care for the lost one in the society is an important aspect. Millions of people need care and help. Also, without care of the human beings the natural world cannot be sustained. The care of the Bridegroom, who gave Himself as a sacrifice for His bride, shall be a model in this regard. Therefore, the bride-bridegroom imagery is very relevant and inspiring in this world that needs justice, peace, and hope to travel forward.

Glossary

Anduthaksa	:	This book comprises the orders of different feasts celebrated in the MOSC.
Bart qyomo	:	Syriac term, literally means the daughter of covenant. In the early Church this term was used to denote those who dedicated themselves for God without marriage or conjugal union of the world. Its masculine is bar qyomo.
Bo'uto	:	This is a title, which means supplications. In the West Syriac tradition certain canonical prayers are denoted by this heading. Especially by Mar Ephrem, Mar Jacob, and Mar Balai.
Chaldean Breviary	:	This is a three-volume set liturgical documents Hudra, Kashkul, and Gaza) for the use of the Chaldean Church. The first volume covers the Annunciation to the Great Fast (Lent), the second Great Fast to Pentecost, and the third Pentecost to the Dedication of the Church. The entire book is only in Syriac, fully vocalized and given in the East Syriac script.
Cor-episcopos	:	*Cor-episcopos* (Syr.) means the bishop of the village. In the early Syrian when the administration of the Church was difficult the episcopo appointed *Cor-episcopos* to assist them in administration of the local churches.
Gehenna	:	In the Syriac literature Gehenna is uses to denote a place of punishment after the death.
Kashtanubhavazhcha Namaskaram	:	This is the Malayalam title of The Order of Passion Week in Malayalam, which is used in MOSC.

Koodashkramangal	:	This is the Malyalam title of *The Order of different sacrament* in Syriac with Malayalam translations side-by-side.
Ktobo d-Takso d-Anoporo	:	Syriac title of *The Order of Book of Anaphora*. This book contains 13 anaphoros in Syriac and its Malayalam translation on the other side.
Ktobo d-zlooto šheemto	:	Syriac title of the *Order of the Common (daily) Prayer* means ordinary or regular. This uses in monasteries and seminaries. Though this is daily prayer usually it would not uses in family. It has prayers for each days in poetic form. Syriac and Malayalam editions are available.
Lilo	:	*Lilo* (Syr.) means night. But used as night prayer.
Madrašo	:	*Madrašo* (Syr.) is a stanzaic verse poem could sing beautifully. It will have different syllable patterns.
Malphono	:	*Malphono* (Syr.) means teacher.
Memero	:	*Memro* (Syr.) means metrical poem. This could probably recite. The Syriac authors of the early and middle centuries like Ephrem, Jacob, etc., wrote this genre of poems as theological oration.
Mosul Penkitho	:	*Penkitho* (Syr.) means a volume or book. *The Mosul Penkitho* contains a set of special prayers comprising seven volumes for the feast days on yearly basis published from Mosul.
Pampakuda Penkitho	:	*Pampakuda Penkitho* (Syr.) is a book of special prayers of the feast days on yearly basis. Published from Pampakuda, Kerala by Malpan Abraham Konat in three volumes.
Prarthanakramam	:	Malayalam title of *Order of Common Prayer*. This is a compilation of canonical, meditational, special feast days, occasional prayers uses in MOSC.
Promiyon:	:	*Promiyon* (Syr.) is a short prayer. Usually *promiyon* is followed by a long prayer called *Sedero*. Here it is used in the sense of a book which contains special *promiyone* for different feasts. The MOSC published four volumes of Malayalam translation from Syriac: From Consecration to departed soul's day, *Promiyone* for Three day's

		fasting and Great Lent, For Passion Week, From Resurrection to Consecration of the Church.
Qurbono	:	*Qurbono* means offerings which is usually used to denote Eucharist in the Syriac speaking Churches.
Rozo	:	Rozo (Syr.) means mystery.
Ruaha d-qudsha	:	(Syr.) Holy Spirit
Savasamskarakramam	:	Malayalam title of *Order of Funeral* uses in the MOSC (For men, women, and children).
Sedro	:	*Sedro* (Syr.) means row and in liturgical prayers it is long prayer followed by *promiyon.*
Sughyotho/ Sugito	:	*Sughyotho* or *Sugito* is a genre of Syriac stnazaic poem. It is ordered like a dialogue, thus commonly called it as dialogue poems.
Vishuddha Qurbanakramam	:	Malayalam title of *Holy Order of Eucharistic Liturgy* (for lay people).
Yoldat aloho	:	Syriac term for Mother of God.

Bibliography

I. Primary Sources

A. ***Acta Martyrum et Sanctorum,* Vols. 1-V, (ed.) P. Bedjan, Paris 1890-1897.** [Reference to these volumes are indicated with the abbreviation *AMS* + Volume no. in Roman numerals + page(s) + lines.

"On Ss. Guria and Shamuna" = "On Ss. Guria and Shamuna," *AMS* I, 131-143; cf. Vol. VIII of the *Ante-Nicene Fathers,* 708-720; *An Oration on Shamuna and Guria, composed by Mar Jacob,* ET by W. Cureton, *Ancient Syriac Documents,* 94-106.

"On Habib the Martyr" = "On Habib the Martyr," *AMS* I, 160-172; E.T. by W. Cureton, *Ancient Syriac Documents,* 86-96.

"On Blessed Mar Ephrem" = "On Blessed Mar Ephrem, the Teacher," *AMS* III, 665-679; Critical Edition + E.T. by J. P. Amar, "A Metrical Homily on Holy Mar Ephrem by Mar Jacob of Serugh," *PO,* 47 (Fascicule 1 No 209), Turnhout 1995.

"Homily on Simeon the Stylite" = "Homily on Simeon the Stylite," *AMS* IV, (repr. Hildesheim: G. Olms, 1968), 650-665; E.T. by S. A. Harvey, in *Ascetic Behavior in Greco-Roman Antiquity: A Source book,* V. L. Wimbush (ed.), (Studies in Antiquity and Christianity), Minneapolis: Fortress Press, 1990, 15-28.

B. ***Epistulae Quotquot Suprnunt* 1.** SARUGENSIS, *Epistulae quotquot supersunt,* (ed.) G. Olinder, Paris 1937, CSCO 110, Louvain, Imprimerie Orinetaliste, Durbecq, 1965. [All references regarding this source in this dissertation is from *CSCO* 110; References to this volume will be indicated with the abbreviation *Ep* +Number of the letter in Roman numerals + page(s) + line(s)].

Brock, "Jacob of Serugh, Letter VII, To the Monks of Sinai" = van Bladel, Kevin Thomas, ET. "Jacob of Serugh, Letter VII (To the Monks of

Sinai)," in *History and Hagiography from the Late Antique Sinai*, Caner, Daniel, (ed.), Liverpool: Liverpool University Press, 2010.

C. ***Homiliae Selectae Mar Jacobi Sarugensis*, Vols. I-V, (ed.) P. Bedjan, Paris-Leipzig 1905-1910.** [References to these volumes are indicated with the abbreviation *HS* + Volume no. in Roman Numerals + Page(s) + Line(s)]. A revised edition: Bedjan, Paulus and Brock, Sebastian P., eds. *Homilies of Mar Jacob of Sarug / Homiliae Selectae Mar-Jacobi Sarugensis* Vols.I-V+VI. Piscataway, NJ: Gorgias Press, 2006.

Bedjan, *HS* I

"On the Descent of the Most High on Mount Sinai and the Mysteries of the Church" = "On the Descent of the Most High on Mount Sinai and the Mysteries of the Church," *HS* I, 3-38, (no 2)

"On the Consecration of the Church and Prophet Moses" = "On the Consecration of the Church and Prophet Moses," *HS* I, 38-48, (no 3).

"On the Serpent of Brass" = "On the Serpent of Brass that Moses Lifted up in the Desert," *HS* I, 49-67 (no 4); ET from HTM, *TV* 6(1990), 38-56.

"On the Three Baptisms" = "On the Three Baptisms, of the Law, of John the Baptist, and of Our Lord," *HS* I, 153-167 (no. 7).

"On the Baptism of our Redeemer in the Jordan" = "On the Baptism of Our Redeemer in the Jordan," *HS* I, 167-193 (no. 8); ET. by T. Kollamparampil, *FH* VI, 159-186.

"On the Holy Baptism" = "On the Holy Baptism," *HS* I, 193-211, (no 9).

"On the Prodigal Son" = "A Homily on the Son Who Squandered his Riches," *HS* I, 267-299 (no. 12); ET. from HTM, *TV* 5.4 (1994), 11-37.

"On the Pharisee and the Publican" = "A Homily on the Pharisee and the Publican, who said Our Lord, went up the temple to pray," *HS* I, 299-319 (no 13); ET. from HTM, *TV* 9 (1991), 18-34.

"On the Workers in the Vineyard" = "On the Parable that Our Lord Said on the Workers of Vineyard," *HS* I, 320-344, (no 14).

"On Zakai, the Tax Collector" = "On Zakai, the Tax Collector," *HS* I, 344-364, (no 15), ET. by Zeki Aydin, "Jacob of Serugh's Memro on Zakai the Tax Collector: A Literary and Theological Analysis," *ParOr* 35 (2010), 77-94.

"On the Rich Man and Lazar" = "On the Rich Man and Lazar," *HS* I, 365-424 (no 16).

"On the Sunday of Hosanna" = "On the Sunday of Hosanna," *HS* I, 445-459 (no 18); ET. by T. Kollamparampil, *FH* X, 246-260.

"Homily on Simon Peter" = "On Simon Peter, When Our Lord said Him, "Get Behind me Satan," *HS* I, 482-506, (no 20), ET. by McCollum, Adam Carter, *MHMJS*, Fascicule 22, 2009.

"On the Commemoration of the Reposed" = "A Homily on the Commemoration of the Reposed, and on the loaf brought for the Eucharist, and that the reposed benefit from the oblations and alms made in their behalf," *HS* I, 531-550 (no 22); ET. from HTM, *TV* 5 (1990), 35-53. Also see R.H. Connolly, *DR* 29 (1910), 260-270.

Bedjan *HS* II

"Jacob of Sarugh's Homily on Malkisedeq" = "That which David said about Our Lord, "Your are the Priest forever, in the in the Resemblance of Malkisedeq," *HS* II, 197-209 (no 41), ET. by Jacob Thekeparampil, *The Harp* 4.1(1993), 53-64.

"On Our Lord is Portrayed as Food and Drink" = "On Our Lord is Portrayed as Food and Drink," *HS* II, 228-244, (no 43).

"On the Samaritan Woman" = "On the Samaritan Woman," *HS* II, 281-312, (no 46).

"On the Three Dead People" = "On the Three Dead People whom Our Lord Raised," *HS* II, 334-347, (no 48).

"On the Transfiguration of Our Lord" = "On the Transfiguration of Our Lord on the Mountain of Tabor and on Moses and Elijah who were Talking with Him," *HS* II, 347-375, (no 49); ET. by T. Kollamparampil, *FH* VIII, 201-230.

"Homily on Ten Virgins" = "Homily on Ten Virgins: Portrayed in the Gospel of Our Savior," *HS* II, 375-401, (no 50); ET. from HTM, *TV* 4.1(1992), 39-62.

"On the Sinful Woman" = "On the Sinful Woman Whom Our Lord Forgiven Her Debts," *HS* II, 402-427, (no 51); ET. by Scott Johnson, *Sobornost* 24.1(2002), 56-88.

"Holy Week, Friday Night" = "Holy Week, Friday Night," *HS* II, 522-554 (no 53.5).

"Holy Week, Friday of Passion" = "Holy Week, Friday of Passion," *HS* II, 554-579 (no 53.6); ET. excerpts from Connolly, *The DR* 27(1908), 285-287.

Holy Week, Saturday Night" = Holy Week, Saturday Night," *HS* II, 580-598, (no 53.7).

"Sunday of Resurrection" = "Sunday of Resurrection," *HS* II, 611-623 (no 54); ET. Kollamparampil, *FH* XIII, 292-305.

"On the Resurrection of Our Lord" = "On the Resurrection of Our Lord," *HS* II 624-635, (no. 55); E.T. by T. Kollamparampil, *FH* XIV, 306-317.

"On the New Sunday and On the Apostle Thomas" = "On the New Sunday and On the Apostle Thomas," *HS* II, 649-669, (no 57); ET. from HTM *TV* 4.2 (1992), 49-66.

"On the Sunday of Pentecost" = "On the Sunday of Pentecost," *HS* II, 670-689, (no 59); ET. by T. Kollamparampil, *FH* XVII, 353-369.

"On Paul the Apostle" = "On Paul the Apostle," *HS* II, 747-769, (no 62); ET. from HTM, *TV* 10 (1991), 57-73.

Bedjan *HS* III

"On the Creation of Creatures: Day One" = "On the Creation of Creatures: Day One," *HS* III, 1-27, (no 71.6); ET. R. D. Young, "Homilies of Six Days of Creation: The First Day," in Trigg, J.W., *Message of the Fathers of the Church* IX, Wilmington: Michael Glazier, 1988, 184-202.

"On the Creation of Creatures: Day Six" = "On the Creation of Creatures: Day Six," *HS* III, 97-128, (no 71.6); FT. by B.P. Sony, in *ParOr*, 11(1983), 172-179.

"On Our Lord and Jacob" = "On Our Lord and Jacob, and the Church and Rachel, and Leah and Synagogue," *HS* III, 208-229 (no 75); ET. from HTM, *TV* 4.4 (1993), 50-64.

"On the Veil of Moses" = "On the Veil of Moses' Face," *HS* III, 283-305, (no 79); ET. Brock, Sebastian, *MHMJS* 1(2009); *Sobornost* 3(1981), 72-84; *Studies in Syriac Spirituality*, Bangalore: Dharmaram Publications, 2008, 177-209.

"Why our Lord Abode upon the earth for Thirty years" = "Why Our Lord Abode upon the Earth for Thirty Years before He Wrought Miracles in the World," *HS* III 321-334, (no 80); ET. from HTM, *TV* 4 (1990), 37-49.

"On the Mysteries of Types and Figures of Christ" = "On the Mysteries of Types and Figures of Christ," *HS* III, 305-321, (no 81); ET. by S. P. Brock, as part of M. St. in Syriac Studies, Oxford, 1991-2; Konat, J. A., *Le Museon* 118 (2005).

"On Kingdom of Heaven Unto Leaven" = "On that which Our Lord Said in the Gospel, that on 'the Kingdom of Heaven is Like Unto Leaven,' which a woman took and hid in three measures of meal, till the whole was leavened," *HS* III 411-424, (no. 86); ET. from HTM, *TV* 3 (1989), 44-57.

"On the Eucharist" = "On the Eucharist," HS III 646-663 (no 95); ET. "A Homily of Mar Jacob of Serugh on the Reception of the Holy Mysteries," by R. H. Connolly, *DR* 27 (1908), 278-287.

"A Homily on Stephen" = "A Homily on Stephen, the Arch Deacon and First-born of the Martyrs," *HS* III 710-723 (no 98); ET. from HTM, *TV* 7 (1990), 38-54.

"On the faith" = "On the Faith," *HS* III, 581-646 (no 94).

"Praises of John the Baptist" = "Praises of John the Baptist," *HS* III, 687-719 (no 97); FT of excerpts by J. Babakan, *Revue de l"Orient Chritien* 19 (1914), 67-68, 1434-1438.

Bedjan *HS* IV

"The Second Homily on Eliasaeus and on the King of Moab" = "The Second Homily on Elissaeus and on the King of Moab who Sacrificed his Son on the Wall," *HS* IV, 282-296 (no. 117); ET. from HTM, *TV* 1 (1989), 51-67.

"On Prophet Jonah" = "On Prophet Jonah," *HS* IV, 368-491 (no 122); ET. of excerpts by Bcheiry, "Repentance and Fasting," in George Anton Kiraz (ed.), *Jacob of Serugh and His Times,* 1-28.

"On Abraham and His Types" = "On Abraham and His Types," *HS* IV, 61-103 (no 109); ET. by R.E. McCarron, *Hugoye* I.1 (1998); and by Thelly, in *The Harp* 24 (2009), 179-88.

"Ezekiel's Vision on Chariot" = "Ezekiel's Vision on Chariot," *HS* IV, 543-610, (no 125); on this see A. Golitzin, in *SVTQ* 46:1-2 (2003), 323-364.

"On the Consecration of the Church" = "On the Consecration of the Church," *HS* IV, 767-789, (no 134); GT. Grill, S., *Jacob von Sarug Die Kirche und die Forschung,* Heiligenkreuzer Studien, 13, 1963.

Bedjan *HS* V

"On Jephthah's Daughter" = "On Jephtha's Daughter," *HS* V, 306-330, (no 159); ET. Susan A. Harvey, "Jacob of Sarugh's Homily on Jephthah's Daughter," Texts from Christian late antiquity 22. *MHMJS*, fascicule 16, 2010.

"A Homily on Samson" = "A Homily on Samson," *HS* V, 331-355 (no. 160); ET. from HTM, *TV* 11 (1992), 50-70.

"On the Presentation of Our Lord in the Temple" = "On the Presentation of Our Lord in the Temple and on the Reception of Him by Simeon," *HS* V, 447-466 (no. 165); ET. by T. Kollamparampil, *FH* V, 138-158.

D. Jacques De Saroug: *Homelies Contre Les Jufis*, M. Albert (ed.) *PO* Tome XXXVIII, (Fac. 1, No 174), Turnhout: Diffusion Mondiale, 1976. [Critical edition with FT. References to these

homilies are indicated with the abbreviation *HCJ* + Number of the homily in Roman numerals + line(s)].

HCJ I	De la Seconde Personne de la Trinite
HCJ II	De la Circoncision et de la Foi
HCJ III	Du Sabbat et de la Typologie
HCJ IV	De la Pedagogie divine

E. **Jacqes De Sarough: *Quarte Homelies Metriques sur La Creation,* Alwan Khalil (ed. & tr.), in *CSCO* Vols 508/509, (Syri 214/215),** [Critical edition with FT, References to these homilies are indicated with abbreviation *QHC* + Number of the homily in Roman Numerals + Line(s) + Page number].

QHC I	*Mêmrô* sur: Dieu dit: "Venez, fasons I'homme à notre image comme à notre resemblance" et sur la naissance du Christ.
QHC II	*Mêmrô* de Saint Mār Jacques sur: Adam a-t-il ete cree mortel ou immortel?
QHC III	De Saint Mār Jacques sur: *Mêmrô* sur la sortie d'Adam du Paradis.
QHC IV	*Mêmrô* de Saint Mār Jacques sur I'agencement d'Adam.

F. **Jacques de Saroug: *Six Homélies Festales en Prose,* (ed.) F. Rilliet, *Patrologia Orientalis* 43 (Fascicule 4, No 196), Turnhout 1986,** [Critical edition with FT; References to these homilies are indicated with the abbreviation *SHF* + Number of Homily in Roman Numerals + Paragraph(s)]; E.T. of the following homilies IV, VII, IX, XI, XII, XV in T. Kollamparampil, *FH.*

SHF I	On the Nativity	= FH IV
SHF II	On the Epiphany	= FH VII
SHF III	On the Forty Days' Fasting	= FH IX
SHF IV	On the Sunday of Hosannas	= FH XI
SHF V	On the Friday of the Passion	= FH XII
SHF VI	On the Sunday of Resurrection	= FH XV

G. ***S. Martyrii, qui et Sahadona, quae supersunt omnia,*** P. Bedjan, (ed.), Paris 1902, [References to this volume are indicated with the abbreviation *SMS* + Page(s) + line(s)]

"On the Perpetual Virginity" = "On the Perpetual Virginity," *SMS*, 639-661 (no. 4); ET. by Puthuparampil, James. *Mariological Thought of Mar Jacob of Serugh* (451–521), Appendix i-xxi; IT. by C. Vona, "Sulla

Santa Generatrice di Dio e Vergine perpetual Maria," Lt (Nova Series) 19(1953), 169-185.

"On the Nativity of Our Redeemer" = "On the Nativity of Our Redeemer According to the flesh," *SMS*, 720-774 (no. 6); ET. by T. Kollamparampil, *FH* I, 37-93.

"The Second Homily on the Nativity" = "The Second Homily on the Nativity," *SMS* 775-790 (no. 7); ET. by T. Kollamparampil, *FH* II, 94-107.

"On the Nativity of Our Lord" = "On the Nativity of Our Lord," *SMS* 790-808 (no. 8); ET. by T. Kollamparampil, *FH* III, 108-127.

"On the Ascension of Our Lord" = "On the Ascension of Our Lord to Heaven," *SMS* 808-832 (no. 9); ET. by T. Kollamparampil, *FH* XVI, 320-352.

H. Other Collections

"An Acrostic Poem on the Soul by Jacob of Serugh," ET. Brock, Sebastian, *Sobornost* 23.1 (2001), 40-44.

"Homily on Spectacle of the Theater," ET. C. Moss, *Le'Muesion,* 48 (1935), 87-112.

Jacob of Serugh Select Festal Homilies, Thomas Kollamparampil, (ET) Rome & Bangalore, Dharmaram Publications, 1997. [References to these homilies are indicated with abbreviation *FH* + Number of the homily in Roman numerals + page(s) + line(s).

"Jacob of Serugh's Verse Homily on Tamar (Gen. 38)," ET. Brock, Sebastian, *Le Museon* 115.3-4 (2002): 279-315.

"The Syrian Orthodox Reaction to the Council of Chalcedon: Jacob of Serugh's Homily on the Council of Chalcedon," E.T. Brock, Sebastian in *Texts and Studies (Athens)* 8-10 (1989-1991), 448-459.

Amar, "A metrical Homily on Holy Mar Ephrem," = Amar, Joseph Phillip, ed. *A Metrical Homily on Holy Mar Ephrem by Mar Jacob of Sarug: Critical Edition of the Syriac Text, Translation and Introduction. PO* 47.1. Turnhout: Brepols, 1995.

Bedjan, *LP*; ET. "Homily on the Blessed Virgin Mary," = Holy Transfiguration Monastery, "A Homily on the Blessed Virgin Mother of God, Mary," in *TV*, 5/1, 17 (1993), 2-28.

Brock, "A Prayer Song by St. Jacob of Serugh Recovered" = Brock, Sebastian, "A Prayer Song by St. Jacob of Serugh Recovered," in George Anton Kiraz (ed.), *Jacob of Serugh and His Times: Studies in Sixth-Century Christianity.* Piscataway, NJ: Gorgias Press, 2010, 29-39.

Brock, "Jacob of Serugh: A Poem on Soul" = Brock, Sebastian P., "An Acrostic Poem on the Soul by Jacob of Serugh," *Sobornost* 23.1 (2001), 40-44.

Brock, "Sleepers of Soul" = "Jacob of Serugh's Poem on the Sleepers of Ephesus." ET. Brock, Sebastian, in *"I Sowed Fruits into Hearts" (Odes Sol. 17:13): Festschrift for Professor Michael Lattke*. (ed.), Pauline Allen, and Majella Franzmann, and Rick Strelan. Early Christian Studies 12. Strathfield, NSW: St Pauls Publications, 2007, 13-30.

Mathews, "Jacob Serugh, Homily on Good Friday" = Mathews, Edward G., "Jacob Serugh, Homily on Good Friday and other Armenian Treasures: First Glances," in George Anton Kiraz, (ed.), *Jacob of Serugh and His Times: Studies in Sixth-Century Syriac Christianity,* Piscataway, NJ: Gorgias Press, 2010, 133-163.

II. SECONDARY SOURCES

AAA = Apocryphal Acts of the Apostles, Vol. I, Wright, W., (ed.), London, 1871; *The Acts of Thomas: Introduction, Text, Commentary*, A. F. J. Klijn, (ET.), Leiden: E. J. Brill, 1962.

Barhadbsabba, *L'histore ecclesiastique* = Barhadbsabba Arbaia, *La seconde partie de l'histore ecclesiastique, de Barhadbasabba Arbaia t controverse de Theodore de Mopsueste avec les Maceedonens,* (ed.), F. Nau, *PO* IX, Paris, 1913.

Chaldean Breviary, III= *Breverium Iuxta Ritum Syrorum Orientalium id est Chaldeaorum*, 3 Vols. Bedjan (ed)., Paris:1887<Reprint Rome:1938>.

CH = Des heiligen Ephraem des Syrers Hymnen contra Haereses, E. Beck, (ed.) CSCO 169-170, Syr. 76-77. Louvain: L. Durbecq, 1957.

Charlesworth, *Odes of Solomon,* = Charleswoth, J.H., *The Odes of Solomon: Edited with Translation and Notes*, Oxford: Clarendon Press, 1973.

Chrysostom, "Instructions to Catechumens" ET. Stephens, W. R. W., *NPNF* Vol. 9, NY: Hendrickson, 1989.

Chrysostom, *Homily on Col.* = S. P. N. Johannis Chrysostomi, Archiepiscopi Constantinopolitani, *Oera Omnia Quæ EjusNomine Circumferuntur,* (ed.), J. P. Migne, *PG* 62, Turnholti, Belium: Brepols Editores Pontifich, (no Year); ET. Saint John Chrysostom, *The Homilies of S. John Chrysostom Arch Bishop of Constantinople On the Epistles of S. Paul the Apostle to the Philippians, Colossians, and Thessalonians*, Oxford: James Parker & Co and Rivingtons, 1879.

Chrysostom, *XIX* = Roth, Catherine P., and David Anderson, ET. *ST John Chrysostom on Marriage and Family Life*, Crestwood, NY: SVS Press, 2003.

CJul = Des heiligen Ephrem des Syrers Hymnen de Paradiso und Contra Julianum, (ed.) E. Beck, CSCO 174/175 (Syri 78/79), Louvain, 1957.

Clement of Alexandria, *Stromateis* = Clement of Alexandria, *Stromateis*, http://www.earlychristianwritings.com/text/clement-stromata-book3-english.html, Online Resource, Retrieved on 1/10/2014.

CNis = *Des heiligen Ephraem des Syrers Carmina Nisibena* I, (ed.) E. Beck, CSCO 218-219, (Syr. 92-93.), Louvain: Secretariat du CorpusSCO, 1961, and *Des heiligen Ephraem des Syrers Carmina Nisibena* II, (ed.) E. Beck, CSCO 240-241, (Syr. 102-103), Louvain: Secretariat du CorpusSCO, 1963.

Crucif = *Des heiligen Ephraem des Syrers Paschahymnen: De azymnis, de crucifixione, de resurrection*, (ed.) E. Beck, CSCO 248-249, (Syri. 108-109), Louvain: Secretariat du CorpusSCO, 1964.

Cureton, W., (ed. & tr.), *Ancient Syriac Document Related to the Earliest Establishment of Christianity in Edessa and the Neighbouring Countries from the Year After Our Lord's Ascension to the Beginning of Fourth Century*, London: William and Norgate, 1864.

Cyprian, "The Epistles of Cyprian" = Cyprian, "The Epistles of Cyprian," in *ANF* Vol. 5, Alexander Roberts and James Donaldson (eds.), Peabody, MA: Hendrickson Publishers, 1994.

Cyprian, *The Treatises of S. Cœlius Cyprian* = *The Treatises of S. Cœlius Cyprian Bishop of Carthage and Martyr*, A Library of Fathers of the Holy Catholic Church, Anterior to the Division of the East and West Vol. III, Translated by the members of the English Church, Oxford: John Henry Parker, J. G. F. and J. Rivington, 1840.

Didascalia = *Didascalia Apostolorum,* (*CSCO* 401-2), Louvain, Washington DC: *Corpus Scriptorum Christianorum Orientalium,* 1979.

Epiph = *Des heiligen Ephraem des Syrers Hymnen de Nativitate (Epiphania)*, (ed.) E. Beck, CSCO 186-187, (Syr. 82-83), Louvain: Secretariat du CorpusSCO, 1959.

Epiphany Hymn: Anonymous Author = Epiphany Hymn: Anonymous Author, in ET. Brock, Sebastian, *The Treasure House of Mysteries,* Crestwood, NY: SVS Press, 2012, 253-258.

Exegesis on the Soul. = Robinson, James M., and Richard Smith, *The Nag Hammadi Library in English*, San Francisco: Harper & Row, 1988. 180-187.

Gospel of Nicodemus = *Gospel of Nicodemus*, Online source, Retrieved on 19/11/ 2013, http://www.sacred-texts.com/bib/lbob/lbob10.htm.

HEcc = *Des heiligen Ephraem des Syrers Hymnen de Ecclesia*, (ed.) E. Beck, CSCO 198-199, (Syr. 84-85), Louvain: Secretariat du CorpusSCO, 1960.

HFid = *Des heiligen Ephraem des Syrers Hymnen de Fide*, (ed.) E. Beck, CSCO 154-155, (Syr. 73-74), Louvain: L. Durbecq, 1955.

HNat = *Des heiligen Ephraem des Syrers Hymnen de Nativitate (Epiphania)*, (ed.) E. Beck, CSCO 186-187, (Syr. 82-83), Louvain: Secretariat du CorpusSCO, 1959.

HPar = *Des heiligen Ephraem des Syrers Hymnen de Paradiso und contra Julianum*, (ed.) E. Beck, CSCO 174-175, (Syr. 78-79), Louvain: Peeters, 1957.

HVir = *Des heiligen Ephraem des Syrers Hymnen de Virginitate*, (ed.) E. beck, CSCO 223-224, Syr. 94-95. Louvain: Secretariat du CorpusSCO, 1962.

Ignatius, *Epistle to Ephesians* = Ignatius, *Epistle to Ephesians,* in *ANF* Vol. 1, *The Apostolic Fathers with Justin Martyr and Irenaeus,* Alexander Roberts and James Donaldson, (eds.), Peabody, MA: Hendrickson Publishers, 2004.

II Clement = *Lactantius, Venantius, Asterius, Victorinus, Dionysius, Apostolic Teaching and Constitutions, 2 Clememt, Early Liturgies* in *ANF Vol. 7,* Alexander Roberts and James Donaldson, (eds.), Peabody, MA: Hendrickson Publishers, 2004.

Irenaeus, *Against Heresies* = *The Apostolic Fathers with Justin Martyr and Irenaeus,* in *ANF* Vol. 1, Alexander Roberts and James Donaldson, (eds.), Peabody, MA: Hendrickson Publishers, 2004.

Justin, *Dial.* = Justin Martyr, "Dialogue with Trypho, a Jew," in *The Apostolic Fathers with Justin Martyr and Irenaeus, ANF* Vol. I., Alexander Roberts and James Donaldson, (eds.), Peabody, MA: Hendrickson Publishers, 2004.

Kashtanubhavazhchayile Namaskarakramam = *Malankara Orthodox Suriyany Kristhyanikalude Kashtanubhavazhchayile Namaskarakramam: Dukhavelliyazhcha šušrooshakal chernnathu (Passion Week Service of the Malankara Orthodox Syrian Christians: Including Good Friday Service*), Kottayam, Kerala: MOC Publications, 2011.

Koodašakramangal = *Malankara Orthodox Suriyani Sabhayile Koodašakramangal* (*Rites of Sacraments in the Malankara Orthodox Syrian Church*), MT. Malankara Malpan Konat Abraham Kathanar, Kottayam, Kerala: MOC Publications, 2014.

Ktobo d-Thakso dAnaphoro = *Ktobo d-Thakso dAnaphoro* (*Book of the Order of Anaphora*) 13 orders Syriac with Malayalam Translation, MT. by Konat Mathan Malpan, Kottayam: MOC Publications, 2011.

Ktobo d-zlooto šheemto= *Ktobo d-zlooto šheemto* (The Book of Common Prayer in Syriac), Kottayam: MOC Publications, 1997.

Mathews, *Armenian Commentary on Genesis* = Mathews, Edward, G., *Armenian Commentary on Genesis Attributed to Ephrem the Syrian,* CSCO 573, Lovanii: Aedius Peeters, 1998.

Mathews, *GenComm.* = Mathew, Edward G., "Commentary on Genesis" in McVey, Kathleen., (ed.), *St. Ephrem the Syrian: Selected Prose Works: Commentary on Genesis, Commentary on Exodus, Homily on Our Lord, Letter to Publius,* The Fathers of the Church, Vol. 91, ET. Edward G. Mathews, Joseph P. Amar, Washington DC, The Catholic University of America Press, 1994.

McCarthy, *CommDiat.* = McCarthy, Carmel, (ET), *Saint Ephrem's Commentary on Tatian's Diatessaron: An English Translation of Chester Beatty Syriac MS 709 with Introduction and Notes,* (Journal of Semitic Studies Supplement 2), Oxford: Oxford University Press, 1993.

McLeod, *Narsai's Metrical Homilies* = *Narsai's Metrical Homilies on the Nativity, Epiphany, Passion, Resurrection, and Ascension*, ed. Graffin, F., ET Frederick McLeod, *PO* 182, Turnhout/Belgique: Brepols, 1979.

McVey, "Letter to Publius" = McVey, "Letter to Publius," *in* McVey, Kathleen, (ed.), *St. Ephrem the Syrian: Selected Prose Works: Commentary on Genesis, Commentary on Exodus, Homily on Our Lord, Letter to Publius,* The Fathers of the Church, Vol. 91, ET. Edward G. Mathews, Joseph P. Amar, Washington DC., The Catholic University of America Press, 1994.

McVey, *Homily on Our Lord* = McVey, *Homily on Our Lord,* in McVey, Kathleen., (ed.), *St. Ephrem the Syrian: Selected Prose Works: Commentary on Genesis, Commentary on Exodus, Homily on Our Lord, Letter to Publius,* The Fathers of the Church, Vol. 91, ET. Edward G. Mathews, Joseph P. Amar, Washington DC., The Catholic University of America Press, 1994.

Mingana, *Commentary of Theodore* = Mingana, A., *Commentary of Theodore of Mopsuestia on the Lord's Prayer and on the Sacraments of Baptism and Eucharist,* Woodbridge Studies VI; Cambridge, Mass., 1933.

Narsai, Dedication of the Church, = Mingana A., (ed.), *Narsai Doctrois Syri Homiliae et Carmina*, 2 Vols. Mosul, 1905.

Origen, *Commentary on the Gospel According to John* = Origen, *Commentary on the Gospel According to John: Book 13-32.* ET. Ronald E. Heine; FC 89; Washington DC: The Catholic University of America Press, 1993.

Parisot, *Demo* = *Aphraatis Sapientis Persae Demonstrationes,* ed. Parisot, in *PO* I&II, Paris, 1894, 1907; Aphrahat, *Demonstrations* I&II, Kuriakose Valavnolickal (ET.), Kottayam: SEERI, 2005.

Pedalion = *The Rudder* (*Pedalion*) *of the Metaphorical Ship of the One Holy Catholic and Apostolic Church of Orthodox Christians*, (ed. & tr.), by Denver Cummings, Chicago: Orthodox Christian Education Society, 1983.

Prarthanakramam= *Malankara Orthodox Suriyani Kristyanikalude Prarthanakramam* (Order of prayer of Malankara Orthodox Syrian Christians), MT. Konat Mathen Malpan, Kottayam: MOC Publications, 2013.

Promiyon I, = *Orthodox Suriyani Kristhyanikalude Penkisa Namaskarangalkkulla Prumiyonukal: Koodoš edtho muthal Aneede Njayarazcha vare,* (*Promiyons for the Feast days of Orthodox Syrian Christians: From the Sunday of Consecration of the Church to the Sunday of Departed*), Kottayam, Kerala: MOC Publications, 2001.

Promiyon II, = Moonu nombileyum Nalpathu nombileyum Promiyonukal (Promiyons of three-day lent and forty-day lent), MT. Baselios Augen I Catholicos, Kottayam, Kerala: MOC Publications, 2006.

Promiyon III, = *Malankara Orthodox Suriyani Kristyanikalude Kashtanubhazhchayile Promiyon* (*Passion Week Promiyon of Malankara Orthodox Syrian Christians*), MT. Mattakal Alexandrayos Kathanar, Kottyam, Kerala: MOC Publications, 2009.

Promiyon IV, = *Orthodox Suriyani Kristhyanikalude Penkisa Namaskarangalkkulla Prumiyonukal: Uyarppu Njayarazhcha muthal Koodoš Edtho vare* (*Promiyons for the Feast days of Orthodox Syrian Christians: From the Sunday of Resurrection to the Sunday of Consecration of the Church*), MT. Baselios Augen I the Catholicos, Kottayam: MOC Publications, 2006.

Resur = *Des Heiligen Ephraem Des Syrers Paschahymnen: De azymnis, de crucifixione, de resurrection,* (ed.) E. Beck, CSCO 248/249, (Syri. 108-109), Louvain, 1964.

Šavasamskarakramam = *Malankara Orthodox Suriyani Sabhayile Savasamskara Šušrushakramam* (*Funeral Rite in the Malankara Orthodox Syrian Church*), MT. Malankara Malpan Konat Abraham Kathanar, Kottyam, Kerala: MOC, 2009.

Tertullian, Against Marcionism, Online Resource, Retrieved on 1/10/2014. http://www.tertullian.org/anf/anf03/anf03-31.htm#19_10,

Tertullian, *Apology* = *Apology of Tertullian, with English Notes and Preface*, Henry Annesley (ed.), Woodham, Cambridge: J. Deighton, 1883.

Tertullian, *To His Wife* = Tertullian, *To His Wife*, in *ANF* Vol. 5, Alexander Roberts and James Donaldson (eds.), Peabody, MA: Hendrickson Publishers, 1994.

The Apostolic Constitutions = *The Apostolic Constitutions*, ET. Clemens Romanus, Edingburgh: T&T Clark, 1870.

The Church Calendar = *Sabha Pangangam*, Kottayam: MOSC, 2013.

The Didascalia Apostolorum in English = *The Didascalia Apostolorum in English,* ET. Margaret Dunlop Gibson, London: C. J. Clay and Sons, 1903.

The *Gospel of Thomas*, = Gospel of Thomas, Online resource, http://www.holybooks.com/wp-content/uploads/Gospel-of-Thomas-Bruce-Version.pdf retrieved on 10/11/2013.

Theodore of Mopsuestia, *Catechetical Homily* = McLeod, Frederic, *Theodore of Mopsuestia*, (The Early Church Fathers), NY: Routledge, 2009.

Thompson, *The Teaching of Gregory* = Thompson, Robert W., *The Teaching of Saint Gregory: An Early Armenian Catechism*, Harvard Armenian texts and studies, Cambridge, MA: Harvard University Press, 1970.

Tonneau, *Gen.et.Exo.*= Tonneau, R. M., *Sanctin Ephraem Syri In Genesim et in Exodum Commentarii,* CSCO 152, Louvain: Peeters, 1955.

Valavanolickal, *Demonstrations* I&II=, Valavnolickal, Kuriakose. (ET.), *Aphrahat Demonstrations* I&II, Kottayam: SEERI, 2005.

Vishuddha Qurbanakramam, = *Malankara Orthodox Suriyani Kristhyanikalude Sleeba-Kyamtha Namaskaram & Vishuddha Qurbanakramam* (Cross-Resurrection (seasons) worship & Holy Order of Eucharist of Malankara Orthodox Syrian Christians), Kottayam, Kerala: MOSC Publications, 2014.

Vööbus, *The Synodicon in the West Syriac Tradition* = Vööbus, A., *The Synodicon in the West Syriac Tradition I*, CSCO 367, 368, Louvain: Secretariate du CopusSCO, 1975.

Voragine, *The Golden Legend* = Voragine, Jacobus de, *The Golden Legend: Readings on the Saints* Vol. I, William Granger Ryan (tr.), Princeton: Princeton University Press, 1993.

Wright, *The Chronicle of Pseudo-Joshua the Stylite* = Wright, William, (ed.), E.T. Trombly, Frank, R., and John, W. Watt, *The Chronicle of Pseudo-Joshua the Stylite,* Liverpool, 2000, 63-64.

III. STUDIES

"Christianity" = "Christianity", in *The New Encyclopedia Britannica*, Vol. 16, 15th edition, Chicago: Encyclopedia Britannica, 331b.

Abbeloos, *De Vita* = Abbeloos, J. B., *De Vita et Scriptis Sancti Jacobi Barnarum Sarugi in Mesopotamia Episcopi*, Lovaini: Universitatus Typographos, 1867, 86-104.

AbouZayd, *Ihidayutha* = AbouZayd, Shafiq, *Ihidayutha: A Study of the Life of Singleness in the Syriac Orient. From Ignatius of Antioch to Chalcedon 451A. D.*, Oxford: ARAM Society for Syro-Mesopotamian Studies, 1993.

Adam, *Making Sense of New Testament Theology* = Adam, A. K. M., *Making Sense of New Testament Theology: "Modern" Problems and Prospects*, Macon, GA: Mercer University Press, 1995.

Adams, *Experiencing World History* = Adams, Paul, V., Eric D. Langer, Lily Hwa, et.al. *Experiencing World History*, NY: New York University Press, 2000.

Anderson, "Adam and Even in *The Life of* Adam" = Anderson, Gray A., "Adam and Eve in The Life of Adam", in Michael E. Stone and Theodore A. Bergen, (eds.), *Biblical Figures Outside the Bible,* Harrisburg, PA: Trinity Press International, 1999, 7-33.

Apple, "Marriage" = Apple, Raymond, "Marriage", *Encyclopedia Judaica Second Edition,* Vol. 13. Lif-Mek, Fred Skolnik (Chief ed.), NY: Thomson Gale.

Arby, *The Beauty of Communion* = Arby, Gregory, *The Beauty of Communion: From and Expression In Hans Urs von Balthasar*, Bangalore: ATC, 2007.

Avis, *Reshaping Ecumenical Theology* = Avis, Paul, *Reshaping Ecumenical Theology: The Church Made Whole*, London: T&T Clark, 2010.

Baab, "Marriage"= Baab, O. J., "Marriage", in George Arthur Buttrick (ed.), *IDB* Vol. 3. Nashville: Abingdon, 1962.

Badger, *The Nestorians and their Rituals* = Badger, George Percy, *The Nestorians and their Rituals: With Narrative of a Mission to Mesopotamia and Coordistan in 1842-1844 and Late Visit to Those Countries in 1850* II, London: Joseph Masters & Co., No Year.

Baker, "Syriac and the Origin of Monasticism" = Baker, Aelred, "Syriac and the Origin of Monasticism", in *DR*, 86 (1968), 343-352.

Baker, and Morris, *Descartes' Dualism* = Baker, Gordon, and Morris, J. Katherine, *Descartes' Dualism*, ebook: Taylor and Francis, 1995.

Batey, *The New Testament Nuptial Imagery* = Batey, Richard A., *The New Testament Nuptial Imagery,* Leiden: E. J. Brill, 1971.

Baumer, *The Church of the East* = Baumer, Christoph, *The Church of the East: An Illustrated History of Assyrian Christianity*, NY: I. B. Tauris & Co., 2006.

Bcheiry, "Repentance and Fasting" = Bcheiry, Iskandar, "Repentance and Fasting from an Ascetical Perspective: A Comparative Reading of Jacob of Serugh and an Unpublished Version of a Collection of Homilies by Severus of Antioch", in George Anton Kiraz (ed.), *Jacob of Serugh and His Times: Studies in Sixth-Century Christianity,* Piscataway, NJ: Gorgias Press, 2010, 1-27.

Beggiani, *Early Syriac Theology* = Beggiani, J. Seely. *Early Syriac Theology with Special Reference to Maronite Tradition,* NY: University Press of America, 1983.

Beggiani, *Introduction to Eastern Christian Spirituality* = Beggiani, Seely, *Introduction to Eastern Christian Spirituality: The Syriac Tradition*, Scranton: University of Scranton Press, 1991.

Belkin, "The Problem of Paul's Background = Belkin, Samuel, "The Problem of Paul's Background", *JBL* 54 (1935), 41-60.

Belkin, "The Problem of Paul's Background" = Samuel Belkin, "The Problem of Paul's Background", *JBL,* 54 (1935), 41-60.

Benin, "Commandments, Covenants, and Jews = Benin, Stephen, D., "Commandments, Covenants, and Jews: In Aphrahat, Ephrem, and Jacob of Serugh", in David R. Blumenthal, (ed.), *Approaches Judaism in Medieval Times,* Chico, CA: Scholars Press, 1984.

Berkouwer, *Studies in Dogmatics* = Berkouwer, G. C., *Studies in Dogmatics: The Person of Christ*, Grand Rapids, MI: Wm. B. Eerdmans Publications, 1980.

Berlin, "Parallelism" = Berlin, "Parallelism", in *The Anchor Bible Dictionary*, Vol. 5, (ed.), David Noel Freedman, New York: Doubleday, 1992, 155-162.

Bickell, *Bibliothek* = Thalhofer, Valentine, and Francis Xavier Reithmayer, *Bibliothek der Kirchenväter: Auswahl der vorzüglichsten patristischen Werke in deutscher Übersetzung*, Kempten: Kösel, 1869.

Biesen, *Simple and Bold* = Biesen, Kees Den, *Simple and Bold: Ephrem's Art of Symbolic Thought*, Piscataway, NJ: Gorgias Press, 2006.

Botha, "Ephrem the Syrian's Treatment of Tamar" = Botha, Phil J., "Ephrem the Syrian's Treatment of Tamar in Comparison to that in Jewish Sources", *Acta Patristica et Byzantina* 6 (1995), 15-26.

Bourg, *Where Two or Three are Gathered* = Bourg, Florence Caffrey, *Where Two or Three are Gathered: Christian Families as Domestic Churches*, South Bend, IN: University of Norte Dame Press, 2004.

Bouyer, *The Church of God* = Bouyer, Louis, *The Church of God: Body of Christ and the Temple of Spirit*, ET. by C. U. Quinn, Chicago: Franciscan Herald Press, 1982.

Brock, "A dialogue Poem on the Sacrifice of Isaac" = Brock, Sebastian, "A dialogue Poem on the Sacrifice of Isaac", *The Harp* 7 (1994), 54-72.

Brock, "Baptismal Themes in the Writings of Jacob of Serugh"= Brock, Sebastian, "Baptismal Themes in the Writings of Jacob of Serugh", in

Symposium Syriacum 1976, OCA 205, Roma: Pontificium Institutum Orientalium Studiorum, 1978.

Brock, "Clothing Metaphors" = Brock, Sebastian, "Clothing Metaphors as a Means of Theological Expression in Syriac Tradition", in M. Schmidt, (ed.), *Typus Symbol Allegorie bei den östlichen Vätern und ihren Parallelen im Mittelalter*, Regensburg: Verlag Friedrich Puset, 1982, 11-40.

Brock, "Come, Compassionate Mother" = Brock, Sebastian, "Come Compassionate Mother…, Come Holy Spirit: A Forgotten Aspect of Early Eastern Christian Imagery", in Brock, Sebastian, *Fire from Heaven: Studies in Syriac Theology and Liturgy*, (Variorum Collected Studies Series), Aldershot/Burlington Ashgate Variorum, 2006, 249-257.

Brock, "Dialogue Hymns of the Syriac Churches" = Brock, Sebastian, "Dialogue Hymns of the Syriac Churches", *Sobornost / Eastern Churches Review* 5.2 (1983), 35-45.

Brock, "Dramatic Dialogue Poems" = Brock, Sebastian, "Dramatic Dialogue Poems", in H. H. W. Drijvers, R. Lavenant, C. Molenberg, et.al., (eds.), *IV Symposium Syriacum 1984: Literary Genres in Syriac Literature*, OCA 229, Rome: Pontificum Institutum Studiorum Orientalium, 1987, 135-147.

Brock, "Jacob of Serugh': A select Bibliographical Guide" = Brock, Sebastian, "Jacob of Serugh': A select Bibliographical Guide", in (ed.), George Anton Kiraz, *Jacob of Serugh and His Times: Studies in Sixth-Century Syriac Christianity,* Piscataway, NJ: Gorgias Press, 2010, 219-244.

Brock, "Jacob's Forgotten *Sughyotho* = Brock, Sebastian, "Jacob's Forgotten *Sughyotho*", in George Anton Kiraz, (ed.), *Jacob of Serugh and His Times: Studies in Sixth-Century Syriac Christianity,* Piscataway, NJ: Gorgias Press, 2010, 39-50.

Brock, "Mysteries in the Hidden Side of Christ" = Brock, Sebastian, "The Mysteries hidden in the side of Christ [Jn 19:34 in Syriac tradition]", *Sobornost* 7.6 (1978), 462-72.

Brock, "Some Important Baptismal Themes" = Brock, Sebastian, "Some important baptismal themes in the Syriac tradition", *The Harp* 4.1-3 (1991), 189-214.

Brock, "Syriac Dialogue Poems" = Brock, Sebastian, "Syriac Dialogue Poems: Marginalia to a Recent Edition", *LeMuseon* 97 (1984), 29-58.

Brock, "Syriac Dispute Poems: The Various Types" = Brock, Sebastian, "Syriac Dispute Poems: The Various Types", in Reinink, Gerrit J. and Vanstiphout, Herman L.J., (eds.), *Dispute Poems and Dialogues in the Ancient and Mediaeval Near East: Forms and Types of Literary Debates in Semitic and Related Literature*, OLA 42. Louvain: Peeters, 1991, 109-119.

Brock, "Syriac Poetry on Biblical Themes…" = Brock, Sebastian, "Syriac Poetry on Biblical Themes, 2. A Dialogue Poem on the Sacrifice of Isaac (Genesis 22)", *The Harp* 7 (1994), 55-72.

Brock, "The Bridal Chamber of the Light" = Brock, Sebastian, "The Bridal Chamber of the Light: A Distinctive Feature of the Syriac Liturgical Tradition", in *The Harp* 18 (2005), 179-191.

Brock, "The Dispute Between the Cherub and the Thief" = Brock, Sebastian, "The Dispute Between the Cherub and the Thief" *Hugoye* 5.2 (July 2002).

Brock, "The Dispute Poem from Sumer to Syriac" = Brock, Sebastian, "The Dispute Poem from Sumer to Syriac" *JCSSS* 1 (2001), 1-10.

Brock, "The Wedding Feast of Blood on Golgotha" = Brock, Sebastian, "The Wedding Feast of Blood on Golgotha. An unusual aspect of John 19:34 in Syriac tradition", *The Harp* 6.2 (1993), 121-34.

Brock, *Bible in Syriac Tradition,* = Brock, Sebastian, *The Bible in the Syriac Tradition,* Kottayam: SEERI Correspondence Course no 1, 1989.

Brock, *Bride of Light* = Sebastian P. Brock, *Bride of Light: Hymns on Mary from the Syriac Churches,* (*Moran Etho* 6), Kottayam, Kerala: SEERI, 2009.

Brock, *Holy Spirit in Syriac Baptismal Tradition* = Brock, Sebastian, *The Holy Spirit in the Syrian Baptismal Tradition* (Syrian Churches Series 9), Kottayam, Kerala, 1979.

Brock, *Hymns on Paradise* = Brock, Sebastian, *Saint Ephrem the Syrian, Hymns on Paradise* (Introduction and Translation), Crestwood, NY: SVS Press, 1990.

Brock, "Sogitha, Syriac Dialogue Hymns" = Brock, Sebastian, *Sogitha,* "Syriac Dialogue Hymns", in Syrian Churches Series XI, Jacob Vellian, (ed.), Kottayam: Jacob Vellian, 1987.

Brock, *Studies in Syriac Spirituality* = Brock, Sebastian, *Studies in Syriac Spirituality*, Bangalore: Dharmaram Publications, 2008.

Brock, The Epiklesis in the Antiochene Baptismal Ordines" = Brock, Sebastian, The Epiklesis in the Antiochene Baptismal Ordines", in Brock, Sebastian, *Fire from Heaven: Studies in Syriac Theology and Liturgy*, (Variorum Collected Studies Series), Ashgate: Variorum, 2006, 183-214.

Brock, *The Treasure House of Mysteries* = Brock, Sebastian (ET) *Treasure House of Mysteries: Explorations of the Sacred Text through Poetry in the Syriac Tradition*, Crestwood, NY: SVS Press, 2011.

Buchan, "Paradise as the Landscape of Salvation in Ephrem the Syrian" = Buchan, Thomas, "Paradise as the Landscape of Salvation in Ephrem the Syrian", in Michael J. Christensen, and Jeffery A. Wittung, (eds.), *Partakers of the Divine Nature: The History and Development of Deification in the Christian Traditions*, Teaneck, NJ: Fairleigh Dickinson University Press, 2008.

Buchan, *Blessed is He Who Brought Adam from Sheol* = Buchan, *Blessed is He Who Brought Adam from Sheol: Christ's Descent to the Dead in Theology of Ephrem the Syrian,* (Gorgias Studies in Early Christianity and Patristics 13), Piscataway, NJ: Gorgias Press, 2004.

Budge, *The Book of the Cave of Treasures* = Budge, E. A. Willas, *The Book of the Cave of Treasures,* NY: Cosimo, 2005.

Bundy, "Language and the Knowledge of God in Ephrem Syrus" = Bundy, David, C., "Language and the Knowledge of God in Ephrem Syrus", in *Dialogue and Alliance*, Winter, 1.4 (1988), 56-64.

Cahill, "Hermeneutical Implications of Typology" = Cahill, P. Joseph, "Hermeneutical Implications of Typology", *CBQ* 44.2 (April, 1982), 266-281.

Carr and Conway, "Constructions of Gender and Bodies" = Conway, "The Divine-Human Marriage Matrix and Constructions of Gender and 'Bodies' in the Christian Bible", in Nissinen, Martti, and Risto Uro, (eds.), *Sacred Marriages: The Divine-human Sexual Metaphor from Sumer to Early Christianity*, Winona Lake, IN: Eisenbrauns, 2008, 275-303.

Chavasse, *The Bride of Christ* = Chavasse, Claude, *The Bride of Christ: An Inquiry into the Nuptial Element in Christianity,* London: Faber and Faber, 1940.

Chesnut, *Three Monophysite Christologies* = Chesnut, Roberta, *Three Monophysite Christologies,* London: Oxford University Press, 1976.

Chukwu, *The Church as the Extended Family of God* = Chukwu, Donatus Oluwa, *The Church as the Extended Family of God: Toward a New Direction for African Ecclesiology*, Bloomington, IN: Xlibris, 2011.

Clark, "The Celibate Bridegroom and Virginal Brides" = Clark, Elizabeth, "The Celibate Bridegroom and His Virginal Brides: Metaphor and the Marriage of Jesus in Early Christian Ascetic Exegesis", *Church History,* 77 (2008), 1-25.

Collins, "Church, Idea of the" = Collins, Raymond E., "Church, Idea of the", in *NIDB* Vol. I, ed. Katharine Doob Sakenfeld, Nashville: Abingdon Press, 2006, 644-455.

Cross, "*Apophatic Theology*" = F. L. Cross & E. A. Livingstone, "*Apophatic* Theology", *Dictionary of the Christian Church,* Massachusetts: Hendrickson Publications, 2007.

Cross, *Ancient Library* = Cross, Frank Moore, *The Ancient Library of Qumran and Modern Biblical Studies*, Garden City, NY: Doubleday, 1958.

Cummings, "Mystical Women and the Eucharist" = Cummings, Owen F., "Mystical Women and the Eucharist", *Antiphon* 5:3 (2000), 11-20.

Daniélou, *Bible and the Liturgy* = Daniélou, Jean, *The Bible and the Liturgy*, Notre Dame: University of Notre Dame Press, 1956.

Daniélou, *The Development of Christian Doctrine*, = Daniélou, Jean, *The Development of Christian Doctrine Before the Council of Nicaea,* Vol. 1: *The Theology of Jewish Christianity,* ET. by J. A. Baker, London: Darton, Longman & Todd, 1964.

Daniélou, *Theology of the Jewish Christianity* = Daniélou, Jean, *Theology of the Jewish Christianity*, ET. by John A. Baker, Chicago: Henry Regnery, 1964.

Davila, "Moriah" = Davila, James, R., "Moriah" in Freedman, David Noel, and Gary A Herion, (eds.), *The Anchor Yale Bible Dictionary*: K-N, NY: Doubleday, 1992.

De Halleux, *Philiene de Mabbog, Lettre aux monies de Senoun = A. de Halleux, Deahalleux Aa, Phyloxene De Mabbog. Lettre Aux Moines De Senoun,* Syr. 99. CSCO Vol. 231, Leuven: Secretariat du CorpusSCO, 1963.

DeConick, "The Great Mystery of Marriage" = DeConick, April, "The Great Mystery of Marriage: Sex and Conception in Ancient Valentine Traditions", in *VC* 57 (2003), 307-342.

Deiss, *Springtime of the Liturgy* = Deiss, Lucien, (ed.), *Spring Time of the Liturgy: Liturgical Texts of the First Four Centuries*, Collegeville, MN: The Liturgical Press, 1979.

DeSimone, *The Bride and the Bridegroom of the Fathers* = DeSemone, Russel J., *The Bride and the Bridegroom of the Fathers: An Anthology of Patristic Interpretations of Song of Songs*, Sussidi Patrisitci 10, Rome: Istituto patristico Augustinianum, 2000.

Dicker, *Descartes* = Dicker, Georges, *Descartes: An Analytical and Historical Introduction*, NY: Oxford University Press, 2013.

Dinno, "Jacob of Serugh, the Man Behind the *memro*" = Dinno, Khalid, "Jacob of Serugh, the Man Behind the *memro*", in George Anton Kiraz, (ed.), *Jacob of Serugh and His Times: Studies in Sixth-Century Syriac Christianity,* Piscataway, NJ: Gorgias Press, 2010, 51-70.

Dulles, *Models of the Church* = Dulles, A., *Models of the Church* (Expanded Edition), Doubleday, NY: Image Books, 1987.

Duncan, *Baptism in the Demonstrations of Aphraates* = Duncan, Edward J., *Baptism in the Demonstrations of Aphraates the Persian Sage,* Studies in Christian Antiquity 8, Washington DC: Catholic University of America Press, 1945.

Eijk, "The Gospel of Philip and Clement of Alexandria" = Eijk, A. H. C. Van, "The Gospel of Philip and Clement of Alexandria: Gnostic and Ecclesiastical Theology on the Resurrection and the Eucharist", in *VC* 25 (1971), 94-120.

Eliade, *Images and Symbols* = Eliade, Mircea, *Images and Symbols: Studies in Religious Symbolism*, ET. by Philip Mairet, London: Harvill Press, 1961.

Empereur and Kiesling, *Liturgy that Does Justice* = Empereur, James L., and Kiesling, Christopher G., *Liturgy that Does Justice*, Collegeville, MD: Liturgical Press, 1990.

Evdokimov, *In the World, of the Church* = Evdokimov, Paul, Michael Pelkon, and Alexis Vinogradov (eds.), *In the World, of the Church: Paul Evdokimov, A Reader*, Crestwood NY: SVS Press, 2000.

Fitzmyer, *Essays on the Semitic Background of the New Testament* = Fitzmyer, Joseph, A., *Essays on the Semitic Background of the New Testament*, Missoula, Montana: Scholars' Press, 1974.

Ford, and Kelly, *Contemporary Moral Theology* = Ford, J. C., Kelly, G., *Contemporary Moral Theology*, Vol. II, Westminster, MD: Newman Press, 1964.

Ford, *Women and Men in the Early Church* = Ford, David C., *Women and Men in the Early Church: The Full Views of St. John Chrysostom*, South Canaan, PA: St. Tikhon's Seminary Press, 1996.

Fragments of Heracleon = *Fragments of Heracleon*, Online, Retrieved on 11/1/2014. http://www.earlychristianwritings.com/text/heracleon.html,

Frankl, *Man's Search for Meaning* = Frankl, Victor, E., *Man's Search for Meaning* (Revised and Updated), NY: Washington Square Press, 1984.

Freedman, "Subat basti" = Freedman, D., "Subat basti: A Robe of Splendor", Journal of the Ancient Near Eastern Society of Columbia University, 4 (1972), 91-95.

Froehlich, *Biblical Interpretation in the Early Church* = Froehlich, Karlfried, ET. *Biblical Interpretation in the Early Church*, Philadelphia: Fortress Press, 1984.

Fruchtenbaum, *The Jewish Wedding System and the Bride of Messiah* = Fruchtenbaum, Arnold, *The Jewish Wedding System and the Bride of Messiah*, 3-4. http://www.arielm.org/dcs/pdf/mbs113m.pdf. Online Source, Retrieved on 26/11/2014.

Gershom, *On the Mystical Shape of the Godhead: Basic Concepts in Kabbalah* = Gershom, Scholem, *On the Mystical Shape of the Godhead,* New York: Schocken Books, 1976.

Gnoli, "Zoroastrianism" = Gnoli, Gherardo, "Zoroastrianism", in *ER,* Vol. 15, Mircea Eliade, (ed.), NY: Macmillan Company, 1987, 579-591.

Golitzin, "Many Lamps are Lighted from the One" = Golitzin, Alexander and Orlov, Andrei, "Many Lamps are Lighted from the One": Paradigms of the Transformational Vision in Macarian Homilies", in *VC* 55 (2001), 281-298.

Golitzin, "Recovering the Glory of Adam"= Golitzin, Alexander, "Recovering the "Glory of Adam": "Divine Light" Traditions in the Dead Sea Scrolls and the Christian Ascetical Literature of Fourth-Century Syro-Mesopotamia," in James R. Davila, (ed.), *The Dead Sea Scrolls as Background to Post-biblical Judaism and Early Christianity,* Leiden: Brill, 2003, 276-308.

Goppelt, "Typos" = Goppelt, "Typos", in *TDNT*, Vol. VIII, 251-256.

Griffith, *Faith Adoring Mystery,* = Griffith, Sidney, *Faith Adoring Mystery: Reading the Bible with St. Ephrem the Syrian*, (The Pere Marquette Lecture in Theology 1997), Milwaukee, MI: Marquette University Press, 1997.

Griffith, "Spirit in the Bread and Fire in the Wine" = Griffith, Sydney H., "Spirit in the Bread; Fire in the Wine": The Eucharist as "Living Medicine" in Ephraem the Syrian", in Sarah Beckwith (ed.), *Catholicism and Catholicity: Eucharistic Communities in Historical and Contemporary Perspectives,* Oxford: Blackwell, 1999, 113-134.

Griffith, "Mar Jacob of Serugh on Monks and Monasticism" = Griffith, Sidney H., "Mar Jacob of Serugh on Monks and Monasticism: Readings in his Metrical Homilies 'On Single", in George Anton Kiraz, (ed.), *Jacob of Serugh and His Times: Studies in Sixth-Century Syriac Christianity,* Piscataway, NJ: Gorgias Press, 2010, 71-90.

Grillmeier, *Christ in Christian Tradition* = Grillmeier, A., *Christ in Christian Tradition, Vol. I: From the Apostolic Age to Chalcedon (AD 451)*, London: Mowbray, 1975.

Guinan, *Eschatology of James* (Jacob) *of Serugh* = Guinan, Michael D., *Eschatology of James* (Jacob) *of Serugh: A Study in Syriac Patristic*

Theology, An unpublished doctoral dissertation, The Catholic University of America, Washington DC., 1972.

Günther, "Bride" = Günther, W., "Bride", in *NIDNT*, Colin Brown, (ed.), Grand Rapids: Zondervan, 1976, 584-585.

Harak, "The Syriac Orthodox Celebration" = Harak, Amir, "The Syriac Orthodox Celebration of the Eucharist In Light of Jacob of Serugh's *Memro* 95", in George Anton Kiraz (ed.), *Jacob of Serugh and His Times: Studies in Sixth-Century Christianity.* Piscataway, NJ: Gorgias, 2010, 91-113.

Harvey, "Bride of Blood, Bride of Light" = Harvey, Susan Ashbrook, "Bride of Blood, Bride of Light: Biblical Women as Images of the Church in Jacob of Serugh", in *Malphono w-Rabo d-Malphone: Studies in Honor of Sebastian P. Brock*, (ed.) by George A. Kiraz, Piscataway, NJ; Gorgias Press, 2008, 177-204.

Harvey, "To Whom Did Jacob Preach?" = Harvey, Susan Ashbrook, "To Whom Did Jacob Preach?", in George Anton Kiraz, (ed.), *Jacob of Serugh and His Times: Studies in Sixth-Century Syriac Christianity,* Piscataway, NJ: Gorgias Press, 2010, 115-132.

Harvey, "Women's Service in Ancient Syriac Christianity" = Harvey, Susan Ashbrook, "Women's Service in Ancient Syriac Christianity", in *Kanon* 16 (2001), 226-41.

Heimpel, "A Catalog of Near Eastern Venus Deities" = Heimpel, Wolfgang, "A Catalogue of Near Eastern Venus Deities", *Syro-Mesopotamian Studies* 4 (1982), 59-72.

Herbert, "The Fertility Cult in Hosea" = Herbert, G. May, "The Fertility Cult in Hosea", *AJSL* 48 (1932), 73-98.

Hertz, *Daily Prayer Book*, = Hertz, Joseph Herman, *The Authorized Daily Prayer Book*, New York, Block Pub. Co, 1984.

Isenberg, *Gospel of Philip* = Isenberg, W. Wesley, *Gospel of Philip.* In *The Nag Hammadi Library in English,* James M. Robinson, (ed.), San Francisco: Harper & Row Publishers, 1981, 131-152.

Jansma, "The Credo of Mar Jacob of Serugh" = Jansma, Taeke, "The Credo of Jacob of Serugh: A Return to Nicea and Constantinople", *Nederlands Archief voor Kerkgeschiedenis* 44.1(1960), 18-36.

Jeremias, "νύμφη, ωυμφίος"= Jeremias, J., "νύμφη, ωυμφίος", *TDNT* Vol. IV, Grand Rapids: WM. B. Eerdmans Publishing Company, 1967.

Jeremias, *The Parables* = Jeremias, Joachim, *The Parables of Jesus,* NY: C. Scribner's Sons, 1963.

Jungmann, *The Early Liturgy to the Time of Gregory the Great* = Jungmann, Josef A, *The Early Liturgy to the Time of Gregory the Great*, ET. by Francis A. Burnner, Notre Dame, IN: University of Notre Dame Press, 1959.

Jurgens, *The Faith of the Early Fathers* = Jurgens, William A., *The Faith of the Early Fathers* III, Collegeville, MN: The Liturgical Press, 1978.

Kelly, *Early Christian Doctrines* = Kelly, J.N.D., *Early Christian Doctrines*, London: Adam & Black, 1960.

Kereszty, Bride and Mother in the *Super Cantica* of St. Bernard = Kereszty, Roch, Bride and Mother in the *Super Cantica* of St. Bernard: An Ecclesiology for Our Time?, *Communio* 20 (Summer 1993), 415-436.

Kilian, "Jesus' Baptism in the Jordan" = Killan, McDonnell, "Jesus' Baptism in the Jordan", in *TS* 56 (1995), 209-236.

Kollamparampil, *Salvation in Christ* = Kollamparampil, Thomas, *Salvation in Christ according to Jacob of Serugh: An Exegetico-Theological Study on the Homilies of Jacob of Serugh (451-521 AD) on the Feasts of Our Lord*, Bangalore: Dharmaram Publications, 2001. See another publication. Kollamparampil, Thomas, *Salvation in Christ according to Jacob of Serugh: An Exegetico-Theological Study on the Homilies of Jacob of Serugh (451-521 AD) on the Feasts of Our Lord,* Piscataway, NJ: Gorgias Press, 2010, 2014.

Konat, "A Metrical Homily of Jacob of Serugh on the Mysteries" = Konat, Johns Abraham, "A Metrical Homily of Jacob of Serugh on the Mysteries, Types and Figures of Christ: Authentic or Compilation?", *LeMuseon* 118.1-2 (2005), 71-86.

Konat, "Christological Insights in Jacob of Serugh's Typology as Reflected in his Memre" = Konat, Johns Abraham, "Christological Insights in Jacob of Serugh's Typology as Reflected in his Memre", in *Ephemerides Theologicae Lovanienses* 77.1 (2001), 46-72.

Konat, "*Old Testament Types of Christ*" = Konat, Johns Abraham, "The Old Testament Types of Christ as Reflected in the Select Metrical Homilies (Memre) of Jacob of Serugh", Th.D. dissertation, Universite Catholique de Louvain, 1998.

Konat, "Typological Exegesis in the Metrical Homilies of Jacob of Serugh" = Konat, Johns Abraham, "Typological Exegesis in the Metrical Homilies of Jacob of Serugh", in *ParOr* 31 (2006), 109-121.

Konat, "Typological Terminology of Jacob of Serugh" = Konat, Johns Abraham, "Typological Terminology of Jacob of Serugh", in *The Harp* 18 (2005), 289-296.

Koonammakal, “Ephrem’s Imagery of Chasm” = Koonammakal, Thomas, “Ephrem’s Imagery of Chasm”, in Symposium Syriacum VII, Upsala University, Department of Asian and African Language, 11-14 August 1996, *OCA* 256, R. Lavenant, (ed.), Roma, 1998, 175-183.

Krüger, *Le caractère monophysite de la troisième lettere de Saroug* = Krüger, *Le caractère monophysite de la troisième lettere de Saroug, in OrSyr,* 6 (1961), 301-308.

Lapinkivi, “The Sumerian Sacred Marriage and its Aftermath” = Lapinkivi, Prijo, “The Sumerian Sacred Marriage and its Aftermath in Later Sources”, in Nissinen, Martti., and Risto Uro,(eds.), *Sacred Marriages: The Divine-human Sexual Metaphor from Sumer to Early Christianity*, Winona Lake, IN: Eisenbrauns, 2008, 7-41.

Lappey, “Marriage” = Lappey, Alice, L., “Marriage”, in *The Collegeville Pastoral Dictionary of Biblical Theology*, Carroll Stuhlmuller, (ed.), Collegeville, MN: The Liturgical Press, 1996.

Lewis, “Light and Darkness” = Lewis, Scott, M., “Light and Darkness”, in *NIDB* Vol. 3, (ed.), Katharine Door Sakenfeld, Nashville: Abingdon Press, 2008, 662-664.

Long, *The Eucharistic Theology of the American Holy Fairs* = Long Kimberly Bracken, *The Eucharistic Theology of the American Holy Fairs*, Louisville, KY: Westminster John Knox Press, 2011.

Lossky, *The Mystical Theology of the Eastern Church* = Lossky, Vladimir, *The Mystical Theology of the Eastern Church,* Crestwood, NY: SVS Press, 1976.

Luther, “Lectures to Song of Solomon” = Luther, Martin, “Lectures to Song of Solomon”, in Jaroslav Pelikan (ed.), and ET. by Ian Siggins, *Luther’s Works*, St. Louis: Concordia Publishing House, 1972.

Maloney, “Apophatic Theology” = Maloney, G. A., “Apophatic Theology”, in *NCE* Second Edition. Vol. 1, Washington DC: Thomson Gale, 2002.

Marsman, *Women in Ugarit and Israel* = Marsman, Hennie, J., *Women in Ugarit and Israel: Their Social and Religious Position in the Context of the Ancient Near East,* Leiden: Brill, 2003.

Matera, “Theologies of the Church in the New Testament” = Matera, Frank, J., “Theologies of the Church in the New Testament”, in Peter C. Phan, (ed.), *The Gift of the Church: A Text Book on Ecclesiology in Honor of Patrick Granfield, OSB*, Collegeville, MN: The Liturgical Press, 2000.

Matter, “Mystical Marriage” = Matter, Ann, E., “Mystical Marriage”, in *Women and Faith: Catholic Religious Life in Italy from Late Antiquity to the Present*, Lucetta Scaraffia and Gabriella Zarri (eds.) Cambridge: Harvard University Press, 1999, 31-41.

Mays, *Hosea: A Commentary* = Mays, James Luther, *Hosea: A Commentary*, The Old Testament Library, Philadelphia: The Westminster Press, 1969.

McCarron, "An Epiphany of the Mystical Symbols" = McCarron, Richard E., "An Epiphany of the Mystical Symbols: Jacob of Serugh's Memra 109 on Abraham and his Types", in *Hugoye* 1.1 (2010), 57-78.

McCarthy, "Becoming One Flesh" = McCarthy, David Matzko, "Becoming One Flesh: Marriage, Remarriage, and Sex", in Stanley Hauerwas and Samuel Wells, (ed.), *The Blackwell Companion to Christian Ethics,* Malden, MA: Blackwell, 2004, 281-283.

McDonnell, "Jesus' Baptism in the Jordan" = McDonnell, Kilian, "Jesus' Baptism in the Jordan", in *TS* 56 (1995), 209-236.

McGrath, *Heresy* = McGrath, Alister, *Heresy: A History of Defending the Truth*, New York, NY: Harper One, 2009.

McGuckin, "Apophaticism"= McGuckin, John Anthony, "Apophaticism", in *The Westminster Handbook to Patristic Theology*, Louisville, London: Westminster John Knox Press, 1989.

McGuckin, "Introduction: The "Great Mystery" of Marital Communion" = McGuckin, J. A., "Introduction: The "Great Mystery" of Marital Communion: Reimaging Orthodox Christian Foundations", in Nicu Dumitraşcu, (ed.), *Christian Family and Contemporary Society,* (Introduction) NY: Bloomsbury T&T Clark, 2014.

Meyendorff, *Marriage: An Orthodox Perspective*, = Meyendorff, John, *Marriage: An Orthodox Perspective*, Crestwood, NY: SVS Press, 1984.

Michalowski, "Presence and the Creation" = Michalowski, Piotr, "Presence and the Creation", in *Lingering Over Words: Studies in Ancient Near Eastern Literature in Honor of William L. Moran,* (ed.), Tzvi Abusch, John Huehnergard, & Piotr Steinkeller, Altlanta: Scholars Press, 1990.

Micinery, "Dualism" = Micinery, R. M., "Dualism", in *NCE,* Vol. 4 (Second Edition), (ed.), Berard L. Marthaler, NY: Gale Thomson, 2003.

Mielziner, *The Jewish Law of Marriage and Divorce* = Mielzner, M., *The Law of Jewish Marriage and Divorce in Ancient and Modern Times and Its Relation to the Law of the State,* Cincinnati: The Bloch Publishing Company, 1884.

Millgram, *Jewish Worship* = Millgram, Abraham Ezra, *Jewish Worship,* Philadelphia: The Jewish Publication Society of America, 1971.

Moffet, *A History of Christianity in Asia* I = Moffet, Samuel Hugh, *A History of Christianity in Asia, Vol. I: From Beginnings to 1500,* NY: Orbis, 2005.

Möhler, *Unity in the Church* = Möhler, Johann Adam, *Unity in the Church, or, the Principle of Catholicism Presented in the Spirit of the Church Fathers of the First Three Centuries*, (ed. & ET.), Peter C. Erb, Washington, DC: CUA Press, 1996.

Moltmann, *The Future of Creation* = Moltmann, Jürgen, *The Future of Creation: Collected Essays*, Philadelphia: Fortress Press, 1977.

Murray, *Symbols of Church and Kingdom* = Murray, Robert, *Symbols of Church and Kingdom: A Study in Early Syriac Tradition*, New York: T & T Clark, 2006.

Murray, "Aramaic and Syriac dispute poems and their connections" = Murray, R., "Aramaic and Syriac dispute poems and their connections", in M.J. Geller, J.C. Greenfield and M. P. Weitxman (eds.), *Studia Aramaica*, (Journal of Semitic Studies, Supplement) 4, Oxford: Oxford University Press, 1995, 157-187.

Murray, "The Lance which Re-opened Paradise" = Murray, R., "The Lance which Re-opened Paradise: A Mysterious Reading in the Early Syriac Fathers", *OCP* 39.1 (1973): 224-234.

Murray, "The Theory of Symbolism in Ephrem's Theology" = Murray, R., "The Theory of Symbolism in Ephrem's Theology", in *ParOr*, 6-7 (1975-1976).

Nedungatt, "The Covenanters of the Early Syriac Speaking Church" = Nedungatt, George, "The Covenanters of the Early Syriac-Speaking Church", *OCP* 39 (1973), 191-215, 419-444.

Nir, *Joseph and Asneth* = Nir, Rivka, *Joseph and Asneth*: *A Christian Book*, Sheffield: Sheffield Phoenix Press, 2012.

Nissinen, Martti, and Uro, Risto, "Sacred Marriages, or the Divine-Human Sexual Metaphor: Introducing the Project", in Nissinen, Martti, and Risto Uro, (eds.), *Sacred Marriages: The Divine-human Sexual Metaphor from Sumer to Early Christianity*, Winona Lake, IN: Eisenbrauns, 2008.

Northrop, *Creation and Recreation* = Northrop, Frye, *Creation and Recreation*, Toronto: Toronto University, 1980.

O'Connell, "*ḥtn*" = O'Connell, Robert, H., "'*ḥtn*", in *NIDOTT,* Vol. 2, Williem A. VanGeneren, (ed.), Cumbria, UK: Paternoster Press, 1997, 325-328.

Olson, "The Book of Judges" = Olson, Dennis, T., "The Book of Judges: Introduction, Commentary, and Reflection", in *NIB,* Vol. II. Nashville: Abingdon Press, 1998.

Pagels, "Pursuing the Spiritual Eve" = Pagels, Elaine, "Pursuing the Spiritual Eve: Imagery and the Hermeneutics of the Hypostasis in the Archons and the Gospel of Philip", in Karen L. King, (ed.), *Images of the Feminine in Gnosticism*, Harrisburg, PA: Trinity Press, 2000, 187-206.

Pagoulatos, *Tracing the Bridegroom in Dura.* = Pagoulatos, Gerasimos, P., *Tracing the Bridegroom in Dura: The Bridal Initiation Service of the Dura-Europos Christian Baptistery as Early Evidence of the Use of Images in Christian Worship.* Piscataway, NJ: Tigris & Gorgias, 2008.

Pannenberg, *The Church* = Pannenberg, Wolfhart, *The Church*, ET. by Keith Crim, Philadelphia: The Westminster Press, 1983.

Pathil, *Theology of the Church New Horizons* = Pathil, Kuncheria, *Theology of the Church New Horizons,* Bangalore: Dharmaram Publications, 2006.

Placher, *A History of Christian Theology* = Placher, William C., and Derek R. Nelson, *A History of Christian Theology: An Introduction*, Philadelphia: The Westminster Press, 1983.

Plastaras, *Creation and Covenant* = Plastaras, James, *Creation and Covenant,* Milwaukee: Bruce Publications, 1968.

Posner, "Marriage Ceremony" = Posner, Raphael, "Marriage Ceremony", *EncJud.* Second Edition, Vol. 13, Lif - Mekm, Fred Skolnik (Chief ed.), NY; Thomson Gale, 2007, 565-568.

Possekel, *Evidence of Greek Philosophical Concepts in the Writings of Ephrem the Syrian* = Possekel, Ute., *Evidence of Greek Philosophical Concepts in the Writings of Ephrem the Syrian*, CSCO 580, Sub. 102, Louvain: Peters, 1999.

Powathil, *Church as the Mystery of Communion* = Powathil, Archbishop, Joseph, *Church as the Mystery of Communion: A Tribute to the Ecclesial Vision of Father Placid Podipara*, Bangalore: Dharmaram Publications, 2014.

Prestige, *God in Patristic Thought* = Prestige, G. L., *God in Patristic Thought*, London: S. P. C. K., 1964.

Puthuparampil, *Mariological Thoughts* = Puthuparampil, James, *Mariological Thoughts of Mar Jacob of Serugh (451–521).* Mōrān' Eth'ō 25. Kottayam, Kerala: SEERI, 2005.

Quasten, *Patrology,* Vol. 2 = Quasten, Johannes, *Patrology* Vol. 2, Westminster, MD: Christian Classics, 1986.

Ras Shamra Parallels = Ras Shamra Parallels: The Texts from Ugarit and the Hebrew Bible, Vol. II. Ed. Loren R. Fisher, *Anelecta Orientalia Commentationes Scientificae De Rebus Orientis Antiqui 50.* Roma: Pontificium Institutum Biblicum, 1975.

Reicke, "Hell" = Reicke, "Hell", in *The Oxford Guide to Ideas and Issues of the Bible,* Bruce M. Metzger and Michael D. Coogan, (eds.), NY: Oxford University Press, 1989.

Reuling, *After Eden* = Reuling, Hanneke, *After Eden: Church Fathers and Rabbis on Genesis 3:16– 21*, Leiden: Brill, 2006.

Robert, "Judges" = Robert, G. Boling, "Judges: A New Translation with Introduction and Commentary", *The Anchor Bible*. Garden City, NY: Doubleday, 1975.

Roberts, "Theology of Christian Marriage" = Roberts, William, "Theology of Christian Marriage", in Bernard Cooke, Kathleen Fischer, et.al., (eds.), *Alternative Future for Worship: Christian Marriage*, Vol. 5, Collegeville, MN: The Liturgical Press, 1987.

Roloff, "εκκλησια"= Roloff, J., "εκκλησια", Exegetical Dictionary of the New Testament, Vol. I, (eds.), Horst Balz and Gerhard Schneider, Grand Rapids, MI: Willim B. Eerdmans Publishing Company, 1990, 410-415.

Rompay, "Humanity's Sin in Paradise Ephrem" = Rompay, Lucas Van, "Humanity's Sin in Paradise Ephrem, Jacob of Serugh, and Narsai in Conversation" in George Anton Kiraz, (ed.), *Jacob of Serugh and His Times: Studies in Sixth-Century Syriac Christianity,* Piscataway, NJ: Gorgias Press, 2010, 199-218.

Ross, "Church as the Mystery and Communion" = Ross, Sophy, *Church as the Mystery (Raza) and Communion (S^{h}awtaput^{h}a) in the East Syriac Liturgical Year*, Kottayam, Kerala: OIRSI, 1997.

Ross, *Extravagant Affections* = Ross, Susan A., *Extravagant Affections: A Feminist Sacramental Theology*, NY: Continuum, 2001.

Rozemond, *Descartes' Dualism* = Rozemond, Marleen, *Descartes' Dualism*, Cambridge, MA: Harvard University Press, 1998.

Rubin, and Kosman, "The Clothing of Primordial Adam" = Rubin, Nissan, and Admiel Kosman, "The Clothing of the Primordial Adam as a Symbol of Apocalyptic Time in the Midrashic Sources", in *HTR* 90.2 (1997), 155-74.

Rush, "Death as a Spiritual Marriage" = Rush, A.C., "Death as Spiritual Marriage: Individual and Ecclesial Eschatology", in *VC* 26 (1972), 81-101.

Russell, "A First Look at the Christology of Ephrem the Syrian" = Russell, S. Paul, "A First Look at the Christology of Ephrem the Syrian", *Symposium Syriacum* VII, (Uppsala University, Department of Asian and African Languages, 11-14 August 1996, *OCA* 256, Ed. Rene Lavenant, Roma: Pontifico Instituto Orientale, 1998, 108-115.

Sacred Texts, Online Resource, Retrieved on 10/18/2013, http://www.sacred-texts.com/ane/sum/sum08.htm.

Samuel, "One incarnate Nature of God the Word" = Samuel, V. C., "One incarnate Nature of God the Word", Fries, Paul, R. & Train Nersoyan, (eds.), *Christ in East and West*, Macon, GA : Mercer University Press, 1987.

Samuel, *The Council of Chalcedon Re-examined* = Samuel V. C., *The Council of Chalcedon Re-examined: A Historical and Theological Survey*, (Indian Theological Library) Madras: The Christian Literature Society, 1977.

Schillebeeckx, *Marriage: Human Reality Saving Mystery* = Schillebeeckx, E., *Marriage: Human Reality and Saving Mystery.* ET. N. D. Smith, NY: Sheed and Ward, 1965.

Schimdst, "εκκλησια" = Schimdst, K. L.,"εκκλησια", in *TDNT* III, Gerhard Kittel, (ed.), Grand Rapids, MI: Wm. B. Eerdmanns Publishing Company, 1965, 501-536.

Schwarz, *Christology*, = Schwarz, Hans, *Christology*, Grand Rapids, MI: Wm. B. Eerdmans Publishing Company, 1998.

Segal, *Edessa, The Blessed City* = Segal, J. B., *Edessa, "The Blessed City"* Oxford: Clarendon Press, 1970.

Sheed, *Theology for Beginners* = Frank Sheed, *Theology for Beginners*, Ann Arbor, MI: Servants Books, 1981.

Shemunkasho, "Jacob of Serugh and His Influence on John of Dara" = Shemunkasho, Aho, "Jacob of Serugh and his Influence on John of Dara as Exemplified by the Use of Two Verse-Homilies", in *Jacob of Serugh and His Times: Studies in Sixth-Century Syriac Christianity*, Kiraz, George Anton, (ed.), Gorgias Eastern Christian Studies 8, Piscataway, NJ: Gorgias Press, 2010, 163-197.

Siegle, *Marriage According to the New Code of Canon Law* = Siegle, Bernard A., *Marriage According to the New Code of Canon Law*, NY: Alba House, 1986.

Smith, "Garment of Shame" = Smith, Jonathan, Z., "Garment of Shame", *HR,* 1.5 (1965), 217-238.

Smith, *Syriac Dictionary,* = Smith, Jessy Payane, (ed.), *A Compendious Syriac Dictionary: Founded upon the Thesaurus Syriaus of R. Payane Smith,* Oxford: Clarendon Press, 1979.

Sokoloff, A Syriac Lexicon = Sokoloff, Michael, *A Syriac Lexicon: A Translation from the Latin, Correction, Expansion, and Update of C. Brockelmann's Lexicon Syriacum,* Winona Lake, Indiana: Eisenbrauns & Piscataway, NJ: Gorgias Press, 2009.

Sony, "La méthode exégétique de Jacques de Saroug" = B. P. Sony, "La méthode exégétique de Jacques de Saroug", in *ParOr* 9 (1979–80), 67-103.

Stevenson, *To Join Together: The Rite of Marriage* = Stevenson, Kenneth W., *To Join Together: The Rite of Marriage*, Collegeville, Minnesota: Liturgical Press, 1987.

Trigg, *Message of the Fathers of the Church* IX = Trigg, J.W., *Message of the Fathers of the Church* IX, Wilmington: Michael Glazier, 1988, 184-202.

Valantasis, "The Nuptial Chamber Revisited" = Valantasis, Richard, "The Nuptial Chamber Revisited: The *Acts of Thomas* and Cultural Intertextuality", in *Semeia* 80 (1987), 261-276.

Valenziano, "Liturgy and Symbolism" = Valenziano, Crispino, "Liturgy and Symbolism", in Anscar J. Chupungco, (ed.), *Fundamental Liturgy: The Pontifical Institute Handbook for Liturgical Studies,* Vol. II, Collegeville, MN: Pueblo, 1998.

Van den Berg, "Bedjan, Paul" = Van den Berg, H. L. Murre, "Bedjan, Paul", in *Gorgias Encyclopedic Dictionary of the Syriac Heritage: With Contributions of Seventy Scholars*, Beth Mardutho: The Syriac Institute, (ed.) Sebastian P. Brock, Aron M. Butts, Geogre A. Kraz, et.al., Piscataway, NJ: Gorgias Press, 2011.

Varghese, "John, Patriarch of Antioch" = Varghese, B., "Jon Patriarch of Antioch Homily on the Consecration of Myron", in *The Harp* (XXVI) 2012, 157-166.

Vatican Council II. *Lumen Gentium,* Dogmatic Constitution on the Church, 21 November 1964, *AAS* 57 (1965), 5-71.

Vatican Council II. *Sacrosanctum Concilium*, Constitution on Sacred Liturgy, 4 December 1963, *AAS* 56 (1964), 97-138.

Vellian, "The Church as the Bride" = Vellian, Jacob, "The Church as the Bride in the East Syrian Liturgy", in Vellian, Jacob, (ed.), *Selected Studies*, Kottayam, Kerala: Deepika Book House, 2006, 496-502.

Villar, "The Plan of God for Marriage and the Family Life = Villar, Jose R., "The Plan of God for Marriage and the Family Life: A Roman-Catholic Perspective", in *Christian Family and Contemporary Society,* London: Bloomsbury, T&T Clark, 2014.

Vööbus, Handschriftliche Überlieferung = Arthur Vööbus, *Handschriftliche Überlieferung der Memre-Dichtung des Ja'qob von Serug, CSCO* 344, 345, 421, 422, Louvain: Secretariat du Corpus *CSCO*, 1973, 1980.

Wakely, "*hᵃtunnâ*" = Wakely, Robin., "*hᵃtunnâ*", in *New International Dictionary of the Old Testament and Theology,* Vol. 2, (ed.), Williem A. VanGeneren, Cumbria, UK: Paternoster Press,1997, 328-330.

Walters, *Hymns on the Unleavened Bread* = Walters, J. Edward., *Hymns on the Unleavened Bread.* Piscataway, NJ: Gorgias Press, 2011.

Ware, and Mother Mary, (ed.), *The Lenten Triodion*, = Ware, Kallistos and Mother Mary, (ed.), *The Lenten Triodion*, London & Boston: Faber and Faber, 1978.

White, "The Historical Roots of Our Ecological Crisis" = White, Lynn, "The Historical Roots of Out Ecological Crisis", in *Science* 155 (1967), 1203-1207.

Wiesenberg, "Nisan," = Wiesenberg, Ephraim Jehudah, "Nisan", in *EncJud.* Second Edition, Vol. 15, Fred Skolnik (Chief ed.), NY: Thomson Gale, 2007.

Wilson, *Our Father Abraham* = Wilson, Marvin R., *Our Father Abraham: Jewish Roots of the Christian Faith*, Grand Rapids, MI: Wm. B. Eerdmans, 1989.

Woolcombe, *Essays in Typology* = Lampe, G. W. H., and Woolcombe, K. J., *Essays in Typology*, Naperville: Allenson, 1957.

Wright, *A Short History of Syriac Literature* = Wright, William, *A Short History of Syriac Literature*, London: Adam and Charles Black, 1894, 13-14.

Young, *From Nicaea to Chalcedon* =Young, Frances M., *From Nicaea to Chalcedon: A Guide to the Literature and its Background*, London: SCM, 1983.

Zimmerman, "The Love Triangle of Lady Wisdom," = Zimmerman, Ruben, "A Triangle of Lady Wisdom: Sacred Marriage in Jewish Wisdom Literature?", in (eds.), Martti Nissinen and Risto Uro, *Sacred Marriages: The Divine-Human Sexual Metaphor from Sumer to Early Christianity,* Winona Lake, IN: Eisenbrauns, 2008.